THE
LONGEST
AUGUST

ALSO BY Dilip Hiro

Nonfiction

A Comprehensive Dictionary of the Middle East *(2013)*

Apocalyptic Realm: Jihadists in South Asia *(2012)*

After Empire: The Birth of a Multipolar World *(2010) (short-listed for Mirabaud Prize, Geneva, 2011)*

Inside Central Asia: A Political and Cultural History of Uzbekistan, Turkmenistan, Kazakhstan, Kyrgyzstan, Tajikistan, Turkey, and Iran *(2009) (on* Financial Times' *List of Best History Books of the Year)*

Blood of the Earth: The Battle for the World's Vanishing Oil Resources *(2007)*

The Timeline History of India *(2006)*

The Iranian Labyrinth: Journeys through Theocratic Iran and Its Furies *(2005)*

Secrets and Lies: Operation "Iraqi Freedom" and After (2004) *(on* Financial Times' *List of Best Politics and Religion Books of the Year; long-listed for the George Orwell Prize for Political Writing)*

The Essential Middle East: A Comprehensive Guide *(2003)*

Iraq: In the Eye of the Storm *(2003)*

War Without End: The Rise of Islamist Terrorism and Global Response *(2002)*

The Rough Guide History of India *(2002)*

Neighbors, Not Friends: Iraq and Iran after the Gulf Wars *(2001)*

Sharing the Promised Land: A Tale of Israelis and Palestinians *(1999)*

Dictionary of the Middle East *(1996)*

The Middle East *(1996)*

Between Marx and Muhammad: The Changing Face of Central Asia *(1995)*

Lebanon, Fire and Embers: A History of the Lebanese Civil War *(1993)*

Desert Shield to Desert Storm: The Second Gulf War *(1992)*

Black British, White British: A History of Race Relations in Britain *(1991)*

The Longest War: The Iran-Iraq Military Conflict *(1991)*

Holy Wars: The Rise of Islamic Fundamentalism *(1989, re-issued 2013)*

Iran: The Revolution Within *(1988)*

Iran under the Ayatollahs *(1985, re-issued 2011)*

Inside the Middle East *(1982, re-issued 2013)*

Inside India Today *(1977, re-issued 2013)*

The Untouchables of India *(1975)*

Black British, White British *(1973)*

The Indian Family in Britain *(1969)*

Fiction

Three Plays *(1985)*

Interior, Exchange, Exterior *(poems, 1980)*

Apply, Apply, No Reply & A Clean Break *(two plays, 1978)*

To Anchor a Cloud *(play, 1972)*

A Triangular View *(novel, 1969)*

THE
LONGEST
AUGUST

The
Unflinching Rivalry
Between India *and* Pakistan

DILIP HIRO

NATION
BOOKS
New York

Published by Nation Books, A Member of the Perseus Books Group
116 East 16th Street, 8th Floor
New York, NY 10003

Nation Books is a co-publishing venture of the Nation Institute and the Perseus
Books Group

Books published by Nation Books are available at special discounts for bulk
purchases in the United States by corporations, institutions, and other organizations.
For more information, please contact the Special Markets Department at the Perseus
Books Group, 2300 Chestnut Street, Suite 200, Philadelphia, PA 19103, or call (800)
810-4145, ext. 5000, or e-mail
special.markets@perseusbooks.com.

Typeset in 11.5 point Adobe Caslon Pro by the Perseus Books Group

Library of Congress Cataloging-in-Publication Data

Hiro, Dilip.
    The longest August : the unflinching rivalry between India and Pakistan /
Dilip Hiro.
      pages   cm
    Includes bibliographical references and index.
      ISBN 978-1-56858-734-9 (hardcover) — ISBN 978-1-56858-503- 1 (e-book)
    1. India—Foreign relations—Pakistan. 2. Pakistan—Foreign relations—
India. I. Title.
    DS450.P18H57 2014
    327.5405491   dc23
                                                              2014045994
    ISBN: 978-1-56858-515-4 (INTL)

10 9 8 7 6 5 4 3 2 1

Contents

Maps   *vii*

Preface   *xi*

Introduction   1

1   The Modish Dresser Meets the Mahatma   9

2   Gandhi's Original Sin: Injecting Religion into Politics   27

3   The Two-Nation Theory: A Preamble to Partition   51

4   A Rising Tide of Violence   75

5   Born in Blood   91

6   The Infant Twins at War   111

7   Growing Apart   134

8   Nehru's "Forward Policy": A Step Too Far   158

9   Shastri's Tallest Order: Pakistan's Nightmare Comes Alive   180

10   Indira Gandhi Slays the Two-Nation Theory   200

11   Zulfikar Ali Bhutto: The Savior of West Pakistan   221

12   Islamist Zia ul Haq, Builder of the A-Bomb   234

13   Rajiv-Benazir Rapport—Cut Short   263

14   Gate-Crashing the Nuclear Club   280

15   General Musharraf Buckles Under US Pressure   309

16   Nuclear-Armed Twins, Eyeball-to-Eyeball   327

17   Manmohan Singh's Changing Interlocutors   341

18   Competing for Kabul   369

19   Shared Culture, Rising Commerce   395

20   Overview and Conclusions   413

Epilogue   433

Notes   *437*

Select Bibliography   *471*

Index   *473*

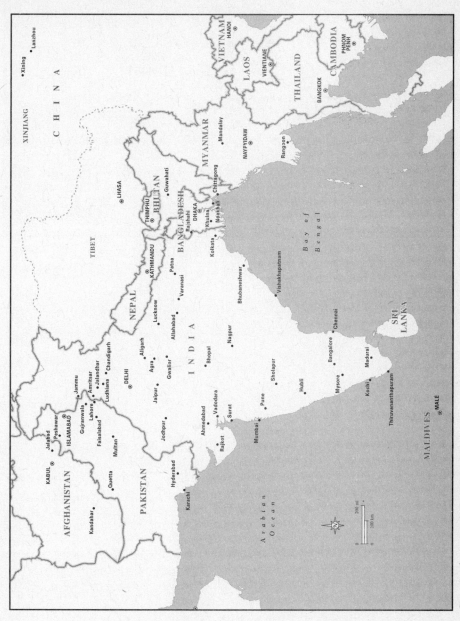

South Asia and Its Neighbors

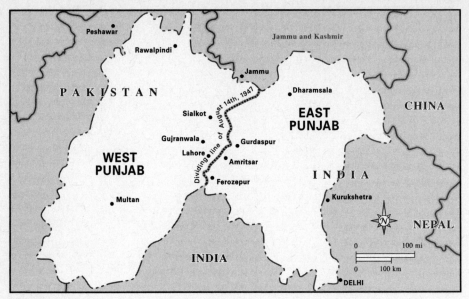

United Punjab in 1946 with the Partitioning Line of August 14, 1947

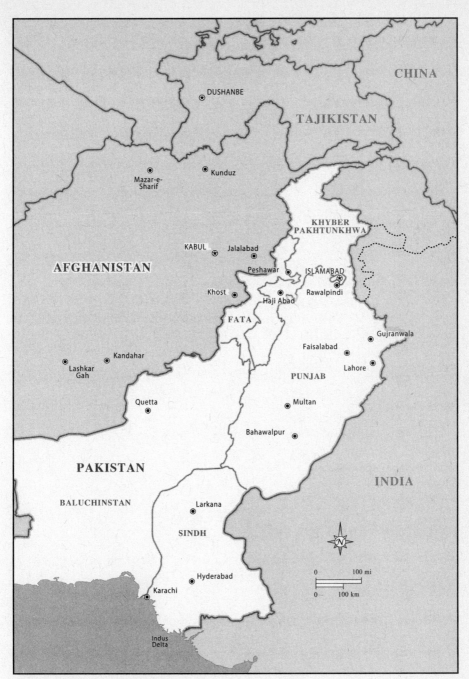

Pakistan Excluding Pakistan-Administered Jammu and Kashmir

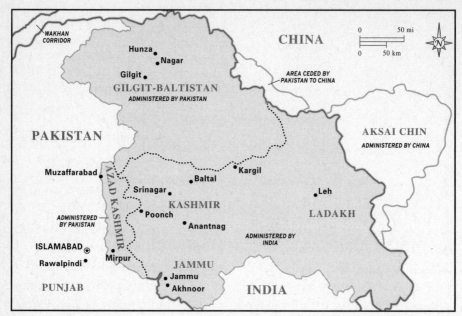

Jammu and Kashmir

Preface

The first colony of the British Empire that was partitioned at the time of acquiring a Dominion status within the British Commonwealth of Nations was Ireland. On December 6, 1922, exercising its right under the Anglo-Irish Treaty of December 1921, Protestant-majority Northern Ireland seceded from the Irish Free State to remain part of the British Empire. It was the historic tension between Protestants and Catholics, dating back to the Battle of Boyne in 1690 between Protestant William III of Orange and Catholic James II, which led to the division of Ireland.

A quarter century after Ireland's partition, the Indian subcontinent became the next colony of Britain to end up divided into the Dominion of India and the Dominion of Pakistan. Irreconcilable tensions between majority Hindus and minority Muslims were the cause of this. The buildup to this partition, its enforcement, and its immediate and later consequences were of far greater import to the region and the world at large than the division of Ireland.

What was common between the two partitions was religious affiliation. In the case of Ireland, it was different sects within Christianity, whereas in united but colonized India it was a clash between polytheistic Hinduism and monotheistic Islam. In sheer numbers, there were 250 million Hindus and 90 million Muslims in the subcontinent on the eve of the partition. Together, they formed nearly one-fifth of the human race.

As a result of the two-way migration of minorities across the new borders created in August 1947, millions of families were uprooted from their hearths and homes of centuries. They left behind their immovable properties and most of the movable goods. The respective governments confiscated the assets of the departed with a plan to compensate those on the other side who had lost their worldly possessions because of the partition. This scheme worked well in the two parts of Punjab and adjoining Delhi, even though the aggregate assets of the Hindus and Sikhs in West Punjab exceeded those of the Muslims in East Punjab and Delhi.

The case of the small province of Sindh differed from Punjab's in two ways. It remained united, and it was spared the communal carnage of Punjab. But in two major cities of Sindh the limited violence against Hindus, who were far better off economically and educationally than Muslims, was enough to cause a steady exodus of Sindhi Hindus. Unlike the Hindus and Sikhs of West Pakistan, however, they did not have a part of Sindh retained by pre-independence India to which they could migrate. As a consequence, traveling in comparatively small numbers over many months by train and ship, they ended up in Indian cities and large towns along an arc in western India, stretching from Delhi to the southern reaches of Bombay province, which was populated solely by the Marathi-speaking people.

My family, based in the Sindhi town of Larkana, belonged to this category of refugees from West Pakistan. We traveled by ship from Karachi to the Port of Okha in north Gujarat and ended up in a sprawling, empty military barracks built during World War II, thirty-five miles southeast of central Bombay. These were now called Kalyan (Refugee) Camps, numbered 1 to 5. Here, in a row of single rooms fronted by a veranda, accommodation was free, with the large room serving as the living-cum-sleeping space, and an area in the veranda allocated for cooking.

Like refugees elsewhere before and since then, we built up our lives slowly. I managed to pursue a university education, thanks to government loans to the children of refugees from Pakistan. There was no hope or wish to return to what had become the "other" country. That door remained shut.

The story of my personal journey from serving as a qualified engineer on a tube well drilling project in Gujarat to becoming a self-taught professional writer in London belongs to another category of my output than the one to which the present work does.

This book on the troubled relations between India and Pakistan chronicles not only political and military events and the principal players, but also trade and cultural links. It covers the involvement of major powers of the globe—the United States, the Soviet Union, and the People's Republic of China—in shaping the relations between these South Asian neighbors, which together form one-fifth of humanity.

In the introduction I explain that the sixty-five-year-old Kashmir dispute has its roots in the tensions between Hindus and Muslims dating back eight centuries. The subjugation of the Indian subcontinent by Britain after 1807 gave rise to Indian nationalism within a century. The aim of the anti-imperialist movement that rose sharply after World War I was open to two different interpretations. One was to end Britain's imperial rule and transform enslaved India into a sovereign state. The other was to end the subjugations that the majority Hindus—three-quarters of the population—had borne since 1192; they were now ready to administer a free India on the basis of one person, one vote. The two interpretations overlapped because the foremost anti-imperialist party, the Indian National Congress, was overwhelmingly Hindu.

In 1915 the return home of Mohandas K. Gandhi, a Gujarati Indian lawyer, from South Africa sowed a seed in national politics that would grow into a tree covering much political space. His rivalry with another Gujarati-speaking lawyer, Muhammad Ali Jinnah, would come to dominate subcontinental politics for three decades. This is the gist of Chapter 1.

A deeply religious man, Gandhi made an alliance with the Muslim leaders of the Khilafat movement, which was committed to the continuation of the caliphate based in Istanbul that had come under threat after the defeat of the Ottoman Empire by the Allied Powers in 1918. The Khilafat leaders backed the noncooperation campaign Gandhi launched in 1920. Its sudden suspension by Gandhi disappointed and bewildered them. The Hindu-Muslim unity forged to oppose the British Raj proved transitory. During the rest of the decade, Gandhi took up the causes of exploited peasants and workers; he garnered much publicity by launching such nonviolent campaigns as making salt from seawater without official permission. In the face of Gandhi's spiraling fame, Jinnah moved his legal practice to London. This analytical narrative forms Chapter 2.

Chapter 3 covers the return of Jinnah from London to take up the leadership of the Muslim League and his articulation of the Two-Nation Theory. Though the League performed poorly in the 1937 elections, the policies of the Congress ministries, composed almost wholly of Hindus, gave a preview of the insensitivity of Congress officials toward the beliefs and mores of Muslims. The non-League Muslim leaders closed ranks with the League. In the 1945–1946 elections, the League won 73 percent of Muslim ballots, a giant leap from the previous 5 percent.

Britain's decision to quit India after World War II intensified the rivalry between the Congress and the League: the former wished to inherit a united India from the British, and the latter resolved to establish a homeland for Muslims by partitioning the subcontinent. Communal tensions turned into violence. The chronology of this period constitutes Chapter 4.

Chapter 5 narrates the communal frenzy that gripped Punjab at the time of the birth of independent India and Pakistan in August 1947 and soon after. As a breakaway political entity, Pakistan faced many hurdles to get established.

Although the communal bloodbath that marked the birth of independent India and Pakistan on August 14–15, 1947, subsided after a few months, the dispute over Kashmir that broke out soon after has continued to vitiate relations between the neighbors. Indeed, their subsequent chronology has been peppered with so many challenges, crises, proxy wars, ongoing attempts to covertly exploit ethnic and other fault lines in their respective societies, hot wars, and threats of nuclear strikes that a historian is moved to encapsulate Indo-Pakistan relations as "the longest August."

The next chapter outlines the fight between India and Pakistan over Jammu and Kashmir, whose Muslim majority was ruled by a Hindu maharaja. When threatened by the incursion of armed tribal irregulars from Pakistan, the maharaja acceded to India, subject to a referendum when normal conditions had been restored. The issue was referred to the United Nations, but it would prove insoluble for many decades.

The two neighboring countries developed differently. Democracy based on a multiparty system and universal suffrage took hold in India. By contrast, political life deteriorated in Pakistan to the extent that General Muhammad Ayub Khan imposed military rule in 1958. His efforts to seek a satisfactory solution to the Kashmir problem in consultation with Indian premier Jawaharlal Nehru got nowhere. Chapter 7 provides the narrative of this period.

Since, according to India, China had occupied a part of Kashmir, Nehru had to deal with the Chinese government, which, independently, disputed the border delineating northeastern India from the Tibet region of China. When Nehru tried to assert India's claim by making military moves, war broke out between China and India in October 1962. It ended a month later, after China, having proved its military superiority, declared a unilateral cease-fire and withdrew its forces to prewar positions. This armed conflict created a bond between China and Pakistan that has endured ever since. This is the essence of Chapter 8.

The succeeding chapter recounts the war that Pakistan started in India-held Kashmir in September 1965. The three-week hostilities failed to deliver what Pakistan had hoped: the destruction of the status quo in

Kashmir. Indeed its failure in this war led to the toppling of Ayub Khan and then to the secession of East Pakistan. Chapter 9 describes the buildup to the war, the actual fighting, and its consequences.

The narrative in the next chapter deals with the run-up to the two-week-long Bangladesh War in December 1971, the combat, and its aftermath. In ideological terms, Indian premier Indira Gandhi slew the two-nation theory of Jinnah by showing that ethnicity overrides religion. This was also a setback for the cause of the Muslim separatists in Indian Kashmir.

Chapter 11 shows how Zulfikar Ali Bhutto salvaged West Pakistan. Even though he held weak cards in his negotiations with Gandhi in Shimla in June 1972, he managed to deprive her of her aim to bring the Kashmir issue to an official closure. In Pakistan, as a result of the rigged election in March 1977, he faced huge protests in the streets, which he failed to curb. This provided an opportunity to his Islamist army chief general, Muhammad Zia ul Haq, to overthrow the government and return Pakistan to a military administration. It lasted as long as Zia ul Haq lived—until August 1988. During his rule he Islamized state and society, thereby moving Pakistan further away from secular India. The Soviet Union's military involvement in Afghanistan turned Pakistan into a front-line state in the Cold War, helping Zia ul Haq accelerate the nuclear weapons program in which China provided Pakistan with vital assistance. In early 1984 it tested an atom bomb assembled in Pakistan at its nuclear testing site.

Rajiv Gandhi's succession in the footsteps of his assassinated mother, Indira, in October 1984, went smoothly. He found a congenial political partner in Benazir Bhutto, a daughter of Zulfikar Ali, after her election to the premiership of Pakistan in December 1988. The bonhomie dissipated as separatist insurgency in Kashmir intensified from 1989 onward, with India resorting to brutish methods to squash it. The protests of Bhutto and her successor Muhammad Nawaz Sharif fell on stony ground. During the premiership of P. V. Narasimha Rao after the assassination of Rajiv Gandhi in May 1991, the international scene changed radically. The disintegration of the Soviet Union in December 1991 signaled the victory of the United States in the Cold War. Delhi strengthened its links with Washington, which saw no need to downgrade its historic ties with Pakistan. Rao accelerated India's nuclear arms program. Chapter 13 relates these events.

Rao's plan to test three nuclear devices in late 1995 was thwarted by US president Bill Clinton, who was committed to stopping the spread of nuclear arms. But to consolidate his thin majority in Parliament, Atal Bihari Vajpayee, leader of the Hindu Nationalist Bharatiya Janata Party (BJP), ordered the testing of nuclear bombs. These tests occurred in mid-May 1998. Two weeks later Pakistan followed suit. With that Pakistan acquired parity with India in its power of military deterrence, thus offsetting its military inferiority in the conventional area. A reassured Pakistani prime minister Sharif welcomed Vajpayee in Lahore in February 1999. Visiting the site where the Muslim League had passed its Pakistan resolution on March 23, 1940, Vajpayee noted that a stable, secure, and prosperous Pakistan was in India's best interests. But once again this proved to be a false dawn. Three months later Pakistan's army chief general, Pervez Musharraf, tried to capture the Kargil region of Indian Kashmir by stealth. He failed. But his surreptitious unveiling of nuclear-tipped missiles was detected by Clinton, who then intervened. Following tense negotiations in Washington, he had Sharif agree to withdraw his troops to the Line of Control (LoC) in Kashmir. Sharif's deal paved the way for his overthrow by Musharraf. This narrative appears in Chapter 14.

The following chapter describes how in the aftermath of 9/11 and the failed terrorist attack on the Parliament House in Delhi three months later, the United States succeeded in getting Musharraf to jettison the Taliban regime in Afghanistan and stop providing military training and weapons to Kashmiri separatists. But the subsequent lowering of Indo-Pakistan tensions in January 2002 did not last. Following the terrorist assault on a military camp at Kaluchak in Kashmir in May, Vajpayee authorized the bombing of training camps in Pakistan-held Kashmir. The lack of enough laser-guided bombs delayed the execution of the order and gave the United States and Britain a chance to douse passions. They ordered their eighty thousand citizens to leave India and Pakistan immediately, cooling Vajpayee's fervor. The nuclear-armed neighbors stepped back from a nuclear brink.

Chapter 17 covers the dealings of Congress prime minister Manmohan Singh from 2004 onward. He and Musharraf set up a back channel to reach an accord on Kashmir. Their personal envoys forged a plan that Musharraf outlined in December 2006. It envisaged "open borders" in Kashmir followed by a phased withdrawal of troops from both sides of the LoC. Since this did not mean changing the present borders, the plan received careful examination by the Indian cabinet. But before it could take a definite stand, Musharraf was forced to step down as army chief prior to being sworn in as a civilian president in November 2007. And in August

2008 he resigned as president to avoid being impeached by Parliament, which was dominated by anti-Musharraf parties. Once again the hopes of resolving the Kashmir conundrum were dashed. Three months later, a sixty-hour siege of luxury hotels in south Mumbai by Pakistani terrorists froze Delhi-Islamabad relations. The freeze lasted two-and-a-half years.

As if the decades-long Kashmir deadlock were not enough, the rivalry between Pakistan and India for dominant influence in Afghanistan intensified as the US-led NATO forces prepared to leave Afghanistan by December 2014. For Pakistani generals brought up on the doctrine of India as the number one enemy, the Indo-Afghan Strategic Partnership Agreement signed in October 2011 was a step toward their worst-case scenario materializing: a simultaneous attack on Pakistan in the east and the west by the Indo-Afghan alliance. This is the gist of Chapter 18.

In contrast to the opposite pulls of geopolitics, the cultures of Afghanistan, Pakistan, and North India—language, cuisine, dress, sports, and the performing arts—continue to have much in common. Bollywood movies and cricket remain popular on both sides of the Indo-Pakistan border. In the economic arena, as signatories of the South Asian Free Trade Area treaty, which specified the reduction of customs duty on all traded goods to zero by 2016 for the eight-member South Asian Association for Regional Cooperation, India and Pakistani started liberalizing mutual trade beginning in 2009. In 2013 they agreed on a nondiscriminatory market access protocol, which was equivalent to most-favored-nation status. Describing all this is the function of the penultimate chapter.

The concluding chapter provides a summary and conclusions.

The epilogue is not indexed.

A word about the changing exchange value of the Indian and Pakistani currencies: the exchange value of the Indian rupee fell from Rs 4.75 in 1947 to US$1 to Rs 60 to US$1 in 2014. The Pakistani rupee has depreciated much more.

My gratitude to Carl Bromley, the now former editorial director of Nation Books, goes beyond the customary thanks. He came up with the idea for a book on India-Pakistan relations. Familiar with my family and professional background, he considered me to be the right author to pen it. And he worked diligently with me to include in the final book proposal an optimum mix of engaging elements.

London
September 2014

Introduction

In March 2013 the air in East Asia was thick with the threat of Armageddon. In retaliation for North Korea's underground nuclear test in mid-February, the UN Security Council imposed further economic sanctions on Pyongyang. Its young, newly installed leader Kim Jong Un threatened to transform Seoul, the prosperous, bustling capital of South Korea with ten million residents, into a "sea of fire" and launch preemptive nuclear strikes on Washington. He declared that his country would no longer recognize the 1953 armistice that ended the war between it and UN forces. The United Nations retorted that the truce could not be abrogated unilaterally.

Yet nothing seemed to change on the ground. The practical outcome of that truce—the demilitarized zone (DMZ) running roughly along the Thirty-Eighth Parallel and divided equally by the military demarcation line—remained intact. So too did the infrastructure at Panmunjom, home of the Joint Security Area (JSA) near the western coast of the peninsula. There was no decrease in the number of busloads of day-trippers from Seoul, an hour's drive from the border through green fields, scrubby mountains, and army observation posts every few hundred yards.

The only danger that a tourist who wished to enter the JSA faced was to sign a voucher to take responsibility for "injury or death as a direct result of enemy action" before boarding a UN bus at Camp Bonifas, with a soldier as tour guide. The JSA has been the site of negotiations between the opposing parties inside the building constructed along the military demarcation line.

The high point for a tourist was to walk around the conference tables where the North Koreans and the UN Command (chiefly South Koreans and Americans) sit on opposite sides. Outside, business remained brisk at the fast food eateries, the amusement park, and souvenir shops selling child-sized military uniforms and DMZ-stamped T-shirts and hats.

The 160-mile-long and 2.5-mile-wide buffer between the two Koreas is hyped as the most heavily fortified and dangerous border in the world—even though it no longer is. That honor goes to the Line of Control (LoC) in Kashmir, the 460-mile-long UN-brokered cease-fire line of 1950 that demarcates the Indian and Pakistan controlled parts of that territory. In March 2000, during a trip to India to defuse tensions in the region, US president Bill Clinton called it "the most dangerous place in the world."[1] Both belligerents possess nuclear weapons and have the means to deliver them. The attempts by Pakistan to change the truce line in Kashmir have led to two wars: one major in 1985 and the other minor, in the Kargil region in 1999.

THE GLOBE'S MOST DANGEROUS PLACE

India started to fence the LoC in the mid-1990s but stopped because of shelling and gunfire from Pakistan, which has opposed any change to the status quo. India resumed the project in 2001 and finished it in September 2004. The end result was a formidable 375-mile-long barrier. Covering all of the 178-mile border in the Jammu region and 197 miles in Kashmir, it passes through dry land, green pastures and valleys, wooded hills, and rugged mountains.

The barrier is terribly intimidating. It consists of a double row of twelve-foot-high wire fencing. The space between the rows is filled with thousands of land mines. At some spots the fence is equipped with thermal imaging devices and motion sensors along with built-in alarm and lighting systems that alert troops of infiltrators from Pakistan-controlled Kashmir. The soldiers themselves are equipped with sensors, thermal imagers, and night vision devices. Only the areas of highest altitude—the 88-mile stretch of glacier running from Kargil at 10,764 feet to the Siachen Glacier at 18,875 feet—have been left unfenced. The total cost of fencing has been an astronomical Rs 1,620 million ($324 million)—$864,000 a mile.[2]

The fence is not strictly along the LoC. It stands about 150 yards to a mile or so away from it—inside Indian-controlled territory. This has created a no-man's-land. And because this area is often dotted with agricultural plots and hamlets, it has become a source of periodic killings of soldiers and civilians, leading to furious accusations and counteraccusations by Delhi and Islamabad.

In some areas, however, the fence cuts through farms or orchards. Such was the case with Touseef Bhat's seven-acre plot near Gurez in the scenic valley of the same name in Indian Kashmir's Bandipora district. "The fence is creating serious difficulties for us," Bhat told the journalist Athar Parvaiz. "Sometimes we have to walk several kilometers to a crossing point just to visit a neighbor who may only be a shouting distance away on the other side of the fence."[3]

Though the latest cease-fire agreement signed in November 2003 held, sporadic infiltration into the Gurez Valley from the Pakistan-administered territory continued despite fortification along the LoC. The bomb shelters built near schools and other public buildings in Gurez, a town of thirty-five thousand souls, testified to the time when artillery exchanges along the LoC were a common feature. For now what worried the residents of Gurez was the sustainability of farming and livestock breeding. "There may be no firing but cattle put out to graze in the area between the fence and the LoC wander off to the Pakistani side and are lost forever," Bhat's neighbor Rashid Lone told Parvaiz. Bhat agreed. "In July [2011], 85 heads of cattle, belonging to my village of Budap, vanished and they were worth at least 50,000 dollars," he said. "We cannot afford to bear such losses and have asked the authorities to help us recover the animals or compensate us."[4]

Consequently there are no day-trippers bussed to the LoC from Srinagar, the summer capital of Indian Kashmir, or Jammu, the winter capital. The nearest the most enterprising Indian journalist can get to this barrier on his own is to arrive at Uri, a town surrounded on three sides by high hills, about two miles from the LoC. Uri lies at the end of a taxi ride of twenty-one miles through green valleys and 8,200-foot-high mountains from Baramulla, thirty-five miles from Srinagar. On arrival he or she would find the settlement swarming with police and informers, since it is situated in an area bristling with separatist militants.

Four hundred thousand heavily armed soldiers and paratroopers are posted on the Indian side. Perpetually fearful of invasion from India, Pakistan has deployed two-thirds of its 610,000-strong army along the LoC. Repeated pleas by the administrations of US presidents George W. Bush and Barack Obama to Islamabad to bolster its troops in the badlands of the Afghan-Pakistan tribal region to help crush the Afghan Taliban by reducing its military deployment in Kashmir have received no response.

The statement by Pakistani president General Pervez Musharraf that "Kashmir runs in our blood" remains as valid today as it did when he made it in January 2002. At that time 700,000 Indian troops and 300,000 Pakistani soldiers faced one another across the LoC in a high state of alert that lasted a whole year.

The conflict in Kashmir between India and Pakistan poisoned relations between the two sovereign states within a few months of their inception in August 1947. The Pakistani government could not bear to see a Muslim-majority area in British India end up as part of Hindu-dominated India. At the core of this conflict, which has remained intractable for almost seven decades, lies the far longer history of unreconciled relations between Hindus and Muslims in the Indian subcontinent.

HISTORIC ROOTS OF DISCORD

Hinduism is polytheistic and centered around idol worship. Islam is monotheistic and forbids graven images. Abraham started with breaking up idols, and Muhammad did the same in Mecca. Hindus worship idols of gods and goddesses. They believe in reincarnation, with the eternal spirit taking different physical forms in an endless cycle of birth, death, and re-birth. Muslims believe that in their afterlife they will be judged by Allah on the Day of Judgment, known only to Allah. Caste is an integral part of Hinduism whereas it has no sanctification in Islam.

In the Indian subcontinent, the Hindu-Muslim antagonism is grounded in eight centuries of history. In 1192 Muhammad Ghori of Afghanistan's army, in a surprise attack before sunrise, defeated the formidable Rajput army of Hindu emperor Prithvi Raj near Delhi and established the Delhi Sultanate, which went on to cover most of north India. In 1526 it fell to a siege by Zahiruddin Muhammad Babur, then ruler of Kabul, who founded the Mughal dynasty. It gave way to the British Raj in 1807.

Unlike the previous foreign rulers of the subcontinent, the British, arriving by sea as fixed-term contracted employees of the trading East India Company, had an island homeland with a distinct identity to which they returned after their tour of duty. This was not the case with their Afghan and Mughal predecessors, who settled down in the conquered land and became an integral part of the indigenous society.

By 1807, Muslims were a quarter of the Indian population, most of them outcaste and lower-caste Hindu converts to Islam, with a sprinkling of the original Afghan and Mughal ruling elite settling at the top of society. In predominantly rural India, Muslims lived in hamlets outside the main villages and had their own wells. In towns and cities, Hindus and Muslims voluntarily lived in separate neighborhoods.

Social intercourse between the two communities was minimal, with intermarriage nonexistent. At the popular level the communal points of friction centered around Hindus' reverence of cows and Muslims' religiously sanctified loathing of pigs and their flesh. In Hindu kingdoms killing a cow was deemed a capital offense since the fourth century CE. To retaliate against Muslims' slaughtering of cows, die-hard Hindus resorted to desecrating a mosque by a stealth depositing of a pig's head or carcass at its entrance, or by playing music or musical instruments outside a mosque during prayers.

During the British Raj, the emerging apartheid between the ruling, white Christian minority and the large, subjugated Indian majority created widespread resentment against foreign imperialists among locals. This sentiment came to dominate the predominantly Hindu Indian National Congress (henceforth Congress Party) formed in 1885 in Mumbai with a modest demand that "the Government should be widened and that the people should have their proper and legitimate share in it."[5]

On the whole, having lost their empire to the British, the Muslim elite sulked, refusing to accept their dramatically diminished circumstances. Contrary was the case with upper-caste Hindus. In the past they had adjusted to the reality of alien rule, learning Persian, the court language of the Muslim dynasties for seven centuries, to administer their rule. With the advent of the British Raj, they switched to mastering English. As such, Hindus started to spawn an English-educated urban middle class. By contrast, Muslims remained divided between the extremes of illiterate peasantry and richly endowed aristocratic landlords.

A minority among the Muslim nobility adapted to the new reality. Prominent among them was Sir Syed Ahmed Khan (1817–1898). A highly educated, pro-British, richly bearded aristocrat, Sir Syed was a political thinker and an educationist who urged fellow Muslims to learn English. He founded the Muhammadan Anglo-Oriental College in Aligarh in 1875. He advised his coreligionists to stay away from the Congress Party and focused on expanding the Muhammadan Educational Conference.

He perceived the Congress Party's demand for a wider role for Indians in the government as the thin end of the wedge for the departure of the British from the subcontinent. "Now, suppose that the English community and the army were to leave India, taking with them all their cannons and their splendid weapons and all else, who then would be the rulers of India?" he asked in a speech in March 1888. "Is it possible that under these circumstances two nations—the Mohammedans and the Hindus—could sit on the same throne and remain equal in power? Most certainly not. It is necessary that one of them should conquer the other. To hope that both could remain equal is to desire the impossible and the inconceivable. . . . But until one nation has conquered the other and made it obedient, peace cannot reign in the land."[6]

Sir Syed's statement reflected the rising friction between the two communities, which he pointedly called "nations." At times these tensions escalated into violence. The first recorded communal riot occurred in the North Gujarat town of Godhra in 1854. Details of the episode are sketchy.[7] More is known about the communal riot in Bombay (later Mumbai) in August 1893. It erupted against the background of the rise of a militant cow protection movement—Gaorakshak Mandali—that many Muslims regarded as provocative and was launched in Bombay Presidency in late 1892. Muslim worshipers leaving the Juma Masjid, a striking mosque in South Bombay, after Friday prayers attacked a nearby temple on Hanuman Lane. In a predominantly illiterate society in a prebroadcasting era, wild rumors spread rapidly over the next two days. The army was drafted to restore control. All together seventy-five people lost their lives.[8]

In December 1906 the Muhammadan Educational Conference meeting in Dacca (later Dhaka) decided to transform itself into a political party, the All India Muslim League. Dominated by feudal lords with a sprinkling of religious scholars and educationalists, it elected Adamjee Pirbhoy as its president. He was followed by Sir Ali Imam and the twenty-three-year-old Sir Sultan Muhammad Shah—popularly known by his title of Agha Khan (or Aga Khan)—in successive years. The League was headquartered in Lucknow. Its primary goal was to promote loyalty to the British crown while advancing Muslims' political rights.

It demanded separate electorates for Muslims when the British government decided to introduce the concept of conferring the right to vote on Indians with the enforcement of the 1892 India Councils Act. It turned the hitherto fully nominated central and provincial legislative councils into partly elected chambers. Nominated municipal boards, chambers of commerce, landowner associations, and universities were authorized to submit lists of elected members from which the viceroy and provincial governors made a final selection of council members. These members, forming a minority, had the right to debate the budget but not vote on it. In popular terms it meant franchise for 2 percent of the adult population, about a third of literate Indians.

Since the League also wanted to promote understanding between Muslims and other Indians, it did not bar Muslim members of the Congress Party from its membership. It soon became a common practice for the League and the Congress Party to convene annual conferences in the same city and around the same time to enable Muslim delegates to attend both assemblies. Among those who did so in 1913 was Muhammad Ali Jinnah (1876–1948), an elegant but skeletal British-trained lawyer with an austere, tapering face—an Edwardian gentleman in hand-tailored suits and starched collars—who had joined the Congress Party seven years earlier.

Those sponsoring Jinnah's membership in the League declared that "loyalty to the Muslim League and the Muslim interest would in no way and at no time imply even the shadow of disloyalty to the national cause to which his life was dedicated."[9] Jinnah was elected to the League's council, where he came to play a leading role.

By then, however, the India Councils Act, amended in 1909, had incorporated the Muslim League's demand for separate Muslim electoral constituencies with reduced franchise qualifications. This concession was made because of the historical reluctance of upper-crust Muslims to discard Persian and learn English, resulting in their reduced socioeconomic standing vis-à-vis their Hindu counterparts. To qualify as voters, Hindus were required to have a minimum taxable income of Rs 30,000, whereas the requirement for Muslims was only Rs 3,000. On the education franchise, a Hindu had to be a university graduate of thirty years' standing, while the figure for a Muslim was only three years. Qualified Muslims were entitled to vote in the general constituencies as well.[10]

Until 1913 the Congress Party, led by lawyers and journalists, had limited itself to petitioning the British government in India, based in Delhi from that year onward (the earlier capital being Calcutta), for modest administrative-political reform. It had welcomed London's concession of letting a minority of the provincial and central legislative council members be elected on a franchise of a tiny 2 percent of the population. It and the Muslim League backed Britain and its allies in their war, which broke out in 1914, against Germany and Ottoman Turkey, whose sultan was also the caliph of Muslims worldwide. Almost

1,441,000 Indians volunteered to join the British Indian army, with 850,000 serving abroad.

They were shipped out from Bombay and Karachi, the main ports on the west coast, to fight in the Middle East and Western Europe. While Delhi was the center of the imperial power exercised by Britain, Bombay, the capital of Bombay Presidency, had emerged as the focal point for domestic politics in which lawyers played a vital role. And it was to this city that Jinnah returned after studying law in London in 1896, and not to Karachi, his birthplace.

Five years earlier, another lawyer, after having been called to the bar in London, arrived in Bombay. He shared with Jinnah Gujarati his mother tongue but not his religion. He was Mohandas Karamchand Gandhi. Jinnah and Gandhi would rise to become titanic public figures and dominate the country's political landscape for three decades.

I

The Modish Dresser
Meets the Mahatma

Muhammad Ali Jinnah was the only son of Jinnahbhai Poonja, an affluent, Gujarati-speaking Ismaili Muslim importer and exporter in Karachi, and Mithi Bai. Poonja had dealings with British trading companies, one of which was headed by Sir Frederick Leigh-Croft. The avuncular Sir Fredrick arranged a business apprenticeship in London for the sixteen-year-old Muhammad Ali. After a brief period of learning the basics of shipping, the young Poonja decided to study law. He qualified as a barrister in 1896 at the age of twenty. He clipped the suffix "bhai" (Gujarati: brother) from his father's name and made Jinnah his surname.

During his time in London, he became an acolyte of Dadabhai Naoroji, a luxuriantly bearded, Gujarati-speaking Parsi Indian businessman and politician who was elected a Liberal member of parliament from a north London constituency in 1892. Jinnah assisted him in his job as an MP and often attended House of Commons sessions.

On his return to India, Jinnah enrolled as an advocate in Bombay's High Court. He rented a room at the Apollo Hotel near the court but struggled to make a living. Recalling those days, he said, "For two or three years before I became a magistrate [in May 1900] I had a very bad time, and I used to go every other day to the Watson's Hotel down the road. It was a famous hotel in those days, and I used to take on to a game of billiards for a wager, and that is how I supplemented my otherwise meager resources."[1] To be appointed a Bombay Presidency magistrate at the age of twenty-four was a remarkable achievement for Jinnah. But he quit that job and returned to his legal career.

He came under the influence of Justice Badruddin Tyabji. Given Tyabji's background as a former Congress Party president, Jinnah came to view the organization with an approving eye. At the 1904 Congress convention, he met and worked with Professor Gopal Krishna Gokhale (1866–1915), a moderate figure in the party. A mustached, spectacled Hindu Brahmin sporting a flat, round hat, Gokhale won the party's presidency in 1905. As in the past, Muslim delegates were thin on the ground: only 20 out of 756, or about 4 percent.[2]

In 1906—when Jinnah's thriving legal practice enabled him to purchase a spacious bungalow in Bombay's upscale Malabar Hills—he attended the Congress Party session in Calcutta (later Kolkata). He acted as private secretary for the aging Naoroji, who, after his return to India, had been elected president of the Congress. In that role, Naoroji explicated the ideal of *swaraj* (Hindi: home rule) for Indians for the first time. As an opponent of separate electoral rolls and seats for Muslims, then being advocated by some Muslim leaders, Jinnah established himself as a noncommunal politician.

In 1909, however, the British government introduced separate Muslim constituencies with reduced franchise qualifications for voters than those for non-Muslim constituencies, classified as "general." Later that year Jinnah defeated Maulavi Rafiuddin, president of the Bombay Muslim League, to represent the Muslims of Bombay Presidency in the viceroy's Imperial Legislative Council. He thus demonstrated his popularity among Muslims while maintaining his opposition to separate Muslim electoral rolls. He attended the Congress session in 1910 but not the ones in the next two years.

However, he remained close to Gokhale. Together with Gokhale, as part of an Indian delegation, he sailed for London in April 1913 to press the case for self-rule for India. After his return home in October, he joined the All India Muslim League at its seventh session in Agra in December. "Jinnah had by now truly come into his own," writes the Indian politician-author Jaswant Singh in his book *Jinnah*. "At this juncture, not only was he taking steps to bring about unity between the League and the Congress, he was also striking a balance between the moderates and the extremists [within the Congress]. In politics now all factions gave him recognition."[3] Jinnah rightly saw himself taking up the legacy of Naoroji and Gokhale as a nationalist leader representing all major communities of the subcontinent.

A year earlier, Gokhale, described by Mohandas Karamchand Gandhi in his autobiography, *The Story of My Experiments with Truth*, as "the most perfect man in the [Indian] political field"[4] had been invited to the Union of South Africa to help invigorate the Indian settlers' protest against racist rules and laws. While there, Gokhale urged Gandhi to return to India to further the cause of home rule there.

Once South Africa had passed the Indian Relief Act in July 1914—abolishing the tax on former Indian indentured laborers and permitting free Indians to enter South Africa as part of the British Empire—Gandhi returned home. When World War I erupted in Europe the next month, he supported the British Empire against Germany and the Austro-Hungarian Empire, which were later to be joined by the Ottoman Empire. Also on Britain's side were the Congress Party, Jinnah, and the Muslim League.

Jinnah and Gokhale were the leading members of the group formed to welcome Gandhi and his unsmiling, diminutive, snub-nosed wife, Kasturbai, on their arrival in Bombay on January 9, 1915. Given his popularity, the local Gurjar Sabha, a Gujarati community council, invited Jinnah to host a garden reception for the Gandhis on the grounds of the spacious mansion of Mangaldas Girdhardas, a leading textile magnate, five days later.

THE CONDESCENDING GANDHI

Speaking in English, Jinnah welcomed Mohandas and Kasturbai Gandhi "not only on behalf of Bombay but of the whole of India." He said that the greatest problem facing them all was "to bring unanimity and cooperation between the two communities [of Hindus and Muslims] so that the demands of India [made on imperial Britain] may be made absolutely unanimously." He added, "Undoubtedly, he [Gandhi] would not only become a worthy ornament but also a real [political] worker whose equals there are very few."[5]

Gandhi replied in Gujarati. He said that in South Africa when anything was said about Gujaratis, it was understood to refer to the Hindu community only, and Parsis and Muhammadans were not thought to be part of it. He was therefore glad to find a Muhammadan a member of the Gurjar Sabha and the chair of the reception.[6]

Leaving aside his mention of the popular perception prevalent in South Africa, Gandhi conveniently overlooked a critical turn of events in his own life. It was a Muslim legal firm, Dada Abdulla & Company,

11

based in the North Gujarat town of Rajkot that had given him a year-long contract in early 1893 to work in their office in Durban, the capital of Britain's Colony of Natal.[7] In any case, to point out the religious minority status of the keynote speaker at an occasion brimming with promise and goodwill was in bad taste, to say the least. It did not augur well for a cordial relationship between him and Jinnah.

Unfortunately, Gokhale died suddenly a month later. His loss grieved Jinnah—"an ambassador of Hindu-Muslim unity" in the words of Gokhale—as much as it did Gandhi, who likened the departed leader to "the Ganges in whose refreshing, holy waters one longed to bathe."[8]

Unlike Jinnah, Gandhi, a novice on his arrival in Durban, had reinvented himself a few times during his twenty-one years in South Africa: a campaigner for Indian settlers' equality with British colonizers, an ally of the British Empire in the 1899–1902 Boer War, an associate of the Natal government's brutal quashing of the Zulu rebellion with an iron hand, the leader of the passive resistance movement against the Asiatic Registration Bill in Transvaal, a political lobbyist in London, the founder of a rural commune to train civil resistors, and the instigator of an Indian miners' strike.

Gandhi's transformation was captured by the way he dressed. In 1893 he arrived in Durban as an attorney, wearing a tight-fitting business suit with a tie around a winged collar and shining shoes. Two decades later, he appeared in a knee-length white shirt, dhoti, turban, and sandals as the leader of the coal miners' strike. In between, he acquired a flair for self-dramatization, a tactic that would serve him well in the struggle for Indian independence. Overall, his South African experiences furnished him with a successful campaigning template he would later deploy on a much larger scale in British India.

ATTORNEY GANDHI TURNS INTO A SATYAGRAHI

Born in 1869, Mohandas hailed from the trading caste. He was the last and fourth child of Karamchand Gandhi, chief minister of the small princely state of Porbandar within Bombay Presidency, and Putlibai. While still at school, the thirteen-year-old Mohandas was married off to Kasturbai Makhanji, an unlettered girl of the same age. He became a father two years later. But the infant died soon after birth. Mohandas scraped through the matriculation examination in 1888, the year when the couple's first healthy baby boy, Harilal, was born. Soon after, his elder brother, Laxmidas, sent Mohandas to London to study law.

A 1889 mug shot of Gandhi shows a young face with jug ears, big, pointed nose, full, sensuous mouth, and eyes dulled by apprehension, the overall impression being of a man without direction. He studied Indian law and jurisdiction. A strict vegetarian, he joined the Vegetarian Society, whose members included the Anglo-Irish playwright and political radical George Bernard Shaw. He introduced the young Gandhi to the works of Henry David Thoreau (1817–1862), a liberal American author and philosopher, and Count Leo Tolstoy (1828–1910), the eminent Russian writer-thinker who was also a vegetarian. Gandhi was called to the bar in June 1891.

On returning to India, he registered as an advocate at the Bombay High Court, five years before Jinnah did. Like Jinnah, he had to struggle to make ends meet. But unlike Jinnah, he soon gave up and left Bombay for Rajkot. There he made a modest living drafting petitions for litigants. That stopped when he ran afoul of a British officer. An offer of a paid job in the Durban office of a local legal firm came as a welcome relief for him.

In June 1893 while he was on his way to Pretoria by rail, a white man, boarding the train at the mountainous Pietermaritzburg station, objected to his presence in the first-class carriage. When he refused to move to the van at the end of the train, he and his luggage were thrown off the compartment. The station staff confiscated his luggage and overcoat. Shivering through the night in the waiting room, Gandhi resolved to stay on in the Colony of Natal beyond his yearlong contract and fight racial discrimination against Indians.[9]

A cofounder of the Natal Indian Congress in 1894, Gandhi was elected its secretary. This gave him an opportunity to build up the institution from the grassroots and in the process develop his organizational skills. Later he would deploy these on a far wider scale in his native land to broaden the base of the Congress Party.

During his visit to India in 1896 to bring his family to Durban, he addressed a meeting in Madras (now Chennai), where he railed against the Natal government for treating Indians as "beasts."[10] Yet he actively sided with the British Empire in its fight with the Dutch settlers in the Orange Free State and the Transvaal Republic in the Boer War: he raised the 1,100-strong Indian Ambulance Corps. The subsequent victory of the British Empire raised his social and professional status. His legal practice thrived to the extent that in 1903 he shifted his successful law firm to Johannesburg, capital of the province of Transvaal.

Despite his material prosperity an element of early asceticism remained part of his character. It came to the fore when he read the book *Unto This Last* by John Ruskin, a British essayist and art critic. That inspired him to live simply. In 1904 he bought a thousand-acre farm among large sugar cane estates near Phoenix, twelve miles north of Durban. Named the Phoenix Settlement, it became the head office of the weekly magazine *Indian Opinion*, founded a year earlier in Durban.

He continued to believe in the benevolence of Britain's imperial rule administered from London. When the Natal government declared martial law in February 1906 to curb a Zulu rebellion led by Bambatha kaMancinza against oppressive British rule, Gandhi urged the colonial government to recruit Indians as a reserve force. In his *Indian Opinion* column he argued that "the British Empire existed for the welfare of the world" and reaffirmed "a genuine sense of loyalty" to it.[11]

In essence, he wanted Indians to ingratiate themselves with the British Empire to win the same rights as white settlers and thus place themselves above the indigenous Africans. The government made a minor concession and let him command a platoon of twenty-one Indian volunteers as stretcher bearers and sanitary aides to treat wounded British soldiers. By the time the ferocious military expedition ended, some three thousand to four thousand Zulus lay dead. In stark contrast, the British lost only thirty-six men.[12]

Across the provincial border, in Transvaal, the government published the draft of the Asiatic Registration Bill in August 1906. It required all Asiatic people to register and carry a registration card, called a "pass," under pain of fine or imprisonment. Gandhi opposed the proposed legislation and urged fellow Indians not to register, but his efforts altered nothing.

The bill became law a year later. Gandhi refused to register and was jailed for two months in January 1908. In his talks with Gandhi, colonial secretary general Jan Smuts promised that if Indians registered voluntarily, he would repeal the law. Gandhi agreed to cooperate. He and other lawbreakers were released. Most Indians followed Gandhi's advice and registered. But Smuts reneged. The law remained on the statute books.

This was *the* pivotal turning point in Gandhi's political evolution. He decided to dramatize noncooperation with the unjust laws of the government in a nonviolent way. On August 16, 1908, some two thousand

Indians of different faiths gathered outside the Hamidiya Mosque in Johannesburg in a protest rally. Gandhi made a bonfire in a cauldron filled with burning paraffin and encouraged the protestors to throw their passes into the roaring flames. The fact that they did was a tribute to his organizational skills.

At the same time, Gandhi remained active at the Phoenix Settlement, which was run on a cooperative basis. There he and his associates in Natal decided to defy the Transvaal Immigration Restriction Act, which banned Indian immigration into Transvaal. Defiance had to be done passively, though. At the same time Gandhi rejected using the adjective "passive," since it resonated with the white settlers' image of "rice-eating" Indian immigrants as weaklings.

That led Gandhi to coin the term "satyagraha," which translates as "truth force" or "force of truth." Those who resorted to satyagraha were called "satyagrahis." What Gandhi did was to synthesize the Hindu concept of *dhama*[13]—squatting in front of a house or office to apply moral pressure on the occupants—with the concept of civil disobedience. Thus satyagraha combined nonviolent resistance against, and noncooperation with, unjust authority.

Each of the potential lawbreakers appeared peacefully at a Transvaal frontier post, courted arrest, and served a jail sentence. Gandhi did the same in October 1908. So he spent a month in prison. Here he reread Thoreau's essay "Civil Disobedience," written in 1849 as tensions over slavery and America's invasion of Mexico were stirring up controversy. Thoreau refused to pay taxes and was jailed. Of the 13,000 Indian settlers in Transvaal before the civil disobedience movement, almost half of them left the province. Of the remaining, at one point as many as 2,500 were behind bars.[14]

Gandhi continued to make a distinction between the nucleus of the British Empire in London and its colonies around the world, and took a benign view of the former. In the second half of 1909 he went to London to highlight the plight of Indian settlers in South Africa. He won the backing of many British liberal and enlightened imperialists and succeeded in getting the Transvaal's Asiatic Registration Act repealed.

Among his white liberal supporters in Transvaal, a rich German architect Hermann Kallenbach stood out, all the more because of his wrestler's physique, handlebar mustache, and pince-nez. In 1910 he purchased 1,100 acres of land at Lawley, twenty miles southwest of Johannesburg, and donated it to the resistors of the unjust laws of Transvaal. Gandhi named the settlement Tolstoy Farm. The idea was to use it as a base to train satyagrahis and their families to live simply in harmony with one another. In other words, it was to be an ashram for the acolytes of Gandhi and his nonviolent civil disobedience movement.

It was at Tolstoy Farm that Gandhi received Gokhale in October 1912. Surprisingly, the government of the two-year-old Union of South Africa, led by Louis Botha (prime minister) and Smuts (defense and interior minister), facilitated Gokhale's tour of the country. They promised him the repeal of the Transvaal Immigration Restriction Act and the £3 annual tax imposed by the Natal government on the freed indentured Indian laborers, who had started arriving from southern India beginning in 1860 to work in mines and on plantations. The tax was introduced to ensure that indentured laborers whose contracts had ended returned home.[15]

But nothing changed. Indeed, South Africa's Immigrant Regulation Act, enforced in August 1913, imposed further restrictions on former Indian indentured laborers wishing to settle in South Africa. Gandhi turned his attention to the tax required of the freed indentured laborers. This mattered particularly to the Indians working in coal mines.

WIELDING THE NONVIOLENT WEAPON AGAINST MINING MAGNATES

Responding to the call by Gandhi and his aides to strike, the Indian miners in Newcastle downed their tools in October 1913. They were joined by others. The strikers were peaceful. Gandhi led a procession of two thousand miners from Newcastle on foot across the Natal border into Transvaal to defy the immigration restriction law. This was a unique but highly effective way to raise popular consciousness.

Remarkably, these marchers, almost all of them Hindus from South India, shouted such religious slogans as *"Dwarakanath ki jai"* (Victory to Lord Krishna) and *"Ramchandra ki jai"* (Victory to Lord Rama). Many sang Hindu devotional songs.[16] Gandhi did or said nothing to cool their religious ardor. The protestors were arrested inside Transvaal, about seventy miles from their destination—Tolstoy Farm—and returned to Natal by train. But on November 11 Gandhi was sentenced to nine months in jail with hard labor.

Nevertheless, by the end of November, the number of strikers soared to sixteen thousand, affecting sixty-six workplaces. The government dispatched extra policemen from Johannesburg and Pretoria, the national capital, to break the strike. Confrontations ensued between them and the strikers. Six Indians were killed by police bullets.

In Delhi Viceroy Lord Hardinge demanded that the South African government appoint a commission of inquiry into the Indians' grievances. London pressured the Pretoria administration. It yielded and released Gandhi in December, and appointed a three-person commission.

In its March 1914 report the commission recommended the repeal of the £3 tax. Four months later the South African parliament passed the Indian Relief Act. It abrogated the £3 tax, cancelled all arrears, and allowed South Africa–born Indians unfettered access to the Cape Colony and free Indians the right to continue to enter South Africa.

Gandhi was basking in this glory as he sailed to Bombay via London. After setting up a makeshift ashram in Ahmedabad in 1915, and receiving the British Empire's Kaiser-i-Hind Gold Medal for his earlier ambulance services, he undertook study tours of the subcontinent.

GANDHI AND JINNAH ON DIVERGENT PATHS

Meanwhile, Jinnah was furthering the cause of Hindu-Muslim unity by nudging the Muslim League and the Congress Party to forge a common platform. The League held its annual conference at the same time—December 1915—and the same city, Bombay, as the Congress Party. Their leaders appointed separate committees to consult one another and produce a program for reforming the colonial government by London.

The result was a common platform adopted by the two parties at the time of their annual conferences in Lucknow in December 1916. Its main points were: "There shall be self-government in India. Muslims should be given one-third representation in the central government. There should be separate electorates for all the communities until a community comes up with the demand for joint electorates. All the elected members of provincial and central legislatures should be elected on the basis of adult franchise."[17]

Following his election as the League's president in December 1916, Jinnah declared, "The Muslim League stands abreast of the Indian National Congress and is ready to participate in any patriotic efforts for the advancement of the country as a whole."[18] He described himself as "a staunch Congressman" who had "no love for sectarian cries."[19]

He appealed to reluctant Congress Party officials to overcome genuine anxiety among Muslims at the prospect of adult suffrage. Forming only a quarter of the population, they feared being swamped by the 70 percent Hindu majority. To still their apprehension, he argued, Congress leaders should concede separate electorates and 33 percent share of power in the central government for Muslims. His proposal was adopted.

At the same time Jinnah led Bombay Presidency's Home Rule League, which demanded the self-governing status of a dominion for India within the empire, as was the case then with Australia, Canada, New Zealand, and South Africa.

In the summer of 1916, Jinnah was invited to vacation in the enchanting hill station of Darjeeling in Bengal at the summer retreat of his friend and client Sir Dinshaw Petit, an affluent Parsi textile magnate. There Jinnah fell in love with Rattanbai (aka Ruttie), the sixteen-year-old daughter of Sir Dinshaw. Fair-skinned, doe-eyed, with a full, fleshy mouth in an elliptical face, she was intelligent and mature beyond her years. She found Jinnah irresistible. But when he approached her father for his permission to marry her, he was rebuffed. Back in Bombay, though, defying her father's stricture to stay away from Jinnah, Rattanbai met him secretly. They decided to wait to marry until she was eighteen.

In politics, Jinnah faced opposition from several Muslim League leaders who were not reassured by the Congress Party conceding separate electoral rolls and enhanced power for Muslims. They were apprehensive that self-rule would lead to Muslims' oppression by Hindus and lack of jobs in government and the Hindu-dominated business world. "Fear not," retorted Jinnah in 1917. "This is a bogy put before you to scare you away from the cooperation and unity [with Hindus] which are essential to self-government."[20]

The December 1916 Congress session in Lucknow proved equally pivotal for Gandhi. He was approached by Pandit Raj Kumar Shukla, the representative of the tenant farmers of Champaran, an outlying district of North Bihar adjacent to Nepal. Shukla seconded the resolution placed before the conference that urged the government to appoint a committee to inquire into the strained relations between the indigo farmers and the European planters in North Bihar. Surprisingly, it was the first time that a Congress session had given a platform to a rural speaker with firsthand knowledge of the state of peasants, who were 80 percent of the population. (Earlier Gandhi had refused to propose the resolution because of his ignorance of the problem, committing himself only to undertaking a study visit later.)

In mid-April 1917, he met the secretary of the Planters' Association, the commissioner of the Tirhut Division (covering Champaran district), and the collector of Muzaffarpur. They told him that since an official inquiry had already started, his visit was unnecessary and he should leave. Disregarding the advice, he proceeded to the nearest town of Motihari[21] to tour the affected area.

The crisis was rooted in the Permanent Settlement Act of 1793 between the East India Company and local landlords in Bengal and Bihar. It invested the latter with permanent ownership of land. So when British planters started acquiring plots to grow sugarcane and indigo, the source of natural blue dye used in the textile industry, they became absolute owners. They rented land to local sharecroppers on the condition that they would grow indigo on 15 percent of the plot—called *teen-katha*, or 3/20, in Hindi—and hand over the crop as rent for the leased land. The Bengal Tenancy Act of 1885 (covering Bihar) codified this practice.

In the early twentieth century the introduction of a chemical substitute for blue dye made the market for indigo unprofitable. This had a devastating impact on the lives of a million tenant farmers and their families. The European planters in Champaran district urged them to abandon indigo crops and in return pay 75 percent more rent than before. Those who refused were beaten by the planters' militia, who harassed them further by confiscating their cattle. Many of them signed new contracts only to find that they could not afford to pay the increased rent. Tensions rose in 1912. Left with no legal recourse, sharecroppers rebelled in 1914 and again in mid-1916. Later in the year they dispatched Shukla, a learned Brahmin, to plead their case before the Congress convention.

Gandhi was no doubt conversant with the historical background as he mounted an elephant, along with two assistants who would serve as interpreters, at nine AM on April 16, 1917, in Motihari and went to interview some tenant farmers in the village of Jasaulipatti. The beast plodded along at the typical pace of a human adult. Around noon he was overtaken by a cyclist. The panting rider turned out to be a police subinspector in plainclothes. He told Gandhi that the collector D. Weston wanted to see him immediately. Gandhi got off the elephant and instructed his assistants to record the testimonies of sharecroppers.

He then boarded a bullock cart procured by the police officer. On their way back to Motihari, they were stopped by the deputy superintendent of police, who was riding in a car. He served Gandhi the collector's notice, ordering him to "leave by the next available train." Gandhi signed the receipt but scribbled on the back that he would not abide by it. He was summoned to court the following day. The news about his brush with officials spread fast.

A couple of hours before his appearance at the court of the district magistrate, W. B. Heycock, several thousand tenant farmers gathered around the place for the *darshan* (Hindi: sight) of the politician who was ready to face incarceration in order to improve their miserable lot.

Gandhi pleaded guilty. "I am fully conscious of the fact that a person, holding in the public life of India a position such as I do, has to be most careful in setting examples," he said. "I have disregarded the order served upon me not for want of respect for lawful authority, but in obedience to the higher law of our being, the voice of conscience."[22]

The magistrate announced a two-hour recess and agreed to release Gandhi on bail. Gandhi refused to furnish the bail, but he was freed nonetheless. When the court reassembled, Heycock said he would announce the verdict three days later. On April 21, following the order of the lieutenant governor of Bihar and Orissa, Sir Albert Gait, the case against Gandhi was withdrawn.

This was the first victory for civil disobedience in India. Gandhi's status was enhanced. The local people started to call him Bapu (Hindi: Father). He kept this struggle strictly economic, divorced from the political demand for self-rule, which could have been construed as treason by the government then empowered with the draconian Defense of India (Criminal Law Amendment) Act of 1915.

By the middle of June, Gandhi and his team, which included several Congress-affiliated lawyers, recorded the testimony of more than 8,000 tenant farmers inhabiting more than 2,800 villages—stories of intimidation and coercion by the British planters and their militia. By then Lieutenant Governor Sir Albert had accepted the suggestion of appointing the Champaran Agrarian Enquiry Committee, and Gandhi had agreed to serve on it. In August 1917 the committee adopted Gandhi's proposal to abolish the 3/20 system. In October, when the committee submitted its report, which favored the tenant farmers' case, the lieutenant governor accepted most of its recommendations. The landlords agreed to forego the rent rise and return a quarter of the increases already collected.[23]

This was a moment of glory for Gandhi.

GANDHI ASCENDANT

Gandhi had resorted to traveling in uncomfortable, overcrowded, third-class train compartments to furbish his image as "a man of the masses." He was riding high when he chaired the First Gujarat Political Conference in Godhra on November 3, 1917. He shared the dais with Jinnah. When Jinnah rose to speak in English, Gandhi interrupted him and asked Jinnah in Gujarati to speak in that language. Jinnah was miffed. He switched to Gujarati but never forgave Gandhi for the slight inflicted on him in public.[24]

For his part, Jinnah too was working tirelessly, albeit behind closed doors, for the welfare of the nation. The newly appointed secretary of state for India, Edwin Montagu, outlined to the British parliament in August 1917 the official policy of "increasing association of Indians in every branch of the administration and gradual development of self-government institutions with a view to a progressive realization of responsible government in India as an integral part of the British Empire."[25] What had driven the British cabinet to this position was the declaration in favor of self-determination for nations by US president Woodrow Wilson after the entry of America on the Allied side of the war four months earlier.

Montagu arrived in India in October to consult its leading figures. Jinnah was a member of the three deputations of leaders who met Montagu and Viceroy Lord Chelmsford, one of these deputations representing the Congress Party and the Muslim League jointly.[26] In these meetings the forty-one-year-old Jinnah cut a dashing figure. "Raven-haired with a mustache almost as full as [Field Marshall Herbert] Kitchener's and lean as a rapier, he sounded like [British actor] Ronald Coleman, dressed like Anthony Eden [a future British prime minister], and was adored by most women at first sight, and admired or envied by most men," noted his American biographer, Stanley Wolpert.[27] A successful barrister who craved luxury, he was formal, fastidious, and often imperious and frosty.

By contrast, the forty-eight-year old mustached Gandhi, dressed in a dowdy dhoti, long shirt, and turban, was accessible and relaxed, with a ready smile. He was used to a Spartan lifestyle at the ashram along the bank of Sabarmati River on the outskirts of Ahmedabad, which he built up properly after the outbreak of plague in the city in August 1917.

To discourage their workers from fleeing to their villages to escape the epidemic, the textile mill owners belonging to the Ahmedabad Mill Owners Association (AMOA), led by Ambalal Sarabhai, gave them an

80 percent "plague bonus." When the deadly disease subsided in January, AMOA announced its intention to rescind the bonus. Workers threatened a general strike. Sarabhai approached Gandhi to help prevent it. Gandhi advised arbitration. It failed. Following sporadic strikes, AMOA declared a lockout on February 22. Workers demanded a 50 percent hike in pay to compensate for high inflation caused by World War I. Gandhi suggested a 35 percent increase. AMOA offered 20 percent and lifted the lockout to employ all those prepared to accept its deal. But most workers opted for Gandhi's figure and leadership.

Gandhi called a total strike on March 12, 1918, but the response was patchy. As employees started to drift back to work, Gandhi undertook a fast on March 15 until all workers stayed out or there was a settlement. This was a novel tactic.

Each day Gandhi published a leaflet to explain his rationale. Stung by the workers' remarks that he was eating "sumptuous meals" while they were suffering "death agonies," he had decided to share their condition, he said. Next, he mentioned "the power of suffering voluntarily for spiritual purpose." He revealed that he had gleaned from "the ancient culture of India . . . a truth which, even if mastered by a few persons here at the moment, gives these few [people] a mastery over the world." On March 17, in his lecture at his ashram, he conceded that there was "a taint of coercion" in his fasting because AMOA feared that he would die of starvation. Later that day Sarabhai capitulated.[28]

The mill owners agreed to pay a 35 percent bonus on the first day, down to 20 percent on the next day, followed by 27.5 percent thereafter until the new arbitration committee came up with its award. Six months later it would prescribe 35 percent.

The greatness of Gandhi lay largely in his tactical innovation to achieve his objectives. As a trained lawyer, he was well placed to argue his case in legal terms. By setting alight registration cards en masse in Johannesburg he dramatized violation of an unjust law. By leading a long land march in South Africa he helped engender political consciousness at the popular level in a manner not seen before. His field research to gather evidence of the oppression of tenant peasants in North Bihar broke fresh ground. To this armory of tactics he added moral coercion through fasting. His wide array of tactics, all nonviolent, set him apart from Jinnah, who remained tied to deploying constitutional means in legislative chambers or meetings held behind closed doors.

In Ahmedabad, besides inadvertently providing Gandhi a new non-violent tactic of fasting—which he would deploy sixteen more times during the next thirty years—the latest episode gave him an urban, industrial base. It would lead to the formation of the twenty-thousand-strong Ahmedabad Textile Labor Association, which practiced moderate trade unionism compared to that advocated by the Communist Party's All India Trade Union Congress. At the same time Gandhi's traditionally cordial relations with textile mill owners and other industrialists enabled him to secure donations from them to fund the running of the Congress Party as it expanded its narrow base. Above all else, the events in Champaran and Ahmedabad gave Gandhi an unprecedented publicity through both the press and, in a 93 percent illiterate society, word of mouth. Other politicians, including Jinnah, envied the renown he had gained within a few years.

When the lieutenant governor of Bihar and Orissa kept his word by signing the Champaran Agrarian Law (Bihar and Orissa Act I of 1918) in March 1918, Gandhi felt vindicated. On April 27 he attended the viceroy's War Conference in Delhi and addressed it in Hindi. Two months later he toured Kaira District in Gujarat to urge young, able-bodied farmhands to enroll in the army and boost the empire's war effort.[29] He reassured women in religious terms: he told them that if their husbands died while performing their duty—dharma—the couples would be together again in their "next incarnation." He urged potential recruits to "fight unconditionally unto death [along] with the British." The skeptical villagers were largely unconvinced.[30]

Whereas Gandhi built up a mass following by getting involved in the economic struggles of peasants and workers, Jinnah's credentials as a nationalist were underscored by his performances as a member of the viceroy's Imperial Legislative Council (ILC) and president of Bombay Presidency's Home Rule League. In early 1918 Bombay Presidency's governor, Lord Willingdon, acknowledged Jinnah's political status when he included Jinnah in a list with Pandit Madan Mohan Malaviya, an eminent Congressman; Bal Gangadhar Tilak (jailed by the British for six years); and Annie Besant (interned in 1917), "who were among those extremists who had no feeling for their duty towards [the] Empire in a crisis."[31]

Jinnah wore this label as a badge of honor. Jinnah married Ruttie Dinshaw, a young nationalist to the core, in April 1918. On converting to Islam, she acquired the name of Maryam, and the wedding took place in South Court, Jinnah's palatial mansion in Bombay, on Mount Pleasant Road in upscale Malabar Hill.

A year later Jinnah vociferously criticized the report by Montagu and Viceroy Lord Chelmsford on reforming the administration of India by introducing diarchy: three of the seven members of the viceroy's executive council would be Indian but charged with such minor ministries as education, health, and agriculture.

Jinnah and other nationalist leaders had expected self-government for India after the Allied victory in November 1918. They had fully backed the British Empire in that armed conflict during which the draconian Defense of India (Criminal Law Amendment) Act, passed in March 1915, was set to remain in force six months after the war.

As the expiration date of this act neared, Viceroy Chelmsford proposed replacing it, indefinitely, with the Rowlatt Act—named after Sir Sidney Rowlatt, chair of the Committee on the Defense of India Act—empowering him to detain or expel any "suspected terrorist" without any charge or trial. While the Indian minority on the ILC rejected the bill, the British majority backed it. In protest, Jinnah resigned from the ILC.

When the Rowlatt Act came into force on March 10, 1919, the Congress Party accepted Gandhi's proposal for satyagraha on the issue by calling for a one-day general strike and the wearing of black armbands, on March 30. The black armband tactic proved very effective—even winning the support of pro-British Indians, when the rumor spread fast in the crowded bazaars that this gesture was in honor of the 62,000 Indian soldiers who were killed in the war. Gandhi later changed the protest date to April 6. But the general strike went ahead in Delhi. Strikers were shot dead by police, further increasing tensions in the capital and Punjab.

On April 6, Jinnah voiced his support for the strike at a rally in Bombay, thus invigorating the protest. Four days later two Congress leaders—a Hindu and a Muslim—were arrested at a rally in the Punjabi city of Amritsar under the Rowlatt Act and taken to an unknown detention area. Their detention sparked protests, which led to an orgy of arson and violence. It left five Europeans dead. Additional troops summoned by Punjab's jug-eared, thin-lipped lieutenant governor, Sir Michael Francis O'Dwyer, arrived in Amritsar under the command of the fifty-five-year-old brigadier general Reginald Dyer. Defying his age, he had retained his haughty looks. O'Dwyer's immediate ban on further assemblies was poorly communicated in the absence of nationwide radio broadcasting, which did not start in India until 1930.

On Sunday, April 13—coinciding with Baisakhi, a spring festival celebrated by Hindus and Sikhs—between five thousand and ten thousand unarmed protestors gathered in Jallianwala Bagh, a park enclosed by walls with only two gateways. After persuading Viceroy Chelmsford to declare martial law in Punjab, Dyer, leading ninety Indian and Nepalese soldiers, marched into the park.

Without warning, he ordered his men to open fire. Finding the troops blocking the larger exit, the terrorized people herded toward the narrower one, while others tried to climb the high walls to escape. By the time Dyer ordered a cease-fire ten minutes later, 1,650 rounds of ammunition had killed 379 (according to the official report, but unofficially 530) people and injured about 1,150. Dyer then withdrew his force. The following day there was more rioting and arson as Dyer advocated a strategy of "frightfulness" to quell disturbances. This episode won Dyer the moniker of the Butcher of Amritsar.[32]

The massacre outraged Indians of all political hues. Though poorly recreated, this episode marks one of the high points in the biopic *Gandhi*, directed by Richard Attenborough. "When the government takes up arms against its unarmed subjects, then it has forfeited its right to govern," declared Gandhi after the massacre. "It has ruled that it cannot rule in peace and justice. . . . Nothing less than the removal of the British and complete self-government could satisfy injured India. . . . [The Battle of] Plassey [in 1758] laid the foundation of the British Empire, Amritsar has shaken it."[33] He suspended the satyagraha on April 18.

In retrospect the massacre in Amritsar proved to be the beginning of the end of the British Raj in the subcontinent.

Congress officials held their annual convention in Amritsar; their Muslim League counterparts did the same. By the time these sessions were convened at the end of December, the British parliament had passed the Government of India Act 1919, which incorporated the diarchy system recommended by Montagu and Chelmsford. It involved restructuring the present single-chamber legislature into a bicameral one, with the upper house, called the Council of State, reviewing the bills passed by the Central Legislative Assembly. At the Congress session Jinnah seconded the resolution that described the 1919 Act as "inadequate, unsatisfactory and disappointing."[34] Gandhi argued against the resolution, but in vain.

At the Muslim League conference, Jinnah was elected president for three years. His place in the sun came at a time when Gandhi's reputation suffered a setback.

Amritsar was also the venue of the Second All India Khilafat Conference, a fledgling body of Muslims that had emerged after October 30, 1918. On that day the defeated Ottoman Sultan-Caliph Mehmet VI—a sad-eyed ruler with a walrus mustache and an astrakhan cap embossed with the Islamic crescent and star—signed an armistice with the victorious Allies. That posed a threat to the future of the caliphate—called khilafat, derivative of *khalifa*, meaning "successor" in Arabic and Urdu, in India—which had been based in Istanbul since 1517. The caliph was recognized as the religious leader of all Muslims in a world where those living in India formed his largest constituency.

2

Gandhi's Original Sin

Injecting Religion into Politics

The seed of the All India Khilafat Conference was planted at the meeting of fifteen thousand Muslims in Bombay in March 1919, when public outrage at the Rowlatt Act was running high. It established the Bombay Khilafat Committee, presided over by Muhammad Chotani, an affluent businessman, who was respectfully addressed as *Seth* (Hindi: merchant or banker) Chotani. It contacted the Muslim League Council. Together they decided to form a broad-based body since the League at the time had only 777 paid-up members, mostly lawyers and religious scholars, called ulema.[1]

What drove the Muslim elite to take this step was its historical perspective. It perceived the fall of the Ottoman Empire as analogous to the downfall of the Mughal Empire in 1807 at the hands of the British—albeit not so precipitately. The Ottomans were brought down by an alliance in which imperial Britain was preeminent. Among those who shared this view, Muhammad Ali Jauhar stood out.

THE ALI BROTHERS

Born in 1878 into an aristocratic family in the princely state of Rampur in the United Provinces—today's Uttar Pradesh—he graduated from Aligarh College and pursued further education at Oxford. Diverting from a study of law, which was then popular with Indians, he opted for history. On his return home he served as education director first in Rampur and then in the much larger princely state of Baroda. In 1911 he moved to Calcutta, then capital of British India, where he founded the weekly *Comrade*. He

27

was a gifted writer and poet with the pen name of Jauhar (Urdu: jewel). His Oxford education, superb mastery of English, and hand-tailored suits marked him as a man of distinction.

When British India's capital was moved to Delhi in 1913, he followed suit. There, assisted by his elder brother Shaukat Ali, he established the Urdu weekly *Hamdard* (Compassionate). With the outbreak of World War I in August 1914, he urged Ottoman Sultan-Caliph Mehmet VI to stay neutral. But when Ottoman Turkey declared war against the Allied Powers in November, he reaffirmed his loyalty to the British crown. At the same time, in a long article he outlined Turkey's grievances against Britain. That was enough to cause the closure of his journal by an official diktat. Later, because he and Shaukat Ali were seen as pro-Turkey, the government jailed them under the Defense of India Act 1915 in an obscure central Indian town, Chhindwara, and held them there until December 1919.

A close study of the Quran in Urdu by the imprisoned Jauhar turned him into a pious Muslim. The same happened to Shaukat Ali. Both of them grew beards and switched to wearing knee-length tunics and baggy pajamas, along with a tall, astrakhan cap. They became known as the Ali Brothers. Jauhar was sometimes invited to deliver the weekly sermon after Friday's congregational prayer at the local mosque. He proved an eloquent speaker with a sense of humor.

While in prison the Ali Brothers were allowed to maintain censored correspondence with friends and allies, and they read newspapers published under wartime censorship. They endorsed the Lucknow Pact of December 1916 between the Congress Party and the Muslim League. Earlier they had heard Ghandi's 1915 address to students in Calcutta, in which he had said, "Politics cannot be divorced from religion."[2] They saw in him a Hindu personage ready to blend religion with politics in order to attract a mass following.

They asked the government to let Gandhi visit them in prison, but in vain. On his part, after attending the viceroy's War Conference in Delhi in April 1918, Gandhi appealed to him to release the Ali Brothers. Lord Chelmsford refused. Gandhi continued to correspond with them in jail, and they supported his Rowlatt Act satyagraha in April 1919.

With the defeat of the Ottoman Empire, gloom descended on the Ali Brothers. Hailing the sultan-caliph as "the personal centre" of Islam, Jauhar warned Britain against reducing the sovereignty of the caliph, the warden of Islam's holiest shrines in Arabia, Palestine, and Iraq, or parceling out his empire, which, Jauhar believed would enfeeble the temporal power of Islam. His views were shared widely by many literate Muslims. This led to the convening of four hundred delegates in Lucknow in September 1919. They decided to set up the Khilafat Committee, with Chotani as its president and the imprisoned Shaukat Ali its secretary.

The Khilafat Committee declared October 17, 1919 (the first anniversary of the armistice signed by Turkey, according to the Islamic lunar calendar), Khilafat Day. It urged Muslims to fast and pray and observe a general strike on that day, and it appealed to Hindus to join them. Gandhi backed their call. Bazaars in major cities remained closed on that day. In Bombay Gandhi addressed a Muslim congregation after weekly prayers. In Delhi a meeting of fifty thousand was addressed by Muslim notables as well as Swami Shradhanand, leader of the Arya Samaj, a Hindu reformist group.[3]

Alarmed at this development, Jinnah advised Gandhi "not to encourage fanaticism of Muslim religious leaders and their followers."[4] Gandhi spurned his advice. The Khilafat Committee was so impressed by Gandhi's spirited advocacy of its cause that it invited him to preside over the First Khilafat Conference in Delhi on November 23–24. Hindu-Muslim unity was a recurring theme in the speeches at the assembly, and due sensitivity was shown to Hindus' opposition to the killing of cows. "The Muslims honor would be at stake if they forget the cooperation of the Hindus," said Maulana Abdul Bari. "I for my part will say that we should stop cow-killing, because we are children of the same soil."[5]

The conference urged Muslims to boycott official peace celebrations scheduled for December. It resolved that Muslims should withdraw cooperation from the government if the settlement with Turkey was unjust. The assessment of what the victorious Allies imposed on Turkey was to be made by a special committee. If it considered the settlement with Turkey unjust, then Muslims would boycott European goods. Gandhi was a staunch supporter of these resolutions.[6]

On the eve of the conference Jinnah had sent a goodwill telegram from Bombay to the conveners, in which he backed the cause of Turkey while lambasting the British Raj for committing atrocities in Punjab.[7] But he strongly disapproved of the adoption of such unconstitutional tactics as boycotting European goods.

The Second Khilafat Conference, convened at the end of December in Amritsar, was dominated by the freshly released Ali Brothers. Their long incarceration had given them the halo of martyrs and earned them the religious title of *maulana* (derived from *mawla*, Arabic: master or learned man). The delegates charged them with drafting the Khilafat Manifesto.

In January 1920, a delegation led by Muslim League president Mukhtar Ahmad Ansari met Viceroy Lord Chelmsford to press the British government not to deprive Sultan-Caliph Mehmet VI of his suzerainty over Muslim holy places. Gandhi was part of the delegation.[8]

Working closely with Gandhi, the Ali Brothers produced the Khilafat Manifesto two months later. It called on Britain not to diminish the status of the caliph and urged Indian Muslims to hold Britain accountable on the caliphate issue. The document also incorporated the concept of nonviolent noncooperation with the government as elaborated by Gandhi for the first time. Such a campaign would consist of ascending levels. Starting with the renunciation of government titles and honors, it would involve boycotting courts, British-supported educational institutions, local council elections, and foreign goods—rising to resignations from the civil service and then the police and military. The final step would be refusal to pay taxes. After issuing the manifesto, Jauhar sailed to Europe as leader of the Khilafat delegation to lobby for Turkey in Paris and London.

The Third Khilafat Conference on April 17 in Madras was chaired by Shaukat Ali. It adopted the Khilafat Manifesto.[9] Between then and early September, when the Special Session of Congress voted for noncooperation, several events helped Gandhi to consolidate his spiraling influence.

At the end of April, Gandhi condemned the resolution of the League of Nations' Supreme Council at its meeting in San Remo, Italy, to let Britain and France decide the nature of the mandates for the non-Turkish parts of the Ottoman Empire. He called for noncooperation to express Indian anger at the San Remo decision.

THE INTERNAL AND EXTERNAL TURNING POINTS

On May 15, 1920, the Allied Powers published the draft of the peace treaty with Ottoman Turkey, proposing the severance of all non-Turkish parts from the Ottoman Empire. Gandhi condemned the document. Domestically, what sharpened anti-British sentiment was the publication on May 28 of the report by an inquiry commission headed by Lord William Hunter: *Report of the Committee Appointed by the Government of India to Investigate the Disturbances in the Punjab, Etc.*

According to the report, there were five thousand to ten thousand people in the Jallianwala Bagh, none of them armed. Brigadier General Reginald Dyer posted twenty-five soldiers on each of the sides on a higher ground. When the firing started, the multitude rushed toward the side of the Bagh with the lowest wall, about five feet high. Dyer ordered his men to aim at that spot. In his own dispatch to the military superiors, he wrote, "*It was no longer a question of merely dispersing the crowd*, but one of sufficient moral effect not only on those who were present, but more especially throughout the Punjab" (emphasis in original).[10] The report criticized Dyer and condemned some aspects of the martial law administration but gave general approval to the martial law policy in Punjab. Gandhi immediately combined protest of the Hunter report with noncooperation with the government as advocated by Khilafat leaders.

However, Shaukat Ali calculated that if Muslims were to resign their civil service posts, these would be quickly filled by aspiring Hindus. He was therefore reluctant to start the noncooperation campaign without the active support of Hindu leaders. Here the intervention of Gandhi, as a leading Hindu, became critical.

Gandhi drew much of his nationalist inspiration from the traditional myths, beliefs, and symbols of Hinduism. As he once explained, "My bent is not political but religious. And I take part in politics because I feel there is no department of life that can be divorced from religion."[11]

In his book *Hind Swaraj*, written originally in Gujarati in 1909—and later translated by him into English with the same title, which means *Indian Home Rule*—he argued that India was one nation long before the British Raj. To support his thesis, he referred to "those far-seeing ancestors of ours who established Shevetbindu Rameshwar in the South, Juggernaut (aka Jagannath) in the South-East, and Haridwar in the North as places of pilgrimage," thus outlining the geographical reach of Vedic Hinduism.[12] These are exclusively Hindu holy sites. Gandhi made no mention of the ancient Buddhist pilgrimage places, much less the shrines of Muslim Sufi saints, scattered all over the subcontinent, some of which are frequented by both Muslims and Hindus. Their shared belief is that by praying at the shrine they will be blessed by the spirit of the departed holy man, who is capable of interceding on their behalf with the Almighty to resolve their worldly problems. (This practice was condemned by orthodox Muslims.)

It is worth recalling that the striking miners in Natal marching behind Gandhi had shouted, "*Dwarakanath ki jai* [Victory to Lord Krishna]," and "*Ramchandra ki jai* [Victory to Lord Rama]." Between the two lead-ing Hindu gods, Rama and Krishna, Gandhi preferred the story of Rama's life, captured in the Hindu epic *Ramayana*, rendered into Hindi by the seventeenth-century poet Tulsi Das. "I regard the *Ramayana* of Tulsi Das as the greatest book in all devotional literature," he asserted in 1919.[13] His fasting during the textile workers' strike in Ahmedabad in March 1918 had given him an aura of a Hindu saint. On the second day of that strike he referred to his gleaning from "the ancient culture of India," which rep-resented Vedic Hinduism before it reformed itself to meet the challenge of Buddhism.[14]

Gandhi's veneration for the cow was legendary. "Cow protection is the outward form of Hinduism," he declared. "I refuse to call anyone a Hindu if he is not willing to lay down his life in this cause. It is dearer to me than my very life."[15]

His lifestyle was saturated with religious practices and pieties. At his ashram near Ahmedabad listening to Hindu devotional songs, called *bhajans*, sung by his co-religionists was part of his morning prayer rou-tine. His saintliness and overt religiosity won him the moniker of Ma-hatma (Sanskrit: Great Soul). Though documentary evidence is lacking, it is widely attributed to Rabindranath Tagore, the eminent writer-philosopher-educationalist.[16] Tagore won the Nobel prize for literature in 1913 and was knighted two years later. A patriot, he would renounce his title in August 1920, responding to a boycott call by Gandhi. In their correspon-dence, Gandhi addressed him as Gurudev (Hindi: Godly Master), and Tagore returned the compliment by calling him Mahatma.

Gandhi's religious persona was reassuring to the leadership of the Khilafat movement, dominated as it was by the ulema. During the Cen-tral Khilafat Committee meeting on June 3, 1920, chaired by Shaukat Ali, Gandhi explained that under his sole guidance noncooperation, starting at a low level, would reach its apex of nonpayment of taxes in four to five months.

He asked to be put in charge of a special noncooperation committee, operating independently—he would be a virtual dictator.[17] Deeply im-pressed by the success he had achieved with this tactic in South Africa, the attendees agreed.

The equivocal Hunter report provided Gandhi a chance to sharpen his attack on the British Raj. "If we are worthy to call ourselves a nation we must refuse to uphold the government by withdrawing cooperation with it," he declared on June 9.[18] Two weeks later he called on Viceroy Lord

Chelmsford to get the humiliating peace terms for Turkey changed by August 1 or resign. He started blending the domestic issue of the continued unrest in Punjab with the demands of the Khilafat movement concerning Turkey, while stressing that the caliphate had priority. But the Allied powers' stance on Turkey remained unchanged.

On August 1, Gandhi inaugurated the noncooperation struggle by returning the three war medals he had been awarded between the Boer War and World War I.

When the Treaty of Sevres, a suburb of Paris, was signed by the Allied powers and Sultan-Caliph Mehmet VI on August 10, keeping the Ottoman dynasty but severing all of the empire's territories in the Arab world, Gandhi condemned it as "a staggering blow to the Indian Mussalmans."[19]

Gandhi and the Khilafat leaders then focused on the upcoming special session of the Congress Party in early September in Calcutta. To underscore their sincerity about forging Hindu-Muslim amity, Khilafat leaders appealed to Muslims to refrain from slaughtering cows for Bakri Eid (Urdu: Festival of Goat)—the Indian term used for Eid al Adha (Arabic: Festival of Sacrifice)—when it is customary to celebrate by killing a goat, sheep, or cow. Determined by the lunar calendar, the festival was due to fall a few days before the Congress convention.[20]

At the special session, Gandhi's resolution was opposed by such stalwarts as Annie Besant, former Congress president, Madan Mohan Malaviya, and Jinnah. Among the weighty arguments Gandhi mobilized was that the Central Khilafat Committee had already launched its noncooperation campaign, and how could the thirty-five-year-old Congress be seen lagging behind the newly born body? He defeated the opposition by 1,886 to 884 votes.

At the simultaneous extraordinary session of the Muslim League on September 7 in Calcutta, Jinnah condemned the Hunter report and Dyer. But his opposition to unconstitutional means remained intact. Though he and Gandhi were in the same nationalist column, they were poles apart on tactics.

During its five-day session in late December in Nagpur, at Gandhi's behest, Congress delegates changed the party's aim to attaining *swaraj* ("home rule") for the people of India by all legitimate and peaceful means. Gandhi forecast that the noncooperation struggle, if conducted nonviolently, would yield *swaraj* within a year. Jinnah struck a note of discord, saying there was no clarity about what *swaraj* meant in practice. "This [noncooperation] weapon will not destroy the British Empire," he predicted. "It is neither logical nor is it politically sound or wise, nor practically capable of being put into execution." He added that though he had no power to remove the cause of India having become Britain's colony, he warned fellow Indians of the dire consequences of such an extreme act as wholesale noncooperation.[21]

But, to his chagrin, even the Muslim League did not agree with his views. At the simultaneous session of the League in Nagpur chaired by its president, Ansari, it also decided to support noncooperation. Its other equally weighty resolution changed its aim to achieving self-rule. The banners at the convention summed up the League's updated ideology: "Be true to your religion" and "Liberty is man's birthright."[22]

Jinnah lost but did not give up. In a letter to Gandhi, he argued that this kind of unconstitutional program appealed only to the illiterate and inexperienced youth and that it was bound to lead to disaster.[23]

GANDHIAN NONCOOPERATION UNLEASHED

Urged by Gandhi, Congress leaders in Nagpur opened party membership to all Indians for a nominal annual subscription of a quarter rupee (equivalent at the time to a quarter British pence or four American cents). They also adopted a new constitution drafted by Gandhi. It set up a hierarchy of committees from the top—the Congress Working Committee—down to the village level, thus turning their amorphous movement into a disciplined organization.

In April 1921 Gandhi launched a campaign to enroll ten million Indians of all classes as Congress members and raise a national fund of 10 million rupees (£1 million) to advance the noncooperation struggle. His cordial relations with Rajasthani finance and industrial capitalists in Calcutta and textile magnates in Ahmedabad helped to shore up the party's coffers.

These efforts led to a vastly enlarged constituency ready to express their feelings against the British Raj in dramatic ways. While Congress officials' withdrawal of their lucrative law practices made newspaper headlines, what caught the popular imagination among urban Indians was the boycott of foreign—primarily British—goods.

Accompanied by Jauhar, Gandhi undertook a six-month-long, nationwide tour by train, surviving on a daily diet of a few slices of toast, grapes, and goat's milk. He stopped at various places to urge his audience to shun foreign clothing and footwear. If they signaled agreement through applause, he urged them to strip off and make a pile of the discarded apparel and shoes. Then, in a repeat of the gesture he first made in Johannesburg on August 16, 1908, he would set the heap alight. He called on the audience to wear homespun clothes to help the *swadeshi* (Hindi: of one's own country) movement. The public burning of foreign textiles extended to unsold stocks of local drapers. As a teetotaler, he preached temperance, which went down very well with Muslim leaders, since Islam forbids consumption of alcohol.

Ad hoc local committees sprung up. Volunteers were deployed to enforce the boycott of courts and British-supported educational institutions. Protestors skirmished with the police. This couldn't have come at a worse time for the British. The victorious Allied powers and their colonies after World War I were experiencing a severe economic downturn—with deflation reaching 15 percent in Britain in 1922. Soon the Congress Party was emboldened with its own volunteer corps, dressed in white homespun uniforms, and the Khilafat movement had one as well.

The newly arrived viceroy, Lord Reading (aka Rufus Daniel Isaacs, First Marquess of Reading), a former chief justice of England and a practicing Jew, was ill-prepared to tackle the turmoil. So for the first half of 1921 he did nothing. Then, to test the waters, he arrested the Ali Brothers for making seditious speeches. The court sentenced them to two years in jail. The subsequent protest was mild, encouraging Reading to focus on suppressing the Khilafat movement.

Gandhi protested. In the September 19, 1921, issue of the weekly *Young India*, he argued, "I have no hesitation in saying that it is sinful for anyone, either soldier or civilian, to serve this government. . . . Sedition has become the creed of Congress. . . . Non-cooperation, though a religious and strictly moral movement, deliberately aims at the overthrow of the government and is therefore legally seditious."[24] In other words, if the Ali Brothers had been seditious, so had been the many thousands who had participated in the noncooperation campaign.

He underscored his alliance with the Ali Brothers in another *Young India* article on October 20: "I claim that with us both the Khilafat is the central fact, with Maulana Muhammad Ali because it is his religion, with me because, in laying down my life for the Khilafat, I ensure the safety of the cow from the Mussalman's knife, that is my religion."[25]

In London, the government decided in July 1921 to send the twenty-six-year-old, handsome Prince of Wales (later King Edward VIII) on a tour of India to let the people express their loyalty to the empire by welcoming him with unbounded enthusiasm and reverence. The viceroy continued to suppress protest. By early November, more than ten thousand Indians, mainly part of the Khilafat movement, were in prison.

On his arrival in Bombay on November 17, the prince was greeted with strikes, rioting, and arson. To restore order during four days of turbulence, police used live ammunition, killing fifty-three people. There were shutdowns in all major cities. In Calcutta, the uniformed members of the Congress and Khilafat volunteer forces took charge of the city, ensuring a total, violence-free strike. At night Calcutta fell into self-imposed darkness—it became the "city of the dead" as described by the British writer Rudyard Kipling.[26]

In early December Jinnah interceded with the viceroy to find a solution to the deteriorating situation. The viceroy expressed his willingness, but Gandhi demanded the release of all prisoners associated with the Khilafat movement as a precondition. The viceroy refused.[27] Indeed, he went on to outlaw the recruiting and organizing of Congress and Khilafat volunteers and the assembly of more than three persons in cities. Defiance of these bans doubled the number of political prisoners to twenty thousand.

FIGHT TO THE FINISH—SUSPENDED

"Lord Reading must understand that the Non-co-operators are at war with the Government," said Gandhi in a manifesto he published in *Young India* on December 21. "We want to overthrow the Government and compel its submission to the people's will. We shall have to stagger humanity, even as South Africa and Ireland, with this exception—we will rather spill our own blood, not that of our opponents. This is a fight to the finish."[28]

The Congress session on December 27–28 in Ahmedabad, presided over by Hakim Ajmal Khan, was like no other. Chairs and tables gave way to carpets on the ground of a huge tent, with most delegates dressed in homespun cotton and donning white, folded-cloth caps, called "Gandhi caps." Sartorially, Jinnah and Gandhi were poles apart. Jinnah appeared in his usual three-piece suit with a stiff collar and a silk tie, his watch firmly in his vest, chain-smoking his fifty Craven-A cigarettes a day. In his continuing drive for a Spartan life, Gandhi had recently discarded his shirt, dhoti, and white cap for a homespun loincloth and a shawl.

Semiclad Gandhi introduced a resolution calling for "aggressive civil disobedience to all Government laws and institutions; for non-violence; for the continuance of public meetings throughout India despite the Government prohibition, and for all Indians to offer themselves peacefully for arrest by joining the [Congress] Volunteer Corps." After much debate, it was passed, with only 10 out of 4,728 delegates dissenting.[29] The conference named Gandhi as the sole executive of the civil disobedience movement.

The most prominent among the dissenters was Jinnah. His speech was interrupted by cries of "Shame, shame" from the audience. When he referred to "Mister Gandhi," many delegates shouted "Mahatma Gandhi."[30] But he stood his ground then—and thereafter, never veering from his "Mr. Gandhi" protocol, as did all British officials. For the moment, though, crestfallen, he left Nagpur on the next train, accompanied by his young wife, Ruttie (Maryam), who had become the mother of their daughter, Dinah, two years earlier. This was to be his last Congress session. In his undeclared competition with Gandhi, he lost by a humiliating margin.

Gandhi chose the Bardoli district, 150 miles north of Bombay in Gujarat, as a testing ground for his civil disobedience movement. On February 1 he announced that he would initiate a refusal to pay taxes in this overwhelmingly rural district. Land revenue was the financial lifeline of the British Raj in the subcontinent's predominantly agrarian society.

A week later the news reached him of a violent episode in the small town of Chauri Chaura in United Provinces, eight hundred miles from Bardoli, on February 5. A long column of marchers protesting rising food prices had passed without incident when some stragglers were hit by armed policemen. When they shouted for help, the protestors turned around to confront the cops. The lawmen fired, killing three men, and then rushed to the police station when their ammunition ran out. There they barricaded themselves. The infuriated mob set the building ablaze. When the terrified twenty-one policemen and their head constable emerged to escape incineration, they were captured and hacked to pieces; and their bodies were fed to the raging flames. Later, of the 225 accused protestors, 72 would be found guilty, with 25 of them hanged.[31]

On hearing the news, Gandhi was horrified. "Suppose . . . the Government had abdicated in favor of the victors of Bardoli, who would control the unruly elements that must be expected to perpetrate inhumanity upon due provocation?" he asked. He said he was unsure he could. He suspended the civil disobedience campaign in Bardoli. And as the sole authorized executive of the noncooperation campaign, he forbade defiance of the government anywhere in India.

Among those who were flabbergasted by his decision and questioned its wisdom were not only the imprisoned Ali Brothers but some of the members of the Congress Working Committee, including Motilal Nehru, former president of the Congress Party and a fabulously successful barrister in Allahabad, United Provinces, whose only son was Jawaharlal. It would later emerge that Viceroy Lord Reading had sent a despairing report to London. "The lower classes in towns have been seriously affected by the non-cooperation movement," he wrote to Edwin Montagu, secretary of state for India, in early 1922. "In certain areas, the peasantry has been affected. . . . The Muhammadan population throughout the country is embittered and sullen."[32]

Responding to the criticism at home, Gandhi said, "The drastic reversal of practically the whole of the aggressive program may be politically unsound and unwise, but there is no doubt it is religiously sound."[33] When push came to shove, Gandhi invoked Hinduism. Who was there to judge whether or not his decision was "religiously sound"? It was all subjective, the judgment resting solely with him. As he once remarked, "Those who say that religion has nothing to do with politics do not know what religion means."[34] In any case, a quarter century later, his injection of religion into politics would lead to undermining the unity of the Indian subcontinent.

Undoubtedly, at the core of Gandhi's faith was orthodox Hinduism, with its prohibition on beef and the killing of cows as an integral part of daily life. His view was aptly summed up by the remark "I yield to none in my reverence for the cow."[35] Like all pious Hindus, he aimed to achieve *moksha* (Sanskrit: liberation) from the endless cycle of birth, death, and rebirth, thus ending the suffering inherent in this cycle. "I am impatient to realize myself, to attain *moksha* in this very existence," he wrote in *Young India* in 1924. "My national service is part of my training for freeing my soul from the bondage of flesh. Thus considered, my service may be regarded as purely selfish. I have no desire for the perishable kingdom of earth. I am striving for the Kingdom of Heaven, which is *moksha*."[36] Elsewhere he said that the path toward moksha was "crucifixion of the flesh," without which it was impossible to "see God face to face" and become one with him. But if such perfection could be attained, the divine would walk on earth, for "there is no point in trying to know the difference between a perfect man and God." Then there would be no limit to his command of his countrymen: "When I am a perfect being, I have simply to say the word and the nation will listen."[37] Around this core of Hinduism was wrapped a layer of Jainism, an offshoot of Hinduism, with its stress on nonviolence, or the nonhurting of any life form.

Following his abandoning of the civil disobedience program, Gandhi undertook a five-day fast of penance as part of his periodic crucifixion of the flesh. All this reinforced his saintly image as a mahatma among the illiterate and deeply religious masses.

There was, however, no letup in his campaign against the British Raj. "How can there be any compromise whilst the British lion continues to shake its gory claws in our face?" he asked. "The rice-eating, puny millions of Indians seem to have resolved upon achieving their own destiny without further tutelage and without arms. . . . The fight that was commenced in 1920 is a fight to the finish."[38]

This article was one of three judged to be seditious, the earlier ones having appeared on September 19 and December 21 of the previous year in *Young India*. Gandhi was arrested on March 10, 1922, found guilty of sedition, and sentenced to six years in prison. As a result of his unexpected surgery for acute appendicitis, he would be freed in February 1924.

During his absence from the political stage, the landscape changed radically.

RETREAT AND REACTION

The shattered hopes for self-government within a year and the abrupt ending of the civil disobedience movement led to disappointment and frustration among the leaders and the led. There was split among Congress dignitaries, with several of them abandoning noncooperation and deciding to participate in elections to be held under the Government of India Act of 1919.

Some at the top who had disagreed with Gandhi's radical agenda started to drift away from the Congress Party. Among them was Madan Mohan Malaviya, who had been the party's president twice. He transferred his loyalty to the All India Hindu Mahasabha (Hindi: Grand Council), a communal organization founded in 1914 as a counterforce to the All India Muslim League. Addressing the Hindu Mahasabha's annual conference in late December 1922, Malaviya detailed the grievances of Hindus. He referred to the atrocities visited on them by Mopila Muslim peasants in the southern Malabar region (now called Kerala) since August 1921.

In the communal rioting in the Punjabi city of Multan in September 1922, Hindus had witnessed the desecration of their temples by Muslim hooligans, he noted. There were similar instances in Amritsar.[39]

On their part, the leaders of the Arya Samaj, a Hindu social reform movement founded originally in 1875 to purge contemporary Hinduism of the caste system and idolatry, started the *Shuddhi* (Sanskrit: purification) movement to return converted Indian Muslims to Hinduism. Some Muslim notables were upset by this effort. Justifying the Shuddhi campaign, Malaviya claimed that during the past year one hundred thousand Hindus had been converted to Islam in Gujarat, an alarming phenomenon. "If when now we are badly treated with a numerical strength of 22 crores [220 million out of 300 million Indians], what would be our condition in future with a much reduced Hindu population if we allow this rate of conversion from Hinduism and do not allow re-conversion into Hinduism?"[40]

Relations between Hindus and Muslims were deteriorating. There was a major outbreak of Hindu-Muslim violence in Calcutta in 1923. To reverse the trend, Congress delegates honored Maulana Muhammad Ali Jauhar by electing him the party's president at their 1923 session within months of his second release from jail. He became the sixth Muslim president of the organization in its thirty-eight-year history. (Five years earlier, when he was still imprisoned, he had been elected president of the Muslim League.)

Jinnah kept well clear of the noncooperation and civil disobedience campaigns. In April 1923 he resigned formally from the Congress Party. In September he was elected a Muslim member representing Bombay in the newly established Central Legislative Assembly, the successor to the old Imperial Legislative Council. In the chamber he continued to press his demand for "a fully responsible government," first promised by Edwin Montagu in 1917.

Gandhi had hardly recuperated fully from his debilitating surgery after his release from jail when he and Khilafat leaders suffered a major political setback. On March 3, 1924, at the behest of the Turkish president, General Mustafa Kemal Ataturk, the Grand National Assembly in Ankara deposed Caliph Abdul Majid and abolished the 1,292-year-old office of the caliph. With that, both planks of Gandhi's noncooperation campaign collapsed.

To Jinnah, a secular public figure, the fate of the caliphate mattered little, if at all. Indeed, he had watched with deepening unease the rising influence of Muslim preachers—bearing the title of *maulavi* (another derivative of *mawla*, Arabic: master or learned man)—in the community on the issue of the caliph and his continued control over Islam's prime holy shrines in Mecca and Medina. With the abolition of the caliphate, Jinnah's stature in the Muslim League rose. Its delegates elected him the party's president in 1924 for a three-year term.

As someone who believed that politics should be the privilege only of the highly educated, he deplored the way Gandhi had opened it up to semiliterate and illiterate agitators. It was this phenomenon that, in his view, had led to the rising tensions between Muslims and Hindus.

On his part, Gandhi tried to reverse this worrying trend. For weeks he listened to both sides and made independent inquiries. The end result was his article "Hindu-Muslim Tension: Its Cause and Cure" in *Young India* on May 29, 1924. Its extraordinary length of six thousand words could not mask its flaws. It summarized the common perceptions of Hindus about Muslims, and vice versa. It examined a few cases of communal rioting. It castigated each community for its seemingly irrational behavior. He recycled his earlier argument that "we [Hindus] say nothing about the slaughter [of cows] that daily takes place on behalf of Englishmen [living in India]. Our anger becomes red hot when a Muslim slaughters a cow. . . . [But] the cows find their necks under the butcher's knife because Hindus sell them."[41] What it did not do was to provide an in-depth analysis of the problem in terms of history, sociology, and economics. In the absence of a fair grasp of these disciplines, the task was beyond his intellectual powers.

As for the cure for this centuries-old malady, he concluded that Hindu-Muslim unity was possible because "it is so natural, so necessary for both, and because I believe in human nature."[42] This circular argument was in essence a cop-out.

Unsurprisingly, his overlong article in English had no impact on the situation on the ground. Periodic rioting continued. But the one that stood out occurred in the town of Kohat (population, forty-four thousand) in North-West Frontier Province (later Khyber Pakhtunkhwa) in September 1924.

The local branch of the Sanatan Dharma Sabha (Sanskrit: Eternal Law Council), a Hindu revivalist organization like the Arya Samaj,[43] published a pamphlet containing a scurrilous poem about Islam purportedly as a riposte to an anti-Hindu poem printed earlier in a Muslim news sheet. This infuriated Muslims, who were 92 percent of the local population. They were not satisfied by the apologies offered by the local Hindu leaders. A three-day rampage, September 9–11, with looting, arson, and violence, left 155 Hindus dead. The authorities evacuated 3,500 Hindus to the town's military cantonment area for their safety.[44]

Fifty-four-year-old Gandhi decided to act in his own peculiar way. In order to "reform" those who loved him, he would fast. This was his attempt to reach out to the belligerents' hearts so that they could share his feelings and react the way he did. On September 17 he announced a twenty-one-day fast in the house of Muhammad Ali Jauhar in Delhi. He was attended by two Muslim doctors. This would show Hindus that their saintly politician trusted Muslims with his life, and that the world would see Mohandas and Muhammad as bosom friends.

On October 8 Gandhi broke his fast with a Muslim preacher reciting the opening verses of the Quran, followed by the singing of the hymn "When I survey the wondrous Cross," and ending with the Hindu hymn, "Raghupati Raghav Raja Ram/ Patita Pavan Sitaram" ("Chief of Raghu's house, King Rama/Uplifter of the fallen, Sita and Rama").[45] It was all very moving and widely publicized. But it made little difference at the popular level.

Gandhi's hunger strike was altogether different from what he had done in Ahmedabad in March 1918. The textile workers' strike was a local issue. The mill owners were a small, cohesive group, apprehensive of Gandhi dying. In stark contrast, the Hindu-Muslim issue existed on a national scale and concerned vast, amorphous social entities even if only their urban members were taken into account. The intercommunal misperceptions and prejudices that had grown over centuries could not be dissipated by an ascetic politician voluntarily abstaining from food.

In late December 1924 in Belgaum, the day after the end of the Congress session he presided over, Gandhi attended the cow protection conference. It decided to found an All-India Cow Protection Organization. His strategy was to persuade Muslims to refrain from killing cows and eating beef voluntarily. "Mussalmans claim that Islam permits them to kill the cow," he wrote in the *Young India* on January 29, 1925. "To make a Mussalman, therefore, to abstain from cow-killing under compulsion would amount in my opinion to converting him to Hinduism by force."[46]

On a contemporary issue such as the rioting in Kohat, Gandhi was unable to reconcile his assessment with Shaukat Ali's. Their joint visit to Kohat to collect evidence had to be scrapped when they were barred from entering the town by the viceroy. They decided to conduct their hearings in Rawalpindi. They ended up viewing the virulent episode from different perspectives. In January 1925, Shaukat Ali declared that arson and the concomitant shootings were accidental, and that there was no preplanned jihad against Hindus. Gandhi, then serving as the Congress Party's president, stated that the Muslim fury was so intense on September 10 that if Hindus had not been evacuated en masse, many more would have been butchered.[47]

GANDHI-JINNAH—PARTING OF WAYS

A disheartened Gandhi now channeled some of his time and energy into a campaign to end untouchability practiced by caste Hindus in their treatment of outcastes. At the same time, to bolster support for *swaraj*, he resorted to presenting its realization in religious terms. He argued that the end of the British Raj would lead to the onset of Ram Raj, the golden age of ancient India, when justice and equity prevailed in a realm ruled by Lord Rama. This scenario mesmerized particularly the unlettered Hindu masses in villages but left Muslims cold and alienated. They could not relate to the Hindu god-king Rama and his kingdom, which supposedly existed around 700 to 300 BCE—two millennia before the founding of Islam.

On his part, Jinnah remained an active participant in the 145-member Central Legislative Assembly. He was elected to the assembly's committee charged with exploring the possibility of establishing a military defense academy in India. In that capacity, he spent several months touring major European countries and North America. Among those who accompanied the committee members during their visit to Sandhurst Military College in Britain was Captain Douglas Gracey—later Sir General Douglas Gracey, commander in chief of the Pakistani Army. Recalling Jinnah's arrogant behavior toward the British officers appearing before the committee, Gracey said, "I had to protest and point out that the officers were giving evidence voluntarily . . . and that they had the right to be treated with courtesy. . . . Once Jinnah was challenged, he became reasonable, and he would never bear malice afterwards."[48]

Despite the leadership Jinnah provided the Muslim League, its membership in 1926 shrank to 1,330.[49] That made him immerse himself further into politics at the cost of neglecting Ruttie. They became estranged.

In November 1927 Lord Birkenhead, secretary of state for India, appointed a seven-member commission of MPs, headed by John Simon, to recommend a revision of the 1919 Government of India Act. The Congress session in December decided to boycott the Simon Commission because it lacked any representatives from India. Guided by Jinnah, the Muslim League's Council followed suit but by a narrow majority, which caused a split in the party. Lord Birkenhead challenged Indian politicians to draft a constitution that would be accepted by the leaders of various communities.

High Congress officials took up the challenge. They invited all non-Congress leaders to an All Parties Conference in Delhi in February 1928. At the second such gathering in May, a committee of ten members was formed to outline broad principles of the constitution. It was chaired by Motilal Nehru, an eminent Congressman. Its nine members included two Muslims—Sir Ali Imam, former Muslim League president, and Shuaib Qureshi—and one Sikh, Mangal Singh. Its unanimously agreed-on draft, called the Nehru Report, was published on August 10. The third All Parties Conference in Lucknow at the end of the month endorsed it.

The salient features of the Nehru Report were as follows. India should be granted the status of a dominion within the British Empire with a federal form of government in which residual powers—that is, the powers not assigned specifically to the center or the provinces—would be vested with the center; Muslims should be given one-quarter representation in the Central Legislature commensurate with their proportion in the population; there should be no separate electorate for any community, but reservation for minority seats could be allowed in the provinces where minorities totaled at least 10 percent; and the official language should be Hindustani, written in Devanagari or Urdu script or in any of the other six major scripts.

The Nehru Report's elimination of separate electorates was rejected by Jauhar, who quit the Congress Party and joined the Muslim League. In late December 1928, two months after his return from a trip to Europe, Jinnah went to Calcutta on the eve of the Congress session to lobby an amendment to the Nehru Report. "Majorities are apt to be oppressive and tyrannical, and minorities always dread and fear that their interest and rights, unless clearly safeguarded by statutory provisions, would suffer," he said. (He could have referred to the way majority-caste Hindus had oppressed the minority Untouchables for centuries.) He warned that the alternative to a settlement might be "revolution and civil war."[50] His plea fell on stony ground. At most, Congress leaders were prepared to raise the Muslim representation from 25 to 27 percent.

"Jinnah was sadly humbled, and went back to his hotel," recalled his Parsi friend, Jamshed Nusserwanjee, who would later become mayor of Karachi. "Next morning . . . at the door of his first-class compartment, he took my hand. He had tears in his eyes as he said, 'Jamshed, this is the parting of the ways.'"[51] Jinnah's statement would prove prophetic: it would be seen in retrospect as marking the first of the three milestones leading to the partitioning of the subcontinent.

At the Congress session, Gandhi proposed a resolution accepting the Nehru Report with a rider that the British government must grant India dominion status within one year. If freedom had not been won under dominion status by December 31, 1929, then "I must declare myself an Independence-wala," concluded Gandhi.[52]

In March 1929 Jinnah came up with his manifesto of fourteen points,[53] the most important of which were the following: India should have a federal form of government in which residuary powers are vested with the provinces; all cabinets at the central or provincial level as well as the Central Legislature should have at least one-third Muslim representation; the separate electorate system should continue; Muslims should be given an adequate share in all the services of the state; and there should be adequate safeguards for the protection and promotion of Muslim education, language, religion, personal laws, and charitable institutions. Despite his position as the Muslim League's president, he failed to win the vote of the League's council for his manifesto. Its meeting in Delhi dissolved into chaotic argument.[54]

Jinnah received this political setback at a vulnerable point in his life. On February 20, 1929, Ruttie, his twenty-nine-year-old, estranged wife, who had developed abdominal cancer, had died of the disease in Bombay while he was lobbying his manifesto in Delhi, where the League was headquartered. He rushed to Bombay and at her burial could not help weeping—for him a rare display of emotion in public.

In June 1929 Labor leader Ramsay MacDonald became the prime minister of Britain. India's viceroy, Lord Irwin, a balding man with a professorial appearance, spent much of the summer in London. On his return to Delhi he stated on October 31 that the British government envisaged a "Round Table Conference" of British and Indian delegates, and added that "the natural issue of India's constitutional progress . . . is the attainment of Dominion status." But when Conservative leaders in Parliament opposed the idea, he backpedaled. In his meeting with top-level Indian leaders on December 23, he said that "he was unable to prejudge or commit the [Round Table] Conference at all to any permanent line."[55] The Indian deputation included Gandhi as well as Jinnah. It would be the last time that the two of them participated in a joint political exercise.[56]

A week later Congress went into session in Lahore. At the stroke of midnight on December 31, 1929, the conference adopted a resolution, moved by the forty-year-old Jawaharlal Nehru, who was presiding over the session: "The British government has not only deprived the Indian people of their freedom, but has based itself on the exploitation of the masses, and has ruined India economically, politically, culturally and spiritually," it stated. "We believe, therefore, that India must sever the British connection and attain *purna Swaraj* or complete independence."[57]

The convention adopted a green-white-saffron flag with a spinning wheel in the middle white strip as the emblem for independent India. It called on its members and friends to withdraw from legislatures, and it sanctioned civil disobedience and nonpayment of taxes. It authorized the Congress Working Committee to decide how and when satyagraha should commence. In practice, the decision rested with Mahatma Gandhi.

SALT OF THE SEA

Gandhi was intent on keeping the civil disobedience campaign strictly nonviolent, particularly when, in his own words, "there was a lot of violence in the air." The most dramatic example of this came in April 1929, when militant nationalists Bhagat Singh and Batukeshwar Dutt threw two handmade bombs from the visitors' gallery inside the Central Legislative Assembly. Gandhi's focus was to be on the refusal to pay taxes.

In February 1922 in Bardoli the tax protest had been tied to land revenue, a primary source for the Raj's treasury. This time around he needed to choose something less vital but at the same time open to a large section of the Indian society. He hit upon the tax on salt, which the British had imposed since the days of the East India Company in the mid-eighteenth century.

The India Salt Act of 1882 specified a government monopoly on the collection, manufacture, and wholesale sale of salt as well as the tax on it. Possessing salt not purchased from the state monopoly became a punishable crime. Under Viceroy Lord Reading, the tax was doubled in 1923. To make his case, Gandhi fired off a long missive to Viceroy Lord Irwin on March 2, 1930, dealing generally with the British Raj's iniquitous taxation system before turning to the salt tax and its deleterious effect on the Indian peasant. "The British system seemed to be designed to crush the very life out of him," Gandhi wrote. "Even the salt he must use to live is so taxed to make the burden fall heaviest on him."[58] He concluded by saying that if the viceroy failed to "deal with this evil," he would proceed with his coworkers at the Ahmedabad ashram to disregard the Salt Acts on March 11. The viceroy ignored the letter.

Gandhi's epic journey on foot started on March 12. He was joined on this 241-mile-long trip by eighty of his followers.

As usual, Gandhi, now sixty-one, wrapped his actions and words in religion. "My feeling is like that of the pilgrim to Amarnath or Badri-Kedar," he said, referring to the Hindu holy places in the mountainous region of northwestern India. "For me this is nothing less than a holy pilgrimage." Motilal Nehru followed suit: "Like the historic march of Ramachandra [Lord Rama] to [Sri] Lanka the march of Gandhi will be memorable."[59] Typically, there was only one Muslim, Abbas Varteji, among the satyagrahis accompanying Gandhi.

Passing through almost three hundred villages, the march ended on April 5 at the village of Dandi, known for its salt pans, 160 miles north of Bombay. At numerous rural stops Gandhi exhorted his audience to wear handspun and handwoven cotton—called *khadi* or *khaddar*—and shun alcohol, child marriage, and untouchability. He made a point of bathing at wells used by local outcastes.

On the morning of April 6, after the ritual of listening to Hindu devotional hymns, he waded into the Arabian Sea and, picking up a handful of salty mud (the salt pans had been stirred up earlier by government agents), symbolically proclaimed his country's full independence as his admirers shouted, "*Kanoon Torhnewala zindabad*" (Hindi: Long live Law Breaker).

Given the long shoreline of India, there were ample opportunities to break the Salt Acts. Mass disobedience followed. After his arrest on April 14, Jawaharlal Nehru was sentenced to six months in prison. The port cities of Karachi, Madras, Calcutta, and Chittagong emerged as major sites of nonviolent protest.

Having stayed in the house of a local Muslim, Shiraz Abdullah, in Dandi, Gandhi moved to a specially built palm-leaf hut. It was there that he was arrested after midnight on May 4, 1930, under Bombay Regulation XXV of 1827, which provided for detention without trial.

With this, the mantle fell on seventy-six-year-old Abbas Tyabji, a retired Muslim judge, whom Gandhi had named as the alternate leader of the satyagrahis. Accompanied by Gandhi's wife, Kasturbai, he led the march on Dharasana Salt Works twenty-five miles to the south of Dandi.

En route, Tyabji was arrested and sentenced to three months in jail. The leadership then passed successively to Sarojini Naidu, an Oxford-educated, outspoken poet, and Maulana Abul Kalam Muhiyuddin Ahmed Azad, who had fallen under Gandhi's spell during the Khilafat movement. By then the number of satyagrahis had soared to two thousand. As they approached the salt plant, they were turned back by police. Frustrated, they resorted to a sit-in, which lasted a couple of days. Hundreds were arrested.

On finally reaching their destination on May 21, some of the sa-tyagrahis attempted to remove the barbed wire surrounding the salt works. The police charged them with steel-tipped staves. Obeying Gand-hi's strict instruction to the nonresistors to "answer organized hooliganism with great suffering," they remained passive.

"Not one of the marchers even raised an arm to fend off the blows," reported Webb Miller, an American correspondent of United Press International.

From where I stood I heard the sickening whacks of the clubs on unpro-tected skulls. . . . Those struck down fell sprawling, unconscious or writhing in pain with fractured skulls or broken shoulders. In two or three minutes the ground was quilted with bodies. Great patches of blood widened on their white clothes. The survivors without breaking ranks silently and dog-gedly marched on until struck down. When every one of the first column was knocked down stretcher bearers rushed up unmolested by the police and carried off the injured to a thatched hut which had been arranged as a temporary hospital.

At times the spectacle of unresisting men being methodically bashed into a bloody pulp sickened me so much I had to turn away. I felt an inde-finable sense of helpless rage and loathing, almost as much against the men who were submitting unresistingly to being beaten as against the police wielding the clubs. . . . Group after group walked forward, sat down, and submitted to being beaten into insensibility without raising an arm to fend off the blows. Finally the police became enraged by the nonresistance. . . . They commenced savagely kicking the seated men in the abdomen and testicles. The injured men writhed and squealed in agony, which seemed to inflame the fury of the police. . . . The police then began dragging the sitting men by the arms or feet, sometimes for a hundred yards, and throwing them into ditches.

On his later visit to the hospital Miller counted "320 injured, many still insensible with fractured skulls, others writhing in agony from kicks in the testicles and stomach. . . . Scores of the injured had received no treatment for hours and two had died."[60]

His first attempts at wiring the story to his agency in London were censored by the British telegraph operators in India. Only after he had threatened to expose British censorship was his report transmitted uncensored. His story appeared in 1,350 newspapers worldwide. And it was read into the official record of the US Senate by Senator John J. Blaine.[61]

Miller's report described the tragic event more graphically than the sequence in Attenborough's biopic *Gandhi*. Like his depiction of the Jallianwala Bagh massacre, which failed to capture the chaos and terror of the victims, the film's recreation of the Salt March was marred by the sanitized appearance of the nonviolent resistors in freshly laundered and pressed white shirts, pajamas, and Gandhi caps, without the faintest notion of even armpit sweat on their clothes in the dusty, subtropical landscape in the sweltering heat of May before the onset of monsoon.

Viceroy Lord Irwin's note to King George V was a case of describing a moonless night as a penumbra. "Your Majesty can hardly fail to have read with amusement the accounts of the severe battles for the Salt Depot in Dharasana," he wrote. "The police for a long time tried to refrain from action. After a time this became impossible, and they had to resort to sterner methods. A good many people suffered minor injuries in consequence."[62]

The mass arrests by the government pushed up the number of political offenders to somewhere between sixty thousand and ninety-two thousand.[63]

In his rivalry with Gandhi as the primary spokesman of Indians, Jinnah had a built-in disadvantage. It was not just that as a Hindu, Gandhi belonged to the majority community, but by invoking the symbols and mythology of the religion, he had given himself a Hindu halo.

By contrast, Jinnah's distaste for street politics remained unabated. He and Gandhi lived in totally different worlds, politically and socially. Temperamentally, Gandhi was a man of heart, skillful in pulling emotional strings, creating and applying "moral pressure." He tried diverse ways to win, particularly when he could not marshal rational argument to support his stance. As his polar opposite, Jinnah was a man of intellect, steeped in logic, unsentimental, a lawyer to his fingertips. He was cold, conservative, constitutionalist, and consistent.

Jinnah realized that the dramatic events of the Salt March and its aftermath, reported worldwide, had overshadowed his efforts at advancing the cause of Indian nationalism through constitutional means. In his political joust he had lost to Gandhi. He decided to quit India. In October 1930 he sailed to London and returned to practicing law.

In stark contrast, Gandhi and other Congress luminaries were languishing in dirty, poorly maintained jails. There was therefore no prospect of them attending the first Round Table Conference on India in London later in the year.

3

The Two-Nation Theory

A Preamble to Partition

When the first Round Table Conference on India opened in London on November 12, 1930, it turned out to be anything but round. The eighty-nine delegates sat around an E-shaped configuration. Among the Muslim representatives, Jinnah stood out because of his distinctive hand-tailored suit and his attention-drawing behavior. "Jinnah did not at the opening of the Conference say what his party [Muslim League] had agreed on, and they are a little sore in consequence," wrote Sir Malcolm Hailey, the Indian government's consultative official, in a private note to Viceroy Lord Irwin. "He declined to give the Conference Secretariat a copy of his speech in advance as all the others had done. But then Jinnah, of course, was always the perfect little bounder."[1]

In his opening speech Jinnah said that there were four parties involved: the British, the princely states, the Hindus, and the Muslims. Thus he made Muslims a distinct group, rather than Indians with special interests and demands. He made explicit what was implicit in his earlier Fourteen Points.

Back in India, the League's acting president, Sir Muhammad Iqbal, also made an original point in his address to the organization's annual conference in Allahabad in late December. A mustached man with a receding hairline and a middle-distance gaze, he was a Cambridge-educated barrister and poet-philosopher. He stressed the distinction of Muslims in a territorial context. "I would like to see the Punjab, the North-West Frontier Province, Sindh and Baluchistan amalgamated into a single state," he said. "Self-government within the British Empire, or without the British Empire, the formation of the consolidated North-West Indian Muslim State appears to me to be the destiny of Muslims, at least of

North-West India."[2] In retrospect, this would prove to be the germ out of which sprouted Pakistan.

In London the conference set up eight subcommittees to deal with different subjects, the most important being the federal structure, provincial powers, and minorities. At the end of the deliberations on January 19, 1931, Prime Minister Ramsay MacDonald said that his government was prepared to "accept devolution of power at the Center if the [central] legislature could be constituted on a federal basis"[3]—and hoped the Congress Party would attend the next conference.

Alert to his superior's cue, Viceroy Lord Irwin released Congress leaders on January 25 on the eve of the party's Purna Swaraj (Full Independence) Day. He invited Mahatma Mohandas Gandhi for talks.

THE GANDHI-IRWIN PACT

Gandhi had a three-and-a-half-hour, one-on-one meeting with the viceroy in Delhi on February 17, a groundbreaking event. According such privilege to the leader of a party committed to ending the British Raj raised hackles among many British politicians, especially Conservatives. Preeminent among them was Winston Churchill, former chancellor of the exchequer and secretary of state for the colonies. He could not bear "the nauseating and revolting spectacle of this one-time Inner Temple lawyer, now seditious fakir, striding half-naked up the steps of the Viceroy's palace, there to negotiate and parley on equal terms with the representative of the King Emperor."[4] The viceroy's game-changing invitation thrust Gandhi into the celebrity stratosphere.

He and Lord Irwin met several times to hammer out an agreement. During one of these sessions, the viceroy asked his interlocutor if he would like tea. "Thank you," replied Gandhi as he adjusted his shawl. Holding up a paper bag, he said, "I will put some of this salt into my tea to remind us of the famous Boston Tea Party." The air rippled with laughter.

During the hard-nosed bargaining, one of the concessions that Gandhi wrung from Lord Irwin was the permission for Indians to make salt on the seacoasts. Overall, though, this turned out to be a token gesture by the viceroy, who compelled Gandhi to accept a future constitution in which Britain would retain control over defense, foreign relations, minority problems, and financial obligations to foreign countries. This was summed up in Article 2 of the pact.[5] Yet, in retrospect, this agreement would prove to be the apogee of Gandhi's political achievement.

In exchange for the Congress Party ending civil disobedience, and agreeing to participate in the next Round Table Conference, Lord Irwin pledged to release all political prisoners and return their confiscated lands.

The Gandhi-Irwin Pact was inked on March 5. Though its terms did not meet the minimum that Gandhi had prescribed for a "truce," he vouched for the sincerity of Lord Irwin, who was set to retire the next month. Despite grumbling from its younger members about Article 2, the Congress Working Committee (CWC, or Congress high command) endorsed the deal. But the special session of the All India Congress Committee (AICC) at the end of March did not. It instructed Gandhi to disown Article 2 at the Round Table Conference.

This hiccup in the Congress camp did nothing to douse the fast-spreading rumor in the predominantly Hindu rural areas of India that the great Mahatma had triumphed over the British king and that Ram Raj was now in the offing.

What transpired at the next conference in London, which opened a fortnight after the collapse of the Labor government of MacDonald, was the exact opposite of the Hindu villagers' expectations.

SECOND AND THIRD ROUND TABLE CONFERENCES

The second Round Table Conference convened on September 7, 1931, against the background of a deepening political crisis in Britain caused by the Great Depression. Mahatma Gandhi was the sole delegate of the Congress Party, claiming to represent 85 percent of all Indians. But he could not sustain his party's claim in the face of 111 other delegates: nearly three-fifths of them from British India, one-fifth from the princely states nominated by the viceroy, and the rest from the British government.

Each of the main issues—the federal structure and the minorities—was taken up by a committee. Gandhi was appointed to both. On the thirty-eight-strong Minorities Committee, however, there were more Muslims (13) than caste Hindus (10), with the remaining seats allocated to the Untouchables (Hindi: *Achhut*)—officially called Depressed Classes, forming 11 percent of the Indian population—along with Sikhs, Christians, Anglo-Indians, Europeans, and women.

Gandhi presented the (Motilal) Nehru Report, which rejected separate electoral rolls for Muslims, as the solution to the contentious Hindu-Muslim problem. He got nowhere. All other groups, except caste Hindus, lined up behind an agreement with separate electorates for different communities at its core.

Challenging the official decision to list the Untouchables as a separate community, Gandhi claimed that he represented all the castes of Hinduism "in my own person." This failed to convince the Untouchables' leader, Bhimrao Ramji Ambedkar. A young, fiendishly articulate law graduate of Columbia University, he slammed Gandhi's practice of calling the Untouchables "Harijans" (Hindi: Children of God), an unworthy example of political posturing. As outcastes, the Untouchables stood apart from caste Hindus, he insisted.

Anticipating failure at the conference, Gandhi spent much time and energy lobbying for India's total independence by trying to convert the British public to his cause. He stressed that quitting the British Empire would not mean severing ties with the people of Britain. He deployed his charm, wit, and self-dramatizing skills to the hilt. Dressed in his trademark loincloth and shawl, with a dangling watch and sandals, he provided an exotically attractive image for British newspapers. He traveled to Manchester, the textile heart of the empire, and Oxford, addressing altogether different audiences. In London he stayed at Kingsley Hall in the impoverished East End.

While Gandhi grabbed newspaper headlines and entertained readers with occasional quips—"You, in your country wear plus-fours, I prefer minus-fours"[6]—Jinnah applied his advocacy talent to enrich himself in London.

Specializing in India-related cases, he practiced law before the Judicial Committee of the (king's) Privy Council. "Contrary to my expectations, I was a success," Jinnah would tell American journalist-author Louis Fischer a decade later, with characteristic British understatement.[7] This success amounted to him earning £25,000 (today's £1.44 million) a year. He lived in a three-story villa in upscale Hampstead with eight acres of garden, where Fatima, his seventeen-years-younger dentist sister acted as his housekeeper and surrogate mother of his daughter, Dinah. He traveled in a chauffer-driven Bentley. In the midst of an economic depression, he purchased several apartments in the posh Mayfair neighborhood.

Following the October 1931 general election, which Labor lost heavily, MacDonald continued as the prime minister of a national government that was dominated by the Conservatives. Sir Samuel Hoare, the new Conservative secretary of state for India, was ill-disposed toward the Congress Party, a feeling shared by Viceroy Lord Willingdon in Delhi. Within weeks the viceroy proclaimed Emergency Powers Ordinances in the Congress strongholds of Bengal and United Provinces.

Yet Sir Samuel showed sufficient sensitivity toward Gandhi's sartorial appearance. When King George V and Queen Mary decided to invite all Conference delegates to a tea party at Buckingham Palace, the king said to Sir Samuel, "What? This little man to be in the Palace without proper clothes on, and bare knees!" Summoning his best diplomatic manner, Sir Samuel persuaded the king not to mention dress restrictions on the invitation cards. After the event, when a journalist asked Gandhi if he had had enough clothes on, he replied, "The King had enough on for both of us."[8]

Joking aside, neither Gandhi nor Jinnah was surprised that the conference failed to resolve the communal issue. MacDonald disbanded the assemblage on December 1, saying that the Indian representatives' failure to reach a communal settlement left his government no option but to make a unilateral decision.

After Gandhi returned to India empty-handed in late December, the CWC decided to renew the civil disobedience struggle. Over the next few months Gandhi and other party leaders were jailed.

On August 16, 1932, MacDonald announced the Communal Award. It granted separate electoral rolls and seats to Muslims, Sikhs, Untouchables, Christians, Anglo-Indians, and Europeans. From a communal perspective, Punjab and Bengal mattered most. In Punjab, Sikhs were a substantial minority, and in Bengal, the miniscule European settler community, dating back to the days of the East India Company (1600–1874), loomed large in British eyes. The government in London proved iniquitous in its allocation of communal representation. In Punjab, it gave Muslims, forming 56 percent of the population, 51 percent of the legislative seats; Hindus, including the Untouchables, 30 percent; and Sikhs 19 percent. In Bengal, it awarded Muslims, constituting 54 percent of the population, 48 percent of the seats; Hindus 32 percent, down 12 percent on their actual proportion; and Europeans, forming a puny 1 percent of the total, beefed up tenfold.[9]

Congress rejected the Communal Award outright. The Muslim League grumbled, prevaricated, and in January 1935 accepted it "until a substitute is agreed upon by the various communities concerned."[10]

The third Round Table Conference, which opened in London on November 17, 1932, was boycotted by the Congress Party. Sir Sultan Muhammad Shah, known popularly as the Aga Khan—the official protégé of the British charged with selecting the Muslim delegates—excluded Jinnah from his list. The attendees were down to forty-six. After scrutinizing and summarizing several reports, they disbanded on Christmas Eve. Their recommendations were incorporated in a white paper published in March 1933. Between then and April 1, 1936, when the Government of India Act 1935 promulgated on August 2 was enforced, there was a succession of momentous events that led to a growing divergence between majority Hindus and minority Muslims.

NOW OR NEVER

As an accomplished barrister and fabulously rich man in London, Jinnah was admired by Indian expatriates, especially Muslims. In early 1933 he was one of the honored guests at a black-tie dinner party given by the Aga Khan at the Waldorf Astoria Hotel in London. At the predinner reception he found himself accosted by Choudhry Rahmat Ali, who pressed on him a pamphlet titled "Now or Never: Are We to Live or Perish Forever?[11] The document included a letter dated January 28, 1933, and addressed to "My Lord," for his opinion on "the proposed solution of this great Indian problem as explained herein."

The author was Rahmat Ali, a tall, powerfully built, thirty-five-year-old bachelor. After graduating from Islamia Madrassa in Lahore and teaching at the prestigious Aitchison College, he had obtained a law degree from Punjab University before moving to Britain in 1930. The next year he enrolled at Emmanuel College in Cambridge.

In his 2,350-word essay, described as an appeal on behalf of "our 30 million Muslim brethren who live in "PAKSTAN—by which we mean the five Northern units of India, viz.: Punjab, North-West Frontier Province (Afghan Province), Kashmir, Sind and Baluchistan" for "your sympathy and support in our grim and fateful struggle against political crucifixion and complete annihilation." It excoriated the Muslim delegates at the Round Table Conferences for agreeing to a constitution "based on the principle of an All-India Federation," which amounted to "nothing less than signing the death-warrant of Islam and its future in India." Like Muhammad Iqbal, a fellow Punjabi, Rahmat Ali focused on the northwestern zone of India, overlooking the Muslim-majority Bengal in the east.

Jinnah responded coolly toward Rahmat Ali and his pamphlet. When Ali and his three cosignatories contrived to meet him to gain his backing for "PAKSTAN," Jinnah replied: "My dear boys, don't be in a hurry; let the waters flow and they will find their own level."[12]

Nonetheless, a decade later, Jinnah, then called Quaid-i-Azam (Urdu: Great Leader) by his admirers, referred to "some young fellows" in a speech to the Muslim League session of April 1943.

What is the origin of the word Pakistan? It was not Muslim League or Quaid-i-Azam who coined it. Some young fellows in London, who wanted a particular part of north-west to be separated from the rest of India, coined a name in 1932–1933, started the idea and called the zone Pakistan. . . . A name was coined. Thus, whatever may have been the meaning of this word at the time it is obvious that language of every civilized country invents new words. The word Pakistan has come to mean the [1940] Lahore resolution [of the League].[13]

While Jinnah thrived financially and socially in London, Gandhi languished in His Majesty's Yerwada High Security Jail in Poona (now Pune). On May 1, 1933, troubled by the continuing stories of caste Hindus' atrocities against the Untouchables, he announced that he would start a twenty-one-day fast a week later as a "heart prayer to God for the purification of myself and my associates for our work to improve the lot of India's untouchable caste."[14] Despite appeals from his worldwide well-wishers to drop the idea, he stuck to his plan. For him, this was a "Now or Never" moment.

Nervous about the consequences of his death in one of its jails, the government released him on the second day of his hunger strike. To the relief of his followers and admirers, he survived the fast, during which he continued to edit the *Harijan*, a weekly he had established a year earlier.

Following a period of suspension, the civil disobedience campaign came to an official end on April 7, 1934—the year Gandhi discontinued his formal membership of the Congress Party and decided to focus on eradicating untouchability. After touring the country for almost a year to uplift the status of the Untouchables, he settled down in a new ashram at Sevagram (Hindi: Village of Service) near the central Indian town of Wardha. From here he mounted his constructive work designed to turn villages into self-reliant settlements, with small-scale, labor-intensive industries such as handlooms. Given his propensity to advertise the latest of his many fads, he used the *Harijan* to hold forth on the virtues of a diet of milk and bananas, his experiments with eating uncooked foods, and the ill effects of machine-polished rice.

Just as Gandhi took a voluntary holiday from active politics, Jinnah was persuaded to reenter the political arena in his homeland.

RETURN OF THE EDWARDIAN DANDY

During his absence from India, the Muslim League, a weak organization lacking a mass base, had atrophied. Muhammad Ali Jauhar, a pillar of the League, died in 1931. Though its titular head, Jinnah refused to sail to India to preside over its annual session in April 1933. In July thirty-seven-year-old Liaquat Ali Khan—a bespectacled, fair-skinned, Punjabi aristocrat, Oxford-educated lawyer with a prematurely receding hairline—called on Jinnah during his honeymoon in Europe. Both Khan and his wife, Raana, urged Jinnah to return home to save the League and the Muslims. Jinnah advised Khan to consult a sample of Muslim politicians. He did and got a positive response.

In April 1934 the Muslim League session named Jinnah president for two years. In the October 1934 election to the Central Legislative Assembly (CLA)—when nationally only 1,415,892 voted, a fraction of the tiny enfranchised minority[15]—the Muslim voters of Bombay elected him to the chamber.

In the 145-strong, partly nominated legislature, Jinnah became the leader of an independent group of 22, with all but 4 being Muslim. The house was evenly balanced between, on the one hand, Congressmen and their allies and, on the other, their pro-British opponents. This enabled Jinnah's group to be the swing voters. He performed skillfully in the chamber and traveled up and down the country, shoring up the League.[16]

In London, the fifty-nine-strong Joint Select Committee of British MPs, Indian CLA deputies, and nominated representatives of the princely states, chaired by Lord Linlithgow, produced a draft bill on constitutional reform in India in February 1935. After eight weeks of debate in the Parliament's two chambers, it was passed as the Government of India Act

1935—shortened to GOI Act 1935—on August 2. It was the longest act the British parliament had adopted in its 676-year history.

One of its major objectives—to establish an All India Federation of the British India Provinces and the Princely States—remained unfulfilled because of the ambiguities about safeguarding the princes' privileges. The act divided the lawmaking powers between the provincial and the central legislatures. The bicameral central legislature was to consist of a partly elected and partly nominated Federal Legislative Assembly and Council of State.[17]

The continuing diarchy in Delhi meant that important ministries such as defense and foreign affairs were run by the nominees of the viceroy, who remained accountable to the British government. He was authorized to dissolve legislatures and rule by decree. The provincial jurisdiction included police, provincial public service, health, and education. (The concurrent list consisted of matters over which both the federal and the provincial legislatures had competence to legislate.) Provincial cabinets were to be responsible to the popularly elected legislature. But provincial governors were given special powers to veto legislation and issue ordinances on law and order, interests of minorities, and the protection of British commerce. Separate electorates were to continue. And Muslims were given one-third representation in the central legislature. Most tellingly, there was no mention of the goal of dominion status for India.

Jinnah was in London when the GOI Act 1935 was passed. On his return home two months later he described it as a law that was "forced upon us," and called on fellow politicians to forge a common response. Things didn't happen that way, partly because Gandhi had taken a backseat, and Jawaharlal Nehru, released from jail only in September 1935, had to rush to the bedside of his thirty-six-year-old, tuberculosis-afflicted wife, Kamala, in a sanatorium in Lausanne, Switzerland.

It was only after her death on February 28, 1936, that a grief-stricken Nehru could focus on the latest law. Presiding over the Congress session in Lucknow on April 23, 1936, he declared that the party would combat the GOI Act inside and outside the legislature in order to kill it. This, he argued, could best be done by participating in those elections in which the executive was accountable to the fully elected legislature. Since this was the case with provincial assemblies, the party decided to contest elections in provinces. Behind the brave talk of undermining the 1935 Act, Congress leaders espied a golden opportunity to propagate their program legally among the electorate.

A week earlier Lucknow had been the site of the annual Muslim League session. Though wary of the provision for the All India Federation, it noted approvingly the retention of separate electorates and one-third Muslim representation in the central legislature. "It is essential that the Muslims should organize themselves as one party, with an advanced and progressive program," stated its leading resolution. "For this purpose the party appointed Mr. Jinnah to form a Central Election Board under his presidency . . . with powers to constitute affiliated Provincial Election Boards."[18] Jinnah did so in June. And the board also drafted the party manifesto.

At the AICC session on December 27 in Faizpur, presided over by Nehru, the party drew a line between contesting elections and taking office in case of victory. The issue on forming ministries was to be settled by the CWC after the polls, taking into account the delegates' bitter opposition to the provincial governor's overriding powers.

1937 ELECTIONS: A BENCHMARK

Of the 30.1 million eligible voters, about half exercised their right in the eleven provincial assembly elections held in January and February 1937. Seventy percent of them favored the Congress, awarding it 707 seats out of 1,585. Of these, 617 were in "general"—that is, non-Muslim—constituencies.[19] The triumph of the Congress was unexpected and striking. The most stunning was its victory in the populous United Provinces (UP). It bagged 133 of the 138 seats it contested, defeating the National Agriculturist Party, a powerful body of landlords, whose 98 candidates managed to eke out 18 seats.[20] Overall, it garnered a clear majority in five provinces and a slim one in Bombay.[21] In Assam, Bengal, and the North-West Frontier Province (NWFP) it emerged as the largest group.

Its stellar performance was the result of three major factors. The adoration and affection in which the preponderant Hindu voters held Gandhi as the Mahatma rubbed off on the party. The grueling, whirlwind election campaign by Nehru, flying hundreds of miles, to lend his charismatic support to local candidates, was another salient element. And the superb organizing skills of the Bombay-based chair of the Congress parliamentary board, Vallabhbhai Patel, equally adept at raising funds from the captains of industry in Bombay and Ahmedabad, was the final factor in the winning formula.

Of the 485 Muslim seats, the Muslim League won only 106. Yet its achievement outshone the Congress's score of 25. Of these, 15 were in the predominantly Muslim province of the NWFP, leaving only 10 Muslims on Congress benches in ten provinces—an unmistakable index of its unpopularity among Muslims. This corresponded with the fact that of its 3.1 million members, only about 100,000 were Muslim, a little over 3 percent.[22] The Muslim League did well in Bombay and UP, gaining 20 out of 29 seats in the former and 29 out of 69 in the latter.[23]

Basking in their success, Congress leaders played hardball with the British. They insisted on an assurance that provincial governors would not use their overriding powers to veto a law or dismiss the council of ministers as a precondition to let their members form ministries where they constituted a majority.

Protracted talks followed. The viceroy agreed to this condition verbally without amending the law. When Congress leaders approached Gandhi for advice, he told them to settle for a gentlemen's agreement. It was early July when Congress legislators assumed office in six provinces and led coalition governments in two.

In Punjab the 18 Congress members were a tiny fraction compared to the Unionist-led coalition of 110. It drew comfort from the fact that the Muslim League won only 2 seats, whereas the Muslim-dominated Unionist Party of landlords, also open to Hindus and Sikhs, gained 89.[24] With only 3 seats to its credit in a chamber of 60 in Sindh, the Muslim League was a cipher there. In Bengal, despite winning 5 seats more than the 35 gained by the (Muslim) Krishak Praja Party (Bengali: "Peasants' People") of Abul Kasem Fazlul Huq, the League ceded the chief minister's office to Huq. By securing the backing of the Europeans (25), and the independent Untouchables and caste Hindus (37), he isolated the 60-strong Congress group.

Jinnah tried to make the most of the League's gains in Bombay and UP. With Congress having a precarious majority in Bombay, he thought that its leader, Bal Gangadhar Kher, would be willing to form a coalition with his party. To achieve his aim, in his message to Gandhi through Kher, Jinnah invoked the cause of forging Hindu-Muslim unity in order to smooth the path to independence. He failed. "I wish I could do something, but I am utterly helpless," wrote Gandhi to Jinnah. "My faith in

Unity is bright as ever, only I see no light out of the impenetrable darkness, and in such distress I cry to God for light."[25]

A year earlier, though, God seemed to have guided Gandhi to lecture his eldest son, Harilal, that converting to Islam would mean breaching his dharma and would be equivalent to putting two swords in the same sheath.[26] His admonition to Harilal provided a rare glimpse of his innermost view about Islam. He faced this situation because the Bombay-based, forty-eight-year-old widower Harilal had fallen in love with Gulab Vohra, a Muslim, and wanted to marry her. He ignored his father's exhortation, converted to Islam, and, to the regret of the Mahatma, became Abdullah Gandhi.

In the electoral arena, rebuffed by Gandhi, Jinnah lowered his sights and discussed a possible Congress-League partnership under Kher. But Patel ruled that League legislators would have to merge with the Congress before any of them could be appointed a minister. The same scenario repeated itself in UP, the main base of Nehru. Here, too, the talks between the two parties broke down in the face of Patel's diktat. To respond to Jinnah's offer to cooperate with the Congress with a demand that he liquidate his party was the height of arrogance on the part of Congress leadership.

For its haughty behavior it would pay dearly a decade later. In that narrative, which ended with the partition of the subcontinent, its rebuffing of the League's friendly gesture in July 1937 would be seen as the second landmark, the earlier one dating back to December 1928 at the Calcutta session of the Congress, which rebuffed Jinnah.

The haughty behavior of the Congress in Bombay and UP toward the League made even neutral Muslim leaders suspicious of its real intentions toward their community. (The example of the sparsely populated NWFP along the Afghan border, governed by the Congress and its allies, was irrelevant to the vast bulk of the Muslim population in the subcontinent.) "When the Congress formed a government with almost all of the Muslim MLAs [members of the legislative assembly] sitting on the Opposition benches, non-Congress Muslims were suddenly faced with this stark reality of near total political powerlessness," wrote Jaswant Singh, a former minister in a Bharatiya Janata Party–led government, in his biography of Jinnah. "It was brought home to them, like a bolt of lightning, that even if the Congress did not win a single Muslim seat, as had happened now [in the 1937 election], as long as it won an absolute majority in the House on the strength of the general seats, it could and would form a government entirely on its own—unless Muslim politicians surrendered altogether their separate political identity, in which case they would hardly be elected in the first place."[27]

JINNAH, SCORNED, HITS BACK

Rebuffed, Jinnah described Congress ministries as the Hindu Raj, in which "Muslims can expect neither justice nor fair play."[28] With khadi-clad ministers in Gandhi caps almost monopolizing the seats of power in eight provincial capitals, it became increasingly difficult for ordinary Muslims as well as non-League Muslim politicians to disagree with Jinnah's assessment. Such was the case with Sir Sikandar Hayat Khan, the Unionist chief minister of Punjab, and Huq in Bengal. Responding to friendly overtures from Jinnah, they decided to associate their parties with the League.

On the other side, unlike Gandhi, Nehru did not view fraught Hindu-Muslim relations as a major hindrance to achieving independence. According to him, the League's leadership, consisting of intellectual landlords and capitalists, was cooking up the problem of Hindu-Muslim disharmony, which did not exist at the popular level.[29] Having spent time in Europe in 1936, which included a trip to Spain in support of the Republican regime in the civil war, Nehru had started to view politics in class terms, ignoring the different stages of economic development in India and in Europe. At the same time he could not overlook the stark fact that his party had contested only one-eighth of the Muslim seats and had an average of one Congress Muslim MLA in ten of the eleven provinces. To rectify this dismal reality, he initiated a program of mass contact with Muslims.

This led the League's leadership to redouble its earlier drive to create a popular base by recruiting members at the rock-bottom annual subscription of one-eighth of a rupee (two US cents).

Jinnah's pioneering appearance in a long coat and tight pajamas at the Muslim League's annual session in Lucknow in October 1937 was more than symbolic. It signaled the beginning of a new chapter in his political career. It rested on two pillars: opposition to the Congress Party and an uncompromising insistence that the League should be recognized as the only authoritative and representative organization of Indian Muslims.

In his speech he blasted the Congress Party for its hypocrisy, "having complete independence on your lips and the Government of India Act

1935 in your hands." Summarizing the scenario under the Congress Raj, he said, "Hindi is to be the national language of all India, and the "Vande Mataram" [aka, "Bande Mataram"; Sanskrit: I bow to Mother] is to be the national song, and is to be forced upon all," and "The Congress flag is to be obeyed and revered by all and sundry." He then turned to possible Congress-League cooperation in the future. "Honorable settlement can only be achieved between equals, and unless the two parties learn to respect and fear each other, there is no solid ground for any settlement," he declared. "Politics means power, and not relying only on cries of justice or fair play or good will." He ended his speech with an appeal to Muslims to join the Muslim League "by hundreds and thousands."[30]

At this conference Sir Sikandar decided to associate his Unionist Party with the Muslim League by agreeing to support the League on national issues while implementing the agenda of his own organization, open to non-Muslims (with Sir Chhotu Ram, a Hindu, being the party's deputy leader), in Punjab. Just before attending the League's session, Huq had found his position weakened when his party split, emboldening the Congress opposition. He therefore joined the League while heading his party's rump. To seal Huq's loyalty, Jinnah had him elected leader of the Bengal Muslim League.

Untroubled by factional politics that plagued Bengal and Punjab, Congress ministries removed restrictions on the press and released most political prisoners. They focused on uplifting rural life by improving irrigation, developing traditional crafts, promoting handspun and hand-woven cloth while paying particular attention to mitigating the plight of Untouchables. Their reform of the land tenancy law benefited all tenant farmers, Hindu and Muslim. But since most of the sharecroppers were illiterate and lacked voting rights, the potential electoral gain for the party was minimal.

Voters living in urban areas felt the most impact. Here schools and colleges underwent change. The Congress ministries introduced the teaching of Hindi; adulation of Mahatma Gandhi; singing of "Vande Mataram," which had been banned by the British Raj; and saluting the Congress flag in government-run educational institutions. These moves ran counter to the beliefs and feelings of Muslims, irrespective of their political leanings.

The six-stanza "Vande Mataram" was the most controversial. It appeared as a song sung by Hindu priests in *Ananda Math* (Bengali: Monastery of Bliss), a novel steeped in Hinduism written by Bankim Chandra Chattopadhyay in 1882. Its fourth stanza reads: "Thou art Durga, Lady and Queen, / With her hands that strike and her swords of sheen, / Thou art Lakshmi lotus-throned, / And the Muse a hundred-toned, / Pure and perfect without peer."

From 1911 onward, Congress leaders had started promoting the poem as the national anthem for free India, the motherland. Over the years their enthusiastic Hindu followers transformed the concept of motherland into Mother India: a matronly goddess with bulging breasts, clad in a colorful sari, holding the tricolor of the Congress Party as if it were a trident held by a militant Hindu god, with a docile calf by her side and embellished with the halo traditionally associated with the goddesses Durga and Lakshmi. Gaudy posters of Mother India were printed by the thousand.

Seven years earlier, Muhammad Iqbal, then a college lecturer in Lahore, had published an anthem for India (Urdu: *Tiran-e Hind*), *Saare Jahan Se Achha Hindustan Hamara* (Urdu: Better Than the Entire World Is Our Hindustan), in the *Ittehad* (Unity) weekly. It was a moving, image-filled ode to the homeland in words that were part of everyday language in North India—a mixture of Urdu and Hindi, called Hindustani, rather than Urdu suffused with Persian words. This patriotic song came to symbolize opposition to the British Raj. Yet it was ignored by Congress leaders.

During the debate on the suitability of "Vande Mataram" as the national anthem for free India in 1937, Rabindranath Tagore in his letter to future Congress president Subash Chandra Bose wrote: "The core of *Vande Mataram* is a hymn to goddess Durga: this is so plain that there can be no debate about it. . . . No Mussalman [Muslim] can be expected patriotically to worship the ten-handed deity as 'Swadesh' [Our Nation]. . . . Parliament is a place of union for all religious groups, and there the song cannot be appropriate."[31]

In Islam, deifying or worshiping anyone or anything other than the One and Only (unseen) God constitutes *shirk* (Arabic: to share)—that is, practicing idolatry or polytheism. Congregational singing of "Vande Mataram" as part of the official protocol during the rule of Congress ministries was one of several points Jinnah broached in his correspondence with Nehru, as Congress president, in 1937–1938. He demanded that this practice be ended.

"It is true that the *Vande Mataram* song has been intimately associated with Indian nationalism for more than 30 years and numerous associations of sentiment and sacrifice have gathered around it," replied Nehru. "During all these thirty or more years *Vande Mataram* was never considered to have any religious significance and was treated as a national song in praise of India. Nor, to my knowledge, was any objection taken to it except on political grounds by the Government. When, however, some objections were raised, the Working Committee carefully considered the matter and ultimately recommended [in October 1937] that certain stanzas, which contain certain allegorical references, might not be used on national platforms or occasions. The two stanzas which have been recommended by the Working Committee for use as a national song have not a word or phrase which can offend anybody from any point of view."[32] Obviously, he and Jinnah were operating on different wavelengths.

As for the national language, Jinnah wanted Urdu to be accorded this status. Nehru pointed out that the policy of the Congress was to make Hindustani, as written both in (Sanskrit) Devnagri and (Persian) Urdu scripts, the national language, and that both scripts should be officially recognized, and the choice left to the people concerned. In practice, to teach Hindustani to a class of Hindu and Muslim pupils required a teacher well versed in two scripts. Such teachers did not exist. So Hindustani was taught in the Devnagri script only.

Within the Congress, Nehru represented the modern, secular trend. Yet he overlooked the conflation of the abstract concept of praise of the motherland into a Hindu goddess called Bharat Mata, and the origins of "Vande Mataram" in Goddess Durga, as pointed out by the nationalist poet-philosopher Tagore. On the other side in the Congress was Patel, a proto-Hindu nationalist with cordial relations with the communalist Hindu Mahasabha. Patel supervised the functioning of the Congress ministries—and did so with an iron rod.

The assuming of power by the Congress Party exposed the fault line between Hindu nationalists and secular nationalists within it. Secular nationalists perceived the anti-imperialist movement as aiming to end Britain's imperial rule and transform the enslaved India into a sovereign state. But Hindu nationalists, who took a longer view of India's history and formed a significant part of the Congress, regarded the party as the vehicle to end the subjugation that the Hindu majority had suffered since 1192, when the Afghan conquerors set up a sultanate in Delhi. Preeminent among the nationalists were Patel and Madan Mohan Malaviya. Indeed, Malaviya, who served as Congress president in 1909–1910 and 1918–1919, was elected president of the Hindu Mahasabha, an unambiguously Hindu nationalist organization, in 1922.

As for Jinnah, he did more than complain to Nehru in his correspondence. A committee chaired by the Muslim League leader Muhammad Mehdi of Pirpur published a document that among other points debunked Nehru's arguments. And, feeling the heat of the hyperactive Congress opposition in Bengal, Huq issued his report in mid-1939, titled "Muslim Sufferings Under Congress Rule."

To the relief of the League's leaders, midway through their five-year tenure, Congress ministries resigned in the wake of the war in Europe.

POINT OF NO RETURN

Exercising his authority as viceroy and commander in chief of India, Lord Linlithgow declared before the CLA on September 3, 1939, that India was at war with Nazi Germany following its invasion of Poland. He promulgated the draconian Defense of India Act 1939.

Protesting vehemently against the viceroy's unilateral decision, the CWC said that it would cooperate with Britain if a new national government was formed and promised India independence after the war. But, it added, first the viceroy must state the war's aims. Lord Linlithgow referred the CWC to the speech by the British prime minister Neville Chamberlain. That, however, only referred to peace in Europe and an adjustment of international relations. The words "freedom" and "democracy" did not appear there or in the viceroy's statements. Therefore, on October 22, obeying the CWC's instruction, Congress ministries in eight provinces resigned. The viceroy imposed direct rule. This left the remaining three provincial cabinets intact.

In stark contrast, Jinnah urged Muslims to cooperate with the British Raj at this "critical and difficult juncture." To poke the Congress in the eye, on December 2 he called on Muslims to observe December 22, a Friday, as the "Day of Deliverance" from the "oppression" of the "Hindu" ministries. He urged them to offer thanksgiving after the congregational prayer and hold public meetings. The widespread response by Muslims heartened him and his colleagues. The high point of the day was a rally in the Bhindi Bazaar (Muslim) neighborhood of Bombay, which was addressed not only by Jinnah but also by the Untouchables' leader, Bhimarao Ramji Ambedkar.

Responding to the dramatic events before and soon after the outbreak of the war, Gandhi ended his semiretirement from politics. The CWC started conferring in Wardha to be near his ashram in Sevagram. Working with Nehru, Gandhi tried to persuade Jinnah to call off the observance of the Day of Deliverance. He pointed out that Nehru had agreed to a third-party review of the League's claims of the Congress Party's mistreatment of Muslims. In return Jinnah demanded that the Congress stop dealing with Muslims unaffiliated with the League. Nehru refused.

Gandhi and the CWC decided to show that the support the Congress enjoyed among Muslims was not insubstantial. At Gandhi's behest, the delegates at the annual session of the Congress in Ramgarh, Bihar, elected Maulana Abul Kalam Muhiyuddin Ahmed Azad president on March 18, 1940.[33] Born of Indian parents in Mecca, he grew up in Calcutta. An Islamic scholar with a well-trimmed mustache and goatee, wearing a black astrakhan cap, he was a poet fluent in Urdu, Arabic, and Persian who had the distinction of being elected Congress president at the age of thirty-five, in 1923.

On March 23 the Muslim League session in Lahore adopted its landmark resolution. It said that since Muslims were "a nation by any definition," the League demanded a constitution whereby "the areas in which the Muslims are numerically in majority as in the North-Western and Eastern zones of India, should be grouped to constitute Independent States in which the constituent units will be autonomous and sovereign."[34] The resolution, proposed by Huq, was adopted unanimously.

Jinnah spelled out his two-nation theory:

It is extremely difficult to appreciate why our Hindu friends fail to understand the real nature of Islam and Hinduism. They are not religions in the strict sense of the word, but are, in fact, different and distinct social orders. . . . The Hindus and Muslims belong to two different religious philosophies, social customs, and literature[s]. They neither intermarry nor inter-dine together, and indeed they belong to two different civilizations which are based mainly on conflicting ideas and conceptions. Their [perspectives] on life, and of life, are different. It is quite clear that Hindus and Mussalmans derive their inspiration from different sources of history. They have different epics, their heroes are different, and [have] different episode[s]. Very often the hero of one is a foe of the other, and likewise their victories and defeats overlap. To yoke together two such nations under a single state, one as a numerical minority and the other as a majority, must lead to growing discontent, and final destruction of any fabric that may be [so] built up for the government of such a state.[35]

In response Gandhi fell back on the argument, popular among Hindus, that since Indian Muslims were "a body of converts and their descendants," they could not claim to be "a nation apart from the parent stock." It was true that most Indian Muslims were originally outcaste or lower-caste Hindus, the estimates varying from 75 percent (according to Jinnah, whose grandfather converted to Islam and whose mother carried a Hindu name, Mithibai) to 95 percent (according to Nehru).[36] The small elite among Indian Muslims—descendants of Afghan, Turkish, and Mughal tribes—were identified in the community as *sharif*, noble. But this argument, rooted in ethnicity and geographic origins, ignored the differences in several other salient elements that together constitute civilization, as pointed out by Jinnah.

Once Winston Churchill, a staunch believer in maintaining the British Empire, became the prime minister of a coalition government in London in May 1940, Britain hardened its position on self-rule for India. In response to the CWC's March 1940 offer of cooperation if the viceroy set up a provisional national government in Delhi, Viceroy Lord Linlithgow made a counteroffer in August. He held up the promise of dominion status for India *after the war* with an immediate plan to expand the present Executive Council with Indian members and form a War Consultative Council. At the same time he ruled out Britain transferring its imperial powers to "any system of government whose authority is directly denied by large and powerful elements in India's national life."[37] This was seen by most observers as giving a veto to the League on any future constitutional reform. Yet Jinnah spurned the offer, as did the Congress.

PRESIDENT ROOSEVELT'S NUDGE

When, following Japan's attack on Pearl Harbor in December 1941, the United States joined the Allies in World War II against the Axis powers—Germany, Italy, and Japan—President Franklin D. Roosevelt became a factor, albeit minor, in Indo-British relations. Four months earlier, he and Churchill had issued an eight-point Atlantic Charter summarizing their war and peace aims, after their meetings in Newfoundland, Canada. The charter included a clause stating that all people had a right to sovereignty and self-determination. Citing this statement, Roosevelt pressed Churchill to win the cooperation of the nationalists in India.

This was bitter medicine for Churchill, whose distaste for Gandhi, and therefore the Congress, had grown since the end of World War I. But to avoid displeasing Roosevelt, whose financial aid Britain needed desperately, he brought up the Muslim factor. He did not wish to let Indian Muslims be governed by "the Congress Caucus and the Hindu priesthood," he told his American benefactor, adding that "there would be great risk in declaring a post-war abdication and exodus [of the British] at this time."[38] He also made a false claim that 75 percent of Indian soldiers were Muslim, more than twice the actual figure.[39]

Roosevelt was not satisfied. He sent a special envoy to London in February 1942, when, in the aftermath of the fall of British Malaya and Singapore to the Japanese, the mood in the British capital was bleak. In response Churchill dispatched Sir Stafford Cripps, a Labor member of the cabinet, to Delhi in March, after the fall of Rangoon to the Japanese, to defuse the political crisis in India.

Cripps offered dominion status for India after the war, with the right to leave the Commonwealth; a constituent assembly, elected by provincial legislatures, except for a proportion nominated by the princely states; and an immediate formation of a national government comprising representatives of the leading parties, with the viceroy retaining his overriding powers. To meet Jinnah's main demand, he agreed to give the provinces the option to secede from the dominion *after* it had been established. This provision was unacceptable to Congress leaders. And Jinnah was not fully satisfied because the plan did not give the "Muslim nation" the right to secede. So he too rejected the package.

DO OR DIE

In May 1942 the Japanese completed their occupation of Burma and planned an invasion of northeast India after the monsoon. That month, inspired by Gandhi's hardening stance, the AICC meeting in Allahabad called on Britain to declare its date of withdrawal from India, failing which the Congress would unleash a nonviolent civil disobedience campaign. At the CWC's meeting in Wardha on July 18, Gandhi won over the skeptics by stating that an independent India would join the Allies as a free nation and offer its soil to their troops to fight Japan. Chakravarti Rajagopalachari, a Tamil Brahmin lawyer from Madras (now Chennai), argued that Britain should and would not leave India at this critical moment. He was not swayed by Gandhi, and resigned from the party. (Later he would emerge as an acutely realistic politician, realizing, for instance, that Britain in the midst of World War II would never quit India.) The CWC authorized Gandhi to take charge of the nonviolent mass movement. Its resolution—known as the "Quit India" call to the British—was approved by AICC delegates in Bombay on August 8, 1942.

In his "Do or Die" speech to launch the civil disobedience campaign, Gandhi made a brief reference to Jinnah. "A day will certainly come when he will realize that I have never wronged him or the Muslims," he said. "I cannot wait till Jinnah Sahib is converted for the immediate consummation of Indian freedom."[40]

Jinnah was furious that Gandhi had decided to launch his campaign without bothering to consult him and that he assumed he alone could deal with Britain and other powers on behalf of India. The League's president perceived the Quit India resolution as "the culminating point in the policy and program of Mr. Gandhi and his Hindu Congress of blackmailing and coercing the British to transfer power to a Hindu Raj immediately."[41]

What followed the instant arrest of Gandhi and top Congress officials was more a rebellion than a nonviolent civil disobedience struggle. In the first week, militant Indians attacked 500 post offices, 250 railway stations, and 150 police stations, and derailed 60 trains. By the end of September, the authorities had arrested sixty thousand agitators—or freedom fighters, in the nationalist lexicon—and shot dead about a thousand.[42]

The viceroy banned the Congress Party. He deployed fifty-seven battalions of regular British soldiers to contain and suppress the civilian revolt. He issued the Revolutionary Movement Ordinance, which further tightened his government's control. "I am engaged here in meeting by far the most serious rebellion since that of 1857, the gravity and extent of which we have so concealed from the world for reasons of military security," Lord Linlithgow informed Churchill in a secret telegram on August 31. "Mob violence remains rampant over large tracts of the countryside."[43] The viceroy's iron fist strategy was applauded by Churchill. "I have not become the King's First Minister in order to preside at the liquidation of the British Empire," he thundered before the House of Commons on November 10, 1942.[44]

By the time the one-eyed Field Marshal Archibald Wavell succeeded Lord Linlithgow in September 1943 as viceroy, British India had been pacified, its jails overflowing with Congress partisans.

The Congress Party's loss proved to be Jinnah's gain, with the League filling some of the vacuum left by the banishing of the country's leading political organization. Within two months of the Quit India campaign, the *Dawn*, founded as a weekly journal in Delhi by Jinnah, was turned into a daily newspaper as the official mouthpiece of the Muslim League.

Jinnah toured the country propagating his two-nation theory. The League made solid gains, winning forty-seven of the sixty-one by-elections in Muslim constituencies between 1937 and 1943, with Congress Muslims securing a derisory four—the remaining seats going to unaffiliated Muslims. Nehru's membership drive among Muslims, and the reelection of Maulana Azad as Congress president in 1941 and 1942, had left most Muslims unmoved. By contrast, in 1944 the League claimed a membership of two million.[45] Part of the reason for Jinnah's mushrooming success was his deliberate decision not to spell out the details of the Muslim homeland he had in mind.

THE LAST THROW OF THE DICE

After the February 1944 death of Kasturbai Gandhi, jailed along with her husband in the Aga Khan Palace in Pune, the government eased off on the bereaved widower. It allowed him to receive Rajagopalachari, who had remained a free man. He discussed with Gandhi a plan for a joint League-Congress demand for a national government based on an understanding that "contiguous Muslim majority districts" could secede following independence, if separation was the preference of their adult populations. Gandhi endorsed this formula.

Rajagopalachari met Jinnah in April and told him that Gandhi was ready to discuss secession. Soon after, Gandhi suffered a near-fatal attack of malaria. He survived. But fearing his death in prison, Viceroy Wavell released him on May 6. After conferring with Gandhi, Rajagopalachari informed Jinnah that Gandhi was favorably inclined toward his formula. Jinnah replied that if Gandhi dealt with him directly, he would refer the plan to the League's Council.

On July 17, Gandhi dispatched a missive in Gujarati, with a copy in English, to Jinnah: "Brother Jinnah . . . Today my heart says that I should write to you. We will meet whenever you choose. Don't regard me as the enemy of Islam or of the Muslims of this country." Jinnah's reply, mailed from Kashmir, where he was on vacation, written in English—"the only language in which I can make no mistake"—read: "Dear Mr. Gandhi . . . I shall be glad to receive you at my house in Bombay on my return. . . . By that time I hope you will have recuperated your health fully. . . . I would like to say nothing more till we meet."[46]

As it was, both of them were old—Gandhi, almost seventy-five, and Jinnah his junior by only seven years—and in poor health. What kept Jinnah, suffering from lingering pneumonia in the base of his lungs, going were calcium injections, tonics, and shortwave diathermy.

From September 9 to 27, they negotiated daily. Their seeming cordiality was captured daily by press photographers: the shorter, bald, jug-eared Gandhi, wearing moon-shaped spectacles and flashing an open-mouth, broken-teeth smile, placing his brotherly arm around the shoulder of the tall, reedy Jinnah, with sunken cheeks and a thatch of thinning gray hair, managing to bare his front teeth. This daily ritual raised hopes.

In the end, nothing came of it. Gandhi proposed that the areas in which Muslims were in majority should be demarcated by a commission appointed jointly by the Congress and the League. Then their wish regarding secession should be tested through a referendum based on adult franchise. But the seceding areas could be consolidated into a separate state according to a treaty only *after* India had become independent, and that such a treaty should specify "an efficient and satisfactory administration of foreign affairs, defense, internal communications, and customs" between the two independent neighbors.

Jinnah wanted the right to secede accorded only to the Muslim nation. That meant giving the right to vote in a referendum only to Muslims in the Muslim-majority areas. Also he proposed partition *before* independence. Aware of the Congress ministries' neglect of Muslims' communal interests, he did not trust Congress-governed independent India to implement the promise of Pakistan. But his proposal was unacceptable to Gandhi. A desperate Gandhi proposed that a third party be selected by them to arbitrate. Jinnah declined.

On the whole, this exercise, conducted in good faith by both titans, raised Jinnah's status. It was Gandhi who came knocking at his door. It was Gandhi who, after much resistance and rhetoric, conceded the principle of secession from the center. It became crystal clear to all that Jinnah now wielded a veto over the future status of India as a political entity.

Within two weeks of the end of World War II in Europe on May 9, 1945, Viceroy Wavell announced a plan to transform his Imperial Executive Council into a national cabinet of Indian leaders. This was to be the first step toward self-rule for India with provisions for separate representation for Muslims and reduced powers for both Hindus and Muslims in their majority provinces.[47] He lifted the ban on the Congress Party and freed its leaders on June 15.

They and their League counterparts were invited to a conference in the summer capital of Simla on June 25. They were charged with nominating their representatives to the proposed national cabinet and discussing the rest of the Wavell Plan. The talks failed. Jinnah insisted on nominating all Muslim members of the cabinet, and Congress president Maulana Azad refused to abandon his party's right to include a Muslim in its list. Earlier Jinnah had pointedly avoided shaking hands with Maulana Azad.[48]

The failure of the Simla Conference scuttled the last viable opportunity for a united India whose chances of independence rose sharply when Britain's Labor Party, led by Clement Attlee, won a two-thirds majority in the general election on July 26.

As leader of the opposition in 1935, Attlee had proposed an amendment to the Government of India Act 1935 providing for a dominion status for the colony, only to see it defeated. Now he, instead of Churchill, had the honor to be among the leaders of the Allied powers to accept the unconditional surrender of Japan on August 14, 1945.

4

A Rising Tide of Violence

Starting in August 1945, the pace of Indian history accelerated. While the Labor government in London set out to withdraw from India against the background of the uncertain loyalty of its Indian military, tensions between the Congress Party and the Muslim League intensified and morphed into savage Hindu-Muslim violence.

Stung by Muhammad Ali Jinnah's manifest discourtesy to him at the Simla Conference, Congress president Maulana Abul Kalam Muhiyuddin Ahmed Azad invited several Muslim groups opposed to the Muslim League to attend the Nationalist Muslim Conference in Delhi on September 8. This was a preamble to establish the Azad Muslim Parliamentary Board to contest elections starting in January 1946.

BRITAIN'S INDIAN MILITARY FOUNDATION SHAKEN

In the interim, public attention turned to the military trials of General Shah Nawaz Khan and Colonels Prem Sahgal and Gurbaksh Singh Dhillon, which started in November. They were ex-officers of the British Indian Army who, as Japan's prisoners of war in Malaya-Singapore, had joined the Indian National Army (INA) led by Subash Chandra Bose, a former Congress president. He had allied with the Axis powers after escaping his house arrest in Calcutta in January 1941. Khan, Sahgal, and Dhillon became the best known faces of the six thousand Indian POWs the British Raj decided to prosecute for treason.

As symbols of Indians' armed resistance to British imperialism, this Hindu-Muslim-Sikh trio mesmerized the public, which had so far been exposed almost exclusively to the virtues of nonviolent struggle against foreign domination.

Reflecting the popular mood, the All India Congress Committee (AICC) session in September had passed a resolution warning that "it would be a tragedy if these officers were punished for the offense of having labored, however mistakenly, for the freedom of India," and demanded their release.[1] The Congress Working Committee (CWC) formed the INA Defense Committee. The proceedings of the trial in Delhi's historic Red Fort took a dramatic turn when Jawaharlal Nehru appeared before the military judges in the barrister's gown he had discarded a quarter century earlier. Jinnah expressed his readiness to defend General Khan if he dissociated himself from the other (non-Muslim) codefendants. Khan declined the offer.

Mahatma Mohandas Gandhi, an apostle of nonviolence, set aside his creed. "The hypnotism of the Indian National Army has cast its spell upon us," he conceded in his article in the *Harijan* of February 24, 1946. "Netaji's [Subash Chandra Bose's] name is one to conjure with. His patriotism is second to none. . . . His bravery shines through all his actions. He aimed high and failed."[2]

By early 1946 the INA's militant nationalism began to resonate among the hitherto loyal ranks of Britain's Indian military. As it was, the discontent about food and working conditions among the enlisted of the Royal Indian Navy (RIN) had been building up. It came to the fore on February 18, when disgruntled naval troops formed a Naval Central Strike Committee, led by M. S. Khan in Bombay. The mutiny at HMS *Talwar*, an onshore signals school, spread to the RIN's seventy-eight ships and twenty on-shore establishments in Bombay, Karachi, Cochin, and Vishakhapatnam (aka Vizag), involving twenty thousand sailors. The next morning they lowered the Union Jack and hoisted the nationalist tricolor on most of the ships and establishments. In Bombay the mutiny on twenty-two ships was backed by workers' strikes and commercial shutdowns. The effort to quell the resulting rioting and violence led to 228 deaths by police fire.[3]

The naval mutiny shook the government of Prime Minister Clement Attlee, who ordered the Royal Navy to quash it. Admiral J. H. Godfrey, the flag officer commanding the RIN, went on air, bellowing "Submit or perish." By then the mutineers' demands had included the freeing of all ex-INA troops.

The Bombay-based Congress leader Vallabhbhai Patel intervened to secure a peaceful end to the mutiny, an enterprise to which Jinnah also made a contribution. By February 21 a British destroyer arrived from Ceylon (later Sri Lanka) and anchored near the Gateway of India in Bombay. The mutiny ended two days later, with the authorities appointing five courts of inquiry to delve into the strikers' demands.[4]

Later, in Delhi, the INA officers' life imprisonment sentences were cashiered by the Indian commander in chief Field Marshal Sir Claude John Auchinleck. His hand was forced by the intensity of the popular protest and barely disguised signs of discontent among serving Indian soldiers.

The decisive roles of the naval mutiny and the widespread disapproval of the INA officers' trials were conceded by Attlee a decade later as a guest of P. V. Chuckraborty, the acting governor of West Bengal. In his letter of March 30, 1976, Chuckraborty wrote:

> I put it straight to him [Attlee] like this: "The Quit India Movement of Gandhi practically died out long before 1947 and there was nothing in the Indian situation at that time, which made it necessary for the British to leave India in a hurry. Why then did they do so?" In reply Attlee cited several reasons, the most important of which were the INA activities of Netaji Subash Chandra Bose, which weakened the very foundation of the British Empire in India, and the RIN Mutiny which made the British realize that the Indian armed forces could no longer be trusted to prop up the British. When asked about the extent to which the British decision to quit India was influenced by Mahatma Gandhi's 1942 movement, Attlee's lips widened in smile of disdain and he uttered, slowly, "Minimal."[5]

By espousing the INA's cause, the Congress garnered the support of those Indians who had little faith in Gandhi's nonviolent strategy. This became apparent in the electoral contests of January through March 1946.

ELECTORAL MANDATES

In the 103-seat election in the Central Legislative Assembly (CLA), the Congress won all of the 51 general (Hindu) seats plus 5 more non-Muslim seats. At the same time the Muslim League roared to victory, winning all 30 Muslim places and polling 86.6 percent of the Muslim vote. These elections were based on the extremely restricted franchise of the 1919 Act, with only 586,647 casting their ballots, representing almost exclusively the propertied classes.

For the provincial elections, spread over late January to mid-March, the electoral base was over 35 million. The turnout of 26 million was an impressive 75 percent. The aggregate count gave the Congress 19 million ballots and the League 4.5 million. The Congress increased its total from 701 seats in the 1937 poll to 923. But the League quadrupled its strength, to 425 out of 485 Muslim seats. To Maulana Azad's profound chagrin, the Nationalist Muslims scored a derisory 16.[6]

Jinnah had masterminded the campaign while staying out of the feuds among provincial leaders. League candidates deployed Islamic symbols and slogans to garner support. In the Muslim-majority provinces they turned, successfully, to such traditional power centers and networks as feudal lords, clan elders, and religious notables. With this, Indian politics came full circle. A generation earlier, Jinnah had warned Gandhi against mixing religion with politics. Now he presided over a political party whose candidates pulled religious strings unashamedly to win electoral contests.

He hammered home the message that every ballot cast for the League was a vote for the welfare of one hundred million Indian Muslims and Islam. "Your votes are not for individuals but . . . for Pakistan," he repeated in his election speeches up and down the country.[7] Oddly, he articulated all this in English, which was translated into Urdu by an assistant. This and his traditional aloofness had become part of the mystique surrounding him, which enhanced his charisma among his coreligionists.

By then the term "Pakistan"—an Urdu compound of *pak*, meaning "pure" and *istan* meaning "place"—had acquired a talismanic quality among Muslims of all classes. It was perceived as a panacea for all the problems Muslims faced. Its exact meaning was kept deliberately vague. "Muslim businessmen foresaw new markets [in Pakistan] free from Hindu competition," notes Alan Hayes Marriam, an American academic. "Landlords hoped for a perpetuation of the *zamindari* system [which guaranteed perpetual ownership of vast, inherited agricultural plots] which the Congress had vowed to abolish. Intellectuals envisioned a cultural rebirth free from the British and Hindus. To the orthodox, Pakistan promised a religious state. . . . To officials and bureaucrats a new nation offered a shortcut to seniority."[8]

After the elections, the Congress formed ministries in eight provinces. As the largest group in Bengal's legislature, the League led the coalition government, with Hussein Shaheed Suhrawardy as chief minister.

In Sindh, where the total electorate was less than one million, the League's 28 seats were equal to those of the Sindh Assembly Coalition Party, comprising 21 Congress lawmakers and 7 dissident Leaguers and Nationalist Muslims, in a chamber of 60, with the remainder being neutral. As "a great sympathizer of Muslims and supporter of the Pakistan cause"—in the words of his secretary, Naseer Ahmad Faruqi[9]—Governor Sir Francis Mudie invited the League leader Sir Ghulam Hussain Hidayatullah to form a ministry. Sir Francis would later be appointed governor of West Punjab by Pakistan's governor-general Jinnah.

But in Punjab Maulana Azad cobbled together a coalition of the Congress (51 seats), the Akali Party of Sikhs (23 seats), and a much reduced Unionist Party (20 seats) under the leadership of Sir Khizr Hayat Tiwana.[10] By depriving the largest group, the League (73 seats), of power, Azad struck a hard blow at Jinnah's conceit. Punjab was at the core of the Muslim League leader's demand for Pakistan in the northwestern region. He found the ignominy of defeat by his bête noire hard to stomach.

The provincial legislatures then elected members to the 300-strong Constituent Assembly in Delhi. The Congress won 150 seats, and the League 79 Muslim places.[11] The latest elections underscored the political dominance of the Congress and the League.

Attlee dispatched a team of three cabinet ministers, led by the seventy-four-year-old Lord Pethick-Lawrence, secretary of state for India, to Delhi on March 22. His colleagues were Sir Stafford Cripps and Albert Victor Alexander. They and Viceroy Archibald Wavell became the quartet charged with finding a formula to transfer Britain's imperial power to Indian representatives.

THE BRITISH QUARTET'S INTRACTABLE TASK

Of the three wise men from London, only Cripps had a full grasp of the complexities of the Indian political scene.

The quartet's talks with Congress and League leaders proved sterile. So on May 16 the cabinet mission, in consultation with Wavell, issued its own Constitutional Award. It rejected Pakistan, as demanded by the League, as well as a smaller version of it. In the League's blueprint, the two parts of Pakistan lay a thousand miles apart, with its western wing being 37 percent non-Muslim and the eastern 48 percent. That would have left the communal minority problem unresolved. The smaller Pakistan, stated the British cabinet ministers, would involve partitioning Assam, Bengal, and Punjab, a step that, in their opinion, "would be contrary to the wishes of a very large percentage of these provinces." Bengal and Punjab, they argued, "each had its own language and a long history and tradition."[12]

The Constitutional Award therefore envisaged a united India, including the princely states, with a federal government in charge of defense, foreign affairs, and communications; a federal parliament, which could pass a major law of racial or religious nature only if a majority of Hindu or Muslim members backed it; and provincial governments with wide powers. A constituent assembly, elected by existing provincial legislatures and charged with drafting a constitution resting on these principles, would convene in Delhi briefly and then divide into three sections. Section A would be Hindu majority, and Sections B and C would comprise the Muslim-majority northwestern region and Bengal-Assam respectively. The aim would be to frame a constitution for three subfederations into which federal, independent India was to be divided.[13]

In order to satisfy the two contending parties—the Congress and the League—the cabinet mission's award included two contradictory clauses. Paragraph 15 stated that "provinces should be free to form groups with executives and legislatures." But Paragraph 19 said that representatives from the groups "*shall* proceed to settle provincial constitutions" and "*shall* also decide whether any group constitution shall be set up for those provinces."[14]

On June 6 Jinnah and the League accepted the Constitutional Award, claiming that the founding of Pakistan was "inherent" in the "compulsory grouping," adding that by implication this document gave a Muslim group "the opportunity and the right of secession."

Congress leaders were of two minds. With the Congress presidency passing from Maulana Azad to Jawaharlal Nehru, a Hindu, in early May 1946, Viceroy Wavell saw an opportunity to satisfy Jinnah's demand that the League should have the monopoly over nominating Muslim representatives to the interim cabinet the viceroy wished to form. On June 16, Wavell announced that he was inviting Jinnah and four of his party colleagues; Nehru and five other Hindu Congress leaders, including one Untouchable; and a Sikh, a Christian, and a Parsi to form the interim government. If the League or the Congress spurned his offer, then he intended to appoint the new cabinet, which, in his view, would be as representative as was possible of those willing to accept the May 16 constitutional statement.

Thus pressed, on June 25 Congress leaders accepted the Constitutional Award, while stressing that Paragraph 15 gave provinces the option to stay out of either of the "Pakistan" groups. But they turned down Wavell's invitation to join the proposed interim government. (The unstated reason was that it deprived them of nominating a Muslim Congressman as a cabinet minister.) They calculated that it would be disastrous for Wavell to appoint a cabinet led by Jinnah. They proved right. Wavell withdrew his offer of June 16, thus depriving Jinnah of his lifelong ambition to be the highest representative of united India.

Jinnah felt cheated. He savaged the viceroy for his betrayal, Pethick-Lawrence and Cripps for their treacherous behavior, and Congress leaders for their dishonesty. What the CWC had done in reality was to win their right to be represented in the viceroy's proposed provisional cabinet and then turn down the chance to exercise it. They had made a fiendishly clever move that stopped Jinnah in his tracks.

Flushed by the crushing of Jinnah's fondest dream and the endorsement of the CWC's decision by 204 to 51 votes at the AICC session in Bombay on July 7, an overconfident Nehru overplayed his hand at the subsequent press conference. He explained that his party had agreed only to participate in the Constituent Assembly and that once convened, the Assembly would have the power to change the Constitutional Award's provisions, if it so wished and that the grouping scheme would most likely not materialize at all.

Nehru's indiscreet, aggressive statement finally and irrevocably killed the scenario of a united, independent India. It led Jinnah to withdraw the League's acceptance of the Constitutional Award. This was the last in a series of three landmark events—all of these wrought by the Congress Party—which culminated in the partition of the subcontinent.

JINNAH ON THE OFFENSIVE

At Jinnah's behest the Muslim League Council meeting in Bombay from July 27 to 29 adopted the path of "Direct Action" to achieve Pakistan. "This day we bid goodbye to constitutional methods," he declared. "[So far] the British and the Congress held a pistol in their hand, the one of authority and arms and the other of mass struggle and noncooperation. Today we have also forged a pistol and we are in a position to use it."[15]

Summarizing his party's recent history, Jinnah said that for the sake of fair play, the Muslim League had "sacrificed the full sovereign state of Pakistan at the altar of the Congress for securing the independence of the whole of India" but had been repaid with "defiance and contempt."[16] The Council named August 16 as the Direct Action Day for the achievement of Pakistan. Thus a quarter century after lambasting Gandhi for resorting to extraconstitutional methods, the seventy-five-year-old Jinnah emulated his rival, but without the Mahatma's stress on nonviolence.

Gandhi was equivocal about the Constitutional Award. "Let us not be cowardly, but approach our task with courage and confidence," he told the AICC delegates in Bombay. "Never mind the darkness that fills my mind."[17] His mind filled with a deeper shade of darkness as he noted a sharp rise in Hindu-Muslim alienation. He blamed Jinnah for this in his long interview on July 17 with Louis Fischer, the American journalist who went on to publish two glowing biographies of the Mahatma.

> GANDHI: The Muslims are religious fanatics but fanaticism cannot be answered with fanaticism. . . . Brilliant Muslims in Congress became disgusted. They did not find the brotherhood of man among the Hindus. They say Islam is the brotherhood of man. As a matter of fact, it is the brotherhood of Muslims. . . . [But] Hindu separatism has played a part in creating the rift between Congress and the League. Jinnah is an evil genius. He believes he is a prophet.
>
> LF: He is a lawyer.
>
> GANDHI: You do him an injustice. I give you the testimony of my 18 days of talks with him in [September] 1944. He really looks upon himself as the savior of Islam.
>
> LF: He pleads a case; he does not preach a cause.
>
> GANDHI: But I don't consider him a fraud. He has cast a spell over the Muslim who is [a] simple-minded man.
>
> LF: Sometimes I think the Muslim-Hindu question is the problem of finding a place for the new Muslim middle class in an underdeveloped India. India is even too underdeveloped to offer a place to the poor. Jinnah won over the middle because he helped it to compete with the other entrenched Hindu middle class. Now he is bridging the chasm between the landlord and peasant. He has done it with Pakistan.
>
> GANDHI: You are right. But Jinnah has not won the peasant. He is trying to win him.

LF: Jinnah told me in 1942 you did not want independence. . . . He said you want Hindu rule.

GANDHI: This is absurd. I am a Hindu, a Buddhist, a Christian, a Jew, a Parsi. . . . He is not speaking the truth. He is speaking like a pettifogging lawyer. . . . Only a maniac resorts to such charges. . . .

LF: What did you learn from your 18 days with Jinnah?

MG: I learned that he was a maniac. A maniac leaves his mania and becomes reasonable at times. I have never been too stubborn. . . . I could not make headway with Jinnah because he is a maniac. . . .

LF: What is the solution?

GANDHI: Jinnah has twenty-five years more to work. . . . Jinnah is incorruptible and brave. . . . If Jinnah stays out of the Constituent Assembly the British should be firm and let us work this plan alone. The British must not yield to [a] Hitler.[18]

With Jinnah pulling out of both plans of the British Raj, Lord Wavell was left with only one Indian partner: Nehru. He approached the Congress president to reconsider his party's stance on an interim government. Once he got a nod from Nehru, the viceroy announced on August 12 that he was inviting him to form an interim cabinet. At Nehru's initiative, Jinnah met him on August 15, on the eve of the League's Direct Action Day. They failed to reach an agreement. Nehru refused to raise his offer of 5 seats out of 14 to the League with Jinnah demanding 7.

Nationally, the League leaders were feverishly planning street action on August 16, a Friday.

A DRAMA ON A DUAL STAGE, ACT I

With Bengal ruled by the Muslim League's Suhrawardy, who was chief minister, the Direct Action Day had official backing. On that morning in Calcutta—a city of 4.2 million, three-quarters Hindu—the two-year-old Muslim League National Guard (MNG), the League's militia, forced Hindu shopkeepers to close their stores in the Muslim majority districts of North Calcutta. The angered Hindus responded by blocking the advance of several small League processions after the Friday congregation prayers toward the commons around Ochterlony Monument in the city center. All the same, between 50,000 and 100,000 Muslims gathered to listen to fiery speeches by League leaders, including Suhrawardy, about achieving Pakistan.

While heading back home after the rally, fired by the political-religious rhetoric of the speakers, some of the Muslims, armed with iron bars and bamboo sticks, attacked Hindus and ransacked their shops. In the main, the anti-Hindu violence was triggered by the MNG, described by Suhrawardy as soldiers of the envisaged Pakistan. Rioting increased as truckloads of Muslims, armed with brickbats and broken bottles, resorted to looting Hindu stores. In retaliation Hindus and Sikhs hit back with a vengeance. They attacked Muslims on streets and shops and even in their homes. With Suhrawardy refraining from pressing the police to quell the rioting, violence spread quickly.

Murder, arson, rape, and looting ravaged the city. The bloody mayhem continued for three days and included several massacres, followed by two days of occasional skirmishes. Its end came on August 21, only after Governor Sir John Burrow intervened and deployed five battalions of British troops, backed by four battalions of Indian soldiers, with orders to use live ammunition to restore order.

The estimated death toll varied between five thousand and ten thousand, with fifteen thousand more suffering injuries. Over one hundred thousand people became homeless. These statistics made it the bloodiest communal riot in India's history. The murdered victims were often mutilated—a pattern that would be repeated on a much larger scale in Punjab a year later. For the first time in communal riots, there were cases of rape, a feature that would become part of such violence later.

According to most accounts, the majority of the victims belonged to the Muslim community, which was by and large poor. "Thus, the massacre could be described as the combination of one large pogrom against poor Muslims by Hindu toughs [called *goondas* in Hindi and Bengali], with one smaller pogrom against poor Hindus by Muslim toughs," concluded Claude Markovits, a researcher of mass violence, in his 2008 study of the dreadful episode.[19] The same conclusion was drawn nearer the time. In his letter to Chakravarti Rajagopalachari on August 21, 1946, Patel wrote: "This [the Calcutta killings] will be a good lesson for the League, because I hear that the proportion of Muslims who have suffered death is much larger."[20] With this horrendous bloodletting and arson, Calcutta lived up to the title "City of Dreadful Night," as it had been named by the British writer Rudyard Kipling.

On August 22 the governor of Bengal dismissed the Suhrawardy government and imposed direct rule. Many of the Muslims who fled Calcutta returned to their villages in Muslim-majority East Bengal. This ramped up interreligious tensions in rural Bengal.

In Delhi the viceroy announced on August 24 that the existing members of his Executive Council had resigned and their successors would be installed on September 2. On that day, a cabinet of twelve ministers—including one Congress and two independent Muslims—was sworn in, with Nehru as vice president of the Executive Council in charge of foreign affairs.[21] As foreign minister Nehru said, "India will follow an independent policy [and] keep away from the power politics of the groups aligned one against another."[22] Soon after the United States decided to upgrade its diplomatic mission in Delhi to the ambassadorial level, Nehru named his erstwhile cabinet colleague, Asaf Ali, a Congress lawyer-politician, ambassador to Washington, where he would take up his post in February 1947.

Meanwhile, Jinnah responded to the inauguration of the interim government by calling on his followers to unfurl black flags as a sign of mourning. He slammed the viceroy for including three Muslims in his cabinet, including Asaf Ali, who lacked the confidence of their coreligionists. His statement triggered communal riots in Bombay and Ahmedabad. This led the viceroy to try to get the Congress and the League to cooperate.

He was helped by Sir Muhammad Hamidullah Khan, the Nawab (aka Nabob) of Bhopal, a friend of Jinnah as well as Gandhi and who was then based at Panchgani, a hill station a hundred miles from Bombay. With Khan's intercession, the two titans met in early October. They managed to come up with a compromise. Gandhi conceded that only the League had "the unquestionable right to represent the Muslims of India," and Jinnah said that the Congress could have "such representatives" in a Congress-League coalition as "it thinks proper."[23]

The five names Jinnah gave Lord Wavell on October 13 included Jogindar Nath Mandal, an Untouchable leader from Bengal. This was his way of getting even with the Congress after it insisted on nominating a Muslim Congressman, Asaf Ali, as a minister. Nehru dropped two independent Muslims and Sarat Chandra Bose (an elder brother of Subash Chandra Bose) from the cabinet and added Jinnah's five nominees, led by his deputy, Liaquat Ali Khan. The reconstituted cabinet took office on October 25. It included Baldev Singh, a Sikh, as defense minister.

By coincidence, October 25 was declared Noakhali Day in the Congress-ruled Bihar by Hindu leaders, many of them affiliated with the Congress Party.

A DRAMA ON A DUAL STAGE, ACT II

They were reacting to the news of violence against Hindus in the predominantly Muslim districts of Noakhali and Tippera districts in the waterlogged delta of the Ganges and Brahmaputra Rivers in East Bengal. Four-fifths of the population in the area was Muslim, whereas most of the agricultural land belonged to Hindu landlords. The religious divide was thus reinforced by gross economic inequity. In light of the recent Great Killings in Calcutta, it was payback for the violence perpetrated against Muslims in the metropolis.

The rioting started on October 10 in Ramganj after a pro-Pakistan rally and spread to ten other settlements. By the time it ended a week later, the number of Hindus killed was likely at least five hundred (official figure) or as many as five thousand—with sixty thousand made homeless. In Tippera district nearly 9,900 Hindus were forcibly converted to Islam, with many of them paraded in the streets wearing caps inscribed with "Pakistan." A larger number were converted to Islam in the Noakhali district. Abducted Hindu women were married to Muslims.[24]

The rumor spread in the adjoining Bihar that fifty thousand Hindus had been slaughtered in the Noakhali-Tippera area. Bihar, a 90 percent Hindu province, was ruled by Chief Minister Krishna Singh, a Hindu Congress leader. Following the declaration of Noakhali Day on October 25, thousands of Hindus, often led by local Congress figures, marched while shouting, "Blood for blood." Murder, arson, and pillage rocked four districts of Bihar, including Patna, for more than a week. The victims were Muslim.

By the time the savagery ended, different estimates of fatalities were published. Congress leaders admitted 2,000. The number mentioned in the British parliament was 5,000. The prestigious Calcutta-based *Statesman* reported 7,500 to 10,000, with the latter statistic accepted by Gandhi. In contrast, Jinnah came up with the figure of 30,000.[25]

To extinguish the fire of communal passion, Nehru, accompanied by the communications minister, Abdur Rab Nishtar, a League nominee, flew to Patna, the capital of Bihar. Escorted by a contingent of the Frontier Force Regiment, he toured the riot-stricken areas in an open jeep. "Murder stalks the streets, and most amazing cruelties are indulged in by both the individual and the mob," he wrote later. "It is extraordinary how our peaceful population has become militant and bloodthirsty. Riot is not the word for it—it is just a sadistic desire to kill."[26] He was so shocked that he threatened to "bomb the rioters."

The horrendous events in rural East Bengal and Bihar demolished the theory of Gandhi and Nehru that communal tensions existed only among the upper echelons of the two communities and that the village folks of different faiths led a peaceful coexistence.

Predictably, contrary was the case with Jinnah. His warnings of persecution of Muslims by the Hindu majority government were being borne out. The League's newspaper *Dawn* called on the surviving Bihari Muslims to "remain united and invincible in the face of Hindu aggression."[27] With the pogrom in Bihar, the slogan of "Islam in danger" in Hindu India gained enhanced credibility. And Jinnah would later tell the Bihari refugees in Karachi that Pakistan became imperative because of the sufferings of the Muslims of Bihar.[28]

THE PENULTIMATE STEP

With the inauguration of the Constituent Assembly on December 9 nearing, Attlee summoned Nehru, Jinnah, Liaquat Ali Khan, Baldev Singh, and Wavell to 10 Downing Street in London on December 2. During four days of meetings, British constitutional experts backed the League's interpretation of the May 16 constitutional statement about grouping. On December 6 Attlee announced that if the Constituent Assembly adopted a constitution without the cooperation of the Muslim League, "His Majesty's Government could not, of course, contemplate . . . forcing such a constitution on any unwilling parts of the country."[29]

While in London, Jinnah said publicly that he expected India to be divided into a Hindu state and a Muslim state. He added that he shared Churchill's apprehensions regarding "civil war and riots in India.[30] Given this, the talks in Downing Street failed.

In Delhi, when the Constituent Assembly convened on December 9, its League members stayed away. The Assembly adjourned to January 20, 1947, to await participation by the League and the quasi-independent princely states. Sporadic communal violence broke out in major cities. By Christmas Eve, for instance, it claimed more than 450 lives in Bombay.

While resisting the constitutional plans of the Congress, League leaders consolidated or expanded their popular base in Muslim-majority provinces. Once the shaky Hidayatullah ministry fell in Sindh in December 1946, the League's Parliamentary Board, headed by Jinnah, focused on winning all of the 35 Muslim legislative seats in the upcoming election.

Jinnah put his friend Ghulam Ali Allana in charge of electioneering. He in turn invited contingents of students from Aligarh Muslim University who narrated the killings of Bihari Muslims in gory detail. Another tactic was to use the network of the caretakers of the Sufi shrines to garner votes. And by giving the League's tickets to leading feudal lords, Allana strengthened the party's electoral card. The League scored all the Muslim seats except 2. With a firm majority in the chamber, the new Hidayatullah government assumed office in mid-February 1947.[31]

The year 1947 unrolled in India with an emergency session of the AICC in Bombay. On January 6 it adopted a resolution by a vote of 99 to 52 to accept the British interpretation of the May 16 statement "under protest," and subject to the qualification that no province or part of it would be forced into a settlement.[32]

On January 20 League members did not turn up for the Constituent Assembly. A week later the League's Council said that since the Congress did not accept the May 16 statement unconditionally, the election to the Constituent Assembly and the Assembly itself had become invalid. In early February intracabinet tensions intensified when the nine non-League cabinet ministers asked the viceroy to demand the resignation of the five League ministers.

In the pivotal province of Punjab, the League's leaders decided to undertake "direct action" to topple the coalition cabinet headed by Sir Khizr, a Unionist luminary. It started on January 24, when the government outlawed the MNG as well as the Rashtriya Swayamsevak Sangh (RSS; Sanskrit: National Volunteer Association), a Hindu militia. League leader and central cabinet minister Ghazanfar Ali Khan contended that proscribing the MNG was tantamount to banning his party's most important activity. Thus challenged, Sir Khizr lifted the ban on January 28. But when the League did not call off its civil disobedience as promised, he jailed its top officials.

While jails filled with the Leaguers defying the ban on public gatherings, their slogans grew more menacing with each passing day. The most popular were *Pakistan ka nara kiya? La illahahillillah* ("What is the slogan of Pakistan? There is no God but Allah") and *Assay leingey Pakistan, jaisey liyatha Hindustan* ("We will gain Pakistan the way we [Muslims] conquered India"). Abusive slogans were coined to insult the chief minister. Increasingly aggressive demonstrators started harassing Hindus and Sikhs and forcing them to fly the Muslim League's green emblem on their stores and vehicles. These slogans and actions made Hindus and Sikhs fearful.

Such activities by the League kept it and Jinnah in the limelight. By contrast, the undramatic reports of Gandhi's intermittent walking tours—alternating between the strife-torn villages in Noakhali, East Bengal, and western Bihar—preaching Hindu-Muslim amity merited less space and attention in the press and All India Radio. Gandhi had an arduous task to perform. In East Bengal, Muslims viewed him as an epitome of the Ram Raj, whereas in West Bihar Hindus saw him as an appeaser of Muslims.

To meet the challenge Gandhi dispersed his dozen-strong retinue to different settlements. He retained only his stenographer, R. P. Parasuram; his Bengali interpreter, Professor Nirmal Bose; and his eighteen-year-old grandniece, Mridula—popularly known as Manuben, Sister Manu—daughter of Jaisukhlal Gandhi, whom he had added to his staff earlier in the year.[33] Gandhi used Mridula as part of his "experiments" in *brahmacharya* (Sanskrit: literally, to follow the Eternal; figuratively, self-imposed celibacy). He had grown up with a notion about the power of semen, originating in ancient Hindu scriptures and summarized in the sentence: "One who conserves his vital fluid acquires unfailing power."[34]

Gandhi's regular sharing of his bed with Mridula had become an embarrassment at best and a scandal at worst. Among others, Patel, in his letter to Gandhi on January 25, 1947, urged him to suspend the experiment, which he called a "terrible blunder" on the Mahatma's part that pained his followers "beyond measure."[35]

On February 1, 1947, in his prayer meeting speech in the village of Amishapara, Gandhi said, "I have my grandniece [Manuben] with me. She shares the same bed with me. The Prophet [Muhammad] . . . welcomed eunuchs made so through prayer by God. This is my aspiration. I know that my action has excited criticism among my friends. But a duty cannot be shirked." His interpreter, Bose, skipped these sentences while translating his speech in Bangali. And the editors of the *Harijan* weekly, Kishorelal Mashruwala and Narhari Parikh, censored them from the published text. But Gandhi was stubborn. "If I don't let Manu sleep with me, though I regard it as essential that she should, wouldn't that be a sign of weakness in me?" he countered. Privately, he had told Manuben, "We both may be killed by the Muslims, and must put our purity to the ultimate test, so that we know that we are offering the purest of sacrifices, and we should now both start sleeping naked."[36]

It transpired that the critical significance Gandhi attached to this "experiment" to control his sexual impulses had a political motive, shorn of any spirituality. Bose once overheard him saying to an associate about *brahmacharya,* "If I can master this [sexual impulse], I can still beat Jinnah."[37] It appears that the Mahatma was secretly, and innovatively, priming himself to get the upper hand in his decades-old rivalry with Jinnah around the time Prime Minister Attlee was drafting a historic statement on India.

5

Born in Blood

On February 20, 1947, British prime minister Clement Attlee announced that Britain would "transfer power into responsible Indian hands by a date not later than June 1948."[1] He added that the British government would have to "consider to whom the powers of British India should be handed over, on the due date, whether as a whole to some form of Central Government or in some areas to existing provincial governments or in such other way as may seem most reasonable."[2] The transition was to be implemented under the viceroyalty of a cousin of King George VI, Lord Louis Mountbatten, who would succeed Lord Wavell.

The immediate and adverse impact of Atlee's historic declaration was felt by the Unionist Party in Punjab, which had a long history of loyalty to the British emperor. Its prestige plummeted. The Muslim League, which had already been agitating in the province, took advantage of this change in status. Since the first letter of the envisioned Pakistan stood for Punjab, local League leaders redoubled their campaign against Chief Minister Sir Khizr Hayat Tiwana.

Unable to bear the label of "traitor to Islam" that League partisans had vociferously pinned on him, he resigned on March 2. But when Governor Sir Evan Jenkins called on League leader Iftikhar Hussain Khan Mamdot to form a ministry, he failed to line up a majority. This was just as well. As chief minister, he would have found it an uphill task to maintain law and order in a province of over thirty-five million, where communal passions were escalating rapidly—with Hindus and Sikhs, forming 45 percent of the population, on one side, and Muslims, constituting 53 percent, on the other.

Nearly six million Sikhs, half as numerous as Hindus, were vehemently opposed to Pakistan, which would have sliced the community into two parts, with one in the Muslim homeland. Their leader, seventy-two-year-old Master Tara Singh, a former Hindu, declared March 11 as Anti-Pakistan Day. To spur fellow Sikhs, he recycled the slogan of the last Sikh guru, Gobind Singh (died 1708), *Raj karega Khalsa, aki rahe na koi* (Punjabi: "The pure Sikhs will rule, no resister will live").[3] Sikhs' animosity toward Muslims was grounded in the defeats that their warlord Maharaja Ranjit Singh (1780–1839) had inflicted on the Mughals, resulting in the rise of the Sikh kingdom, which covered most of northwestern India.

Incendiary speeches stoked hatred between Sikhs and Muslims. The militant Muslim League National Guard and Muslim ex-servicemen attacked Sikhs. Within days communal violence spread to the villages of Rawalpindi and Multan districts. In the former, Sikhs were butchered. "In many villages they were herded into houses and burnt alive," noted Governor Sir Evan Jenkins in his report of April 16. "Many Sikhs had their hair and beards cut, and there were cases of forcible circumcision. Many Sikh women who escaped slaughter were abducted."[4] Pillage and arson accompanied the murder of an estimated 3,500 Sikhs. More than 40,000 displaced Sikhs were sheltered in hastily established refugee camps.

In polar contrast to the condoning of this mass violence by the League's leaders, General Sir Frank Messervy, then posted in the province, was horrified. "Having served for 34 years, mostly in the Punjab and with Punjab troops, I would never have believed that agitation could have aroused the normally chivalrous and decent Punjabi Muslim peasant to such frenzied savagery as was widely prevalent," he wrote. Besides the major communal factor, he mentioned two minor causes.

> The first is the economic element. Scarcity of cloth and some items of food, such as sugar, have been exploited by the Hindu-Sikh *bania* [shopkeeper] community to profiteer and indulge in black-market operations. The government controls were also mostly in the hands of Sikh or Hindu agents and clerks. The Muslim peasant and laborers were only too ready to get some of their own back when they got the chance. The second is the "goonda" [goon] element in every community, which is always ready to take full advantage of such disturbances to practice arson, loot and dacoity [armed robbery].[5]

In retrospect this carnage would prove to be the rumbling of a volcano that would erupt with searing ferocity five months later.

PARTITION BECOMING INEVITABLE

It was this Cyclopean convulsion in Punjab that awaited Lord Louis Mountbatten—tall and handsome in his naval white uniform, embellished with an impressive array of decorations and orders—along with his slim, gangling wife, Edwina, when they arrived in Delhi on March 22.

The next day, the seventh anniversary of the Muslim League's Lahore resolution, Jinnah warned that "terrific disasters" awaited India if there were no Pakistan. On March 27, Finance Minister Liaquat Ali Khan presented his first budget, proposing a business profit tax, a capital gains tax, and a higher duty on tea. In their criticism, instead of describing his budget as antibusiness or socialistic, and likely to be seen as progressive, opponents accused him of grinding his communalist axe.

Khan was indignant. "If I present a budget which according to me is the budget which consists of principles which I believe India should follow, they [critics] say now here is Pakistan." He regretted that the budget was seen as an attempt by him to "ruin the economic life of the country and then go away to Pakistan."[6]

On March 31, Viceroy Mountbatten had the first of six meetings with Gandhi that stretched over the next twelve days. He had an equal number of face-to-face conversations with Jinnah. On April 12, he deliberately allowed his meeting with Gandhi to overrun because his next interviewee was Jinnah. He hoped that if these two estranged political titans could be induced to speak to each other, progress might be made. Arriving on time, Jinnah occupied a large leather armchair as distant from Gandhi as possible. Both of them lowered their voices as they spoke to the viceroy. He acted as the common interlocutor. He suggested they meet separately. They agreed.

Since Gandhi was staying in the insalubrious quarters of the Untouchables, their meeting could only take place at Jinnah's spacious bungalow surrounded by a neatly maintained garden on Aurangzeb Road in New Delhi. At the end of a three-hour-long "friendly" talk on April 15, they disagreed on partitioning India. But they issued a joint communiqué, deploring "the recent acts of lawlessness and violence that have brought the utmost disgrace to the fair name of India" and denouncing "the use of force to achieve political aims."[7] Characteristically, Gandhi signed the statement in Hindi, Urdu, and English, whereas Jinnah did so only in English. Their appeal received no response.

Relations between Congress and League members of the interim cabinet were so fraught that Congress ministers could not fill a post or transfer an official with the consent of their League colleagues. There was a food shortage in the country, but polarization in the government and bureaucracy blocked remedial action. Frustrated by the internecine war within his cabinet, Jawaharlal Nehru declared on April 21: "The Muslim League can have Pakistan if they wish to have it, but on condition that they do not take other parts of India which do not wish to join Pakistan."[8]

Gandhi saw the writing on the wall. "The Congress has accepted Pakistan and demanded the division of the Punjab and Bengal," he said during his prayer meeting on May 7. "I am opposed to any division of India now as I always have been. . . . The only thing I can do is to disassociate myself from such a scheme."[9]

MENON'S ASTUTE PLAN

Now the practicalities of the transfer of power had to be worked out. Here a senior Indian civil servant bearing the title of reforms commissioner, Vapal Pangunni Menon, proved innovative. He proposed that power be transferred to two central governments, one each in India and Pakistan, which should simultaneously be accorded the status of Dominion within the British Commonwealth of Nations (British Commonwealth, for short). The provincial assemblies in Punjab and Bengal should decide partition or continued unity. Instead of waiting for a new constitution to be framed by the present Constituent Assembly, Britain should pass on power immediately to the new central governments, which would operate under the Government of India Act 1935 until the declaration of their own constitutions.

Mountbatten had a meeting with Jinnah and Liaquat Ali Khan on May 17 as he prepared to fly to London for urgent meetings there, starting with Attlee. They concurred with the Menon Plan. Nehru had earlier accorded it an informal nod.

By the time Mountbatten was summoned by Attlee on May 18, he could claim a provisional acceptance of the Menon Plan by the two Indian principals. He took Menon with him. In London, he lobbied the Menon Plan successfully first with Attlee, then his cabinet, and lastly Sir Winston Churchill, leader of the opposition Conservative Party. This kept him busy for ten days.

On May 25 in Delhi, keenly aware that the final die was being cast in London, Nehru urged Gandhi, then preaching Hindu-Muslim amity in East Bengal, to rush to Delhi to join him at the center-stage of history. But instead of boarding the special aircraft offered to him, Gandhi stuck to traveling by train.

Mountbatten and his party returned to Delhi on May 31. Two days later, in the pale gray office at the viceroy's house, he chaired a meeting of seven Indian leaders. On his left sat Jinnah, flanked by Liaquat Ali Khan, next to Abdur Rab Nishtar with his jet black walrus mustache and a white turban with upright, pleated top, and on his right was Nehru, next to the bald-headed, leathery-faced home minister Vallabhbhai Patel; Jiwatram Bhagwandas Kripalani, the mustached, skeletal Congress president; and defense minister Baldev Singh, a robust, turbaned Sikh. Mountbatten briefed the august assembly on the details of the transfer of power. He let the assorted leaders consider the details overnight and give their opinion the next day.

Soon after the end of this meeting and the departure of the leaders, Gandhi was ushered into his office. Being Monday, it was the Mahatma's weekly day of silence. After sitting down without uttering a word, he informed the viceroy of his vow of silence in his scrawling handwriting. He did not comment on the Menon Plan. Instead, he referred to the cabinet mission's May 16 statement, which had rejected partition.[10]

That evening Mountbatten left a dinner party early for a one-on-one dialogue with Jinnah. He gave an account of this crucial meeting in his speech, titled "Transfer of Power in India," to the Royal Empire Society in London, on October 6, 1948. "The Congress leaders agreed that they would accept partition to avoid civil war," he told his audience. But they refused to let large non-Muslim areas go to Pakistan. "That automatically meant a partition of the great provinces of the Punjab and Bengal," so their non-Muslim areas would not be incorporated into Muslim Pakistan.

> When I told Mr. Jinnah that I had their [Congress leaders'] provisional agreement to partition, he was overjoyed. When I said that it logically followed that this would involve partition of the Punjab and Bengal he was horrified. He produced the strongest arguments why these provinces should not be partitioned. He said that they had national characteristics and that partition would be disastrous. I agreed, but I said how much more must I now feel that the same considerations applied to the partitioning of the whole of India. He did not like that, and started explaining why India had to be partitioned. So we went round and round the mulberry bush until finally

he realized that either he could have a United India with an un-partitioned Punjab and Bengal or divided India with a partitioned Punjab and Bengal. And he finally accepted the latter solution.[11]

When the seven Indian leaders met again on June 3, they formally endorsed the Menon Plan, which meant the Congress giving up its demand for a transfer of power and the framing of a constitution *before* partition. It also meant a smaller Pakistan than the one envisaged by Jinnah. At the end, Mountbatten produced a communiqué to be signed by the attendees. Jinnah refused to do so, giving his assent only with a nod.[12]

That evening, as the viceroy, accompanied by Nehru, Jinnah, and Baldev Singh, waited in the studios of All India Radio (AIR), Attlee announced the details of the handover to the House of Common. In his speech on AIR, Mountbatten said that "if" there is partition—implying that it depended on the vote in the Punjab and Bengal Assemblies.

In his broadcast, Jinnah stated that the final decision on the British plan rested with the Muslim League Council, scheduled to meet on June 9. After paying tribute to the viceroy's "fairness and impartiality," he referred to the referendum to be held in the Congress-ruled North-West Frontier Province (NWFP) whether to join Pakistan or Hindustan. He called on the provincial League leaders to end the civil disobedience campaign they had launched there. He signed off with the slogan "Pakistan *zindabad*" ("Long live Pakistan").[13]

At the press conference on June 4, Mountbatten said, "I think the transfer [of power] could be about the 15th of August." Soon after, under his chairmanship, he set up the four-member Partition Council, two each from the Congress (Patel and Rajendra Prasad) and the League (Jinnah and Liaquat Ali Khan). Their tasks were to supervise the division of civil servants and military personnel as well as governmental assets—from typewriters to locomotives, including the treasury of British India—into the two successor states.

With the Congress-majority government in Delhi regarding the imminent partition as secession of some parts from the center, the (Muslim) officials opting for Pakistan found themselves ejected from their offices. Therefore the planning for Pakistan was carried out in tents. Later, with the population and the area of Pakistan estimated respectively at 17.5 percent and 20 percent of the India of the British Empire (British India and 562 princely states), it was to be allocated 18.75 percent of the assets of the existing political entity.

Thus Jinnah got what he called a "maimed, moth eaten" Pakistan, with its eastern and western wings separated by one thousand miles of Indian soil, hanging like two lobes on either ear of the body of India. Of its seventy-seven million inhabitants, forty-one million were concentrated in the eastern wing, occupying only one-sixth of the national territory.

The members of the League's Council assembled in New Delhi's Imperial Hotel on June 9. By a vote of 300 to 10 they adopted a resolution stating that though the Council could not agree to the partition of Bengal and Punjab, it considered the transfer-of-power plan as a whole and decided to give full authority to Quaid-i-Azam Jinnah to accept its basic principle as a compromise, and left it to him to work out the details.[14] The Council's meeting in the ballroom on the first floor was distracted by a band of fifty Khaksars, a militant Muslim group demanding the inclusion of Delhi in Pakistan. They were thrown out by uniformed Muslim League National Guard volunteers before they could reach the ballroom.[15]

On June 15 the All India Congress Committee (AICC) passed a resolution by 153 to 29 votes to accept the June 3 plan. To sweeten the bitter partition pill, Maulana Abul Kalam Muhiyuddin Ahmed Azad, the former longest serving Congress president, said: "The division is only of the map of the country and not in the hearts of the people, and I am sure it is going to be a short-lived partition."[16]

As expected, the legislative assemblies of Bengal and Punjab opted for division, with the latter doing so on June 23. With Hindus lacking majority in any district of Sindh, that provincial assembly decided to join the Pakistan Constituent Assembly. In Baluchistan the same decision was reached by the local tribal leaders, appointed by the British Raj, and the nominees of Quetta's municipality.

In the July 6–7 referendum in Sylhet, the Muslim-majority district of Assam, 239,600 favored joining East Bengal, while 184,000 voted to stay with the Hindu-majority Assam.[17] Sylhet and East Bengal together formed East Pakistan. Three days later, it was announced that Jinnah would be the governor-general of Pakistan.

In the highly strategic NWFP, the Congress Party called for a boycott of the referendum held between July 6 and 17 under the supervision of British officers of the Indian Army. Of the 572,800 eligible voters, 51 percent participated, and 99 percent opted for the Pakistan Constituent Assembly. With the total votes cast in the referendum being only 25 percent less than in the 1946 provincial assembly election, the call of the Congress for a boycott had proved virtually ineffective.[18]

On July 18, King George VI signed the Indian Independence Act 1947. The government in Delhi informally split into two cabinets, with the one for Pakistan led by Liaquat Ali Khan.

A week later Mountbatten addressed the issue of the future of the princely states (aka, native states), which had signed treaties with Britain accepting the paramountcy of the British crown. More than 560 such entities occupied a third of India under the British Empire, their sizes varying from a few square miles to eighty-thousand-plus square miles in the case of Hyderabad and that of Jammu and Kashmir.

In his speech to the Chamber of Princes, the viceroy offered them the chance of signing an instrument of accession with India or Pakistan: it would ensure their continued autonomy and access to their "privy purses"—part of the taxes due to them for their royal upkeep—in lieu of letting the new dominion conduct their international relations and defense. Referring to his blood relationship with the British monarch, Mountbatten stated that the emperor of India would be offended if they did not accede to one or the other dominion under the British crown. The native rulers were also aware of Nehru's warning that any independent state would be considered an enemy by the Indian Dominion—as well as the declaration by the Congress Working Committee in June that the end of the British paramountcy did not mean sovereign independence.

Little wonder that signed instruments of accession to the "Indian Union"—which was yet to emerge—landed on Mountbatten's desk thick and fast just as the Congress-dominated interim government set up a "States Department" under Patel assisted by Menon.[19] But the Muslim Nizam of Hindu-majority Hyderabad and the Hindu Maharaja of Muslim-majority Jammu and Kashmir sat on the fence.

The decision of the Muslim ruler of the Hindu-majority Junagarh, measuring twenty-three square miles along the coast of north Gujarat, to accede to Pakistan could not be implemented. But this was a trivial matter compared to the complexities of Punjab.

BLOOD-SOAKED DIVISION OF THE LAND OF FIVE RIVERS

In British India, the five tributaries of the Indus that gave the province its name Punjab (Urdu: *Punj*, five; *aab*, water) were, from east to west, Beas, Sutlej, Ravi, Chenab, and Jhelum. In terms of religion, the western sector beyond the Chenab River was clearly meant to go to Pakistan and the sectors between Sutlej and Jamuna (later Yamuna) in the east to India. The populous central zone, rich and strategically important, was in dispute. Here the lives of Muslims, Hindus, and Sikhs were intricately integrated. There were also conflicting demands on holy shrines, railways, defensive frontiers, and irrigation facilities.

Baldev Singh's acceptance of the June 3 plan was challenged by militant Sikh leaders. In July they submitted a memorandum to the Boundary Commission, chaired by the eminent British lawyer Sir Cyril Radcliffe, which proposed using the Chenab River to divide Punjab in order to keep 90 percent of its Sikhs in India. Since this would have further reduced the "maimed, moth-eaten" Pakistan Jinnah had reluctantly agreed to, the proposal was summarily rejected.

The Sikhs grew apprehensive. Militancy rose steeply in a community that had once been classified by the British as one of the "martial races" of India. Agitated Sikh leaders convened political assemblies in their *gurdwaras*, or temples, to plan anti-Muslim strikes. They recruited ex-servicemen and armed them with private stockpiles of revolvers, rifles, shotguns, tommy guns (aka, Thompson submachine guns), and light machine guns as well as grenades, spears, and axes. They decided to avenge the earlier anti-Sikh carnage in northern Punjab with unremitting vengeance in the central Punjab districts of Lahore and Gurdaspur. Their savage assaults were conducted with military precision. Terrified Muslims struggled to defend themselves.

When Muslims sighted an armed Sikh squad, they would rush to their roofs and beat gongs to alert neighboring Muslim settlements. The gun-toting Sikhs targeted their prey as other members of the attacking party threw grenades over compound walls to force the residents into the street, where the attackers, armed with tridents, spears, and sharp, small swords—called *kirpans*, carried as a religious obligation—slaughtered them. Finally, the older members of the Sikh squad set alight the village with outriders ready with spears and *kirpans* to hack the escapees.

In his fortnightly report to the viceroy, Punjab governor Jenkins noted on August 4 that he was witnessing nothing less than a "communal war of succession" in the province as competing groups struggled "for the power we are shortly to abandon. . . . Moreover, there is very little doubt that the disturbances have in some degree been organized and paid for by persons or bodies directly or indirectly under the control of the Muslim League, the Congress, and the [Sikh] Akali Party."[20] His chief investigator of crimes, Gerald Savage, personally informed Mountbatten that his intelligence showed the militant Sikhs of the Akal Fauj (Punjabi: Eternal Army) planning bombings and train derailments.

To cope with the expected surge in stomach-churning violence, Field Marshall Sir Claude Auchinleck, commander in chief of the British Indian Army, transformed the Fourth Indian Division into the Punjab Boundary Force under Major General Thomas Pete Rees on July 17. Rees was given four brigadiers (two Muslim, one Hindu, and one Sikh) as advisors. It started functioning on August 1.[21]

But reports of an exponential rise in bloodletting and arson piled up by the time Jinnah flew from Delhi to Karachi, the temporary capital of Pakistan, on August 7. Before boarding Lord Mountbatten's silver Dakota along with his sister Fatima, he rued: "I suppose this is the last time I'll be looking at Delhi."[22] He was received in Karachi as the governor-general designate of Pakistan. Four days later the inaugural session of the Pakistan Constituent Assembly gave emergency powers to Jinnah as well as electing him president of the Assembly.

Officially, Sir Cyril Radcliffe's decision on the demarcation of boundaries in Bengal-Assam and Punjab was to be announced on August 16. But leaks started much earlier.

On August 8, the sketch map of the Radcliffe Line, showing the allotment to Pakistan of the *tehsils* (subdistricts) of Ferozepur and Zira forming the Ferozepur salient east of the Sutlej River, was leaked to Nehru and Patel by Radcliffe's Indian assistant secretary.[23]

Radcliffe informed the civil, military, and police officers of the central districts of Punjab to make advance police and troop deployments. In Delhi this news leaked through other sources, including Mountbatten's Indian administrative staff. This demarcation was equivalent to pointing a dagger at the core of the Sikh heartland. It also meant Nankana Sahib, the birthplace of Guru Nanak Dev (1469–1539), the founder of Sikhism, going to West Punjab. Sikh militants were furious.

On the night of August 9 they unleashed a war of attrition. A squad of Sikhs, using electronic devices, derailed the Pakistan Special No. 1 train carrying senior Muslim civil servants who had opted for Pakistan, along with their families, from Delhi to Lahore near the border of the princely state of Patiala in East Punjab. Several passengers were killed.

"Feeling in Lahore city is now unbelievably bad and Inspector General [of Police] tells me that Muslim League National Guard appearing in uniform and that Police are most unsteady," read Governor Jenkins's wire to the viceroy on August 12. The next day he reported the murders of nearly four hundred people in Punjab, and flames ravaging Amritsar. "General situation deteriorating," concluded his telegram.[24] The cauldron that had been boiling since March now spilled over, with ghastly consequences.

Among others, Jinnah was horrified by the heart-wrenching butchery being perpetrated in Punjab. This was the background against which he addressed the seventy-nine-member Pakistan Constituent Assembly on August 11. "I know there are people who do not quite agree with the division of India," he said. "But in my judgment there was no other solution and I am sure future history will record its verdict in favor of it. . . . Maybe that view is correct; maybe it is not; that remains to be seen." He added that his ambition was that Pakistan should become a nation in which there were no distinctions of "color, caste or creed":

> You are free, you are free to go to your temples. You are free to go to your mosques or to any other places of worship in this State of Pakistan. You may belong to any religion or caste or creed that has nothing to do with the business of the State. . . . We are starting in the days when there is no discrimination, no distinction between one community and another, no discrimination between one caste or creed or another. We are starting with this fundamental principle that we are all citizens and equal citizens of one State. . . . Now, I think we should keep that in front of us as our ideal and you will find that in course of time Hindus would cease to be Hindus and Muslims would cease to be Muslims, not in the religious sense, because that is the personal faith of each individual, but in the political sense as citizens of the State.[25]

Extracts of this speech were widely disseminated in the hope that these would dampen the bloodthirsty frenzy that had gripped Hindus, Muslims, and Sikhs alike in Punjab and the NWFP. The tactic had little, if any, impact on the horrendous barbarity that was being perpetuated on the plains of Punjab.

A COMMUNAL HOLOCAUST

As India and Pakistan gained, respectively, their independence on August 14 and 15, 1947, the communal holocaust, the likes of which had never been witnessed before, continued. By the time it was over toward the end of October, it had claimed the lives of two hundred thousand to one million people. More recent research has gravitated toward a consensus around a death toll of five hundred thousand to six hundred thousand, divided almost equally between Muslims and non-Muslims.[26]

In economic terms, the losses of the comparatively better-off Hindus and Sikhs who moved to India far exceeded those of the Muslim migrants arriving in Pakistan. The 4.35 million Muslims who migrated to Pakistan from East Punjab left behind 4.7 million acres of land, whereas the 4.29 million Sikhs and Hindus who moved to India from West Punjab had to part with more fertile 6.7 million acres.[27] Moreover, as majority residents of urban areas in West Punjab, non-Muslims possessed assets that far exceeded those of Muslims in East Punjab. In Sindh, forming only a quarter of the population, Hindus owned almost three-quarters of the moveable and immovable property.

The unbridled savagery consisted of attacks by marauding mobs on villages, railway stations, trains, long caravans of displaced persons on the move, and refugee camps. These assaults involved mass murder, castration, mutilation, rape, looting, arson, abduction, and derailing of trains followed by the slaughtering of passengers. The most commonly used weapons were axes, scythes, swords, spears, and clubs, with revolvers, rifles, and light machine guns playing a minor role. Throwing the hapless members of the local minority into wells, the sole source of potable water in the subcontinent's villages, was a special feature of communal frenzy. Sexual assault of women became a dramatic means to highlight the victim community's vulnerability and the humiliation of its men folk.

On August 13 Lord Mountbatten and Edwina flew to Karachi. As a secondary school student in Karachi at the time, I had witnessed the building of barracks-like structures on the vast empty plots of the city to serve as Pakistan's sprawling secretariat, posthaste, with construction workers laboring around the clock. On August 14, along with many thousands of other spectators, I saw the skeletal Jinnah, in *salwar* and long coat topped with a black karakul hat, and Viceroy Mountbatten, dressed as an admiral, standing side by side in an open-roofed Rolls Royce as their vehicle traveled slowly from the provincial governor's residence to the Constituent Assembly.

In stark contrast to Punjab, the small province of Sindh, with a little over five million inhabitants—a quarter of them Hindus—was peaceful. The half million residents of its capital, Karachi, were divided almost equally between Hindus and Muslims. On the birthday of Pakistan, there was a carnival atmosphere in the capital. This atmosphere was heightened by the authorities' decision to make travel by buses and trams free. The pleasant sea breeze of the port city was filled with hope and exuberance. The milling crowds inhaling it were in high spirits—unmindful of the human blood flowing into the soil of Punjab, or the fact that the coming influx of Urdu-speaking Muslims from adjoining Gujarat and Rajasthan, as well as distant United Provinces (UP) and Bihar, into the city would turn the local Sindhi- and Baluchi-speaking Muslims into a minority.

After addressing the Pakistani Constituent Assembly, Mountbatten boarded his Dakota at noon. As his plane flew over the plains of Punjab on its way to the Indian capital, the viceroy saw many of the province's seventeen thousand villages in flames. Mindful of the dreadful violence ravaging neighboring Punjab, the authorities in Delhi cancelled formal, colorful ceremonies. Instead, they settled for speeches from the ramparts of the seventeenth-century Red Fort. The walls of the streets were re-painted and banners hung, with fences and trees wired with countless orange, green, and white lights—the colors of the national flag—while horse carriage drivers painted the legs of their animals in the national colors, and cloth merchants did a roaring trade, selling tricolored saris.

At eleven PM Nehru started addressing the mammoth crowd outside the Red Fort. "At the stroke of the midnight hour," he said, "India will awake to life and freedom. A moment comes, which comes but rarely in history, when we step out from the old to the new, when an age ends, and when the soul of a nation, long suppressed, finds utterance." But the loudest applause that stirred the air on that momentous day came when Viceroy Mountbatten declared, "At this historic moment let us not forget all that India owes to Mahatma Gandhi—the architect of her freedom through nonviolence. We miss his presence here today and would have him know how he is in our thoughts."[28] That remark earned Mountbatten popular goodwill on the eve of becoming the governor-general of the Dominion of India.

Unreconciled to the partition of the subcontinent, which he called "a spiritual tragedy," Gandhi had stayed away from the official ceremonies in Delhi. A week earlier, arriving in Calcutta, he had lodged himself in the mansion of a Muslim widow in the suburb of Belliaghatta along with Hussein Shaheed Suhrawardy, praying and fasting to bring about Hindu-Muslim amity.[29]

UPSURGE IN CATHARTIC BLOODLETTING

Just as Indians were celebrating their first day of independence, a Pakistan Special train heading for Lahore was derailed near Amritsar by Sikh extremists. There were two similar derailments over the next couple of days. In retaliation, enraged Muslim mobs ambushed three overcrowded India-bound trains in the Wazirabad-Sialkot area and massacred the passengers.[30] The frenzied crowds vented their primeval religious hatred and animosities, bottled up during the past many generations, in an orgy of cathartic bloodletting.

Though the fatalities caused by the wholesale murder of packed trains were a fraction of the grand total, the novelty of this sort of mind-numbing carnage left a lingering mark on the popular psyche. This was brought home by Khushwant Singh (1915–2014), the author of the classic novel *Train to Pakistan*. One sunny summer day in 1947, when this thirty-two-year-old, turbaned and spectacled Sikh lawyer was being chauffeured from his home in Lahore to his family's summer residence in Kasauli at the foothills of the Himalayas, he encountered a jeep carrying Sikhs, armed with rifles and blood-covered spears, on an unusually empty road. The Sikhs stopped his car and triumphantly described in grisly detail how they had butchered in cold blood all the inhabitants of the nearby Muslim village. The attackers' gratification in indulging their blood lust left a deep mark on Khushwant Singh's secular psyche. It became the seed out of which grew his novel, published in 1956.[31]

The story is set in an imagined Indian village of Mano Majra near a railway bridge on the Indo-Pakistan border, a settlement mainly of Sikhs and Muslims, coexisting peacefully in their separate quarters. When the local Hindu moneylender is killed, suspicion falls on Juggat Singh, a brawny Sikh convict on parole, who holds a secret rendezvous with Nooran, the nubile daughter of the near-blind mullah. When a train arrives at the village railroad station carrying the corpses of Sikhs from Pakistan, tension escalates rapidly. The police are unable to cope with spiraling communal violence. The government orders all Muslims to leave by a special train at night. A Sikh gang plans to ambush it and kill its passengers. Aware that the train is carrying Nooran, pregnant with his child, Juggut Singh foils the marauding scheme and in the process gets killed by the Sikh band. The novel admirably captures the gritty reality and spine-chilling horror of the partition memorably.

Factual accounts of the time describe Nehru, deeply shaken by the horrifying events, flying to Lahore, where the Hindu-Sikh population had shrunk from three hundred thousand to ten thousand, on August 17 to meet his Pakistani counterpart, Liaquat Ali Khan. They appealed for peace in their broadcasts—but to no avail.

During the rest of August, Nehru made forays into East Punjab three times, talking to people on both sides of the newly created border, to take stock of the rapidly worsening situation. Sadly, he concluded, "Both sides have been incredibly inhuman and barbarous."[32]

As Hindu and Sikh refugees from West Punjab started pouring into Delhi, to be herded into makeshift refugee camps, anti-Muslim sentiment rose steeply, reaching fever pitch by late August. Soon the Indian capital would become the crucible for the murderous passions consuming the adjoining Punjab.

On August 31 the eighteen-day peace in Calcutta, mediated by Gandhi, broke down when one thousand Hindu youths brought a wounded Hindu to his house in Belliaghata, claiming that he had been stabbed by Muslims. Gandhi faced the angry, screaming mob with folded arms. A stick thrown at him failed to strike. That ended the showdown. But the Mahatma was troubled. On September 2 he started to fast. Within a day leaders of all faiths and parties came to plead with him to end it while Hindu and Muslim goons turned up to apologize with tearful eyes. Calm returned to the city. On September 4 he ended his hunger strike.

In Delhi, the unending stream of Hindu and Sikh refugees pouring into the capital energized the cycle of reprisals and revenge. Their narratives, often exaggerated and embellished, fed the anti-Muslim mania already on the upswing. On September 4 serious rioting erupted in Delhi, with Muslims bearing the brunt. Two days later, a bomb thrown into New Delhi's railway station, packed with Muslims departing for Pakistan, killed many.

On September 7, looters descended on the Connaught Circus, the huge plaza in the capital's heart. "The dead [Muslims] lay rotting in the streets, because there was no one to collect and bury them," noted General Hastings Ismay, the viceroy's chief of staff. "The hospitals were choked with [the] dying and wounded, and in imminent danger of attack because of the presence of Muslim staff and Muslim patients. Arson and looting were widespread. . . . The Muslim members of the Delhi police had either deserted or were disarmed: the Hindu members had either been suborned or were afraid to do their duty."[33]

The government imposed a curfew, called the army, and issued a shoot-to-kill order. In his September 9 radio broadcast, Nehru said, "We are dealing with a situation that is analogous to war, and we are going to deal with it on a war basis in every sense of the word."[34] By the time law and order was restored, 10,000 Muslims were dead, and 330,000, forming a third of the city's total population, had fled their homes out of fear.[35]

Nehru rose to the occasion with exemplary courage and conviction. He turned the vast garden of his official residence into a campsite of tents for Muslim refugees. He walked into the streets fearlessly and conversed with common folk. He single-handedly challenged the rioters and looters. His spontaneous forays into the street to confront violent hooligans were sufficiently dramatic to warrant a moving sequence in Richard Attenborough's *Gandhi.*

Behind closed doors, Patel and Prasad—both members of the Partition Council—advocated the dismissal of all Muslim officials and argued that there was little point in deploying Indian soldiers to protect Muslim citizens. By contrast, Nehru personally rushed to Connaught Circus and Old Delhi to stop murder and pillage, and to assure Muslim families that they could rely on the protection of his government. To him—in the words of Sunil Khilnani, an Indian chronicler—"partition was above all, however, a test of the Indian state's sovereignty, its capacity to protect its citizens, keep order, and justify its territorial ownership."[36]

Shocked by the tales of violence against the Hindus and Sikhs of Punjab, almost half of Nehru's cabinet, led by Patel, seemed inclined to opt for a "Hindu Pakistan." Nehru put his foot down. "As long as I am at the helm of affairs, India will not become a Hindu state," he declared. "The whole idea of a theocratic state is not only medieval but also stupid."[37] He was not prepared to remain the prime minister for a single day if that was the price he had to pay for Hindu India.[38]

Nehru, a staunch secularist, thus proved his mettle in the face of a gargantuan challenge at a most crucial moment in India's history. In the acute crisis of explosive proportions, he remained clear-eyed, resolute, and perceptive. He described the situation in India as "a ship on fire in mid-ocean with ammunition in hold."[39] He ignored the argument that Prasad advanced in his letter of September 17: the use of the army to save Muslims was making the government unpopular. Disagreeing with Patel,

Nehru said that he did not want to exact a price from Muslims for having supported the Pakistan movement in the past. If for that reason he was to be dubbed "Maulana Nehru," so be it.

He was helped by the timely arrival of Gandhi from Calcutta on September 10. The Mahatma had intended to proceed to Punjab to break the murderous cycle of revenge and counterrevenge, but Patel dissuaded him: the situation there was far too explosive. So instead of setting up his modest office in the Untouchables' colony, as he had done before, he chose the safe address of the Birla House, the spacious mansion of the textile millionaire Ghanshyam Das Birla, his long-time patron and financier. Gandhi argued that besides looking after the Hindu and Sikh refugees from Pakistan, the Indian government should take care of the internally displaced Muslims in the capital's assorted refugee camps, including such historic sites as the dilapidated Old Fort.

With population exchange across the newly created Indo-Pakistan increasing in speed by the day, the number of refugees swelled. The ad hoc refugee colonies burst at the seams. The only way to register the size of this unparalleled exodus was to survey the scene from the air. So that was what Mountbatten did, together with the most senior cabinet ministers.

CARAVANS OF DESPAIR

On September 21 Mountbatten took Patel and Nehru along with a few aides on a round trip in his Dakota to "view the Punjab migration." Near Ferozepur in the vicinity of the Indo-Pakistan border, they noticed the first caravan of non-Muslim refugees—and continued to see it for fifty miles without finding its source.[40]

Earlier, on September 2, a press report from Lahore headlined, "Gigantic Exchange of Two Million People Begins in the Punjab," referred to a sixty-mile-long caravan of non-Muslims. Consisting mainly of those possessing bullock carts or pack animals, it took thirty-six hours to cross the Sulaimanki Barrage Bridge over the Sutlej River in West Punjab.[41] These groups were part of the biggest mass migration in history.

An insight into the creation of such seemingly endless caravans—which dwarfed the biblical exodus of the Israelites from Egypt—was provided later by the father of Dalvinder Singh Grewal, a retired colonel born in the village of Rattan in Lyallpur (now Faisalabad) district, West Punjab. As part of a caravan, the senior Singh had kept a diary.

On September 4, 1947, a train from India arrived at Gojra, thirty miles from Rattan, stacked with corpses and hideously injured Muslims. Local Muslims were enraged and vowed to avenge the massacre. The inhabitants of the almost exclusively Hindu-Sikh village of Rattan began to seriously consider migrating to the Indian Punjab. They resolved to leave when they heard of the appearance of another train, drenched with Muslim blood, at the nearby Pakka Anna station.

On September 10 the Hindu and Sikh households in Rattan started loading their essential possessions, including food and clothing, on bullock carts. They let loose their cattle. The next afternoon all non-Muslim families quit their ancestral settlement, reducing it to three Muslim households. While the carts carried children, the elderly, and the infirm, adult men and women walked. In the evening they reached Dhaipai, where they became part of a bigger caravan, which included the non-Muslim residents of six other villages.

The long caravan started trudging before sunrise and was escorted by a squad of mounted young Sikhs carrying rifles to secure its flanks, front, and rear. When its members reached the Theekriwala Canal Rest House in the evening, they camped along the canal. They fed fodder collected from the nearby fields to the oxen and had their first meal after covering fifteen miles in fourteen hours. They obtained water from local pumps and wells, even though some wells, containing corpses, were polluted. At the next stop at Sudhir they were instructed by the district commissioner to stay put to avoid a brutal attack by a band of enraged Muslims. They did—for three days. They suffered from water scarcity because the nearby ponds and wells were polluted by floating corpses.

It was only when they reached Lyallpur that local Sikhs provided them food and water. On September 19, when the caravan was a mile short of Balloki Head, it was fired on by an armed band of Muslims. Its mounted Sikh guards responded in kind. Nonetheless, a Hindu resident of Rattan was killed. (Instead of being cremated, he was buried in an open field.) The episode heightened fear among the refugees, surrounded as they were by burning villages and intermittent cries of *"Allah-u-Akbar"* ("God is great"). After they had crossed the Ravi River and camped along its other bank, the Sikh men armed all women, Sikh and Hindu, with a sheathed *kirpan*, held by a strip of cloth across the torso. If assaulted, the women were to kill the attacker, failing which they were instructed to turn the deadly weapon on themselves. Mercifully, such an eventuality did not come to pass.

After four more days of dreary marching, and the deaths of many children and elderly people from diarrhea caused by drinking polluted water, the caravan crossed the unmarked Indo-Pakistan border at Khem Karan on September 25. That was the end of their two-week-long life-saving trek.[42]

Earlier, the displaced Muslims from East Punjab and the neighboring areas trekking their way on foot or in caravans to West Punjab had faced the additional strain of observing the daytime fast during the month of Ramadan, which started on July 19. Because of the delayed monsoon rains, the temperature was often 100 degrees Fahrenheit in the shade.

"There is another sight I am not likely to easily forget," reported the Punjab correspondent of the Madras-based, English-language weekly *Swatantra*:

> a five mile long caravan of 20,000 Muslim refugees crawling at a snail's pace into Pakistan over the Sutlej Bridge, with bullock carts piled high with pitiful chattels, cattle being driven alongside, women with babies in their arms and wretched little tin trunks on their heads. 20,000 men, women and children trekking into the promised land—not because it is the promised land, but because bands of Hindus and Sikhs in Faridkot [Princely] State and the interior of Ferozepur district had hacked hundreds of Muslims to death and made life impossible for the rest.[43]

During Governor-General Jinnah's visit to Lahore, his rehabilitation minister, Mian Iftikharuddin, and editor of the *Pakistan Times*, Mazhar Ali Khan, flew him over the divided Punjab. On sighting the endless streams of people pouring into and out of West Punjab, he reportedly struck his forehead with a hand in a sign of remorse and said, "What have I done?"[44]

It was not until the end of October that the population exchange in the partitioned Punjab was completed. And it was not until a year later that there was a one-way exodus of a million Hindus from Sindh to different parts of India. By then an equal number of Hindus had moved to West Bengal from East Pakistan. According to India's 1951 census of displaced persons, 7.226 million Muslims migrated to East and West Pakistan from India, while 7.249 million Hindus and Sikhs moved in the other direction.[45]

Daunting though these challenges were for Nehru's cabinet, they paled before the steep hurdles Jinnah and his government had to surmount at the birth of Pakistan.

PAKISTAN: YEAR ZERO

When Pakistan's finance minister Ghulam Muhammad arrived in his Karachi office for his first day's work on August 15, 1947, he found it bare except for a single table. Everything else dispatched by train from Delhi had been looted en route.[46] As for his treasury, it had only Rs 200 million on hand. Pakistan was entitled to 18.75 percent of the current cash balances in Delhi, a little over Rs 4,000 million, amounting to Rs 750 million (worth $2.4 billion today), to be paid in two installments. For the present, Pakistan's available cash was barely enough to pay the Pakistani army for four months. Its outstanding debts amounted to almost Rs 400 million.

Jinnah, who had a flair for handling his own money skillfully, deployed all means to keep Pakistan solvent. His entreaty to the Nizam of Hyderabad, Sir Osman Ali Khan, resulted in an eagerly welcomed loan of Rs 200 million. Patel and his cohorts in Nehru's government were determined to strangle the nascent Muslim homeland at birth. Jinnah's appeals to other members of the British Commonwealth, including Britain, for financial assistance drew a blank. "Every effort is being made to put difficulties in our way by our enemies to paralyze or cripple our State and bring about its collapse," he complained to Attlee in his letter of October 1. "It is amazing that top-most Hindu leaders repeatedly say that Pakistan will have to submit to the Union of India. Pakistan will never surrender."[47]

Besides serving as the governor-general, president of the Constituent Assembly, and president of the Pakistan Muslim League, Jinnah took charge of dealing with the princely states and the tribal agencies of the NWFP. He also laid out foreign policy guidelines. Pakistan, he stressed, should develop friendly relations with the United States and Britain while projecting itself as a buffer zone between communist Soviet Union and dubious India, and a vantage point between China, then in the midst of a bloody civil war, and the Middle East.

Once Paul H. Alling had been named the US ambassador to Pakistan on September 20, Jinnah directed his appeal for funds to Washington. But before the State Department got around to sanctioning $10 million (Rs 48 million) as aid to the nascent nation in December 1947,[48] Jinnah found himself faced with a political-ideological challenge of enormous import—in Jammu and Kashmir. At the center of this crisis was Maharaja Sir Hari Singh.

6

The Infant Twins at War

Born in Jammu as the only child of General Sir Amar Singh and Rani Chib Devi, Hari Singh showed promise as a teenager. After attending the Princes' Mayo College in Ajmer, he graduated from the Indian Defense Academy in 1915 at the age of twenty. He was immediately appointed commander in chief of the Jammu and Kashmir state armed forces by Maharaja Partap Singh, his richly bearded, heavily turbaned uncle. His big-boned, muscular frame, topped by a jowly face, lent him gravitas beyond his age.

Fourteen years before Hari Singh's birth, Jammu and Kashmir became the largest princely state in India, at 84,470 square miles. Its constituent vassal territories of Gilgit Wazarat and Ladakh Wazarat, occupying three-quarters of its area, were sparsely populated because of high mountains, creating an inhospitable climate with an arid, treeless terrain. In 1941 only 311,500 people lived there. By contrast, the Jammu Province, abutting Punjab, was home to almost 2 million souls and the Kashmir Province to nearly 1.75 million. Overall, the state was 85 percent Muslim. The Jammu region, predominantly Muslim in the west, contained a Hindu-Sikh majority in the east. But in Kashmir, non-Muslims were a puny minority of 6 percent.[1]

SIR HARI SINGH VERSUS SHAIKH ABDULLAH

After the death of the childless Partap Singh in 1925, Hari Singh ascended the throne in Srinagar. The tension between this autocratic Hindu ruler and the largely Muslim population came to the fore with the formation of the Muslim Conference in 1932. Presided over by Shaikh Muhammad Abdullah, it demanded an end to the discrimination against Muslims in civil service. Two years later, responding to popular discontent, the maharaja established a State Assembly of 75 members, with only 30 members elected by a limited franchise.[2] In 1939 he raised the number of elected representatives to 40. But the gesture was meaningless since the Assembly lacked power.

The rising star in Kashmiri politics was Shaikh Abdullah. Since his father died soon after Abdullah's birth in a village near Srinagar, he grew up in poverty.[3] Yet he managed to obtain a master's degree in science from Aligarh Muslim University. He was a gangling young man, six-foot-four, oval-faced, with a sharp straight nose and a middle-distance gaze. He made his living as a schoolteacher.

In 1937, the thirty-two-year-old Abdullah was introduced to Jawaharlal Nehru in the waiting room of the Lahore railway station while the latter was en route to a tour of the North-West Frontier Province (NWFP). Their cordial talks became so engrossing that Nehru asked Abdullah to accompany him to Peshawar. He did. Nehru—a descendant of Kashmiri Brahmins who was born in the north Indian city of Allahabad—told Abdullah that he regarded himself a Kashmiri and advised him to open the Muslim Conference to all Kashmiris.[4] As a result of Abdullah's lobbying, the Muslim Conference's General Council changed the name to the National Conference in June 1939 and opened its doors to all those living in Kashmir. The dissidents, led by Ghulam Abbas, retained the original title of the party.

During World War II, thanks to Sir Hari's active encouragement of his subjects to join the British Indian Army, 71,667 signed up. Seven-eighths of them were Muslim, chiefly from the Poonch-Mirpur area of the Jammu region.[5] Aware of this, and the maharaja's military background, Prime Minister Sir Winston Churchill invited him to a meeting of the War Cabinet in April 1944. He felt honored.

After his return to Srinagar later in the year, he was presented with the National Conference's manifesto, titled "Naya Kashmir" (Urdu: New Kashmir), by Shaikh Abdullah. It demanded a fully democratic government with a constitutional monarch. Its economic blueprint called for the abolition of *zamindari* (Urdu: landlordism) under the slogan "Land to the Tiller." The autocratic Sir Hari rejected the manifesto summarily.

In the summer of 1944, when Muhammad Ali Jinnah was vacationing in Kashmir, he was invited to receptions by both the National Conference and the Muslim Conference. After meeting Shaikh Abdullah, Jinnah expressed ambivalent views about his party. But he was unequivocal in his comment on the Muslim Conference. "The Muslims have one platform, one *kalma* (Islamic creed), and one God," he said. "I would request the Muslims [of Kashmir] to come under the banner of the Muslim Conference and fight for their rights."[6]

Once World War II ended, Shaikh Abdullah tried to rally Kashmiris around the democratic model outlined by the New Kashmir manifesto. The pompous maharaja—given to decking himself in a much decorated military uniform—showed no sign of surrendering any of his powers.[7] That led Abdullah to emulate the Congress Party's 1942 Quit India movement and launch the Quit Kashmir campaign in May 1946. Its aim was to secure the resignation of the maharaja. Hundreds of people, including Abdullah, courted arrest.

Nehru, accompanied by another Congress leader, Asaf Ali, a lawyer, entered Kashmir by road with the intention of defending Abdullah in court. Nehru was arrested and deported instantly. Abdullah was sentenced to three years imprisonment.

Unsurprisingly, Jinnah dismissed the Quit Kashmir movement as "an agitation carried out by a few malcontents to create disorderly conditions in the State."[8] He urged the Muslim Conference to stay away from the campaign.

Like the pro-British Unionist politicians in Punjab, Sir Hari was shocked to hear Prime Minister Clement Attlee's February 1947 plan to quit India. He tried to distract himself from this news by indulging further his passion for polo and golf as well as poaching and wild game hunting.

As Britain's withdrawal gathered momentum, Sir Hari—influenced by his anti-Nehru prime minister, Ram Chandra Kak, who was married to a British woman—tilted toward declaring independence in order to maintain friendly relations with both India and Pakistan. In military-strategic terms, the chief of staff of the state's armed forces, Major-General H. L. Scott, could see merit in an independent Kashmir. In addition, the maharaja's astrologer, who claimed clairvoyant powers, declared that Maharaja Gulab Singh (ruled 1846–1857), the founder of the state, favored the inauguration of a sovereign Kashmir.

On the other hand, during his four-day stay in Srinagar in mid-June, Viceroy Lord Mountbatten advised Sir Hari to choose India or Pakistan before August 14. On the last day of his sojourn, when the maharaja was expected to convey his decision to the viceroy, Sir Hari feigned an attack of colic and cancelled the meeting. All the same, as promised, the British Raj returned the leased area of Gilgit Wazarat to the maharaja in July.

Nehru decided to fly to Srinagar but was dissuaded by Vallabhbhai Patel, who was in charge of the States Department. Instead, Mahatma Mohandas Gandhi was dispatched. During his meeting with Hari Singh and his pro-India wife, Tara Devi, on August 1, Gandhi repeated what the viceroy had told the Chamber of Princes a week earlier. By signing an instrument of accession with India he would continue to enjoy autonomy and receive his privy purse in exchange for surrendering foreign relations and defense to the imminent Dominion of India. Sir Hari, however, was disconsolate at the thought of Nehru settling old scores with him about his unceremonial ejection from the state a year earlier. Nevertheless, accepting Gandhi's advice and buttressed by his wife's inclination, he sacked the pro-independence Kak on August 10.

Two days later the newly appointed prime minister Major-General Janak Singh sent telegrams to the Pakistani and Indian governments offering a standstill agreement. Pakistan agreed; India did not. As for Gandhi's plea for the release of Abdullah, as part of his overarching counsel to the maharaja not to act against the wishes of his people, Sir Hari put it in his "pending" tray. He was not yet ready to make peace with long-time bête noire.

POST-MIDNIGHT BIRTHS OF TWINS

In July, noticing signs of discontent in the Muslim-dominated western Jammu Province, which had supplied tens of thousands of recruits to the Indian Army during the war, the maharaja urged ex-servicemen to surrender their arms to the local police. The response was lackadaisical. To the maharaja's alarm, many Muslim farmhands, working for Hindu landlords, defiantly displayed Pakistan's green flag, emblazoned with the star and crescent, after August 14.

This was a preamble to the anti-maharaja revolt by Muslims in the Poonch-Mirpur area of western Jammu, leading to the killing of some Hindus and displacement of many more. Sir Hari responded by unleashing his Hindu troops to quell the rebellion. They resorted to a scorched-earth policy. They fired on crowds, set alight houses and whole villages, looted, imposed curfews, and carried out wholesale arrests. There were many instances of collective punishment when, for instance, they burnt a whole village because of the rebellious act of just one family.[9]

"Within a period of about 11 weeks, starting in August, systematic savageries [in Jammu] . . . practically eliminated the entire Muslim element in the population, amounting to 500,000 people," wrote Ian Stephens, editor of the Calcutta-based *Statesman*, in his book *Pakistan*. "About 100,000 just disappeared, remaining untraceable, having presumably been butchered or died from epidemic or exposure. The rest fled to West Punjab."[10]

The maharaja's iron-fist policy inflamed the local Muslims, who joined the militia organized by the Muslim Conference, later to be called Azad Fauj (Urdu: Free Army) or Azad Army, with a claimed strength of fifty thousand, most of them being ex-servicemen. It would later come under the command of one General Tariq, the pseudonym of Brigadier Muhammad Akbar Khan of the Pakistan Army. "A few weeks after partition, I was asked by Mian Iftikharuddin [the minister for refugee rehabilitation] on behalf of [Prime Minister] Liaquat Ali Khan to prepare a plan for action in Kashmir," he would reveal in his interview with the Karachi-based *Defence Journal* published in the June–July 1985 issue. "I was called to a meeting with Liaquat Ali Khan at Lahore where the plan [of mine] was adopted, responsibilities allocated and orders issued. Everything was to be kept secret from the Army."[11] While remaining in charge of the princely states and the tribal areas, Jinnah had assigned Ali Khan the task of dealing with Kashmir.

On September 4, the Lahore-based *Civil and Military Gazette* reported an uprising in the Poonch area. And four days later the *Times* (of London) followed suit. By September 22, despite inadequate supplies of arms and ammunition, and poor communications, the Azad Army was doing so well that the outgoing Major General Scott, commanding only three brigades, informed the maharaja that his soldiers scattered in small pickets over a large area were finding it hard to control the situation against the much larger size of the insurgents. Brigadier Rajinder Singh Jamwal, who succeeded Scott, was inclined to be pro-India.

Frantic diplomatic moves were afoot in Karachi, Delhi, and Srinagar. By spurning Jinnah's offer, made in mid-September, to meet him in Srinagar, Sir Hari upset Pakistan's highest official. The offended Jinnah retaliated by imposing a loose blockade in early October, depriving the state of such essentials as salt, edible oil, sugar, kerosene, gasoline, and cloth. He was helped by the fact that the Muslim truck drivers from West Punjab were vulnerable to attacks by Hindu and Sikh militants in Jammu.

On the Indian side, there was rapid upgrading of communications between Kashmir and India by post and telegraph, telephone, wireless, and roads. "The metaling of the road from Jammu to Kathua is also proceeding at top speed," reported the Lahore-based *Pakistan Times* on September 27. "The idea is to keep up some sort of communication between the State and the Indian Union, so that essential supplies and troops could be rushed to Kashmir without having to transport them through Pakistani territory."[12] The building of a boat bridge over the Ravi River near Pathankot was meant to improve access from Gurdaspur in East Punjab.

On September 27 Nehru wrote to Patel that the maharaja should make friends with the National Conference so that "there might be popular support against Pakistan." (A day earlier the imprisoned Abdullah had expressed his written allegiance to the maharaja in a letter that was widely publicized.) Sir Hari released Abdullah on September 29. During their subsequent meeting Abdullah reportedly offered the maharaja a few gold coins as a tribute, thus accepting his paramountcy.

Abdullah's release created another track of diplomacy. On October 1 a Pakistani delegation, headed by Dr. Muhammad Din Taseer, an academic friend of Abdullah who had later settled in Lahore, conferred with Abdullah and his colleagues in Srinagar. Abdullah agreed to meet Jinnah but only after he had seen Nehru in Delhi. Nonetheless, his friend, Ghulam Muhammad Sadiq, accompanying Taseer, traveled to Lahore where Bakshi Ghulam Muhammad, another colleague of Abdullah, had arrived earlier. Their various meetings with Pakistani officials climaxed with one with Ali Khan on October 8.

In Delhi, in his talks with Abdullah, Nehru reiterated Mountbatten's terms to the princely states that they would have to surrender only defense, foreign affairs, and communication to the Indian Union. In addition, he assured Abdullah that those living outside Kashmir would be barred from owning property in the state, as had been the case during the British Raj. Abdullah demanded that these guarantees be written into the Indian constitution. Nehru agreed. Referring to the reports that feudal lords in West Punjab were eyeing to buy agricultural land in Kashmir, Nehru pointed out the commonality between the Congress Party's commitment to abolish *zamindari* and the New Kashmir manifesto.

From early October, reports of rapid deterioration in law and order in Kashmir started appearing in the *Civil and Military Gazette*. By October 7 the Kashmir government had arrested the correspondent for the Associated Press of India, a major source of news about the state; imposed "rigorous pre-censorship on all news and views" published in the local press; and banned the import of four daily newspapers from West Punjab. Protesting at the official order not to print matter advocating Kashmir's accession to Pakistan, the editor of the *Kashmir Times* ceased publication.[13]

The situation changed abruptly when the maharaja replaced Prime Minister Janak Singh with Mehr Chand Mahajan, an Indian judge, on October 15. Mahajan immediately ordered A. K. Shah, Pakistan's joint secretary of foreign affairs and states, who had tried to persuade Janak Singh to opt for Pakistan, to leave Srinagar.

But this left intact the two-pronged scheme the Pakistani premier had devised earlier: to take charge of the Azad Army created by the local Muslim Conference and to forge an independent plan to secure Srinagar by deploying armed irregulars from the tribal areas.

LIAQUAT ALI KHAN, THE PRIME PLOTTER

On September 21 Liaquat Ali Khan chaired a top-secret planning meeting on Kashmir in Lahore. It was attended by civilian and military officials, including the chief ministers of Punjab and the NWFP—Iftikhar Hussain Mamdot and Abdul Qayyum Khan respectively—as well as Mian Iftikharuddin, (Retired) Major Khurshid Anwar, and Brigadier Muhammad Akbar Khan, who was in charge of the weapons and equipment department at general headquarters in Rawalpindi. The agreed-on strategy involved intensifying the insurgency in the Poonch-Mirupr area and opening a new front in western Kashmir to be accomplished by the tribal irregulars led by Anwar. Akbar Khan was charged with arming these fighters without his British commander detecting the loss from the armory.

A native of a princely state in Punjab, Anwar became a high-ranking official in the civil supplies department in Delhi. Because of the close association of this department with the military during World War II, he gained the rank of major. After being discharged from the army for suspected bribe-taking while supplying scarce goods to civilians, he joined the Muslim League in Punjab. He was appointed commander of the

Muslim National Guards (MNG; aka Muslim League National Guard) for the "Pakistan" provinces. He set up the MNG headquarters in Lahore. During the League's civil disobedience campaign against the Unionist-led ministry, he went underground and kept the agitation going. After the fall of the Unionist government in March 1947, he turned his attention to the NWFP. There he worked with Qayyum Khan and other League officials to launch direct action against the Congress ministry. Operating incognito, he remained active while other leaders served prison sentences.

Though the voters opted for Pakistan in a referendum in mid-July, the cabinet of Abdul Jabbar Khan (aka Dr. Khan Sahib), a Congress ally, maintained its majority in the legislature. And yet Jinnah ordered NWFP governor Sir George Cunningham to dismiss the ministry of Dr. Khan Sahib on August 22. That dismissal led the Muslim League's Qayyum Khan, a Pashtun of Kashmiri origin, to form the next cabinet.

Anwar claimed to have gotten clearance from Ali Khan in late August to turn his attention to Kashmir. He and Qayyum Khan set about raising a force of tribal men from the Tirah region and North and South Waziristan Agencies. The number of volunteers rose quickly. By early October about five thousand armed men from the Afridi and Mahsud tribes, embedded with a few hundred Pakistan soldiers on leave, would be assembled in the NWFP city of Abbottabad.

Inside Kashmir, by mid to late October, the Azad Army controlled large parts of Poonch and Mirpur, while much of the Muzaffarabad subdistrict was being cleared of non-Muslims in reprisal for the continued violence against Muslims in eastern Jammu.

On the diplomatic front, Kashmir's prime minister Mahajan sidestepped Jinnah's offer of an impartial inquiry by a third party to investigate his government's allegation of armed infiltration into Poonch by Pakistan. Instead, on October 18 he sent Jinnah a telegram threatening to ask for "friendly" assistance by India if the Pakistanis continued their armed infiltration into Poonch while blockading the border for transport of goods and persisted in their anti-maharaja propaganda.[14]

Jinnah responded by sending a telegram to the maharaja. "The real aim of your Government's policy is to seek an opportunity to join the Indian Dominion through a coup d'état by securing the intervention and assistance of that Dominion," he said. Then he offered to invite his prime minister to visit Karachi "to smooth out the difficulties and adjust matters in a friendly way."[15]

On October 20 relations between Karachi and Srinagar deteriorated when the maharaja's soldiers assaulted four villages inside West Punjab with mortars, grenades, and automatic fire, causing heavy casualties.[16]

That day, as previously planned, the tribal warriors began marching from Abbottabad toward Kashmir. So far Sir George, the governor of NWFP, had been in the dark about the preparations Anwar had made with the cooperation of his chief minister, Qayyum Khan. When he learned about the march the following day, he immediately informed Prime Minister Ali Khan.

"On October 21, Liaquat Ali Khan told me in a state of unusual excitement that a tribal *lashkar* [Urdu: army], some thousands strong, was on the way to Kashmir," wrote Chaudhri Muhammad Ali, the chief secretary of Pakistan, in his book *The Emergence of Pakistan*. "I asked him if he had informed the Quaid-i-Azam and he said, 'Not yet,' as he had just received the report."[17]

Did the prime minister mislead his topmost civil servant? The answer is to be found in Anwar's statement, as cited later by his friend M. Yusuf Buch, a Pakistani expert on Kashmir since 1947. "The old man never gave it the green light," Anwar told Buch after he had retired and set up an ice factory in Rawalpindi. "The old man" was Jinnah, who had not been kept fully briefed by Ali Khan.[18]

THE DENOUEMENT

After crossing into western Kashmir along the Jhelum Valley road on October 22, (Retired) Major Anwar launched Operation Gulmarg by leading a convoy of two hundred trucks filled with sturdy Pashtuns armed with small weapons and mortars. His strategy was to advance along the axis of Muzaffarabad, Domel, Uri, and Baramula to capture the Srinagar airfield and the city, and then proceed to secure the Banihal Pass to block the road from Jammu and cut off the state from the rest of India. Following his capture of two outposts, the Muslim companies of the state's army started defecting to his side.

When the news of the tribal attack reached the maharaja on the afternoon of October 22, he ordered Brigadier Jamwal to fight the invaders to the last man and the last bullet. Jamwal's company of 150 men encountered the raiders at Garhi, forty-five miles west of Uri, in the early hours of the next day. Heavily outnumbered and weakened by the earlier defection of the Muslim units, he withdrew to Uri after blowing up the bridge. That delayed the attackers by one day. His soldiers then fought them at Baramulla, straddling the Jhelum, thirty miles east, on October 24. They were all killed in action.

That day, the local insurgents in the Poonch-Mirpur region formed the independent government of Azad Jammu and Kashmir—shortened to Azad Kashmir—under the presidency of Muhammad Ibrahim Khan of the Muslim Conference in Palundari. Announcing the aim of his government as liberation of the rest of the state, he appealed to Pakistan for assistance.

The Indian government learned of the extent of the invasion on the evening of October 24, when Kashmir's deputy prime minister, R. L. Batra, arrived with letters addressed to Nehru and Patel and seeking military assistance. The next morning, October 25, the defense committee of the Indian cabinet met under Governor-General Lord Mountbatten. He argued that sending troops to a neutral state would be a great folly in the eyes of the world.

The committee then dispatched Vapal Pangunni Menon, along with civil and military officials, to Srinagar to assess the situation on the ground and find out whether or not the maharaja was prepared to accede to India.

After his meeting with Prime Minister Mahajan, Menon and Mahajan conferred with the maharaja, who was in a nervous state. Giving credence to the rumors that some invaders had infiltrated Srinagar, Menon advised the maharaja to drive to the winter capital of Jammu posthaste.

In retrospect, the precaution proved unnecessary. According to Operation Gulmarg, the tribal warriors should have reached Srinagar by October 25 to celebrate Eid al Adha in the city along with local Muslims. As a result of unexpected delays, on that day they found themselves in Baramulla. Home to fourteen thousand people, it was the commercial gateway to the Vale of Kashmir, with a high proportion of non-Muslims. The population included the staff and patients at Joseph's College, Convent, and Hospital, built on a hill, some of them being European.

Before being recruited, the tribal men had been told by Anwar that in the absence of any remuneration upfront, they were entitled to loot the properties of infidels in the conquered parts of Kashmir. Now, given the opportunity, the invaders went beyond pillaging non-Muslim possessions. They snatched jewelry from local women (irrespective of their religion), plundered the bazaar and homes, and vandalized Hindu and Sikh temples. They shipped their plunder back to Abbottabad in trucks. They used the local cinema as a rape center. Among those they shot dead were Lieutenant Colonel D. O. Dykes and his English wife, ready to leave the hospital that day with their newborn baby, and two European nuns. They abducted hundreds of girls, Hindu, Sikh, and Muslim alike. They ignored the pleas of Anwar to advance to Srinagar, only thirty miles away along a level road. In desperation, Anwar led a few bands of regular Pakistani soldiers in civilian clothes to the capital.

The two days' delay by the main force in order to indulge in an orgy of plunder, rape, and murder made all the difference between success and failure of this armed venture.

After the maharaja along with his entourage and valuable possessions fled to Jammu in a convoy of cars around two AM on October 26, Menon and his party, accompanied by Mahajan, boarded a Dakota to fly to Delhi. Once Menon had apprised the Defense Committee of the dire situation in Kashmir, a debate followed. Mountbatten pointed out that Indian soldiers could not be dispatched to the state until and unless the maharaja had signed the Instrument of Accession. He added that he would accept the accession subject to ascertaining the will of the people in a plebiscite after law and order had been restored. Nehru, Patel, and other members of the committee agreed.

Menon flew back to Jammu. At the royal palace he woke up the maharaja, slumbering after a night-long drive from Srinagar. Maharaja Sir Hari Singh signed the instrument of accession, which specified autonomy for the state. (Later, an article in the Indian Constitution would specify that the Indian parliament would need the state government's agreement to apply laws in other administrative areas to the state's territory.) In his forwarding letter to Governor-General Mountbatten, he said that, following the acceptance of the accession, he would ask Shaikh Muhammad Abdullah, lodged in a Delhi hotel as an official guest for the previous week, to form an interim government.

That evening Defense Minister Baldev Singh sent a message to the military command in Delhi to airlift troops to Srinagar early the following morning. Overnight, supported by the swift acquisition of all civilian aircraft by Patel, about a hundred civilian and air force planes were mobilized to ferry men, weapons, and ammunition to Srinagar. The first airplane carrying Indian soldiers arrived at ten thirty AM on October 27 at the unguarded Srinagar airport, eight miles from the city center.

While accepting the Instrument of Accession by the maharaja on October 27, Lord Mountbatten wrote in his cover letter:

In the circumstances mentioned by Your Highness, my government has decided to accept the accession of Kashmir State to the Dominion of India. In consistence with their policy that in the case of any State where the issue of accession has been subject to dispute, the question of accession should be decided in accordance with the wishes of the people of the state, it is my government's wish that, as soon as law and order have been restored in Kashmir and its soil is cleared of the invaders, the question of the state's accession should be settled by a reference to people.[19]

On October 28 Nehru sent a long telegram to his Pakistani counterpart. After summarizing the background to the signing of the Instrument of Accession by the maharaja, he added: "In regards to accession, it has been made clear that it is subject to reference to people of the State and their decision. The Government of India have no design to impose any decision and will abide by people's wishes. But those cannot be ascertained till peace and law and order prevail." Two days later Ali Khan replied by telegram. He alluded to the killings of Muslims in Poonch and their massacres in Jammu, and how those atrocities and the earlier butchering of Muslims in East Punjab had inflamed feelings among the tribes. "When there was evidence that there was to be repetition of that in Kashmir as in East Punjab, it became impossible wholly to prevent the tribes from entering Kashmir without using troops which would have created a situation on the frontier that might well have got out of control," he explained. "The Pathan [aka Pashtun] raid did not start until 22 October. It is clear therefore that Kashmir's plan of asking for Indian troops . . . was formed quite independently of this raid, and all evidence and action taken shows [that] it was pre-arranged."[20]

The sharply divergent ways in which the two leaders presented their respective cases on Kashmir foreshadowed the severity of the challenge the neighboring nations would face in resolving this dispute over the next many decades.

Jinnah noted with growing anxiety the events in Kashmir. When Indian soldiers flew into Srinagar, he ordered his commander in chief General Sir Frank Messervy to dispatch troops to Kashmir. Messervy was a subordinate of the Delhi-based Field Marshal Sir Claude Achinleck, the supreme commander of the British forces remaining in India and Pakistan.[21] His superior ruled out such a move because that would have resulted in British officers commanding their respective Indian and Pakistani contingents fighting one another. Messervy therefore refused to implement Jinnah's order, arguing that the presence of the Indian forces in Kashmir was justified since the maharaja had acceded to India and that introducing Pakistani forces into Kashmir would compel him to withdraw all British officers from Pakistan's military. Thus Jinnah, a lawyer by training, found his hands tied. His subsequently tense relations with Messervy would lead the general to take an early retirement, in February 1948.

THE DAY AFTER

On October 30 Pakistan said that since Kashmir's accession to India was based on "fraud and violence," it could not be recognized. That day Jinnah met Mountbatten in Lahore. They failed to agree on the modalities of the plebiscite on the state's future. In his broadcast to the nation on November 2, Nehru reiterated his promise to hold a plebiscite in the state under international auspices after law and order had been established. Two days later Ali Khan responded in a broadcast from Lahore, describing Kashmir's accession as immoral and illegal.

Once Shaikh Abdullah—popularly called Sher-i-Kashmir (Urdu: Lion of Kashmir)—formed an interim administration as its chief administrator, on October 30, his party activists greeted the incoming Indian soldiers with slogans such as *Hamlavar Khabardar, Hum Kashmiri Hai Tayar* (Urdu: Invaders beware, we Kashmiris are ready), and *Sher-i-Kashmir Ka Kya Irshad, Hindu Muslim Sikh Ittihad* (Urdu: What's Lion of Kashmir's guidance—Hindus, Muslims, Sikhs are united).

On October 31 the vanguard of Azad Kashmir's army reached the outskirts of Srinagar and engaged Indian troops. They fared badly. Once the Indian force had retaken Baramulla on November 8 and cut off the supply lines of the enemy forces, their opponents withdrew.

The recaptured Baramulla, now a deserted town of a thousand people, was opened to local and foreign journalists. "The once lovely town . . . was heaped with rubble and blackened with fire," wrote Margaret Bourke-White, a reporter-photographer for *Life* magazine, in her book *Halfway to Freedom*, published in 1949. "The deserted [St. Joseph's] Convent on the hill was badly defaced and littered. . . . We made our way into the ravaged Chapel, wading through the mass of torn hymnbooks and broken sacred statuary. The altar was deep in rubble." She described what happened when the town was raided by the armed tribesmen:

The nuns, their hospital patients, and a few stray townspeople who had taken refuge at the Mission were herded into a single dormitory and kept under rifle guard. On one of these days, after an air attack from the Indian Army had left the tribesmen in a particularly excited and nervous mood, six of the nuns were brought out and lined up to be shot. [But] one of their chiefs arrived; he had enough vision to realize that shooting nuns was not the thing to do, even in an invasion, and the nuns were saved.[22]

On November 11 the Indian soldiers recaptured Uri, and the raiders withdrew from the nearby towns of Gulmarg and Tanmarg. On the other side, Azad Kashmir forces intensified their campaign and captured Mirupr on November 26.

That day the Joint Defense Council of India and Pakistan meeting in Delhi decided to maintain the council, despite London's decision to close down the Joint Supreme Command (JSC) of the British forces in India and Pakistan on November 30.

On December 8, Mountbatten and Nehru attended the meeting of the Joint Defense Council in Lahore. Nehru argued that letting the tribal raiders use Pakistani territory to attack India was tantamount to an act of war by Pakistan, and that it should call on the raiders to return home. Ali Khan contended that such an appeal by him would lead to the fall of his government. Mountbatten then suggested that the United Nations may be invited to mediate between India and Pakistan. His idea merited serious consideration. And Nehru would later accept it.

As foreign minister Nehru had pursued a policy of nonalignment by sending his sister Vijay Lakshmi Pandit as ambassador to the Soviet Union on the eve of independence to balance the appointment of cabinet minister Asaf Ali as the Indian ambassador to Washington six months earlier. He was therefore confident of not falling afoul of the United States or the Soviet Union at the UN Security Council.

Nehru referred the turmoil in Kashmir to the UN Security Council on January 1, 1948, in the form of a complaint against Pakistan under Chapter VI of the UN Charter (Pacific Settlement of Disputes), Article 35. Along with the preceding article, this one authorizes the Security Council to investigate any dispute in order to determine if it was "likely to endanger international peace and security."[23] Pakistan had armed and abetted the tribal men from its territory to attack Kashmir, and that should vacate the gains of its aggression, argued India's representative to the United Nations.

Two weeks later Pakistan filed a countercomplaint. It alleged that India had persistently attempted to undo the partition scheme; launched a preplanned, wide-scale genocide of Muslims in East Punjab and Punjab's princely states; and secured Kashmir's accession by fraud and violence. It referred to Delhi's nonpayment of Pakistan's share of the cash balances.[24] Earlier, quite independently, in his report to Prime Minster Attlee on the eve of the closure of the JSC of the British forces in India and Pakistan, Auchinleck had said that he had "no hesitation in affirming that the present Indian Cabinet are implacably determined to do all in their power to prevent the establishment of the Dominion of Pakistan on a firm basis."[25]

APOSTLE OF NONVIOLENCE FELLED BY GUNSHOTS

At Pakistan's inception,[26] India paid it Rs 200 million as the first installment of its share of the cash balance in Delhi. But before the remaining balance was due—Rs 550 million—war broke out in Kashmir. India held back this payment, arguing that Pakistan would use it in its ongoing armed conflict in Kashmir. Jinnah complained to India's governor-general, Lord Mountbatten. When he failed to convince Nehru and Patel to meet India's legal obligation, he turned to Gandhi. The Mahatma agreed with him.[27] In a prayer meeting speech in mid-December he publicly urged the Indian government to honor its moral and legal financial agreement with Pakistan.

On December 22 he referred to the shrine of the Sufi saint Khwaja Qutb-ud-din Chishti in the village of Mehrauli, twelve miles from central Delhi, which tens of thousands of Muslims and non-Muslims visited annually. It was "subjected to the wrath of Hindu mobs" in September, he regretfully informed his audience. As a result, the Muslims living in its vicinity for the past eight hundred years had fled. "Now though Muslims honor the shrine, no Muslim can be found anywhere near it," he said. "It is the duty of Hindus, Sikhs and the officials of the government to open the shrine, and wash this stain off us. The same applies to other shrines and religious places of Muslims in and around Delhi."[28]

When Gandhi's plea went unheeded, he began a fast on January 13, 1948. "I will terminate the fast only when peace has returned to Delhi," he declared. "If peace is restored to Delhi it will have an effect not only on India but on Pakistan." Later, he explained that his fast was "against the Hindus and Sikhs of India, and against the Muslims of Pakistan."[29]

Addressing a mammoth rally in Delhi in January 17, Maulana Abul Kalam Muhiyuddin Ahmed Azad explained that people of all faiths should be able to move around the capital without fear and that the Muslims who had been chased out of the city should be advised to return. The next day a collective of political and religious leaders issued a joint statement signed in Gandhi's presence:

> We take the pledge that we should protect the life, property and faith of Muslims and [that] the incidents that have occurred in Delhi shall not happen again. We want to assure Gandhiji that the annual fair held at Khwaja Qutb-ud-din's shrine will be held this year as before. . . . The mosques which have been left by Muslims and are now in the possession of Hindus and Sikhs will be returned. We shall not object to the return to Delhi of Muslims who had migrated. All these things will be done by our personal effort and not with the help of the police and military.[30]

While many community leaders were urging Gandhi to end his fast, militant Hindu demonstrators marched past Birla House, his base, shouting "Let Gandhi die!" They mocked him as "Muhammad Gandhi." Their hatred of Gandhi intensified on January 15, when, heeding his appeal, the Indian government announced that it was transferring Rs 550 million (worth $1.6 billion today) due to Pakistan forthwith.[31]

At his prayer assembly on January 19, held in the garden of Birla House, Gandhi told his audience that an official of the communalist Hindu Mahasabha had repudiated his endorsement of the earlier Hindu-Muslim amity pledge. Hindu Mahasabha was a counterforce, albeit a weak one, to the League's communalism. It was allied with the Rashtriya Swayamsevak Sangh (RSS), a Hindu militia.

The next day, as he spoke at the prayer meeting, a handmade bomb, placed on the wall about seventy-five feet behind Gandhi's podium, exploded. It was ignited by Madan Lal Pahwa, a refugee from West Punjab, who had learned to make grenades as an employee of a fireworks factory in Bombay. A strong woman in the audience grappled with Pahwa until others rushed forward. He was part of a plot to create panic during which Gandhi was to be shot by two of the seven-strong assassination team that had traveled from Poona and Bombay to Delhi. By the time Pahwa led the police to the two hotels where the rest of the gang were staying, they had fled in a hurry. In a room at the Marina Hotel, they found a few clothes carrying the initials "NVG." Gandhi, who had remained calm during the episode, refused to restrict access to his daily prayer assembly as advised by the police.

Once the police heat was off, NVG—Nathuram Vinayak Godse—a sturdy man of medium height with owlish eyes and a jowly face, carried out repeated reconnaissance of the Birla House and its environs.

Meanwhile, Gandhi was troubled by reports of increased tensions between Nehru and Patel, who among other things had disapproved of Nehru's complaint about Kashmir to the UN Security Council, which in turn had led to Pakistan filing an unwieldy countercomplaint. Gandhi decided to mediate. On January 30 he addressed a letter to Nehru to bridge his differences with Patel. That day at four PM Gandhi had a meeting with Patel on the same subject. Their talk went on beyond the scheduled hour.

Among those who had gathered in the front row of the congregation for the prayers was Godse. Gandhi emerged from the building. He passed through the garden, leaning, as usual, on the shoulders of Abha Gandhi, his granddaughter-in-law, and Manu Gandhi, his grandniece. As he ascended the four steps leading to the prayer marquee, Godse, wearing a loose jacket over his cotton shirt and pajamas, approached him. Standing about six feet from Gandhi, he pressed his palms together in reverence. Gandhi returned his salutation. "You are late today for the prayer," remarked Godse as he bowed to touch the Mahatma's feet as a further sign of respect. "Yes, I am," Gandhi replied. Godse pulled out his six-chamber Beretta M 1934 semiautomatic pistol from his jacket pocket. He fired three shots near Gandhi's heart. It was 5:12 PM. Gandhi collapsed, but his consorts held him up. He was taken to his room, where he died fifteen minutes later.[32]

Godse was seized by those around him and beaten. When the police arrested him, he described himself as editor of the Poona-based *Hindu Rashtra* (Marathi: Hindu Nation), a weekly journal of the Hindu Mahasabha. He was a former member of the RSS, spawned by the Mahasabha, which believed in Hindu supremacy.[33] At his trial he would say that he killed Gandhi for "weakening India" by insisting on payments to Pakistan.

Heartbroken, Nehru wept openly; he had established a son-father relationship with Gandhi. Patel felt guilty for having failed to provide adequate security to the Mahatma and for the ineptitude of the Intelligence Bureau in unearthing the assassination plan in the making. He banned the Hindu Mahasabha and the RSS, whose members he had described three weeks earlier as "patriots who love their country."[34] The searing tragedy brought the leading Congress officials together and strengthened the Nehru-led secular wing in the party.

An emotional tide washed over the Indian nation while condolences poured in from around the globe. Among them was one from Jinnah, who ordered the closure of all government offices in Pakistan the following day. Describing him as "one of the greatest men produced by the Hindu community, and a leader who commanded their universal confidence and respect," he sincerely sympathized with "the great Hindu community and his family in their bereavement at this momentous, historical and critical juncture." (This was payback for Gandhi's remark in 1915 of finding a Muslim like Jinnah as head of the multi-religious Gurjar Sabha in Bombay.[35]) It was only the last sentence—"The loss to the Dominion of India is irreparable"—that did not tie Gandhi to the Hindu community.[36]

Reversing his earlier rejection of the advice of his military aide-de-camp, General Muhammad Akbar Khan, Jinnah quietly ordered that the low compound wall of the Government House, his base in Karachi, be raised, ostensibly to make him and his office safe from a bomb thrower.

A far more important reversal from Jinnah was his stance on the future constitution of Pakistan, which he had expressed publicly almost a week earlier. His change of position was caused by recent developments in the subcontinent and elsewhere. In Delhi Patel had resorted to demanding that India's Muslim leaders should vociferously support the government's military intervention in Kashmir, thereby raising communal tension. And the Indian move in Kashmir had weakened the position of the Hindus in Pakistan, with the Muslim majority there viewing them as unpatriotic. Lastly, Washington's decision in December to award $10 million in financial assistance to Pakistan gave Jinnah a badly needed economic boost, which, in turn, encouraged him to harden his ideological position.

"I cannot understand the logic of those who have been deliberately and mischievously propagating that the Constitution of Pakistan will not be based on Islamic Sharia." Jinnah said in his address to the Sindh Bar Association in Karachi on January 25. "Islamic principles today are as much applicable to life as they were 1300 years ago." He added that Pakistan's constitution would be based on the Sharia canon to make it "a truly great Islamic state."[37]

Jinnah reiterated this message in his speech to the Fifth Heavy and Sixth Light Ack Ack Regiments based at Malir, a suburb of Karachi, on February 21, a fortnight after the early resignation of General Messervy:

"You have to stand guard over the development and maintenance of Islamic democracy, Islamic social justice and the equality of manhood in your own native soil."[38] It is worth noting that it was the first time in modern history that the term "Islamic democracy" was used by a leading Muslim politician.

JINNAH'S TERMINAL ILLNESS

Once General Messervy was succeeded by General David Gracey, and the remaining four thousand British troops in India had sailed away on February 28, Jinnah felt freer to commit regular troops in Kashmir. As it was, on October 31 the Gilgit Scouts, led by British officers who had all opted for Pakistan, arrested the maharaja-appointed governor and set up a provisional administration that affiliated with the Azad Kashmir government. Three days later the ruler of Chitral signed the Instrument of Accession with Pakistan. This amounted to Pakistan controlling directly or indirectly, through the Azad Kashmir government, most of the sparsely populated areas of Kashmir except Ladakh. But the coveted prize of the Vale of Kashmir—measuring 6,160 square miles at an average altitude of 6,000 feet—had escaped Jinnah. "The turn of events in Kashmir had an adverse effect on the Quaidi Azam's health," wrote Chaudhri Muhammad Ali. "His earlier optimism gave way to a deep disappointment. 'We have been put on the wrong bus,' he remarked."[39]

After a lull in the fighting in Kashmir caused by winter snows, the Indians geared up to recapture the lost area, particularly in the populous Kashmir region, which was partly controlled by Azad Kashmir forces. Fearing a breach of Pakistan's border in the course of India's offensives, Jinnah ordered the deployment of Pakistani troops in early April. By so doing he risked Delhi's refusal to deliver the bulk of the 18.75 percent share of the 165,000 tons of ordnance stores, which had been allocated to Pakistan by the Partition Council.[40]

At the United Nations, having listened to both sides, the Security Council passed Resolution 47 on April 21, 1948. It stated that to ensure the impartiality of the plebiscite on the state's future, Pakistan must withdraw all tribesmen and nationals who entered the region to fight, and India should leave just enough troops to maintain civil order. Since it was passed under Chapter VI of the UN Charter, it was nonbinding and lacked mandatory implementation.[41] Only resolutions passed under

Chapter VII ("Action with Respect to Threats to the Peace, Breaches of the Peace and Acts of Aggression") require mandatory enforcement.

Jinnah demanded that both sides withdraw their forces simultaneously. Delhi rejected this. So the state of war between the two neighbors continued, both of them deciding to ignore the Security Council's call for an immediate cease-fire.

For administrative purposes, Jinnah established the Ministry of Kashmir Affairs in Karachi. Across the border, pressured by Delhi, the maharaja had replaced his Hindu prime minister, Mahajan, in March with Shaikh Abdullah, the erstwhile chief administrator, thus making his government appear more representative of the Muslim majority.

In Karachi, Jinnah by now was too ill to use his desk in the Government House office as his workplace. He could perform his job only while lying down on a sofa, surrounded by documents, newspapers, and endless news-bearing telex tape. In June he and his sister-carer Fatima moved to cooler Quetta. Black dispatch boxes, stamped with the initials "M.A.J.," were airlifted daily from Karachi for his attention and action. He still managed to muster enough energy to address the cadets at the local Command and Staff College. "You, along with the other forces of Pakistan, are the custodians of the life, property and honor of the people of Pakistan," he told them.[42] He would have hardly predicted that a decade later the military leaders would prove more than mere custodians and that they would seize total power and send all politicians packing.

Jinnah flew to Karachi on July 1 to inaugurate the State Bank of Pakistan. On his return to Quetta some days later, he was advised to move to the hill town of Ziarat seventy miles away. He did so, and he continued to work ceaselessly. Toward the end of the month, Colonel Dr. Illahi Bux, who had been invited to Ziarat by Fatima Jinnah, told his patient and Fatima that Jinnah's lungs were afflicted with tuberculosis and cancer. The news was withheld even from Prime Minister Ali Khan when he arrived in Ziarat.

Invited by Bux and Fatima Jinnah, the British nursing superintendent of Quetta's civil hospital, Sister Phyllis Dunham, arrived in Ziarat on July 29 to give Jinnah professional nursing care. Despite the strict secrecy, the public knew vaguely that their Quaid-i-Azam—Great Leader—was ill and resting in Ziarat in the hills of Baluchistan. On Eid al Fitr, which fell on August 7, public prayers were offered in mosques for his recovery. Two days later Jinnah, now reduced to 79 pounds from an earlier 120 pounds, his face shrunken to hollow cheeks and blank stare, was moved back to Quetta. To maintain a semblance of official normality, on the eve of Independence Day, August 14, the government broadcast a ghostwritten message from him.

Belying a slight improvement in his health, on August 29 a tearful Jinnah said to Bux, "You know, when you first came to Ziarat, I wanted to live. Now, however, it does not matter whether I live or die."[43] It was imperative for political stability that he should return to Karachi while he was still alive. Being vain, Jinnah did not want to be seen arriving in the capital on a stretcher. When he developed pneumonia on September 9, however, he had no option but to fly to Karachi to receive better medical treatment.

On Saturday morning, September 11, Jinnah's Viking touched down at Quetta's airport. Ali Khan was informed but told not to come to the Mauripur Airport located ten miles from the Government House in Karachi. At four fifteen PM, Jinnah's plane was met by his state-owned Cadillac, an army ambulance, and a truck for luggage and servants. Jinnah, lying on a stretcher, was placed in the ambulance, which moved slowly. Almost halfway to his destination, it broke down. When the driver failed to get it moving again, Jinnah's military secretary was sent off to fetch another ambulance.

Jinnah could not be transferred to the Cadillac as he was too weak to sit up in the backseat, and the stretcher could not be fitted into the automobile. Since the ambulance was not carrying the governor-general's flag, nobody in Jinnah's party could stop any of the buses or trucks passing by. It was hot and close inside the ambulance. Jinnah was perspiring even when Sister Dunham fanned him vigorously with a piece of cardboard. In gratitude, the speechless Jinnah touched her arm with his hand and smiled weakly. It was an excruciatingly long hour before the next ambulance arrived. The party reached the Government House at 6:10 PM.[44] Jinnah was put to bed. He died at 10:25 PM.

The government announced three days of mourning. On September 12 almost a million people gathered for the funeral service of Quaid-i-Azam Jinnah, who was succeeded by Khwaja Nazimuddin, the Bengali president of the Pakistan Muslim League. The state of mourning was announced in Delhi on that day, and flags flew at half-mast on all official buildings.

Nehru said:

Jinnah did mold history in India in the wrong way, it is true, and let loose forces which have done so much evil. How shall we judge him? I have been very angry with him often during these past years. But now there is no bitterness in my thought of him, only a great sadness for all that has been. . . . Outwardly he succeeded in his quest and gained his objective, but at what a cost and with what a difference from what he had imagined. What must he have thought of all this, did he feel sorry or regret for any past action? Probably not, for he had wrapped himself in a cloak of hatred and every evil seemed to flow from those whom he hated. Hatred is poor nourishment for any person.[45]

In his evaluation of Jinnah, Nehru showed no sign of self-examination. Nor did he attempt to apportion blame for the tragic partitioning of the subcontinent. It was all the fault of malevolent Jinnah. Self-righteousness remained a salient feature of Nehru's character until his death while prime minister sixteen years later.

With the exit of Jinnah and Gandhi, the giants of subcontinental politics for three decades, an era came to an end. Jinnah's death just a year after the birth of a new nation he had conceived deprived it of strong moorings at a critical moment. And top policymakers in independent India, focusing on rapid economic development with a stress on industrialization, found Gandhi's utopian ideas of self-sufficient village communities outdated.

Whereas a Hollywood biopic on Gandhi was produced in 1982 and proved a critical and box office success, a movie on Jinnah, carrying his name, materialized only in 1998. The Hindi version of *Gandhi* helped enormously to establish him as an iconic figure, particularly among the younger generations. *Jinnah*, produced and directed by the London-based Jamil Dehlavi, cast the British horror movie actor Christopher Lee in the lead role. Its Urdu version did well in Pakistan; its impact elsewhere was negligible.

TRUCE IN KASHMIR

Following Jinnah's death, Ali Khan bore the full burden of shepherding the fledgling Pakistan. His aristocratic background, formalized in his title of Nawabzad (Urdu: Son of Nabob) from Punjab, his profession as an

Oxford-trained attorney, and many years in politics made him feel at ease with Nehru, a Cambridge-educated lawyer.

On Kashmir, he opted for the "harder diplomatic" track by downgrading the military option that his government was finding too expensive to continue—a policy he had failed to sell to Jinnah earlier. Nehru's administration was also feeling the adverse effect of the drain caused by the war in Kashmir. With winter snows freezing the battle lines, the two neighbors decided to silence their guns by agreeing to a truce brokered by the UN Commission for India and Pakistan. Despite unpublicized disapproval by the top military brass at the general headquarters in Rawalpindi, the cease-fire went into effect on January 1, 1949. It was decided that a free and impartial plebiscite would be held under UN supervision.

Pakistan controlled 37 percent of Jammu and Kashmir, later divided into Northern Areas and Azad Kashmir, with its capital in Muzaffarabad. To monitor the cease-fire line, the Security Council appointed the UN Military Observer Group in India and Pakistan. Crucially, India retained control of the eighty-five-mile-long and twenty-mile-wide Vale of Kashmir, which lies between the Pir Panjal and Karakoram mountain ranges of the Himalayas. Guarded by snow-capped peaks, carpeted with verdant forests of fir and pine trees along with wildflowers of riotous colors in the spring, and irrigated by the Jhelum River and its tributaries, it has been described by poets and people alike as "Paradise on Earth."

On the eve of their independence the two Dominions had decided to allow free movement of goods, persons, and capital for one year. But because of the rapid deterioration in relations after the Kashmir conflict, this agreement broke down. In November, Pakistan levied export duties on jute, which was processed in the mills of Calcutta. India retaliated with export duties of its own. The trade war escalated to a crisis on September 19, 1949, when Britain devalued the pound against the US dollar by 30.5 percent, to $2.80. Both the Indian rupee and the Pakistani rupee were pegged to the British pound. India followed Britain's lead, but Pakistan did not. That made Pakistani exports almost a third more expensive. Delhi terminated its trade relations with Karachi.

7

Growing Apart

The rupture in Indo-Pakistan trade links ended the export of Hindi movies to Pakistan. These films often starred Punjabi actors endowed with good looks and fluency in Hindustani—an amalgam of Urdu and Hindi. West Pakistanis thus found themselves deprived of their staple in mass entertainment. The studios in Lahore produced only nine movies a year, compared to Bombay's output of seventy-five.

Whereas most Muslim businessmen and professionals in the Muslim-minority provinces of British India migrated to Pakistan to escape competition from their more advantaged Hindu counterparts, this was not the case with the socially liberal and politically progressive Muslims in Bombay's thriving movie industry. As scriptwriters, lyricists, directors, and producers, they stayed in Bombay—all except Sadat Hassan Manto.

SADAT HASSAN MANTO

A bespectacled, oval-faced native of Samrala near Ludhiana in East Punjab, Manto was a prolific short story writer in Urdu who made a comfortable living penning screenplays. He made his debut as a writer with "Tamasha" (Urdu: Show), a short story based on the 1919 Jallianwala Bagh massacre in Amritsar.

After partition, the thirty-five-year-old Manto migrated to Lahore. Faced with a lack of demand for movie scripts, he had to rely exclusively on publishing short stories in literary magazines or newspaper supplements for paltry sums. His sexually explicit tales fell afoul of the socially conservative readership of Urdu publications. Because he wrote freely about social and sexual issues considered taboo in Indo-Pakistan society, he was charged with obscenity six times, three times in India and three times in Pakistan. Though he was not convicted, he switched to writing a regular newspaper column. It provided him with an outlet for drawing pen-portraits of leading Indian actors and writers as well as Muhammad Ali Jinnah. (His eye-opening essays on working in the Hindi movie industry—at turns nostalgic, acerbic, poetic, and gossipy—are collected in a remarkable collection *Stars from Another Sky*.) The constant struggle to support his wife, Safiya, and their three daughters drove him to cheap, illicitly brewed alcohol—and an early death in 1955 from cirrhosis.

He left behind twenty-two collections of short stories, a novel, and five collections of radio plays as well as three of essays. Yet it was only on January 18, 2005, the fiftieth anniversary of his death, that he was commemorated on a Pakistani postage stamp and awarded the Nishan-e Imtiaz (Urdu: Order of Excellence), the highest official honor.

Some months before his demise he published a satirical tale, "Toba Tek Singh." Set in 1950, when India and Pakistan exchanged the inmates of their lunatic asylums, "Toba Tek Singh" has become a classic because it captures the demented logic of the partition. The story is based on the premise that the inmates of these asylums were largely unaware of the dramatic events in the subcontinent.

Bishan Singh, an old Sikh lunatic in Pakistan, had owned land in his hometown, Toba Tek Singh (the name of an actual town, which remains unchanged), before going mad and was known as Toba Tek Singh among his fellow lunatics. On the day of the exchange of mad men, when Bishan Singh's turn comes to give his personal details for the records before being transferred to India, he asks the official, "Where's Toba Tek Singh? In India or Pakistan?" The official laughs and answers, "In Pakistan, of course." Hearing this, Bishan Singh turns and runs back to join his companions in Pakistan. The Pakistani guards catch hold of him and try to push him across the line to India. Bishan Singh refuses to budge. "This is Toba Tek Singh," he announces. In order to persuade him to cross the border into India, he is told falsely, repeatedly, that Toba Tek Singh is in India, or very soon will be. But he remains unconvinced. When they try to drag him to the Indian side, he resists. Since he is a harmless old man, the officials leave him alone for the time being and proceed with the rest of the exchange. Engrossed in the demanding task of accomplishing the exchange, the guards forget about him. At dawn they hear a heart-rending scream. They find Bishan Singh's corpse, face down and sprawled between two barbed pens—one of Indian lunatics and the other of their Pakistani counterparts—on a land without name.[1]

As it was, in real life, a no-man's land had come into existence along some sections of the Indo-Pakistan cease-fire line in Kashmir—an issue that continued to exercise the United Nations Commission for India and Pakistan (UNCIP) as well as the military representatives of India and Pakistan during 1949.

NEHRU'S NONALIGNMENT IRRITATES WASHINGTON

That year witnessed the twin dominions drifting apart in such vital areas as foreign affairs. In pursuit of his policy of nonalignment with either power blocks—led respectively by the Soviet Union and the United States—Jawaharlal Nehru transferred his sister Vijay Lakshmi Pandit from Moscow to Washington as India's ambassador in August. She set the scene for her brother's visit to America two months later.

Nehru started his four days of official visits and conferences in Washington with a meeting with President Harry Truman on October 13. He then addressed the US House of Representatives. "I have come here on a voyage of discovery of the mind and heart of America and to place before you our own heart," he said. "Thus we may promote that understanding and cooperation which, I feel sure, both our countries earnestly desire." He assured his audience that "where freedom is menaced or justice threatened or where aggression takes place, we cannot be and shall not be neutral." Then he rushed to the Senate, temporarily meeting in the old Supreme Court Chamber, to deliver the same speech.[2]

As the leader of a newly independent nation of 360 million people with a legacy of ancient civilization, Nehru was treated as a political superstar. "Washington's hopes for a democratic rallying point in Asia have been pinned on India, the second biggest Asiatic nation, and the man who determines India's policy—J L Nehru," said the *New York Times* in its editorial on October 14, 1949. *Time* chimed in by featuring a flattering portrait of Nehru on the cover of its October 17 edition. He then undertook a three-week tour of the United States, visiting cities on the East and West Coasts and the Midwest.

In June 1950, as one of the six nonpermanent members of the UN Security Council, India backed its Resolution 82, calling on North Korea to withdraw immediately to its border with South Korea. A few days later it supplied a medical unit to the UN Command charged with reversing North Korea's aggression.

But later, as the United States embarked on a policy of encircling the Soviet Union with a string of regional defense treaties, Nehru parted company with Washington in defense matters. In early October 1949, Truman signed the Mutual Defense Assistance Act to complement the Economic Cooperation Act (the Marshall Plan) of April 1948, both aimed at Europe. In 1951 these two acts were merged into the Mutual Security Act under the Mutual Security Administration, charged with overseeing all foreign aid programs, military and nonmilitary, to bolster the defense capability of Washington's allies. This step integrated the mutual security pacts and the concept of security assistance with the US-led Western world's global strategy of containing the Soviet Union.

However, Washington's modest economic aid to India, which started after Nehru's sojourn to America, continued. In January 1952 India and the United States inked a five-year Technical Cooperation Agreement, with Washington providing funds for specific technical projects.

The outbreak of war between North Korea and South Korea in June 1950 drew America's attention toward Asia and heralded globalization of its security policy. Six months earlier India had recognized the People's Republic of China (PRC), which came into existence on October 1, 1949, with the military defeat of the Republic of China. India thus became the first noncommunist country to recognize the PRC. (Its ambassador K. M. Pannikar arrived in Beijing in April 1950.)

In October 1950 the PRC stepped into the Korean War to ensure that the US-led UN forces did not reach its frontier. At the UN India disagreed with America in February 1951 and refused to censure Communist China as an aggressor in the ongoing war. Washington considered Delhi's stance an example of communist appeasement. India's refusal to join the US-sponsored 1951 Treaty of Peace with Japan—a pact designed among other things to recruit Japan as an ally against communist successes in Asia—signaled further divergence between the two nations.

With India refusing to ally with America, the Truman administration focused on Pakistan, which had been courting the United States since its inception under Jinnah, who was paranoid about the Kremlin's ambitions in South Asia. Little wonder that it was fifteen months after his death that, following the establishment of Pakistan's diplomatic ties with the Soviet Union, the first Pakistani ambassador arrived in Moscow.

President Truman laid out the red carpet for Ali Khan at the airport in Washington on May 3, 1950. After their meeting the next day, the Pakistani leader addressed the two chambers of Congress separately. He reemphasized the importance of his country's geostrategic location adjacent to Afghanistan, which shared a long border with the Soviet Union. He lined up with America to meet the Soviet menace.[3] To achieve this common aim, he asked for military aid, which Truman promised to consider. Then, emulating Nehru, he toured the United States for more than three weeks.

Soon after, he backed the UN use of force to reverse North Korea's invasion and occupation of part of South Korea. And, unlike Nehru, he supported Washington's peace treaty with Tokyo.

Once the Mutual Security Act came into force in 1951, it became comparatively easy for Washington to combine its military and nonmilitary aid to Pakistan. But Truman was cautious about granting Ali Khan's request for arms, fearing that he would use US weapons against India in Pakistan's ongoing dispute in Kashmir. On his part, frustrated by Truman's prevarication, Ali Khan established diplomatic relations with the PRC on May 21, 1951.

The divergence of the two neighbors in foreign policy was reflected in their bilateral commerce. Following India's virtual suspension of trade with it in early 1950, Pakistan tried to forge trade links with America. The outbreak of war in the Korean peninsula in June 1950 helped. The subsequent hike in the prices of such raw materials as jute, leather, and cotton benefited Pakistan, being a supplier of raw materials. The trade rupture with India also accelerated the building of cotton and jute mills in Pakistan by newly arrived Indian Muslim businessmen, whose backing of the Muslim League prepartition was premised on the hope that one day, in a Muslim state, they would no longer face competition from Hindu industrialists. These new factories reduced Pakistan's dependence on India for finished goods. And an increased demand for raw materials enabled it to diversify its foreign commerce.

NEHRU-ALI KHAN INTERLUDE

At home the Liaquat Ali Khan government resolved to crush the Communist Party in East Pakistan, where it had substantial support among Untouchable Hindus. During a police raid to arrest communists in the

Untouchables' settlement of Kalshira in mid-December 1949, a policeman was killed. In retribution, a contingent of armed policemen and troops raided Kalshira on December 20, beat up the villagers, and let neighboring Muslims loot their properties, kill some men, and abduct women. All except three homesteads were razed. The nearby Hindu villages suffered a similar fate. Some of the refugees from Kalshira arrived in Calcutta. Their tales of woe were publicized in the West Bengal press, inflaming the feelings of local Hindus. The result was communal rioting in Calcutta. The exaggerated reports of these events in East Pakistan's newspapers strained fragile Hindu-Muslim relations.

In early February the Speaker of the East Pakistan Assembly disallowed discussion of the incidents in Kalshira, which had been demanded by the Congress Party members, all of them Hindu. The simmering communal tensions escalated into violence in the capital, Dacca (later Dhaka), following a February 10 rally in which speakers delivered anti-Hindu tirades.

The dispersed crowd of Muslims went on a spree of looting Hindu shops and housing, setting some of them alight. An estimated 50,000 Hindus out of 80,000 among the city's 417,000 residents became homeless during seven hours of murder, pillage, and arson. "What I saw and learnt from firsthand information was simply staggering and heart-rending," wrote Jogendra Nath Mandal, the (Untouchable) law minister of Pakistan.[4]

The weak government of Chief Minister Nurul Amin proved unequal to the task of curbing the rioting. It also failed to instruct the authorities in district capitals to take precautionary measures. As a consequence, communal violence spread to several district capitals and rural areas. It included looting, murder, rape and abduction of women, and forcible conversions to Islam. By collating detailed information, Mandal concluded that the total Hindu deaths in Dacca and elsewhere were "in the neighborhood of 10,000," with the district of Barisal accounting for a quarter of the figure.[5] Large-scale exodus of Hindus from East Pakistan started in the second half of March.

Reprisals followed in West Bengal with attacks on Muslims. In one instance more than one hundred Muslim workers of a jute mill were murdered in Howrah in late March. Nearly two hundred thousand Muslims from the bordering villages of West Bengal were driven into East Pakistan.[6]

Both Nehru and Ali Khan realized that if they failed to act urgently in unison to stem the tide of communal violence, there would be a nightmarish reprise of divided Punjab at the time of the partition. Nehru invited his Pakistani counterpart to Delhi. Ali Khan arrived with a large delegation. After six days of intensive negotiations, on April 8 the prime ministers signed major documents on minorities' rights, resolving disputes through peaceful means, and trade, with commercial links to be restored in February 1951.[7]

The two leaders agreed to set up a Ministry for Minority Affairs to be headed by a member of the minority community. The newly established Minority Commission in each country was charged with ensuring that the refugees were allowed to return unmolested to sell their property, the pillaged possessions were returned to the owner, the abducted women repatriated, and forced conversions nullified. Even so, by the end of 1950, more than one million Hindu refugees migrated from East Pakistan to West Bengal. In contrast, of the seven hundred thousand Muslims who left West Bengal because of communal turbulence, five hundred thousand returned later.[8]

On the eve of the 1951 census, East Pakistan had nine million Hindus, forming 22 percent of its population of forty-one million. In polar contrast, West Pakistan had only one million Hindus, almost all of them in Sindh. Altogether Hindus were nearly 13 percent of Pakistan's population. And Muslims in India constituted a minority of 10 percent.

ALI KHAN AND HIS ASSASSIN KILLED

On the afternoon of October 16, 1951, Ali Khan was the star speaker at a huge public rally held at the Company Park in Rawalpindi. At 4:10 PM, as he opened his speech with the welcoming words "*Braadran-e-Millat*" (Urdu: Brothers of the nation), two shots fired from a Mauser pistol from a distance of six feet hit him in the chest. He collapsed, muttering the Islamic creed in Arabic, "*La ilaha illallah, Muhammad ur rasul Allah*" ("There is no god but Allah, and Muhammad is messenger of Allah").

The weapon was fired by the twenty-nine-year-old Saad Akbar, a resident of Abbottabad, where he had settled as a political refugee from Afghanistan in 1944 and survived on a modest government stipend. Intriguingly, he had arrived a few hours before the event and had assisted the volunteers of the Muslim League National Guard to fix the dais and make other arrangements for the rally.

In the melee that followed his murderous act, Akbar was hit by five shots fired by police subinspector Muhammad Shah Gul. His fatal injuries did not spare him further stabbings, breaking of his arms, and gouging of his eyes by those who pounced on him. Meanwhile, Ali Khan was rushed to the hospital, where he died at 4:50 PM.[9]

The inquiry commission led by Justice Muhammad Munir, in its report on August 17, 1952, said that it had not been possible to decide definitively whether the assassin, Akbar, had acted as an individual or as the agent of a conspiracy. The known facts and documents tended to suggest that he was "the conscious or unconscious tool of some clever third party."[10] The matter rested there, enveloped in mystery—the first in a series that dogged the history of Pakistan, the other unsolved cases being those of General Muhammad Zia ul Haq and Benazir Bhutto.

Thus within four years of its birth, Pakistani lost its two prime cofounders, known respectively as the Quaid-i-Azam and Quaid-i-Millat (Urdu: Leader of the Nation). Since none of the succeeding politicians had the charisma or popularity of either one, the politics of the fledgling state started to unravel.

Contrary was the case in India. There Nehru went from strength to strength. In Delhi the Constituent Assembly adopted a new constitution in November 1949 that came into effect two months later. The newly inaugurated Republic of India (Bharat in Hindi), with Rajendra Prasad as its president, was able to maintain its membership in the British Commonwealth thanks to the change in Britain's law. With the December 1950 death of Vallabhbhai Patel, who represented the Hindu nationalist trend within the Congress, the grip of the Nehru-led secular wing in the ruling party tightened.

The first general election for the directly elected lower house of the national parliament, called the Lok Sabha (Hindi: People's Council), was held with universal suffrage between October 1951 and February 1952. The Congress Party won three-quarters of the 491 seats. As in the past, the party's star vote-puller was Nehru, who undertook a whirlwind tour of the country. He continued as the prime minister and foreign minister, assiduously pursuing his nonalignment policy.

By contrast, Ali Khan's successor, Khwaja Nazimuddin (in office October 1951–April 1953) kept up the practice of periodically dispatching a delegation to Washington to seek arms. His chances brightened when (Retired) General Dwight Eisenhower followed Truman into the White

House in January 1953 and appointed the rabidly anticommunist John Foster Dulles as his secretary of state.

By then the two neighbors in South Asia had consolidated their positions in Kashmir.

CONSOLIDATION IN KASHMIR

Following the truce on January 1, 1949, the Azad Kashmir government became the administrative authority for the territory west of the cease-fire line, including Gilgit Agency—composed of Gilgit, Hunza, and Nagar—and Baltistan. Later in 1949, Pakistan imposed direct rule on Gilgit Agency and Baltistan after merging them and named the new entity Northern Areas. Next year it issued an ordinance, "Rules of Business of the Azad Kashmir Government," which served as the basic law for the territory. The supreme head of this government functioned under the watchful eyes of the Ministry of Kashmir Affairs. Pakistan retained control of defense, foreign policy, and dealings with the United Nations, while Azad Kashmir authorities continued to administer the territory and develop it economically.

In March 1950 the UNCIP gave way to the UN representative charged with the task of bringing about demilitarization in both parts of Kashmir. The first such representative, Australian judge Owen Dixon, reported that since Delhi would never agree to demilitarization, two other alternatives should be considered. One: hold four regional plebiscites—in Jammu, Kashmir Valley, Ladakh, and the Northern Areas. Two: partition the state, with some areas to India and others to Pakistan, and hold a plebiscite only in the Kashmir Valley.

Nehru showed interest, but Ali Khan rejected Dixon's proposals. He insisted on a plebiscite to decide the fate of all of Jammu and Kashmir, confident that its Muslim majority would opt for accession to Pakistan. This was the earliest of several missed opportunities to peacefully resolve the dispute, which has since then proved intractable.

Forced by Delhi, Maharaja Sir Hari Singh abdicated in favor of his eighteen-year-old son, Karan Singh, in 1949, while Shaikh Muhammad Abdullah remained the state's chief executive. Article 370 in the secular Indian constitution accorded Kashmir the right to have its own constitution. Elections for the 75-member Constituent Assembly were scheduled for August through September 1951. In the end polls were held only in four constituencies because those opposing Abdullah's National Conference, concentrated in the Jammu region, were told that they had all filled their nomination papers "incorrectly" and could therefore not contest the election! Such tactics were the staple of a one-party dictatorship rather than a multiparty democratic entity.

By so doing, Abdullah accentuated the traditional animosity that had existed between the Hindus in Jammu who had identified with the maharaja and the Muslims in Kashmir who loathed the Hindu ruler. Now the Hindus in Jammu began protesting against "Kashmiri domination" and demanding closer ties with India. Abdullah agreed to give the Indian president power to "declare state of emergency" in Jammu and Kashmir in the event of external aggression. This did not satisfy the staunchly pro-India elements in Jammu. Led by the communalist Bharatiya Jan Sangh (Hindi: Indian People's Union), they launched an agitation for "One constitution, one flag, and one president" in late 1952. This caused apprehension among Kashmiri Muslims, who saw in this a threat to the special status conferred on the state by the Indian constitution.

It was in this atmosphere of escalating tension and suspicion in the state that a plan to arrest Abdullah was hatched in Delhi by a Nehru-guided cabal, which included Bakshi Ghulam Muhammad, deputy of Abdullah; Durga Prasad Dhar, a Hindu colleague of Abdullah; and Karan Singh. What spurred them into action was the letter by President Prasad to Nehru on July 14, 1953, in which he wrote that on his return from a visit to Kashmir, Vice President Dr. Sarvepalli Radhakrishnan told him that "even Shaikh Abdullah thought that we would lose in a plebiscite."[11]

On August 9, 1953, on the order of Karan Singh, Abdullah was arrested under the state's Public Security Act and detained "for the time being."[12] His incarceration ended briefly in January 1958.

Much changed during the intervening period in Pakistan, domestically and externally.

PAKISTAN IN WASHINGTON'S ORBIT

The Eisenhower-Dulles duo set out to build a ring of containment around the Sino-Soviet bloc, and Pakistan was a key part of that ring. Washington viewed Pakistan as a strategically located country with "a volunteer army of 300,000," which was "not neutral but [was] anti-communist." It was "extremely well-disciplined, professional, well trained armed forces whose morale and bravery are unquestionable."[13]

Muhammad Ali Bogra, the prime minister of Pakistan, had previously served as his country's ambassador to the United States from February 1952 to April 1953. On April 2, 1954, the United States signed a Mutual Defense Assistance Agreement with Pakistan, capped by a separate pact to meet Congressional requirements on May 19.

"I send you this personal message because I want you to know about my decision to extend military aid to Pakistan before it is public knowledge, and also because I want you to know directly from me that this step does not in any way affect the friendship we feel for India," wrote Eisenhower to Nehru on February 24.

> What we are proposing to do, and what Pakistan is agreeing to, is not directed in any way against India. I am confirming publicly that if our aid to any country, including Pakistan, is misused and directed against another in aggression I will undertake immediately . . . appropriate action, both within and without the U.N., to thwart such aggression. . . . We also believe that it is in the interest of the free world that India should have a strong military defense capability, and have admired the effective way in which your government has administered your military establishments. If your government should conclude that circumstances require military aid of a type contemplated by our mutual security legislation, please be assured that your request would receive my most sympathetic consideration.[14]

Nehru declined Eisenhower's offer. "You are, however, aware of the views of my Government and our people in regard to the matter," replied Nehru on March 1. "Those views and policy which we have pursued after most careful thought are based on our desire to help in the furtherance of peace and freedom. We shall continue to pursue that policy." By making this suggestion, he observed, "the President has done less than justice to us or to himself. If we object to military aid being given to Pakistan, we would be hypocrites and unprincipled opportunists to accept such aid ourselves."[15]

On that day Nehru publicly denounced Washington's military assistance to Pakistan as "intervention" in Indo-Pakistan affairs. As such, his government was no longer prepared to accept the American members of the UN observers' team in Kashmir as neutral. Domestically, by leading the denunciation of the Pakistan-US pact in its demonstrations and rallies, the Congress Party preempted any chances of the right-wing Bharatiya Jan Sangh or the Communist Party of India exploiting the issue to shore up its popular following.

Before Nehru's open disagreement with Eisenhower, his administration had made use of its neutrality to end the war in Korea. During his spring 1953 global tour, Dulles visited Delhi, where he paid tribute to "India's efforts at the UN to end the war in Korea." He also said that Washington would aid India's First Five Year Plan for economic development.[16]

When the negotiations for a cease-fire in the Korean War became deadlocked on the issue of the repatriation of prisoners of war, a solution was found in establishing the Neutral Nations Repatriations Commission, headed by India. It was mandated to interview in a neutral setting individual prisoners who refused repatriation and have them choose their side. That process finally led to the signing of the truce on July 27, 1953.

By strange coincidence, it was during that month that, overriding America's objections, India went ahead with a shipment of thorium nitrate—a substance with potential for use in nuclear industry—to Communist China. To qualify for receiving any aid from the United States, Delhi had to abide by its End User Agreement, which incorporated its Export Control Act of 1949. That act restricted export of certain strategic or military items to the Soviet bloc and covered a wide range of materials needed for the production of weapons, with particular focus on anything that could aid atomic weapons research and construction. In 1953, when Washington learned of India's impending export of thorium nitrate to Communist China, which it considered part of the Soviet bloc, it pointed to its acts to abort the shipment. Keen to assert his country's newly won independence, Nehru refused to accept any US-imposed restrictions on India's trade. Breach of the US law would have led to the termination of aid by Washington. Realizing that cutting off all aid to India would do more harm than good, Dulles negotiated a compromise whereby India agreed to send only one shipment to Communist China.[17]

This minor concession to India left untouched the Eisenhower-Dulles strategy to cordon off the Sino-Soviet bloc. Four months after signing the Mutual Security Assistance Agreement, Pakistan attended a meeting of eight nations in Manila to form the South-East Asia Treaty Organization (SEATO).[18] This was followed by Pakistan joining Iran, ruled by the shah Muhammad Reza Pahlavi, and Turkey, a member of the North Atlantic

Treaty Organization (NATO), to form the Central Treaty Organization (CENTO) in 1955.

After the signing of the US-Pakistan military pact, hundreds of Pakistani officers were sent to the Pentagon's military academies for advanced training. The US Military Assistance Advisory Group set up its office at Pakistan's Army Headquarters in Rawalpindi.

With US military aid of $266 million in 1955 rocketing to $1.086 billion the following year,[19] the budget and the popular standing of Pakistan's armed forces rose sharply. By contrast, the prestige of politicians sank ever lower.

In the March 1951 elections in Punjab during Ali Khan's premiership, the Muslim League fared well. But it failed to repeat the performance in the North-West Frontier Province (NWFP) election in December. Its achievement in the legislative election in Sindh in May 1953 was lackluster. And in the populous East Pakistan in March 1954 it suffered a humiliating defeat by the United Front of Bengali nationalists.

Reflecting this dramatic development, Governor-General Ghulam Muhammad dissolved the Constituent Assembly on October 24, 1954, saying it had become unrepresentative. This in turn led Bogra to form a new cabinet. He appointed Major-General Iskander (also spelled Sikander) Ali Mirza to be his interior minister and the chief of army staff, Major-General Muhammad Ayub Khan, as his defense minister, a post held until then by civilian premiers. When the ailing Muhammad spent two months in Britain for medical treatment, Mirza served as the acting governor-general.

A month later Bogra announced a plan to merge the western wing's four provinces, former princely states and tribal agencies into one unit, to be called West Pakistan. It came into being in October 1955. A new Constituent Assembly of 80, with its members divided equally between West and East Pakistan, was elected by the members of their respective legislatures in April.

When the terminally ill Muhammad resigned as governor-general in August 1955, Major-General Mirza succeeded him, a sign of the ascending power of the military in administering Pakistan. As an ethnic Bengali, he considered it politically unwise to have another Bengali, Bogra, continue as the prime minister. So he dispatched him back to Washington as Pakistan's ambassador.

PAKISTAN LOSES ITS CONSTITUTION AND
GAINS A MILITARY RULER

Mirza called on Chaudhri (also spelled Chaudhry) Muhammad Ali, a Punjabi bureaucrat turned Muslim League leader, to form the next government. Thanks to his determined push, the new Constituent Assembly adopted a republican constitution with a provision for universal suffrage on February 29, 1956. It prescribed a parliamentary form of government, with Islam as the state religion and Urdu, English, and Bengali as the state languages. However, objecting to the absence of regional autonomy, the sixteen members of the East Pakistan-based Awami League, led by Hussein Shaheed Suhrawardy, walked out. The constitution came into force on March 23, 1956—the sixteenth anniversary of the Lahore Resolution of the All India Muslim League—with Major-General Mirza unanimously elected as the first president of the Islamic Republic of Pakistan by its National Assembly.

With its republican constitution, Pakistan caught up with India. But by having a retired major-general as its president, Pakistan set itself apart from its bigger neighbor, where all power rested with elected civilians. Moreover, the constitutional article in Pakistan that "the ministers shall serve at the pleasure of the president" accorded the president a most powerful lever. Mirza used this authority freely to dismiss ministries at the center and in the provinces. He constantly misused his clout to promote political intrigue and horse-trading.

When the Muslim League group in the National Assembly split and the defectors joined other politicians to form the Republican Party, Muhammad Ali resigned in September 1956. He was followed by Suhrawardy, who led a coalition of his Awami League and the Republican Party. He was married to Vera Tiscenko, a Moscow-born Russian actress who had found refuge for herself and her infant son from the impending war in Europe by moving from Rome to Calcutta in the late 1930s. As a result Suhrawardy had become keenly interested in international affairs.

Within weeks of becoming the premier and defense minister, Suhrawardy, accompanied by his foreign minister, Firoz Khan Noon, visited Beijing. They told Prime Minister Zhou Enlai (Chou Enlai) that Pakistan had made its choice to stand with the United States, and hoped Communist China would move toward more friendly relations with Pakistan as well as America.[20] Zhou lent them a sympathetic ear. He paid a return visit to Karachi in December. By happenstance, during that month Nehru visited Eisenhower at his Gettysburg Farm.

The coveted prize for Suhrawardy was a meeting with Eisenhower. This materialized on July 10, 1957, at the White House. In return for US civilian and military aid to Pakistan of $2.142 billion in the previous year, Eisenhower asked for secret intelligence and military facilities on the Pakistani soil. Suhrawardy agreed, according to Syed Amjad Ali, a former Pakistani ambassador to Washington.[21] The United States was allowed to fly its high altitude U-2 reconnaissance planes over the Soviet Union from the Pakistani Air Force's section of the Peshawar airport. In return Eisenhower agreed to include F-104 fighter jets and Patton tanks, both superior to India's weapons, in Washington's arms shipments.

After lengthy negotiations, the two governments signed a ten-year agreement in July 1958. It provided the six-year-old US National Security Agency (NSA) a base at Badaber, ten miles from Peshawar.

The agency's task was to monitor communications at the sites of ballistic missiles and nuclear tests in Soviet Central Asia, and other related exchanges.[22]

At home Suhrawardy came under pressure to confirm March 1958 as the date for the general election under the new constitution. Arguing that he needed two years to implement his program, he advanced that date to the end of 1958. President Mirza feared that Suhrawardy's success as premier would weaken his hand. So he fired Suhrawardy in October. He called on Ismail Ibrahim Chundrigar, a Gujarati-speaking contemporary of Jinnah, to head the new government. Chundrigar failed to assemble a cabinet.

Mirza's next choice fell on Noon, a Punjabi feudal lord and leader of the Republican Party. Noon headed a coalition of five groups, including the Muslim League, which assumed office in mid-December 1957. It was during Noon's tenure that the NSA started building the Peshawar Air Base complex, with Washington's overgenerous aid to Pakistan running at $1.5 billion annually.[23] Known locally as Little America, the completed Badaber complex included technical infrastructure, residential quarters, and sports facilities, with access to it controlled by the United States.

Domestically, Mirza reveled in political intrigue. As a result the Muslim League withdrew from the coalition. On September 28, 1958, its leaders threatened to dislodge Noon's government through extraconstitutional means, if necessary.

That gave Mirza a convenient rationale to scrap the constitution on October 7, 1958. He claimed it was unworkable because of dangerous compromises. He dismissed the national and provincial cabinets, dissolved the national and provincial legislatures, and banned all political parties. He imposed martial law and appointed Major-General Ayub Khan as the chief martial law administrator.[24]

When he and Ayub Khan could not work out the modalities of power sharing, Mirza unilaterally appointed Ayub Khan prime minister and selected a cabinet of technocrats for him. Ayub Khan protested Mirza's high-handedness. An arch manipulator, Mirza tried to gain support of Ayub Khan's rivals within the military. Informed of Mirza's chicanery, Ayub Khan, backed by the high command, dispatched three generals to the presidential residence in the middle of the night on October 26–27 to put Mirza on a plane to London. Ayub Khan became the sole ruler. By abolishing the post of prime minister, he became the president.

He explained to the nation that Pakistan needed stability that could only be achieved by turning out "the inefficient and rascally" politicians responsible for political instability and letting the army play a central role in administering the republic. Since day-to-day administration remained with civil servants, it led to an alliance between the upper ranks of bureaucracy and the military.

With that an era ended in Pakistan. It now stood starkly apart from India, where the second general election in 1957 had returned the Congress Party and Nehru to power. By then the stances of the two neighbors on Kashmir had become unbridgeable.

Military ties between Karachi and Washington were reinforced as a consequence of the Joint Resolution to Promote Peace and Stability in the Middle East passed by the US Congress in March 1957. It authorized the president to use the armed forces to assist any nation or group of nations in the Middle East against armed aggression from any country "controlled by international communism."[25] Washington treated Pakistan as part of the Middle East by virtue of its defense alliance with Iran and Turkey under CENTO.

KASHMIR ISSUE HARDENING

In the wake of their bilateral meeting in London during the Commonwealth prime ministers' conference in June 1953, Bogra and Nehru decided to continue their dialogue on Kashmir and other issues. During his three-day visit to Karachi toward the end of July, Nehru was received warmly at the official and popular levels, with Bogra repeatedly referring to him as "my elder brother." They parted with an agreement to meet in Delhi in October.

But Shaikh Abdullah's overnight arrest in early August led to a change in the timing. Anti-India protests in the Kashmir Valley at Abdullah's detention were suppressed with a heavy hand by his successor, Bakshi Ghulam Muhammad. Across the border, Abdullah's incarceration turned him into a hero. The demonstrators in major Pakistani cities demanded urgent and strong action by their government on Kashmir.

Pressed by Bogra, Nehru agreed to meet in Delhi on August 16. Their joint communiqué referred to a fair and impartial plebiscite agreed to "some years" ago and a lack of progress because of certain "preliminary issues." It was decided to appoint committees of military and other experts to advise the prime ministers to resolve the "preliminary issues" as a preamble to appointing the plebiscite administrator by the end of April 1954. The administrator would then outline preparations for holding a plebiscite in "the entire State [of Jammu and Kashmir]."[26]

This communiqué went down badly in West Pakistan. Its critics denounced the sidelining of the United Nations, the proposed replacement of Admiral Chester Nimitz of the United States as the plebiscite administrator, and the possibility of zonal plebiscites. Popular disapproval and the lack of unanimous backing by his cabinet tied Bogra's hands. His initial enthusiasm died when Nehru repudiated his agreement about the return of refugees to their homes because of "practical difficulties." That meant disfranchising hundreds of thousands of Muslim refugees from the Jammu region who had migrated to West Pakistan out of fear.

As US arms poured into Pakistan, Nehru, in his letter to Bogra on December 3, 1953, said that American military aid would have direct bearing on the Kashmir issue, and advised the Pakistani government to stay away from power blocs. Later, when the delegates of the two countries met in Delhi to discuss demilitarization, the Indians insisted that the issue of US military assistance be discussed first. The Pakistanis refused. The meeting ended with the agenda untouched.

In his letter of March 29, 1954, Bogra explained to Nehru that Washington's military aid had nothing to do with either the Indo-Pakistan dispute over Kashmir or the right of self-determination for Kashmiris. Nehru ignored the argument. Two weeks later he informed Bogra that the situation had changed as a result of the US-Pakistan military pact and that the deadline of appointing the plebiscite administrator by the end of April had become redundant. "It is with profound regret that I have been led to the conclusion that our talks regarding Kashmir have failed," concluded Bogra in his letter of September 21.[27]

If, by some miracle, Bogra would have seen the note Nehru addressed to Kashmir's prime minister Abdullah on August 25, 1952, from Sonamarg in Kashmir, he would have concluded that his "elder brother" was just going through ritualistic motions about a plebiscite. In it Nehru virtually conceded that he had decided against a plebiscite "towards the end of December 1948." He had accepted the UN Commission for India and Pakistan's plebiscite proposals on December 23, 1948, in order to achieve a cease-fire, since the Indian Army had reached the desired line on the ground. He was determined to maintain "the status quo then existing" by force. "We are superior to Pakistan in military and industrial power," he wrote. "But that superiority is not so great as to produce results quickly either in war or by fear of war. Therefore, our national interest demands that we should adopt a peaceful policy towards Pakistan and, at the same time, add to our strength."[28] In short, Nehru, a self-righteous moralizer, sacrificed morality and legalism on the altar of power politics.

Compared to this sensational admission, his revelation in April 1956 that about a year earlier he had made an unsuccessful offer to Bogra involving a permanent de jure partition of Kashmir along the cease-fire line was bland.[29]

NEHRU'S HENCHMAN IN SRINAGAR

While Nehru conducted diplomatic dialogue with Bogra, in Srinagar Bakshi Ghulam Muhammad proved more pro-India than Indians themselves. Led by him, 64 of the 74-strong Constituent Assembly members ratified the state's accession to India on February 15, 1954. "We are today taking the decision of final and irrevocable accession to India and no power on earth could change it," declared Bakshi Muhammad.[30] Later that year he said that Shaikh Abdullah would be "detained as long as the future of Kashmir remains undecided."[31]

In Moscow, the communist leadership was alarmed by the way the US-led alliance was circling the USSR with regional defense pacts. It noted that Pakistan had the distinction of belonging to both SEATO and CENTO. By contrast, Nehru was unswervingly committed to his doctrine of nonalignment. After the death of Soviet premier Joseph Stalin in March 1953, relations between Moscow and Delhi had improved, with the two nations inking a trade pact at the end of the year. In 1954 the Kremlin agreed to build a steel plant in India's public sector. Four months later, Nehru undertook a sixteen-day official tour of the Soviet Union.[32] Nikita Khrushchev, first secretary of the Communist Party of the Soviet Union, and Marshal Nikolai Bulganin, the Soviet premier, paid a return visit to India from November 18 to December 1.

To register their disapproval of Pakistan's foreign policy, the Soviet dignitaries visited Srinagar. "The people of Jammu and Kashmir want to work for the well being of their beloved country—the Republic of India," said Khrushchev. "They do not want to become toys in the hands of the imperialist powers. This is what some powers are trying to do by supporting Pakistan on the so-called Kashmir question. . . . That Kashmir is one of the States of the Republic of India has already been decided by the people of Kashmir."[33] While the Soviet leader's statement was thunderously lauded in Delhi, the disillusioned top officials in Karachi called it "extraordinary."

Bogra and his succeeding prime ministers rejected anything less than a plebiscite. They were confident that in any fair plebiscite the predominantly Muslim population would opt for Jammu and Kashmir acceding to Pakistan.

This point was conceded, implicitly, by Arthur Lall, India's representative to the United Nations, in his private meeting with James W. Barco, counselor in the US delegation at the United Nations, in New York in early January 1957. "Lall maintained that the only way Pakistan could win [the plebiscite] would be on religious issue and this would fan religious tensions among Moslems in India and could produce another round of communal riots," read the telegram sent by the American mission at the United Nations to the Department of State on January 10.[34]

Working in close cooperation with Delhi, Muhammad used bribes, repression, and election rigging to consolidate his power. On November 17, 1956, the Constituent Assembly adopted the state's constitution, which came into effect on January 26, 1957. Section 3 stated that "the State of Jammu and Kashmir is and shall be an integral part of the Union of India." This section was declared immune from any amendment in the future.

Responding to Pakistan's lobbying of SEATO, three of its members—the United States, Britain, and Australia—submitted a resolution at the UN Security Council on February 20, 1957, backing its proposal for the deployment of "a temporary United Nations force in connection with demilitarization" in Kashmir. It won 9 out of 11 votes, but the Soviet Union vetoed it, arguing that the two contending parties had not exhausted bilateral means of resolving the dispute.[35] As a result, the prestige of the Soviet Union in India rocketed. In October it was boosted further with Moscow's successful launch of the world's first artificial satellite, named *Sputnik*.

In March 1957, in a blatantly rigged election in Indian Kashmir, the National Conference won 68 of the 75 seats in the Legislative Assembly.

Shaikh Abdullah was released from house arrest in January 1958. He became the chief patron of the Plebiscite Front. Formed by his deputy Mirza Afzal Beg during his incarceration, the Front demanded a referendum under the aegis of the United Nations to decide the issue of Kashmir's sovereignty. Abdullah blasted Muhammad's government as one composed of goons, opportunists, and thieves. Delhi attributed his uncompromising stance to contacts with Pakistan, which was allegedly funding him. He was rearrested in late April and charged, along with twenty-two others, of hatching a conspiracy to bring down the government through chaos and violence. Livid at Abdullah's rearrest, Muslim Conference activists from Azad Kashmir decided to cross the cease-fire line into Indian Kashmir. President Mirza did not want to provoke India. So the Pakistani authorities arrested hundreds of Muslim Conference volunteers and their leaders.

The trial against Abdullah and others, which started in March 1959, involving 223 prosecution witnesses and nearly three hundred exhibits, would drag on until early 1964, when it would be withdrawn.

DIFFERING PRIORITIES

Ayub Khan's first priority was to consolidate and legitimize his authority at home. He set in motion a process to draft a new constitution. At the same time he needed to assure the military and the public that he was not neglecting the emotionally and ideologically charged issue of Kashmir.

In March 1959 he cosigned the Pakistan-US Cooperation Agreement. After stating that the United States "regards as vital to its national interests and to world peace the preservation of independence and territorial integrity of Pakistan," Article 1 added that "in case of aggression against Pakistan . . . the United States of America . . . will take such appropriate action, including the use of armed forces, as may be mutually agreed upon, and as is envisaged in the [March 9, 1957] Joint Resolution to Promote Peace and Stability in the Middle East in order to assist Pakistan in its requests."[36]

In Delhi, escalating tensions between India and China on their border dispute, which had been building up since 1954, had made Nehru pliable to discuss the Kashmir dispute with Pakistan and set aside his objections about the Pakistan-US Cooperation Agreement.

Thus, on September 1, 1959, Ayub Khan, now a self-promoted field marshal, stopped over at New Delhi's Palam airport on his way from Rawalpindi to Dacca to meet Nehru. (On that day Indian newspapers splashed the news of the resignation of the chief of army staff, General K. S. Thimayya, in protest of the government's tepid response to China's inroads in the Aksai Chin region of Kashmir.) The Nehru–Ayub Khan communiqué stated that "there was need to conduct their relations with each other on a rational and planned basis, and not according to the day-to-day exigencies as they arose, and that their outstanding issues and other problems should, in mutual interest, be settled in accordance with justice and fair play in a spirit of friendliness, cooperation and good neighborliness."[37]

The conciliatory approach led to a successful end to the long, tortuous negotiations on the distribution of the waters in the Indus River basin. In May 1948 the two neighbors had signed the Inter-Dominion Accord on apportioning the waters of the Indus basin, whereby India agreed to release sufficient waters to West Pakistan for an annual payment. This was a temporary arrangement. When it came to negotiating a permanent accord, Pakistan realized anew that with the source of all six major rivers of the basin being in India, it held weak cards. Yet it insisted on perpetuating its prepartition right to the waters of all the Indus tributaries, arguing that the absence of this resource would turn the eastern zone of West Punjab into a desert. India maintained that the previous distribution of waters should not determine future allocation. Pakistan suggested referring the matter to the International Court of Justice. India rejected the idea.

Instead, in 1952 both agreed to invite the World Bank initially to offer advice on the technical aspects of the problem. Two years later, however, the World Bank came up with its own award. It offered India the three eastern tributaries of the basin—Sutlej, Beas, and Ravi—and Pakistan the remaining three western ones: Indus, Jhelum, and Chenab. To compensate Pakistan for ceding its (partial) rights to the eastern tributaries,

India was required to build canals and storage facilities to transfer water from the eastern Indian rivers to West Pakistan. Whereas Delhi was amenable to the bank's proposal, Karachi rejected it.

Bilateral negotiations reached a breaking point but were not called off. The successive short-term Pakistani governments realized that ending the talks would raise tensions with India to a boiling point, which they could not risk. In the absence of a permanent treaty, Delhi was forced to put on hold large development projects in the Indus basin area.

Now that he headed a stable military government in Pakistan, President Ayub Khan was able to clinch the deal on Indus waters once the World Bank persuaded America and Britain, along with Australia and New Zealand, to finance the construction of canals and storage facilities in India to transfer water from the eastern Indian rivers to West Pakistan.

Ayub Khan proposed Karachi as the site for the formal signing of the accord by Nehru and him. Nehru concurred. On September 19, 1960, more than one hundred thousand people greeted Nehru at the Karachi airport. The ten-mile route from the airport to the Presidential House was lined by crowds shouting, "Nehru *zindabad*" (Urdu: Long live Nehru), at the slow moving motorcade led by Nehru and Ayub Khan in an open car. There was a ceremonial signing of the Indus Waters treaty at the President's Office. In the evening, after a reception attended by a thousand invited guests on the spacious, manicured lawns of the Presidential House, Nehru hailed the treaty as "memorable" because "in spite of the problem and harassing delays, success has come at last." He described it as "a symbol of unity and cooperation between two neighboring countries."[38]

The successful solution to this critical economic conundrum encouraged Ayub Khan to try to resolve the pivotal political issue of Kashmir. To discuss the thorny dispute in a salubrious climate, Ayub Khan flew Nehru to the Presidential Lodge in the hill station of Murree on September 21. But their one-on-one talks proved sterile.

Six months later, on the sidelines of the Commonwealth Heads of Government conference in London, Ayub Khan chatted with Rajeshwar Dayal, his friend of prepartition days who later served as India's high commissioner in Karachi. "*Woh mujhe hiqarat ki nazar se dekhta hain*" (Urdu: He looks at me with contempt), he told Dayal, referring to Nehru and their meeting in Murree. The Pakistani president added that being the head of a large state, he should not have been treated that way. "Ayub Khan revealed that when he tried to open a conversation about Kashmir, Nehru simply stared out of the window at the scenery and 'shut up like a clam.'"[39] By then Nehru had made it a standard practice to turn his gaze to open space or stare at his feet when any foreign leader mentioned Kashmir in their conversation.

As an intellectual who had authored *Glimpses of World History*—a thousand-page tome written during his imprisonment in 1931–1933—without reference to any library as well as *The Discovery of India*, penned in five months during his incarceration from August 1942 to June 1945, Nehru was disdainful of leaders of lesser knowledge. In his public life he had dealt mainly with lawyer-politicians, often trained in Britain. Of the five Pakistani prime ministers Nehru met or corresponded with, all except one was a lawyer or an Oxbridge graduate, or both. Though Ayub Khan had a distinguished career in his own right, he did not fall into any of these categories.

Born into the household of Mirdad Khan, an ethnic Pashtun non-commissioned officer of the British Indian Army, in a village near Haripur in NWFP, Ayub Khan had the distinction of being the first nonwhite cadet at the Royal Military Academy at Sandhurst, England. He graduated as a second lieutenant and joined the British Indian Army. During World War II he was promoted to colonel. In 1947, when he opted for the Pakistan army, he was the tenth ranking senior officer. Further promotions made him the chief of army staff four years later. A bluff, broad-shouldered man with a clipped mustache, he was a contrast to the slight figure of Nehru.

While unable to mask effectively his disdain for Ayub Khan, Nehru summarized his talk with him in Murree in fifteen paragraphs penned on September 21, 1960. "He [Ayub Khan] spoke at some length on this subject [of Kashmir] and laid stress on as speedy a solution as possible," noted Nehru. "In dealing with Kashmir we had to take a realistic view of the situation. Not to do so would land us in greater difficulties. It would be most unfortunate for us to try to take a step which might create numerous upsets and emotional upheavals."[40] Nehru was a master of obfuscation when it suited him.

In his memoirs, *Friends Not Masters*, published in 1967, Ayub Khan referred to the Murree meeting and Kashmir. "Mr Nehru finally asked what, accepting the fact that there was need for peace between the two countries and also that the room for maneuver for settlement of the Kashmir dispute was limited, I thought should be our first step," wrote Ayub Khan. "I told him that this would depend on the objective we had before us. Once the objective was determined, an organization could be established to work out the method. Mr Nehru said that he foresaw serious political opposition in his country. He mentioned that Indian public opinion had reacted violently to Chinese 'occupation' of [the] 'Indian territory.'"[41]

Having used the external factor of the US-Pakistan Mutual Security Pact as his excuse to renege on the holding of a plebiscite in Kashmir earlier, Nehru now shifted his argument to the domestic scene. In essence, he had come to subscribe to the idea of turning the cease-fire line into a de facto partition of Kashmir, which he first mentioned to his Pakistani counterpart, Bogra, in May 1955. This was unacceptable to Pakistan because it would have legitimized Delhi's control of the Vale of Kashmir, the coveted prize in the increasingly bitter struggle.

By then China had become an integral factor in the Indo-Pakistan equation because of its occupation of a part of Jammu and Kashmir, as alleged by Delhi. Unsurprisingly, therefore, at the Murree meeting, Nehru raised the issue of Pakistan's boundary with China. Ayub Khan recalled:

> He asked me whether we had approached the Chinese to demarcate the border and I informed him of the position. He wanted me to show him the map on which we were basing our claim and wanted to know exactly the area to which our claim extended. I told him quite frankly that we had no intention of claiming any area which we did not honestly believe to be covered by the actual line of control as determined by our experts. We might ask for certain areas beyond the line of control to provide facilities for the local population. . . . As soon as he went back to India, he started criticizing us for having approached the Chinese to demarcate the border. He mentioned the map I had shown him and said that we did not even know where the border was and that we were acting in a childish manner. That was Mr Nehru's style, he quite forgot the spirit in which we had discussed the matter and used the whole thing as a debating point.[42]

It was this sort of diplomacy that had brought relations between India and China to a breaking point within six years and that would lead to a war between them in the autumn of 1962.

8

Nehru's "Forward Policy"

A Step Too Far

In earlier centuries, given the inaccessibility of desolate tracts in remote high mountains along their common borders, the dispute between British India and China centered on the zone or tract rather than the line in their eastern and western sectors. Notably, the North-East Frontier Agency in British India was originally called the North-East Frontier Tract.

The modern-day boundary is the end result of a process that starts with delimitation—defining the boundary in writing, in treaties or agreements—and then proceeds to delineation, sketching the boundary in maps after joint boundary surveys. The final stage, called "demarcation," establishes the boundary line on the ground with pillars, chains, or other markers. By this criterion, China's southern border lacked line boundaries not only with India (and later Pakistan as well) but also Burma (renamed Myanmar) and Nepal.

TIBET, A BUFFER BETWEEN CHINA AND BRITISH INDIA

In the wake of the fall of the Qing Dynasty in China in early 1912, the claim of Tibet, ruled by the Dalai Lama, to be an independent entity clashed with the 1904 treaty it had signed with London following its defeat by the British Indian Army. That treaty ceded Tibet's foreign relations and trade rights to Britain, and entitled it to an indemnity of Rs 2.5 million.

In 1913, British India's foreign secretary, Sir Henry McMahon—a tall, slim man with a long, lean face embellished with a mustache—conferred with the Chinese plenipotentiary Chen Ivan and Tibetan

158

Lonchen Shatra in Simla (later Shimla) to discuss Tibet's new status. Their final Simla Convention document of July 3, 1914, referred to a small-scale map. It showed lines separating China from "Inner Tibet"— roughly today's Tibet Autonomous Region—administered by the Dalai Lama government under the "suzerainty" of China and separating "Inner Tibet" from "Outer Tibet." This map lacked an initial or signature of Chen.[1] After Beijing had repudiated the first draft of the Simla Convention on April 28, McMahon and Shatra attached a note denying China any privileges under the agreement and signed it as a bilateral accord. The McMahon Line ran 550 miles east from the northeastern border of Bhutan along the Himalayas, across the great bend in the Brahmaputra River, then southeast to Burma.

In 1935, Olaf Caroe, deputy secretary of British India's Foreign and Political Department, discovered the documents of the Simla Convention while dealing with the case of a Briton's illegal entry into Tibet through the Tawang tract. He convinced his superiors to include the McMahon Line on official maps, which had not been the case so far.

Seven years later, to withstand the Japanese offensive during World War II, the Assam government undertook a number of forward policy measures to tighten its hold on the semiautonomous North-East Frontier Agency (NEFA), covering 23,165 square miles. In 1945 it extended its administrative control over that part of the Tawang tract that lay south of the Se-La Mountain Pass. The subsequent Assam Rifles contingent posted at Dirang Dzong expelled the Tibetan tax collectors from the territory but left the Tibetan authorities in control of the area north of the Se-La Mountain Pass, which contained the town of Tawang with its four-centuries-old Buddhist monastery.

As the successor of the British Empire in India, Nehru's government inherited these privileges. When the long-running Chinese civil war ended with the founding of the People's Republic of China (PRC) in October 1949, this necessitated a fresh treaty between Delhi and Beijing on Tibet.

In Delhi a Tibetan delegation met the Chinese ambassador, General Yuan Zhongxian, on September 16, 1950. Yuan passed on his government's proposal that in return for Tibet agreeing to be part of China, and letting Beijing handle its defense and foreign relations and trade, China would respect its internal autonomy and social system under the Dalai Lama. The government of Tenzin Gyasto, the eighteen-year-old fourteenth Dalai Lama, in Lhasa rejected the offer. As a consequence, the

Chinese troops of the People's Liberation Army (PLA) entered Tibet in October and defeated its army in Chamdo.

Protracted negotiations followed. On May 23, 1951, the Tibetan delegation in Beijing signed a Seventeen-Point Agreement with the Chinese government, accepting China's rule in Tibet, including the posting of the PLA there.[2]

The turmoil in Tibet provided the background against which Major Ralengnao Khathing led an Assam Rifles column to Tawang in February 1951 and took control of the remainder of the Tawang tract from the Tibetans. That signaled the end of Tibet's historic control of the area.[3] At that time the Chinese government was too preoccupied with getting the Dalai Lama to accept the reduced status of Tibet to protest India's seizure of the territory north of the Se-La Pass.

On the western sector of the Sino-Indian border, the southern part of the PRC's Sinkiang-Uighur Autonomous Region—later, Xinjiang Autonomous Region—abuts the Ladakh province of Jammu and Kashmir. There the Aksai Chin region became a bone of contention between India and China. The 1931 volume of the annual *Aichison's Treaties*, published by the government in Delhi, stated that "the northern as well as the eastern boundary of the Kashmir State is still undefined."[4] The Survey of India maps published in the 1920s and 1930s showed wide blank spaces between Kashmir and Xinjiang and between Kashmir and Tibet.[5] In 1945, guided by Olaf Caroe, promoted to foreign secretary of India, new Survey of India maps marked the Aksai Chin as "Boundary Undefined." That was what the Nehru government inherited from the British.

But on March 24, 1953, Nehru decided to establish, unilaterally, a nonnegotiable line for the 2,015-mile Sino-Indian border along the Himalayas, including the Aksai Chin area in the Ladakh province of Jammu and Kashmir, which was at the center of poisoned relations between India and Pakistan. "It was a fateful decision," noted A. G. Noorani, an Indian commentator, in his book *India-China Boundary Problem, 1846–1947: History and Diplomacy*. "Old maps were burnt. One former Foreign Secretary told this writer how, as a junior official, he himself was obliged to participate in this fatuous exercise."[6]

While negotiating a fresh treaty with China on India's relations with Tibet—ostensibly in good faith—Nehru followed the strategy he had dictated earlier to N. Raghavan, the Indian ambassador in Beijing. "Our attitude to the Chinese Government should always be a combination of friendliness and firmness," he stated in his secret memorandum to

Raghavan on December 10, 1952. "If we show weakness, advantage will be taken of this immediately. This applies to any development that might take place or in reference to our frontier problems between Tibet and Nepal, Bhutan, Sikkim, Ladakh and [the] rest of India. In regard to this entire frontier we have to maintain an attitude of firmness. Indeed there is nothing to discuss here and we have made that previously clear to the Chinese Government."[7]

Nehru practiced what he preached. Soon afterward, at his initiative, the agents of the Intelligence Bureau started helping in every possible way Gyalo Thendup, the anticommunist brother of the Dalai Lama, and other Tibetan refugees, then living in and around Kalimpong on the border of India and Sikkim.[8]

SUBVERSION IN THE SHADOW OF PEACEFUL COEXISTENCE

On April 29, 1954, India signed an agreement with China on "Trade and Intercourse Between the Tibet Region of China and India," which, in its preamble, included the famous *Panchsheel* (Sanskrit: "five virtues"), the Five Principles of Peaceful Coexistence: "Mutual respect for each other's territorial integrity and sovereignty; mutual nonaggression; mutual non-interference in each other's internal affairs; equality and mutual benefit; and peaceful coexistence."[9] India gave up the extraterritorial rights and privileges in Tibet it had inherited from the British Indian government, and recognized Tibet as an integral part of China.

But that did not stop Nehru from playing the Machiavellian. A week before the suave, fifty-six-year-old Chinese premier Zhou Enlai was to visit Delhi on June 25—when he would be greeted by adoring crowds shouting "*Hindi Cheeni Bhai Bhai*" (Hindi: Indians, Chinese, Brothers, Brothers)—Nehru addressed a note on Tibet and China to the three top bureaucrats at the Foreign Ministry. "No country can ultimately rely upon the permanent goodwill or bona fides of another country, even though they might be in close friendship with each other," he wrote on June 18.

It is conceivable that the Western Atlantic alliance might not function as it was intended to and there might be ill-will between the countries concerned. It is not inconceivable that China and the Soviet Union may not continue to be as friendly as they are now. Certainly it is conceivable that our relations with China might worsen, although there is no immediate likelihood of that. . . . If we come to an agreement with China in regard to Tibet, that is not a permanent guarantee, but that itself is one major step to help us in the present and in the foreseeable future in various ways. . . .

Of course, both the Soviet Union and China are expansive. They are expansive for evils other than communism, although communism may be made a tool for the purpose. Chinese expansionism has been evident during various periods of Asian history for a thousand years or so. We are perhaps facing a new period of such expansionism. Let us consider that and fashion our policy to prevent it coming in the way of our interests or other interests that we consider important.[10]

During five apparently cordial sessions over three days, Nehru and Zhou discussed the situation in Southeast Asia, South Asia, and the Middle East, and other subjects. Nehru did not raise the boundary issue with his Chinese counterpart.

A week after these talks, Nehru sent a long, secret memorandum to his most senior mandarins at the Foreign Ministry. It contained three operative paragraphs, 7 to 9. All old maps should be replaced with new ones, which should no longer show "any un-demarcated territory." The subsequent frontier "should be considered a firm and definite one which is not open to discussion with anybody." To consolidate that position on the ground, "it is necessary that the system of check posts should be spread along this entire frontier. More especially, we should have check posts in such places as might be considered disputed areas," such as Demchok and Tsang Chokla, "considered by the Chinese as disputed territories."[11]

On the first day of Nehru's twelve-day return visit to China starting on October 19, more than a million people lined the twelve-mile route from the airport to the Forbidden City in Beijing to greet him riding an open car along with Zhou. Besides his sessions with Zhou, Nehru had two friendly meetings with Mao Zedong, chairman (chief of state) of China, on October 19–20. "Between India and China there is no tension, there is no psychological war," stated Mao. "We do not spread psychological war among the people." Nehru agreed, having declared earlier that "peace is an absolute necessity."[12] Neither these paramount leaders nor anybody else present at these sessions would have imagined then that India and China would go to war eight years later to the day.

Despite Nehru's cordial exchange of views with Mao, his government soon published maps on which the legend "boundary undefined" in the

Western (Kashmir) sector was dropped in favor of a firm continuous line to show India's frontier.

Delhi's clandestine backing of Tibetan refugees continued as before. "Regarding the spirit of resistance in Tibet, the Prime Minister [Nehru] was of the view (after the 1954 agreement with China) that even if these refugees helped their brethren inside Tibet, the government of India would not take any notice and, unless they compromised themselves too openly, no Chinese protest would be entertained," wrote B. N. Mullik, director of the Intelligence Bureau, in his memoirs.[13] India resorted to supplying arms secretly to the Tibetan rebels. This was a clear violation of mutual noninterference in each other's internal affairs enshrined in the doctrine of *Panchsheel*, which India had ostensibly adopted along with China.

By 1956, knowingly or unwittingly, secret agents of America and Taiwan, operating mainly from Kalimpong, were engaged in the same activity as their counterparts from India and the Soviet Union—recruiting and arming Tibetan émigrés to organize a separatist rebellion in Tibet against Beijing, with the Khampa tribes in eastern Tibet providing the initial thrust. The subversion strategy progressed as planned. The rebellion, which started modestly in the east in 1956–1957, spread to the west.

On August 21, 1958, Nehru protested against China's "cartographic aggression," which showed parts of India as Chinese territory. In his reply on December 14, Zhou wrote, "These maps were doubtless reproductions of old maps, but it [the PRC] had not yet undertaken a survey of [the] Chinese boundary nor consulted the countries, and pending such surveys and consultations, it would not make changes in the boundary on its own."[14] Zhou's statement applied as much to India as it did to Burma and Nepal.

Replying on the same day, Nehru quoted from the records of their discussions in 1954 and 1956 in which Zhou had "proposed" to recognize the McMahon Line. "I wish to point out that the Sino-Indian boundary has never been formally delimited," shot back Zhou on January 23, 1959.

Historically no treaty or agreement on the Sino-Indian boundary has ever been concluded between the Chinese Central Government and the Indian Government. So far as the actual situation is concerned, there are certain differences between the two sides over the border question. . . . The latest case concerns an area in the southern part of China's Sinkiang-Uighur Autonomous region, which has always been under Chinese jurisdiction.

Patrol duties have continually been carried out in the area by the border guards of the Chinese government. And the Sinkiang-Tibet Highway built by our country in 1956 runs through that area. Yet recently the Indian government claimed that the area was in its territory. All this shows that border disputes do exist between China and India.[15]

By December 1958 the anticommunist partisans had become active in western Tibet. In early March 1959 an estimated twenty thousand Tibetan guerrillas engaged PLA troops in the northeastern and southern environs of Lhasa. As the Chinese commanders prepared to shell the Dalai Lama's palace and the surrounding administration complex on March 15–16, the Dalai Lama prepared to escape along with an entourage of twenty aides. They did so on March 17. In the three days of fighting between the Tibetan rebels and the Chinese army in Lhasa, an estimated two thousand people died.[16]

After trekking for fifteen days, the Dalai Lama and his aides crossed into NEFA. Within days, Nehru granted asylum to the Dalai Lama and his companions. "We have no desire whatever to interfere in Tibet, but at the same time we have every sympathy for the people of Tibet, and we are greatly distressed at their helpless plight," he told the Lok Sabha, the lower house of the Indian parliament.[17]

At his press conference on April 18 in the Assamese city of Tezpur, the Dalai Lama repudiated the Seventeen-Point Agreement between Tibet and China signed in May 1951. By so doing he stoked the hostility of the Chinese government toward him and, by implication, soured its relations with Nehru.[18] Consequently, the controversy over the Sino-Indian border sharpened. When China's ambassador Pan Tsue-li warned Nehru of India's possible two-front estrangement (with Pakistan and China) in May 1959, Nehru rebuffed him.

EARLY SKIRMISHES

As friction escalated between the two Asian giants, an armed clash occurred between their troops on August 25, 1959. Following the arrest of one of their comrades, a squad of Indian soldiers at Longju crossed the McMahon Line and fired at the Chinese guards stationed at the Tibetan village of Migyitun for several hours.[19] In retaliation, the Chinese killed some Indian troops. This incident received massive publicity in India, with

Nehru stoking popular sentiment by infusing the clash with "national pride . . . self-respect . . . and . . . people's passions."[20] The upside for Nehru was that his peroration earned China censure not only by the West but also by the Soviet Union.

On October 21 the western sector flared up. That day India's Central Reserve Police Force lost ten policemen when it challenged an incursion by Chinese border guards in Aksai Chin.[21] This territory, described by Nehru as "a barren, uninhabited region without a vestige of grass, and 17,000 feet high," had no strategic value for India, and it had left the area unpatrolled.

In the larger diplomatic arena, though unhappy at the increasing warmth between Delhi and Moscow, the United States continued to give India economic aid, including food grains under Public Law 480 of 1954. That legislation allowed Washington to sell agricultural commodities at a discount and accept the bulk of payments in the recipient country's currency. In India's case, it reimbursed 80 percent of the amount to Delhi in grants and loans for development projects, using the remainder to maintain its embassy and consulates in the country. Washington wished to see India win the economic race against communist China and illustrate the superiority of Western-style democracy to communism for the benefit of the other Afro-Asian nations.

China emerged as the chief villain for both America *and* the Soviet Union when it refused to subscribe to the concept of "peaceful coexistence" between socialism and capitalism—as agreed to by US president Dwight Eisenhower and Soviet premier Nikita Khrushchev at their meeting in Camp David, Maryland, in October 1959. Two months later Eisenhower received a rousing reception on the streets of Delhi against the background of rising tensions between India and China.

To resolve the border dispute peacefully, Zhou spent almost a week in Delhi in April 1960. In the first of his meetings with Nehru he presented his case in six points, the most important being number 4.

"Since we are going to have friendly negotiations, neither side should put forward claims to an area which is no longer under its administrative control," it stated. "For example, we made no claim in the eastern sector to areas south of the McMahon Line, but India made such claims in the western sector. It is difficult to accept such claims and the best thing is that both sides do not make such territorial claims." He suggested that each side should keep to the line of actual control in all sectors, eastern, western, and middle. Nehru disagreed. "Our accepting things as they are would mean that basically there is no dispute and the question ends there; that we are unable to do," he argued. He proposed a radical alternative. "We should take each sector of the border and convince the other side of what it believes to be right."[22]

Such an approach in international diplomacy is unheard of. Instead, the two sides examine the differences that exist in their respective positions and then try to reduce the gaps until they reach a point of concurrence. In this case, each had its vital, nonnegotiable interest securely under its control. India held fast to the McMahon Line, while China had built the Xinjiang-Tibet Highway passing through Aksai Chin in Ladakh in 1957.

Recalling his last meeting with Nehru on April 25, 1960, Zhou told the Soviet ambassador in Beijing on October 8, 1962, that Nehru rejected out of hand all his proposals. "We suggested that bilateral armed forces respectively retreat for 20 km on the borders and stop the patrols to escape conflicts. They did not accept the suggestion. Later, we unilaterally withdrew for 20 km and did not appoint troops to patrol in the area in order to evade conflicts and help negotiations develop smoothly. However, India perhaps had a wrong sense that we were showing our weakness and [we] feared conflicts. . . . India is taking advantage that we withdrew for 20 km and did not assign patrols, and has invaded as well as set up posts."[23]

It was this stalemate that led Nehru to raise the subject of Pakistan's boundary with China with President Field Marshal Muhammad Ayub Khan in September 1960. But instead of learning from the Pakistani leader's successful handling of the issue with Beijing, Nehru mocked him by saying that the Pakistanis "were acting in a childish manner."[24]

In his conflict with China, Nehru found himself being cosseted by both Moscow and Washington. On the eve of the US presidential elections in early November 1960, the Democrat candidate Senator John F. Kennedy described India as representing "a great area for affirmative action by the Free World" in his interview with Walter Cronkite of CBS News. "India started from about the same place that China did. The Chinese Communists have been moving ahead the last 10 years. India . . . has been making some progress, but if India does not succeed with her 450 million people, if she can't make freedom work, then people around the world are going to determine, particularly in the underdeveloped world, that the only way they can develop their resources is through the Communist system."[25]

NEHRU'S CLENCHED FIST: FORWARD POLICY

By July 1961 the Chinese had advanced 70 miles west of their Xinjiang-Tibet Highway passing through Aksai Chin, thus occupying 12,700 square miles of India's claimed territory. Nehru's resolve to implement his country's territorial claims in the eastern and western sectors had turned the frontier areas into conflict tracts, resulting in periodic clashes.

On November 2, 1961, a high-level meeting of Indian officials, chaired by Nehru, adopted the "Forward Policy" on the Sino-Indian border issue. That is, Delhi decided to establish forward military posts north of the McMahon Line in the eastern sector and behind the Chinese posts in the Aksai Chin region of Ladakh. It planned to set up five new all-weather posts of eighty to a hundred soldiers each behind nine existing forward Chinese posts in Ladakh. These outposts were to be located strategically to sever the supply lines of the targeted Chinese posts and starve their personnel with the aim of seizing these posts. From there Indian patrols planned to probe the Xinjiang-Tibet Highway.[26]

From November 5 to 19, Nehru was away, touring America, Mexico, and Britain. He started his itinerary with a visit to the United States, where he was warmly welcomed by President Kennedy in Newport, Rhode Island, where he maintained a family mansion.

On his return home, Nehru presented his Forward Policy on the Chinese border issue to the Lok Sabha. "They [the Chinese] are still in areas which they occupied [in Ladakh] . . . but progressively the situation has been changing from the military point of view and from other points of view in our favor," he told the chamber on November 28. "We shall continue to take steps to build up these things so that ultimately we may be in a position to take action to recover such territory as is [now] in their possession." In other words, Nehru publicly declared his intention to achieve his aim by force. He seemed to rest his strategy on the hypothesis that an armed conflict between India and China would escalate into a world war. His thinking was dangerously flawed. Astonishingly, he was unfamiliar with Henry Kissinger's groundbreaking book *Nuclear Weapons and Foreign Policy* published in 1958. In it Kissinger argued that, given the "balance of terror" between nuclear-armed America and the Soviet Union—with its scenario of Mutually Assured Destruction—it was incumbent on Washington to develop the doctrine of limited wars. "Is it imaginable that a war between India and China will remain confined to these two countries?" Nehru asked rhetorically while addressing the Rajya Sabha (Hindi: States'

Council), the upper house of Parliament, on December 6. "It will be world war and nothing but a world war."[27]

In Beijing, Chairman Mao concluded that since India was rejecting his government's repeated reiteration of a policy of peaceful coexistence, it should be given a taste of "armed coexistence." When peaceful means deployed by China had failed to bring about a reversal in Delhi's Forward Policy, Mao ordered that the PLA must "undertake a long period of armed coexistence."[28]

On June 26, 1962, during the clandestine talks between the ambassadors of the United States and China in Warsaw, Poland, the American envoy received instructions to secretly assure his Chinese counterpart that Washington would not support any attempt by the Nationalist government (of the Republic of China) based in Taiwan to invade the mainland.[29] This allowed PLA generals to move some troops posted along the coastline to the Sino-Indian border. They added two divisions to the six already posted in Tibet to fight the local rebels.

Along the disputed border the Dhola post had been held by the Indians since June. It lay opposite the Thagla Ridge north of the McMahon Line at its western extremity. On September 8 sixty Chinese soldiers appeared at the Thagla Ridge opposite this post with orders to use threats to induce the Indians' withdrawal without engaging into a fight. Briefed by government officials, the Indian media inflated the size of the Chinese contingent by a factor of ten, to six hundred.

Nehru, then attending the Commonwealth Heads of Government conference in London, told the media that the British Indian Army had instructions to "free" India's territory under Chinese occupation. On September 11 it was decided to give permission to all forward posts and patrols to fire on any armed Chinese who entered India's claimed territory. Overall, India had established sixty forward posts, forty-three of them north of the McMahon Line, and occupied four thousand square miles of Chinese territory. Its eastern command upgraded this order on September 20 to "engage" any Chinese patrols within range of their weapons. This radical step was tantamount to a declaration of war.

On October 3 China sent its final diplomatic warning coupled with a plea for immediate, unconditional negotiations. Nehru rejected the offer. Before leaving for a trip to Ceylon (now Sri Lanka) on October 12, he told the media he had ordered the armed forces to clear the Chinese from NEFA. Excepting the Communist Party of India (CPI), he had the unanimous and raucous backing of the opposition as well as the press.

On the ground, however, Nehru's lordly order resulted in two lightly armed and poorly clothed and shod India battalions posted in the plains marching through mud, mountains, and rains at an altitude of thirteen thousand feet to accomplish the mission. All the same, Nehru's declaration was unambiguous. "We don't want a war with India," said Zhou. "But Nehru has closed all roads. This leaves us only with war."[30]

Addressing the meeting of the Politburo of the Communist Party of China on October 18, Chairman Mao said, "Now that Nehru is determined to fight us, we have no way out but to keep him company. As the saying goes, 'from an exchange of blows, friendship grows.' Maybe we have to counter-fight them before we can have a stable border and a peaceful settlement of the boundary question. However, our counter-attack is only meant to serve a warning to Nehru and the Government of India that the boundary question cannot be resolved by military means."[31]

At the other end of the globe, October 18, 1962, marked the beginning of the thirteen-day-long crisis between the White House and the Kremlin on the installation of Soviet nuclear missiles in Cuba.

NEHRU BATTLES MAO; KENNEDY CHALLENGES KHRUSHCHEV

On October 20, 1962, under cover of ear-splitting mortar fire, two heavily equipped Chinese divisions, armed with medium machine guns, launched simultaneous offensives in Ladakh and across the McMahon Line. In a rerun of their fight in the Korean War (1950–1953) against the American and South Korean troops, they attacked in waves. In NEFA they advanced on the Chumbi Valley between Sikkim and Bhutan, and further east to Tawang. Outnumbering the Indians by five to one, they quickly captured twenty of their outposts in NEFA and eight in Ladakh.

Geography coupled with their military engagement in Tibet favored the Chinese. They approached the battle fronts from the fairly flat Tibetan plateau, which was conducive to road building and troop movement. They had also been fighting the armed rebels in Tibet since the mid-1950s and were used to combat in mountains. (India's troops with high-altitude fighting experience were posted in Kashmir along the border with Pakistan.) By contrast, Indian soldiers had to ascend very steep hills covered with thick vegetation in wet weather. Their outmoded .303 rifles were no match for the Chinese troops' automatic weapons.

During the war, Zhou and Nehru corresponded daily. On October 24 Zhou offered a cease-fire package. In principle, each side should withdraw twelve miles from the Line of Actual Control (LAC) and disengage, he proposed. If India agreed to this, then China would withdraw its frontier guards in the Eastern Sector north of the LAC and disengage. Zhou offered to visit Delhi to seek a friendly settlement of the dispute. "What is the Line of Actual Control?" retorted Nehru. He rejected Zhou's proposal.[32] The next day the Chinese occupied Tawang and stopped there.

Nehru sent off frantic appeals for military assistance to the leaders of America, Britain, and the Soviet Union. John Galbraith, the gangling, gaunt-faced US ambassador in Delhi, and Sir Paul Gore-Booth, the short, plump high commissioner of the United Kingdom—nicknamed Laurel and Hardy by the diplomatic corps—got frantically busy. In his memoirs, *Ambassador's Journal*, Galbraith described the Indian leader on October 28 as "frail, brittle and seemed small and old. He was obviously desperately tired."[33] Washington and London rushed vital arms and ammunition to India by gigantic transport aircraft, to Pakistan's distress.

What concerned Kennedy and British prime minister Harold Macmillan—not to mention Nehru—was Pakistan opening a new front against India in Kashmir. "The Pakistanis continue to make pro-Chinese noises, and three Indian divisions are being kept along the Pakistani border," noted Galbraith in his memoirs. "This upset the Indians."[34] His counterpart in Pakistan, Walter McConaughy, intervened, urging the Pakistani foreign minister Muhammad Ali Bogra that his country should not do anything to embarrass India.

Unsurprisingly, President Ayub Khan spied a golden opportunity to squeeze Nehru on the Kashmir issue. He told McConaughy that Pakistani neutrality in the Sino-Indian War could be assured only by Delhi's concessions on Kashmir. The unmistakable inference was that an Indian refusal would induct Pakistan into the war, thus forcing India to fight on two fronts. "My concern was about equally divided between helping the Indians against the Chinese and keeping peace between the Indians and the Pakistanis," wrote Galbraith. "The latter had grievances against the Indians which they considered, not without reason, to have substance. The nightmare of a combined attack by Pakistan and China, with the possibility of defeat, collapse and even anarchy in India, was much on my mind."[35]

Later, when McConaughy was instructed to approach Ayub Khan to assure Nehru that "they wouldn't do anything to embarrass the Indians in their time of trouble," the Pakistani president preferred a letter to that effect from Kennedy.[36] He received one soon after. At the same time Washington urged Nehru to provide Pakistan with data on Indian troop movements in Kashmir and send a friendly message to Ayub Khan. He complied.[37] Only then did Ayub Khan finally give the assurance that Nehru sought anxiously.

As for the more ominous superpower confrontation, to the relief of the world at large, Kennedy and Khrushchev resolved their eyeball-to-eyeball nuclear confrontation on October 29. The Kremlin agreed to withdraw its missiles from Cuba in exchange for the White House removing its Jupiter intermediate-range ballistic missiles from Turkey. Nehru sent congratulatory letters to Kennedy and Khrushchev, hoping that they would both now pay greater attention to pulling India out of the quagmire it had fallen into.

In Delhi, while a record 165 members participated in the parliamentary debate on the war from November 8 to 15, patriotic fervor gripped the nation. In the four leading Indian cities young men lined up at army recruitment centers. In normal times these offices were open only twice a week, and most volunteers failed the physical test. Now the lowering of the strict physical requirements induced by the national emergency drew multitudes of casual laborers, factory hands, and jobless graduates, who were attracted by the prospect of assured food and accommodation, not to mention a worthwhile purpose to their wayward existence that would come with a military uniform.

The Chinese broke the lull on the battlefield on November 15 by assaulting Walong at the easternmost point of the McMahon Line. The Indian regiments retreated in disarray, many of their ranks getting mowed down by the enemy and others throwing away their arms and fleeing. The dazed Indian commanders could not decide where to make their last stand. Finally, they settled for the fourteen-thousand-foot-high Se-La Mountain Pass, fifteen miles south of Tawang. But their ranks failed to hold Tawang. This compelled their officers to order a withdrawal toward Bomdi La, ninety miles inside NEFA. The relentless advance of the Chinese continued, with Bomdi La being their latest prize. Panic gripped the adjoining Assam province. Its large Tezpur settlement turned into a ghost town.

Consternation spread to Delhi and struck Nehru. "Late that night [November 20, 1962] Nehru made an urgent, open appeal for the intervention of the United States with bomber and fighter squadrons to go into action against the Chinese," stated Neville Maxwell, a British journalist and author. "This appeal was detailed, even specifying the number of squadrons required—fifteen."[38] Nehru's strategy was to bomb the supply lines of the Chinese as well as their gasoline dumps, with the warplanes of the US Seventh Fleet stationed in the Bay of Bengal to provide air cover for the major cities of India. The Indian embassy in Washington received this message at nine PM local time on November 19, after President Kennedy had retired for the day. "So you couldn't last out even two weeks," mocked Kennedy's special assistant. "Churchill fought the war without American weapons for two years."[39]

Suddenly the crisis passed. At midnight on November 20, having established its superiority in weaponry, strategy, communications, logistics, and planning, China declared a unilateral cease-fire, and added that after their withdrawal the Chinese frontier guards would be "far behind their positions prior to September 8, 1962." Beijing's decision was in line with what Mao had told the Politburo on October 18: "However, our counterattack is only meant to serve a warning to Nehru and the Government of India that the boundary question cannot be resolved by military means."[40] India accepted the cease-fire without saying so explicitly. On November 22 the Chinese pulled back to the north of the McMahon Line and in Ladakh to the positions they held before the war.

Overall, this was a limited war between Asia's mega-nations. Neither side deployed its air force. China lost only 722 troops. And India's loss of 3,100 soldiers included 1,700 who went missing—that is, froze to death in snow drifts or collapsed in wet forests.

India's defeat, illustrated by the humiliating disproportion in its battlefield fatalities, was implicitly dramatized in the Bollywood movie *Haqeeqat* (Hindi: Reality). During the Sino-Indian war in Ladakh, an Indian platoon, considered dead, is rescued by the locals. When it is ordered to retreat from its post, surrounded by the Chinese, an Indian captain and his Ladakhi girlfriend hold the enemy at bay to facilitate the platoon's safe withdrawal. In the process, they die. But the retreating troops find themselves heavily outnumbered and get killed to the last man. The movie was meant to highlight the patriotic fervor that filled Indian soldiers. It was released in 1964 after the death of Nehru in May.[41]

NEHRU'S OBSTINACY ON KASHMIR

Within a month of the end of the Sino-Indian War, Kennedy and Macmillan agreed to provide Delhi with $120 million worth of emergency military aid. To fulfill the US-UK obligation to Ayub Khan for staying his hand during the Sino-Indian conflict, US special envoy Averell Harriman and British foreign minister Duncan Sandys urged Nehru to enter into talks with Pakistan.

At first Nehru refused to include Kashmir, but later he relented. On November 30 he and Ayub Khan issued a joint statement that effort must be made to resolve outstanding differences between the two countries on "Kashmir and other related matters." But characteristically Nehru told the Lok Sabha the next day that to upset the present arrangements regarding Kashmir would be harmful to future Indo-Pakistan relations.[42]

The Indian delegation led by Foreign Minister Swaran Singh met its Pakistani counterpart led by Muhammad Ali Bogra in Rawalpindi in mid-December, with the resident US and British envoys monitoring the talks by staying in the same building. The two sides decided to hold a second round in Delhi in late January 1963. By then Bogra would be dead, and Zulfikar (aka Zulfi) Ali Bhutto would succeed him as Pakistan's foreign minister. The talks in Delhi led nowhere. Bhutto suggested third-party mediation to Galbraith and Gore-Booth. Nehru rejected this promptly.

On the eve of the next round in Karachi on February 8, 1963, Ayub Khan in his interview with an American reporter repeated his statement of March 22, 1961: Pakistan was open to a solution other than a plebiscite in Kashmir, but such a proposal should come from India.[43] The latest session between the two delegations ended with a joint communiqué that referred to "various aspects relevant to the settlement of the Kashmir problem."

On March 2, 1963, following two years of negotiations, the Ayub Khan government signed a border demarcation treaty with China that involved Pakistan-administered Kashmir. Unlike India, Pakistan renounced previous claims based on obsolete British India maps. China reciprocated by ceding 750 square miles of the territory it had been administering. Beijing acquired legitimacy over its control of the Khunjerab Pass in the Karakoram mountain range on the northern border of Pakistan's federally administered Gilgit-Baltistan. This mountain pass was of vital, strategic importance to the China's Xinjiang Autonomous Region.

When India objected to the Pakistan-China treaty, Bhutto asserted that his country had not ceded any territory to China. Responding to the pressure of Galbraith and Gore-Booth, the Indian and Pakistani delegations kept up the ritual of talking to each other. The Kennedy administration intervened directly. It referred Nehru to the growing demand by the US Congress to tie its military aid to India to the resolution of the Kashmir dispute. Two more sessions followed in April and May. Unsurprisingly, nothing happened.

Despite this lack of progress, after their meeting at Macmillan's country house in Sussex, Kennedy and Macmillan decided to give India an Anglo-American air umbrella to familiarize the Indian air force with supersonic fighter bombers and draft plans to assist the bolstering of India's defenses against the threat of a renewed Chinese attack. The Pentagon agreed to modernize some mountain army divisions of India.[44] The tightening of these defense ties alarmed Pakistani leaders, who could do no more than lodge written protests.

The Washington-London military aid enabled India to double its army divisions to twenty-two and expand its air force and navy.[45]

The US Central Intelligence Agency (CIA) helped India raise a secret Special Frontier Force (SFF) composed of dissident Tibetans under the command of Brigadier Sujan Singh Uban to harass the Chinese troops in Tibet.[46] The SFF was renamed Establishment 22 (so called because Uban was the commander of 22 Mountain Regiment during World War II), located next to the headquarters of the Defense Ministry in Delhi.

The Anglo-American bounty to Delhi left Ayub Khan and the fiery Bhutto fuming. The goodwill Kennedy had generated among Pakistanis by welcoming Ayub Khan with grand gestures evaporated. In July 1961 Kennedy had honored the Pakistani president with a ticker-tape parade on New York's Fifth Avenue and a state dinner at Washington's Mount Vernon. In September 1962 the US president hosted him at his family mansion in Rhode Island and at his farm in Middleburg, Virginia.

But bolstered by the generous US-UK military aid to India, Nehru put the Kashmir question on the backburner, leaving Ayub Khan to wring his hands in frustration.

On the other hand, defeat at the hands of the Chinese left Nehru a shattered man. His health suffered. In the summer and autumn of 1963 he spent considerable time in the salubrious climate of Kashmir to repair his failing physical and mental powers.

THE PROPHET'S MISSING HAIR: A TURNING POINT

The people in the troubled state were transfixed by the "Kashmir Conspiracy" case involving Shaikh Muhammad Abdullah and twenty-three others accused of plotting to overthrow the government. Initiated in 1958, the case dragged on for years, against the background of the return to power of Bakshi Ghulam Muhammad's team. As a result of a glaringly rigged election in February–March 1962, his National Conference garnered 70 of the 75 Assembly seats. In September the special magistrate trying the accused transferred the case to a higher court.

Over the years, the corruption and tyranny of Muhammad's regime, mitigated somewhat by a generous food subsidy and rapid expansion in educational facilities funded by Delhi, had become unbearable. In October 1963, under the guise of implementing a plan to reinvigorate the Congress Party and its allies (which included the National Conference), Nehru got several chief ministers, including Muhammad, to resign and take up party work.

His successor, Khwaja Shamsuddin, had hardly settled in his job when the Kashmir Valley was rocked by massive antigovernment demonstrations that followed the disappearance of a hair of Prophet Muhammad's beard from Srinagar's Hazratbal shrine on December 26. The missing hair provided a trigger for popular disaffection, which had been building up since Shaikh Abdullah's arrest a decade earlier, to burst into the open like a volcanic eruption. Protestors took to the streets on a massive scale in the Vale of Kashmir. This shook a fast-aging, perpetually tired Nehru.

Until then, thanks to the complicit press's grossly biased reporting on Kashmir, Indians in general had been complacent about the situation there. Most of them associated their northernmost state with images of snow-capped mountains, gushing cold streams, and cypress and poplar trees, which provided an idyllic background to the duets sung by a heart-broken hero and the love of his life—stunningly shot in such Bollywood movies as *Kashmir Ki Kali* (Hindi: Kali of Kashmir) and *Mere Sanam* (Hindi: My Love). Cinema, which arrived in the subcontinent in 1913, when only one in sixteen Indians was literate, had become a vital tool to mold popular perceptions and culture. As for radio broadcasts, the popular medium for news, these were controlled by the Ministry of Information and Broadcasting. State-run television news would start in Bombay and Amritsar only a decade later.

Though the missing relic in Srinagar was recovered on January 4, 1964, popular agitation did not subside even after Shamsuddin stepped down in favor of the older, more experienced Ghulam Muhammad Sadiq almost two months later. He and Nehru decided to withdraw the "Kashmir Conspiracy" case against Abdullah in April and released him and the others.

Abdullah was invited to Delhi by Nehru as a personal guest and lodged in his official residence. The two discussed the Kashmir problem. During a cabinet session, attended by Abdullah, Nehru told fellow ministers that he wanted to resolve the Kashmir issue during his lifetime. In the course of his meeting with Pakistan's high commissioner in Delhi, Abdullah received an invitation from Bhutto to visit Pakistan's capital. Nehru recommended acceptance. After consulting several other Indian leaders outside of Delhi, Abdullah returned to Nehru's residence on May 20.

Abdullah and his party boarded the special plane sent by Ayub Khan on May 23. Eleven years of incarceration by the Indian government had transformed Abdullah from a traitor to Islam and Kashmiri Muslims in the eyes of Pakistanis into a fearless champion of Kashmiris. He received a hero's reception in Rawalpindi.

On May 25, a Friday, he addressed a rally of almost two hundred thousand people, presided over by his lifelong rival, Chowdhury Muhammad Abbas of the Muslim Conference.[47] The next day, during his long session with the Pakistani president, Abdullah broached the idea of a quadrangular confederation of the subcontinent, India–West Pakistan–Kashmir–East Pakistan, which had earlier interested Nehru. After this meeting, he announced that Ayub Khan would hold talks with Nehru in Delhi in mid-June to resolve the Kashmir dispute.

On May 27, as Abdullah was on his way in an official convoy to Muzaffarabad, the capital of Azad Kashmir, news came that following a stroke, Nehru had died in the early afternoon of a heart attack. When Abdullah heard the news, he broke down and sobbed. Nehru's death killed any chance of India's amicable settlement with Pakistan on Kashmir.

At the open-air cremation of Nehru's corpse on the banks of the Jamuna (aka Yamuna) in Delhi, Abdullah leapt on the platform and, crying unashamedly, threw flowers onto the funeral pyre. Later, in his autobiography *Aatish-e Chinar* (Urdu: Flames of the Chinar), Abdullah would sum up his rocky relationship with Nehru: "Pandit Nehru's love for Kashmir was more like love for a beautiful woman whom he wanted to possess and that he had come to regard me as a rival in love—for the possession of this beautiful valley."[48]

NEHRU'S LACKLUSTER SUCCESSOR

Lal Bahadur Shastri, who succeeded Nehru, had neither the charisma nor the popularity needed to win the approval of Parliament for an agreement with Pakistan, which would have inevitably involved some territorial concessions to Pakistan and/or letting Kashmiris exercise their right of self-determination for the state as a whole or by region. In polar contrast to the aristocratic background of handsome Nehru, a child of the fabulously rich lawyer Motilal Nehru and his wife, Swaruprani Thussu, the diminutive, jug-eared Shastri, mild-mannered and soft-spoken, was born into the household of a schoolteacher who died when he was a year old. He grew up as a staunch member of the Congress Party and served in Nehru's cabinets from 1952 onward, his latest ministry being home affairs.

Realizing the dramatically altered political scene, Shaikh Abdullah openly called for a plebiscite, something he had not done before. This had an unsettling effect on Sadiq, who had simultaneously to cope with Muhammad's maneuvers in the State Assembly against his recently formed cabinet. He was therefore driven to rely even more heavily on Delhi than Muhammad to stay in power. He actively cooperated with the Shastri government to integrate Kashmir further into the Indian Union.

On December 21, the president of India acquired powers, hitherto denied him, to take over Kashmir's administration if he felt that the constitutional machinery had broken down. Three weeks later it was announced that the National Conference would be dissolved and that the Congress Party would establish a branch in Kashmir. The opposition declared January 15 Protest Day, when Shaikh Abdullah demanded a plebiscite to decide the state's future.

The next month, accompanied by his wife, Akbar Jahan, and a senior deputy, Abdullah went on a hajj—a pilgrimage to Mecca—with plans to visit a few other Arab countries as well as Britain and France. In Algiers he had an unscheduled meeting with Zhou Enlai. According to his memoir, *Flames of the Chinar*, they discussed China's agreement with Pakistan over the northern frontier of Gilgit. Zhou said, "At present, Gilgit is under the control of Pakistan, and therefore we entered into an agreement stipulating that the agreement shall remain valid only as long as Gilgit is under the control of Pakistan." Abdullah revealed that he sent a summary of his conversation with Zhou to the Indian ambassador to China.[49] But the news of Zhou's invitation to Abdullah to visit China disconcerted the Shastri government.

In March, while Abdullah was abroad, the legislature, guided by Sadiq, amended Kashmir's constitution to alter the title of head of state from *Sardar-i-riyasat* (Urdu: president of province) to governor, and *Wazire Azam* (Urdu: prime minister) to chief minister, thus removing the constitutional distinction between Kashmir and other Indian states. In short, the leading features of the "special relationship" that had existed all along between Jammu and Kashmir and the Indian Union were annulled.[50]

In April Abdullah published an essay in the prestigious, New York–based *Foreign Affairs* journal in which he argued that India, Pakistan, and Kashmiris should devise a solution that would grant Kashmiris "the substance of their demand for self-determination but with honor and fairness to both Pakistan and India."[51] He thus put India and Pakistan on a par.

OPERATION DESERT HAWK: A DRY RUN

The moves by the Sadiq-Shastri duo whipped up anti-India sentiment in Pakistan, leading to armed clashes between the two neighbors in the Rann (Desert) of Kutch along the Arabian Sea. Measuring about 2,900 square miles of sparsely inhabited marshland, originally part of the princely state of Kutch, its upland islets were used as pasture plots. It was one of the few un-demarcated tracts between Pakistan and India, each of which maintained a few armed police posts on scattered islets.

On April 9, 1965, the Pakistani army captured an Indian police post near the Kanjarkot fort and claimed all of the Rann of Kutch. Delhi deployed its army in the area to recover the lost posts. In turn, on April 24, Pakistan mounted Operation Desert Hawk by deploying an infantry division and two armored regiments equipped with superior US-supplied Patton tanks and field guns. Four inches of steel armor plating on the forty-six-ton Patton made it immune to all fire except at a very close range.[52] Pakistan captured four more posts and claimed the entire Kanjarkot tract. Given their poor logistics and inferior military hardware, the Indians had no option but to withdraw after offering token resistance. To contain the fighting between two Commonwealth members, British prime minister Harold Wilson intervened. A temporary truce followed at the end of April.

But the Kashmiri background to this crisis worsened in May, when Abdullah returned home. He was arrested and interned in the hill station of Ootacamund, two thousand miles from Kashmir. The anti-India feeling that had been bubbling in the Kashmir Valley during March and April boiled over. Streets filled with huge protest demonstrations. These were crushed with a heavy hand.

The truce in the Rann of Kutch broke down. Hostilities resumed on June 15 on the eve of the weeklong Commonwealth Heads of Government conference in London. Once again Wilson intervened. A formal cease-fire was signed on June 30. Later the border issue was referred to a three-member arbitration committee.[53]

The purpose of Pakistan's Operation Desert Hawk was threefold: to assess India's military preparedness, to draw its troops away from Punjab and Kashmir, and to determine the extent of Washington's seriousness about enforcing its ban on the use of its superior military hardware, including F4 jet fighters, in a war with India. Despite Delhi's repeated protests, no effective action was taken by the Lyndon Johnson administration to inhibit Pakistanis' use of US-made weaponry.

Field Marshal Ayub Khan was buoyed by his victory in the armed sparring he had with India in the Rann of Kutch. An inkling of his upbeat mood was provided by Lakshmi Kant Jha, the principal secretary to Shastri, who was present when the two South Asian leaders met on the sidelines of the Commonwealth conference in London. "You know, your chaps tried to commit aggression on our territory, our chaps gave them a few knocks and they began to flee," Ayub Khan reportedly said. "Mr President, do you think if I had to attack Pakistan, I would choose a terrain where we have no logistic support and you have all the advantages?" asked Shastri. "Do you think I would make such a mistake or any of my generals would allow me to make that mistake?"[54]

Little did Shastri realize that in the previous month Ayub Khan had scrutinized a military presentation on Operation Gibraltar and that at his behest an assault on Akhnoor in India-held Kashmir was included in the subsequently code-named Operation Grand Slam. Following that, Ayub Khan approved Operation Gibraltar. Soon after, however, he had second thoughts about executing the grand plan. The hawks within his cabinet, led by Bhutto, pounced on this and put it about that the president did not want to disturb the status quo because that would jeopardize the freshly acquired riches of his family. That forced Ayub Khan's hand. At the end of July, he addressed the force commanders of Operation Gibraltar as a preamble to the actual launch.[55]

9

Shastri's Tallest Order

Pakistan's Nightmare Comes Alive

Operation Gibraltar[1] grew out of Zulfikar Ali Bhutto's memorandum to President Muhammad Ayub Khan in early May 1965. In it he warned that as a consequence of the ramped-up Western military assistance to India, the balance of power in South Asia was tilting rapidly in Delhi's favor. He recommended "a bold and courageous" move in Kashmir to create "greater possibility for a negotiated settlement."[2] The end purpose of the complex Operation Gibraltar was to enable the Pakistani military to capture territory in Kashmir while making it appear that it was the Kashmiri people who had finally mounted an armed rebellion to end the unbearably oppressive rule of India.

OPERATIONS GIBRALTAR
AND GRAND SLAM

Devised conceptually by the Kashmir Cell of the Ayub Khan regime, it was passed on to Major General Akhtar Hussain Malik, the Murree-based commander of the Twelfth Infantry Division. Along with the Azad Kashmir Armed Force, this division guarded the cease-fire line in Kashmir. The strategy was to have a sizable force of trained guerrillas and saboteurs infiltrate India-held Kashmir to carry out sabotage to destabilize the state government and spark an anti-India rebellion by Kashmiris.

If it failed to achieve the desired aim, then the complementary Operation Grand Slam was to be launched by the Pakistani military. It envisaged a rapid strike by armored and infantry units from the southern tip of the cease-fire line to Akhnoor, a town along the Pathankot-Jammu-Srinagar highway. The capture of Akhnoor would sever the critical supply line for the bottled-up Indian forces in the Vale of Kashmir, providing Pakistan with several options, one or more of which could be exploited.

Major General Malik, a tall, hefty, mustached man with receding gray hair, worked with Brigadier General Riaz Hussain, director-general of the Inter-Services Intelligence (ISI) directorate, to recruit volunteers for a new force, Mujahid Companies. Armed and trained as guerrillas and sab-oteurs, it was to be led by Pakistani officers. Malik formed six task forces, each five hundred strong, and gave them names of outstanding Islamic generals of the past. Each contingent consisted of Azad Kashmir troops and Mujahedin irregular volunteers, all in civilian clothes. Their tasks were to blow up bridges, cut communication lines, raid supply dumps, and attack military units as a prelude to an armed uprising scheduled for August 9, 1965. That day would coincide with the twelfth anniversary of the first arrest of Shaikh Muhammad Abdullah and was chosen by Plebiscite Front leaders to protest his latest incarceration.

According to this plan, Mujahideen ranks were scheduled to cross the cease-fire line in small groups between August 1 and 5, and assem-ble at prearranged places to set up camps as a preamble to infiltrating the Kashmir Valley at many points during the following three days. This phase would be facilitated by Pakistani troops firing along the truce line to distract their Indian adversaries.

The envisaged capture of Srinagar airport and radio station by the Ghaznavi Task Force on August 9 would set the scene for the declaration of the establishment of a Revolutionary Council, which would proclaim the liberation of Jammu and Kashmir.

In practice, however, on August 5 a shepherd boy informed the police of the presence of strangers, wearing green *salwar kameez* in the border town of Tanmarg, twenty-four miles from Srinagar, who offered bribes for information. He led the police to the base camp of the Salahuddin Task Force. The same day a local man in Mendhar, sixty miles from Srinagar, informed the nearby army brigade headquarters of a few foreigners who sought intelligence from him. But it was not until August 8 that the army troops arrested two commanders of the infiltrators near Narain Nag, five miles from Srinagar, that they learned about Pakistan's plan.[3]

By then, however, the Ghaznavi Task Force had managed to reach a suburb of Srinagar. Gunfights soon broke out in the capital. Taken by surprise, the Kashmiri authorities urged Delhi to declare martial law in the valley. But the Lal Bahadur Shastri government refrained from doing so. The sabotage and shootings by the armed infiltrators in Srinagar continued until August 12–13. "The streets in Srinagar were deserted," noted Lieutenant General Harbaksh Singh, the commanding officer of India's Western Command. "There were visible signs of anxiety and tension on the faces of the residents gaping through the windows."[4]

All India Radio broadcast the confessions of the two captured officers outlining Pakistan's extensive plan.[5] The Indian government protested through diplomatic channels. Pakistan replied that Kashmir was a disputed territory and violent disturbances there could not be attributed to it. On the other hand, as preplanned, Pakistan's state-run radio broadcast on August 9 that a rebellion had broken out in India-occupied Kashmir. It added that, according to the Voice of Kashmir radio station, a Revolutionary Council had assumed full power over the state.

In Delhi, the chief of army staff (COAS) General Joyanto Nath Chaudhuri informed the Emergency Committee of the Cabinet that though the infiltrators were being apprehended, further sabotage could still be carried out by those at large. Indeed shoot-outs and subversive activities in Indian Kashmir continued until August 13.

On that day, Shastri authorized the army to cross the cease-fire line to destroy the infiltrators' bases. If regular Pakistani troops intervened, then the army would be free to retaliate at any suitable place of its choice, he added. In his August 15 Independence Day speech from the ramparts of the Red Fort in Delhi, he declared that the "resort to the sword will be met with the sword."[6] His valiant words helped portray him as a resolute leader. That day the Indian soldiers crossed the cease-fire line in the eastern Kargil region.

India's far more ambitious objective was to cut off Pakistan's main infiltration route into the Kashmir Valley. It passed through the 8,652-foot-high Haji Pir Pass on the western Pir Panjal mountain range three miles inside Azad Kashmir. The operation required meticulous planning and execution over several days. On August 24 the Indians prepared to capture the Haji Pir Pass.

That day, Major General Malik sought permission of the Rawalpindi-based general headquarters to launch the preplanned Operation Grand Slam. The director of military operations, Brigadier Gul Hassan, passed on the request to the COAS, General Muhammad Musa Khan. When nothing happened, Hassan reminded the COAS the next day. The COAS needed to get the permission of President Field Marshall Muhammad

Ayub Khan, who was then vacationing in the picturesque Swat Valley two hundred miles away. So Musa Khan dispatched Foreign Minister Bhutto to Swat. Pakistan was on the verge of an all-out war, but the COAS, a Baluch by ethnicity, was unwilling to make decisions while the Pashtun executive president was on vacation. On August 29 Malik received the green light. By then the Indians had captured the Haji Pir Pass and bolstered their forces by adding three infantry units and an artillery regiment in that sector. Following a further thirty-six-hour delay at the headquarters, the launch of Operation Grand Slam started at five AM on September 1.

AYUB KHAN'S MIDSTREAM SOMERSAULT

When Malik advanced the Twelfth Infantry Division, he had a six-to-one advantage over the Indians in armor, with his Patton tanks being hugely superior to the enemy's lesser (American) Shermans and (French) AMX-13s. He enjoyed a similar advantage in artillery. His infantry was twice the size of the Indians'.[7] It was no surprise, then, that before the day was over, the Pakistanis had captured all their targets. Outnumbered and outgunned, the Indians suffered heavy losses. They withdrew rapidly, while the strategic Akhnoor remained lightly defended by four infantry battalions and a squadron of tanks.

At this point an inexplicable change of command occurred in Pakistan. General Musa Khan arrived at the theater of operations in a helicopter and transferred the command of the Twelfth Division from Malik, a Punjabi, to Major General Agha Muhammad Yahya Khan, then commander of the Seventh Infantry Division. A burly, double-chinned, bushy-browed, slothful Yahya Khan was, like Ayub Khan, an ethnic Pashtun. Malik was asked to leave with Musa Khan in his helicopter.

Yahya Khan altered Malik's strategy and thus lost more time. Malik had planned on bypassing strongly defended Indian positions and subordinating everything to capturing the bridge over the Chenab River at Akhnoor with the least possible delay. But Yahya Khan opted for a different route. He crossed the Tawi River and went straight into Troti, thereby losing crucial hours.

Why did Ayub Khan change horses midstream? He was overconfident of the glorious victory that Operation Grand Slam would deliver and wanted the kudos to go to his fellow Pashtun, Yahya Kahn, rather than Malik, who had masterminded the interlinked operations Gibraltar and Grand Slam.

Ayub Khan's egregiously unprofessional decision allowed India to shore up its defenses of Akhnoor. Its military high command deployed warplanes to blunt the attack at a time when the enemy was about ten miles from Akhnoor. The air strikes destroyed a number of Pakistani Pattons and slowed the advance of the rest. In response, the Pakistani planes targeted India's air bases not only in Kashmir but also in Punjab.

On September 3 the UN secretary-general U Thant conveyed to the Security Council the gist of the report he had received from the head of the UN Military Observer Group in India and Pakistan (UNMOGIP). There had been a series of cease-fire line violations in Kashmir from the Pakistani side by armed men in civilian clothes for "the purpose of armed action on the Indian side."[8] Three days later the Council passed a resolution authorizing the secretary-general to strengthen the UNMOGIP and inform it on the situation in the area. U Thant dashed to the capitals of the warring nations.

On the battlefield, the Indian generals concluded that the Pakistani tank advance could not be halted by air strikes alone. So the Emergency Committee of the Cabinet pondered the question: Should we attack Pakistani soil across the international border to compel its military high command to redeploy its forces away from the Kashmir front? The ultimate decision lay with Shastri. He said, "Go!"

THE SHORTEST LEADER'S TALLEST ORDER

On September 6, when the Pakistan Army was only three miles from Akhnoor, the Indians opened a new front by attacking the Lahore and Sialkot sectors inside Pakistan. This compelled headquarters in Rawalpindi to rush its men and weaponry from the Kashmir front to blunt the Indian incursion toward Lahore, only fifteen miles from the border. For all practical purposes that move marked the end of Operation Grand Slam. "The [Indian] Army could never forget the tallest order from the shortest man," remarked Lieutenant General Harbaksh Singh later.[9]

Actually, Shastri had made a more critical, but super-secret, decision in November 1964 by giving the go-ahead to India's nuclear weapons program—a fact that became known only a decade later. This was Shastri's response to the successful testing of an atomic bomb by China near Lop Nor, Kansu, in the previous month. That groundbreaking event in China had been the result of Mao Zedong's order to accelerate his country's nuclear arms program in light of the military and diplomatic backing that both Washington and Moscow accorded Delhi during the Sino-Indian War.

On the Pakistani side, addressing his compatriots on September 7, Ayub Khan said, "[The earlier] Indian aggression in Kashmir was only a preparation for an attack on Pakistan. Indian rulers were never reconciled to the establishment of an independent Pakistan where the Muslims could build a homeland of their own. . . . But their defeat was imminent because the 100 million people of Pakistan whose hearts beat with the sound of '*La ilaha illallah, Muhammad ur rasul Allah*' ['There is no god but Allah, and Muhammad is messenger of Allah'] will not rest till India's guns are silenced."[10]

In the diplomatic arena, as soon as the Indians penetrated the Indo-Pakistan frontier, Ayub Khan and Bhutto appealed to Washington to honor the 1959 Pakistan-US Cooperation Agreement to assist their country in resisting Indian aggression. President Lyndon Johnson's administration pointed out that the concord referred to armed aggression from any country "controlled by international communism" and that India did not belong to that category.[11] Johnson suspended military aid to both Delhi and Rawalpindi. That hurt Pakistan, solely dependent on Washington, more than India. (Britain followed suit.) Pakistan's appeal to the South-East Asia Treaty Organization (SEATO) headquarters in Bangkok also failed because it was not a victim of communist aggression.

PATRIOTIC SURGE IN WARRING NATIONS

In Pakistan, patriotic emotion gripped the nation—from Karachi to Lahore to Dacca, with people attending huge rallies in support of the army. "Every Pakistani wanted to contribute," recalled Mahmood Shaam, then a reporter with the Lahore-based daily *Nawa-e-Waqt* (Urdu: New Times).

> Poets wrote nationalist poetry. The radio became the medium of the masses. Television was accessible only in Lahore. Popular singer Malika-e-Tarnoom (Queen of Melody) Nur Jahan went to the Lahore television station, requesting them to allow her to sing for Pakistan. . . . Outside the Lahore radio station a post box was kept in which people would submit patriotic poetry. . . . A poem I wrote for the Pakistan Air Force became very popular: *Yeh hawa ke rahion / Yeh badalon ke sathion / Harfan shan Mujahideen / Apni*

jaan pe khel kar / Tum bane salamati (Oh guides of the air / Oh companions of clouds / You glorious Mujahedin/Playing with your own life / You become robust). Rulers and opposition were united. . . . It was the first time we gave blood for our borders. From 1947 to 1965 . . . we were struggling to become a nation. But during the 1965 war all of us were one: Pakistanis. Hostility and enmity against India solidified.[12]

For the Pakistani public, this was the first full-scale war with India, the 1947–1948 conflict in Kashmir having been a minor affair and confined to that princely state. This time the antagonists deployed two-thirds of their total tank arsenals (Pakistan, 756; India, 620). What followed were some of the most intense armored battles since the end of World War II, often in sugarcane fields along the Punjab border. To boost morale, the public was bombarded with stories of victories on the battlefield embellished with heroism of individual soldiers and their units.[13]

The battle around the small town of Khem Karan, a few miles from the international border inside Indian Punjab, gripped popular attention on both sides. The Pakistani armor and infantry had seized it on September 7. The Indians resolved to retake it against heavy odds. They could marshal only three armored regiments equipped with a mishmash of inferior tanks against Pakistan's six armored regiments driving versatile Pattons. But they compensated for their disadvantage in hardware with superior tactics, surprising the enemy force and encircling it.

Their field commander, Major General Gurbaksh Singh, arrayed the tanks in a U-formation in unharvested sugarcane fields outside the village of Asal Uttar during the night of September 9–10. Then he flooded the surrounding area. The next morning the advancing Pakistani armor divisions got trapped within the enemy's horseshoe formation and found it hard to turn around because of the marshy terrain. The Indian gunners opened fire from their camouflaged locations only when the Pakistani tanks came close, thereby managing to penetrate the Pattons. By the time the fierce battle was over, India had lost thirty-two tanks while destroying or capturing ninety-seven of Pakistan's tanks, including seventy-two Pattons.[14] "So many tanks lay destroyed, lying in the battlefield like toys," wrote Lieutenant General Harbakhsh Singh in his memoir *In the Line of Duty*.[15]

On the opposing side, Pakistanis were regaled with their army's capture of Khem Karan on September 7. "We were also taken to Khem Karan," recalled Mahmood Shaam four decades later. "We felt proud to see the battleground where we won. Even *Time* magazine reported that 'despite claims from both sides the awkward fact is Khem Karan is under Pakistan administration.'"[16] What followed next—a debacle—was censured.

While censuring such news as enemy warplanes bombing targets in Peshawar and Dacca, Radio Pakistan announced raids on the famed Chandni Chowk shopping area of Delhi—a mood-enhancing tonic for Pakistanis. "When I went to Rawalpindi in January 1966 to cover a ministerial conference between India and Pakistan, Pakistani journalists asked me how badly Chandni Chowk . . . [had] been damaged by bombs," wrote Kuldip Nayar in his book *India: The Critical Years*. "My reply that not a single bomb had been dropped in Delhi was greeted with derisive laughter."[17]

Equally, Indian journalists were in a triumphalist mode. At the daily press briefings in Delhi, the most frequent questions were: "Has Lahore airport fallen? Is Lahore radio station under our control?"[18] The reality was that though India's tanks had reached Batapur near the Allama Iqbal international airport—halfway between the international border and the city center of Lahore, twenty miles from the Wagah border post—causing an exodus, its generals had no intention of seizing the city of one million. It would have involved hand-to-hand fighting and later burdened the occupying army with the taxing tasks of maintaining law and order and feeding the people.

Overall, a comforting belief had taken hold in Pakistan that the war was going well and that Hindu India was paying a punishing price for its unprovoked attack on their hallowed territory. The popular perception clashed with reality on the ground, as noted by general headquarters in Rawalpindi. By the third week of hostilities, it became evident to Field Marshal Ayub Khan and his close aides that the army's supply of bombs, bullets, fuel, and food was dangerously low, and that no military assistance by a foreign power was in the offing.

DIPLOMATS AT WORK

Following the rebuffs from the United States and SEATO, Pakistan ruled out approaching Moscow, given its close ties with Delhi. On his part, however, in early April 1965, Soviet premier Alexei Kosygin had welcomed Ayub Khan and Bhutto during their eight-day tour of the Soviet

THE LONGEST AUGUST

Union in a move to counterbalance the influence America and China enjoyed in Pakistan. The Kremlin then hosted Shastri on a weeklong trip in mid-May to highlight the Indo-Soviet friendship forged by Jawaharlal Nehru.

In the war, China resolutely backed Pakistan. It warned Delhi against any Indian incursion into Pakistan's territory. And when that happened, it condemned India's move. In its message to the Shastri government in Delhi on September 16, it stated that it would go on supporting Pakistan in "its just struggle" as long as Indian aggression against it continued.

Facing a dire situation on the battlefield, on the night of September 19–20, Ayub Khan and Bhutto flew from Peshawar to Beijing for a clandestine meeting with top Chinese leaders. Mao Zedong coupled his earlier promise of assistance with advice that Ayub Khan should prepare contingency plans to withdraw his army to the hills and fight a long guerrilla war against India.[19] Such counsel washed over the Sandhurst-trained Ayub Khan and the Berkeley-educated lawyer Bhutto. In practice, all Beijing did was to threaten to open a second front against India.

In the leading world capitals there was considerable apprehension that any direct Chinese involvement in the conflict would draw other powers into the conflict. Western ambassadors therefore kept pressing Pakistan not to encourage China to go beyond rhetorical statements. Equally they pressured India not to attack East Pakistan, which would have drawn Beijing into the bilateral war.

After his shuttle diplomacy in South Asia, U Thant reported to the UN Security Council on September 16 that each of the warring countries had expressed its desire to cease hostilities under certain conditions that were unacceptable to the other side. Among the few suggestions he made to the Council was a request to the leaders of the sparring nations to meet in a mutually friendly country to discuss ending the present conflict and other outstanding differences. On September 18 Kosygin addressed letters to Ayub Khan and Shastri to meet in Tashkent in Soviet Uzbekistan or any other Soviet city for negotiations on the Kashmir issue, and offered to attend the bilateral meeting if so wished by both sides. Shastri accepted the suggestion on September 22 and informed the parliament. Ayub Khan prevaricated, replying a week later that such a meeting would not be fruitful "at present."[20]

Meanwhile, at the Security Council the United States and the Soviet Union worked together to draft a resolution. As a result, Resolution 211

188

secured a swift and unanimous passage on September 20.[21] It called for a cease-fire at 0700 hours GMT (Greenwich Mean Time) on September 22, 1965, negotiations to settle the Kashmir dispute, and a subsequent withdrawal of "all armed personnel" to the positions held before August 5. India accepted the resolution on September 21. Addressing the Security Council on September 22, Bhutto described the resolution as unsatisfactory but accepted it for the sake of international peace. The guns fell silent at 0330 hours on September 23, Indian Standard Time (IST)—2200 hours GMT on September 22.

Unsurprisingly, the claims made by Delhi and Rawalpindi regarding their losses and gains were out of sync. According to Pakistan, 8,200 Indians were killed or captured, and 110 of India's aircraft and 500 of its tanks were destroyed or seized. Herbert Feldman, an academic specialist on Pakistan, put India's losses as follows: fatalities, 4,000 to 6,000; tanks, about 300; and aircraft, 50. The statistics for Pakistan were 3,000 to 5,000 dead and losses of 250 tanks and 50 planes.[22] Delhi admitted a loss of 75 aircraft, which chimed with neutral observers' figure of 60 to 76. But their estimate of India losing 150 to 190 tanks was well below Feldman's. Whereas Delhi claimed that 5,260 Pakistanis were killed or captured, the neutral commentators settled for 3,800. And their estimate of Pakistan losing 200–300 tanks was in line with Feldman's 250. India's claim of destroying 43 to 73 Pakistani aircraft was way above the neutral observers' 20.

According to David Van Praagh, a Canadian academic, India gained 710 square miles of Pakistan, including a third of the total in Azad Kashmir. By contrast, Pakistan acquired 210 square miles of the Indian soil, all except 19 square miles being in Kashmir.[23] Pakistan's gain in the Indian Punjab was restricted to the environs of Khem Karan.[24]

What was the end result of the war? This question is best answered by stating the primary objective of each protagonist. The aim of Pakistan, the instigator, was to change the status quo in Kashmir by force. It failed to do so. India's objective was merely to frustrate its adversary's goal. It succeeded. In a way, Delhi won by not losing. In stark contrast, Rawalpindi gained nothing from a war it initiated. Indeed, catastrophic results came to pass in domestic politics. This armed conflict set in motion trends that culminated in the downfall of Ayub Khan's regime, followed by the breakup of Pakistan, with its eastern wing seceding to form the sovereign state of Bangladesh.

WHEN THE GUNS FELL SILENT

Most Pakistanis could not figure out why their generals had signed a cease-fire when they were vaunting glowing victories on the battlefield. The credibility of Ayub Khan's government suffered a precipitous fall from which it never recovered, even though the president addressed several gatherings rationalizing his decision.

His defensive posture contrasted sharply with Bhutto's. "Pakistan will fight, fight for a thousand years," he declared at a press conference in October. "If India builds the [atom] bomb, we will eat grass or leaves, even go hungry, but we will get one of our own. We have no alternative . . . bomb for bomb."[25] Bhutto's statement was a signal to India that Pakistan was aware of its clandestine nuclear weapons program. He had garnered that information from Munir Ahmad Khan, a senior technician at the eight-year-old International Atomic Energy Agency, a UN watchdog, during Bhutto's visit to Vienna earlier in 1965. Later, during Bhutto's presidency in 1972 Ahmad Khan would be appointed head of the Pakistan Atomic Energy Commission.

During the three-week conflict with India, East Pakistanis realized to their consternation that their province was woefully short of troops to assure their security. Whereas the military consumed 60 percent of the nation's budget, only 7 percent of its ranks came from East Pakistan, which accounted for 54 percent of the country's population.

In India there was disgruntlement among its soldiers, who would have preferred to keep on destroying Pakistan's armor. After flamboyantly posing for cameras on top of a captured Patton tank, Shastri addressed the troops at the garrison border town of Ferozepur. He explained that he agreed to a truce because of pressure from America, on which India was dependent for food and economic aid.[26] This would become abundantly clear later in the year, when a steep drop in US economic aid forced Delhi to liberalize its restrictions on foreign trade and devalue its currency by a staggering 57.5 percent.[27]

After the cease-fire no progress was made on the belligerents' withdrawal to their positions of August 5 as required by Resolution 211. This situation required mediation by a great power. Kosygin repeated his earlier proposal for an Indo-Pakistan summit in Tashkent in his letters on November 21. Shastri responded positively. In Rawalpindi, the wily Bhutto finagled an immediate invitation for a state visit by the Kremlin as a means to pressure the United States before the scheduled December 10

Ayub Khan–Johnson meeting in Washington. Ayub Khan and the president dashed to Moscow on November 23, and two days later Ayub Khan accepted Kosygin's proposal.

SOVIETS' SUCCESS AS PEACEMAKERS

On January 4, 1966, the Tashkent Conference at the grand municipal hall opened with an address by Kosygin, a sixty-two-year-old leader with deep-set eyes and sparse graying hair. Besides officials from India, Pakistan, and the Soviet Union, his audience included three hundred representatives of the international media.

The Indian delegation, headed by Shastri, wanted the restoration of the prewar cease-fire line, except the mountain passes its army had seized in the Haji Pir, Poonch-Uri, and Kargil regions, and the signing of a no-war pact with Pakistan. Its counterparty, which included the pugnacious Bhutto, had no intention of ceding the mountain passes, which were the main infiltration points into India-held Kashmir, or entering into a no-war agreement.[28]

When the Indian side insisted on a no-war pact, the Pakistanis responded that they would agree only if there were a built-in mechanism to discuss resolving the Kashmir issue. Reiterating that Kashmir was an integral part of their country, the Indians refused. A stalemate ensued.

In his private talks with Shastri, Kosygin told him that if India refused to withdraw fully from the captured territories completely, as demanded by Resolution 211, the Kremlin would not use its veto against possible UN sanctions against Delhi. That softened up Shastri. At the same time Soviet foreign minister Andrei Gromyko convinced the Pakistani delegates that it was futile to try to achieve gains at the negotiating table that they had failed to obtain on the battlefield.[29]

As the last throw of the dice, on the morning of January 9 Kosygin took Ayub Khan on an unscheduled tour of the vast warplanes manufacturing plant in Tashkent, aware that Washington had cut off supplies of military hardware to Pakistan. Ayub Khan, a lifelong soldier, was impressed—all the more as he was bombarded by Kosygin with jaw-dropping statistics of the number of tanks and warplanes the Soviet Union produced annually. A bond grew between the two leaders. Kosygin adroitly interweaved his narrative with his viewpoint that, lacking resources, developing countries like Pakistan and India should avoid resolving their differences through use of force. Ayub Khan got the mes-sage.[30] In the evening the nine-point draft of the Tashkent Declaration was finalized.[31]

"They [The prime minister of India and the president of Pakistan] re-affirm their obligation under the UN Charter not to have recourse to force and to settle their disputes through peaceful means," read Article 1 of the Tashkent Declaration, signed on January 10, 1966. "They considered that the interests of peace in their region . . . were not served by the con-tinuance of tension. . . . It was against this background that Jammu and Kashmir was discussed, and each of the sides set forth its respective posi-tion." Two other articles specified a February 25 deadline for the armed personnel of the two countries to be withdrawn to the positions they had held prior to August 5, and "both sides shall observe the cease-fire terms on the cease-fire line." The last article stated that "both sides will continue meetings at the highest and at other levels on matters of direct concern to both countries. Both sides have recognized the need to set up joint Indian-Pakistan bodies, which will report to their Governments in order to decide what further steps should be taken."[32] A day earlier, answering a question by Bhutto, Kosygin replied, "Jammu and Kashmir is disputed and naturally you have a right to bring this up under Article 9."[33]

The absence of a reference to a plebiscite in Jammu and Kashmir seemed to satisfy the Indian delegates. "The Indians were jubilant and smiling," wrote Air Martial Asghar Khan, a member of the Pakistani delegation. "Tashkent Declaration was for Pakistan a statement of sur-render. The Indians were all over the room shaking any hand that they could grasp. It was as if India had defeated Pakistan in hockey at the Olympics."[34]

Khan was unaware that the head of the Indian delegation, Shastri, was hardly in a buoyant mood. His consultations first with Kosygin on the text of the declaration and then with his foreign and defense minis-ters to judge how the joint communiqué would be received in India had dragged on until three AM on January 10. His sleep was brief—too brief for his ailing heart.

DEATH IN THE LINE OF DUTY

During the morning of January 10 Shastri held a series of meetings with his ministers and senior bureaucrats as well as Soviet officials to fine-tune the declaration, and also work on his speech. He signed the historic document in the afternoon. Then, turning immediately to the accompanying Indian press corps, he said: "I am in your hands; if you write favorably, the country will accept it."[35] In the evening he attended the farewell party given by the Soviet hosts.

The journalists accompanying Shastri retired to their rooms in a hotel located some distance from the dacha where Shastri and his party were lodged. "'Your Prime Minister is dying'": that was what Kuldip Nayar, part of the Indian press team in Tashkent, heard the Russian female concierge saying as she tried waking up the journalists on her floor. Nayar and the Indian press attaché rushed to Shastri's dacha by taxi. "At the dacha, we met Kosygin, a picture of grief," wrote Nayar. "He could not speak and only lifted his hands to indicate that Shastri was no more."[36]

After the farewell reception, Shastri had reached his dacha at about ten PM. "Shastri told [his personal servant] Ram Nath to bring him his food which came from Ambassador [T. N.] Kaul's house, prepared by his cook, Jan Mohammed," continued Nayar. "He ate very little: a dish of spinach and potatoes and a curry." Venkat Raman, one of Shastri's personal assistants in Delhi, called him to say that the general reaction to the Tashkent Declaration in the capital had been favorable, except by opposition leaders, who objected to the withdrawal of Indian troops from the Haji Pir Pass. Keen to know the reaction of his close family members, Shastri phoned to know the opinion of his eldest daughter, Kusam. She replied in Hindi, "We have not liked it." Shastri asked, "What about [your] Amma [Hindi: mother]?" She too had not liked it, came the reply. This upset Shastri. "If my own family has not liked it, what would outsiders say?" he remarked.

Agitated, he started pacing the room, something he often did while giving interviews to the press. He drank some milk as a preliminary to retiring to bed. But he could not sleep, and resumed pacing the room. He asked for water, which Ram Nath served him from the thermos flask on the dressing table. Soon after midnight he asked Ram Nath to retire to his room and rise early for a flight to Kabul.

In another room Shastri's personal secretary, Jagan Nath Sahai, and two stenographers finished packing their luggage at 1:20 AM. Suddenly they found the prime minister standing at their door. "Where is the doctor sahib?" he inquired with some effort. Astonishingly, there was no emergency bell or buzzer in Shastri's spacious room. Dr. R. N. Chugh was sleeping at the back of the room. Sahai woke up Chugh. While the doctor dressed, Sahai and the stenographers helped Shastri to walk back to his room. (In retrospect this was a fatal move by someone who had suffered a severe heart attack, according to Nayar in his book *India: The Critical Years*. Shastri had previously survived two mild heart attacks.)

In his room, a racking cough convulsed him. He was given water to drink and put to bed. After touching his chest, he fell unconscious. Dr. Chugh arrived, felt his pulse, gave him an injection in the arm, and later put the syringe needle into his heart. There was no response. He then gave the dying Shastri mouth-to-mouth resuscitation, but it failed.

Chugh said to Sahai, "Get the local doctors." The security guard at the dacha acted promptly. A Soviet doctor arrived within ten minutes, with others following. They declared Shastri dead. The exact time of his death on January 11 was 1:32 AM Tashkent time, or 2:02 AM IST.

Ayub Khan was informed instantly, and he arrived at Shastri's dacha at four AM. He looked downcast. "Here is a man of peace who gave his life for amity between India and Pakistan," he remarked. Later he would tell Pakistani reporters that Shastri was one Indian leader with whom he had hit it off. "Pakistan and India might have solved their differences had he lived," he remarked.[37] When Aziz Ahmad, the foreign secretary of Pakistan, called Bhutto to inform him of Shastri's death, Bhutto was half asleep and grasped only the word "died." "Which of the two bastards?" he asked;[38] the other "bastard," according to him, being Ayub Khan.

Any opposition to the Tashkent Declaration in India died with Shastri. Parliament endorsed it. Indira Gandhi, the forty-nine-year-old minister of information and broadcasting, was installed as prime minister by Congress Party barons as a stop-gap measure. The sole, but largely neglected, child of Jawaharlal and Kamala Nehru, Indira had grown up as an insecure and defensive woman. With her long, sharp nose and a broad forehead, she was a cross between the refined, sinewy features of her father and the bloated visage of her mother. She fell in love with an outgoing, articulate Zoroastrian intellectual and Congress Party activist named Feroze Gandhi. At the age of twenty-five, disregarding the opposition of her father and Mahatma Mohandas Gandhi, she married Feroze Gandhi according to Hindu rituals. Since Zoroastrianism does not accept converts, there was no question of Indira adopting the religion of her husband. Following the breakdown of her marriage after Indian independence, she ran her father's household. Using his unchallenged power and personality, Nehru got her elected president of the Congress

Party in 1959. That was how she was parachuted into mainstream Indian politics. The ruling party's presidency gave her insight into the weaknesses of the main political players, an asset she would successfully use later to outmaneuver those who had earlier privately derided her as a "dumb doll" (Hindi: *goongi guddia*).

AYUB KHAN PASSES ON THE RULER'S BATON

The state-controlled press in Pakistan was inhibited from airing the public letdown about the Tashkent Declaration. Even then popular anger burst into street demonstrations. The protestors felt that their president had sold Kashmir to the Hindu babus (Urdu: petty clerks) and warlords and that he had given away his battlefield gains in the negotiations. Police gunfire killed two protesting students in Lahore. Angry demonstrators, marching along the main thoroughfare of Karachi, set ablaze the US Information Service Library.

Referring to the disturbance in his radio broadcast on January 14, Ayub Khan said, "There may be some amongst us, who will take advantage of your feelings and will try to mislead you."[39] He was referring to his political adversaries, whose ranks and temper had been bolstered by Bhutto's undisguised opposition to the Tashkent Declaration. Indeed Bhutto resigned as foreign minister five months after the signing of this declaration, and started planning the birth of a political party of his own.

However, a more robust opposition was growing in East Pakistan with material as well as cultural causes. Under Ayub Khan's presidency, power became concentrated in the hands of the military, bureaucratic, and commercial-industrial elites, among whom Bengalis were only marginally represented. The war in Kashmir, in which they had minimal interest or attachment, was thrust on them without consultation. During the seventeen days of its duration, they remained helpless observers. In March 1966, they were shocked to hear Bhutto state, during a National Assembly debate in Dacca,[40] that during the Indo-Pakistan War the government had confidently assumed that, in the event of an attack on East Pakistan, China would come to its defense.[41] If, in the final analysis, Beijing was responsible for the defense of East Pakistan, then there was no advantage in the eastern wing remaining a part of Pakistan. As an independent nation, most Bengalis concluded, they might be able to safeguard it more effectively. These factors swelled the ranks of the Awami League, led by Shaikh Mujibur Rahman. Its six-point platform, centered around a federal Pakistan, envisaged a weak central government, lacking taxation powers and control over external trade, with its jurisdiction reduced to foreign affairs and defense.

Looking back, Ayub Khan regretted his decision to go to war with India. In April he told his cabinet: "I want it understood that never again will we risk 100 million Pakistanis for 5 million Kashmiris—never again."[42] But the plunge in his popular standing proved irreversible.

Four months after resigning from the cabinet in June 1966, Bhutto announced the creed of his forthcoming Pakistan People's Party (PPP): "Islam is our Faith; Democracy is out Policy; Socialism is our economy. All power to the People." While serving as a cabinet minister for eight years, he had impressed his colleagues with his extensive knowledge, wit, and brilliance, and had acquired a base of his own. He expanded it by coopting leftists in West Pakistan with a sprinkling of communists from East Pakistan to establish the PPP in Lahore in November 1967. Notably, its founding charter referred to "jihad against India" because of its continued refusal to hold the promised plebiscite in Jammu and Kashmir. A prematurely balding man with a sharp nose in a buttery face, he was charismatic and glib, with a penchant for catchy slogans. His slogan "Bread, Clothing, and Shelter" for all clicked with the public, as did his cries of "Down with zamindars [landlords]" and "Equal rights for peasants." Through seductive demagoguery and awe-inspiring self-confidence, he rapidly built up popular support for the PPP.

Beginning in the autumn of 1968, opposition to the government, expressed through demonstrations and strikes, escalated. It became so acute that in March 1969 Ayub Khan abrogated the constitution he had unveiled in 1962, reimposed martial law, and resigned. He handed over power to the COAS, General Yahya Khan.

In August Yahya Khan welcomed US president Richard Nixon in Lahore. He paid a return state visit to Washington at the end October 1971, when the crisis in East Pakistan became acute, requiring consultations with Nixon. He followed this up with a meeting with Zhou Enlai in Beijing on November 14. At home one of his early decisions was to expand the Inter-Services Intelligence (ISI) directorate and assign it the task of gathering political intelligence in East Pakistan.

THE RISE OF THE ISI AND RAW

The ISI had come a long way from its modest inception in 1948, when Deputy COAS Major General Robert Cawthorne established it as part of military intelligence. Two years later he turned it into an independent agency under his direct command. In the 1950s COAS General Ayub Khan used the ISI to keep increasingly fractious politicians under surveillance. Its authority grew when he seized power in 1958, and in effect it became the military's political arm. Following its intelligence failures in the Indo-Pakistan War in September 1965, he reorganized it. He set up a Covert Action Division inside the ISI. Its early assignment was to assist ethnic minority insurgents operating under such names as the All Tripura Tiger Force and the National Democratic Front of Bodoland in northeast India that were demanding independence.

Delhi countered this when, in September 1967, Indira Gandhi established a foreign intelligence agency initially as a wing of the main Intelligence Bureau (IB) with the innocuous title of Research and Analysis Wing (RAW) but reporting directly to the prime minister's office. It immediately acquired the assets of the Special Frontier Force, a secret army set up five years earlier and trained by the CIA to carry out subversive actions, originally aimed at Chinese troops in Tibet.[43]

Before establishing the new agency, Indira Gandhi had secured the assistance of the CIA through President Lyndon Johnson. Since their White House meeting in March 1966, he had maintained cordial relations with her. He disapproved of the close relationship Pakistan was developing with China. This opened the way for senior RAW and IB officials to be trained by the CIA. RAW was made an independent agency in 1968 under Rameshwar Nath Kao, who had headed the IB's foreign intelligence division. Its activities were to be concealed not only from the public but also from Parliament. To counter the growing intelligence and military links between Pakistan and China, the prime minister instructed Kao to cultivate links with Israel's foreign intelligence agency, Mossad, which also functioned as a department of the prime minister's secretariat.[44] This was at a time when Delhi had no diplomatic relations with Tel Aviv and took a strongly pro-Palestinian stance in the Palestinian-Israeli conflict.

When Yahya Khan announced elections for the provincial and national assemblies in October 1970 on the unprecedented basis of adult franchise, he mandated that the national parliament should act as a constituent assembly and adopt a new constitution. Aware of the popularity of the Awami League, led by Shaikh Rahman, in East Pakistan, Yahya Khan instructed the ISI chief Brigadier Muhammad Akbar Khan to deny the Awami League a majority in the elections, and allocated some funds for the purpose. This project did not get very far.

The ISI had an active rival in East Pakistan: RAW. The Indian agency devised ways to fund the Awami League because its election manifesto, demanding a federal constitution with only the center dealing with defense and foreign affairs, suited Delhi. As a result of hurricane and floods in East Pakistan, elections in the province were postponed for two months.

Later, RAW agents operating in Dacca (later Dhaka) would warn their handlers in Calcutta of an upcoming army crackdown on the Awami League in February 1971 irrespective of the election results. They advised Shaikh Rahman to leave Dacca, but to no avail.[45]

In the general election held on December 7, the Awami League won a stunning 288 of the 300 seats in the provincial legislature and 160 out of 162 places allocated to East Pakistan in the National/Constituent Assembly of 300. Earlier, in West Pakistan, Bhutto's PPP had gained 81 of 132 National Assembly seats and 144 of the 300 in the Provincial Assembly. The voter turnout was 63 percent. When on December 17 Shaikh Rahman reiterated his six-point demand for a loose federation of Pakistan, Bhutto rejected the proposal and declared that no constitution could be framed or government run from the center without his party's cooperation.[46]

The tenuous geographical linkage between the two wings of Pakistan was highlighted when, in the aftermath of Kashmiri militants hijacking an Indian aircraft headed to Lahore and blowing it up in January 1971, India banned Pakistan's flights over its air space. This compelled the Pakistani authorities to reroute air traffic between the two wings via Colombo, Sri Lanka—an expensive, time-consuming alternative.

In its assessment of Pakistan, RAW painted an alarming picture of its military capabilities—which were duly reproduced in the Indian media—quantifying its troops and weaponry, and concluding that Islamabad had achieved "a good state of military preparedness for any confrontation with India." It judged "the potential threat" of an attack on India "quite real, particularly in view of the Sino-Pakistan collusion." Besides, it added, the constitutional crisis in East Pakistan might encourage the generals to undertake a diversionary adventure, to begin, as in August 1965, with "an infiltration campaign in Jammu and Kashmir."[47]

The opening of the National/Constituent Assembly in Dacca on March 3 was postponed indefinitely by Yahya Khan when Bhutto threatened a general strike in West Pakistan if the Assembly met as scheduled.

On March 2 Shaikh Rahman called a five-day general strike in East Pakistan. It was followed by a campaign of noncooperation by the Awami League. Yahya Khan settled for the inaugural of the National/Constituent Assembly on March 25.

On March 7 Shaikh Rahman declared that the Awami League would attend the National/Constituent Assembly only if martial law was immediately revoked and power transferred to the elected members of the Provincial Assembly. That day, Yahya Khan appointed the mustached, unsmiling, leathery faced General Muhammad Tikka Khan as military governor of East Pakistan. He then ordered the airlifting of troops from West Pakistan to Dacca, albeit in civilian clothes, to shore up the thirty-thousand-strong force, of which eighteen thousand were Bengalis, most of whom would defect or be disarmed. Once that was accomplished, he flew to Dacca on March 15 to work out a compromise between Shaikh Rahman and Bhutto. Five days later, when he announced a plan to introduce an interim constitution that would end martial law on March 20, Bhutto rejected it.

Behind the scenes, Yahya Khan and Tikka Khan finalized plans for a military takeover in East Pakistan to overcome the resistance offered by the Bengalis of the East Bengal Regiments, East Pakistan Rifles, and police as well as nationalist students and other civilians. On March 23 Shaikh Rahman issued a "declaration of emancipation" for East Pakistan. And when, as anticipated, the final round of talks between him, Yahya Khan, and Bhutto broke down at ten PM on March 25, Tikka Khan mounted Operation Searchlight to crush the popular upsurge. He sent the sixty-five-thousand-strong army to accomplish the atrocious task.

He outlawed the Awami League, flew the arrested Shaikh Rahman to West Pakistan to be tried for treason, expelled foreign journalists from East Pakistan, and imposed censorship.[48] This was the opening phase of violent turbulence that culminated in the ground war between Islamabad and Delhi in East Pakistan eight months later.

10

Indira Gandhi Slays
the Two-Nation Theory

The run-up to the Indo-Pakistan war in East Pakistan in 1971 went through three phases: March to May, June to September, and October to November 21. These were determined as much by political-diplomatic developments as by the weather in the eastern part of the subcontinent. The end of monsoon—June to September—is a preamble to the harvest season, spanning October and early November. The transportation of crops to urban centers clogs up the railways, which are needed for mass transport of heavy military hardware from garrison towns to the front lines.

It was left to India's chief of army staff (COAS) General Sam Hormusji Framji Jamshedji Manekshaw to explain the linkage between harvesting a seasonal crop and preparing the army for war. A slim, blimpish Zoroastrian with a walrus mustache, Manekshaw also pointed out that with the approaching winter closing the mountain passes in the Himalayas, Chinese leaders would be inhibited from intervening in the fight on the side of Pakistan. The cabinet agreed.

The buildup to this armed conflict—called the Bangladesh War or Bangladesh Liberation War—and its duration witnessed complex diplomatic maneuvering—unrivaled in history since World War II. Besides India and Pakistan, it involved the United States, the Soviet Union, and the People's Republic of China (henceforth China). Following the expulsion of the Republic of China (i.e., Taiwan) from the United Nations, China acquired a permanent seat on the UN Security Council on October 25, 1971. This was a consequence of the clandestine trip to Beijing on July

10–11 by US National Security Adviser Henry Kissinger, primarily to discuss the fate of Taiwan.

OVERARCHING AIM OF THE "BUTCHER OF BENGAL"

General Tikka Khan mounted Operation Searchlight on March 25, 1971, to decimate intellectuals, the wellspring of Bengali nationalism, as a prelude to a more ruthless goal. According to Anthony Mascarenhas, an assistant editor of the Karachi-based *Morning News*, the official policy consisted of three elements. "One: the Bengalis have proved themselves unreliable and must be ruled by West Pakistanis," he reported in mid-June. "Two: the Bengalis will have to be re-educated along proper Islamic lines. The Islamization of the masses—this is the official jargon—is intended to eliminate secessionist tendencies and provide a strong religious bond with West Pakistan. Three: when the Hindus have been eliminated by death and fight, their property will be used as a golden carrot to win over the underprivileged Muslim middle-class."[1] Though Hindus were only one-seventh of East Pakistan's population of seventy-five million, they disproportionately owned far more property.

Pakistani troops singled out the university in Dacca as well as Hindu neighborhoods for their attacks. On March 31 the Indian parliament passed a resolution in support of the "people of Bengal." In Delhi, open interference in the internal affairs of Pakistan went hand in hand with feverish activity by Research and Analysis Wing (RAW) agents operating in Calcutta. They played a central role in helping the Awami League leaders who had escaped the army's dragnet establish a government-in-exile in Calcutta on April 17.

Calling itself the provisional government of Bangladesh, with Shaikh Mujibur Rahman as its president, it soon formalized the assorted groups of armed resistors to the regime inside East Pakistan under the generic term of Mukti Bahini (Bengali: Liberation Army). Placed under the command of (Retired) Colonel Muhammad Ataullah Gani Osmani, the Mukti Bahini was organized, funded, armed, and trained by the Indian government. In its secret correspondence it started describing the events in East Pakistan as the "struggle for Bangladesh [Bengali: Bengali Nation]."

Like the regime in Islamabad, China viewed the Indian move with ill-concealed concern. "The Chinese Government holds that what is happening in Pakistan at present is purely an internal affair of Pakistan which can only be settled by the Pakistani people themselves and brooks no foreign interference whatsoever," wrote Chinese premier Zhou Enlai to President Yahya Khan on April 21. "Your Excellency may rest assured that should the Indian expansionists dare to launch aggression against Pakistan, the Chinese government and people will, as always, support the Pakistan Government and people in their just struggle to safeguard state sovereignty and national independence."[2]

On April 7 the bright-eyed, oval-faced, clean-shaven Lieutenant General Amir Abdullah Khan Niazi, a veteran of several battles since World War II, was dispatched to Dacca to assist General Tikka Khan. With that, the uprising in East Pakistan intensified—and so did India's involvement, covert and overt.

On Niazi's advice, Tikka Khan coopted the Islamist Jamaat-e Islami (Urdu: Islamic Society), popular among Urdu-speaking Bihari Muslim immigrants. Its leaders declared a jihad against the Bengali liberation forces and their Indian backers. This chimed with Islamabad's claims, widely publicized in the media, that the Awami League had close ties with Bengali Hindus and that they were part of "an Indo-Zionist plot [hatched] against Islamic Pakistan."[3] The latter statement had a nugget of truth in it, as later revelations would show.

Jamaat-e Islami's student wing joined the military government's move in May to set up two paramilitary counterinsurgency units. This arrangement was formalized by Tikka Khan under the East Pakistan Razakar Ordinance on June 1. It stipulated the creation of a trained, voluntary force to act as auxiliaries to the regular army.

"A separate Razakars Directorate was established," wrote Niazi in his memoirs *Betrayal of East Pakistan*.

Two separate wings called Al Badr and Al Shams were recognized. Well educated and properly motivated students from schools and madrassas were put in Al Badr wing, where they were trained to undertake "Specialized Operations" while the remainder were grouped together under Al Shams which was responsible for the protection of bridges, vital points and other areas. The Razakars were mostly employed in areas where army elements were around to control and utilize them. . . . This force was useful where available, particularly in the areas where the rightist parties were in strength and had sufficient local influence.[4]

Al Shams also supplied logistics and intelligence to the army. Its members often patrolled Bengali nationalist strongholds in jeeps, arrested suspects at random, and took them to local torture centers.

This strategy was implemented after the army's first round of violence had overpowered the local nationalist forces, consisting of militant civilians and Bengali army deserters (described as "miscreants" by the authorities), in major cities by mid-May. To inform the outside world of its success, the government in Islamabad selected eight journalists, including Mascarenhas of the *Morning News*, for a ten-day guided tour of East Pakistan.[5]

On their return home in early June, seven of these journalists produced pro-government reports, which were published after military censors had cleared them. Mascarenhas, a square-faced, mustached man with soulful eyes behind his glasses, stalled. "He told me that if he couldn't write the story of what he'd seen he'd never be able to write another word again," his wife, Yvonne, would reveal later. He told her that if he wrote what he had seen he would be shot. Pretending that his London-based sister, Ann, was seriously ill, he flew to London. There he met Harold Evans, editor of the *Sunday Times*. Even the earlier exposure to the outrages committed in East Pakistan had not prepared Evans to hear what he did from Mascarenhas. The Pakistani journalist told Evans that "what the Army was doing was altogether worse and on a grander scale," and that he had been an eyewitness to a huge, systematic killing spree, and had heard army officers describe the killings as a "final solution." Tikka Khan, the architect of Operation Searchlight, would acquire the sobriquet of the "Butcher of Bengal."

But Evans could run this spine-chilling account only after the eyewitness's wife and five children had left Pakistan. Once that was accomplished through a ruse, and the Mascarenhas family had arrived in London on June 12, the *Sunday Times* ran a three-page report by Mascarenhas the next day under the headline "GENOCIDE." "I have witnessed the brutality of 'kill and burn missions' as the army units, after clearing out the rebels, pursued the pogrom in the towns and villages," he reported. "I have seen whole villages devastated by 'punitive action.' And in the officers' mess at night I have listened incredulously as otherwise brave and honorable men proudly chewed over the day's kill. 'How many did you get?' The answers are seared in my memory."[6]

The sensational, meticulously recorded, firsthand account by a long-established Pakistani journalist was quoted worldwide. It played a vital role in turning international opinion against the military junta in Islam-abad. According to Evans, Indian premier Indira Gandhi told him that the article had shocked her so deeply it had set her "on a campaign of personal diplomacy in the European capitals and Moscow to prepare the ground for India's armed intervention."[7]

In stark contrast, this distressing reportage left topmost American officials unmoved. The stance of President Nixon was aptly encapsulated in his scribbled note on a memorandum from Kissinger on April 28, 1971, in which the latter suggested that the future of East Pakistan was "greater autonomy, and perhaps eventual independence": "To all hands, don't squeeze Yahya at this time." Nixon was unaffected by the letter Indira Gandhi sent him in May about "the carnage in East Bengal" and the flood of refugees burdening India. The declassified transcripts of the White House tapes released in June 2005 contained the following snippet of conversation between Nixon and Kissinger on May 26, 1971:

KISSINGER: They are the most aggressive goddamn people around there.
NIXON: The Indians?
KISSINGER: Yeah.
NIXON: Sure.[8]

On June 22 the *New York Times* ran a report by Ted Szulc, headlined "US Military Goods Sent to Pakistan Despite the Ban." It revealed that to circumvent the Congressional ban on arms to Pakistan since the September 1965 Indo-Pakistan War, the Nixon administration was shipping weapons to Pakistan via Iran and Turkey.

At that time Kissinger and Nixon were pursuing a plan for Kissinger to visit Beijing secretly to exploit the virtual breakdown in Beijing-Moscow relations. The deterioration started with a series of border clashes between the communist neighbors, originating in March 1969, and escalated in October with a military alert by Beijing following a failed meeting between Zhou and Soviet premier Alexei Kosygin in September. The number of Soviet divisions deployed along the Chinese border rose to thirty in 1970 amid rumors that the Kremlin was planning a surgical strike on the Chinese nuclear testing site in Xinjiang.[9]

As the military buildup by both sides continued in 1971, Nixon and Kissinger saw an opportunity for the United States to seek rapprochement with China, using Pakistan as a courier, to reinforce its leverage over its primary adversary, the Soviet Union.

WARMING UP PHASE

On June 28 Yahya Khan announced plans for the drafting of a new con-stitution, proposing that the task should be completed in four months. A month later he claimed that normality had returned to the eastern wing. His assertion clashed with the fact that the first India-trained, 110-strong Bengali guerrilla unit managed to infiltrate East Pakistan to reach its central town of Madaripur in July.[10] It destroyed tea gardens, riverboats, and railway tracks—acts that tied down Pakistani troops, undermined local industry, and destroyed communications between Dacca and two important provincial cities.[11]

The concerned governments tried diplomacy to grapple with the deepening crisis. In his meeting with his Soviet counterpart, Andrei Gromyko, in Moscow in June, India's foreign minister, Swaran Singh, re-marked that China was the only country to give "all out, full, unequivocal support" to the military regime in Islamabad. "The Chinese are against everything the USSR stands for," said Gromyko. "Any cause we support invites their opposition, and anything which we consider unworthy of our support secures their support."[12]

The two ministers discussed a treaty initially suggested by Gromyko's ministry to Durga Prasad Dhar, the Indian ambassador in Moscow, to act as "a strong deterrent to force Pakistan and China to abandon any idea of military adventure." This led to Singh meeting Premier Kosygin, who endorsed the proposal. Following an exchange of drafts, the Indo-Soviet Treaty of Peace, Friendship and Cooperation, valid for twenty years, was finalized. It was signed on August 9 in New Delhi by Singh and Gromyko.[13]

"Each of the High Contracting Parties" to the treaty declared that it would maintain "regular contact with each other on major interna-tional problems affecting the interests of both the states," that "it shall not enter into or participate in any military alliance directed against the other Party," and that "in the event of either Party being subjected to an attack or a threat thereof, the High Contracting Parties shall immedi-ately enter into mutual consultations in order to remove such threat and to take appropriate effective measures to ensure peace and the security of their countries."[14]

This historic document was inked a month after Kissinger's clan-destine visit to Beijing, where he met Zhou Enlai. "In our opinion, if India continues on its present course in disregard of world opinion, it will continue to go on recklessly," Zhou told him. "We, however, support the stand of Pakistan. This is known to the world. If they [the Indians] are bent on provoking such a situation, then we cannot sit idly by." Kissinger told Zhou that Washington's sympathies also lay with Pakistan.[15]

Nixon's perception of the Indian diplomats as "slippery, treacherous people" was enhanced when he learned of the Indo-Soviet Treaty. He viewed it as an undisguised collusion between Delhi and Moscow—and an extension of Soviet power in South Asia. During the latter half of August, Nixon told a meeting of the Washington Special Action Group (WSAG), formed to discuss the South Asia crisis, that while the Pakistanis were "straightforward" if sometimes "extremely stupid," the "Indians are more devious, sometimes so smart that we fall for their line." He stressed that "the US must not—cannot—allow India to use the refugees as a pretext to break up Pakistan."[16]

The unending flow of refugees from East Pakistan—the figure touching six million by August, with three-quarters of them Hindu—surviving in ramshackle camps in West Bengal and surrounding states, was creating an unsustainable burden on Delhi's resources. On the other hand, these camps became an abundant source of volunteers keen to be trained as guerrillas.

In the formation of the Mukti Bahini, RAW cooperated with the Indian Army. By acquiring the nine-year-old Establishment 22 (aka Special Frontier Force) as its armed wing, it had gained experience in training volunteers as guerrillas and saboteurs. A liaison between it and the army was maintained through the military advisor to RAW's director and the Military Intelligence Advisory Group. By then, RAW had developed sophisticated signals intelligence and photo-reconnaissance capabilities, thanks to CIA assistance.

At the conclave of the Bengali officers held in Calcutta from July 11 to 17 under the joint aegis of the Indian Army and RAW, East Pakistan was divided into eleven sectors. The Liberation Force was separated into regular troops and guerrillas supported by intelligence volunteers. The guerrillas' tasks were to raid and ambush military targets, sabotage factories and power plants, and disrupt communications systems. They were also taught how to compel the Pakistani forces to scatter in small units, thus making them vulnerable to lethal attacks.[17]

POSTMONSOON PERIOD

By September, India was processing twenty thousand guerrillas a month in ten camps, with eight Indian soldiers appointed to coach a hundred volunteers each.[18] As monsoon rains tapered off, infiltration by Mukti Bahini guerrillas rose steeply.

On the other side, intent on showing that normalcy had returned to East Pakistan, Yahya Khan declared a general amnesty in early September and replaced Tikka Khan with a moderate politician, Abdul Malik, as governor. Tikka Khan was reassigned to lead the Multan-based Corps II in West Pakistan. Lieutenant General Niazi succeeded Tikka Khan as the commander of the Eastern Command.

On the diplomatic front, after signing a friendship treaty with Delhi, the Kremlin did not alter its earlier stance on East Pakistan. In pursuance of its policy to befriend Pakistan after the 1966 Tashkent Conference, it had started supplying arms to Islamabad. Now it maintained that the conflict in East Pakistan was an "internal problem" of the Islamabad regime.

To persuade the Kremlin to alter its policy, Indira Gandhi flew to Moscow in late September. There she reiterated her argument that the nonstop flow of refugees from East Pakistan was severely straining the limited resources of her government. Because of the wretched living conditions in the camps people were dying in droves, she added. The subsequent Indo-Soviet communiqué referred to the need for all necessary measures to stop and reverse the refugee exodus, now touching eight million.[19]

From mid-October, the Indian troops started using artillery fire to give cover to Mukti Bahini infiltrators. To their disappointment, these partisans were rarely able to hold their ground when the Pakistan Army counterattacked. As a result, the Indians' shelling along the India–East Pakistan frontier became more intense, and the size of the infiltration by Mukti Bahini ranks swelled.

India Gandhi's diplomatic drive continued, with a focus on highlighting the ongoing flow of refugees from East Pakistan. Her three-week tour of the capitals of Western Europe and North America ended in Washington on November 4.

She was welcomed by Nixon with full military honors on the South Lawn at the White House. During their meeting Nixon made a case for avoiding a new war and offered to fix a time limit for Yahya Khan to reach a political settlement in East Pakistan. Emulating the response of her father, Jawaharlal Nehru, to the mention of the Kashmir dispute by a foreign leader, Indira Gandhi listened "with aloof indifference," according to Kissinger, who was present. By refraining from making any comment on Nixon's presentation, she successfully created an invisible yet impenetrable wall between her and Nixon. On his part, the American president said next to nothing about the millions of refugees who had sought haven in India.

After Gandhi's departure from the White House on November 5, Nixon reviewed her visit with Kissinger. "We really slobbered over the old witch," said Nixon according to the documents declassified by the State Department in June 2005. (This was apparently a reference to the praise he showered on her when in his welcoming speech he said that Indira Gandhi had "the unique distinction, through the parliamentary system of India that more people have voted for her leadership than for any leader in the whole history of the world."[20]) "The Indians are bastards anyway," remarked Kissinger. "They are starting a war there." He added, "While she was a bitch, we got what we wanted too. She will not be able to go home and say that the United States didn't give her a warm reception and therefore in despair she's got to go to war."[21]

By a strange coincidence, on November 5 Zulfikar Ali Bhutto was in Beijing as head of a Pakistani delegation to seek China's backing. But the Chinese leaders avoided making a firm commitment to side with Pakistan militarily. Five days later, Nixon instructed Kissinger to ask the Chinese to move some troops toward the Indian frontier. "Threaten to move forces or move them, Henry, that's what they must do now." Kissinger conveyed the message to Huang Hua, China's freshly appointed ambassador to the United Nations.[22]

Beijing had to take into account the eight mountain divisions that India had deployed along the Indo-Tibetan border. Nonetheless, it amassed soldiers on India's frontier. Delhi threatened to bomb the Lop Nor nuclear facility in Xinjiang, so Beijing redeployed its troops.[23] To balance that move, it decided to shore up West Pakistan's defense capabilities. It was aided in this enterprise by the existence of the five-year-old Karakoram Highway, which traversed the Khunjerab Pass. Each day one hundred trucks, carrying civilian and military goods, arrived in Gilgit from the Chinese city of Kashgar.

India's military planners had finessed a strategy that integrated the secret Establishment 22 forces into the fight being waged against Pakistan.

According to the selective leaks from the classified official history of the Bangladesh war on its fortieth anniversary, by early November 1971 about 51,000 Mukti Bahini fighters were active in East Pakistan. By operating mainly along the frontier with India, they had succeeded in drawing the Pakistani troops forward to the India border, thereby easing the way for regular Indian soldiers' eventual thrust to Dacca.[24] As it was, during November units of regular Indian soldiers resorted to conducting over-night guerrilla actions inside East Pakistan and then withdrawing across the frontier.

GROUND WAR IN EAST PAKISTAN

On the night of November 21, discontinuing their earlier practice of re-turning to Indian soil after pinprick attacks in East Pakistan, India's forces stayed put. Two days later Yahya Khan declared a state of emergency in all of Pakistan and called on Pakistanis to prepare for war with India. By November 25 several Indian Army divisions had attacked key border regions of East Pakistan, using armor and artillery fire. To divert Pakistani soldiers from major population centers, RAW's director, Rameshwar Kao, pressed into action the CIA-trained dissident Tibetans. Armed with hastily imported Bulgarian assault rifles and US-made carbines, and commanded by Brigadier Sujan Singh Uban, they poured into the Chittagong Hill tracts, inhabited by East Asian tribes. They tied down Pakistani troops in low-grade border skirmishes.[25]

Niazi had sixty-five thousand troops under his command. He faced Lieutenant General Jagjit Singh Aurora, the commanding officer of India's Eastern Command in Calcutta, with nearly four times as many soldiers. This compelled Niazi to adopt a defensive strategy. He withdrew his forces from scattered border pickets and assembled them in fortified defensive positions at major urban centers in the interior. "The whole nation is proud of you and you have their full support," read the message he received from General Abdul Hamid Khan, chief of staff, on November 30. That day the military high command in Rawalpindi decided to launch Operation Chengiz Khan (Genghis Khan) on the western front of India on December 2, later postponed by twenty-four hours, without informing Niazi.[26]

At 5:40 PM on Friday, December 3, Pakistan bombed eleven Indian airfields near its western frontier and mounted artillery attacks on

India-held Kashmir. When Indira Gandhi was informed of this move, she remarked, "Thank God, they have attacked us."[27] This meant that India would not be accused of aggression, since its eleven-day-old military moves in East Pakistan were considered by outsiders as part of the nationalist Bengalis' ongoing clandestine armed struggle. At midnight Indira Gandhi declared war on Pakistan.

HOT WAR, FRENZIED DIPLOMACY

On December 4, India launched an integrated ground, sea, and air invasion of East Pakistan of such might that it won the moniker of a "blitzkrieg without tanks." Accompanied by Mukti Bahini fighters, Indian troops penetrated the East Pakistani frontier at five points and advanced on Dacca from the north, east, and west. Niazi's forces tried to slow down the enemy's advance by blowing up bridges. Aided by Mukti Bahini guerrillas already inside East Pakistan, the invading forces cut off communications between the capital and other important cities. And by capturing vital railheads they immobilized the defenders. The Indians responded to Pakistan's air and ground assaults on their soil with attacks on targets in West Pakistan.

The third Indo-Pakistan war unleashed a diplomatic frenzy. At the UN Security Council, George Herbert Walker Bush, the American ambassador to the United Nations, introduced a resolution calling for an immediate cease-fire and the withdrawal of armed forces by India and Pakistan. It was vetoed by the Soviet Union. The CIA chief, Richard Helms, told Nixon that while Gandhi hoped China would not intervene from the north, the Kremlin had warned her that the Chinese were still able to "rattle the sword" in the Ladakh region of Kashmir.

On December 6 India recognized the Calcutta-based provisional government of Bangladesh. Yahya Khan responded by forming a civilian administration with Nurul Amin, a Bengali from East Pakistan, as prime minister and Bhutto as deputy prime minister and foreign minister.

By December 9, the Indians had blunted Pakistan's offensive on their western front and destroyed its oil storage tanks in Karachi.

On December 10 Kissinger met Huang at the United Nations. "If the People's Republic were to consider the situation on the Indian subcontinent a threat to its security, and if it took measures to protect its security, the US would oppose efforts of others to interfere with the People's

Republic," he told Huang. "We are not recommending any particular steps; we are simply informing you about the actions of others. The movement of our naval force is still east of the Straits of Malacca and will not become obvious until Sunday evening [December 12] when they cross the Straits." Kissinger then offered Washington's assessment of the military situation on the subcontinent. "The Pakistani Army in the East has been destroyed," he said. "The Pakistani Army in the West will run out of what we call POL—gas and oil—in another two or three weeks, two weeks probably, because the oil storage capacity in Karachi has been destroyed. We think that the immediate objective must be to prevent an attack on the West Pakistan Army by India. We are afraid that if nothing is done to stop it, East Pakistan will become a Bhutan and West Pakistan will become a Nepal. And India with Soviet help would be free to turn its energies elsewhere."[28]

Both Washington and Beijing feared that India's invasion of West Pakistan would lead to Soviet domination of South Asia, a prospect they were determined to abort. Nixon encouraged China to further increase its arms shipments to Pakistan.

Bhutto arrived at the United Nations on the evening of December 10 to shore up Pakistan's case.

What happened on the diplomatic front during the next crucial days was captured in the message Kissinger sent to Zhou Enlai on December 17. According to Kissinger, on December 12 the United States urged the Soviet Union through its embassy in Washington to pressure India to end the war. The next day Soviet ambassador Anatoly Dobrynin informed the White House that the Kremlin was consulting India and would inform it of the result. "Early Tuesday morning, December 14, the Soviet Union sent a message which, in addition to some standard Soviet views on the South Asian situation, relayed firm assurance that the Indian leadership had no plans of seizing West Pakistan territory or attacking West Pakistan armed forces." Later that morning, instructed by Nixon, Deputy Secretary of State General Alexander Haig met Soviet chargé d'affaires Yuli Vorontsov and told him that the president and Kissinger had found the Soviet message imprecise on India's intentions in West Pakistan and wanted clarification on two points: Did the Soviet note include Azad Kashmir, and did it involve a return to the exact borders before the outbreak of hostilities? Vorontsov expressed his personal understanding that this was precisely the Soviet view.

Haig stressed that the United States wanted the Kremlin to move promptly to halt the fighting and that delays could have the most serious impact on US–Soviet relations.[29] "Nixon and Kissinger had to rely on Moscow's word that India would not attack West Pakistan," noted Dobrynin in his memoirs, *In Confidence*, and added that "the Soviet Union's diplomatic intervention helped prevent the military conflict from spreading."[30]

When Henry Kissinger and Prime Minister Zhou met in the Great Hall in Beijing on June 20, 1972, they reviewed the events of the tumultuous days in December. Among the topics discussed was a series of articles about the "US tilt" toward Pakistan, published in January 1972 by columnist Jack Anderson, based on the classified minutes of the WSAG.[31] In hot pursuit of forging friendly ties with China, Nixon and Kissinger ignored the rising condemnation and anger of American commentators at the brutal atrocities committed by the Pakistan Army in East Pakistan. Tellingly, the early protest of their stance of "See no evil" had come from the US consulate in Dacca. A telegram headlined "Dissent from US Policy on East Pakistan," signed by twenty officials from the consulate and other American development agencies and sent from Dacca by the consul-general, Archer K. Blood, on April 7, 1971, referred to "selective genocide" in East Pakistan.[32]

> PM [ZHOU]: They [Pakistanis] were not clear about the situation because Mr. Bhutto himself was not a military man and Yahya Khan had boasted about the military situation. So I believe Mr. Bhutto on the 11th [December] thought that the military situation in Pakistan at that time was indeed very well.
>
> HK [KISSINGER]: Bhutto arrived in New York on Friday the 10th our time, 11th your time. . . . You called us in the morning of the 12th and we were going to the meeting with [French President] Pompidou [in Azores] so we sent General [Alexander] Haig. But between the time we got the phone call and picked up the message we didn't know what it was. And since Huang Ha had taken a very tough line, not knowing the situation I thought your message to us was that you were taking military measures. And since we were going to the Azores before [the meeting with Huang], we had to give instructions [to Haig]. If your message was, you were taking military measures our instructions were that if the Soviet Union moved against you we would move against the Soviet Union.
>
> PM: Why did the newspapers publish what had been discussed step by step in the Washington Special Actions Group with respect to the East Pakistan situation?

HK: Well first, the PM has to understand that the Washington Special [Action] Group implements decisions, it does not make decisions. The reason I had to take such a strong stand in this group was because the vast majority of our bureaucracy was pro-India and pro-Soviet.

PM: Pro-Soviet?

HK: More Pro-Soviet than Pro-Chinese. I came under the most violent attack. . . . What happened is that a disloyal member of our bureaucracy gave these documents to newspapers and they printed them in order to destroy us and they came very close.

PM: But after reading the records that were published, it seemed to me that the members of that group came from quite a lot of quarters.

HK: Yes, they were almost unanimously against our policy.

PM: Especially toward India?

HK: They didn't understand our overall strategy. If they had understood we were getting ready to take on the Soviet Union then what happened was mild compared to what would have happened. The reason we moved our Fleet into the Indian Ocean was not because of India primarily—it was as pressure on the Soviet Union if the Soviets did what I mentioned before.

PM: And they also closely followed you down into the Indian Ocean.

HK: Yes but what they had we could have taken care of very easily.

PM: What they were trying to do was to create more noise in East Bengal. They openly passed through the Tsushima straits and then through the Malacca Straits.

HK: Yes but not with a force that could fight ours.

PM: Yes, but you know they could surface in such a way their support to East Bengal.

HK: Oh yes, it was used for that purpose. Actually, the Pakistan Army in the East surrendered five days later [on December 16], so it would have been too late for you to do anything.

PM: Also Yahya Khan had sent his order in preparation for such a measure on the 11th or the 12th.[33]

China's message to the United States on December 12 apparently expressed support for an immediate cease-fire. That day, Washington requested the reconvening of the Security Council. While the Council deliberated, the military situation for Pakistan deteriorated rapidly.

Within a week of the hostilities, Indian warplanes had grounded the entire air force of East Pakistan by raiding four major air bases and had gained almost total control of its air space. By attacking the three main ports of East Pakistan, India's warships severed the escape routes for the stranded Pakistani troops.

The lightning progress of Delhi's forces owed much to the success Indian code breakers had in breaking Pakistan's military cipher. They furnished India's military intelligence with real-time information on the enemy's strategic decision making, according to the selective leaks from India's classified official history of the 1971 war.[34] Among other things, the Indians' interception of Pakistan's military communications aborted its high command's decision to evacuate its troops in five vessels disguised as merchant ships.

On land, the Indian troops advancing along Dacca-Chittagong Highway were forced to halt twenty miles southeast of Dacca when they encountered a broken bridge across the Meghna River. "The Pakistani forces thought they had cut us off after they blew up a bridge over the Meghna River," recalled Lieutenant General Aurora later. "But we took them by surprise and crossed it at night with the help of the local people. That was the turning point [in the war]."[35] With that, on December 13 Dacca became vulnerable to the invaders' artillery fire.

NIAZI'S UNCONDITIONAL SURRENDER

"You have fought a heroic battle against overwhelming odds," read the dispatch to Niazi from general headquarters in Rawalpindi. However, the message continued, "you have now reached a stage where further resistance is no longer humanly possible nor will it serve any useful purpose. . . . You should now take all necessary measures to stop the fighting and preserve the lives of armed forces personnel, all those from West Pakistan and all loyal elements."[36]

Later, when controversy broke out in Pakistan about the actual events on those crucial days, some critics accused Niazi of acting unilaterally. "I swear on oath that I was given clear-cut orders from Yahya to surrender, but still I was determined to fight till the end," Niazi asserted. "I even sent a message that my decision to fight till the end stands. However, General Abdul Hamid Khan and Air Chief Marshal Rahim [Khan] rang me up, ordering me to act on the [headquarters'] signal of December 14, 1971 because West Pakistan was in danger. It was at this stage that I was asked to agree on a cease-fire so that the safety of the troops could be ensured."[37]

On December 15 Niazi approached the American consul-general in Dacca, who contacted the appropriate authority in Delhi. The next day Lieutenant-General Aurora, the joint commander of India's Eastern Command and the Bangladesh Forces of the Provisional Government of Bangladesh, flew into Dacca to accept the instrument of surrender signed by Niazi.

In Delhi, within hours of learning about Niazi's decision to surrender, Manekshaw called on Indira Gandhi. He reportedly asked her if the military high command had the permission to "finish the job." This meant overrunning West Pakistan. She replied that the cabinet would consider his suggestion.[38]

She summoned a cabinet meeting. By the time she had briefed her colleagues about the secret intermediary role the Kremlin had played between her and Nixon, and that the Kremlin had ruled out even attacking Azad Kashmir, any enthusiasm for Manekshaw's gung-ho proposal harbored by some of her ministers vanished. The session ended with a unanimous decision to declare a unilateral cease-fire on December 17 on the western front as well. Such level-headed decision making had a parallel during the September 1965 Indo-Pakistan War, when the Cabinet Committee on Security, headed by Prime Minister Lal Bahadur Shastri, voted against attempting to capture Lahore, which would have been defended fiercely.

In Dacca, Aurora met Niazi at the ornate administrative office of the Ramna Race Course, the former exclusive club of the British officers stationed in Dacca Cantonment, overlooking the race course and the surrounding park. It was here that in his historic speech on March 6, 1971, Shaikh Mujibur Rahman had declared: "This time the struggle is for our freedom." Now, surrounded by a large group of uniformed officers and civilian bureaucrats, the bearded Aurora, wearing a starched, striped turban, countersigned the instrument of surrender signed by clean-shaven Niazi, sporting a beret.

As the Indian and Pakistan officers emerged from the site of the signing ceremony, they were greeted by a cheering crowd. Jubilant young men and boys and girls in colorful clothes held aloft Bangladeshi and Indian flags as vehicles played loud music. They threaded their way slowly through the jostling assemblage. Shouts of *"Joi Bangla"* (Bengali: "Victory to Bengal") interspersed with anti-Pakistan and pro-India slogans stirred the wintry air. Before their eyes the officers witnessed the celebrating multitude grow exponentially.

The victorious and the vanquished senior army officers struggled to reach their jeeps to repair to the officers' mess in the cantonment. Once there, while drinking whiskey and soda, they exchanged anecdotes about their time at the Indian military academy, where they had trained together before the partition.

COUNTING THE COST

For the moment, they set aside the fate of the 90,370 Pakistani POWs acquired by the nascent Bangladeshi government but held by the Indian military. Of these, 56,370 were military personnel, 22,000 paramilitaries and policemen, and the rest civil servants and their families. The war on both fronts cost India the lives of 3,850 servicemen and Pakistan 9,000. Predictably, Pakistan's claim of destroying 130 Indian warplanes was rebutted by Delhi, which put the figure at 45. Equally, India's claimed score of 94 enemy warplanes was scaled down to 42 by Pakistan. India's tank loss of 82 was a fraction of Pakistan's 226.[39]

The estimate of the deaths by violence in East Pakistan from March 26 to December 16, 1971, has varied wildly—from twenty-six thousand to three million. Going by the records of Pakistan's Eastern Command, seen by the Hamoodur Rehman Inquiry Commission, the military killed twenty-six thousand people in action, with the commission noting that the officers always gave a low count.[40] The figure of three million—five times the estimate for the unparalleled communal butchery in Punjab during 1947—first mentioned by Shaikh Rahman in his interview with British TV personality David Frost in January 1972 after his return to Dacca as a free man is now universally regarded as excessively inflated.[41] The statistic given by Indian officials to Richard Sisson and Leo E. Rose, authors of *War and Secession: Pakistan, India, and the Creation of Bangladesh*, was one hundred thousand.[42]

In her study of the subject, published as *Dead Reckoning: Memories of the 1971 Bangladesh War*, Sarmila Bose, a Bengali-speaking research scholar at Oxford University, undertook extensive field research. After selecting the worst of the alleged atrocities, she reconstructed and quantified these by interviewing the participants in Pakistan and Bangladesh—mainly retired Pakistani officers, the survivors of the brutalities, and their relatives in Bangladesh, as well as members of the non-Bengali and non-Muslim minorities. Her case-by-case estimation gave her a total of 50,000 to 100,000 dead.[43] In their analysis of the data from the world health survey program, covering fifty years of violent war deaths from Vietnam to Bosnia, Ziad Obermeyer and fellow researchers mentioned a figure of 269,000.[44]

In the excitement over the lightning triumph of the Indian and Bangladeshi forces, however, the statistics of those who perished in East Pakistan did not engage popular attention. The appearance of jubilant crowds in the cities of Bangladesh and West Bengal was a striking contrast to the angry demonstrations that rippled through the streets of West Pakistani cities. Such was the thoroughness with which the military junta controlled the media that the public at large believed that their forces were winning the war in the East while clobbering the Indians along the border with West Pakistan.

When exposed to the sights and sounds of Niazi signing the instrument of surrender on TV and radio on December 16, West Pakistanis went into instant denial. They blamed the battlefield debacle on Yahya Khan's heavy drinking and womanizing. That night in a broadcast, Yahya Khan, his voice slurred with drink, declared bravely that though a battle had been lost, the war would go on. The next day he accepted Delhi's unilateral offer of a cease-fire in West Pakistan.

Senior military officers outside Yahya Khan's immediate clique thought that he would accept responsibility for the nation's humiliating defeat and that he and the top generals would step down. Instead, on December 18 he announced he was going to promulgate a new constitution, while furious demonstrations demanding the regime's resignation had erupted all over the country. There was a real danger he might call on the army to restore order, which would have resulted in civilian bloodshed in West Pakistan.

To avert such a scenario, several commanders at divisional headquarters outside Rawalpindi jointly issued an ultimatum to Yahya Khan to step down by eight PM on December 19. That morning their representatives, Colonels Aleem Afridi and Javed Iqbal, flew to Rawalpindi and repeated the message to General Gul Hassan, chief of the general staff, in the afternoon. After high-level consultations, Hassan told them that Yahya Khan would see them at seven PM. Meanwhile his immediate boss, General Hamid Khan, tried to shore up support for the president by phoning several generals. He drew a blank. Shortly before the deadline of eight PM, a news broadcast said that President Yahya Khan had decided to hand over power to the elected representatives of the people.[45]

General Hassan, Air Marshal Rahim Khan, and Pakistan People's Party leader G. M. Khar collectively phoned Bhutto—then sitting out the crisis in Rome, unsure of his fate on his return home—advising him to fly back to Rawalpindi. On arrival there on December 20, he headed for the presidential residence. His talk with Yahya Khan lasted a few hours. At the end of it, the forty-three-year-old wily politician found himself president, commander in chief, and chief martial law administrator of Pakistan.

In his rambling address to the nation, Bhutto promised "a new Pakistan" and added that "our brothers in East Pakistan" would have the support of the rest of Pakistan in "liberating" themselves from "foreign domination." He announced the retirement of all the generals in Yahya Khan's inner clique, saying that he was doing this "in accord with the sentiments of the Armed Forces and the younger officers."[46]

EUPHORIA IN INDIA

Whereas the people, politicians, and soldiers in West Pakistan sank into deep depression after their initial shock and disbelief, their counterparts in India exploded instantly into unbounded joy. After the drubbing their motherland had received from the Chinese nine years earlier, Indians savored their victory over Pakistan with relish and special prayers.

The celebratory feeling was palpable in urban streets and markets all over India. Notwithstanding their secular constitution, and the rededication of their politicians to secularist values, the predominantly Hindu Indians tapped into their religious mythology to crown their triumph. They conferred the sobriquet of Goddess Durga (Sanskrit: "Inaccessible") on Indira Gandhi. This went down particularly well with Bengali Hindus, whose colorful worship of Goddess Durga is legendary. According to Hindu lore, Durga—portrayed as a beautiful woman clad in a colorful sari, with eight arms carrying different weapons, riding a lion or tiger—is an outstanding warrior goddess whose energy becomes lethal when she targets forces of evil. In that role she slays the buffalo-demon Mahisasura. In the present context, as a clone of Durga, Indira Gandhi decapitated the evil of the two-nation theory on which Muhammad Ali Jinnah had built Pakistan with its two far-flung wings.

Now Jinnah's Pakistan had lost more than half of its population, as well as its main source of foreign exchange earned by the export of jute from its eastern wing. Far more importantly, the breakaway of East

Pakistan undercut the founding doctrine of two nations inhabiting the Indian subcontinent and upheld the view of Congress Party leaders that the partition was a pragmatic resolution of its conflict with the Muslim League rather than an ideological defeat. The secession of East Pakistan proved that a common religion was not a strong enough glue to hold together two societies with different languages, cuisines, cultures, and historical backgrounds. The trumping of religion by ethnic nationalism was a bitter pill to swallow not only for West Pakistani people and politicians but also for those in Indian Kashmir who advocated accession to Pakistan.

West Pakistanis also lamented the fact that for the first time in eight centuries Hindus had defeated Muslims in the Indian subcontinent. In mid-December 1971 their independent existence hung in the balance. It was ultimately saved by Nixon's strong intervention, the restraining hand of the Soviet leader Leonid Brezhnev, and the cool-headed deliberation of the Indian cabinet.

The third Indo-Pakistan war, fought almost a quarter century after the traumatic partition of the subcontinent, closed a tumultuous period in the postindependence history of South Asia. Among other things, it gave enough confidence to a few moviemakers in India to dwell on the acute dilemma the Muslims in India had faced on the eve of the partition.

CAPTURED ON CELLULOID

One controversial result was the making of a low-budget movie *Garm Hava* (Hindi: Hot Wind) in Hindustani in 1972 under the direction of Mysore Shrivinas Sathyu. The screenplay, based on an unpublished short story by Bombay-based Ismat Chughtai (1911–1991), a leftist Muslim writer, focused on the postpartition trials and tribulations of Salim Mirza, owner of a shoe factory in Agra, the site of the Taj Mahal, a glittering example of Islamic architecture.

The bank refuses him an overdraft, and the orders for shoes decline sharply. When the prospective husband of his daughter, who migrated to Pakistan after his engagement, returns to marry her, he is arrested as a suspected spy. That drives Mirza's daughter to suicide. In despair he, his wife, and his college-age son leave for the railway station to move to Pakistan. But their horse-driven carriage is blocked by a flag-waving procession whose marchers are shouting slogans for communal harmony.

Impetuously, the son jumps off the carriage and joins the demonstrators. Salim Mirza follows the son, as does his wife.

Astonishingly, the Censor Board concluded that the story was likely to "instigate communal dissension" and denied the producer a license to exhibit it. When Sathyu showed the film to many officials and journalists, they disagreed with the board. Their pressure led the censors to lift the ban. The movie was a critical and commercial success on its release in 1973. It won a prestigious award for its contribution to "national integration" and later found its place in the top twenty-five Bollywood movies of all time according to film critics.[47] Yet it had no chance of being shown in Pakistan because, after the 1965 war, the Indo-Pakistan trade had virtually ceased.

Whereas their triumph in the Bangladesh War boosted the confidence of the people of India, the Pakistani Army's disgraceful surrender left the nation shell-shocked. The Herculean task of restoring its collapsed morale fell on Zulfikar Ali Bhutto.

II

Zulfikar Ali Bhutto

The Savior of West Pakistan

Zulfikar Ali Bhutto achieved supreme power in a country with a disgraced military, shattered government, and bewildered and demoralized public. Born into the household of a feudal lord, Sir Shah Nawaz Bhutto, in Larkana, Sindh, he went along at the age of fourteen with an arranged marriage to his cousin Amira, but only after receiving a cricket bat as a gift. Five years later he enrolled at the University of California and graduated with a degree in political science in 1950. He then studied law at Oxford University. During the next summer break, while in Karachi, he met and married twenty-two-year-old Nusrat Ispahani, a tall, slender, high-cheek-boned daughter of Iranian parents who had moved to Karachi from Bombay, where Nusrat had received higher education. The young couple then departed for Oxford. After acquiring a law degree from Oxford University, Bhutto was called to Lincoln's Inn, London. He was twenty-five and the father of a daughter named Benazir (Urdu/Sindhi: Peerless).

On his return to Karachi he practiced as a barrister and taught law at Sindh Muslim Law College. Three years later he was appointed a member of Pakistan's delegation to the United Nations. In that capacity he addressed the Conference on the Freedom of the Seas.

After his military coup in 1958, General Muhammad Ayub Khan appointed Bhutto minister of water and power. He advised Ayub Khan on the Indus Waters Treaty with India, which was signed in September 1960. The military ruler then promoted him to minister of commerce. His real opportunity came when, at age thirty-five, he took charge of the foreign ministry after the death of Muhammad Ali Bogra in January 1963. By the time he quit Ayub Khan's government in mid-1966, he had been a cabinet minister for eight years. That had enabled him to acquire a base in the political-bureaucratic landscape of Pakistan. His founding of the Pakistan People's Party (PPP) and its rapid rise have been narrated earlier (see Chapter 9).[1]

Intent on becoming the prime minister, even though the PPP was way behind the Awami League led by Shaikh Mujibur Rahman, Bhutto played the spoiler. Knowingly or inadvertently, he was instrumental in the breakup of Pakistan. Yet neither he nor the people and political and military leaders, traumatized by a military defeat and the loss of the eastern wing, were in a frame of mind to rake up the recent past.

On December 22, 1971, he transferred Shaikh Rahman from solitary confinement to house arrest at a government guest house near Rawalpindi, where he was still deprived of news. A few days later, Bhutto visited the Bengali leader to inform him of his supreme office. He tried to extract a promise from Rahman that Bangladesh and Pakistan would maintain some links. Shaikh Rahman refused.[2]

Pressure from assorted foreign leaders, including President Richard Nixon, mounted for the release of Shaikh Rahman. To divert popular attention away from the fate of the much-loathed Bengali icon, Bhutto issued a series of ordinances, including one on January 1, 1972, to nationalize ten basic industries. Five days later he coupled his decision to place Yahya Khan under house arrest with the release of Shaikh Rahman, who was put on a plane to London. He appointed an inquiry commission under Justice Hamoodur Rahman into Pakistan's military defeat in East Pakistan. These actions of Bhutto resulted in Washington resuming its aid to Pakistan in February.

Bhutto rushed to pursue his pet project of arming Pakistan with an atom bomb. On January 20, 1972, he convened a secret meeting of the officials of the Pakistan Atomic Energy Commission (PAEC) and other scientists under a canvas awning in the spacious garden of a feudal lord friend in Multan, Punjab. He delivered an inspiring speech in which he referred to fate placing him in a position from which he could lead Pakistani into a nuclear arms race. "Can you give it [the bomb] to me?" he asked. When the senior scientists hemmed and hawed, Bhutto turned to the younger ones, who included Sultan Bashiruddin Mahmood and Munir Ahmad Khan. Mahmood rose to his feet. "Yes, it would be possible," he said. "But how long would it take?" inquired an insistent Bhutto. "Maybe, five years." Bhutto held up three fingers. "I want it in three."[3] Ironically, it would be Bhutto's bête noire, India, that would detonate a nuclear device before his deadline.

In February he traveled to London.

BACK CHANNELS TO A TORTUOUS SUMMIT

During that visit Bhutto told former British prime minister Sir Alec Douglas-Home, a fellow alumnus of Christ Church (College), Oxford, that he wanted to start a new page in the prickly Indo-Pakistani relations. This would require a summit with Indira Gandhi. As victor of the recent war, she could afford to be magnanimous and invite him for talks.

When Gandhi was told that Bhutto was in a chastened and realistic mode, back channels were set up. Bhutto used Mazhar Ali Khan, then editor of the prestigious daily *Dawn* and a former member of the (banned) Pakistan Communist Party, to contact one of his prepartition fellow travelers from the Communist Party of India (CPI). He chose Sajjad Zaheer, based in Delhi. They met in London in the third week of March to settle the agenda. Khan confirmed to Zaheer that Bhutto wanted to forget the past, and added that it was in India's interest to help him consolidate power—otherwise the generals and religious right would coalesce and overthrow him. (Indeed, this would happen five years later.) Zaheer passed on the gist of his talk to a fellow traveler of the past, Parmeshwar Narayan Haksar, now a close aide to Gandhi.

They agreed to hold a summit in Shimla (previously, Simla), capital of Himachal Pradesh, in late June 1972. The overarching purpose was to forge a set of principles to guide relations between India and post-1971 Pakistan.

President Bhutto, dressed in a well-cut white, double-breasted cotton suit was greeted by Prime Minister Gandhi, wearing a bright-colored sari with a very broad border in the salubrious weather of Shimla. Bhutto had arrived with a large delegation, which included the bedazzled nineteen-year-old Benazir, then a student of Radcliffe College. She and her father stayed at the state governor's guest house. Gandhi had gone out of her way to visit the house and, after ordering fresh furniture, had supervised its arrangement before the summit on June 28.

M. K. Kaw, a senior civil servant, was charged with looking after Benazir Bhutto. He was assisted by Veena Datta, an officer of the Indian Foreign Service. He and his colleague had to improvise to keep Benazir occupied while her father conducted high diplomacy. "Veena helped me keep Benazir in a good mood," wrote Kaw in his memoir, *An Outsider Everywhere: Revelations by an Insider*, after his retirement.

Benazir's first priority turned out to be to watch the recently released Bollywood movie *Pakeezah* (Urdu: Pure), which, given the virtual absence of Indo-Pakistan trade, could not be exhibited in Pakistan. There were no DVDs or VHS tapes in those days. Benazir's choice underscored the addiction to movies among Pakistanis and Indians irrespective of gender, class, or religion. *Pakeezah* is the story of a Mughal court courtesan, well versed in dance, music, and social etiquette, played by Meena Kumari, a Muslim film star whose life would end in tragedy. A special showing was arranged for Benazir at the local Ritz Cinema. "There were only three of us in the cinema hall: Benazir, Veena and myself," wrote Kaw. "Benazir enjoyed the film immensely."[4] It was Benazir's love for movies that fifteen years later would lead to her marriage to Asif Ali Zardari, whose father, Hakim Ali, owned Bambino Cinema in Karachi—one of the few that showed foreign films and was therefore frequented by her.

However, in Shimla now, the real-life drama was between Benazir's father, Zulfikar Ali, leader of a vanquished nation, and Indira Gandhi, the victor. She had risen to supreme power at home by exploiting the weaknesses of her detractors in the ruling Congress Party who had initially nicknamed her *goongi guddia* (dumb doll) because of her lack of articulation. In marked contrast, Bhutto was a soaring orator in public and an entertaining raconteur in private. A lawyerly approach to negotiations had become second nature to him. Gandhi, on the other hand, never finished her study of modern history at Somerville College in Oxford. Both of them were strong-headed, though, and monopolized power once they reached the apex. They felt offended at the merest slight. They nursed grudges and delighted in trouncing their adversaries. In order to beat her political enemies and counter their evil intentions, Gandhi was known to sponsor outlandish religious rites conducted by self-styled Hindu gurus. She regularly consulted astrologers and holy men.

On the positive side, while conducting day-to-day administration, both maintained a long-term strategic vision beneficial to their nations. Bhutto's self-regard was unbounded. "My name and my reputation are safe in the custody of the people and in the heart of history," he wrote at the end of a chapter in one of his books.[5] Statements such as these led Gandhi to describe him as "unbalanced." Intensely emotional, he was given to theatrical gestures, such as tearing up his speech at the UN Security Council on hearing of the Pakistani Army's surrender to India on December 16, 1971. In stark contrast, Gandhi was remarkably serene in crisis; she displayed this serenity to much acclaim during the run-up to the Bangladesh War.

At the Shimla summit her primary aim was to bring the Kashmir dispute to an official closure. Given Bhutto's weak bargaining position, her chances of success were high. Intense and tortuous negotiations between the two delegations reached a dead end when Gandhi insisted on including "the final solution of the Kashmir problem" in the joint communiqué. Bhutto disagreed. He wanted the Kashmir issue listed as an ongoing dispute that remained to be settled. Earlier, the two sides had agreed on converting the 1949 UN cease-fire line into the Line of Control (LoC). To save the summit from failure, Bhutto and Gandhi held a one-on-one meeting on the evening of July 2.

There are conflicting reports of what transpired during that session. One version has it that Bhutto, using all his lawyerly logic and immense charm, convinced Gandhi that after the disastrous loss of East Pakistan in the recent war, if he were to abandon Pakistan's claims to Kashmir in peace, he would be booted out by the military. According to another account, the Bhutto-Gandhi bargaining boiled down to converting the present LoC into an international border. Bhutto reportedly agreed verbally. "Is this the understanding on which to proceed?" Gandhi asked. "Absolutely," Bhutto is said to have replied. "*Aap mujh par bharosa kee jiye* [You should trust me]."[6]

In the end a compromise on Kashmir ensued. The agreed-on document said that "in Jammu and Kashmir, the Line of Control resulting from the ceasefire of December 17, 1971, shall be respected by both sides without prejudice to the recognized position of either side. Neither side shall seek to alter it unilaterally, irrespective of mutual differences and legal interpretations." Also, both sides undertook "to refrain from threat or the use of force in violation of this Line." The final draft included India's wording that the two countries would settle all their differences "by peaceful means through bilateral negotiations or by other peaceful means mutually agreed upon." This ruled out third-party mediation. Article VI of the agreement listed a final settlement of Jammu and Kashmir "as one of the outstanding questions awaiting settlement."[7]

The Shimla Agreement laid down the principles to govern future relations between India and Pakistan as well as steps to normalize them. Though it is dated July 2, 1972, the accord was signed at 12:40 AM on July 3, 1972. Since then the cease-fire has largely held, except during the 1999 Kargil armed confrontation. And bilateralism has become the defining feature of Indo-Pakistan relations, with no quarter given to third-party mediation or arbitration. Overall, the 1972 Shimla Accord has been the basis of all subsequent Indo-Pakistan talks.

POST-SHIMLA AGREEMENT

Following detailed negotiations to determine the line of demarcation in Kashmir, India and Pakistan completed the mutual withdrawal of their troops on December 20, 1972. They exchanged POWs resulting from their hostilities along India's western frontier. And Delhi returned over five thousand square miles of West Pakistani territory to Islamabad.

The Shimla Agreement did not refer to the 90,370 Pakistani POWs. They were under the jurisdiction of Bangladesh but held inside India because of the insufficient financial and administrative resources of the newly established sovereign state, which was not recognized by Pakistan.

Repatriation of these POWs was a high priority for Bhutto. But he could recognize Bangladesh only after the introduction of a new Pakistani constitution, which took into account the reduced area of the country. It was the National Assembly that had the authority to prepare a fresh constitution. The PPP enjoyed a comfortable majority there. Guided by Bhutto, the committee charged with drafting the constitution got to work.

In return for cooperating with the PPP on this task, the ruling National Awami Party (NAP) in Baluchistan demanded greater autonomy. Bhutto refused to envisage any reduction in his powers. The simmering civil unrest intensified. In February 1973 he dismissed the NAP government and dissolved the provincial assembly. The protests in Baluchistan turned violent. Bhutto dispatched the army to crush the insurgency and maintain order. This assignment restored the morale of the military, badly shaken by its debacle in East Pakistan. Its emboldened generals called for an expansion of the ranks, which Bhutto granted enthusiastically, hoping thus to reinforce his popularity among the twelve corps commanders. On the other hand, Bhutto unwittingly eased the army's path toward resuming its earlier centrality in running the country.

Under Bhutto, the Pakistani military's traditional doctrine that India was enemy number one remained intact. It was politically expedient for him to promote the idea of Pakistan facing a foe. This provided a strong incentive for the populations of the four Pakistani provinces to subordinate their linguistic, subnational loyalty to the overarching patriotism of Pakistan sharing borders with a powerful adversary.

Released of its linkage with the subcontinent's eastern zone, post-1971 Pakistan started looking westward to the Persian Gulf region, including Saudi Arabia, the birthplace of Islam. The dramatic prosperity of the Gulf monarchies stemming from the quadrupling of oil prices in 1973–1974 created an unprecedented demand for the Muslim workers of Pakistan. That in turn strengthened religious sentiment in their native land and pushed Indian and Pakistani societies further apart.

Pakistan's new constitution, finished in March 1973, described Islam as the country's official religion, thus highlighting Bhutto's commitment to the doctrine of Islamic socialism. (As it was, with the loss of a substantial Hindu population in East Pakistan, the proportion of Hindus in the rest of Pakistan had declined sharply to a tiny 2 percent.) It stipulated parliamentary government. A provision barred any change in the constitution, which was unveiled on August 14, 1973. With that Bhutto became the prime minister of the Islamic Republic of Pakistan.

By then Bangladesh had its first general election under its own constitution and returned Shaikh Mujibur Rahman as prime minister.

In February 1974 the Islamic Conference Organization in Lahore provided an opportunity to reconcile two leading Muslim nations, Pakistan and Bangladesh. A special delegation flew to Dhaka (the renamed Dacca) and returned to Lahore, along with Shaikh Rahman. The Pakistani parliament then authorized Bhutto to recognize Bangladesh. After doing so, he traveled to Bangladesh and laid a wreath at its war memorial at Savar Upazila, fifteen miles northwest of Dhaka—a gesture warmly appreciated by Bangladeshis but controversial in Pakistan.

Once India had signed a supplementary agreement with Pakistan, the repatriation of the Pakistani POWs followed. With this event, Bhutto could rightly claim that he had wiped off the last vestige of humiliation suffered by the pre-1971 Pakistan.

Bhutto quietly moved toward converting the LoC in Kashmir into an international border in 1974. He incorporated the Northern Areas into Pakistan. And his government assumed direct authority to administer Azad Kashmir, which was tantamount to Pakistan incorporating the territory—something Delhi had done earlier in the case of India-held Kashmir.

Meanwhile, in India, Shaikh Muhammad Abdullah, then under house arrest in Delhi, was ruminating on the 1971 Bangladesh War. He concluded that it was better to end the politics of confrontation, which had the potential of causing further breakups in Pakistan and India. "Our

227

quarrel with the Government of India is not about accession but about the quantum of autonomy," he said in February 1972. He was released later in the year. Protracted talks between the appointed personal representatives of Abdullah and Gandhi led to the signing of the Kashmir Accord in November 1974. "The State of Jammu and Kashmir which is a constituent unit of the Union of India, shall, in its relation with the Union, continue to be governed by Article 370 of the Constitution of India," read the accord.[8] In the end, Abdullah settled for genuine self-rule in the state by a government elected in free and fair elections. He became the chief minister of Kashmir in February 1975 after disbanding the Plebiscite Front and reviving the moribund National Conference.

These developments signaled a lowering of Indo-Pakistan tensions on the Kashmir problem. But there was no progress on any of the subjects listed in Article III of the Shimla Agreement on normalization of relations: establishing greater communications through all available means, promoting travel facilities, resuming trade and economic cooperation, and making exchanges in science and culture.

INDIA'S PEACEFUL "SMILING BUDDHA"

In any case, Bhutto and Gandhi got distracted by turmoil on the domestic political scene. Bhutto faced insurgency in Baluchistan. And the quadrupling of oil prices in late 1973 and early 1974 spiked inflation in India, whose foreign reserves fell dangerously low because of the hard currency payments it had to make for oil imports. Nonviolent mass protest gathered momentum, and Gandhi's Congress Party was blamed for corruption and misrule.

To divert popular attention, Gandhi authorized an underground explosion of "a peaceful nuclear device"—code-named Smiling Buddha—at the Pokhran military firing range, located between the Rajasthani cities of Jodhpur and Jaisalmer, on May 18, 1974. Its yield was put at twelve kilotons. The official statement said that further experiments would be conducted to perfect "nuclear devices," adding that it was all "for peaceful purposes."[9]

This detonation was the climax of a process initiated by the research of Homi J. Bhabha, an Indian nuclear physicist, in 1944 at the Tata Institute of Fundamental Research in Bombay. He lobbied officials and leading politicians in Delhi to sponsor nuclear research. Among those who agreed with him was Jawaharlal Nehru. "I have no doubt India will develop its scientific researches and I hope Indian scientists will use the atomic force for constructive purposes," Nehru said in June 1946. "But if India is threatened, she will inevitably try to defend herself by all means at her disposal."[10] As the prime minister, Nehru set up the Indian Atomic Energy Commission in 1948 under Bhabha. Six years later the Bhabha Atomic Research Center in Trombay, a suburb of Bombay, purchased a research reactor code-named CIRUS (Canadian-Indian Reactor, US) using heavy water (deuterium oxide) supplied by the United States.[11] It went critical only in July 1960. After China's defeat of India in the October 1962 war, Bhabha publicly called for developing nuclear weapons as a means of deterring potential Chinese aggression. His proposal got the official green light after Beijing tested its atomic bomb two years later, when Lal Bahadur Shastri was prime minister.[12] The nuclear test at Pokhran used plutonium derived from the reprocessed spent fuel from the CIRUS reactor. The nuclear program had so far cost India $1 billion, with its current annual budget running at $140 million.[13] However, it would be only in 1980 that India would be able to put its nuclear weapon into service.

Unsurprisingly, the government in Islamabad did not accept Delhi's pronouncement of peaceful intentions. At a press conference, Bhutto declared that Pakistan would not be threatened by India's "nuclear blackmail." Returning to the same subject three weeks later, he claimed that India's nuclear program was designed to intimidate Pakistan and establish "hegemony in the subcontinent" and that Pakistan would develop a nuclear program in response to India's nuclear test.[14]

The Pokhran explosion marked the start of a nuclear arms race between the two traditional rivals, with Bhutto—having secured financial assistance for his nuclear enterprise from a few oil-rich Arab states, including Libya under Colonel Muammar Gaddafi—coining the catchy term "Islamic atom bomb." He argued that the possession of a nuclear weapon by Christian, Jewish, and Hindu countries had highlighted the deficiency of a Muslim nation in this regard. In his argument there was apparently no place for China, ruled by the atheistic Communist Party of China, but that mortal flaw in his argument did not bother him.

To burnish his Islamic credentials at home, Bhutto rejected the Ahmadi minority's pleas in 1974 that they were Muslim, and declared them non-Muslim.[15] He did so to placate the ulema (religious scholars). He had often felt susceptible to the Islamist groups' attacks on him for being a son of a Hindu mother, Lakhi Bai. They willfully overlooked her conversion to Islam and name change to Khurshid before marrying Sir Shah Nawaz Bhutto. Nor did they take note of the fact the founder of Pakistan, Muhammad Ali Jinnah, had married a Zoroastrian who converted to Islam.

As a symbol of socialism, Bhutto started wearing a cap worn by Mao Zedong as well as an open-collar Mao jacket. Crucially, he nationalized all banks and insurance companies and seventy other industrial enterprises, including some medium-sized factories, thus breaking the power of the top twenty-two families who dominated Pakistan's nonfarm economy.

Simultaneously, his program to expand the military continued. Despite the loss of more than half of its citizens following East Pakistan's secession, Pakistan expanded its armed forces from 370,000 in 1971 to 502,000 in 1975.[16] As a result of a series of Sino-Pakistan agreements signed by the Bhutto government, China became the main supplier of military hardware to Pakistan. Ties between the two became stronger and extended to the nuclear industry following Bhutto's visit to Beijing as leader of the high-level Pakistani military and scientific delegation in June 1976. China agreed to revive the nuclear reactor in Karachi originally sold by Canada in 1965. More importantly, it contracted to supply Pakistan uranium hexafluoride, UF6—commonly called "yellow cake"—a compound used as feedstock in the uranium enrichment process that produces fuel for nuclear reactors and weapons.[17]

In July 1976 work started on the Engineering Research Laboratory (renamed Kahuta Research Laboratory in 1983), code-named Project 706, in Kahuta, a village twenty-five miles southeast of Rawalpindi, the twin city of Islamabad. Bhutto placed it under the joint authority of Lieutenant General Zahid Ali Akbar of the Army Corps of Engineers and Abdul Qadeer Khan, a nuclear scientist, who had convinced Bhutto to pursue a uranium enrichment path, instead of plutonium (which India had done), to build an atom bomb. Bhutto gave Qadeer Khan the deadline of seven years to assemble one. The scientist would meet that challenge, thanks to the active assistance of China.

Born in the central Indian city of Bhopal, Qadeer Khan was sixteen when his parents migrated to Pakistan. After graduating in physical metallurgy from Karachi University, this oval-faced Pakistani with an intense gaze, a clipped mustache, and raven black hair pursued further studies in West Berlin; Delft, Holland; and Leuven, Belgium, between 1962 and 1971. He obtained undergraduate and postgraduate degrees in metallurgy and engineering. In between, he married Hendrina Donkers, a Dutch woman, and they had two daughters. This pointed to his acquiring Dutch citizenship. In March 1972 he got a job with an engineering company, Physical Dynamics Research Laboratory (acronym in Dutch: FDO), in Amsterdam as a metallurgist.

Qadeer Khan's fluency in English, Dutch, and German proved a great asset to FDO when it got a subcontract to develop a better version of centrifuges for enriching uranium from URENCO,[18] a consortium of Britain, Holland, and West Germany formed in 1970 to manufacture centrifuges to produce enriched uranium for use in power plants and nuclear weapons. He thus got free access to the design and manufacturing of centrifuges and the suppliers of various parts and materials. His declaration to his employers that he intended to take up Dutch citizenship eased his way to getting security clearance.

Enraged by the explosion of the "Smiling Buddha" by India, he addressed a letter to Bhutto in which he explained that he had gained expertise in centrifuge-based uranium enrichment technologies at URENCO's laboratory in Almelo, Holland. On his arrival in Karachi with his family in December 1974, he was whisked off to Islamabad. He explained to Bhutto that producing fuel for one atom bomb through uranium enrichment would cost a paltry $60,000. Bhutto was convinced. Once Pakistan's uranium enrichment program got going in early 1975, Qadeer Khan started channeling secret technical information from URENCO to Sultan Bashiruddin Mahmood, head of Project 706. With the 1976 Chinese agreement to supply yellow cake to Pakistan, Bhutto's dream started to turn into reality.

"We were on the threshold of full nuclear capability when I left the government to come to this death cell," wrote Bhutto in his memoirs, *If I Am Assassinated*, published posthumously in late 1979. "We know that Israel and South Africa have full nuclear capability. The Christian, Jewish and Hindu civilizations have this capability. The Communist powers also possess it. Only the Islamic civilization was without it, but that situation is about to change."[19]

DOMESTIC SETBACKS FOR BHUTTO-GANDHI DUO

In India, any feel-good sentiment among its nationals, sparked by the nuclear device explosion in May 1974, soon vanished as continued high inflation and scarcity of essential goods showed no sign of abating. In Gujarat the protest movement initiated by university students spread so quickly that it caused the downfall of Gandhi's Congress Party ministry there. By the end of the year, all opposition parties except the CPI rallied around Jaya Prakash Narayan, a nonparty personality of high, unblemished caliber. Its demands now included eradication of corruption in politics and government bureaucracy and an overhaul of the inequitable electoral system corrupted by the Congress Party. In the midst of this turbulence, in June 1975, a court invalidated Gandhi's parliamentary seat won on the corrupt practice of using government facilities and resources during her 1971 election campaign. Instead of stepping down, she had the president, Fakhuruddin Ali Ahmad, declare an emergency. She started ruling by decree.

In Pakistan, Bhutto turned nationalization into a political tool and extended it to all wheat-milling, rice-husking, and cotton-ginning units in 1976 to enfeeble his opponents. His autocratic manner alienated many left-wingers and others who had joined the PPP in droves at its birth.

On the eve of the general elections in March 1977, all opposition factions and disempowered interest groups coalesced to form the nine-party Pakistan National Alliance (PNA), covering both religious and secular elements, to challenge the PPP.

This caused consternation in PPP circles. It led to vote rigging, carried out by the all-powerful district commissioners in rural areas, to an undetermined extent. The electoral officials declared the PPP had won 155 of 200 seats—76 percent of the total, up from 58 percent in the previous general election in 1970—with the PNA getting only 36. Bhutto's opponents cried foul. Massive protest demonstrations led by the Islamic parties within the PNA followed. Bhutto responded with martial law and gunfire by army troops.

When these methods proved ineffective, he made concessions to the religious camp. He announced that Islamic Sharia law would be enforced within six months. He banned alcohol and gambling and closed night clubs. He declared Friday, the holy day in Islam, as the weekly off-day instead of the traditional Sunday.

Bhutto's compromises failed to satisfy the opposition. That provided General Muhammad Zia ul Haq with a rationale to stage his Operation Fair Play at four AM on July 5, 1977. He overthrew the civilian government and imposed martial law. He placed Bhutto under house arrest in the hill station of Murree. Zia's operation code-name implied that he wanted to disengage the hostile camps and conduct a fresh election, but that never happened.

In Delhi, on the other hand, Gandhi, assured of the electoral success of her Congress Party by the Intelligence Bureau (IB), ordered a general election in January 1977. The IB proved disastrously wrong. The Janata Alliance, a coalition of the main opposition parties, trounced the Congress Alliance, led by Gandhi, by 345 to 189 seats. Morarji Desai, a former conservative Congress leader, became the prime minister. A long-time adversary of Gandhi, he attempted to move as far away from his predecessor's foreign policy as he could. To balance Gandhi's strong pro-Soviet tilt, he tried to improve ties with China, with his foreign minister Atal Bihari Vajpayee visiting Beijing in February 1979. Desai went on to formalize the decade-long covert cooperation between RAW and Israel's Mossad. At the same time he reiterated India's peaceful intentions toward Pakistan.

Zia ul Haq reneged on his promise to hold a National Assembly election because the Inter-Services Intelligence (ISI) chief told him that based on the information collected by his agents, the PPP would win a free and fair contest. Ironically, it was on the recommendation of General Ghulam Jilani Khan, the ISI head, that Bhutto had promoted Lieutenant General Zia ul Haq to chief of army staff in March 1976 above the heads of four more senior generals. Also, given Zia ul Haq's well-known piousness and lack of interest in politics, Bhutto had concluded that he could count on the unfailing loyalty of a general whose religiosity would add a pro-Islamic hue to his political persona.

When General Ayub Khan had seized power in 1958, the standing of politicians had collapsed, and the once-powerful Muslim League had splintered into squabbling factions. By contrast Zia ul Haq had overthrown Bhutto, who for all his faults had mesmerized a very substantial part of the public and whose PPP, built from scratch, had acquired fairly deep roots in society. He therefore faced a daunting challenge: to dispel the Bhutto magic and smash the PPP.

12

Islamist Zia ul Haq,
Builder of the A-Bomb

As personalities, Muhammad Zia ul Haq and Zulfikar Ali Bhutto stood poles apart. Zia ul Haq came from a modest home in the East Punjab city of Jalandhar, his very religious father, Muhammad Akbar Ali, being a junior clerk in the British Indian Army in Delhi. Born in 1924, he graduated from the city's prestigious St. Stephen's College[1] and then joined a cavalry regiment of the army. In 1947 he opted for the Pakistani military. He rose through the ranks but did not cease to be reverential to those who were socially superior to him. He remained strictly religious. "Drinking, gambling, dancing and music were the way the officers spent their free time," he recollected. "I said prayers, instead. Initially, I was treated with some amusement—sometimes with contempt—but my seniors and my peers decided to leave me alone after some time."[2] As a colonel in 1962, he underwent two years' training at the US Army Command and General Staff College in Fort Leavenworth, Kansas. Here too he stayed away from drinking and dancing. During the 1965 Indo-Pakistan War he was a tank commander. And as Brigadier Zia ul Haq, he trained soldiers in Jordan from 1967 to 1970. He was promoted to major general in 1973 and put in charge of the First Armored Division in Multan.

Two years later he rose to lieutenant general and took command of the Second Strike Corps, also based in Multan. He invited Premier Bhutto to his base and asked him to hit a target. The egotistical Bhutto scored with the first shot, much to his surprise and satisfaction. Turning on his obsequiousness to the fullest, Zia ul Haq exuded his loyalty to Bhutto, who noticed how meticulous the general was in offering his daily Islamic prayers.

Now, in July 1977, having toppled his benefactor and assumed supreme power as the chief martial law administrator, Zia ul Haq called himself "a soldier of Allah." He projected himself as a moderator, promising a free and fair election in ninety days, with both the Pakistan People's Party (PPP) and the Pakistan National Alliance (PNA) contesting. He released Bhutto on July 28.

Among those who accepted his word at face value was India's Ministry of External Affairs (MEA). "He [General Zia] has categorically stated on several occasions that takeover was necessary to prevent civil war, his prime objective being to supervise political solution," said Foreign Secretary J. S. Mehta, the highest bureaucrat in the ministry, in his cable to all of India's foreign missions, according to declassified documents. "His 90-day plan makes it incumbent on him to arrange polls in October. All public indications so far suggest that he means what he says."[3]

This was not to be. Bhutto's rallies proved hugely popular, and he capped his domestic activities with a tour of friendly Arab countries. Knowing Bhutto's record of punishing his enemies, Zia ul Haq calculated that after his expected electoral victory, Bhutto would wreak vengeance. Therefore he rearrested him on September 3 because of his alleged involvement in the murder of Muhammad Khan Kasuri, a Punjabi politician who, because of his differences with Bhutto, had quit the PPP in 1974. Bhutto would be found guilty and hanged in April 1979.

ZIA'S ARTFUL DECEPTION

India's ambassador in Islamabad,[4] however, continued to present Zia ul Haq in a favorable light. "Gen Zia ul Haq is said to be devout but not a fanatic and is professional in outlook," wrote Mehta, the former foreign secretary of the MEA in Delhi. The Pakistan-Afghanistan division of the MEA agreed. "The concessions to Islamic Sharia Law and *Nizam-i-Mustafa* [Urdu: Rule of Prophet Muhammad] are doubtless meant to neutralize any serious opposition to the unconstitutional takeover of government by the armed forces, but not necessarily an indication of ambition to continue in power. It also incidentally gains for the regime the support of orthodox political elements."[5]

In reality, Zia ul Haq started monopolizing power once the Supreme Court had invoked the "doctrine of necessity" in October to legitimize the coup. It also allowed him to suspend the 1973 constitution. As the chief martial law administrator, he presented a provisional constitution that authorized him to amend the 1973 document at will. But he pursued Bhutto's project of building an atom bomb with much greater vigor while keeping Project 706 under wraps, with the innocuous sounding Engineering Research Laboratory (ERL) stealthily enriching uranium.

To get an inkling of what transpired inside the ERL, India's Research and Analysis (RAW) agents collected discarded hair from nearby barber shops and sent them to the Bhabha Atomic Research Centre, Trombay, for analysis. It found traces of uranium in the hair, indicating uranium enriching activity at the ERL.[6]

A past master in speaking with a forked tongue, Zia ul Haq responded warmly to friendly overtures by Indian premier Moraji Desai. They maintained direct contact through periodic telephone conversations until mid-1979, when, following a split in the ruling Janata Alliance, Desai had to step down. In early 1978, according to Bahukutumbi Raman, former head of RAW's Counter-Terrorism Division, in an unguarded moment Desai told Zia ul Haq that he was well aware of Pakistan's nuclear weapons program.[7] Predictably, Zia ul Haq denied any contraband activity. Pakistan's Inter-Services Intelligence (ISI) went into overdrive to winkle out all foreign spies and their agents from the ERL area.

Zia ul Haq was well aware of Washington's policy of discouraging non-nuclear states to acquire nuclear arms. In 1976, US senator Stuart Symington's Amendment to the Foreign Assistance Act of 1961 specified ending aid to any country that imported uranium enrichment technology. The following year Senator John Glenn's Amendment to the Foreign Assistance Act stipulated the termination of aid to any country that imported reprocessing technology, which is used to recover fissionable plutonium from irradiated nuclear fuel for nuclear weapons.[8] The US Congress passed the Nonproliferation Act in March 1978. It barred any country from receiving American assistance if it tested a nuclear weapon, and imposed sanctions against a state that attempted to acquire unauthorized nuclear technology.

While acknowledging the construction of a uranium enriching facility, Zia ul Haq said that it would be used solely for generating electricity and declared that no Pakistani government could compromise on the nuclear issue under American pressure. In his meeting with Cyrus Vance, US secretary of state, in October 1978, Pakistan's foreign minister Agha Shahi said, "You don't have to be a nuclear weapons expert to understand the strategic importance of having one. The value lies in its possession, and not in its use."[9]

In geopolitical terms, however, what caused a major shift in Indo-Pakistan relations was the coup by Marxist military officers against Afghan president Muhammad Daoud Khan on April 27, 1978. Daoud Khan was killed in the fighting at the presidential palace, and his official positions of president and prime minister went to Nur Muhammad Taraki. The military leaders renamed the country the Democratic Republic of Afghanistan. The coup turned Afghanistan into a frontline state in the Cold War between the White House and the Kremlin.

This was a second seismic change in five years in Afghanistan. In July 1973 Prime Minister General Daoud Khan had overthrown his cousin King Muhammad Zahir Shah and declared Afghanistan a republic. To consolidate his power he revived the issue of Pashtunistan, an independent state to be carved out of parts of Pakistan's North-West Frontier Province (NWFP) and Federally Administered Tribal Agencies (FATA). His officers started training twelve thousand irredentist Pashtun and Baluch volunteers to harass Pakistan's army. In return, Bhutto sponsored an anti-Daoud Khan coup, fronted by the Afghan Islamist leader Gulbuddin Hekmatyar, in July 1975. It failed. But Bhutto allowed Peshawar, the capital of NWFP, to become a base of Afghan Islamist groups. Mediation by the shah of Iran eased Islamabad-Kabul tensions by 1977. But normalization of relations between the two neighbors was disrupted by the subsequent Marxist military officers' coup.

RIPPLES OF THE MARXIST COUP IN KABUL

The Marxist takeover in Kabul alarmed the administration of US president Jimmy Carter (in office 1977–1981). It hastened to resume development aid to Islamabad that it had stopped earlier. Washington's ban on the sale of US weapons and parts to Pakistan after the 1965 Indo-Pakistan War remained in place until 1975, when it was lifted by President Gerald Ford.

On the other side, the Kremlin dispatched its military advisers to Kabul. At the same time Alexander Puzanov, the Soviet ambassador in Kabul, advised President Taraki in June to initiate dialogue with his Pakistani counterpart to resolve their mutual differences.[10]

Taraki invited Zia ul Haq to Kabul. Instead, they met in Paghman, sixteen miles from the capital, on September 9.[11] Their starkly opposing ideologies came into sharp focus. Taraki proudly informed his interlocutor that his regime had given land to eleven million Afghans. Zia ul Haq remarked that all property belonged to Allah and human beings were no more than His custodians. "All land belongs to the tiller," retorted Taraki.[12]

Desai and other Indian politicians would have agreed with Taraki's statement. They had carried out land reform in India, albeit in fits and starts. Unsurprisingly, therefore, Delhi's historically close ties with Kabul were unaffected by the political upheavals. The Taraki regime's signing of a Treaty of Friendship and Cooperation with Moscow in December 1978 followed India's example in August 1973.

By then the government of President Zia ul Haq had provided Afghanistan's Islamist insurgents, called mujahedin (Arabic: those who wage jihad), with covert training bases—an enterprise in which the CIA participated actively under its Operation Cyclone.

At home, on December 2, 1978, the Islamabad government announced that the Islamic law concerning theft (cutting off of hands), drinking (seventy-four lashes), and adultery (death by stoning) would be enforced from the birthday of Prophet Muhammad the following year. Pakistan's lurch toward Islamization went unremarked by the Carter White House. Finding itself deprived of its strategic alliance with Iran after the overthrow of its staunch ally Mohammad Reza Pahlavi Shah by the rabidly anti-American Ayatollah Ruhollah Khomeini in February 1979, the United States tightened its links with Zia ul Haq's military regime.

It decided to upgrade its backing for the Afghan mujahedin by authorizing the CIA to start supplying them with weapons. Initially the CIA armed them with Soviet-made arms partly from its own stores built up during the previous regional conflicts and partly by procuring them from Egypt, a one-time ally of Moscow. This enabled the mujahedin to claim that they had secured these firearms by attacking the armories of the government.

In Kabul the Marxist regime split into two factions, leading to the killing of Taraki and the rise of Hafizullah Amin as president in September 1979. He in turn was toppled by Babrak Karmal in December. Karmal invited Soviet troops to help him stabilize the political situation. They arrived on Christmas Day. Overnight this transformed Zia ul Haq from a despicable dictator to an unblemished ally in the US-led global campaign against Soviet communism.

Delhi and Islamabad reacted differently to the events in Afghanistan. Indian diplomats recommended negotiations between the contending

Afghan parties. In stark contrast, Zia ul Haq presented Moscow's move as "a push towards the warm waters of the Arabian Sea," implying that Pakistan would be the next target of the Soviet Union's aggressive expansion. Carter readily accepted his interpretation.

The Cold War between the White House and the Kremlin intensified. But the Carter administration realized that killing Soviet troops in Afghanistan with CIA-supplied arms would be very provocative and raise the prospect of direct Moscow-Washington confrontation. Therefore it decided to work through a proxy—Pakistan's Inter-Services Intelligence (ISI) directorate—to be able to exercise "plausible deniability." Out of this emerged the Washington-Islamabad-Riyadh alliance, whereby the United States, the overall coordinator, became the sole supplier of weapons, bought with American and Saudi cash, to be channeled exclusively through Pakistan. In this scheme, the ISI acquired a pivotal role.

It then operated from a drab, unmarked red-brick building behind high stone walls on Khayaban-e-Suhrawardy in Islamabad. About one hundred military officers maintained an internal and external intelligence network of thousands of agents and freelance spies. Like the rest of the military, ISI officers and agents underwent religious education, as mandated by Zia ul Haq. Equally compulsory became the offering of prayer by soldiers led by officers.

With the new, ambitious assignment in Afghanistan and a vastly increased budget, the ISI would expand its staff and agents, engaging Pakistanis fluent in Persian and Pushtu as well as thousands of Afghans with promises of money and domicile for their families in Pakistan. That would push the total number of ISI employees, full- and part-time, to almost one hundred thousand by early 1988.[13] Zia mandated that the ISI collect foreign and domestic intelligence; coordinate intelligence functions of the three military services; conduct surveillance over foreigners, the media, politically active Pakistanis, diplomats of other countries based in Pakistan, and Pakistani diplomats serving abroad; intercept and monitor communications; and conduct covert offensive operations.

While relations between Islamabad and Moscow turned frosty, the Delhi-Moscow embrace became warmer. In May 1980, Indian officials signed contracts for the purchase of MIG-25 aircraft, attack boats, and advanced T-72 tanks, to be produced later in India.

In June 1980 Zia ul Haq set up Sharia courts at the high court level in the provinces and the appellate Sharia bench at the Supreme Court level. They were authorized to decide whether a particular law was Islamic or not.[14] These official measures were buttressed by the promotion of Islam through mosques and the media. A review of all textbooks was undertaken and the ones regarded as un-Islamic were removed.

As a consequence, the social, cultural, and ideological distance between rapidly Islamizing Pakistani and secular Indian societies grew wider than before.

ZIA'S CAT-AND-MOUSE GAME ON NUCLEAR WEAPONS

By late 1978, the Carter administration had solid evidence of Pakistan's uranium enrichment program at the ERL in Kahuta. It broached the subject with Islamabad. Dissatisfied with the response he received, Carter cut off economic and military assistance, except food aid, to Pakistan in April 1979 under the Symington Amendment. He reiterated that the aid would be resumed only if he certified that Pakistan would not develop or acquire nuclear arms or assist other nations to do so.[15]

Relations between Islamabad and Washington remained stalemated when Indira Gandhi was returned to power on January 14, 1980—within a few weeks of Soviet troops arriving in Afghanistan. She was keen to dissuade Zia ul Haq from approaching the Carter administration to restore military and economic aid to his country because of the Soviet military presence in Afghanistan. In April she dispatched Swaran Singh, former foreign minister, as her special envoy to Islamabad to reassure Zia ul Haq that her government would not take advantage if he decided to move his troops away from the Indian border to the Afghan frontier. But by the time the back channel contacts between the two leaders built up to schedule a visit to Islamabad by the Indian foreign minister Pamulapartu Venkata Narasimha Rao in March 1981, the political scene in Washington had altered—to the detriment of Gandhi.

Republican Ronald Reagan (in office 1981–1989) moved into the White House in January 1981. His description of the Soviet Union as the "evil empire" would become his signature. It was with this reprehensible regime that the Gandhi government had signed a major agreement to boost India's energy sector and to double bilateral trade between 1981 and 1986 during the December 1980 visit of the Soviet leader Leonid Brezhnev to Delhi.

While Reagan lacked Carter's intelligence, he was a superb communicator, having spent many years as a tall, robustly built actor in Hollywood.

His persuasive manner helped him to overcome congressional resistance to his policies. Alexander Haig, his secretary of state from January 1981 to July 1982, described Pakistan's nuclear program as "a private matter." All he wanted was that it should not detonate an atom bomb, thus emulating the example of Israel, which had refrained from testing its nuclear weapons first acquired in 1966.

The Reagan administration worked with Congress to give Pakistan a five-year waiver of the Symington Amendment because of its role in funneling US aid to the mujahedin in Afghanistan. In May 1981, the Senate Foreign Relations Committee reversed its previous stance and sanctioned $3.2 billion aid to Islamabad over the next six years, divided equally between civilian and military assistance. The White House argued that supplying Pakistan with modern US weaponry would reduce the chance of its pursuing the nuclear option. In reality, nothing of the sort happened. Islamabad forged ahead on both armament fronts, conventional and unconventional. The Senate adopted its committee's bill in December 1981.[16]

Reagan appointed William Casey as CIA director. A bald, corpulent man with a rubbery face and oversize spectacles, he had started his working life with the CIA's predecessor, Office of Strategic Surveys, and established himself as an unconventional operator, callous and combative in equal measure. Now, personal rapport quickly developed between him, ISI director Lieutenant General Abdur Rahman Khan, and Prince Turki bin Faisal, head of Saudi intelligence. The Afghan insurgency picked up.

Since the United States did not want to create a paper trail of money transactions, which would give Moscow evidence of its involvement in Afghan affairs (thus raising the specter of a regional conflict with international potential), all money dealings were in cash. This gave ample opportunities to the ISI to siphon off foreign funds and funnel them into the nuclear program.

As 1982 unrolled, Pakistan received from China the complete design of a twenty-five-kiloton nuclear bomb and sufficient weapons-grade uranium for two bombs. Beijing went on to provide Islamabad with the design of one of its warheads.[17] Little wonder that Islamabad-Moscow relations turned bitter. In his speech at the banquet in honor of the visiting Indira Gandhi on September 20, 1982, Brezhnev publicly advised India against accepting Zia ul Haq's offer of a no-war pact. Behind closed doors, he explained to Gandhi that after inking a no-war pact with India, the Pakistani leader would shift the bulk of his troops from the Indian border to the one with Afghanistan and threaten the Kremlin-backed regime in Kabul. Gandhi took his advice. She made a counterproposal for a peace and friendship treaty, which failed to interest Zia ul Haq.

During her talks at the Kremlin, Gandhi privately advised a pullout of Soviet troops from Afghanistan. But her counsel was spurned.[18] By then India's defense industry was tied so closely to its Soviet counterpart that she lacked any cards to play in her dealings with the Kremlin.

As a result of India's continued cordial relations with the Marxist regime, links between RAW and the Afghan intelligence agency, KHAD, run by the Ministry of State Security, became tighter. Both worked closely with the KGB, the Soviet Union's main security and intelligence agency. Among other things, the KGB and KHAD supplied vital information to RAW on the activities of Sikh separatists in Pakistan's tribal region.

In the state of Punjab, formed in 1966, Sikhs were 60 percent of its fifteen million inhabitants, the rest being almost wholly Hindu. Militants in the Sikh community had resorted to violence from October 1981 in their demand for Khalistan—the homeland for Sikhs—sandwiched between Pakistan and India. Sikh separatists argued that their community was the victim of discrimination by Hindus. However, the founder of Sikhism, Guru Nanak (1469–1539), was born a Hindu, and his faith emerged out of his attempt to reform Hinduism by getting rid of its caste system. Since the inception of Sikhism, relations between Hindus and Sikhs had been cordial, with Sikhs celebrating such Hindu festivals as Divali (Hindi: festival of light). Interfaith marriages were tolerated by both communities. Now, by resorting to attacking Hindus in Punjab, the advocates of Khalistan created tension between Sikhs and Hindus. Crucially, their demand for a homeland on the basis of religion, the seed that had flowered into Pakistan, struck at the very foundation of India's secular constitution. It was ruled out of hand by the authorities in Delhi.

This subject was therefore off the agenda during the hour-long meeting Gandhi had with Zia ul Haq on November 1, 1982, when he stopped in New Delhi on his way to Malaysia. They decided to authorize their foreign ministers to proceed with talks leading to the establishment of the South Asian Association for Regional Cooperation (SAARC).[19]

FIVE PLAYERS IN SOUTH ASIA'S NUCLEAR GAME

Behind the scenes, Gandhi fretted about Zia ul Haq's clandestine drive to build an atom bomb by using weapons-grade uranium, and she considered ways of terminating his scheme. She knew that Israeli warplanes had destroyed the French-equipped Osirak nuclear reactor under construction eighteen miles south of Baghdad on June 7, 1981. The daring, surprising raid by Israel inspired her to initiate a project in the autumn code-named Osirak Contingency under Air Marshall Dilbagh Singh, chief of air staff.

The Indian Air Force's planes practiced low-level flying runs with two-thousand-pound bombs. But neutralizing the strong air defenses of the Kahuta facility, including surface-to-air missiles, proved too great a challenge for India's military. But because of the links between RAW and Mossad, it did not take long for Israel to offer its expertise in jamming advanced communications systems at Kahuta. Its move was in line with its policy of blocking any Muslim nation from possessing nuclear weapons.

Thus in 1982 Israel became the fifth player in South Asia's nuclear game—after India, Pakistan, China, and America. Their alignments were full of contradictions. India forged a daring plan against Pakistan with Israel, a country with which it lacked full diplomatic links. Though committed by law to the doctrine of nonproliferation of nuclear arms, the Reagan White House chose to turn a blind eye to the ongoing assistance that Beijing, a nonsignatory to the nuclear Non-Proliferation Treaty (NPT), was giving to Islamabad in its nuclear weapons program. Israel, the long-established staunch ally of the United States in the Cold War, now arrayed itself against Pakistan at a time when that country had become the key element in Washington's campaign to defeat the Soviet Union in Afghanistan.

In marked contrast, China remained singularly consistent in its strategy to offset India's hegemony in South Asia by aiding Pakistan to overcome its inherent weakness compared to its mighty neighbor in conventional weapons and armed personnel. By eagerly assisting Pakistan to construct a nuclear weapon, Beijing aimed to raise it to parity with India in defense matters, thus frustrating India's ambition to become a hegemonic power in South Asia.

Delhi accepted the assistance of Israel's hawkish defense minister, Ariel Sharon. By the end of 1982, a joint Indo-Israeli plan was hatched to raid Pakistan's Kahuta nuclear facility. Indian military officers traveled to Tel Aviv clandestinely in February 1983 to purchase electronic equipment to jam Kahuta's air defenses. Tellingly, on February 23, 1983, Gandhi accused Pakistan of "covertly attempting to make nuclear weapons," and three days later Raja Ramanna, head of the Bhabha Atomic Research Center, revealed that India too was developing a uranium-enriching facility.[20]

Bizarrely, this was the backdrop to the cordial meeting between Gandhi and Zia ul Haq on the sidelines of the Seventh Nonaligned Movement from March 7 to 12, 1983, in Delhi. They signed an agreement on normalizing relations by setting up the Joint Indo-Pakistan Commission, with subcommissions for trade, economics, information, and travel.

During 1983, China helped Pakistan with triggering devices for an atom bomb. These were either conventional charges or electronic trigging circuits. The Pakistani experts, led by Abdul Qadeer Khan, started conducting cold tests in a tunnel in the Chagai Hills of northwest Baluchistan to perfect a triggering device. Success came only at the end of more than twenty trials. That was the final step to assembling an atom bomb. They did so by the end of the year. At that point the Engineering Research Laboratory was officially renamed the Kahuta Research Laboratory.

In Washington a (later) declassified US government assessment in 1983 concluded that "there is unambiguous evidence that Pakistan is actively pursuing a nuclear weapons development program. . . . We believe the ultimate application of the enriched uranium produced at Kahuta is clearly nuclear weapons."[21]

Yet no action was taken against Pakistan. The Reagan White House had equated hurting Pakistan by imposing sanctions on it with aiding the Kremlin. So when faced with the choice of expelling the Soviets from Afghanistan by all possible means or stopping Islamabad from building an atom bomb, it opted for hemorrhaging the "evil empire." It was so unwaveringly committed to this policy that it deployed underhand tactics to squash the irrefutable evidence that State Department officials would periodically furnish to show Islamabad inexorably racing to produce a nuclear weapon.

The Indo-Israeli plan to raid the Kahuta facility did not remain secret for long from the ISI. In the autumn of 1983 its chief Lieutenant General, Rahman Khan, sent a message to his counterpart in RAW, Nowsher F. Suntook. This led to a meeting between Munir Ahmad Khan, head of the Pakistan Atomic Energy Commission (PAEC), and Ramanna in a Vienna hotel. Ahmad Khan warned Ramanna that if India alone, or in collusion with Israel, attacked Kahuta, Pakistan would hit India's nuclear facility in Trombay on the outskirts of Mumbai, with horrific consequences for millions of that mega-city's residents.[22] Faced with such a scenario, Gandhi hesitated.

Meanwhile, the links between RAW and Mossad had grown so tight that Mossad equipped RAW's two Boeing 707s belonging to its Aviation

Research Center with specialist equipment to gather signals intelligence.[23] It was against this background that in late 1983 Sharon offered to carry out the raid from Jamnagar in Gujarat by entering Pakistan beneath the radar and following the mountains in Kashmir to reach Kahuta. It was then that, with the connivance of the Reagan White House, the CIA station chief in Islamabad reportedly tipped off Zia ul Haq about Sharon's proposal to Gandhi, hoping to de-escalate the dangerous tit-for-tat between India and Pakistan.[24]

Zia ul Haq acted. At his behest, Qadeer Khan gave long interviews to two leading local newspapers in January and February 1984. His core message was that "Pakistan could build the bomb if it needed to. And if Kahuta is destroyed, more than one such plant can be rebuilt." To leave nothing to chance, Pakistan's ambassador in Delhi told India's External Affairs Ministry that his country would rain fire in retaliation for an attack on Kahuta.[25] Zia ul Haq's aim was twofold: to show that Pakistan's nuclear program was unstoppable in order to gain international acceptance, and to warn Gandhi that Pakistan was ready to strike back if she decided to raid Kahuta. He succeeded. In March Gandhi revoked her earlier go-ahead to Sharon.

The year 1984 was the pivotal one for Pakistan's nuclear program. After receiving an atom bomb assembled in Kahuta in January, the Chinese detonated it successfully at their test site at Lop Nor in Xinjiang province in March.[26] This led to discreet jubilation among top officials in Islamabad and Kahuta. Having thus acquired parity with India in defense, Pakistani leaders were now equipped to challenge India's claim to regional hegemony. This super-secret event at Lop Nor, however, would reach the CIA and RAW two years later, and others much later. Meanwhile, Zia ul Haq, a master in dissimulation, would only admit that his country had acquired a very modest uranium enrichment capability for peaceful purposes.

In late 1984, Qadeer Khan said he was ready for a hot test in Baluchistan, but Zia ul Haq ruled it out. He did not wish to embarrass the Reagan administration, which had been overly generous to his government and had repeatedly overlooked its transgressions in its nuclear arms program.

Zia ul Haq had another major reason to be cautious. In April 1984 the US Senate's Foreign Affairs Committee had adopted a restrictive provision, proposed by Larry Pressler and two other senators, to tie the continuation of economic assistance and military sales to Islamabad. The president needed to certify that Pakistan did not possess a nuclear explosive device, and to add that fresh aid to it would reduce significantly the risk that it would possess such a weapon. It was not until August 1985 that this provision, called the Pressler Amendment, was attached to the Foreign Assistance Act, covering fiscal 1985–1986. In the House of Representatives, Stephen Solarz's amendment stipulated a ban on *all* military and economic aid to those nonnuclear nations that illegally procured or tried to procure nuclear-related materials from America.

But there was an overriding opt-out provision that applied to all such amendments. The US president was authorized to waive these if he thought it was in the national interest to do so. Reagan did not use that option, though. Instead, while incontrovertible evidence from several sources piled up, showing Pakistan's unflinching drive to produce an atom bomb, year after year Reagan certified to the contrary. He did so to keep the US military and economic aid flowing into Pakistan while its government boosted the destructive power of the mujahedin insurgents in Afghanistan.

SOFT BELLIES OF INDIA AND PAKISTAN

Reagan's unqualified backing and the deadly effectiveness of the Afghan mujahedin's insurgency emboldened Zia ul Haq to implement his pet policy of pinpricks against India to weaken it. This meant providing material aid to any irredentist movement that arose there. The violent agitation of militant Sikhs for an independent Khalistan was one such. It gathered steam in the early 1980s. With many Sikh immigrants in Britain and North America backing the movement, it became comparatively easy for the ISI to contact their leaders.

At home, Zia ul Haq's rule came under pressure in early 1983. The PPP-led coalition of ten parties, called the Movement for the Restoration of Democracy (MRD), demanded elections and restoration of the 1973 constitution by August 14, Independence Day, on pain of starting a nonviolent campaign against the military dictatorship.

Zia ul Haq failed to heed the call, describing the MRD as a tool of India. His allegation gained traction when Indira Gandhi endorsed the movement in a comment in the lower house of India's parliament. Because the MRD was particularly strong in Sindh, the traditional bastion of the PPP, the military government charged that the MRD had the agenda of securing the secession of Sindh from Pakistan in protest of the Punjabi-dominated administration in Islamabad. Sindhi villagers dismissed the official propaganda. They backed the MRD's campaign so staunchly that Zia ul Haq dispatched three army divisions to quell it. The army arrested fifteen thousand people and killed sixty to two hundred protestors.[27]

In early October Gandhi inaugurated the World Sindhi Conference, a human rights advocacy organization registered in Welwyn Garden City, United Kingdom, in New Delhi. "We are for democracy and shall ever be so," she declared. "We have to oppose injustice everywhere. We want that there should be democracy everywhere, and there is nothing bad or improper in saying so." The conference passed a resolution for the immediate withdrawal of troops from Sindh and the restoration of constitutional rights of the people. All India Radio started broadcasting in Sindhi, which had been added to the list of recognized languages in the constitution in 1967 but never accorded the status of radio broadcasts before. When the news of these developments was conveyed to the Sindhi nationalist leader Ghulam Murtaza Syed, he was overjoyed.[28]

Zia ul Haq latched on to these events. On October 22 he asserted that the MRD was working in league with a foreign power: "As soon as the MRD began agitating, a foreign power, as agreed before, came out in its support." There was no second-guessing as to who this "foreign power" was. Referring to Indians, he said, "They are not really reconciled to the existence of Pakistan."[29] This was the age-old refrain that still remained potent in Pakistan. On his part, in 1984, the Pakistani leader instructed ISI officers to establish contacts with the representatives of the Jammu and Kashmir Jamaat-e Islami (JeI) and the secular-nationalist Jammu and Kashmir Liberation Front (JKLF).

SIKH INSURGENCY CLAIMS INDIRA GANDHI

In the Sikh-majority Punjab, a peaceful campaign for a larger share of irrigation water for the state in August 1982 was repressed by the Congress ministry. It arrested thirty thousand protesting Sikhs, and police shootings killed more than one hundred, in less than three months. During the run-up to the Asian Games in Delhi, held from November 19 to December 4, all Sikhs from Punjab traveling to Delhi were searched as a precaution against terrorist attacks during the event. Sikhs felt humiliated and alienated from the Hindu community. This swelled the ranks of the thirty-five-year-old firebrand religious leader Jarnail Singh Bhindranwale. His inordinately long, raven-black beard and deep blue turban made him stand out in a crowd.[30]

Along with several hundred armed acolytes of his, Bhindranwale planted himself in the Golden Temple—officially called Harmandir Sahib—a complex of forty-two buildings, many of them glittering shrines. They felt safe there because, as a rule, security forces did not enter places of religious worship. In his interviews with foreign TV channels, Bhindranwale called for the establishment of an independent state of Sikhs to be called Khalistan. He gained the backing of many affluent Sikhs settled in Britain and North America. Their donations enabled the Bhindranwale camp to arm themselves with Pakistan-made rifles smuggled across the 150-mile-long Punjab border.

Bhindranwale threatened his Sikh opponents. In a sensational act, his partisans killed police deputy inspector general Avtar Singh Atwal in April 1983. The security situation deteriorated. Following the murder of six Hindu bus passengers in October, the Gandhi government in Delhi declared a state of emergency and imposed central rule. But there was no letup in violence. During the first five months of 1984, it claimed 298 victims in Punjab and spread to the contiguous Haryana and its neighbor, Delhi.

Gandhi decided to launch a military assault to gain control of the Golden Temple, which had become the bastion of Bhindranwale and his six hundred armed followers. As a preamble to the attack by army troops and armed policemen—code-named Blue Star—a thirty-six-hour curfew in Punjab on June 3 brought all movement to a standstill. Strict censorship of news was imposed while seven army divisions were deployed in the state. Security forces, equipped with heavy artillery, tanks, and armored personnel carriers, stormed the Golden Temple on the night of June 5. They gained full control by the morning of June 7 after fierce fighting with the heavily armed insurgents, who had been arrayed in strategic positions in more than forty buildings of the complex by a retired Sikh general.

The official fatality statistics of 136 security personnel and 357 insurgents and other civilians were widely believed to be unreliable. The number of suspected terrorists was put at 1,592. And there was a reference to 1,600 "missing" people. Bhindranwale was killed.[31] Unofficial estimates of the dead ranged between 1,500 and 5,000. The *Chicago Tribune* on June 12 published a figure of 2,000. Military helicopters reported marches on Amritsar by tens of thousands of Sikhs in defiance of the emergency.

More seriously, some 4,000 Sikh soldiers in garrison towns of Punjab defected, killed their officers, and marched on Amritsar. They were stopped by armed policemen, and many lost their lives.[32]

In two subsequent military operations, code-named Shop and Woodrose, security forces raided rural Punjab to capture suspected extremists and scan the countryside. This dragnet campaign forced nearly three thousand young Sikhs to cross into Pakistan. They were arrested as aliens entering the country without proper documents.[33] In its "White Paper on the Punjab Agitation," published on July 10, 1984, the Indira Gandhi government referred to Pakistan's involvement in backing the Khalistan movement, which was directed against India's strength, unity, and secularism.[34]

The Indian military's ferocious assault on their most sacred shrine traumatized Sikhs all over India. They viewed this onslaught as an attack on their religion and identity. There were reports of Sikh civil servants and army officers resigning in protest and others, including the famous writer-columnist Khushwant Singh, returning their official honors.

In their eyes, Indira Gandhi became evil incarnate. On the morning of October 31, 1984, as she passed a wicket gate between the garden of her official residence and her office to give an interview to Irish TV, she paid the ultimate price. Her assassins were none other than her Sikh bodyguards, twenty-five-year-old subinspector Beant Singh and twenty-one-year-old constable Satwant Singh Bhakar. Beant Singh aimed three shots from his .38-caliber revolver into Gandhi's chest and abdomen. As she fell to the ground, Bhakar pumped all thirty rounds from his submachine gun into her bleeding body.

They threw their weapons on the ground and were immediately apprehended by the commandos and taken to the guardhouse. Indira Gandhi was dead on arrival at the All India Institute of Medical Sciences. In the evening her forty-year-old son, Rajiv, a junior member of the lower house of Parliament, was sworn in as prime minister. Three days of official mourning followed.

During that time an anti-Sikh pogrom in greater Delhi and elsewhere was carried out by organized gangs. By the time the mob fury had spent itself, between six thousand and eight thousand Sikhs were killed—stabbed, burned, or beaten to death. More than one hundred Sikh temples were set alight, and thousands of shops and homes were pillaged. Altogether Sikhs lost property worth Rs 300 million ($6 million).[35] To save his life, Khushwant Singh, who opposed the Khalistan movement, sought refuge in the Swedish embassy. "I felt a refugee in my own country," he moaned.[36]

With Indira Gandhi's demise, India lost a politician who during her fifteen years of premiership had proved to be a strong leader, although her decision to impose a state emergency in 1975–1977 was wrongheaded and authoritarian. In her handling of domestic politics she was manipulative and vengeful—traits that, in the final analysis, lay at the root of the rise of Sikh irredentism. It was she who had bolstered an upstart Bhindranwale to rival an established Sikh leader she disagreed with. Later Bhindranwale morphed into a Frankenstein and turned against her.

In Pakistan, the government declared three days of mourning. Zia ul Haq rushed to Delhi to attend the cremation of Gandhi on the banks of the Yamuna River.

In the wake of Indira Gandhi's assassination, RAW secured the services of a senior officer of Israel's domestic intelligence agency, Shin Beth, to tighten up its prime minister's security system. Indo-Israeli links tightened during her successor's rule, much to the apprehension of Pakistani leaders.

UNTUTORED RAJIV AND DUPLICITOUS ZIA

In the wake of the assassination of his mother, a wave of popular sympathy favored Rajiv Gandhi's Congress Party in the parliamentary election that followed. It garnered 404 of the 515 seats at stake.[37] This was a truly remarkable achievement for the tall, robustly built, moon-faced Rajiv, who had entered politics reluctantly in 1981 after the death of his younger, politicized brother, Sanjay, in a flying accident. Though he studied engineering at Trinity College, Cambridge, from 1962 to 1965, he did not graduate. He met and dated Antonia Edvige Albina Maino, an Italian, who had come to Cambridge to learn English and worked as a part-time waitress. On his return to India in 1966, Rajiv trained as a pilot and joined the state-owned Indian Airlines. Two years later he married twenty-one-year-old Maino according to Hindu rites in Delhi. She changed her name to Sonia. After the birth of their two children, Rahul and Priyanka, the couple settled down to a humdrum domestic life, with Rajiv showing no interest in politics.

Thus India came to be ruled by a public figure lacking experience in politics, administration, diplomacy, or strategy. Personable and sincere in his utterances, he was bereft of the guile of a politician, an attribute Zia ul Haq, though trained as a soldier, possessed in spades. The two leaders met in Moscow on March 13, 1985, during the funeral of Soviet leader Konstantin Chernenko. Whereas Gandhi was still struggling to find equilibrium in his exacting job, the Pakistani president was sure-footed.

By holding a "party-less" general election to the National Assembly, Zia ul Haq had pacified his critics in the United States. And by a sleight of constitutional hand he had acquired the power to appoint one of the elected members of this Assembly as the prime minister. He picked Muhammad Khan Junejo for the post. US financial assistance, which had been running at $60 million annually since 1981, shot up to $300 million a year in 1985.[38] The sly Pakistani general went along with Gandhi's proposal to try to establish good relations between their countries.

Their bilateral summit took place in mid-December 1985. After his overnight stay at the sprawling Indian president's estate, Rashtrapati Bhavan, in Delhi, Zia ul Haq conferred with his host in the Yellow Room, used earlier by Lord Mountbatten for his high-level talks with the leaders of British India. Their one-on-one meeting lasted two hours.

"The most important aspect [of our meeting] is that we have decided not to attack each other's nuclear facilities," Zia ul Haq declared at the joint press conference. Gandhi described the agreement as "a first step in establishing confidence." India then had three nuclear reactors, five smaller research reactors, and three major nuclear power plants with two more under construction. Pakistan had a nuclear power plant, a research reactor, and one uranium enrichment facility. Neither nation had signed the 1968 NPT. Both claimed their nuclear programs were for peaceful purposes. Gandhi expressed his doubts about the peaceful nature of Pakistan's nuclear program diplomatically. "We have not reached an agreement on the nature of nuclear programs." he said.[39]

The two leaders instructed their defense secretaries to meet to discuss recent border clashes on the inhospitable twenty-thousand-foot-high Siachen Glacier, measuring one thousand square miles, in a region of Kashmir where the frontier had not been clearly defined. The glacier had been captured by the Indians in April 1984. In addition, they announced, the foreign secretaries of India and Pakistan would meet in the third week of January 1986 to reopen talks on Delhi's proposal for a peace and friendship treaty and Islamabad's offer of a no-war pact.

Zia ul Haq said the Indian premier had repeated his accusation that his county was sheltering, training, and arming Sikh terrorists from Indian

Punjab. "Pakistan is totally against all kinds of terrorism," he declared. In turn he referred to his complaint of cross-border subversion by India. "We have agreed that we will look into this problem in a more detailed manner," he said, without elaborating.[40]

Once the emergency was lifted in Punjab and state elections held in September 1985, the exclusively Sikh Akali Dal party emerged victorious. A modicum of normalcy returned to Punjab. But the Rajiv Gandhi government's failure to fulfill its promise to transfer Chandigarh—the joint capital of Punjab and Haryana—to Punjab by the end of January 1986 led to the revival of Sikh extremism.

INDIA'S OPERATION BRASSTACKS

On January 26, 1986, the militant Sikhs who had gathered in the Golden Temple backed the resolution proposed by the leaders of the All India Sikh Students Federation and the late Bhindranwale's Damdami Taksal, a fundamentalist sect within Sikhism, favoring the establishment of Khalistan. But it was only three months later that the troops of the border security force and the "Black Cat" commandos of the National Security Guards[41] were sent into the Golden Temple by the Akali Dal chief minister Surjit Singh Barnala to flush out the armed militants. Their Operation Black Thunder I resulted in the capture of three hundred armed militants and caches of firearms originating in Pakistan's tribal belt, where the production of small arms flourished.

While publicly complaining about Pakistan's role in igniting Sikh irredentism, Rajiv Gandhi instructed RAW to take countermeasures. RAW set up its Counter Intelligence Team-X and Counter Intelligence Team-J to target Pakistan and the Khalistani groups respectively. These clandestine units of RAW used cross-border traffickers to ship weapons and cash across the long, porous Indo-Pakistan frontier, just as the ISI had been doing in the opposite direction.

In Afghanistan, the CIA shipped 150 shoulder-held, US-made Stinger surface-to-air (SAM) missiles to the ISI for the Afghan mujahedin in the spring of 1996, followed by three hundred British-made Blowpipe missiles in the summer. The mujahedin started firing them extensively in the autumn, downing sixty Soviet helicopter gunships by year-end, thus finding them more effective than the Soviet-designed SAM-7s, clandestinely procured from Egypt and China by the CIA, which they had used before.[42] The blunting of the most effective tool in Moscow's armory to decimate the insurgents turned the war in favor of the mujahedin.

In January 1987 the Moscow-backed Afghan government declared a unilateral cease-fire for six months, which was to be followed by a unilateral withdrawal of six thousand Soviet troops in August.

Among other things, this further raised the spirits of Zia ul Haq, who was savoring good tidings from Washington. Disregarding the solid evidence that US intelligence services had provided President Reagan about the 1984 explosion of a Pakistani-produced nuclear bomb, he issued a certification of "no atom bomb made by Pakistan" in October 1986 to clear the way for generous economic and military aid. His decision put Rajiv Gandhi in a spin.

The next month Gandhi gave the go-ahead to his assertive chief of army staff (COAS) Lieutenant General Krishnaswamy Sundararajan, often called Sundarji (in command February 1985–May 1988), to stage the war game code-named Brasstacks he had conceived in July. It was designed to test the scholar-soldier's innovative concept of combining mechanization, mobility, and air support, using computers for operating tanks and running command centers, as well as electronic warfare equipment that had been installed in the past few years. Along with the chief of naval staff, Radhakrishna Hariram Tahiliani, he had submitted a draft of the nuclear weapons doctrine to the defense minister in 1985.

Operation Brasstacks involved mobilizing nearly three-quarters of the Indian army in Rajasthan bordering Sindh, where irredentist Sindhi nationalism was gaining momentum, and putting them on high alert. It was the largest war game ever seen on the subcontinent, involving 1,300 tanks, 1,000-plus armored vehicles, and 400,000 troops barely thirty miles from the Pakistani frontier. It was the model for a full-scale invasion and revived the long-held fear of Pakistani leaders of their country being annihilated by India.

The mobilization of the Indian military, involving nine army divisions and five independent armored brigades, in western Rajasthan gave "the assembled forces the capability to launch a piercing strike into Pakistan to cut off northern Pakistan from the southern part," according to Abdul Sattar, then Pakistan's foreign secretary. "Contrary to an existing understanding, the Indian army chief did not inform his Pakistani counterpart of the location, schedule and scale of the exercise. . . . Three wars, chronic tensions rooted in unresolved disputes, inadequate or unreliable intelligence, and deep-rooted mutual suspicions fuelled worst-case assumptions."[43]

As Pakistan's COAS, General Zia ul Haq extended his army's winter exercises in Punjab and then in December mobilized the Fifth Corps in Karachi as well as the Southern Air Command while deploying mechanized divisions and artillery along the Indian border. The Indians perceived his moves north of the Sutlej River and west of the Ravi River in Sialkot district as part of a pincer to squeeze Indian Punjab, where the Sikh insurgency had revived.

The crisis deepened in January 1987, with Delhi calling Pakistan's moves "provocative." In return Islamabad pointed its finger at the massive Indian military buildup in Rajasthan, not far from its frontier. The mood at the annual Army Day Parade in Delhi on January 15 was bullish. The tension between the two neighbors became explosive three days later. That night Pakistani foreign minister Zain Noorani conveyed President Zia ul Haq's personal message to the Indian ambassador, S. K. Singh: in the event of a violation of Pakistan's sovereignty and territorial integrity by India, Pakistan was "capable of inflicting unacceptable damage on it."[44] This, however, did not dissuade Sunderarajan from ordering the airlifting of troops into Indian Punjab.

In Islamabad top Pakistani officials met in an emergency session on January 20. The next day Prime Minister Junejo telephoned Rajiv Gandhi and proposed defusing the crisis. After consulting the four other members of the Cabinet Committee on Security, Gandhi agreed. As a result, the foreign secretaries of India and Pakistan met in Delhi on January 31. They signed an agreement on February 4 to deactivate forward air bases and then withdraw ground troops from frontline positions in stages.

ZIA UL HAQ'S HIGH-WIRE ACT

That there was a menace lurking behind Zia ul Haq's claim—"capable of inflicting unacceptable damage" on India—would become clear some weeks later. Known to only a select few, Zia ul Haq was engaged in a high-wire act. His overarching aim was to dissuade the Indians from starting a conventional war with a nuclear-armed Pakistan without providing evidence that contradicted President Reagan's assertion that Islamabad was not pursuing a nuclear weapons agenda.

At his behest, Qadeer Khan gave an interview to Indian journalist Kuldip Nayar on January 28, 1987, in Islamabad. "We have it [an atom bomb,] and we have enriched uranium," he said. "Weaponized the thing. Put it all together." Nayar said, "If you have tested, it would be a tremendous warning for India." Qadeer Khan stared at the interviewer coldly. "Mr Nayar, if you drive us to the wall, we will use the bomb," Qadeer Khan said. "You did it to us in East Bengal. We won't waste time with conventional weapons. We will come straight out with it."[45]

Nayar sent his scoop to the London-based weekly newspaper *Observer*, whose editor, Donald Trelford, withheld publication for four weeks while he tried to get the story authenticated by different sources. During the hiatus, the content of the interview leaked.

To lower tensions, Rajiv Gandhi hit on the idea of using the upcoming cricket test match between India and Pakistan in the Reliance World Cup Cricket tournament in Rajasthan's capital of Jaipur. He invited Zia ul Haq to witness the second day's play in the five-day match on February 22, 1987, as part of the "Cricket for Peace" diplomacy. Cricket is extremely popular in India and Pakistan, with test matches attracting up to three hundred million television viewers. On such occasions, streets and bazaars in both countries are deserted as most people sit glued to their TVs— or their radios before the arrival of television. Predictably, the Pakistani leader accepted Gandhi's invitation.

But, sitting next to his host, Gandhi, at the cricket ground, Zia ul Haq reportedly said, "If your forces cross our border by an inch, we are going to annihilate your cities," indicating that if necessary, his military would not hesitate to use atom bombs first to defend Pakistan.[46] In a pro forma statement, Pakistan denied the statement attributed to its president.

After a long wait, on March 1, 1987, the *Observer* splashed the story: "Pakistan Has the A-Bomb." It quoted Khan: "What the CIA has been saying about the atom bomb is correct. They told us Pakistan could never produce the bomb and they doubted my capabilities, but they now know we have it."[47]

The story, published around the globe, embarrassed Zia ul Haq. He launched a vigorous damage limitation effort. Qadeer Khan claimed he had been tricked by Nayar, who had quoted him out of context. In the Pakistani media, Nayar was pilloried as "a scummy RAW agent." Zia ul Haq asserted that "Pakistan has neither the desire, nor the intention, nor the capacity to develop a nuclear weapon."[48] Following the *Observer* revelation, the Indian government stated that the disclosure was "forcing us to review our option." It was a meaningless statement, as India had been manufacturing atom bombs since 1980.

Despite the controversy and the news headlines, the public diplomacy of mending fences by the protagonists remained on track. On March 2 the two foreign secretaries, meeting in Islamabad, agreed to a phased troop withdrawal to peacetime positions. Two days later the Indian defense ministry arranged a guided tour of the front line in Rajasthan for local and foreign journalists as well as military attachés, including the one from Pakistan. "This is not a third-world army," a Western diplomat told the *New York Times* correspondent Steven R. Weisman. "This is a modern army, fully competent for any mission, easily as good as the Chinese, the Koreans or the French." India's superiority in conventional warfare "might be motivating Pakistan to turn to nuclear weapons as a deterrent," according to some analysts.[49] This was an understatement.

In reality, a bomb built by Pakistanis had been tested in China in early 1984, and three years later Pakistan was all geared up to assemble one at home. From March 1988 it became commonplace in the Indian media to say that the Pakistanis were "within a turn of a screwdriver" of assembling an atom bomb.

PROXY WARS ON TRACK

While the overtly conducted war games and diplomacy ended satisfactorily, the proxy war by India and Pakistan through RAW and the ISI intensified in 1987. In Afghanistan KHAD and the KGB increased their training and arming of the Baluchi nationalists for subversive activities in Baluchistan. The separatists' aim of establishing an independent Baluchistan would have meant reducing Pakistan by a hefty 43 percent and was therefore resisted bitterly by the government in Islamabad. As part of the KHAD-RAW-KGB triad, RAW's Counter Intelligence Team-X became an active participant in stoking subversion in Pakistan. It coordinated its activities with KHAD. The result was a low-level but steady campaign of bombings in Karachi, Lahore, and Multan. According to the US State Department, more than half of the 835 terrorist incidents worldwide in 1987 were in Pakistan.[50]

Indian Punjab remained on the boil. In Amritsar, militants had started creeping into the Golden Temple from the summer of 1986. Their takeover was complete in June 1987, when Darshan Singh Ragi, the Sikhs' supreme leader opposed to violence, was forced to flee the shrine because of serious threats to his life. This was a signal for the Delhi government to impose central rule in Punjab. (It would continue until February 1992.)

To ensure that the proxy war did not escalate to the extent that it made hot war inevitable, Zia ul Haq conceived the idea of a clandestine meeting between the heads of the ISI and RAW. But he needed an obliging but influential intermediary with extraordinary finesse to achieve this aim. During his military assignment in Jordan, he had cultivated a friendship with Crown Prince Hassan bin Talal, whose Cambridge-educated, Pakistani wife, Sarvath Ikramullah, was born in Kolkata and was a niece of Hussein Shaheed Suhrawardy, the former Pakistani premier. Hassan bin Talal agreed to act as go-between. He succeeded in contacting Rajiv Gandhi's office.

With the authorization of their respective leaders, Lieutenant General Hamid Gul, director general of the ISI (in office March 1987–October 1989), and RAW chief A. K. Verma met in Amman to discuss their mutual problems. In exchange for the phased handing over of the nearly three thousand militant Sikhs who had crossed into Pakistan, Verma promised to de-escalate the bombing campaign in Pakistani cities in stages.[51] They met again in the Swiss town of Interlaken, this time focusing on the India-occupied Siachen Glacier in Kashmir, but made no progress.

In Indian Punjab, operating from the safety of the Golden Temple, the armed militants of the Bhindranwale Tiger Force and the Khalistan Commando Force of the Pakistan-based Paramjit Singh Panjwar[52] would go out to murder prominent Punjabi politicians, police, and army officers, as well as suspected informers and innocent Hindus. Equally, the security forces carried out extrajudicial killings, attributing them to fake "encounters." The photographs of these Sikh "martyrs" adorned the walls of many buildings in the Golden Temple complex.[53]

Militant Sikhs operated in an environment in which Sikh and Hindu communities were alienated. With the terrorists increasingly carrying deadly AK-47 assault rifles, smuggled from Pakistan from May 1987 onward, armed policemen, lacking this weapon, found themselves at a crippling disadvantage. Since a section of Sikh police officers sympathized with the Khalistan cause, there were instances when underarmed Sikh policemen fled when encountering extremists. The morale of the law enforcement agencies plummeted.[54]

Terrorism by Sikh militants intensified, claiming 173 victims, many of them Sikhs suspected as police informers, in January 1988, including 30 extremists. "Today, young Sikh militants with AK-47 assault rifles, shotguns and handguns of all kinds roam the [Golden Temple] complex at will, often carrying their weapons under blankets and robes," reported Marc Kaufman of the *Philadelphia Inquirer* in February 1988. "Scores of militants—many of whom proudly say that large rewards have been offered for their capture—now live in small rooms that ring the Holy Pool, the most sacred area of the complex."⁵⁵

In a nine-day operation in May 1988, code-named Black Thunder II, India's security forces, commanded by Punjab's director general of police, imposed a strict blockade of the Golden Temple complex and then moved in with blazing guns. In the resulting firefight forty-one militants were killed. Nearly two hundred Sikh extremists surrendered.

The authorities claimed that interrogations of arrested militants revealed that many of them had been trained in camps inside Pakistan and that sophisticated firearms and ammunition had been smuggled across the Pakistani border. "Pakistan is perhaps the largest supporter of terrorism on the globe," said Rajiv Gandhi at a press conference in New York after addressing the special UN session on disarmament on June 13, 1988. "We have given [the Pakistanis] a detailed list of training camps, of people who are carrying out the training, the type of training that has been carried out in the camps," he added, demanding that Islamabad stop the aid. "We have given them maps of where the camps are located."⁵⁶

As before, Zia ul Haq denied the charge and condemned terrorism. He was in an upbeat mood. Good tidings reached him from Afghanistan. Following the Soviet leader Mikhail Gorbachev's agreement with the UN special envoy in February 1988, the first phase of Soviet pullout from Afghanistan was completed in April. Also, his strategy of weakening Delhi's grip over Kashmir in stages, conceived in early 1987 and conveyed to the leaders of the Jammu and Kashmir JeI, had gained traction. What had so far been viewed by India and Pakistan as a territorial dispute was now placed into a wider ideological context of Islamism by Zia ul Haq.

Ironically, some months later, Zia ul Haq would become a victim of terrorism in Pakistan.

A CRATE OF EXPLODING MANGOES

On August 17, 1988, Pak-One, a C-130 Hercules turbo-prop transport plane, equipped with a sealed, air-conditioned capsule and carrying a four-man crew and twenty-seven passengers, crashed at 3:52 PM, eighteen miles from the Bahawalpur airport. Besides Zia ul Haq, the dead included Pakistan's chair of the Joint Chiefs of Staff, General Abdur Rahman Khan; US ambassador Arnold Raphel, head of the US military aid mission to Pakistan; General Herbert M. Wassom; and a dozen other Pakistani generals. After lurching up and down in the sky, Pak-One plunged into the soil with such force that its propellers churned the ground for several feet. It then exploded, the crash igniting twenty thousand pounds of fuel, which burned for hours. The plane was on its return journey to Islamabad after top Pakistani and American officials had finished witnessing the performance of the newly supplied US M1 Abrams tank at the firing range of Tamewali, which was located several miles from the Bahawalpur airport.

Pak-One was seen off by Lieutenant General Mirza Aslam Beg, the vice COAS, at the Bahawalpur airport. He boarded a smaller turbojet to take him to the Dhamial Army Aviation Airbase in Rawalpindi. On his way to his destination, his pilot overheard a helicopter pilot telling the control tower about the crash. He diverted his turbojet to the site, saw the blazing wreckage on the ground, and resumed his journey. After arriving at the Dhamial Airbase, General Beg rushed to the general headquarters of the army and assumed the rank of the COAS.

On hearing the news, Ghulam Ishaq Khan, chair of the Senate since 1985 and a confidante of Zia ul Haq, drove to army headquarters, well aware that a provision in the constitution entitled him to become the acting president in case of a power vacuum. Once he had bonded with General Beg, he assumed the presidency. That evening, as army units moved swiftly to cordon off official residences, government buildings, television stations, and other strategic locations in Islamabad, Ishaq Khan addressed the nation on television. He declared ten days of official mourning.

In Delhi the government announced three days of mourning. Indian president Ramaswamy Venkataraman attended Zia ul Haq's funeral on August 19. And Rajiv Gandhi cancelled the celebration of his birthday on the twentieth.

Three major published documents have dealt with the possible perpetrator of this terrorist act. The official board of inquiry, assisted by six US Air Force experts, submitted its report in November 1988. Edward Jay Epstein, an American journalist, investigated the case and published his account in the September 1989 edition of *Vanity Fair*.

Finally, the findings of Barbara Crossette, former South Asia correspondent of the *New York Times*, appeared in the fall 2005 issue of the

World Policy Journal. Her star interviewee was Bahawalpur-based General Mahmud Ali Durrani, who was in charge of the tank field tests at the testing site of Tamewali. (The US-made M1 tank designed for desert warfare failed the field trial chiefly because its filters got choked by the local dust, which was a mixture of sand and clay, according to Durrani.) After arriving in Pak-One at the Bahawalpur air port, Zia ul Haq had flown to Tamewali and conferred with Durrani, who presented Zia ul Haq with two crates of mangoes, a local specialty. The president took the crates in his helicopter on his return flight to the Bahawalpur airport to be transferred to Pak-One. These mangoes were checked, one by one, by security, according to Durrani. "I believe some mangoes were also loaded at Bahawalpur which were presented [to Zia ul Haq] by the local military and civilian leadership," he told Crossette. He had no control over those mangoes or other baggage put on the plane.[57]

Pakistan's board of inquiry ruled out mechanical failure mentioned by Lockheed, the manufacturer of the plane. It concluded that "the accident was most probably caused through the perpetuation of a criminal act or sabotage." It added that the explosives found in the wreckage and "the use of ultra-sophisticated techniques" indicated "involvement of a specialist organization well versed with carrying out such tasks and possessing the means and abilities for its execution."[58]

Epstein's inquiry established that President Zia ul Haq's security staff had gone through the standard procedure for his safety. Pak-One had done the 310-mile flight to and from Bahawalpur the day before. The pilot, Wing Commander Mashood Hassan, had been chosen by Zia ul Haq himself and cleared by air force intelligence. A Cessna security plane did the final check of the area and gave the all clear before Pak-One was allowed to take off. Once the wreckage was sifted and samples of soil taken, the recovered parts of the victims' bodies were sent in body bags to the Bahawalpur Military Hospital on the night of August 17 and stored there for autopsies by a team of Pakistani and American pathologists.

The following afternoon, however, the hospital authorities were ordered to return the bags to the coffins for immediate burial. The key evidence of what happened, particularly to the pilot and copilot, thus got buried.[59] Durrani explained to Crossette that all the victims were reduced to bits of charred flesh and that they could be identified only by clothing or stray pieces of identification. Zia ul Haq was nothing more than his jawbone. The Pakistani authorities lacked the technical expertise to deal with that sort of contingency.[60]

An analysis of the chemicals in the wreckage by the laboratory of the Bureau of Alcohol, Firearms and Tobacco in Washington found traces of pentaerythritol tertranitrate (PNET), a high explosive used by saboteurs as a detonator, and antimony sulfide used in fuses to set off a device. By using these chemicals, Epstein explained, "Pakistan ordinance experts reconstructed a low-level explosive detonator which could have been used to burst a flask the size of a soda can which probably contained an odorless poison gas [most likely VX] that incapacitated the pilots."[61]

Murtaza Bhutto, the elder son of Zulfikar who had led the Al Zulfikar group in Kabul but later moved to Damascus, had the self-confessed motivation. He had admitted that the guerilla group had tried to assassinate Zia ul Haq on five previous occasions. Once in 1982 a missile it fired had narrowly missed hitting Pak-One.[62]

The Al Zulfikar group, Epstein claims, took credit for the Pak-One explosion in a call to the BBC, but the Damascus-based Murtaza retrieved it once it became public that the US ambassador had been killed.[63] Zia ul Haq's son Ijaz ul Haq told Crossette in mid-1989 that he was "101 percent sure" that Murtaza Bhutto was involved.[64] But he failed to provide any evidence. His unsubstantiated claim ran counter to what Fatima Bhutto, daughter of Murtaza, had to say in her memoir. "Officially, Al Zulfikar, inactive in the years since [Murtaza's] brother Shahnawaz's murder [in 1985], was disbanded," she noted. "I know my father would have loved knowing that AZO [Al Zulfikar Organization] was among the many groups whose names popped up in regard to General Zia's plane crash, but their symbolic resistance to the dictator's tyranny had ended."[65]

The KGB working with KHAD had the reach and the expertise. The State Department blamed KHAD for many terrorist attacks in Pakistani cities in 1987 and 1988. In a few cases, Radio Kabul even announced the bombings before they occurred.[66]

Israel's Mossad too was highly motivated. Israel had repeated its earlier offer of a joint attack on the Kahuta nuclear facility to Rajiv Gandhi in 1987. He had declined it. Mossad had bombed, blackmailed, and threatened many European suppliers to the Kahuta Research Laboratory because Zia ul Haq had promised to share nuclear bomb technology with other Muslim nations. Among those who suspected the involvement of Mossad was Washington's ambassador to India, John Gunther Dean. Later, in his interview with Crossette, he went on to qualify his statement by saying Israel could have been part of a multinational plot involving India and the Soviet KGB.[67]

RAW's involvement in the crash was less likely, since Indian leaders were unsure who would succeed Zia ul Haq. The accusing finger at the CIA seemed unconvincing, since the US ambassador was scheduled to accompany the Pakistani president. And that schedule, finalized on August 13, according to Durrani,[68] was known to the CIA.

But none of the above would have had the means to abort the chances of a postmortem of the pilots. "Any foreign intelligence service or even Murtaza [Bhutto] might have had the motive and even the means to bring down Pak-One but they would not have had the ability to stop planned autopsies at a military hospital in Pakistan, stifle interrogations or, for that matter, keep the FBI out of the picture," concluded Epstein. "Nor would they have much of a reason for making the whole thing seem like an accident rather than an assassination. Only elements inside Pakistan would have an obvious motive for making the death of Zia, Rahman and 28 others look like something more legitimate than a coup d'état."[69]

As for the means deployed, the most plausible explanation seems to be that the mango crate loaded directly at the Bahawalpur airport, which by design or accident went unchecked, contained a canister of nerve gas with a timer, which, when dispersed by the plane's air-conditioning system, killed both pilots, sending the plane out of control.

At least that possibility inspired Mohammed Hanif, a London-based journalist and a former Pakistan Air Force pilot, to title his novel on the subject as *A Case of Exploding Mangoes*, published two decades after the event. His satirical work of imagination attacked militarism, false piety, and overregulation of personal life—as epitomized by Zia ul Haq.[70]

13

Rajiv-Benazir Rapport—Cut Short

On hearing of the air crash near Bahawalpur, Benazir Bhutto privately rejoiced at Muhammad Zia ul Haq's violent death as just retribution for having her father, Zulfikar Ali Bhutto, hanged on trumped-up charges. In public, though, she described the incendiary event as an "act of divine intervention." Pressured by the Ronald Reagan administration, Zia ul Haq had allowed her to return to Pakistan in 1986 from her self-exile in London.

Born into the household of a super-rich feudal lord in Larkana, Sindh, Benazir was educated at the Convent of Jesus and Mary in Murree and Karachi, and then, at age sixteen, sent to study politics at Radcliffe College. In the absence of a chauffeur-driven car at home, she had to walk to her classes for the first time in her life. By the time she traveled to Shimla along with her president father, "Pinky"—as she was nicknamed—was a Westernized teenager who dressed in clothes from Saks Fifth Avenue and led the life of a doted-on daughter of an affluent foreign leader.

Following her graduation from Harvard in 1973, she enrolled at Oxford University for further studies. She drove around in a yellow two-seater MG. Her famed parties were liberally lubricated with alcohol, and she loved to dance. "Her Oxford lifestyle was almost a parody of the rich Islamic girl released from the constraints of a rigid Muslim home," recalled a male contemporary of hers in Oxford. "When she stood for the presidency of the Oxford Union, she skillfully used the rumors about her un-Islamic activities. . . . At the same time she rallied the feminists with the suggestion that she would be held back by the male chauvinists and reactionaries—even though they were the kind of men with whom she enjoyed her leisure time."[1] Endowed with fair skin and high cheekbones in an oval face, the svelte Bhutto had an appealing persona. Yet at her first attempt at the Union presidency she ended up in third place. But after graduating in 1976 with a second in politics, philosophy, and economics, she stood again while pursuing studies in international law and diplomacy at St. Catharine's College, aiming to join Pakistan's diplomatic service. She won, becoming the first Asian woman to hold the presidency in the Union's history.

Soon after her return home in 1977, her prime minster father was removed from office in a military coup. A few months after his hanging in April 1979, she and her mother, Nusrat Begum, then chair of the Pakistan People's Party (PPP), were charged with offenses under martial law. She spent much of the next five years in solitary confinement in dingy prison cells or under house arrest—with a brief respite in 1982 to undergo an ear operation in London. She went into self-exile in January 1984, taking up residence in a London apartment.

On her return to Lahore on April 10, 1986, she was greeted by two million people. She married Asif Ali Zardari in December 1987, thus overcoming the popular prejudice against older, unmarried women in Pakistan.

Once Acting President Ghulam Ishaq Khan had announced the election for the National Assembly on November 16, she and Nusrat Begum Bhutto started campaigning furiously for the PPP.

On the opposite side, the triad of Ishaq Khan, Chief of Army Staff (COAS) General Mirza Aslam Beg, and the Islamist chief of the Inter-Services Intelligence (ISI), Lieutenant General Hamid Gul, resolved to stop the PPP bandwagon. They sponsored the forming of a coalition of conservative and Islamist parties as the Islami Jamhoori Ittihad (Urdu: Islamic Democratic Alliance; IJI), headed by Muhammad Nawaz Sharif. Gul coached IJI candidates to stress that Western-educated Benazir Bhutto, being a close friend of America, was a security risk for Pakistan's nuclear program. In its leaflets IJI questioned if a woman could become the prime minister of an Islamic state. Posters titled "Villains in Bangles" showed faces of Benazir and Nusrat superimposed on the photos of models riding cycles in swimsuits. The photo of Nusrat Bhutto dancing with President Gerald Ford during the Bhuttos' visit to Washington in 1975, discovered by Brigadier Imtiaz Ahmed of the ISI, was exploited to the hilt.

FROM PARTY GIRL TO PRIME MINISTER

Yet of the 207 contested seats in the National Assembly on November 16, the PPP scored 94, far ahead of the IJI's 56. Benazir Bhutto won because of being the daughter of the PPP founder, Zulfikar Ali, who was accorded the captivating honorific of Shaheed (Urdu: Martyr), and because the bulk of Pakistanis, who followed the tolerant Sufi version of Islam, yearned to be freed from the puritanical Islamic rigidity imposed on them by dictator Muhammad Zia ul Haq.

Despite emerging as the leader of the largest group in the National Assembly, it was not until December 1 that Ishaq Khan called on her to form the government. He did so only after he had her accept his conditions conveyed to her by an intermediary: stay away from the nuclear issue; retain Zia ul Haq's foreign minister, Shahzada Yaqub Khan; and respect the army.

Benazir Bhutto led a coalition government that included the recently formed Muhajir Qaumi Mahaz (Urdu: Migrant National Movement; MQM), a party of Urdu-speaking Muslim immigrants from India. At the age of thirty-five, she became the first executive prime minister of a Muslim country. She also headed the defense and finance ministries.

Within a month of Bhutto assuming office, Rajiv Gandhi, accompanied by Sonia and their two children, arrived in Islamabad to attend the summit of the South Asian Association for Regional Cooperation (SAARC) from December 29 to 31. As SAARC hostess Bhutto invited Rajiv and Sonia Gandhi to dinner, attended by Asif Ali Zardari and Nusrat Begum.

Since all the diners were nonvegetarian, the dishes they consumed did not deviate from the regular fare at the Pakistani couple's dinner table. They shared the cuisine of the northern Indian subcontinent. Equally, the wardrobes of Benazir and Sonia had much in common, with Benazir having more pairs of *salwar* kameez than saris and blouses, and Sonia the other way around. The division of the subcontinent's northern zone had left intact the common cuisine, dress, and language.

Recalling the dinner, Rajiv later told his close aides that while Benazir seemed nervous about the possibility of the ISI having bugged the dining room, Zardari was uninhibited in his conversation.[2] Zardari would have been even more relaxed if Rajiv had contrived to move the conversation to Bollywood movies, telling him and Benazir about the up-and-coming

Bollywood actors Aamir Khan, Salman Khan, and Shah Rukh Khan[3]—all born in 1965, the year of the Second Indo-Pakistan War. After all, it was movies and a movie theater that had brought Benazir and Asif Ali together. The Bambino Cinema in Karachi, owned by Asif Ali's father, Hakim Ali, was remarkable on two counts. Its flashing blue neon sign with an image of a woman dancer with gyrating hips glowed all night. Its staple fare was foreign films, patronized among others by Benazir, an aficionado of foreign movies. And it was at this theater that Asif Ali Zardari had first set his eyes on his future wife.

In terms of social hierarchy, Hakim Ali Zardari, who besides the cinema and the floors above it owned a modest house in rural Sindh, was way below the celebrated Bhutto family. But in a society in which brides were always five to ten years younger than grooms, Asif Ali opted to marry a woman two years his senior in order to boost his social status.

During their one-on-one meeting with Rajiv the next day, Benazir Bhutto promised to choke off Pakistan's aid to Sikh separatists. In a 2007 interview, she said, "Does anyone remember that it was I who kept my promise to Prime Minister Rajiv Gandhi when we met and he appealed to me for help in tackling the Sikhs? Has India forgotten December 1988? Have they forgotten the results of that meeting and how I helped curb the Sikh militancy?" In return, Rajiv Gandhi promised to withdraw Indian troops from the disputed Siachen Glacier, a commitment he later moved forward to a period after the 1989 general election, which he lost.[4] Benazir Bhutto reportedly handed over a dossier of names containing the covert identities of Pakistan's agents among radical Sikhs who were masterminding the Sikh insurgency. That aided RAW enormously in tracking down the Sikh terrorists and destroying their network—a process that lasted nearly five years.

On December 31, 1988, Bhutto and Gandhi formalized the informal understanding between Zia ul Haq and Gandhi from three years earlier about nuclear sites, and signed the "Agreement on Prohibition of Attack Against Nuclear Installations and Facilities." It went into effect on January 27, 1991, and has held ever since.

Another accord between the two neighbors that has remained in force since 1960 is the World Bank–brokered Indus Waters Treaty (see Chapter 7, p. 155). The treaty is monitored by the Permanent Indus Commission, with a commissioner appointed by each country. Despite several crises and wars, the two sides continued to exchange pertinent data and maintain a cooperative spirit—elements starkly missing from their stances on Kashmir.

RAJIV-BENAZIR RAPPORT FADES

The Gandhis and Bhutto-Zardari met again in Paris on the bicentenary of the French Revolution on July 14, 1989. Here British prime minister Margaret Thatcher subconsciously fell into the role of a nanny, chaperoning her two subcontinental wards, who seemed to get along famously.

On his return journey Rajiv Gandhi stopped in Moscow for a meeting with Soviet leader Mikhail Gorbachev and then flew to Islamabad to be received as a state guest on July 16 at the Chaklala airport. "Bedecked like a bride, the Chaklala overflows with people," reported Madhu Jain in *India Today* magazine. "The Gandhis greet Benazir and husband Zardari like long lost friends—though it's not been quite 24 hours since they last met in Paris." At the state banquet, Rajiv Gandhi said, "When an Indian and a Pakistani meet as human beings in a human encounter there is an instant mutual recognition, an embrace that transcends the passing passions of politics. . . . Why must we go round to meet each other? Why can't we meet in each other's hearths and homes?"[5]

Bhutto had broached the subject of working out a trade agreement. But in their joint communiqué issued on July 17 she and Gandhi merely expressed their desire to work toward a comprehensive settlement to reduce the chances of conflict and the use of force. It turned out to be a pro forma statement that changed little on the ground.

By early 1989 the image of Rajiv Gandhi as Mr. Clean was tarnished because of the scandal surrounding his government's $1.3 billion deal for 410 field howitzers from the Swedish company A B Bofors in March 1986. He did what US Republican president Richard Nixon had done when the illegal break-in of the Democratic Party offices in Washington's Watergate apartments came to light in 1974: devise an elaborate cover-up plan to sustain the myth that the Bofors payments were not commissions paid to acquire the much-coveted contract. His ploy failed. In October, a month before the general election, the prestigious *Hindu* published the facsimile of the secret part of the report by the Swedish National Audit Bureau, which concluded that the Bofors payments were "entirely proven commission payments to [the receiving] companies' accounts in Switzerland in relation to the Bofors FH-77 deal."[6] That was the smoking gun that destroyed Gandhi's credibility and led to the electoral defeat of the Congress Party by the National Front, an unwieldy alliance of opposition parties. One of these was led by Vishwanath Pratap Singh, who became prime minister.

In Pakistan Benazir Bhutto narrowly survived a no-confidence motion in the National Assembly in October 1989. She had proved to be an abysmal administrator. She faced charges of corruption leveled not just at her cabinet colleagues generally but specifically at Asif Ali Zardari, appointed minister for investments. He soon earned the nickname of "Mr. 10 Percent"—that being the percentage he allegedly charged for government contracts, which was paid to his father.

KASHMIR OVERSHADOWS ALL

Islamabad's relations with Delhi turned frosty because of events in Indian Kashmir. By placing the Kashmir issue into a wider ideological context of Islamism, Zia ul Haq had provided an opportunity for non-state jihadist organizations to wade into the dispute. Among others the Lashkar-e Taiba (Urdu: Army of the Righteous; LeT), the armed wing of the charity organization of the Jamaat-e Islami (Urdu: Islamic Society; JeI), supported by the ISI, became an active player in the ongoing Kashmir drama. The conditions seemed ripe for it in Delhi-controlled Kashmir. On India's Republic Day, January 26, 1989, Kashmiris went on a protest strike. During that year, one third of all working days were lost because of strikes. This warmed the cockles of Pakistani leaders' hearts. For many years their efforts to foment strikes in Indian Kashmir had failed. Now they loudly welcomed the Kashmiris' nonviolent protest, which they had mounted on their own.

Between early 1988 and late 1989 many young Kashmiri Muslims crossed over to Pakistan-held Kashmir to receive military training. It was provided by the armed wing of the Jammu and Kashmir JeI, popularly known as Hizb ul Mujahideen (Arabic: Party of Mujahedin), as well as the LeT—and other organizations associated with the ISI. These included the secular, nationalist Jammu and Kashmir Liberation Front. On their return home with arms and ammunition, they trained others clandestinely.

Kashmiri militants went on the offensive. The number of bomb blasts and assassinations increased in 1989. So too did the intimidation of pro-India National Conference activists, with the aim of forcing them into retirement and bringing about the collapse of the political process. In January 1990, V. P. Singh's administration appointed Jagmohan as governor of Kashmir and imposed direct rule, which would continue until

October 1996—a record. Given Jagmohan's anti-Muslim bias, Delhi made a colossal mistake. Kashmiri Muslims' alienation from India widened and deepened.

Benazir Bhutto's government protested volubly but in vain. Her domestic problems were multiplying, and she proved unequal to the daunting task. On August 6, 1990, President Ishaq Khan dismissed her cabinet on account of corruption, incompetence, and failure to maintain law and order in Sindh, as well as the use of official machinery to promote partisan interests. He dissolved the National Assembly and the Provincial Assemblies in Sindh and North-West Frontier Province (NWFP), and declared an emergency, citing external aggression and internal disturbance. Bhutto denounced his action as "illegal and unconstitutional"—to no effect.

Gandhi and Bhutto, the two rising stars in the subcontinent, met the same fate. But the manner of their fall illustrated a sharp contrast in the political cultures of the neighboring countries. In India it was voters who refused to give Gandhi a fresh mandate once irrefutable evidence of his involvement in the Bofors graft was established by the prestigious daily the *Hindu*.[7] In Pakistan it was the decision of the president, who, acting at the behest of top military leaders, sealed Bhutto's fate without providing evidence of the charges of misrule he laid against her. The president had been given this power by the eighth amendment to the constitution, passed by the bicameral parliament in November 1985. This provision had turned Pakistan's parliamentary system into a semipresidential one, thereby making Pakistan stand apart from India in political administration.

In the National Assembly election that followed in October 1990, the ISI, headed by Lieutenant General Asad Durrani, intervened directly. It once more brought together nine chiefly right-wing parties, led by Nawaz Sharif's Pakistan Muslim League (PML-N), under the banner of the IJI. It also channeled funds to Nawaz Sharif through Mehran Bank to finance the IJI's election campaign, a clandestine action that would come to light twelve years later in a case filed by Asghar Khan, a former air marshal of Pakistan, in the Supreme Court.[8] The IJI and its ally, the MQM, trounced the PPP-led People's Democratic Alliance, whose strength plunged to 44 versus the IJI's 106 and the MQM's 15. Nawaz Sharif, a Lahore-based industrialist, became the country's thirteenth prime minister.

A rotund, balding man with a pudgy face, the forty-one-year-old Nawaz Sharif was a protégé of Zia ul Haq. After the 1985 nonparty elections, urged by Washington but boycotted by the PPP, Zia ul Haq appointed him finance minister of Punjab and then promoted him to chief minister. Now, on becoming the prime minister, Nawaz Sharif, who had made liberating Kashmir an important and emotional theme in the election campaign, backed his mentor's strategy of subversion in Indian Kashmir.

Pakistan's formal contacts with India at the highest level, however, continued. Meeting on the margins of the SAARC summit in Male, the capital of the Maldives, in November 1990, Sharif and Indian prime minister Chandra Shekhar decided to set up an additional hotline between them, the earlier one dating back to 1972. They also agreed to resume foreign-secretary-level talks between their republics.

Around that time Indian intelligence sources claimed that some ten thousand Kashmiri Muslims had gone to Pakistan for arms training and that there were forty-six safe houses in Pakistan-held Kashmir, where militants were trained how to handle weapons and explosives. In its 1991 report on global terrorism, the US State Department referred to credible reports of Islamabad's support for Kashmiri militant groups, involving military training and supplies of arms and ammunition. By then the ISI was busily aiding Pakistani and other foreign militants, including veterans of the anti-Moscow jihad in Afghanistan, to infiltrate Indian Kashmir.

This raised the prospect of Washington naming Pakistan as a state that sponsors terrorism. US law mandated strict sanctions on such a country, including restrictions on bilateral commerce and vetoing of financial assistance by the International Monetary Fund and the World Bank. In his letter to Sharif in May 1992 American secretary of state James Baker referred to the reliable information he had received regarding the ISI and others continuing to provide material aid to terrorist groups, added that "US law requires that an onerous package of sanctions apply to those states found to be supporting acts of international terrorism."[9]

After discussing this missive with his top officials, Sharif decided to channel aid to Kashmiri separatists exclusively through "private channels" consisting of such organizations as JeI and its subsidiary, LeT. In his response to Baker, he offered the assurance that any clandestine assistance by his government to anti-India militants would cease forthwith.[10] Such duplicity would become the norm in Islamabad's relations with Washington in the coming decades.

DEMOLITION OF A HISTORIC MOSQUE IN INDIA

On May 21, 1991, during the election campaign for the lower house of Parliament, Rajiv Gandhi's motorcade headed to a rally for a local party candidate, Maradadam Chandrashekhar, in Sriperumbudur, a town twenty-five miles southwest of Chennai. Carnival lights twinkled around the open-air gathering of several thousand people, mostly men, in a meadow. Men were dressed in sarongs and sport shirts, and women in cheap, colorful saris. Security was nonexistent, with knots of people milling around the platform, albeit calmly, even though Rajiv Gandhi was late by two hours that evening.

Gandhi, who had been talking to two foreign correspondents sitting in the back of his modest India-made Ambassador car during his ride, sought quick advice from Chandrashekhar about the subject he should cover in his speech. "Village development" was her crisp reply. Gandhi's car stopped twenty-five yards from the dais. He got out, followed by the other occupants of his car. As he walked toward the short stairs to the platform, a young woman—later identified as Thenmozhi Rajaratnam, a Sri Lankan Tamil militant—garlanded him. She then stooped to touch his feet as a sign of respect and pressed the button of her suicide belt containing RDX explosive and thousands of tiny steel balls.

"As Mrs Gopal [of the *Gulf News*, Dubai] and I followed [Gandhi] there was a sudden burst of what sounded like firecrackers and then a large boom, an explosion and a cloud of smoke that scattered people all around," reported Barbara Crossette in the *New York Times*. "It was over in a matter of seconds."[11] It was 10:10 PM. Gandhi was dead, and so were fourteen others. All that survived of his body were his head and his feet, shod in expensive running shoes. Rajaratnam was part of a conspiracy.[12]

Gandhi had earned fanatical hatred of the Liberation Tigers of Tamil Eelam (LTTE) by dispatching an Indian peacekeeping force into Sri Lanka in 1987 to assist the Colombo government in squashing LTTE insurgents fighting for an independent Tamil state. His mother, Indira Gandhi, lost her life battling Sikh irredentists at home, while he ended up sacrificing his own in the cause of averting the partition of India's small neighbor in the Arabian Sea. His scant remains were cremated on the banks of the Jamuna (aka Yamuna) River in Delhi.

The privilege of leading the Congress Party fell on P. V. Narasimha Rao, a seventy-year-old, lackluster, diminutive lawyer and a party veteran from the southern state of Andhra Pradesh. His party's 244 seats were

18 short of bare majority. This compelled him to rope in small groups to be able to govern. He succeeded.

With the disintegration of the Soviet Union in December 1991, the United States emerged triumphant in the Cold War. The world became unipolar, with America as the sole superpower. With the counterpull of the Kremlin gone, the friendship between Delhi and Washington became warmer, much to the discomfort of Islamabad.

Continuing the past practice of using regional and international gatherings to hold bilateral talks with the Pakistani leader, Narasimha Rao had three meetings with Nawaz Sharif between October 1991 and September 1992. During that period the 120-strong opposition Hindu nationalist Bharatiya Janata Party (Hindi: Indian People's Party; BJP) took advantage of the weakness of Narasimha Rao's government.

The BJP had raised its popularity substantially by recycling the narrative of the marauding Muslim tribes of the past butchering native Hindus of the Indian subcontinent. It then targeted the mosque built by Emperor Babur in 1527 in the northern town of Ayodhya, claiming that it stood at the site of an ancient temple built at the birthplace of Lord Rama. The fact that there was no evidence about the existence of King Rama of Ayodhya in recorded history did not matter a jot to the BJP leadership.

It launched its campaign just as the armed insurgency by separatist Muslims in Kashmir, aided by foreign jihadists, was intensifying. The jihadists equated assisting Kashmiri Muslims to achieve self-determination by expelling Indian troops from their state with their earlier, successful guerrilla actions against Soviet forces in Afghanistan. The BJP's campaign took off. In other words, insurgency in Kashmir helped spark Hindu revivalism.

Before obtaining official permission to hold a rally in front of the Babri Mosque on December 6, 1992, the nationalist Hindu organizers assured the Supreme Court that the mosque would not be touched. Yet on that day, nearly two hundred thousand Hindu militants, working in cahoots with BJP leaders, stormed the barricades erected around the mosque. Armed with pickaxes, ropes, and sledgehammers, some four thousand demonstrators demolished the historic structure within four hours. The Narasimha Rao government's later decision to block off the site and heavily increase security around it was a classic example of shutting the stable door after the horse had bolted. Indian Muslims felt stunned and enraged in equal measure. When they protested in the streets in various cities of India, they were attacked by militant Hindus. The subsequent rioting left more than two thousand people, mostly Muslims, dead.

Pakistan promised to appeal to the United Nations to pressure India to protect the rights of Muslims. Sharif's call for a nationwide strike on December 8 was observed universally. Opposition leader Benazir Bhutto outdid him by blaming the tragedy on his flawed foreign policy, claiming that such an event would not have occurred if she had been in power.[13] She had realized that there was political capital to be made by adopting a hard line toward India.

For three days Muslim mobs in Pakistan went on a rampage, shouting "Death to Hinduism" and "Crush India." In Karachi they attacked five Hindu temples and hurled rocks at and set ablaze twenty-five temples in towns across Sindh, where 85 percent of Pakistan's 1.5 million Hindus lived.[14]

The demolition of the Babri mosque put India at a disadvantage in the international arena, although the ransacking of the Indian consul-general's house in Karachi brought Pakistan a notch or two down from its moral high ground.

Far more significantly, Pakistan had to deal with the prospect of being added to the list of states supporting terrorism maintained by the United States. Such a prospect sharpened after a bomb exploded in the basement of the World Trade Center in New York on February 26, 1993. The hand of terrorists based in Pakistan was suspected. A nervous Nawaz Sharif dispatched his foreign secretary, Akram Zaki, to Washington in early April to reassure the State Department that he would curb extremists at home. The ISI drastically reduced direct support for Kashmiri militants but continued it indirectly, through the JeI and the LeT.

On April 18 President Ishaq Khan sacked Nawaz Sharif for alleged maladministration, corruption, graft, and nepotism. Sharif challenged this decision in the Supreme Court. Stalemate ensued. COAS General Wahid Kakar intervened. He compelled both of them to resign in July. Ishaq Khan was succeeded by Wasim Sajjad, chair of the Senate, as acting president.

REELECTED BHUTTO PLAYS HARDBALL WITH INDIA

In the October 1993 parliamentary election, Benazir Bhutto's PPP emerged as the largest group but fell short of a majority by 23 seats. So she ended up heading an unwieldy coalition, which included the Islamist Jamiat Ulema-e Islam (Urdu: Association of Islamic Religious Scholars;

JUeI), led by Fazlur Rahman. Along with the JeI, the JUeI had been a leading participant in the Afghan jihad.

Spurred by Rahman, Bhutto gave the green light to Lieutenant General Pervez Musharraf, then director general of military operations, to dispatch ten thousand new jihadists to Indian Kashmir. Under her watch, Islamabad's annual budget for the insurgency in India-held Kashmir spiked to $100 million.[15]

In a candid interview with the Delhi-based *Tehelka* magazine after Benazir Bhutto's assassination in December 2007, Retired Lieutenant General Gul said, "She was rather protective of the jihadis in the past. Benazir was never soft on the Kashmir issue, let me tell you that. I served as the ISI director-general under her [December 1988 to October 1989]. The Taliban emerged during her second tenure in office and captured Kabul when she was the prime minister. Her interior minister [General Naseerullah Babar] used to patronize them openly."[16]

She ruled out a meeting with her Indian counterpart, Narasimha Rao, until Delhi ended its brutish violations of human rights in Kashmir. This was not in the cards.

Actually, behind the scenes, to get even with Islamabad, the Indian RAW's Counter Intelligence Team-X (CIT-X) and Counter Intelligence Team-J (CIT-J) worked furiously to subvert Pakistan and eliminate the Khalistani groups respectively. The aim of the CIT-X Team was to exploit the ethnic fault lines in Pakistan—between Sindhis and the Urdu-speaking immigrants, called Muhajirin, in Sindh, between nationalist Baluchis and the Punjabi-dominated federal government, and between irredentist Pushtuns in the NWFP and Islamabad. Widely published reports in Pakistan alleged that between 1983 and 1993, as many as thirty-five thousand RAW agents entered Pakistan: twelve thousand in Sindh, ten thousand in Punjab, eight thousand in the NWFP, and five thousand in Baluchistan.[17]

As for the CIT-J Team, it had helped undermine the Sikh insurgency in Punjab sufficiently to let the Delhi government end its direct rule and return the state to democratic rule in February 1992. Following the election, the Congress Party's Beant Singh became the chief minister. Remnants of Sikh militancy continued, however, for another year or so. During the decade-long violence, more than twenty thousand people lost their lives in Punjab.[18]

Across the border, it became standard practice in Islamabad to blame RAW for all ethnic and intersectarian conflicts. Relations between

majority Sunnis and minority Shias became strained during the Islamization process unleashed by Zia ul Haq because of different interpretations
of Islamic jurisprudence by their respective religious scholars. The situation worsened when funds from Saudi Arabia, home of the puritanical
Wahhabi subsect of Sunni Islam, turned extremist Sunni organizations in
Pakistan murderously anti-Shia. That in turn led Shia radicals to hit back.
In 1994, the violence between sects and between radical Sindhi nationalists and militant Muhajirin in the country's largest city, Karachi, claimed
eight hundred lives. Unable to reduce the bloodshed, the Bhutto government resorted to blaming RAW. It closed down the Indian consulate in
the city. But there was no letup in Sunni-Shia bloodletting.

In Kashmir, the appointment of K. V. Krishna Rao, former COAS
with counterinsurgency experience in the rebellious northeast of India,
as governor in 1993 led to the infiltration of militant factions by RAW
agents. The strategy was to cause splits in militant organizations. As part of
its Operation Chanakya, RAW also sponsored the founding of fake radical groups with names almost akin to the existing genuine ones, thereby
confusing ordinary Kashmiris. Thus RAW and the ISI came to confront
each other directly in India-administered Kashmir. RAW gained the upper hand. By 1996, whereas the estimate of Indian security forces was put
at 210,000 to 600,000, the figure for the militants declined sharply to
6,000 from a peak of 20,000 to 25,000.[19]

INDIA'S ABOMINABLE RECORD ON TORTURE

India had achieved this outcome by beefing up its security forces in Kashmir and violating human rights on an industrial scale.

By the summer of 1990, a pattern had become established. Armed insurgents' assaults on specific targets, resulting in reprisals by security forces
with arrests and cordon-and-search operations to flush out guerrillas and
discover arms and ammunition, lead to Kashmiris heeding the militants'
calls for shutdowns.

The Delhi parliament passed the Armed Forces (Jammu and Kashmir) Special Powers Act 1990 (AFJKSP) in July. It authorized the state
government to declare Jammu and Kashmir or part of it as a "disturbed
area," where the AFJKSP Act applied. It allowed an armed forces officer
to shoot any person who was acting in contravention of "any law" or was
in possession of deadly weapons, to arrest without a warrant anyone who

was suspected of having committed any offense, and to enter and search any premise to make such arrests. This law gave military officers legal immunity for their actions.[20] It was carte blanche for security forces to do what they wished without worrying about accountability. Thereafter they carried out arbitrary arrests, torture, rape of women and men, extrajudicial killings, and arson to crush the raging insurgency.[21] By mid-1991 Indian military and paramilitary personnel totaled 150,000. The estimates of the armed militants ranged widely, from 10,000 to 40,000.

The list of those who were tortured or killed in extrajudicial executions by the Indian security forces grew by the week. Torturing suspects became routine. "They took you out to the lawn outside the building," a torture victim, "Ansar," told the Kashmiri journalist Basharat Peer, years later, after getting assurance that his real name would not be used. "You were asked to remove all your clothes, even your underwear. They tied you to a long wooden ladder and placed it near a ditch filled with kerosene oil and red chili powder. They raised the ladder like a seesaw and pushed your head into the ditch. It could go on for an hour, half an hour, depending on their mood." Other times the torturers would tie the fully clothed suspect to a ladder, tie his long pants near the ankles, and insert mice inside his pants. "Or they burnt your arms and legs with cigarette butts and kerosene stoves used for welding," Ansar continued. "They burn your flesh till you speak." He rolled up his right sleeve above the elbow to show an uneven dark brown patch of flesh.[22]

The brutal ways of the Indian security forces in Kashmir were widely and prominently reported in Pakistan, ruled by a democratically elected government after Zia ul Haq's death in 1988. Equally, the switch from dictatorship to democracy made no difference in Islamabad's policy on Kashmir, implemented in essence by the ISI. In November 1995 the BBC aired a documentary showing evidence of the JeI's support in Azad Kashmir camps, where fighters, openly expressing their intent to wage jihad in Indian Kashmir, were being trained.[23] This was a clear violation of the 1972 Shimla Agreement between India and Pakistan.

While Delhi refused to state the total strength of its security forces in Kashmir, it publicized the amount of weapons its security forces and Kashmiri police had seized between 1989 and 1995: 13,450 AK-47 Kalashnikovs, 1,682 rockets, 750 rocket launchers, and 735 general-purpose machine guns. With better intelligence they retrieved 590 bombs in 1995—almost twice the figure for 1994. As for fatalities, the unofficial estimate of forty thousand during the period 1988–1995 was three times the official figure. The London-based Amnesty International mentioned seventeen thousand, plus several thousand unaccounted deaths.[24] Of these almost half were believed to be militants.

This was the backdrop to elections in Kashmir in September and October 1996. On the eve of the election, Prime Minister Haradanahalli Doddegowda Deve Gowda unveiled a hefty package of financial aid of Rs 3.52 billion ($100 million) to improve infrastructure and wrote off outstanding loans of up to Rs. 50,000 ($1,400) per person—a flagrant example of electoral bribing.[25]

Reversing his previous stance, the late Shaikh Muhammad Abdullah's son, Farooq Abdullah, head of the National Conference, decided to contest the elections. "People like to see *azadi* [independence] but they don't see the consequences of that azadi," he said. "We are landlocked with powerful neighbors of China and Pakistan. If we get independence and India quits, I am sure Pakistan will march in overnight and take over."[26] It was better to take the plunge and see how best to alter the situation, rather than let the situation stagnate with no public involvement, he argued. In marked contrast, leaders of the separatist All Parties Hurriyat Conference (APHC) stuck to their stance of a boycott of the vote held under the Indian constitution.

In the face of dire threats by the militants, the candidates sought and secured bulletproof vehicles and security personnel as bodyguards. Very few people voted voluntarily in the Kashmir Valley. Many more were pressed to go to the polling booths by the security forces, who warned citizens of "consequences" if they failed to show indelible ink on their index fingers, used at the polling stations, in the evening. Unsurprisingly, the National Conference won 59 seats out of 87. Abdullah became chief minister.

THE SIMMERING NUCLEAR ISSUE

In her interview with British TV personality David Frost in November 1994, Benazir Bhutto said, "We have neither detonated nor have we got nuclear weapons. Being a responsible state and a state committed to non-proliferation, we in Pakistan, through five successive governments, have taken a policy decision to follow a peaceful nuclear program."[27] It was true that the military leaders kept the nitty-gritty of the nuclear project from Bhutto, but she was well briefed about the nature of the overall program and had traveled to North Korea a year earlier to facilitate the purchase of missiles suitable for delivering nuclear warheads.

During her visit to Washington in April 1995 to meet President Bill Clinton, she pressed him to alter the Pressler Amendment to the US foreign aid program. She argued that while it was "a veto in the hands of India, a tool and a club in the hands of those who stood against America and with the Soviet Union for 50 years," it rewarded "Indian intransigence" and punished "Pakistani loyalty and friendship" with America. At her press conference she offered "to go anywhere, at any time" to sign the nuclear Non-Proliferation Treaty if her Indian counterpart did the same. "I will joyfully agree to a treaty to ban nuclear weapons in South Asia, to create a missile-free zone in South Asia, to stop the production of fissile material in South Asia, as long as the only proven nuclear power on the subcontinent adheres to the same treaties."[28]

Her spirited performance in Washington made no mark on her increasingly vocal critics at home. The law and order situation in Karachi remained dire. It provided sufficient rationale to President Farooq Leghari, a PPP stalwart, to dismiss her government in November 1996, citing such grounds as maladministration, nepotism, and corruption.

Six months earlier the government in Delhi had changed too, but through the ballot, not by the fiat of the president. The general election in India had resulted in a hung parliament. There were two prime ministers belonging to different constituents of the United Front in as many years.

By the time Inder Kumar Gujral became prime minister in Delhi in April 1997, his counterpart in Islamabad was Nawaz Sharif, leader of the PML-N. Sharif had romped to success with a historic two-thirds majority in the National Assembly.

Born in the West Punjab town of Jhelum in British India, Gujral was a graduate of Forman Christian College, Lahore. A tall, lean, balding man with a graying goatee and oversized spectacles, he was a contrast to the rotund Sharif. As fellow Punjabis equally fluent in Urdu, however, they clicked the moment they met on the margins of the SAARC summit in Male in May 1997.

Unlike Rajiv Gandhi and Benazir Bhutto in 1988, they were seasoned politicians. They decided to reactivate the hotline and form working groups on several contentious issues. Crucially, Sharif agreed to adopt "an integrated approach" to resolving mutual differences, instead of focusing on Kashmir. During their interaction Gujral accepted Pakistan's position that Kashmir was a dispute that would require resolution. But according to Mushahid Hussain, the information minister of Pakistan, this was made public only "on June 23, 1997 when an Agreement was announced between the Foreign Secretaries on the establishment of joint working groups on outstanding issues between India and Pakistan with a separate working group on Kashmir. This was the first time in 50 years that India had agreed to this."[29]

With the Sikh emergency in Punjab over, Gujral ordered the disbanding of RAW's CIT-J. In Kashmir, the combined strategies of RAW and Governor Krishna Rao had reduced the size of the insurgents to a fraction of their peak of twenty to twenty-five thousand. With Farooq Abdullah installed as the elected chief minister in Srinagar, Gujral saw no reason to maintain RAW's CIT-X, mandated to subvert Pakistan, as a quid pro quo for stoking insurgency in Indian Kashmir. He disbanded it.

Following talks between their foreign secretaries in June 1997, India and Pakistan agreed to form joint working groups on eight subjects: Peace and Security, Jammu and Kashmir, Siachin Glacier, Wullar Barrage, Sir Creek, Terrorism, Commerce, and Promotion of friendly exchanges in various fields. But a week later Gujral ruled out a joint working group on Kashmir, which for Pakistan was "the core issue."[30]

In early September 1997 Sharif declared that "Pakistan's nuclear capability is now an established fact. Whatever we have, we have a right to keep it."[31] There was no prize for guessing what this "capability" was.

Sharif and Gujral met on the margins of the UN General Assembly in New York in late September and on the sidelines of the Commonwealth Heads of Government Meeting in Edinburgh a month later. But they failed to end the stalemate on the significance of the Kashmir dispute.

Gujral's minority government fell in December. And following the next parliamentary election in February 1998, the BJP-led thirteen-party National Democratic Alliance (NDA) won a slim majority.

14

Gate-Crashing the Nuclear Club

The 286 seats won by the National Democratic Alliance (NDA) in the latest parliamentary election gave it a majority of only 13. As leader of the 182-strong Bharatiya Janata Party (BJP) within the NDA, Atal Bihari Vajpayee became the prime minister on March 19, 1998. His immediate task was to consolidate the loyalty of the remaining twelve NDA constituents. This, he realized, was best done by raising the popular standing of his freshly formed government with a dramatic decision—something that would capture the nation's imagination and raise its self-confidence. That led him to order nuclear explosions within three weeks of taking office.

VAJPAYEE'S LONG-NURTURED NUCLEAR DREAM

To seasoned observers, though, this move by the seventy-three-year-old Vajpayee fitted his political persona to a tee. The white-haired Hindu nationalist politician—a broad-shouldered man with chubby cheeks in a jowly face—had been a proponent of nuclearization of India ever since China tested its atom bomb in 1964. Back then, he was a junior member of parliament representing the Bharatiya Jan Sangh (Hindi: Indian People's Union; BJS), an exclusively Hindu party.

Born into the Brahminical household of Krishna Bihari Vajpayee, a schoolteacher in the central Indian city of Gwaliar, Atal Bihari grew up as a devout Hindu. At the age of seventeen he attended the officers' training camp of the Rashtriya Swayamsevak Sangh (RSS), a Hindu chauvinist organization modeled after the Italian Fascist Party.

Its members met daily, wearing a uniform of a white shirt, baggy khaki half-pants, and belt; they drilled, played games, and attended sessions of political discussion and indoctrination.[1] After obtaining a master's degree in political science from Kanpur University, a public university in Uttar Pradesh, he became a full-time worker for the RSS in 1947. To devote himself fully to the RSS, he spurned the idea of marrying his college female friend Raj Kumari. He emerged as the only prime minister of India who was a lifelong bachelor, although by no means celibate. A teetotaler in public, he was rumored to drink on the sly.

While working for the RSS, he edited a Hindi magazine promoting Hindu revivalism until 1951, when the RSS set up the BJS as its political arm. As an MP, he proved an effective speaker in Hindi. On the death of Deen Dayal Upadhaya, a BJS cofounder, in 1968, he was elected the party's president. The BJS developed as an opponent of the Congress Party, decrying its perceived pampering of Muslims. During the national emergency, imposed by Indira Gandhi in mid-1975, Vajpayee and other BJS leaders were jailed. Their eighteen-month incarceration gave them the aura of political martyrdom. Their participation in the cabinet of Prime Minister Morarji Desai, leader of the Janata Alliance an anti-Congress coalition that included the BJS and won the 1977 general election, enhanced their popular standing. Vajpayee served as foreign minister.

After the breakup of the Janata Party, the BJS transformed itself into the BJP and opened its membership to non-Hindus. In practice, however, its RSS-rooted anti-Muslim ideology remained intact. The BJP became the political face of the Rama Janam Bhoomi Mandir movement, initiated by the RSS, to build a temple to Lord Rama at the site of the Babri Mosque in Ayodhya. Musing on the demolition of the Babri Mosque in December 1992 by a clandestinely organized four-thousand-strong group of militant Hindus, Vajpayee wrote: "Now, I think, the Hindu society has been regenerated which was the prime task of the RSS. Earlier, Hindus used to bend before an invasion but not now. . . . So much change must have come with the new-found self-assertion."[2]

In its campaign manifesto for the general election in April and May 1996, the BJP referred to India exercising "the option to induct nuclear weapons" and declared that "India should become an openly nuclear power to garner the respect on the world stage that India deserved."[3] As leader of the largest group in Parliament (187 seats), Vajpayee was invited to form a government on May 16 with the proviso of securing the MPs' vote of confidence within two weeks. He immediately ordered nuclear tests.

Three nuclear devices were rushed to the Pokhran Military Firing Range in Rajasthan, ninety-three miles from the Pakistani border, and placed in the test shafts. On May 28 Vajpayee concluded that he lacked majority support in Parliament and resigned. But before doing so, he rescinded his authorization for the nuclear explosions.

INDIAN CONSENSUS ON NUKES

Actually, what Vajpayee did was nothing more than complete the process inaugurated by Rajiv Gandhi in 1988, with his order to upgrade the nuclear testing site in Pokhran, first used in 1974, to make it suitable for a detonation on short notice. In 1995, his successor, P. V. Narasimha Rao, decided to conduct an underground test on a nuclear device. Preparations built to a climax in early December. The telltale signs were recorded by four powerful US spy satellites.

On December 15 the *New York Times* quoted unnamed officials of the Clinton administration that Washington had recorded activity at the Pokhran test site in recent weeks. Instructed by the State Department, the US ambassador to India, Frank Wisner, showed satellite photographs to top Indian officials to dissuade them from testing. In a telephone call, Clinton urged Narasimha Rao to abandon the plan. Rao assured Clinton that India would not act "irresponsibly"—nothing more. On December 18 the Indian government declared that it would not succumb to external pressure. The next day Foreign Minister Pranab Mukherjee denied that any nuclear tests had been planned. In the end, Narasimha Rao abandoned the project but instructed nuclear scientists to be ready for tests within a month of receiving an executive order.[4]

Two subsequent prime ministers, H. D. Deve Gowda and Inder Kumar Gujral, continued this state of readiness. According to Gujral, "the nuclear file was on our table all the time."[5] With the exception of the two communist factions, all major political parties favored acquiring nuclear weapons. The reason was contained in a much-quoted Gujral-Clinton exchange on September 22, 1997, on the margins of the UN General Assembly session in New York, as recounted by the Indian leader. He told Clinton about an ancient saying from the subcontinent that holds that an Indian is blessed with a third eye. "I told President Clinton that when my third eye looks at the door of the UN Security Council chamber it sees a little sign that says 'Only those with economic power or nuclear weapons are allowed.'" Having grabbed Clinton's attention, Gujral added, "It is very difficult [for India] to achieve economic wealth."[6] The moral was that in the absence of India becoming a heavy-weight economy, its only way to getting a permanent seat at the UN Security Council was to become a state with nuclear arms. It is chastening to recall that it was this logic that drove Zulfikar Ali Bhutto to urge his Pakistani scientists at a top-secret gathering in Multan a quarter century earlier to build the bomb within three years.[7]

After its denouement with the United States in December 1995, India changed the pattern of work at the Pokhran site radically to escape the all-seeing eyes of American spy satellites.

The army's Fifty-Eighth Engineer Regiment resorted to operating mostly at night and returned its equipment to its original location at the end of the work shift to make it seem that it had been stationary all along. Its personnel wore civilian clothes. Members of the regiment as well as civilians dug shafts under camouflage netting, and the excavated sand was made to look like natural dunes. The cables for sensors were covered with sand and concealed under vegetation. Those who were hired to work at the site traveled to destinations other than Pokhran and were then picked up by the army's vehicles. At the end of their shift the workers left the site in twos or threes.

To hoodwink Washington's National Security Agency (NSA), which was monitoring telephone conversations, the army devised a code. When the Delhi-based Defence Research and Development Organization (DRDO), charged with implementing the project, asked an officer manning the operations room in Pokhran, "Has the store arrived?" followed by "Is Sierra serving whisky in the canteen yet?," his decoded messages were: "Have the scientists started working on the nuclear devices?" and "Have the nuclear devices been lowered in the special chamber in the shaft codenamed Whiskey?"[8]

"Today, at 15.45 hours, India conducted three underground nuclear tests in the Pokhran range," Vajpayee told journalists at a hastily assembled press conference on May 11, 1998. "The tests conducted today were with a fission device, a low yield device and a thermonuclear [aka fusion] device. These were contained explosions like the experiment conducted in May 1974. I warmly congratulate the scientists and engineers who have carried out these successful tests."[9] Then, under the same code name of Operation Shakti (Hindi: Power), the DRDO conducted two more tests of smaller, subkiloton yield on May 13.

Indian officials claimed that the tests were a matter of national security, a precaution against Pakistan's nuclear development, and a deterrent to China's rising military might. As a nonsignatory to the nuclear Non-Proliferation Treaty (NPT), India did not violate any international treaty. Predictably, Islamabad immediately condemned the tests.

The objective of the Indian tests was threefold: to test the newly built fusion (aka hydrogen) bomb with a yield of forty kilotons (kT); to check the effectiveness of a fifteen-year-old fission bomb with a yield of twelve kT; and to determine whether or not the three freshly assembled tactical weapons with a yield of less than one kT would produce a chain reaction when activated. All fission bombs were plutonium based. As evidence of successful tests, the Indian government would release pictures of the five sites, each one a 160-foot-deep shaft, on May 17.

These tests caught Washington by surprise, with many red faces at the headquarters of the CIA in Langley, Virginia, just across the Potomac River. CIA director George J. Tenet immediately appointed Admiral David Jeremiah, a former vice chair of the Joint Chiefs of Staff, to lead a ten-day investigation into the intelligence community's failure to detect preparations for the tests at Pokhran.[10]

In marked contrast, Indian officials were elated at having fooled the all-knowing CIA. At the popular level the BJP and the RSS were quick to demonstrate their fervent support for Vajpayee's bold decision by holding public rallies and demonstrations. They were not alone. "It was a matter of national pride that the country's scientists had once again proved that they were second to none in the area of high technology, adding that they had all along turned every denial into an opportunity to make India a reckonable power in spheres of space and technology," noted the influential *Hindustan Times* in its editorial on May 13.[11] To make the point, the Vajpayee government declared May 11 National Technology Day.

Summarizing his wide-scale survey of the reactions in India to the tests, Thomas Blom Hansen, an American academic, noted that "the response from newspapers seemed even more positive, opinion polls indicated overwhelming support to the decision, and the BJP could now appear on the domestic scene in its much-desired role as the most resolute defender of India's national pride and its national interest."[12]

In the area of party politics, however, opinion was divided. The opposition Congress Party spokesman, Salman Khurshid, attributed Vajpayee's decision to the political consideration of consolidating the BJP's influence by rallying strong nationwide pro-nuclear sentiment. Eager to make his point, Khurshid conveniently overlooked the fact that the Congress premier Narasimha Rao was on the verge of presiding over nuclear tests in December 1995. Communist MPs argued that Vajpayee's unsheathing of the nuclear sword would lead to Pakistan doing the same, which it did. The subsequent nuclear arms race between two of the poorest countries in the world would retard their economic development, they argued.

In Washington Clinton swiftly invoked the 1994 Nuclear Proliferation Prevention Act. He blocked all aid, banned loans by American banks and export of products with military use such as computers, and curbed military technology exports to India. His decision covered $500 million of pending US loans or loan guarantees to Delhi.

INDIA, 5; PAKISTAN, 6

Clinton then turned his attention to dissuading Pakistani premier Muhammad Nawaz Sharif from following Vajpayee's example. Given the dire straits of his country's economy, Sharif was vulnerable to economic sanctions by Washington, which would have extended to the International Monetary Fund (IMF) and the World Bank. Karachi's stock exchange reacted nervously to the Indian tests, losing a record one-third of its value. Sharif was compelled to dither while Clinton kept up pressure in telephone calls, even from the British city of Birmingham, where he had gone to attend the G8 Summit from May 15 to 17.

But once the Islamist parties in Pakistan mobilized tens of thousands of their supporters on the streets on May 15, Sharif found it hard to sit on the fence. As if the raucous demand of the Islamist camp were not enough, Benazir Bhutto weighed in. On May 18 she vowed to "take to the streets" at the head of mass demonstrations in a bid to force Sharif from office if he did not authorize nuclear tests.[13]

Little did Bhutto know that following the decision a day earlier by the Defense Committee of the Cabinet to conduct nuclear tests, Sharif had conveyed his order to Ishfaq Ahmed, sixty-eight-year-old chair of the Pakistan Atomic Energy Commission (PAEC), in crisp Urdu: "*Dhamaka kar do*" ("Conduct the explosions").[14] The bespectacled, jug-eared Ahmed, endowed with high cheekbones and long, snow-white hair, assured Sharif that all would be ready for testing in ten days.

The detonations were mainly to occur in a 0.62-mile-long, 9-foot-diameter, steel-covered tunnel bored into the granite Koh Kambaran

Mountain in the Ras Koh range in Chagai district of Baluchistan, thirty miles from the Iranian border. Constructed in the form of a fishhook by the PAEC in 1980, it was a PAEC asset. Its fishhook form ensured that following an explosion, the mountain would move outward and the tunnel would collapse and seal the entrance. It was capable of withstanding an explosion of twenty kilotons, the same magnitude as the one dropped on Nagasaki, Japan, in August 1945.

Taking this into account and the fact that the PAEC had conducted more cold tests on nuclear weapons than the Kahuta-based Khan Research Laboratories (KRL), the government had opted for the PAEC.[15] At an earlier, expanded meeting called by the government, the nuclear scientist Abdul Qadeer Khan had argued that given the KRL's record as the first to enrich uranium and design its own atom bomb and conduct cold tests on its own, it should be given the opportunity to carry out Pakistan's first nuclear tests. But his plea fell on deaf ears. He complained to Chief of Army Staff (COAS) General Jehangir Karamat. The COAS called Sharif. As a result, Sharif decided that KRL personnel should be involved in preparing the test sites as well as be present at the time of testing.

On May 19 two teams of 140 PAEC scientists, engineers, and technicians were flown from Islamabad and other locations to Turbat airport in Baluchistan on their way to the test site in the Koh Kambaran Mountains.

It took five days to assemble the five nuclear devices containing weapons-grade, highly enriched uranium. The PAEC's Samar Mubarakmand supervised the assembly personally, checking and rechecking each device, while trudging through the stuffy tunnel five times. Then diagnostic cables were laid through the tunnel to the telemetry station, which communicated with the command post six miles away. Next, a complete simulated test was carried out by radio link.

It was now May 25.

Unlike the latter-day Pokhran military firing range in India, the test site in Pakistan was an open book for the US spy satellites, which were focused on their target day and night. On May 25 an American intelligence official said, "At this point, they could conduct a nuclear test at any time." The CIA kept Clinton informed on an hourly basis.

By the time the tunnel was sealed with six thousand bags of cement, it was the afternoon of May 26. Once the cement had dried within twenty-four hours, the engineers declared that the site was ready. This was conveyed to Sharif via the military's general headquarters (GHQ). All told, various official agencies of Pakistan had performed a gargantuan task with admirable speed, coordination, and calm confidence.

In Washington officials predicted the testing occurring "within hours." On the night of May 27 (Islamabad time), Clinton made the last of his four calls to Sharif. According to his spokesman Mike McCurry, it was a "very intense" twenty-five-minute conversation in which Clinton implored Sharif not to conduct a test.[16] It proved futile.

Recalling the intense pressure he was subjected to during that crisis twelve years later, Sharif revealed that Clinton offered as much as $5 billion of aid to Pakistan in return for abstinence from testing nuclear weapons. But, added Sharif, it was more important for him to implement the national will, which demanded those tests.[17] Another version of that crucial telephone conversation is that Sharif sought explicit US security guarantees, which Clinton was unable or unwilling to offer.[18] Most likely, both points were discussed.

As if this were not enough, India and Israel cropped up in Pakistan's unfolding drama. On May 27, the Indian Army's Signals Intelligence Directorate intercepted a coded telegram alerting the Pakistan High Commission in New Delhi that Pakistan had "credible information" that India was all set to mount a predawn attack on its nuclear installations.[19]

And as Pakistan prepared to test its nuclear devices, its military spotted US-made F16s in the surrounding airspace. It was aware that Israel used two-seater F16s, equipped with advanced reconnaissance equipment, which at forty-five thousand feet could take pictures of objects many miles away. It feared that this was part of an Indian-Israeli plan to launch a preemptive strike at its test site in Baluchistan. It alerted both the United States and the United Nations. They in turn contacted the Israeli government immediately, which assured then that it had no such plan.[20] Pakistan was not reassured. Its president, Muhammad Rafiq Tarar, would suspend the constitution and declare a state of emergency as a result of threats of unspecified "external aggression" soon after Sharif's TV speech.

"Today, we have settled a score and have carried out five successful nuclear tests," announced Sharif at 15:00 GMT on May 28 on Pakistani TV. His declaration received the jubilant applause usually reserved for a batsman who has smashed the ball over the boundary by cheering crowds at cricket matches.

Elaborating his dramatic statement later at a press conference, Sharif said, "Pakistan today successfully conducted five nuclear tests. The results were as expected. There was no release of radioactivity. I congratulate all Pakistani scientists, engineers and technicians for their dedicated team work and expertise in mastering complex and advanced technologies. The entire nation takes justifiable pride in the accomplishments of the Pakistan Atomic Energy Commission, Dr. A. Q. Khan Research Laboratories and all affiliated organizations." Blaming "the present Indian leadership's reckless actions," he added that "our decision to exercise the nuclear option has been taken in the interest of national self-defense . . . to deter aggression, whether nuclear or conventional."[21]

There was instant jubilation in the streets. Karachi, for instance, was paralyzed by traffic jams as tens of thousands headed for the city center to join the festivities. In Lahore crowds burned effigies of Vajpayee while chanting slogans in praise of Sharif, Karamat, and Qadeer Khan.[22]

Those attending Friday prayers heard sermons thanking Allah for making Pakistan the first Muslim nation to acquire nuclear weapons. The Islamist parties were euphoric about the successful testing of the Islamic atom bomb—a term coined by Zulfikar Ali Bhutto, their bête noire—for two reasons. It gave Pakistan parity with India in defense that it lacked when facing its bigger and more powerful neighbor in conventional terms. Second, mastering the production and testing of such a weapon was a triumph of the marriage between Islam and modern technology. What they overlooked was the fact that Pakistan had assembled a uranium-based atom bomb by pilfering parts and materials from Western sources and obtaining the design from the atheist government of the communist People's Republic of China.

Gohar Ayub Khan, a hawkish foreign minister close to the generals, was decidedly bullish, brimming with newborn confidence. "We have nuclear weapons, we are a nuclear power," he declared. "We have an advanced missile program," he added, warning that Pakistan had acquired the capacity to retaliate "with vengeance and devastating effect" against Indian attacks.[23]

After half a century of uncertainty about the continued existence of Pakistan because of the hostility of the militarily mightier India, its leaders now possessed an effective deterrent against any attempt by Delhi to break up their republic or absorb it.

Moreover, intent on beating India in the numbers game, Sharif ordered a further test, code-named Chagai II, on May 30 at Kharan, a flat desert valley ninety-five miles southwest of the Ras Koh Range. The site was an L-shaped shaft three hundred feet deep and then seven hundred feet long horizontally, and the device was plutonium-based. The officially announced yield of eighteen to twenty kT was disputed by independent assessors, with the *Bulletin of Atomic Scientists* coming up with the figure of two kT. Equally exaggerated were the statistics about the cumulative total of the five devices detonated earlier under the codename of Chagai I. Pakistan's claimed figure of forty to forty-five kT stood in sharp contrast to the estimate of eight to fifteen kT by the *Bulletin of Atomic Scientists*.[24]

Scientists make a distinction between a nuclear weapon test and an explosion. According to them, India had conducted three nuclear tests, including the one in 1974. In May 1998 at Pokhran there were two tests: one involving two simultaneous blasts and the other three synchronized explosions.[25] By the same token, Pakistan's five simultaneous explosions at Chagai Hills counted as the first test, with the next single blast at Kharan as the second. So the final test score was: India, 3; Pakistan, 2.

While ordinary Pakistanis were in a celebratory mood on May 29, the affluent among them fell into deep depression. The Sharif administration issued an emergency order, freezing $11.5 billion in private foreign currency deposits in Pakistani banks and suspending the licenses of foreign exchange dealers. Fearing a rush to withdraw foreign currencies in view of the impending economic sanctions, the government acted instantly, nervously aware that its central bank had only $1.6 billion in foreign exchange reserves. At $32 billion, Pakistan's foreign debts were a whopping 64 percent of its GDP. It announced a 50 percent cut in all expenditures except development projects.[26]

The only foreign leader Sharif shared his top-secret decision to conduct atomic tests with was Crown Prince Abdullah bin Abdul Aziz, the de facto leader of Saudi Arabia. In appreciation of this gesture, Abdullah offered to supply Pakistan fifty thousand barrels of oil per day, about one-seventh of its total consumption, for an indefinite period and on deferred payment terms. This helped to relieve to a certain extent the ill effects of the sanctions by the United States and the European Union.[27] Saudi Arabia was one of the two countries that congratulated Pakistan for taking the "bold decision," the other being the United Arab Emirates.

Domestically, the political upside for Sharif was a dramatic turnaround in his popularity, from a slow, irreversible decline to a meteoric surge. Vajpayee too gained in the esteem of the public, which saw him as a staunch upholder of India's security. This uptick in their popular standing made the two leaders amenable to cease saber rattling and mend fences.

POSTBLAST THAW

They did so by sticking to the long-established practice of meeting on the margins of the annual South Asian Association for Regional Cooperation summit. In July 1998, it was hosted by Sri Lanka. News of this event encouraged Clinton to consider easing sanctions against the two South Asian neighbors.

More substantial progress was made during the cordial parley between Sharif and Vajpayee in New York on the sidelines of the UN General Assembly session on September 23. Sharif stated that in a nuclear weapons environment neither side could even contemplate the use of force.[28] They decided to revive dialogue between their respective foreign secretaries on the eight outstanding issues and to break new ground: resume bus service between Delhi and Lahore to encourage people-to-people contact. This in turn led Clinton to withdraw his opposition to the IMF loan to Pakistan.

Welcome though the news from Washington was to Sharif, it was not enough to reverse the economic downturn in Pakistan, which had deepened in the aftermath of sanctions by Washington and other Western capitals. Among those suffering were the military's corporate interests. COAS Karamat lamented the deteriorating internal situation and proposed the formation of the National Security Council, including military leaders, to institutionalize decision-making.

Sharif interpreted this as an attempt to curtail the constitutional rights of the prime minister. He challenged Karamat either to take over the administration or resign. Unlike Sharif, Karamat was not confrontational. So he stepped down in July 1998, three months before his scheduled retirement date.

Sharif promoted General Pervez Musharraf. A square-faced, bespectacled man of medium height with a neatly trimmed mustache, he was third in seniority among the three-star generals. Sharif figured that Urdu-speaking Musharraf, a native of Delhi, leading the predominantly Punjabi-Pushtuns corps commanders, would lack the clout to pressure a civilian government led by a Punjabi. This would turn out to be a fatal assumption.

As for Islamabad-Delhi relations, during their meetings in October and November, foreign secretaries Krishnan Raghunath and Shamshad Ahmad made progress on procedural matters as a step toward institutional contacts. Starting mid-December they focused on drafting a mutually agreed-on document to be presented to their respective premiers.

In an interview published on February 3, 1999, Sharif said, "Why can't we talk directly? Why do we have to go on approaching each other via *Bhatinda* [a Punjabi metaphor for circuitous approach]?" He added that if Vajpayee responded positively, he would be more than willing to "take the initiative" to invite him to Pakistan.[29] Vajpayee responded positively. And Sharif invited him to Lahore on the inaugural fourteen-hour Delhi-Lahore bus journey on February 20, 1999. Vajpayee boarded the bus.

BUS DIPLOMACY

That afternoon, Sharif rolled out the red carpet for Vajpayee at the Wagah border crossing, fifteen miles from Lahore, in the full glare of international media. He was accompanied by senior cabinet ministers as well as Information Minister Mushahid Hussain, who was designated liaison minister-in-waiting with Vajpayee—but not the defense chiefs. They had declined Sharif's invitation to join him at Wagah, arguing that they did not wish to be seen in public welcoming the leader of "an enemy nation." After inspecting a guard of honor, Vajpayee and Sharif boarded a helicopter. It flew them to where the Indian premier was to stay overnight—the palatial, opulent Governor's House in Lahore, decorated with crystalline chandeliers in many rooms, in the midst of eighty acres of immaculately tended lawns.

"When the helicopter landed on the lawns of the Governor's House he [Vajpayee] was received by the three Service Chiefs led by the Chief of the Army Staff, General Pervez Musharraf, who saluted him and extended his hand," Hussain revealed later in an interview with *Frontline*, an Indian magazine. "So did the Air Chief Marshal, Pervez Mahdi Qureshi, and Admiral Fazi Bukhari, Chief of the Navy Staff. Then we all went inside the drawing room . . . for a tête-à-tête over tea. They [Service Chiefs] returned to Islamabad because [Foreign Minister] Sartaj Aziz was hosting the same night a banquet for the visiting Chinese Defense Minister, and the three Service Chiefs had to be there."[30]

According to Hussain, "When the formal talks began between Mr. Vajpayee and Mr. Sharif, Mr. Sharif began by smilingly thanking Mr. Vajpayee, saying 'You provided us an opportunity for becoming a nuclear power, because had you not gone nuclear, we would not have probably tested. So, it was India's tests, India's initiative on becoming a nuclear power by coming out of the closet that forced Pakistan to respond in kind.' . . . Mr. Vajpayee merely smiled faintly at that."[31]

Sharif went out of his way to ensure that Vajpayee did not encounter hostile crowds in the city. To abort the chance of their removal, the welcome banners for Vajpayee were displayed along the main thoroughfare, the Mall, only late at night on February 19. Whereas the mainstream political parties, including Bhutto's Pakistan People's Party (PPP), welcomed the visit, the Jamaat-e Islami (JeI) called a general strike in Lahore on February 20. It was noteworthy that it was at the behest of Major General Ehsan ul Haq, the director-general of Military Intelligence, that JeI leader Qazi Hussein Ahmad had given the call for protest. And it was at his house in Rawalpindi that Ahmad hid to avoid arrest[32] while hundreds of his followers were detained. This provided evidence of linkage between the intelligence agencies of the military and the Islamist groups. The origins of this unholy alliance went back to the rule of General Muhammad Zia ul Haq, who resorted to using Islamist organizations and their armed wings first against the Marxist regime in Kabul and then against Delhi in the Indian Kashmir.

Several ambassadors invited to the state banquet for Vajpayee at the historic Lahore Fort were blocked by the protesting demonstrators.

To leave nothing to chance, the next morning a helicopter flew Vajpayee and his party to the lawns of the Iqbal Park, the site of the Minar-e Pakistan, barely two miles from the Governor's House. A fluted, tapering column of white marble, two hundred feet high, it rose from a marble cupola resting on a high platform—the result of eight years of expert workmanship in the 1960s—ringed by fluttering green-and-white national flags. This was the site where, on March 23, 1940, the All India Muslim League passed its resolution for a homeland for the Muslims of India.

Accompanied by his adopted daughter, Namita, Vajpayee read the printed legend, which stated in part: "This session of the Muslim League emphatically reiterates that the scheme of federation embodied in the Government of India Act, 1935, is totally unsuitable and unworkable in the peculiar conditions of this country and is altogether unacceptable to Muslim India." In the visitors' book Vajpayee expressed "the deep desire for lasting peace and friendship'" that the people of India nursed toward Pakistan. "A stable, secure and prosperous Pakistan is in India's interest. Let no one in Pakistan be in doubt. India sincerely wishes Pakistan well."[33]

Vajpayee's highly symbolic visit to the Minar-e Pakistan was meant to reassure Pakistanis that even Hindu nationalists in India no longer questioned Pakistan's right to exist. This was a preamble to the signing of the Lahore Declaration by the two prime ministers. It stated that the possession of nuclear weapons by both nations required additional responsibility to avoid conflict and promote confidence-building measures. To avoid accidental or unauthorized use of nuclear weapons, the signatories agreed to give each other advance notice of ballistic missile flight tests and accidental or unexplained use of nuclear arms in order to stave off nuclear conflict. They also agreed to discuss their nuclear doctrines and related security issues.[34] After the signing ceremony, Sharif hoped that "Pakistan and India will be able to live as the United States and Canada."[35]

At the civic reception given by the city's mayor, Khwaja Ihsan Ahmed, the Indian prime minister said in Hindustani, "There has been enough of enmity. Now we must forge friendship. Achieving friendship will require difficult decisions. For the sake of friendship we have to talk about Kashmir."[36] These words were music to his listeners. Consequently, his trip was covered in glowing terms by the Pakistani media.

Across the border, too, politicians and the press welcomed the easing of bilateral tensions that had intensified in the wake of the nuclear tests. Had a Congress prime minister undertaken such a trip and held out an olive branch to Pakistan, he or she would have been mauled by the BJP for being "soft" on the unfriendly neighbor. It was left to India's foreign minister, Jaswant Singh, a BJP leader, to encapsulate the significance of Vajpayee's historic visit. He averred, rightly, that "like Richard Nixon's visit to China [in 1972], it was a kind of gesture that only a leader with strong conservative credentials could get away with."[37]

President Clinton was quick to commend Vajpayee and Sharif for "demonstrating courage and leadership by coming together and addressing difficult issues that have long divided their countries."[38] What he did not know was that during the last of their three meetings, held on a one-on-one basis after the signing of the Lahore Declaration, the two premiers secretly agreed to open a backchannel to devise a mutually satisfactory formula on Kashmir, also agreeable to Kashmiris.

On February 28, Sharif used the hotline to inform Vajpayee that he was ready to receive his nominee, Rishi Kumar Mishra—a sixty-seven-year-old founding chair of the Observer Research Foundation, a Delhi-based think-tank—in Islamabad to talk to his principal secretary, Anwar Zahid, on Kashmir. Mishra and Zahid met on March 3.

But a week later Zahid was dead. Sharif replaced him with Niaz Ahmad Naik, a former foreign secretary. During his five-day stay in Delhi toward the end of March, Naik and Mishra hammered out a four-point set of guidelines. One of these points required Vajpayee and Sharif to refrain from asserting their official positions—India's insistence that there is nothing to discuss about Kashmir, a settled issue, and Pakistan's reference to the UN Security Council Resolution 47. They also decided to resolve the Kashmir dispute before the advent of the new millennium.

Unknown to them and their principals, however, Pakistan's military brass had other ideas.

STAB IN THE BACK

While overt and covert diplomacy was in train to resolve the bitter Kashmir dispute, the Pakistan Army's top generals had secretly embarked on a plan to break the status quo in Kashmir in Islamabad's favor. The initiative seemed to have come from Lieutenant General Muhammad Aziz Khan, chief of the general staff, distinguished by his elegantly trimmed, salt-and-pepper beard and a fixed, middle-distance gaze, in charge of operations and intelligence. As leader of the Sudhan clan dominant in the Poonch district of Pakistani-held Kashmir, he was emotionally interested in loosening Delhi's grip over 48 percent of Kashmir.

During and after the anti-Soviet jihad, Aziz Khan had supervised the establishment of training camps for the radical Harkat ul Ansar—renamed Harkat ul Mujahedin after being listed as a terrorist organization by Washington in 1997. It was committed to securing all of Kashmir for Pakistan. His idea was adopted immediately by General Musharraf, who turned it into his brainchild. Keen to keep it super-secret, he did not even share it with his friend Air Marshal Qureshi, chief of air staff.

Musharraf's coteries focused on capturing the Kargil region in the east-central part of India-held Kashmir as a means of diverting Indian troops from the western front abutting Pakistan-administered Kashmir. The plan was code-named Operation Badr. The sole highway linking Srinagar with Leh, the regional capital of Ladakh, passed through the Kargil region lying close to the Line of Control (LoC). Here jagged peaks soared to 16,500 feet, and average winter temperatures dropped to an incredible −60° Celsius (−76° Fahrenheit). Such harsh conditions had led India and Pakistan to reach an understanding in the mid-1970s to leave their pickets unmanned in the area from mid-September to mid-April.

In early spring 1999 Pakistan violated this informal agreement. Under cover of heavy artillery and mortar fire, Aziz Khan launched Operation Badr. He airlifted one thousand troops of the Northern Light Infantry into the Dras sector of Kargil and provided them with the logistical support of a further four thousand. They in turn recruited several hundred local volunteers, described as mujahedin, to perform logistical tasks. Later, the combat forces would increase to five thousand. They succeeded in occupying 132 Indian posts along the seventy-five-mile frontline, which had a depth of five to ten miles, covering three hundred square miles. Their tactical aim was to dominate the Indians' supply line to the Siachen Glacier and force them to withdraw from there.

In early May the returning Indian soldiers found Pakistanis occupying mountaintops overlooking the Kargil highway. The discovery came within weeks of the fall of the Vajpayee government on April 17, following its failure to win a vote of confidence in the lower house of Parliament by a single ballot. When the opposition failed to assemble a majority in the house, President Kicheri Raman Narayanan dissolved Parliament on April 26 and appointed Vajpayee caretaker prime minister. With fresh elections scheduled for September (after monsoons), Vajpayee found it politically profitable to take a tough line with Pakistan.

Delhi protested Islamabad's action in Kargil. But Pakistan claimed that it was the local Kashmiri freedom fighters—the mujahedin—who had occupied Kargil. On May 22 India launched air strikes at the enemy-occupied territory as part of its Operation Vijay (Hindi: Victory). But aerial bombing amid jagged peaks was only partly effective.

India then bolstered its infantry in the battle zone by moving troops from the Kashmir Valley—not the western front line, as Musharraf and his senior commanders had anticipated—to expel the Pakistanis from the occupied posts. The reported exclusion of Air Chief Qureshi from the original planning seemed to be the reason for his refusal to deploy warplanes or lend them to Musharraf, thus tying Musharraf's hands.[39]

During the seven-week war, Vajpayee and Sharif made repeated use of their hotline. And as early as June 3, President Clinton wrote to the two premiers to act with restraint. Pakistan's foreign minister Sartaj Aziz arrived in Delhi on June 11 with a plan to de-escalate the conflict by finding a way of seeking safe passage for the Kashmiri mujahedin.

Unluckily for Pakistan, that day India released intercepts of the telephone conversation between Musharraf, then visiting Beijing, and Aziz Khan in Rawalpindi. By so doing, Delhi demolished Pakistan's repeated assertions of noninvolvement in the occupation of Kargil. The origins of this intelligence coup have been open to speculation. The claim of India's Research and Analysis Wing (RAW) to have recorded the intercepts is suspect. It is most likely that Washington's lavishly funded NSA, working with the CIA, intercepted all of Aziz Khan's conversations and passed on the relevant ones with Musharraf to India's RAW as instructed by the White House. Clinton was keen to see the conflict end.[40]

Having indisputably established the Pakistani Army's occupation of Kargil, Vajpayee said in his third telephone conversation with Sharif on June 13: "You withdraw your troops and then we are prepared for talks." The next day Vajpayee received a call from Clinton advising him against escalating the conflict by opening a new front in Kashmir. On June 15 Clinton telephoned Sharif urging him to withdraw his forces from Kargil. He found Sharif's response unsatisfactory.

Sharif was caught between a rock and a hard place. The senior generals had kept him in the dark, as he claimed later repeatedly. Amid much speculation on the subject, it could be deduced that they presented the plan to him long after mounting the offensive. It happened only on May 17—a fact confirmed by the presenter, Lieutenant General Jamshaid Gulzar Kiani, who described the briefing as "perfunctory."[41] With the two armies engaged in a hot war, Sharif was faced with a fait accompli. He could not disengage himself from the ongoing armed conflict, thereby highlighting his humiliating lack of control over the military high command.

To add to his woes, Sharif lost out to Vajpayee on the diplomatic front. The Indian leader won the backing not only of America but also of China, which called for the withdrawal of forces to prewar positions along the LoC and settling Indo-Pakistan border issues peacefully. Both Sharif and Vajpayee maintained ongoing contact with Clinton, but it paid better dividends to Vajpayee than Sharif.

At Vajpayee's behest, Clinton lobbied the G8 Summit—a meeting of a group of eight industrialized nations—in Cologne, Germany, on June 19 to take a stand on the Kargil War. Its communiqué issued the next day stated: "We regard any military action to change the status quo [in Kashmir] as irresponsible. We therefore call for an immediate end to these actions [and] restoration of the Line of Control."[42] Predictably, Vajpayee welcomed the G8 statement, and Sharif and his generals did not.

As the strain between Delhi and Islamabad intensified, Clinton dispatched General Anthony Zinni, commander in chief at US Central Command, and Gibson Lanpher, deputy assistant secretary of state, to

Islamabad on June 22. While India declared that it would not be the first to use nuclear weapons, Pakistan's information minister Hussain, appearing on the BBC World's *HARDtalk* program on June 23, refused to give the same guarantee, describing the idea of a nuclear war as "too far fetched."[43]

On the ground, the Indian forces, using Swedish-made Bofors self-propelling artillery guns and laser-guided aerial bombs, were making headway, rising up the heights steadily to make a final assault to wrest the peaks from the enemy. An insider view of Pakistan's position was provided fourteen years later in *Yeh Khamoshi Kahan Tak?* (Urdu: How Long This Silence?), a book by (Retired) Lieutenant General Shahid Aziz, then head of the analysis wing of Inter-Services Intelligence (ISI). He wrote that the Pakistani troops were told by their commanders that no serious response would come from the Indians. "But it did—wave after wave, supported by massive air bursting artillery and repeated air attacks," he noted. "Cut off and forsaken, our posts started collapsing one after the other, though the [commanding] general publicly denied it."[44] As the lead military planner, Musharraf took a decisive first step in Kargil, but, fatally, he had no exit strategy—an unforgivable failing.

Sharif feared that, faced with an imminent defeat, Musharraf would open new fronts in Kashmir, resulting in robust responses from Delhi, which would escalate to a full-fledged war with India—a disastrous scenario he felt compelled to avoid. As for Musharraf, having considered the worst scenario in the case of an all-out war with India, he started preparing for the deployment of the nuclear option—without even bothering to inform Sharif. He seemed unaware that he could not mask the activity he had unleashed at Sargodha Air Force Base where nuclear-tipped missiles were stored, from Washington's spy satellites.

The White House was monitoring the battle between the nuclear-armed neighbors closely. Just as India prepared to launch a three-pronged offensive to capture the mountaintops in Kargil on July 2, a nervous Sharif telephoned Clinton appealing for "American intervention immediately to stop the fighting and to resolve the Kashmir issue." Clinton was equivocal. So Sharif used his Saudi card. He made an urgent call to Prince Bandar, Saudi Arabia's ambassador to the United States since 1983, to help. Bandar intervened on behalf of Sharif, who made yet another call to the White House.[45]

In Washington, Clinton had been alarmed to read the intercepts of satellite overheads obtained by the NSA showing that Musharraf had ordered the unveiling of nuclear-tipped missiles at Sargodha Air Force Base for possible use in a wider war with India, most likely without the knowledge of Nawaz Sharif.[46] This was confirmed by Bruce Riedel, then senior director at the National Security Council and special assistant to Clinton on South Asia, in a policy paper he presented almost three years later.[47]

Eager to prevent a nuclear holocaust in South Asia, Clinton summoned Sharif and Vajpayee to Washington for talks. Mentioning previous commitments, Vajpayee declined, aware that a tripartite meeting in the United States on Kargil would compromise the long-held Indian position that Kashmir was a bilateral, not an international, issue. He had his eye fixed unflinchingly on the general election in September.

At Rawalpindi's Chaklala airport, Sharif was seen off by Musharraf, implying that the prime minister's mission had the backing of the military. TV viewers had no idea that Sharif was traveling to Washington with his family. When they arrived at Dulles Airport on July 3, they were picked up by Prince Bandar. On his way to the prince's electronically guarded, sprawling mansion on the outskirts of Washington, Sharif reportedly told his host that he was worried about his life and that he had brought his family along because he was not sure whether he would be the prime minister by the end of his mission.

FOURTH OF JULY 1999 AT BLAIR HOUSE
LIKE NONE BEFORE

"Gentlemen, thank you very much for gracing our Independence Day." This is how Clinton, straining to smile, greeted Sharif and his team at Blair House, the presidential guest house, on July 4, 1999.[48] Neither Clinton nor any of his team, which included National Security Advisor Sandy Berger and Bruce Riedel, was pleased by having had to tackle urgently a war-and-peace issue in South Asia on the most celebrated secular holiday in the American calendar.

Progress was slow because the counterparty—Vajpayee—was missing. Without his say-so, a cease-fire—the ultimate objective of the Blair House meeting—could not be achieved. So fax machines were put to work. As the draft of a joint communiqué by Clinton and Sharif went through several stages, heavy fax traffic ensued between Blair House and the Indian prime minister's office.

As Riedel noted:

The Prime Minister [Sharif] told Clinton that he wanted desperately to find a solution that would allow Pakistan to withdraw with some cover. Without something to point to, Sharif warned ominously, the fundamentalists in Pakistan would move against him and this meeting would be his last with Clinton. . . . Clinton asked Sharif if he knew how advanced the threat of nuclear war really was? Did Sharif know his military was preparing their nuclear tipped missiles? Sharif seemed taken aback and said only that India was probably doing the same. The President reminded Sharif how close the US and the Soviet Union had come to nuclear war in 1962 over Cuba. Did Sharif realize that if even one bomb was dropped . . . Sharif finished his [Clinton's] sentence and said it would be a catastrophe.

(This warranted a pause for everyone in the room to digest the ghastly consequences.)

The President was getting angry. He told Sharif that he had asked repeatedly for Pakistani help to bring Osama bin Laden to justice from Afghanistan. Sharif had promised often to do so but had done nothing. Instead the ISI worked with bin Laden and the Taliban to foment terrorism. [Clinton's] draft statement would also mention Pakistan's role in supporting terrorists in Afghanistan and India. Was that what Sharif wanted, Clinton asked? Did Sharif order the Pakistani nuclear missile force to prepare for action? Did he realize how crazy that was? You've put me in the middle today, set the US up to fail and I won't let it happen. Pakistan is messing with nuclear war.[49]

During the session, as the drafting of the communiqué inched forward with continued inputs from Delhi, Sharif whispered to Clinton, "They will get me, Mr President." Clinton was unmoved. "Yours is a rogue army," he rejoined. "Keep them under civilian oversight." To which came a quick response from Sharif: "It is not the army. It is [a] few dirty eggs. They will meddle to cover up the Kargil debacle."[50] These "dirty eggs" were the so-called Dirty Five: Musharraf; Aziz Khan; Lieutenant General Mahmood Ahmed, a broad-shouldered man with a walrus mustache who commanded the Tenth Corps in Rawalpindi; and Aziz Khan's immediate subordinates, Lieutenant General Aziz, director-general (DG) of Operations, and Major General Ehsan ul Haq, DG of Military Intelligence (MI).

The negotiating teams broke for lunch and rest. While Clinton stayed at Blair House, Sharif went to his hotel. That gave Clinton a chance to have a proper conversation with Vajpayee over the phone.[51]

When the two principals met again, Clinton placed a statement on the table. Sharif left the room to consult his advisers. He agreed to his troops' withdrawal to the LoC. "The mood changed in a nanosecond," recalled Riedel. "Clinton told Sharif that they had tested their personal relationship hard that day but they had reached the right ending."[52] Later they posed for photographs at the White House.

The Clinton-Sharif statement said that steps would be taken to restore the unspecified LoC, thus facilitating a cease-fire that would follow as a preamble to the resumption of bilateral talks as the best forum to resolve all Indo-Pakistan disputes. Sharif parted with Clinton saying he felt he had done "the right thing for Pakistan and the world," but he was not certain "the Army would see it that way."[53] His hunch would prove prescient, leading to his overthrow three months later.

There was of course no mention of the secret deal struck between Clinton and Sharif during their separate one-on-one parley after the formal talks. Clinton agreed to ease US economic sanctions against Islamabad and recommend to the IMF not to withhold its next loan to Pakistan. In return, Sharif promised to actively cooperate with Washington in apprehending bin Laden.[54]

On his return home, Sharif announced the Pakistan Army's withdrawal from Kargil while justifying Operation Badr, which, he argued, had drawn the attention of the international community to the Kashmir dispute. The pullback started on July 11, when the cease-fire became effective. Three days later Vajpayee declared Operation Vijay a success. The Kargil Way war consumed the lives of 527 Indian soldiers (versus Pakistan's claim of 1,600) and 450 Pakistani troops (versus India's claim of 700). The loss of one Indian aircraft was puny.

All along Vajpayee was fixated on the general election, when he wanted to present himself as a resolute leader committed to having peaceful relations but only on India's terms. In the final analysis, Pakistan's withdrawal to the LoC was achieved through the intervention of a US president. But Vajpayee and his defense and foreign ministers attributed it exclusively to Delhi's strong military response to the occupation of Kargil, combined with secret diplomacy conducted through the confidantes of the two prime ministers. Breaking with protocol, Vajpayee revealed that on June 27 he had told Sharif's emissary Naik in Delhi that "unless Pakistani forces leave Kargil, no discussions on any matter can take place."[55] These tactics ramped up the electoral chances of the BJP-led NDA.

A SPATE OF POPULAR WAR DRAMAS IN INDIA

In India, the public perception of the latest fight with Pakistan was formed differently from the earlier armed conflicts. In the past it was shaped exclusively by the broadcasting media run by the Ministry of Information and Broadcasting. But following the Supreme Court's ruling ending the state monopoly in broadcasting in 1995, this changed. The subsequent competition between several private Indian radio and TV channels, specializing in news and comment, led to the sensationalizing of war news. As a consequence, Vajpayee's announcement of Operation Vijay defeating Pakistan's Operation Badr received thunderous coverage.

The situation in Pakistan was starkly different. With its monopoly over the broadcasting media, the government controlled the news about the Kargil upheaval, attributing the fighting there to the mujahedin of Kashmir, who had taken up arms. But given the arrival of satellite and cable television in their country, Pakistanis had the option of seeking news from non-Pakistani sources. Their choices covered not only the BBC and All India Radio but also privately run Indian TV channels. Besides the accuracy (or otherwise) of the reports from the frontline, their presentation was far more engaging than the staid fare being offered by the state-controlled electronic media of Pakistan. With the complicity of Pakistani forces in Kargil becoming public knowledge, and Sharif agreeing to military withdrawal to the LoC, the credibility of Pakistan's media fell steeply.

Commenting on the media coverage of the Kargil War a decade later, Major General Muhammad Azam Asif lamented the fact that the Pakistani media gave up without putting up a fight against enemy media invasion. The Indian media created war hysteria using cricketers, film actors, and popular personalities to boost the morale of their troops. "Pakistan decided to withdraw due to low morale of troop's heavy causalities and mounting international pressure," he added. "It [Pakistani media] lacked offensive posture and well coordinated and planned themes to raise the morale of the troops or to shield them against Indian propaganda."[56]

In India, the Kargil conflict led to a spate of songs, documentaries, movies, and stage dramas. Within months of the war's end, the five-year-old, Mumbai-based, foursome rock band Pentagram released India's first exclusive-to-Internet song, "The Price of Bullets," about the conflict. It featured famous Muslim poet and lyricist Javed Akhtar. Sahara TV aired a series, titled *Mission Fateh: Real Stories of Kargil Heroes*, chronicling the Indian Army's missions in a triumphalist mode.

In February 2002, Mumbai was the venue of *Fifty Day War*, a 15 million rupees ($330,000) gigantic theatrical production with one hundred performers, about the Kargil conflict. It was presented in a six-hundred-seat outdoor theatre-in-the round, with seats that revolved 360 degrees around the action of the play. Directed by Aamir Raza Husain, the play featured vast sets along with brilliant lighting, thundering sound, and the smell of gunpowder produced by actual explosions, and recreated the frontlines of the Kargil war in three dimensions—an extraordinary feat in the history of theater. "The play tries to break the conventional paradigms of time and space by transposing audiences from one set to another," Husain told the *Financial Express*.[57]

As before, Bollywood producers tried to capitalize on India's successful military venture. In 2003, *LoC Kargil*, a four-hour-long Bollywood film, recreating many events of the war, set another record.

Unlike earlier war movies, which were in essence recruitment tools for the Indian Army, the fictionalized account of the Kargil conflict, as depicted in the expensively produced *Vaishya* (Hindi: Aim), released on the fifth anniversary of the Kargil War, broke new ground. Its protagonist was a wayward young man, Karan Shergill—played by superstar Hrithik Roshan—who realizes that the aim of his life is to join the army and retake a post captured by Pakistan-backed Kashmiri freedom fighters in the strategic heights of the Indian Kashmir. "All this is quite well done, without the usual excessive jingoism," noted Ihsan Aslam, a Cambridge-based Pakistani historian, after seeing the movie. "There is, of course, a certain feel-good factor for the Indian viewers, but the Pakistanis don't come out entirely bad. . . . The latter part of the film has a very newsy feel because of [the lead female] Priety Zinta's role as a TV war reporter. The war scenes, all shot in the dark, are realistic as is the depiction of death and injury."[58] The script was written by the renowned Javed Akhtar and directed by his son, Farhan. It was a box office hit, making a profit of almost $1 million, a colossal sum in India.

There was nothing comparative produced in Pakistan. All that happened was that the actor-director-producer Abdul Rauf Khalid devoted the last of the twenty-seven episodes in the state-run Pakistan TV's *Laag* (Urdu: Roaming) series (1998–2000), centered on the trials and tribulations of the Kashmiris living in India-held Kashmir, to the Kargil War.[59] This was partly because, unlike in India, there was no unanimity in Pakistan about the end result of the Kargil War. Far more importantly, that conflict heralded a new chapter in the rocky history of democracy in Pakistan.

THE SHARIF-MUSHARRAF BATTLE

While Sharif was on his way back home on July 5, 1999, after several hours of tense talks with Clinton, Musharraf expressed his disapproval of "the surrender" by Sharif in his comments to leading newspapers. What had been gained on the military front had been lost on the political front, he claimed, without providing incontestable evidence to that effect.

Overall, though, Sharif's agreement to withdraw the Pakistani forces from Kargil without consulting the military high command angered the generals. He thus violated the cardinal principle guiding Pakistan since the deaths of its founding figures—Muhammad Ali Jinnah and Liaquat Ali Khan—that the ultimate authority for forming and implementing national security policies lay exclusively with the corps commanders. This paved the way for his downfall. In the words of an unnamed high military officer, "Sharif brought disgrace to the Pakistani army by bowing down before the US administration for an abrupt pullout from Kargil. In the aftermath of the Kargil crisis we went through almost a revolt in the army as the rank and file thought that the government had betrayed them."[60]

In a way this was a repeat of what had happened after the 1971 Bangladesh War. The only difference was that whereas the Pakistani commander in East Pakistan signed the surrender document in the Indian-occupied Dacca, this time the DGs of Military Operations of the two sides signed the cease-fire agreement at the Attari border post in Indian Punjab.

Sharif could do little to counter the prevailing feeling in the army ranks that he had let them down. And his promise to Clinton to pressure the Taliban, whose government in Kabul had been recognized by Pakistan, had not gone down well with Musharraf and other generals.

On August 7, 1999, huge bombs exploding at the US embassies in Nairobi and Dar es Salaam killed 227 people. Washington blamed bin Laden, then living in Kandahar, Afghanistan, as the mastermind. On the night of August 8 two planeloads of teams from the CIA's Special Activities Division arrived in Peshawar and Quetta to infiltrate Afghanistan, with the help of ISI agents, to capture bin Laden. But when Al Jazeera leaked the story on television, the project was aborted.

On August 20 Clinton ordered strikes at six terrorist training camps in Afghanistan, a landlocked country. Executing that order from the *Abraham Lincoln* aircraft carrier in the Arabian Sea required firing cruise missile through Pakistani airspace. Since bin Laden was not present at any of these venues, the strikes missed their prime target. Washington's action upset Sharif. "Prime Minister Nawaz Sharif told President Clinton that the unilateral US action constituted violation of the sovereignty and territorial integrity of independent states," said an official Pakistani statement. "This attack has caused anguish and indignation in Pakistan."[61] The casualties caused by the American attack on a training camp near Khost included members of the ISI-backed Harkat ul Mujahedin, a militant Kashmiri group. This evidence of the ISI's indirect links with Al Qaida deeply embarrassed Sharif.[62]

To placate Clinton, for whom capturing or killing bin Laden was top priority, Sharif dispatched ISI chief Lieutenant General Ziauddin Butt to Washington in early October 1999 to coordinate the next move to seize the Al Qaida chief. And to contradict the rumors of a falling-out between him and Musharraf, on September 30 he confirmed the remaining two years of Musharraf's term as the COAS and also appointed him the chairman of the Joint Chiefs of Staff Committee, amid much fanfare. This was meant to signify a truce between the two protagonists. Sharif capped this by inviting Musharraf and his wife, Sehba, to dinner, where the prime minister's father, Muhammad Sharif, welcomed Musharraf as "my third son," his second son being Shahbaz, the chief minister of Punjab.

Several earlier narratives of the run-up to the October 12 coup have to be revised in light of the revelations made by the coplotter Lieutenant General Aziz in his book published in October 2013. According to Aziz, during the last days of September Musharraf chaired meetings at the Army House in Rawalpindi to decide the right moment to oust Sharif's government in order to preempt the prime minister's anticipated move to replace the general as the COAS. The pivotal role was played by the MI's Ehsan ul Haq, who provided Musharraf and others close to him with up-to-date information on Sharif's plans.

It was vital for the two rivals to show that it was "business as usual." But before departing for Colombo to attend the October 9 celebrations of the fiftieth anniversary of the Sri Lankan Army, he told Lieutenant Generals Aziz Khan, Mehmood Ahmed, and Aziz: "All three of you would be individually authorized to issue orders for the removal of the government. I hold you three responsible for this [to act and remove the government]."[63] As the DG for Military Operations, Aziz issued written orders to the commander of the Rawalpindi-based Brigade 111 to be ready for the critical operation.

Musharraf's return flight from Colombo by the Pakistan International Airline (PIA) got delayed—twice. In Islamabad, Sharif realized that his words and deeds were being monitored by the military's intelligence apparatus. Therefore, accompanied by one of his sons and Lieutenant General Butt dressed in civilian clothes, he flew to Abu Dhabi on October 10 to confer with Butt in an espionage-free environment. After a courtesy call on the UAE ruler, Shaikh Zayed bin Sultan al Nahyan, followed by the fine-tuning of Butt's rise to the COAS, Sharif's team returned home the same day. This vital information was conveyed to Musharraf in Colombo by Ehsan ul Haq.

DRAMA IN THE AIR

As finalized in Abu Dhabi, Sharif prepared to announce the promotion of Butt as the COAS on October 12. Just as the PIA flight, carrying two hundred passengers including Musharraf took off at three PM (Pakistan time) from Colombo for Karachi, Sharif appointed Butt as the COAS at the prime minister's official residence in Islamabad in a fitting ceremony. This was aired on the sole state-run Pakistan TV.

But at the GHQ in Rawalpindi, twelve miles from the capital, Lieutenant General Aziz Khan, chief of the general staff, denied Butt the control of GHQ. Spiked at this level, Butt's orders could not go further down the chain of command. This was coupled with the refusal of Lieutenant General Mahmood Ahmed, commander of the Rawalpindi-based Tenth Corps, to accept Butt's authority.

Around four PM Sharif's office announced that General Musharraf had retired. An hour later soldiers from the 111 Brigade of the Tenth Corps rushed to Islamabad in trucks. Arriving there, they started pouring out onto the streets. Watched by curious onlookers, they seized the state television station and switched off the signal.

This compelled Butt and Sharif to stop the airborne Musharraf from reaching Karachi. They were unaware that at the GHQ in Rawalpindi, Aziz Khan had phoned Lieutenant General Muzaffar Usmani, commander of the Fifth Corps in Karachi, to ensure Musharraf's safe return to the city. The PIA flight from Colombo approached Karachi airport around six thirty PM, but air traffic control refused permission for the plane to land.

High drama followed. Sharif ordered air traffic controllers to redirect the flight to the airport in Nawabshah, southern Sindh, where Sharif had dispatched his own plane and a security team to arrest Musharraf. Inside the PIA aircraft, Musharraf entered the cockpit. He instructed the pilot to keep circling the Karachi airport while he personally urged the air traffic controllers to let the plane land.

They refused—until the control tower was seized by troops of the Fifth Corps. By the time Musharraf touched down on Pakistani soil, it was 7:47 PM, with the now stationary PIA airliner having only seven minutes of fuel left. He was instantly whisked away by officers of the Fifth Corps.[64]

In Islamabad, soldiers of the 111 Brigade disarmed the security force at Sharif's official residence. Soon Lieutenant General Ahmed arrived and asked Sharif to resign or rescind his order promoting Butt. Sharif refused both options. He was then escorted out by soldiers and detained at a government guest house near the airport. By now the troops controlled all TV stations, administrative offices, and the power and communications infrastructure throughout the country. They placed the entire cabinet under guard and cut international telephone lines.

At 10:15 PM the military restored television broadcasts. Minutes later an announcement running across the bottom of the screen announced the dismissal of Prime Minister Nawaz Sharif. Musharraf's prerecorded message to the nation at 2:50 AM on October 13 cited Sharif's attempts to divide the army as one of the chief reasons for the coup. "This is not martial law, only another path towards democracy," he added. "The armed forces have no intention to stay in charge any longer than is absolutely necessary to pave the way for true democracy to flourish in Pakistan."[65]

This was the fourth power grab by the military in Pakistan's fifty-two-year history. It was triggered by its involvement in the Muslim separatist insurgency in India-held Kashmir and the fate of bin Laden. It highlighted the fact that the military was the final arbiter of power in Pakistan. There were historical, ethnic, and socioeconomic reasons for this state of affairs. The armed conflict over Kashmir came within a few months of the birth of the new country. That accorded the military the highest priority. Most of the ranks and officers of the army have come from Punjab, which accounts for 55 percent of the national population. The resulting ethnic homogeneity imparts the military extra strength. In a predominantly agrarian, largely illiterate or subliterate society, the army stands out as a paragon of discipline and order. And unlike all other institutions, it has remained almost free of corruption. As a consequence, it is held in high esteem by the public at large.

By a strange coincidence, it was on October 13, 1999, that Vajpayee was sworn in as prime minister. As leader of the 303-strong NDA, he enjoyed a comfortable majority in the 545-seat lower house of Parliament.[66] The contrast between India and Pakistan could not have been starker.

MUSHARRAF, THE "CHIEF EXECUTIVE"

Two days later Musharraf declared an emergency, suspended the constitution, and assumed supreme power as the chief executive. He closed down the prime minister's secretariat while leaving in place the incumbent Muhammad Rafiq Tarar as president. On October 17, during his second nationwide TV address, he announced the formation of a seven-member military-civilian council under his chairmanship.

Washington was quick to condemn the coup and urged a return to democracy. The reaction in Delhi, however, was mixed. "He is the man who attacked us in Kargil," said Jyotindra Nath Dixit, former foreign secretary and advisor to the National Security Council. "We should be much more alert about General Musharraf." Having just taken the oath of office, Vajpayee was diplomatic. "We are willing to talk to any regime in Pakistan," he told reporters. "It is for Pakistan to create a climate for resumption of dialogue between the two countries." Unsurprisingly, the response of pro-Pakistan Kashmiris was euphoric. "It is good to see military rule in Pakistan but the step was delayed," said a spokesman of the Hizb ul Mujahedin. "It should have come earlier at the time of the Kashmir [Kargil] war when Nawaz Sharif betrayed us."[67]

Following the Kargil debacle, the separatist Hizb ul Mujahedin and Harkat ul Mujahedin stepped up their attacks on the security forces in Indian Kashmir. Harkat ul Mujahedin hit the headlines in the international media when five of its militants, armed with pistols, knives, and hand grenades, hijacked an Indian Airlines (aka Air India) aircraft flying from Katmandu to New Delhi on the morning of December 24. After refusals by several airports in Pakistan, Afghanistan, Oman, and the United Arab Emirates, the plane landed at the Kandahar airport in the early hours of Christmas Day with 155 passengers and crew.

The hijackers demanded the release of thirty-six Kashmiri prisoners and a £125 million ransom. After refusing to deal with them, the Vajpayee government entered into staggered negotiations through the Taliban authorities in Kabul. As days passed, the passengers, crew, and hijackers cooped up inside the plane kept warm in the freezing temperature of an Afghan winter by the power generated by the plane's engines. The Indians managed to bring down the hijackers' demand to just three names from the top of their list.

By the time they arrived at the Kabul airport, accompanied by the Indian foreign minister Jaswant Singh, it was December 31. The released men included Maulana Masoud Azhar, a Pakistani cleric whose brother, Muhammad Ibrahim, was one of the hijackers. Azhar had gone to Indian Kashmir to conciliate the two feuding factions of Harkat ul Ansar (later renamed Harkat ul Mujahedin) and was imprisoned. One of the remaining two freed men was Ahmad Umar Shaikh, a Pakistan-based British national involved with the separatist movement committed to separating Kashmir from India. At Kandahar airport, the gun-toting hijackers along with the released militants boarded a van provided by the Taliban, whose government refused them asylum. It let the van cross the Afghan-Pakistan border, with its passengers disembarking in Pakistan to shelter in safe houses briefly before going underground.

Within days, Maulana Azhar surfaced in Karachi. Surrounded by bodyguards in camouflage-colored clothes and brandishing automatic rifles, he delivered an incendiary speech to ten thousand supporters assembled in front of a central Karachi mosque. "I have come back and I will not rest in peace until Kashmir is liberated," he declared.[68] The Musharraf government had stated earlier that the hijackers would be arrested if they stepped into Pakistan. But there was no effort to detain Azhar or stop him from addressing a rally.

This hijack drama, the longest in the world to date, pushed Indo-Pakistan relations to their lowest ebb in peace times at the turn of the century.

15

General Musharraf
Buckles Under US Pressure

The strengthening alliance of Musharraf-ruled Pakistan with the Taliban government in Afghanistan caused grave concern in Washington. President Bill Clinton was also well aware of Musharraf's masterminding of the military campaign in the Kargil region of the Indian Kashmir and his reckless preparation for a nuclear attack on India. The general had then capped his dangerously surreptitious actions with toppling the democratically elected government of Prime Minister Muhammad Nawaz Sharif.

Though Pakistan's withdrawal to the Line of Control (LoC) in Kashmir was completed by the end of July 1999, the deaths of India's security personnel caused by the insurgents in Indian Kashmir more than doubled from the previous year's figure, to 425 in 1999. The loss of life among the armed militants, however, was almost three times as much.[1] The long, tortuous cease-fire line passing through assorted terrains had proved immune to being sealed thoroughly by India, which was at the receiving end of the violence committed by young Kashmiris who, after crossing the LoC, had received training and arms in Pakistani Kashmir.

It was this state of affairs that led Clinton to call the LoC arguably "the most dangerous place in the world today"[2] as he prepared for a week-long trip to Bangladesh, India, and Pakistan in mid-March 2000.

FIVE DAYS IN INDIA, FIVE HOURS IN PAKISTAN

After a brief visit to Dhaka, Clinton arrived in Delhi on March 20 and spent five days in the country, touring Agra to see the Taj Mahal, the pink

309

city of Jaipur, the village of Nayala, Hyderabad, and Mumbai. His time in India equaled the combined total spent earlier by three US presidents: Dwight Eisenhower, Richard Nixon, and Jimmy Carter. Wherever he went, he witnessed Clinton-mania, which pleased not only him but also his daughter, Chelsea, and his mother-in-law, Dorothy Rodham, who accompanied him.

At the end of a series of meetings with top Indian officials and a speech to the joint session of Parliament, he signed agreements on commerce and science and technology while acknowledging India's potential as an information technology superpower. Along with Indian premier Atal Bihari Vajpayee he issued a statement spelling out a new "vision" for Indo-American ties. He spoke of institutionalizing mutual dialogue up to the highest level and continuing talks on the nuclear issue. At the joint press conference, Vajpayee said, "We have a problem of cross-border terrorism, but there is no threat of war." During his visit to Nayala, ten miles from Jaipur, Clinton got a glimpse of democracy at work at the village level in India when he talked to elected representatives, some of them women in colorful Rajasthani dresses. The overall result of Clinton's extended sojourn in India was to raise the level of Delhi-Washington engagement to a higher level, particularly when compared to Islamabad-Washington ties.[3]

This became dramatically evident within hours of Clinton's departure for Islamabad. Arriving at the Mumbai airport on the morning of March 25, he walked toward the Presidential Air Force One C-17, giving the impression of planning to board this plane. He paused briefly to bid farewell to Richard Celeste, the US ambassador to India. But then he did not make the expected move. Air Force One left the airport without Clinton, who, unknown to onlookers, had sneaked into the adjoining small, unmarked Gulfstream III, which took off a little while later.

Clinton played this hide-and-seek game at the insistence of his Secret Service. Its chief had warned him that Pakistan's security forces were so thoroughly penetrated by terrorists that extremist groups, possibly Al Qaida, would be privy to his travel route from their sympathizers within the Inter-Services Intelligence (ISI) directorate and would attempt to shoot down the presidential plane.

The Secret Service's ruse did not stop at the safe arrival of the Clinton-bearing Gulfstream III at Islamabad's Chaklala airport. On its way to the office of Pakistani president Muhammad Rafiq Tarar, Clinton's motorcade stopped near an underpass, where he changed cars.[4] To leave nothing to chance, the Pakistani government emptied out the center of its capital on the eve of his arrival. It was in the midst of this fortified ghost town that Clinton addressed Pakistanis on TV, a precondition for his visit, which would last all of five hours.

"Now we are in the dawn of a new century, and a new and changing world has come into view," Clinton began. "Clearly, the absence of democracy makes it harder for people to move ahead. . . . Democracy cannot develop if it is constantly uprooted before it has a chance to firmly take hold. . . . The answer to flawed democracy is not to end democracy, but to improve it." Clinton then turned to terrorism. "We [Americans and Pakistanis] have both suffered enough to know that no grievance, no cause, no system of beliefs can ever justify the deliberate killing of innocents," he stated. "Those who bomb bus stations, target embassies or kill those who uphold the law are not heroes. They are our common enemies, for their aim is to exploit painful problems, not to resolve them." Next he focused on the region. "For India and Pakistan this must be a time of restraint, for respect for the Line of Control, and renewed lines of communication," he said. "There is no military solution to Kashmir. International sympathy, support and intervention cannot be won by provoking a bigger, bloodier conflict. On the contrary; sympathy and support will be lost. And no matter how great the grievance, it is wrong to support attacks against civilians across the Line of Control." As for the United States, "We cannot and will not mediate or resolve the dispute in Kashmir. Only you and India can do that, through dialogue."[5]

To emphasize his strong disapproval of Musharraf's military role, he ensured that his handshake of the dictator was not recorded by cameras. During his one-on-one meeting with Musharraf he raised the issues of terrorism and a road map for democracy in Pakistan but found him non-committal.

Then, to the surprise of Clinton and many others, the Supreme Court of Pakistan stepped in to dictate its own road map. In mid-May the twelve-member bench unanimously coupled its justification of the coup on the grounds of corruption, maladministration, and the faltering economy with an instruction to Chief Executive Musharraf to hold elections within three years from the date of the coup—that is, October 12, 2002.[6]

DELHI-WASHINGTON BONDING
SOFTENS MUSHARRAF

During his state visit to Washington in mid-September Vajpayee warmed up relations between the largest and the most powerful democracies of the globe. He addressed a joint session of Congress. The next day he was received by Clinton with full state honors on the South Lawn of the White House. In his talk with his host he did not veer from his previous stances on terrorism ("India was a victim of cross-frontier terrorism from Pakistan"), reviving the Lahore Declaration process ("It was up to Pakistan to stop aiding Kashmiri insurgents as a precondition for reconciliation"), and the nuclear agenda ("India had no attention of subscribing to the Comprehensive Test Ban Treaty which the US Senate had rejected in 1999"). "I took the bus to Lahore, but the bus went to Kargil," repeated Vajpayee at every opportunity.[7]

In his public utterances, Clinton was relentless in his praise of India. He was more eloquent about the virtues of Mohandas Gandhi than Vajpayee was when the latter unveiled a bronze image of the seminaked, striding Mahatma, armed with a long walking stick, on the triangular island along Massachusetts Avenue across the road from the Indian embassy. Mahatma Gandhi thus became the first South Asian personage to be so honored in the American capital.

The convergence between India and the United States went beyond geopolitics. The service India's software companies provided to US corporations to immunize their computer systems from crashing on January 1, 2000, opened a new chapter in the Indo-American commercial-industrial arena. And the 6.5 percent expansion in India's GDP in fiscal 1999 showed the country breaking out of its traditional growth band of 3 to 5 percent. This encouraged US companies to invest in India.

Critics who argued that Vajpayee's visit to Washington at the very end of the Clinton administration was badly timed missed the point that the burgeoning economic links between the two nations were unrelated to the tenure of an American president.

Among those who fretted about the ever-tightening concord between Delhi and Washington was Musharraf. By establishing the National Accountability Bureau, headed by Lieutenant General Syed Mohammad Amjad, Musharraf had cracked down hard on corruption. That won him much popular acclaim and helped him consolidate his power. He was now ready for a meeting with the Indian prime minister. His chance would have come if the biennial meeting of the South Asian Association for

Regional Cooperation (SAARC) had taken place in 2000. Because of Vajpayee's refusal (expressed privately) to share the SAARC platform with dictator Musharraf, the biennial conference was postponed.

It was only in mid-March 2001 that an opening appeared for Musharraf because of the South Asia visit by UN secretary-general Kofi Annan. After meeting Musharraf and his foreign minister, Abdul Sattar, in Islamabad on March 11, Annan explained to journalists that since UN resolutions on Kashmir were not passed under the self-enforcing Chapter 7 of the UN Charter, these needed the cooperation of the concerned parties for their implementation. He urged Pakistan and India to start a fresh dialogue on Kashmir.[8]

On arriving in Delhi four days later, Annan said, "You and Pakistan have too much in shared heritage by way of history, as well as family and cultural ties, not to resolve your differences. . . . It is time to begin healing the wounds." Following his meeting with Vajpayee, he stressed the need for Indo-Pakistan dialogue on the dispute over Kashmir.[9]

Since the Vajpayee-Sharif summit had been held in Pakistan, it was the Indian leader's turn to invite his Pakistani counterpart to India. They agreed on a three-day visit starting July 15.

FLEXIBLE MUSHARRAF MEETS INFLEXIBLE VAJPAYEE

A few weeks before the summit, Pakistan's president Tarar resigned in favor of Chief Executive Musharraf. That was why President Musharraf arrived at the Delhi airport in civilian dress to be welcomed by his Indian counterpart, K. R. Narayanan. For the fifty-eight-year-old Musharraf, to return to the city of his birth after fifty-four years was an intensely moving experience. When he visited his ancestral home in the Daryaganj neighborhood, called Nehra Wali Haveli, he had a tearful reunion with an old servant who remembered him as a little boy.

Musharraf became the first Pakistani leader to pay homage to Mahatma Gandhi. After laying a wreath at the site containing the Mahatma's ashes, he and his chubby, short-haired wife, Sehba, elegantly dressed in an embroidered purple *salwar kameez*, showered rose petals at the memorial—an honoring ritual common among Pakistanis and North Indians. "Never has the requirement of his ideals been so severely felt than today, especially in the context of India-Pakistan relations," he wrote in the visitors' book. "May his soul rest in peace."[10]

Musharraf did his best to live down his reputation as the mastermind of the failed Kargil campaign in Kashmir. He repeatedly asserted that his government accepted the Shimla and Lahore Declarations. "We must not allow the past to dictate the future" became his refrain in the way "I took the bus to Lahore, but the bus went to Kargil" had become Vajpayee's in Washington.

Pakistan's high commissioner in Delhi, Ashraf Jahangir Qazi, invited leaders of the major political parties of India as well as Kashmir, including the separatist All Parties Hurriyat Conference (APHC), to a reception at his residence in the evening. Ignoring his hosts' advice, Musharraf held a closed-door meeting with APHC leaders. But, to his credit, in the several statements he made off and on the record, he never mentioned APHC or the UN resolutions on Kashmir. In the hour-long informal tête-à-tête he had with invited Indian journalists, academics, and former diplomats before the reception, he came across as an unpretentious, affable man— and a professional staff officer who spoke clearly, being largely unfamiliar with the diplomatic niceties and obfuscations. "My English is not very good," he remarked at one point. "So if India has problems with the phrase 'Kashmir dispute,' let us just call it an 'issue' or a 'problem.'" On the contentious subject of whether or not "Kashmir is the core issue," he said, "Let us find another word, another adjective. What I mean is that this is the [only] issue on which we have fought wars."[11]

In short, Musharraf was being flexible, whereas earlier in the day in his meetings with Home Minister and Deputy Prime Minister Lal Krishna Advani and Foreign Minister Jaswant Singh he had been presented with a list of cross-frontier acts of terrorism.

The next day the scene shifted to Agra, the city of the Taj Mahal, the gem of the Indo-Islamic architecture and a shining symbol of the apogee of Mughal power in the Indian subcontinent. The two sessions of talks were described by the host's spokesperson as "very constructive." The following day was spent on finding common ground and preparing a version acceptable to both sides. But after a delay of nine hours, in which several draft proposals were exchanged, the two delegations failed to produce a document that Vajpayee and Musharraf were willing to sign.

The Agra summit ended in smoke. Its failure set it apart from the ones in Shimla (1972) and Lahore (1999), but there was another major difference: the coverage by the media. In 1972 the Indian government monopolized broadcasting. It was the same with Pakistan in 1999. Two years later in Agra, thanks to the proliferation of privately owned broadcasting companies in India, there was a massive presence of invasive electronic media with a battery of TV cameras and roving commentators at work throughout the day and well into the night. Given the cutthroat competition in the industry, the newsreaders and field reporters tried frantically to engender exciting headlines for each successive half-hour news bulletin with the endless—and often meaningless—lead of "Breaking News." In this cornucopia of exposure, Pakistanis got an ample chance to express their viewpoint on Indian TV channels eager to feed their viewers with something unfamiliar. The Pakistanis marshaled competent spokespersons. In the absence of studio editing, they offered coherent arguments—a refreshing change for Indian viewers.

After the event, there was much debate as to who was responsible for the failure of the summit. As often happens in long-running disputes, cause and effect get mixed up. The Indians' fixation on cross-border terrorism paralleled the Pakistanis' insistence on treating Kashmir as the core problem. Keen on quashing terrorism by all means, India's top officials missed the logical point that terrorism stemmed from the fact that because of Delhi's obduracy the Kashmir dispute had remained unresolved for sixty-odd years. It followed that cross-frontier terrorism and the unresolved Kashmir problem could not be treated on par. The cause had to precede the result. This plain logic was unacceptable to BJP ministers.

The BJP had been in the forefront of forging strong ties with Israel, which had won Delhi's diplomatic recognition in 1992. During his visit to Israel in June 2000, the BJP home minister Advani had said, "Defeating the designs of our neighbor [Pakistan] who has unleashed cross-border terrorism, illegal infiltration, and border management are concerns that have brought me to Israel."[12]

His trip prepared the ground for India's purchase of Israel's surveillance equipment, including thermal sensors and night-vision devices, for use mainly in Kashmir. Later a team of senior Israeli counterterrorism officials toured Indian Kashmir and other areas of endemic antigovernment violence. According to the August 14, 2001, issue of the United Kingdom–based *Jane's Terrorism and Security Monitor*, Israel had posted "several teams" in the Kashmir Valley to train Indian counterinsurgency personnel.[13]

The next month's shattering attacks on the World Trade Center (WTC) in New York and the Pentagon in Washington strengthened the hands of BJP leaders in Delhi at the expense of Musharraf.

9/11: A GEOPOLITICAL EARTHQUAKE

The sensational crashing of three passenger aircrafts into two World Trade Center skyscrapers and the Pentagon, along with the failed but fatal hijacking of a fourth plane, on September 11, 2001, led to almost three thousand deaths. It was the most lethal assault from a foreign source the United States had suffered on its mainland. "The deliberate and deadly attacks that were carried out against our country yesterday were more than acts of terror," said President George W. Bush on September 12. "They were acts of war."[14] He immediately formed a war cabinet.

Among Afghanistan's neighbors, Pakistan mattered most to the United States. Indeed, it was the key state. In the absence of land bases in an adjoining country sharing long borders—which Pakistan did—the Pentagon's options would be severely limited. That in turn would diminish the prospect of a short, successful campaign, which, given the very real prospect of inflaming Muslim opinion worldwide, was essential.

As it happened, on September 11 the ISI head, Lieutenant General Mahmood Ahmed, was having a business breakfast with Congressman Porter Goss and Senator Bob Graham—respective chairs of the House and Senate Intelligence Committees—when the airplanes struck the towers. Ahmed assured his interlocutors that, when pressured, Taliban leader Mullah Muhammad Omar would hand over Osama bin Laden to the United States.

Goss and Graham were dubious about Ahmed's loyalties. They knew that he had refused to cooperate with an earlier CIA plan to subvert the Taliban by bribing local commanders to desert.[15]

The next day, accompanied by Maheela Lodhi, Pakistan's ambassador to the United States, Ahmed found himself facing Richard Armitage, deputy secretary of state, in the latter's office. According to Lodhi, "The two of them were very tense. Armitage started out by saying, 'This is a grave moment. History begins today for the United States. We are asking all our friends—you're not the only country we're speaking to—we're asking people whether they're with us or against us.'"[16] He then handed Ahmed a list of official demands. Washington's wish list—later published in *The 9/11 Commission Report*—read:

1. Stop Al Qaida operatives at its border and end all logistical support for bin Laden. 2. Give the United States blanket overflight and landing rights for all necessary military and intelligence operations. 3. Provide territorial

access to US and allied military intelligence and other personnel to conduct operations against Al Qaida. 4. Provide the United States with intelligence information. 5. Continue to publicly condemn the terrorist attacks. 6. Cut off all shipments of fuel to the Taliban and stop recruits from going to Afghanistan. 7. If the evidence implicated bin Laden and Al Qaida, and the Taliban continued to harbor them, to break relations with the Taliban government.[17]

Armitage's document was actually a follow-up to the urgent phone calls that the Bush White House had made earlier to Musharraf, who had agreed to come on board. In his television address on September 13, Musharraf said, "I wish to assure President Bush and the US government of our fullest cooperation in the fight against terrorism." He immediately froze the assets of the Taliban regime in the State Bank of Pakistan as well as the accounts being used by various Pakistani organizations to fund the Taliban.[18]

Musharraf's swift and sudden abandoning of his erstwhile policy of sustaining and aiding the Taliban while professing to have scant influence over them was a severe blow to the fundamentalist Islamic regime in Kabul. Since its inception, Pakistan had been not only the chief provider of military supplies, fuel, and food to the Taliban's armed forces, but also the sole supplier of officers to act as its military planners. It had allowed sixty thousand students, mainly from madrassas (religious schools), to participate in many Taliban offensives at one time or another.[19]

Having received Washington's list of demands, Musharraf called a meeting of a dozen top military commanders at the general headquarters in Rawalpindi on September 15. The atmosphere was somber. Musharraf outlined his proposal to support America fully in its imminent war against the Taliban and bin Laden–led Al Qaida. He explained that failure to opt for the United States would not only result in Washington cutting off its economic funding, including loans from the International Monetary Fund, but most likely make Pakistan its potential target for punishment. He was challenged by Lieutenant General Ahmed, who led the opposition, consisting of Musharraf's other coconspirators in the 1999 coup—General Muhammad Aziz Khan and Lieutenant General Muzaffar Hussein Usmani—as well as General Jamshaid Gulzar Kiani, now commander of the powerful Tenth Corps in Rawalpindi. "Let the US do its [own] dirty work," remarked Ahmed. "Its enemies are our friends."[20] Musharraf then argued that this was a strategic opportunity to manipulate the situation for Pakistan's benefit, just as General Muhammad Zia ul Haq had done in 1979. Among other things that alliance had shored up Pakistan's cash-strapped treasury: "We should offer up help and, mark my words, we will receive a clean bill of health."[21] In subsequent years Pakistan would be upgraded to a non-NATO ally (in 2004), which entitled it to purchase advanced US military hardware, and would receive a total of $10 billion in economic and military assistance for participating in Washington's counterterrorism campaign. But, at this pivotal, highly charged meeting, the dissenters remained unconvinced.

In desperation, Musharraf played his strongest card. He revealed that on September 13 Delhi had offered the use of Indian soil for US military strikes against Afghanistan—a decision kept secret by the Vajpayee government so as not to inflame Muslim opinion in India.[22] Because of a lack of common borders with Afghanistan, India's offer could not match Pakistan's. All the same, for the Islamist Pakistani generals, more anti-India than pro-Taliban, such a prospect was taboo. Reluctantly, they went along with Musharraf.

Indeed, in his TV address to the nation on September 19 to justify his U-turn on the Taliban and lining up solidly with Washington, he played up the Indian angle. "They [Indians] have readily offered all their bases, facilities, and logistic support to the United States." He said. "They want the United States . . . to declare Pakistan a terrorist state. They also want our strategic assets—nuclear and missiles—and our Kashmir cause to be harmed."[23]

PAKISTAN'S DIRE ECONOMY

At $38 billion, Pakistan's foreign borrowings were half of its GDP. Servicing these and domestic loans consumed 65 percent of government revenue. Another 25 percent of its annual treasure was spent by the military. Islamabad's foreign reserves at $1.7 billion were barely enough to pay for essential imports for two months. Therefore the bilateral talks conducted behind closed doors were focused on working out the modalities of a graduated deal, with economic concessions to Islamabad moving up gradually—from the lifting of US sanctions imposed because of Pakistan's nuclear tests to easier rescheduling of foreign loans, more bilateral and multilateral credits, and better access to the American market for Pakistani goods in exchange for Islamabad implementing US demands, culminating in the dismissal or retirement of the pro-Taliban, Islamist generals.[24] In return, Musharraf extracted a promise from Washington that it would not promote the anti-Taliban Northern Alliance, which had been supported by Russia, Iran, and India—a pledge the United States would break with impunity.[25]

On the other side of the international border, once Delhi backed Bush's campaign in Afghanistan, the United States restored its military ties with India, which had been suspended after the 1998 nuclear tests.

Though Musharraf airily dismissed the opposition to his alliance with America as representing no more than 15 percent of the population, a later Gallup Poll would show 62 percent against Pakistan joining the US-led global coalition.[26]

Having done the deal with the Bush administration, Musharraf tried to persuade Mullah Omar to hand over bin Laden to the United States. During their eight-hour meeting in Kandahar, the Pakistani military delegates, led by Lieutenant General Ahmed, warned Omar that if his government did not turn over bin Laden to Washington, he would face an attack by the US-led coalition. He remained obdurate.

The Pentagon's relentless air campaign started on October 7 and ended on November 14, with Kabul falling to the Northern Alliance, led by Ahmad Shah Masoud, in the wake of the Taliban's overnight flight from the capital. Reneging on its pledge to Musharraf, the Bush administration had actively bolstered the Northern Alliance, whose original backers included India.

By contrast, Musharraf delivered on his most secret promises to the United States about the hard-line Islamist generals in the military's high command a day after he had extended his own term as president indefinitely, "in the larger interests of the country," on October 7. He forced Lieutenant General Ahmed to resign. India claimed a secret role in the downfall of Ahmed.

Lieutenant General Ehsan ul Haq, who replaced Ahmed as ISI chief, was expected to purge those ISI officers who had helped the Taliban in the past. Musharraf removed General Kiani from the command of the Tenth Corps and appointed him adjutant general, the chief military administrative officer—a desk job. He "promoted" Aziz Khan to a largely ceremonial position of chair of the Joint Chiefs of Staff Committee, with no direct command of troops. By so doing he weakened the hand of the ambitious Islamist vice COAS Lieutenant General Muzaffar Hussein Usmani. In protest, Usmani resigned. His job went to a moderate, Lieutenant General

Muhammad Yusaf Khan. These moves by Musharraf satisfied the Bush administration while making his refurbished top team line up fully behind him, conceptually and strategically.

INDIA'S ELEVATED MORAL GROUND

Meanwhile, a daring terrorist attack on the Kashmir State Assembly in Srinagar on October 1 highlighted India's condition as a victim of cross-frontier terrorism. A suicide attacker drove a hijacked government jeep loaded with explosives to the main entrance of the Assembly complex and exploded it. In the mayhem that followed, two militants in police uniform slipped into the main Assembly building, firing their weapons and throwing hand grenades at security forces. At the end of a several-hour gun battle, interspersed with grenade explosions, thirty-eight people were dead. The Pakistan-based Jaish-e Muhammad (Urdu: Army of Muhammad; JeM), founded by Maulana Masoud Azhar in March 2000, claimed responsibility for the lethal assault and named Wajahat Hussein, a Pakistani national, as the suicide bomber.[27]

The storming of the legislature in Srinagar proved to be a precursor of something far more sensational in which JeM was involved. On December 13, five gunmen in commando uniforms went past the perimeter entrance gate to the mammoth, circular Parliament House in Delhi—built on a high platform with chambers for both houses of the central legislature—in a white car, carrying bulky bags filled with grenades, Kalashnikov rifles, and explosives, with a red flashing beacon on the roof, used typically by members of Parliament.

The vehicle crossed gate number 1, a sandstone portico. Fortuitously, the driveway was blocked by the motorcade of Vice President Krishna Kant, presiding official of Parliament's upper house, ready for a swift departure. When the driver of the gunmen's car tried to bypass the motorcade, he crashed into the vice president's car. The five attackers scrambled. As they rushed up the steps firing, they wounded an unarmed sentry guarding the huge carved door. Despite his injury, he managed to close the door and raise the alarm on his walkie-talkie. Swiftly the other eleven entrances to the building were shut. The ensuing gun battle between the attackers and security personnel on the steps of the Parliament House lasted half an hour. In the end, all the assailants lay dead, as did eight security guards. The terrorists had planned on massacring many of the eight hundred–odd Indian MPs, with their focus on the front benches of the Lower House, occupied by cabinet ministers.

It transpired later that, aside from the car accident and the ensuing mayhem, the terrorists' plan had gone awry as a result of the quintessentially Delhi experience of sudden power cuts. Electricity failure that morning deprived Muhammad Afzal (aka Afzal Guru)—a Kashmiri Muslim, arrested later as the suspected sixth coplotter—of his task: to sit at home to watch all-news television and inform the terrorist team by mobile phone of the arrival of cabinet ministers, including Vajpayee.

So Afzal did not know that the Lower House had adjourned five minutes after opening (because of the noisy protest by the opposition over a Defense Ministry scam of paying excessive sums for soldiers' coffins) and that Vajpayee had therefore decided to stay at his official residence. When Afzal informed the terrorists' leader in the car of his failure to access the twenty-four-hour television news, the latter got angry and went ahead with the assault.

Later that day Vajpayee chaired an emergency meeting of the five-strong Cabinet Committee on Security comprising defense, home, foreign, and finance ministers. The government described the event as "an attack on not just the symbol, but the seat, of Indian democracy and on the sovereignty of the Indian people." This daredevil raid stirred the people, politicians, and the media into a fury.

The US embassy called it "an outrageous act of terrorism" and "a brutal assault on the heart of Indian democracy."[28] The next morning, US ambassador Robert Blackwill, a bearlike man with a jowly visage who, as a history professor specialized in the study of the 1962 Cuban missile crisis, attended the memorial service at Parliament House for those who had fallen in the line of duty. Facing a battery of TV cameras after the somber service, Blackwill declared: "The United States and India are as one in this outrage. The tragic event that occurred yesterday and that was perpetrated by terrorists was no different in its objective from the terror attacks in the United States on September 11th."[29]

Delhi blamed the Pakistan-based JeM and Lashkar-e Taiba (LeT) for the audacious assault. It accused the LeT's Hafiz Muhammad Saeed of being the mastermind. It called on Musharraf to outlaw the two organizations and freeze their assets. Pakistan condemned the attack, but, claiming that it had never allowed its soil to be used for terrorism, it rejected

India's demand. Protesting Islamabad's foot-dragging, India reduced its diplomatic staff in Pakistan and unilaterally suspended the bilateral rail and bus links.

Official circles in Pakistan had a radically different take on the Parliament House assault. During his meeting with the visiting undersecretary of the US Army, Les Brownlee, on December 24, Vice COAS General Yusaf Khan said that he suspected India's manipulation in this attack. He was expressing a unanimously shared view in Islamabad that it was Delhi's policy to use its intelligence agencies to stage-manage terrorist assaults periodically to impress the international community.[30]

In sharp contrast to Islamabad's laid-back attitude toward the JeM and LeT, the United States went on to ban the two groups, which, according to later White House briefings to American reporters, had been responsible for 70 percent of the recent attacks in Indian Kashmir.[31]

OPERATION PARAKRAM

Following a full cabinet meeting, Vajpayee ordered the Defense Ministry to mobilize all three wings of the military for an offensive war. It did so on December 20 under the code-name of Operation Parakram (Sanskrit: Valor). The Indian Air Force was ready to strike at training camps inside Pakistan-held Kashmir. But mobilization of half a million army troops under COAS General Sundararajan Padmanabhan could not be achieved as rapidly as the government wished. In line with common practice in the modern military, only a part of the Indian army was organized as a strike force.

Delhi's overarching strategy was directed at both Islamabad and Washington; it was well aware that, as the aggrieved party, it held the high moral ground. While the Bush administration, committed to eradicating terrorism worldwide, had no option but to side with India, it could not afford to get too tough on Musharraf. He had played a pivotal role in the overthrow of the Taliban regime in Afghanistan, and his continued cooperation was essential in destroying the remnants of the Taliban and Al Qaida.

At the same time, the Bush White House could not deflect the argument Delhi offered. India equated Pakistan's support for the LeT and the JeM, along with its earlier backing for the Taliban, with the ISI's Kashmir and Afghan cells, which had been the primary engines behind these jihadist entities. It reasoned that Islamabad could not wage war on terrorism on its western frontier (Afghanistan) while supporting it on its eastern border (Kashmir).

Specifically, India demanded that Pakistan hand over twenty wanted terrorists living within its boundaries, six of them being its citizens. The list included Muhammad Ibrahim Azhar, one of the hijackers of the Indian Airlines plane two years earlier. In the absence of an extradition treaty between the two nations, Islamabad refused to do so. It called on Delhi to give it the evidence against the Pakistani nationals for further action.

By early January 2002, India had mobilized some five hundred thousand soldiers and three armored divisions along its 1,875-mile-border with Pakistan, including Kashmir. It placed its navy and air force on high alert and moved its nuclear-capable missiles closer to the border. In response, Pakistan's Yusaf Khan did the same. His orders resulted in the mobilization of over three hundred thousand Pakistani soldiers. This was the largest buildup on the subcontinent since the 1971 war.[32]

What particularly worried Washington was Yusaf Khan's decision to redeploy seventy thousand army troops, constituting the Pentagon's "anvil," to capture bin Laden on the run from his hideout in Afghanistan into the tribal belt along the Afghan-Pakistan border to the LoC in Kashmir.

Despite the deepening crisis, on January 1, 2002, India and Pakistan exchanged lists of nuclear installations and facilities under the terms of a confidence-building agreement designed to ensure that such sites were not attacked during any conflict. "For the eleventh consecutive year, India and Pakistan today, through diplomatic channels, simultaneously at New Delhi and Islamabad, exchanged lists of nuclear installations and facilities covered under the Agreement on the Prohibition of Attack Against Nuclear Installations and Facilities between India and Pakistan," read the press release by the Ministry of External Affairs in Delhi.[33]

This was all the more remarkable in view of the authoritative report in the *New Yorker* by prize-winning investigative journalist Seymour Hersh on November 5 that India, working with the United States and Israel, was planning preemptive strikes to prevent nuclear weapons falling into the hands of fundamentalist generals. On his part, fearful of US strikes, Musharraf had started moving critical nuclear components within forty-eight hours of the 9/11 attacks to six new locations, away from air bases, the Pentagon's most likely targets.[34]

Given the crucial need to maintain Islamabad as an active member of Bush's coalition to wage "war on terror," Washington could not afford to pressure Musharraf publicly to rein in the anti-India terrorist organizations in his country.

Privately, though, no diplomatic effort was spared. The United States was provided a window of opportunity by the foresighted decision of General Padmanabhan. He and his planners believed that Pakistan had an interest in escalating conventional warfare to a nuclear flashpoint as soon as possible. In a newspaper interview after his retirement a year later, Padmanabhan revealed that in order to avoid creating Pakistan's desired situation, it was essential to have Indian forces in place who could rapidly secure war objectives. "When December 13 [the Parliament House attack] happened, my strike formations were at peace locations. At that point, I did not have the capability to mobilize large forces to go across [the border]."[35]

According to Armitage, his boss, US secretary of state Colin Powell, a retired, four-star general born in New York to Jamaican immigrant parents, in his repeated "general-to-general" telephone conversations urged Musharraf to take visible steps to end his military's support for jihadists in Kashmir. Powell appealed to Jaswant Singh, his counterpart in Delhi: "Please don't undermine our war in Afghanistan."[36] This would have happened as a result of Pakistan moving its troops from the Afghan border to the Indian frontier.

Responding to the Indian demand to see the evidence that Musharraf was dismantling the infrastructure supporting cross-border terrorism, his aides told the *New York Times* on January 2, 2002, that he had ordered the dissolution of the ISI section assisting pro-Pakistan armed groups in Indian Kashmir. They added that in future Islamabad would limit its support for the Kashmiri freedom struggle to the groups rooted in the territory and rely on Kashmiris to conduct their armed struggle on their own while getting only moral and political backing from Pakistan.[37]

Despite the deepening crisis, Vajpayee and Musharraf decided to attend the eleventh SAARC summit in Katmandu on January 5–6, 2002. Toward the end of his speech, to the surprise of all, Musharraf turned to Vajpayee and said, "As I step down from this podium, I extend a genuine and sincere hand of friendship to Prime Minister Vajpayee. Together we must commence the journey for peace, harmony and progress in South Asia." As he moved toward the Indian leader, the latter extended his hand to Musharraf—to the thunderous applause of the assembly. In return, at the end of his speech, Vajpayee said, "I have shaken his hand in your presence. Now President Musharraf must follow this gesture by not permitting any activity in Pakistan or any territory it controls today which enables terrorists to perpetrate mindless violence in India." Earlier Musharraf pointed out that Pakistan had joined the international coalition against terrorism. But he added that the antiterrorism campaign must also identify and examine the causes that breed terrorism, driving people to violent desperation: "We cannot address only the symptoms and leave the malaise aside." He also argued that a distinction should be made between acts of resistance and freedom struggles and acts of terrorism.[38] As a start, the foreign ministers of India and Pakistan held a bilateral meeting in Katmandu.

Returning to Delhi, Vajpayee found his cabinet ministers in two minds about an attack on Pakistan. Their attention turned to the upcoming visit of the hawkish home minister Advani to Washington, ostensibly to discuss "ways to give effect to our common resolve to defeat terrorism decisively and speedily." During his meeting with Powell, he was shown the early draft of the speech Musharraf was scheduled to deliver on television in a few days. He compared the document against his set of demands for Musharraf: categorical renunciation of terrorism, closing of jihadist training camps and ending assistance to terrorist, stopping infiltration of men and materiel into Indian Kashmir, and handing over twenty Pakistan-based terrorists. He discovered that Musharraf was conceding the first three of his demands.

Advani's high point came when Bush dropped by during his meeting with National Security Adviser Condoleezza Rice at the White House on January 10. He had a brief conversation with Bush. At the subsequent press conference Advani referred to Bush's statement expecting Musharraf to abandon terror (as was clear from the draft of his forthcoming speech that Bush had read) and said that he felt reassured.[39] No doubt Advani telephoned Vajpayee and briefed him on Musharraf's impending address to the nation.

On the other hand, in a rare press conference on January 11, General Padmanabhan referred to Pakistani leaders, stating that "they will use nuclear weapons first should the necessity arise." Alluding to Musharraf, he added that "if he is man enough—correction—mad enough . . . he can use it." But "should a nuclear weapon be used against India, Indian forces, our assets at sea, economic, human or other targets, the perpetrators of that outrage shall be punished so severely that their continuation thereafter in any form or fray will be doubtful."[40]

MUSHARRAF BITES THE BULLET

Compared to Padamnabhan's words, the hour-long TV address by Musharraf on January 12 was a long sermon of peace and goodwill. "Pakistan rejects and condemns terrorism in all its forms and manifestations," he declared. "Pakistan will not allow its territory to be used for any terrorist activity anywhere in the world. . . . No organization will be allowed to indulge in terrorism in the name of Kashmir." He then added that Pakistan would not surrender its claim to Kashmir. "Kashmir is in our blood. No Pakistani can afford to sever links with Kashmir. We will continue to extend our moral, political and diplomatic support to Kashmiris."[41] He banned five extremist organizations, including the LeT and the JeM. While maintaining his backing for self-determination for Kashmiris—the principle that, when applied to the Muslims in British India, had resulted in the creation of Pakistan—Musharraf disengaged Kashmir from the pan-Islamist movement, as was done first by Zia ul Haq and then by bin Laden.

Washington welcomed Musharraf's speech. After brief equivocation, Delhi responded positively. It noted approvingly his closure of 390 offices of the banned organizations and the detention of about three thousand of their activists under the Maintenance of Public Order Ordinance, which authorized the police to detain a suspect for thirty days without charge. In the end, none was charged, and by March they were all released. The proscribed extremist organizations resurfaced under different names.

Equally, there was no change of heart on the part of India's policy makers. They remained wedded to their simplistic strategy: crush terrorism through brute force. The link between cross-border terrorism and widespread Kashmiri alienation from India, which transformed into local hospitality to "guest" militants from Pakistan-held Kashmir, escaped them. Though aware that a purely military solution to terrorism was not possible, they plowed on with that strategy.

The Bush administration remained equally committed to maintaining a delicate balance in its relations with Islamabad and Delhi. It made sure not to express publicly its shock at discovering that most of the literature on guerrilla training that the Pentagon and the CIA seized at fifty sites in post-Taliban Afghanistan pertained to the training of jihadists for liberating Kashmir under the supervision of Musharraf as Pakistan's director general of Military Operations.[42] Powell persisted in pursuing the two neighbors to pull back from the brink of war. He succeeded, but the resulting thaw proved transient.

16

Nuclear-Armed Twins,
Eyeball-to-Eyeball

The Indo-Pakistan thaw ended on May 14, 2002. On that day three armed Kashmiri militants in Indian army fatigues boarded a bus at Vijaypur in the Jammu region destined for Jammu city. Just before the army camp at Kaluchak, they stopped the vehicle and sprayed it with gunfire, leaving seven people dead. Then they entered the army residential camp and killed thirty more by lobbing hand grenades and firing their automatic weapons, before they were shot dead. This daring attack on a military facility roiled the Indian government as never before.

EYEBALL-TO-EYEBALL

On May 19 the Indian chief of army staff (COAS), General Sundararajan Padmanabhan, centralized command of the paramilitary forces, including the Border Security Force, posted along the international frontier, and the Central Reserve Police Force. That same day the Indian Navy took operational control of the coast guard. All Indian merchant ships were placed "on alert" and directed to file daily location reports to the navy. Soon after, the navy redeployed its warships from their eastern fleet home base in Vishakapatnam to the Arabian Sea, closer to Pakistan. Delhi's strategic aim was to assert total control of the sea and deny movement to Pakistani ships and submarines.

On May 22 Indian premier Atal Bihari Vajpayee asserted that the time for a "decisive fight" had come and that India needed to be ready for sacrifices while reassuring his fellow citizens that it would be a fight to victory.[1] He ordered the air force to hit training camps inside Pakistan-held Kashmir. He was told that the military lacked enough laser-guided bombs and night-vision pods to accomplish the task. His government approached the United States for fresh supplies. But President George W. Bush, anxious to cool the dangerous upsurge in the already fervid Delhi-Islamabad relations, refused to oblige. Vajpayee then turned to Israel, which agreed. But it was June 5 by the time these munitions and night-vision pods arrived in three C-130J Hercules transporters at Delhi's Palam airport, along with Amos Yaron, the director-general of Israel's defense ministry.[2]

Alarmed by Delhi's military moves, Bush publicly called on Pakistani president General Pervez Musharraf on May 25 to stop infiltration into Indian Kashmir. He resorted to public diplomacy after the brush-off that Colonel David Smith, the US Army attaché in Islamabad, repeatedly received from Pakistan's generals. They would often tell him: "We are the only ones that you can rely on to get these guys in Afghanistan—you can't do it without our help, and we're helping you in every way we can. You're putting tremendous pressure on us, and you're doing nothing on the Indian side."[3] Bush's tactic worked. He got an assurance from Musharraf that the militants' infiltration into Indian Kashmir had ceased. The White House passed on the message to Delhi. Two days later Musharraf repeated his promise to curb jihadist organizations. But Vajpayee's cabinet had lost trust in his word.

By the end of the month, Padmanabhan had moved eight of the ten strike divisions of the army to jumping-off points near the border. The Twenty-First Strike Force had advanced toward Akhnoor in the Jammu region and set up a forward command post. Each of the Fourteenth, Fifteenth, and Sixteenth Corps stationed in Kashmir was reinforced with additional armored and infantry brigades to be able to switch from a defensive posture to an offensive one. While maintaining nine divisions in a holding formation, Musharraf and Vice COAS General Muhammad Yusaf Khan moved an attack force of armored and motorized infantry divisions into combat readiness positions. They redeployed two infantry divisions based in Baluchistan and the North-West Frontier Province to the eastern borders. They augmented the Kashmir front by deploying two brigades of the Rawalpindi-based Tenth Corps. Equally, they reinforced the troops along the Indian border in Punjab and Sindh.[4]

ANGLO-AMERICAN EXODUS: AN EFFECTIVE DAMPER

Washington feared that India's impending cross-border attacks on the extremists' training camps in Pakistani Kashmiri would escalate to an exchange of nuclear missiles by the warring neighbors. Its fears were justified. The leaders of these sparring nations lacked reliable, comprehensive knowledge of each other's nuclear doctrine—that is, under what circumstances the highest official would unleash atom bombs. Soon after the attack on India's Parliament House in December 2001, John McLaughlin, the deputy director of the CIA, informed Bush's War Cabinet that intelligence analysts believed that given the confusion among decision makers in Delhi and Islamabad as to when and how a conventional war could escalate to nuclear confrontation, there was a serious risk of the first nuclear strike since August 1945.[5]

The statements made so far by Indian and Pakistani leaders did not add up to a coherent, comprehensive nuclear doctrine. "We have formally announced a policy of Non-First-Use," Vajpayee said in December 1998. "We are also not going to enter into an arms race with any country. Ours will be a minimum credible deterrent, which will safeguard India's security, the security of one-sixth of humanity, now and into the future."[6] This was in contrast to the stance taken by Pakistan during the May–July 1999 Kargil War, when its spokesmen refused to give the same guarantee.[7]

On August 17, 1999, the National Security Advisory Board on Indian Nuclear Doctrine, appointed by Vajpayee, issued a draft doctrine. "The fundamental purpose of Indian nuclear weapons is to deter the use and threat of use of nuclear weapons by any State or entity against India and its forces," it stated. "India will not be the first to initiate a nuclear strike, but will respond with punitive retaliation should deterrence fail." The comprehensive document covered nuclear forces, credibility and survivability, command and control, and security and safety.[8] But in his interview to the *Hindu* on November 29, foreign minister Jaswant Singh said that it was "not a policy document" of the government because the advisory board's authority was legally nebulous. All the same, he went on to explain that "minimum credible deterrence" mentioned in it was a question of "adequacy," not numbers. He described the concept as "dynamic," which was "firmly rooted in strategic environment, technical imperatives and national security needs."[9]

On his part, Musharraf tried to project a moderate stance on nuclear arms. "Pakistan, unlike India, does not have any pretensions to regional or global power status," he said in May 2000. Three months earlier he had established the Strategic Plan Division in the National Command Authority and appointed Lieutenant General Khalid Kidwai its director-general. Kidwai became the official spokesman on Islamabad's nuclear policy. In October 2001 he outlined its nuclear doctrine with the preamble that "It is well known that Pakistan does not have a 'No First Use Policy.'" Nuclear weapons were aimed solely at India, he declared. In case that deterrence failed, they would be used if India attacked Pakistan and conquered a large part of its territory (spatial threshold); or it destroyed a large part of either its land or air forces (military threshold); or it proceeded to strangle Pakistan economically (economic threshold); or it pushed Pakistan into political destabilization or created a large-scale internal subversion (domestic destabilization threshold).[10] Among these scenarios, the most likely was the spatial threshold. This situation was open to wide-ranging speculation, and the uncertainty caused as much anxiety in Delhi as it did in Washington.

A report by Washington's Defense Intelligence Agency in early May 2000 estimated that in the worst-case scenario, an Indo-Pakistan nuclear war could result in eight to twelve million fatalities initially, followed by many more millions later from radiation poisoning.[11] Alarmed by this scenario, the United States and Britain advised around sixty thousand Americans and twenty thousand Britons, including many thousands of business executives, to start leaving India beginning on May 31. Most diplomats and their families departed for home. The American embassy and the British high commission in Islamabad gave the same advice to their nationals in Pakistan.

The prospect of Delhi being hit by a Pakistani atom bomb was considered so plausible that the aides of US ambassador Robert Blackwill investigated building a hardened bunker in the embassy compound to survive a nuclear strike. But when they realized that those in the bunker would be killed by the effects of the nuclear blast, they abandoned the idea.[12]

As Vajpayee flew to Almaty, Kazakhstan, on June 3 to attend the first summit Conference on Interaction and Confidence-Building Measures in Asia, the Defense Ministry in Delhi said, "India does not believe in the use of nuclear weapons." That day, answering questions by reporters in Almaty on whether he would rule out the first use of nuclear arms, Musharraf said that "the possession of nuclear weapons by any state implies that they will be used under some circumstances." He failed to spell out these circumstances. At the summit, exchanging stony stares across a table, Vajpayee and Musharraf angrily blamed each other for five-and-a-half decades of conflict between their countries. "Nuclear powers should not use nuclear blackmail," remarked Vajpayee stiffly. Concerted efforts by Russian president Vladimir Putin and Kazakh president Nursultan Nazarbayev to bring about a meeting between the feuding protagonists failed, with the Indian leader insisting that Pakistan had to end its sponsorship of cross-border terrorism first.[13]

The acute gravity of the crisis was summed up by White House press secretary Ari Fleischer. "Progress is going to be measured day by day," he said on June 5. "In a tense situation, lack of war is the goal. Reduction of tension is the goal. And while it remains tense, it remains delicate. War is not inevitable."[14]

That day the United States and Britain urged their citizens to leave India and Pakistan *immediately*. The raised travel alert came in the wake of Islamabad rejecting Delhi's offer of joint border patrols in Kashmir. Stock markets in India and Pakistan fell precipitately. That shook the two governments, more so the one in Delhi. The pro-business, center-right cabinet led by the Bharatiya Janata Party (BJP) wanted very much to propel the country beyond the sluggish GDP expansion rates of the past. The abrupt loss of Western confidence in the improving health of the Indian economy gave Vajpayee pause.

Later, Brajesh Mishra, a Vajpayee loyalist who served as the national security adviser, put a spin on the premier's retreat from starting an armed conflict with Pakistan: "We almost went [to war] in May 2002, but Prime Minister Vajpayee, when he faced the final step, concluded that, at the end of a long political career, he wanted to be remembered as a man of peace." For many Pakistani senior commanders, Vajpayee's decision offered cast-iron evidence that nuclear deterrence works. "Suppose Pakistan had been non-nuclear in 2002," a Pakistani general told Steve Coll of the *New Yorker*. "There might have been a war."[15]

On June 6, Jaswant Singh said that his country would not use nuclear weapons first, whereas Musharraf reiterated that he would not renounce Pakistan's right to use nuclear weapons first. For India and other nations, the crucial unknown was the spatial threshold that would trigger Pakistan's activation of its atom bombs. Many defense experts surmised it would be the impending loss of Lahore, only fifteen miles from the Indian border. Others put the red line for the spatial threshold at Pakistan's sprawling Indus River basin.

BACK FROM THE NUCLEAR BRINK

On June 15 Delhi accepted Musharraf's public pledge to end militant infiltration into India. It did so after the intercepts by its intelligence agencies showed that the Rawalpindi-based army general headquarters had ordered the Tenth Corps commander to stop infiltration across the Line of Control (LoC) in Kashmir. There were confirmed reports of the Musharraf government closing some militant training camps in Pakistan-held Kashmir. In return, India ordered its warships to sail away from the Pakistani shoreline and started reducing the presence of its army troops along its international border with Pakistan. On June 26 Washington officially announced that the high tension of late May and early June had subsided.[16]

Since then, no threat of armed conflict on such a grand scale has emerged again, even though the underlying causes of the 2001–2002 eyeball-to-eyeball confrontation—jihadist terrorism, abiding mutual distrust, and an ill-defined system of mutual nuclear deterrence—remain in place.

Those who put a positive spin on this frightening episode argued that the 2001–2002 war scare was a rerun of the three-week Cuban missile crisis between the United States and the Soviet Union in October 1962. Just as in the wake of the Cuban missile crisis period, the two superpowers ground nuclear deterrence into a mix of military restraint, diplomatic patience, and negotiations about underlying differences, so too did the nuclear-armed India and Pakistan after the Kaluchak crisis. In other words, Indian leaders learned to react defensively, by nonmilitary means, when faced with continuing jihadist terrorist strikes.

There was a major difference between the events in October 1962 and May–June 2002. In the earlier case President John F. Kennedy negotiated directly by a hotline with the Soviet leader Nikita Khrushchev. But in the confrontation between the nuclear-armed Delhi and Islamabad, the negotiations between the rivals were channeled through Washington.

The United States enjoyed the goodwill of both—albeit for diverse reasons. Pakistan was an almost indispensable member of Bush's coalition to defeat global terror, which stemmed from Afghanistan and the tribal belt along the Afghan-Pakistan frontier, whereas India was a long-time victim of terrorism. Unsurprisingly, therefore, in early May India and America carried out a weeklong joint naval exercise code-named Exercise Malabar in the Arabian Sea off the southern seaport of Kochi, far away from Pakistan.[17]

In the Bush team, Colin Powell played the lead role in defusing the near-combustible relations between the two leading South Asian nations. This became clear when at his press conference in Delhi on July 28 he referred to his third trip to the city in ten months. "I take note that the situation has improved considerably over the past month," he said. "We have been able on the US side, to return our families who had temporarily moved back and we have also been able to change our alert levels or caution levels to a point where we are now hopeful that more American tourists will return to India and more businessmen and women will come and find ways to enhance trade between the United States and India." At the same time he noted that both armies remained mobilized. "So we look to India to take further de-escalatory actions as Pakistan makes good on its pledges to permanently cease support for infiltration." However, he conceded that though the infiltration had declined, it had not ended.[18]

In his subsequent meeting with Musharraf in Islamabad, Powell found him "more positive" about his commitment to ending all infiltration. But when he raised the closing of the camps training terrorists, Musharraf's response was "they will be dealt with in due course." Powell expressed Washington's inability to independently verify the state of infiltration. And yet America's role remained pivotal. "It took US intervention for Pakistan to leave Kargil," said an unnamed State Department official in Washington. "And don't forget, Musharraf's pledge [to end cross-border terrorism] was made to the US and not to India. So we have to guarantee it."[19]

However, India's leaders were realistic enough to realize that it was in Pakistan's interest to create fear in India-held Kashmir during the run-up to the elections from September 19 to October 9. As before, the secessionists in Kashmir were opposed to the exercise. Infiltrations from Pakistan continued. As a result, during the electoral campaign, over eight hundred militants, civilians, election candidates, and security personnel were killed.

Despite the allegations of vote rigging and low turnout of 43 percent, the election produced an astonishing result. The Delhi-loyalist National Conference was reduced to 28 seats, followed by the Congress Party at 20. The newly launched People's Democratic Party (PDP) of Mufti Muhammad Sayeed—calling on India to have "an unconditional dialogue" with Kashmiris to end the long-running crisis—won 16 seats, and the People's Democratic Forum (PDF), opposed to the National Conference, 7. The coalition of the Congress and the PDP, backed by the PDF, formed the government in mid-October, turning the National Conference into the opposition for the first time.[20] This invested the coalition government with some legitimacy among Kashmiris.

Two days later Delhi announced that it would withdraw troops from its international border with Pakistan. Islamabad reciprocated. On the eve of the first anniversary of the December 13, 2001, attack on the Parliament House, the Vajpayee government decided to end the high-alert state of its military. Pakistan followed suit.

The yearlong mobilization of its armed forces cost India Rs 75 billion ($1.63 billion), including Rs 10 billion ($0.21 billion) for deploying and redeploying the navy, coast guard, and air force. It was an important contributory factor to produce the low GDP growth of 4.3 percent in fiscal 2002. The corresponding buildup of the Pakistani forces consumed $1.4 billion, a much higher percentage of its budget than India's.[21]

This nail-biting episode taught India's politicians and military a lesson to make certain basic changes to the composition and equipment of its land forces to cope with similar challenges in the future. After Padmanabhan's retirement at the end of 2002, his successor, General Nirmal Chandar Vij, implemented an ambitious modernization of the ground troops with new weapons systems, enabling each corps a limited offensive capability of its own. And the reequipment of the special forces augmented their ability to operate behind enemy lines for a considerable time.[22] These changes were to be incorporated into a new armed forces doctrine that the Vajpayee government instructed military leaders to formulate.

Meanwhile, on January 4, 2003, India's Cabinet Committee on Security summarized the nuclear doctrine. While reiterating the "No First Use" of nuclear weapons, it said that "nuclear retaliation to a first strike [by the enemy] will be massive and designed to inflict unacceptable damage." In the case of "a major attack against India, or Indian forces anywhere, by biological or chemical weapons, India will retain the option of retaliating with nuclear weapons." It stated that the Nuclear Command Authority (NCA) comprised a Political Council and an Executive Council. The Political Council, chaired by the prime minister, was the only body to authorize the use of nuclear weapons. The function of the Executive Council, headed by the national security advisor, was to provide inputs for decision making by the NCA and implement the orders given to it by the Political Council.[23]

POLITICIZED MUSHARRAF TURNS PRAGMATIC

A succession of major Indo-Pakistan dramas in Kargil (May–July 1999), the hijacking of the Indian airliner by Pakistan-based jihadists (December 1999), and the terrorist attack on the Parliament House in Delhi (December 2001) were covered widely and engagingly by privately owned Indian electronic media. Over time these TV channels had garnered a large audience among Pakistanis with access to satellite and cable television and bored by the bland, sanitized fare offered by the state-owned Pakistan television, PTV. Given tens of thousands of cable operators, it was impossible for the Musharraf government to enforce its ban on accessing Indian TV channels.

To counter the inexorably growing input of the Indian media in molding public opinion in Pakistan, Musharraf decided to liberalize the electronic media while making sure to set the political agenda and regulate private outlets on the sensitive subject of national security. On January 16, 2002, his government established the Pakistan Electronic Media Regulatory Authority (PEMRA) to license privately owned radio and TV stations.

Pakistanis with subscriptions to cable or satellite services were already receiving two private channels in Urdu. These were ARY, set up by Pakistani businessman Abdul Razzak Yaqoob in Dubai in 1997, and Geo TV,[24] run by the Karachi-based Independent Media Corporation, broadcasting from Dubai and London.[25]

The Geo TV channel, established in Karachi in May 2002, did its test transmission on Independence Day, August 14. Its regular transmission started on October 1, nine days ahead of the general election held by the Musharraf government as ordered by the Supreme Court. It broke new ground by airing debates between candidates and giving ample time to opposition parties—in contrast to state-run television. Geo TV would astonish its viewers by announcing election results hours before PTV. Over the years, however, the fiercely competing Urdu language channels tried to outdo one another in their biased reporting and analysis of India as well as America, perceived to be empathizing with its rival because of the shared feeling of being a victim of extremist Islamist terrorism.

Musharraf had prepared well for the electoral contest. Following his instructions, the loyalist Inter-Services Intelligence (ISI) chief, Lieutenant General Ehsan ul Haq, set out to create a pro-Musharraf party. His starting point was to cause a serious split in the Pakistan Muslim League (Nawaz Sharif)—PML (N). The defectors were then led to coalesce with pro-Musharraf groups and independents. The end result was the birth of the Pakistan Muslim League (Quaid-i-Azam)—PML (Q)—on July 20, 2002. Its leader was Zafarullah Khan Jamali, a bland Baluchi tribal chief. In exchange for the Islamist camp's backing of Musharraf to remain the COAS while serving as president, he encouraged the formation of a six-party coalition of six Islamist parties, called the Muttahida Majlis-e-Amal (Urdu: United Council of Action; MMA).

On September 1 the authorities allowed the election campaign to start with a ban on street rallies and use of loudspeakers. Besides the PML (Q), those who entered the race included the PML (N), the Pakistan People's Party (PPP), and the MMA. For the PML (Q), the campaign did not go as well as the Musharraf government had wanted. It became nervous. "Pakistani journalists are of two categories," said Lieutenant General Javed Ashraf Qazi, the minister of communications and a former head of the ISI. "The left-wing, liberal journalist can be bought by India for two bottles of whisky while the right-wing journalists are patriotic. The job of the 'purchased' journalist is to pick up disinformation published in India and print it in Pakistan as his own investigative work."[26] India came in handy as the ultimate malevolent player in denying Musharraf unfettered power.

The official figure of 40 percent voter participation was far above the generally agreed 25 percent.[27] In the 342-strong National Assembly, the PML (Q) garnered 103 seats, the PPP 80, the MMA 59, with the rest going to small factions and independents.[28] The entry of the Islamist MMA, which demanded the application of the Sharia Islamic canon and ran a vigorously anti-American campaign, into the political mainstream was a new development. This worried Washington as much as Delhi. In its election campaign the MMA attributed the 9/11 attacks to the machinations of the CIA and the Israeli foreign espionage agency Mossad, and equated "war on terrorism" with "war on Islam." Intriguingly, Musharraf had turned a blind eye to the MMA's violation of the ban on street meetings and loudspeakers.

It took Musharraf's military overseers nearly six weeks to cobble together a coalition of 170 members with Jamali as the prime minister. He reiterated continued good relations with Washington while bemoaning the fact that Delhi had not responded positively to Islamabad's offers of talks.

This was as well. The Vajpayee government had noted that within a year of their proscription in January 2002, the five extremist Pakistani organizations were back in business under different names. Lashkar-e Taiba (LeT) reemerged as the Pasban-e Ahl-e Hadith and Jaish-e-Muhammad as Al Furqan. Moreover, the shadowy ISI paid substantial sums to such jihadist leaders as Hafiz Muhammad Saeed of the LeT and Maulana Masoud Azhar of the JeM to persuade them to keep a low profile for an unspecified period.[29] With many of their cadres released from prison within months, there was only a minor dip in the activities of these and other jihadist factions.

All this was very much part of the Pakistani military's unchanging doctrine: India is the foremost enemy of Pakistan. So it is incumbent on Islamabad to balance Delhi's superiority in conventional defense by following a dual strategy: build up Pakistan's nuclear arsenal, and encourage periodic terrorist acts against targets in India as well as the Delhi-friendly government in Kabul. To offset any advantage that India might gain in Afghanistan after the ultimate withdrawal of the US-led NATO forces from that country, Islamabad must sustain and bolster the Afghan Taliban as its proxy.

The downside of this two-track strategy was that Pakistan remained a very risky country for Western corporate investment, which its fragile economy needed desperately. This realization started to seep into the Musharraf administration as the standing of its finance minister since the coup, Shaukat Aziz, a former Citibank executive, started to rise. With that, a glimmer of normalization of Indo-Pakistan relations appeared. In May 2003 the two neighbors restored full diplomatic ties after a break of eighteen months.

Feeling the economic pain of maintaining its forces across the LoC on high alert, Pakistan saw salvation in easing tensions in Kashmir. In his speech at the UN General Assembly in New York on September 24, Musharraf invited India to join Pakistan in "a sustained dialogue" aimed at resolving the Kashmir issue. Musharraf proposed that both countries should announce a cessation of violence in Kashmir, involving "reciprocal obligations and restraints on Indian forces and on the Kashmiri freedom fighters," he proposed.[30] Vajpayee let Musharraf's offer lapse.

Two months later, however, India and Pakistan agreed to a comprehensive cease-fire, covering the international border and Kashmir. This coincided with the start of the Eid al Fitr, which marks the end of the Muslim holy fasting month of Ramadan. And on December 1 the two neighbors restored air links that had been cut off two years earlier.

Meanwhile, Musharraf's active involvement in Washington's campaign against Al Qaida and the Taliban had led him to deploy large forces in the semiautonomous Federally Administered Tribal Agencies along the Afghan-Pakistan border. This had alienated the traditional tribal leaders, some of whom were reportedly harboring the deputy leader of Al Qaida, Ayman Zawahiri, and Taliban's Mullah Muhammad Omar. In turn, Al Qaida leadership made Musharraf their number one target. Its first attempt to kill him in Karachi in April 2003 failed.

On December 14, Musharraf narrowly escaped a well-planned assassination attempt, when five bombs exploded under a bridge in Rawalpindi soon after his black Mercedes had passed over it. "When I came back from my tour of Sindh and as I was going home [in Islamabad] from Chaklala [airbase near Rawalpindi] and we crossed the Ammar Chowk Bridge, there was an explosion just half a minute or one minute after we crossed," he told PTV. "I felt the explosion in my car. That is all that I know, except of course that it was certainly a terrorist act and certainly it was me who was targeted."[31] He was saved by a CIA-supplied radio-jamming device to block all wireless communications within a radius of 650 feet fitted into his car. That blocked the use of a remote-controlled device to detonate the explosives while his car was on the bridge.

But that was not the end. A second attempt to kill him came on Christmas Day at 1:20 PM. Two suicide bombers in cars targeted him just 650 feet from the site of an earlier attempt on his life. In a TV speech Musharraf, visibly shaken, referred to one suicide bomber driving out of a gas station toward his car and a policeman attempting to stop him when a bomb exploded. "We increased the speed but another bomb exploded at another petrol pump a few yards ahead of the first explosion," he continued. He assured his audience that these blasts had given "new strength" to his resolve to eliminate terrorists and extremists from the country.[32] It transpired later that these attacks were masterminded by Al Qaida's Amjad Farooqi and Abu Faraj al Libbi. Farooqi, who was also involved in sheltering 9/11 plotter Khalid Shaikh Mohammed, would be killed by Pakistani security forces during a raid in 2004. And al Libbi would end up in American custody.[33]

Between these two survivals, on December 17 Musharraf said his government was prepared to drop its long-standing demands for the implementation of UN resolutions on Kashmir in order to end the fifty-six-year-old dispute. This required both sides to be flexible, he added.[34]

Predictably, this was welcomed by Kashmir's chief minister Mufti Sayeed. And it was savaged by the leader of the separatist All Parties Hurriyat Conference, Maulavi Abbas Ansari, who said that Pakistan had no right to drop the vital issue for which the UN had conferred the right of self-determination to the people of Kashmir.[35]

In Islamabad, backed by Finance Minister Aziz, Musharraf had convinced his military high command that only by pursuing a peace process with India could Pakistan achieve political stability and badly needed economic expansion by attracting foreign investment.

BACK TO DIALOGUE

This was the background over which Vajpayee rolled into Islamabad, whose administrative heart had been turned into a fortress, to attend the twelfth South Asian Association for Regional Cooperation summit from January 4 to 6, 2004.

On January 5 he paid a "courtesy call" on Musharraf. It lasted an hour. The following day the two leaders issued a joint statement stating that their foreign secretaries would meet the following month to kick-start the stalled Indo-Pakistan talks on all outstanding issues. At the subsequent press conference, Musharraf referred to the key linkages in the joint communiqué: the continuation of the normalization process, the start of a dialogue that included Kashmir, and Pakistan's commitment to preventing the use of its territory by terrorist groups. He was effusive in his praise for Vajpayee. "I would like to give total credit to his vision, to his statesmanship, which contributed so significantly towards settlement, for coming to this joint statement," he said. To be even-handed he stated that "I would like to commend the flexibility of the negotiators on both sides."[36]

Vajpayee, who as foreign minister had inaugurated the Indian chancery in Islamabad in 1979, laid the foundation stone for its extension over a ten-acre site. "A quarter of a century has passed in a jiffy, and every year has thrown up new questions for which new answers are being sought," he said. "Our dialogue with Pakistan must continue and we must strive together to find solutions by understanding each other's concerns and difficulties."[37]

In practical terms what mattered far more were the "significant meetings" that his national security adviser, Mishra, had with high Pakistani officials, away from the prying eyes of the media. The most important was his talk with ISI chief Lieutenant General Haq. Instructed by their principals, they agreed to revive a back channel on Kashmir that Vajpayee had established with Prime Minister Nawaz Sharif five years earlier.[38]

After their talks in Islamabad, Shashank and Riaz Khokar, respective foreign secretaries of India and Pakistan, announced on February 18 the modalities and timeframe for discussing all subjects included in the composite dialogue. They agreed to meet in May and June for talks on peace and security, including confidence-building measures, and Jammu and Kashmir. Negotiations on the Siachen Glacier, Wullar Barrage, Sir Creek, terrorism and drug trafficking, economic and commercial cooperation, and promotion of friendly exchanges in various fields were scheduled for July.

But before these meetings could be held, there was a change of government in Delhi. In the general election held between April 20 and May 10, the center-right, BJP-led National Democratic Alliance (134 seats) lost to the Congress Party–led United Progressive Alliance (226 seats). As a result, Congress leader Manmohan Singh, a seventy-two-year-old Sikh and economist turned politician, with a well-groomed, salt-and-pepper beard and a trademark sky-blue turban, became the prime minister.

On the eve of the vote, however, India's military high command, charged with refining the concept of surgical destruction of targets inside Pakistan, finalized its new strategy of blitzkrieg, called "Cold Start."

The Cold Start doctrine envisioned the formation of eight division-size Integrated Battle Groups (IBGs), each consisting of infantry, artillery, armor, and air support, which were able to operate independently on the battlefield. In the case of terrorist attack from or by a Pakistan-based group, the IBGs would rapidly penetrate Pakistan at unexpected points and advance no more than thirty miles beyond the border, disrupting the command and control networks of its military while staying away from the locations likely to trigger nuclear retaliation. The overall aim was to launch a conventional strike swiftly but to inflict only limited damage in order to deny Pakistan justification for a nuclear response.[39]

The effectiveness of this strategy was based on the dodgy assumption that the thirty-odd-mile penetration by India would not lead the Pakistani high command to launch nuclear attacks on Indian targets. In any case, the existence of this plan was sufficient to keep alive the fear and loathing of India by Pakistan's people and their civilian and military leaders.

17

Manmohan Singh's
Changing Interlocutors

The return of the secular, center-left Congress Party as the leader of the United Progressive Alliance, headed by Manmohan Singh, augured well for ending the Kashmir deadlock. To further the objectives of the February 1999 Lahore Declaration, foreign and defense secretaries of India and Pakistan met in mid-June 2004 to discuss nuclear crisis management, strategic stability, and risk reduction. Both neighbors decided to continue their moratorium on nuclear weapons testing, which had been maintained since June 1998.

A preliminary understanding reached in mid-2001, requiring both countries to give advanced notification of missile tests, had failed to graduate to a formal concord because of the December 2001 terrorist attack on India's Parliament House. During the latest session the two sides agreed to stay with the original undertaking. Further progress was inhibited for two main reasons: India and Pakistan had only limited command and control structures in place, and neither possessed the technology to recall a nuclear-tipped missile fired by mistake. Meanwhile, in a far simpler context, they decided to install a new telephone hotline between the most senior officials in Delhi and Islamabad and upgrade the existing secure hotline between their senior military commanders to alert each other to potential nuclear risks.[1]

MANMOHAN SINGH–MUSHARRAF RAPPORT

The two subsequent rounds of talks between the Indian and Pakistani foreign ministers—Kunwar Natwar Singh and Khurshid Mahmood

Kasuri—in Delhi and Islamabad in July and early September 2004 paved the way for a one-on-one session between Prime Minister Singh and President General Pervez Musharraf at the United Nations in New York on September 24. After their parley Singh declared that any proposal to resolve the Kashmir dispute would be acceptable so long as it was not based on religious division or the altering of India's boundaries. Remarkably, the first condition reflected the view of Congress Party leaders before independence. And the second condition was the reiteration of the position Prime Minister Jawaharlal Nehru had publicly adopted in 1955.[2]

Unknown to the rest of the world, Singh and Musharraf agreed to encourage the secret talks that had been initiated between their respective national security advisers—Tariq Aziz and Jyotindra Nath Dixit—with a mandate to hammer out a detailed document on Kashmir. Aziz and Dixit started meeting secretly in hotels in Dubai, London, and Bangkok almost every other month.

In October the Singh government allowed a group of Pakistani journalists to visit Indian Kashmir. To their astonishment, they were free to interview anybody they wished. In June 2005 Delhi would permit a delegation of the separatist All Parties Hurriyat Conference to travel to Pakistani-administered Kashmir.

On October 25, in an informal address at a breaking-the-fast dinner during Ramadan, Musharraf invited debate on the alternatives to the plebiscite in Kashmir. He saw the need for it because Pakistan was unprepared to accept India's proposal to transform the Line of Control (LoC) into the international border, and India saw no need for a plebiscite as envisaged by UN Security Council Resolution 47 in April 1948. He argued that Jammu and Kashmir consisted of seven regions with different languages and sects, with two—Azad Kashmir and the Northern Areas—being with Pakistan and five with India.[3] He proposed that the linguistic, ethnic, religious, geographic, political, and other aspects of these regions be reviewed to find a peaceful solution to the Kashmir problem.[4] A tidal wave of protest rose in Pakistan. Musharraf back-pedaled. He explained that his statement was not a substitute for the official position about holding a plebiscite, which—in reality—he had abandoned almost a year earlier.

However, Musharraf's public retraction did not derail Aziz's clandestine talks with Dixit. Following the death of Dixit in January 2005, his job went to Satinder Lambah, India's former high commissioner in Pakistan.

On March 10, 2005, Singh informed the lower house of Parliament that he had invited Musharraf to Delhi to watch a cricket match the following month. "I must say that nothing brings the people of our subcontinent together than our love for cricket and Bollywood cinema," he said.[5] Singh was referring to the One Day International (ODI) between India and Pakistan on April 17. Musharraf agreed.

After the ODI at the Feroz Shah Kotla Stadium in Delhi on April 17, Singh declared that that the "peace process [between India and Pakistan] can no longer be reversed." Musharraf outlined the agreed-on guidelines for the process: "India's insistence that no boundaries can be redrawn; Pakistan's refusal to accept the Line of Control; and the two countries' agreement that borders must become less important." In pursuit of the last option, he referred to the bus service that had been started between Srinagar and Muzaffarabad, capital of Azad Kashmir, ten days earlier. Following his parley with Singh, the two of them agreed to increase the frequency of the bus service and also let trucks ply the route in order to boost trade. The news was warmly welcomed by Kashmiri families on both sides of the LoC.[6]

On October 8, a 7.6 Richter scale earthquake, with its epicenter near Muzaffarabad, wreaked havoc in the region. It killed as many as seventy-nine thousand people, including at least three thousand in Indian Kashmir, and rendered two million homeless. Following an appeal by the Azad Kashmir government for cooperation with India to improve relief, Musharraf agreed to open the LoC temporarily. India reciprocated. This was the first instance of Delhi and Islamabad cooperating actively in disputed Kashmir.

In an unprecedented move, the Pugwash Conferences on Science and World Affairs, based in Pugwash in Nova Scotia, Canada, sponsored a seminar, "Prospects for Self-Governance in Jammu and Kashmir, and Present Status of Cooperation and Communications Across the LOC," in Islamabad in March 2006. It was attended by serving and former officials of Azad Kashmir and several leading Pakistani journalists, as well as officials of assorted political parties and organizations from Indian Kashmir.

Inaugurating the seminar, Musharraf proposed step-by-step demilitarization combined with self-governance as a practical solution to the Kashmir dispute. This, he argued, would make the LoC irrelevant—and with it any redrawing of borders. Demilitarization would be a huge confidence-building measure and, by providing relief to Kashmiris, would help undercut support for militants.[7] His proposal failed to get off the ground primarily because the policy makers in Delhi figured that the reduction of security forces in Indian Kashmir would allow the separatists to broaden their popular base.

In any case, Singh knew as well as Musharraf that hard-knuckle bargaining was going on in the secret meetings between Lambah and Aziz in five-star hotels far from Kashmir.

In his book *In the Line of Fire: A Memoir*, published in September 2006, Musharraf formalized his ideas into a four-point program. One, identify the regions of Kashmir that need resolution. Two, demilitarize the identified region or regions and curb all militant aspects of the struggle for freedom. Three, introduce self-governance in the identified region or regions. Four, most importantly, have a joint management mechanism with Pakistani, Indian, and Kashmiri members to oversee self-governance and deal with residual subjects common to all identified regions as well as those beyond the scope of self-governance. Describing this plan as "purely personal," he recognized the need for selling it to the public by all the involved parties.[8]

By late autumn of 2006 the Aziz-Lambah negotiations had inched forward to the point at which Musharraf felt it was time to test popular opinion. In his interview with Delhi-based NDTV in early December 2006, he outlined a four-point plan. One, Pakistan would give up its claim to Indian-administered Kashmir if people from both regions had freedom of movement through open borders. Two, neither part of Kashmir could become independent, but both could have a measure of autonomy. Three, there would be phased withdrawal of troops from both sides of the LoC. Four, a "joint mechanism," consisting of representatives from India, Pakistan, and Kashmir, would be formed to supervise the issues affecting people on both sides, such as water rights.[9]

MUSHARRAF'S DOWNFALL

In the final analysis, on the Kashmir issue what mattered most at the official level in Islamabad was the opinion of the top generals, including Lieutenant General Ashfaq Parvez Kayani, then director-general of the Inter-Services Intelligence (ISI) directorate. Since Musharraf continued to be the chief of army staff (COAS), it was tricky for his subordinate commanders to disagree with him even in private.

So when the secret document between Aziz and Lambah was finessed by early 2007, Musharraf presented it formally to his twelve corps commanders, including his vice COAS, General Muhammad Yusaf Khan, and Foreign Minister Kasuri, for review.[10]

Soon after, the attention of the Pakistani elite turned to the spat between Musharraf and the independent-minded chief justice, Iftikhar Muhammad Chaudhry. When Musharraf suspended Chaudhry as the chief justice on March 9, the latter challenged his order in the Supreme Court. Popular protest broke out in the streets in which the major opposition parties of Benazir Bhutto (Pakistan People's Party; PPP) and Muhammad Nawaz Sharif (Pakistan Muslim League–N; PML-N) joined hands. On July 20, ten of the thirteen judges ruled that Chaudhry should be reinstated. When Musharraf refused to do so, the protest intensified. At the same time, following the military's July 10–11 storming of the Red Mosque complex, a bastion of jihadists in Islamabad, Islamist terrorists began a violent backlash.[11] In desperation, Musharraf declared an emergency on November 3, soon after winning the most votes in the provincial and national legislatures in a controversial presidential election. He suspended the constitution and Parliament, and placed all judges under house arrest. But any protection he achieved by this ploy would prove temporary.

In Delhi, though profoundly interested in devising a peaceful solution to the long-running Kashmir dispute, the Indian interlocutors had to ponder three major unknowns. Did Musharraf have the generals on board on this vitally important issue, which had played a central role in raising the prestige and budget of the military since the birth of Pakistan? What was the likelihood of Musharraf being overthrown by his military high command, as had happened to General Ayub Khan in 1969? What were the chances of the post-Musharraf regime, military or civilian, abiding by the provisional deal struck with Delhi by Musharraf?

The answer to the first question came on November 28, 2007. On that day Musharraf was compelled to resign as the COAS on constitutional grounds before being sworn in for a second term as civilian president. (On the eve of his resignation as the COAS, Musharraf promoted Kayani to that post.) The answer to the second poser came on August 18, 2008. The poor performance of his Pakistan Muslim League–Q in the general election in February 2008 was a barometer of Musharraf's rapidly declining popularity. With the PPP's Yusuf Raza Gilani becoming the prime minister, he had a powerful political adversary to contend with. By resigning as president on August 18 he spared himself the ignominy of impeachment by the National Assembly, which was dominated by two anti-Musharraf parties in the aftermath of the general election in February. As stipulated in the constitution, the Speaker of the Senate, Muhammad Mian Soomro, became the acting president.

PAKISTANI JIHADISTS STRIKE BACK

The slow but definite movement toward a peaceful resolution of the Kashmir dispute unsettled the jihadist organizations in Pakistan, particularly the Lashkar-e Taiba (LeT) and the Harkat al Jihad Islami (Arabic: Movement for Islamic Jihad; HuJI). Though formally banned in 2002, the LeT had continued to exist under the guise of an Islamic charity. The LeT's Indian cohorts succeeded in carrying out three bombings in Delhi, killing sixty-one people, in October 2005. Such an audacious terrorist attack in the Indian capital foreshadowed yet another period of soured relations between India and Pakistan.

Finding that Musharraf had resolved not to let Pakistan-based jihadist groups export terror to India, LeT and HuJI leaders decided to sponsor a self-sufficient Indian jihadist organization. They achieved their objective by coopting young Indian Muslims with expertise in extortion, ransom, and bank robbery. Such gangs existed in Mumbai and Kolkata. Also, with Dubai, populated largely by South Asians, emerging as a thriving financial center and entrepôt, the earlier, tenuous links between organized crime in Pakistan and India, involved partly with money laundering, strengthened. The end result was the establishment of the Indian Mujahedin (IM) in 2005. IM terrorists targeted markets and movie theaters, as well as Hindu temples, to maximize fatalities. They resorted to sending highly provocative emails containing abusive comments on Hindus and Hinduism to intensify Hindu-Muslim tensions.

Sixteen synchronized bomb blasts on July 26, 2008, in Ahmedabad killed thirty-eight people. Five minutes before the explosions, the IM emailed a fourteen-page document, signed by "Al Arabi Guru al Hindi," to the media. It contained several verses from the Quran along with an English translation. "O Hindus! O disbelieving faithless Indians!" ran the text. "Haven't you still realized that the falsehood of your 33 crore [330 million] dirty mud idols and the blasphemy of your deaf, dumb, mute idols are not at all going to save your necks, Insha Allah [God willing], from being slaughtered?"[12] This was a reference to the Hindu myth that there are 330 million gods and goddesses; Islam forbids worship of idols, icons, or images. The IM's bombing campaign would reach a peak in September 2008, two months before the LeT-sponsored terrorist attacks, planned in association with an ISI officer, in Mumbai on November 26.

In Pakistan LeT leaders found their cadres defecting to join such organizations as Al Qaida with an agenda for global jihad. This caused concern among the top officials of not only the LeT but also the ISI. Focused on destabilizing Indian Kashmir, the ISI leadership did not want the Kashmiri-based groups integrating with the wider jihad-based factions, thereby weakening its Kashmir campaign.[13] That was how the aims of the LeT and the ISI converged. Mounting a gigantic operation against India was expected to enhance the radical image of the LeT and stem the outflow from its ranks.

The LeT-ISI plan was unaffected by the new civilian coalition government in Islamabad in April 2008. The PPP had emerged as the largest group in the National Assembly after a general election in which Asif Ali Zardari rode the sympathy wave generated by the assassination of his wife, Benazir Bhutto, by militant jihadists. Zardari succeeded Musharraf as president.

LeT leaders realized that in their ranks they had one Pakistani-American whose dedication to the cause was equaled by the training he had received at LeT camps. He was Daood Sayed Gilani, born in 1960 in Washington to Sayed Salim Gilani, a Pakistani diplomat, and Serrill Headley, a Pennsylvania-born secretary at the Pakistani embassy.

After his education at an elite military school near Islamabad, Gilani went to live with his divorced mother in Philadelphia to help her run a bar. He carried two passports, one American and the other Pakistani. His drug smuggling took him to Pakistan and led to his arrests, first in 1987 and then in 1998, when he became an undercover agent for the US Drug Enforcement Administration (DEA). Soon after 9/11, the DEA sent him to Pakistan, even though it had been informed of his pro-Islamist views. In December 2001, attracted by the LeT's banner advertisement at a mosque in Lahore where he prayed, he joined the organization. Between 2002 and 2005 he received training in small arms and countersurveillance at the camps run by the LeT. He was intent on participating actively in jihad and awaited a move by LeT leaders. When that failed to materialize, he set out for the Pakistan-Afghan border on his own and crossed into tribal territory without an official permit for entry. He was arrested by an ISI officer.

Once Gilani established his LeT bona fides, the officer handed him over to "Major Iqbal" (aka Mazhar Iqbal) of the ISI in Lahore. Major Iqbal became his minder. Taking his advice, Gilani changed his name to David Coleman Headley in 2006 during his stay in the United States. Through one of his LeT trainers, Abdur Rahman Hashim (aka Pasha), a retired officer of the Sixth Baluch Regiment, Headley established contact with Ilyas Kashmiri, who was linked to Al Qaida. The ISI gave him $25,000 to open a US visa facilitation office in Mumbai as a front. After scouting for targets in the city, he handed over flash drives to the LeT and the ISI. He went through the images with Zaki ur Rahman Lakhvi, the LeT's military operations chief. In 2007 Headley made six trips to Mumbai, two of them with his Moroccan wife, Faiza Outalha, when they stayed at the Taj Mahal Palace Hotel. In September 2007 his LeT minder instructed him to focus on that hotel.

In April 2008 Headley hired boats to scout landing sites and passed on GPS coordinates to the LeT high command. Major Iqbal, working as the LeT's planner, supervised the model of the Taj Mahal Palace Hotel and arranged the communications system for the attack. Between June and August 2008, the LeT high command upgraded the operation from an assault on the Taj Mahal Palace Hotel, with the two or three attackers escaping, to a mission involving several targets and the operatives' role changed to suicide bombers. These were to be the attacks by the *fidayeen* (Arabic: self-sacrificing volunteers), with the overarching aim of highlighting the suffering of the Kashmiri Muslims under the Indian yoke as a step toward liberating them.

Ten LeT recruits, selected from a group of twenty-five, were then indoctrinated for this holy task by Lakhvi. (After being proscribed in January 2002, the LeT functioned under its political arm, the Jamaat ud Dawa.) Among them was Muhammad Ajmal Amir Kasab, a short, chubby, baby-faced man of twenty-one, from Faridkot village near Deepalpur in eastern Punjab. During his trip to Rawalpindi, he had joined the LeT in December 2007 and ended up at the organization's base camp near Lahore. His subsequent training was at a camp near Muzaffarabad in Pakistani-administered Kashmir. It included learning Hindi. During the visit to Faridkot in May 2008, he sought the blessing of his mother after telling her that he was going to engage in jihad to liberate Kashmir.[14]

In October 2008 the LeT *fidayeen* were ensconced in a safe house in Azizabad near Karachi airport, where they were taught how to navigate an inflatable boat. Their first foray by boat from Karachi failed because of choppy waters. It was their second attempt that succeeded and made a spectacular mark in the history of global terrorism.

THE MOST DOCUMENTED SIXTY HOURS EVER

Dressed in navy-blue T-shirts and jeans, and armed with revolvers, AK-47 assault rifles, ammunition, hand grenades, explosives, mobile and satellite phones, and dried fruit, the LeT attackers left Karachi on an inflatable dinghy on a 310-mile voyage to Mumbai. During their journey, once past the Indian port of Porbandar, they seized an Indian fishing trawler, *MV Kuber*. After killing its crew of four, they forced the captain, Amar Singh Solanki, to sail to Mumbai, the commercial capital of India. As they neared their destination, they murdered Solanki.

Guided by the GPS coordinates on their "old used Garmin set,"[15] they landed safely at the Gateway of India in South Mumbai on a rubber dinghy. It was eight PM on November 26. Their main targets were the Chhatrapati Shivaji Railway Terminus (CSRT)—popularly called VT, the acronym for Victoria Terminus named after Queen Victoria—the landmark Taj Mahal Palace Hotel, the Oberoi-Trident Hotel, and the Nariman House, a Jewish community center. LeT planners wanted to hit the commercial elite of India staying at the most prestigious hotels of Mumbai and the visiting Israelis using the Nariman House, and create mass panic and confusion by slaughtering ordinary Indians at a busy railway terminus. They had instructed their charges to familiarize themselves with the locations of their targets by using Google Earth maps.

At the crowded passenger hall of the CSRT, while Kasab sprayed his submachine gun, his companion, the twenty-five-year-old Abu Dera Ismail Khan, threw hand grenades. They killed 58 people, including 22 Muslims, and injured 104 in fifteen minutes. They then hijacked a car and went on a shooting spree. When they encountered a police barricade near the beach, they tried to turn around. In the subsequent gun battle, Khan was killed, and Kasab was apprehended alive. This proved to be an invaluable asset for the Indian authorities. Eager to save his life and limb, Kasab readily provided vital information, including the fate of the fishing trawler, which proved authentic.

Armed with the layouts of their respective targets, the remaining eight terrorists split up, with four assaulting the Taj Mahal Palace Hotel in Apollo Bunder with its 560 rooms and 44 suites. Once there, they fired their AK-47s in marble hallways and broke down doors, mowing down those hiding behind them. The remainder of the terrorist gang headed for the luxury Oberoi-Trident Hotel and the Nariman House. According to radio transmissions picked up by Indian intelligence, the terrorists were told by their handlers based in the LeT office in Karachi that the lives of Jews were worth fifty times those of non-Jews.[16]

The gunmen were directed by their handlers from inside Pakistan via mobile phones and Voice over Internet Protocol. "Inflict maximum damage," a controller in Pakistan urged the attackers at the Oberoi-Trident Hotel. "Keep fighting. Don't be taken alive."[17] As the Indian intelligence agents managed to listen and record the conversations between the terrorists and their handlers in Pakistan, they realized that the attackers were monitoring broadcasts by Indian and foreign television channels and garnering vital information. So the Indian authorities blocked the TV feeds to the Taj Mahal and Oberoi-Trident Hotels. But that still left their handlers in Karachi free to monitor telecast news and inform the gunmen.

Taken by surprise, the state and central governments stumbled badly before mobilizing the local police, the National Security Guard (NSG), and Marine commandos, as well as the Rapid Action Force troops. By the morning of November 27, the NSG secured the Nariman House and the Oberoi-Trident Hotel.

After a briefing to the media by Home Minister Shivraj Patil at eleven AM on November 27, describing the attacks as "very disturbing," there was no official announcement until a TV broadcast by Prime Minister Singh at seven thirty PM, which had been originally scheduled for four thirty PM. The delay of three hours ratcheted up public anxiety; people were eager to know how the authorities were reacting to the events being telecast by droves of Indian and foreign TV channels. Singh was measured in his address, which lacked a strong message and failed to reassure the people that their government was in control of the situation.

As it was, ending the siege of the Taj Mahal Hotel, where the terrorists had resorted to lining up the guests to single out the Americans and Israelis as their quarry, proved far more arduous. The captors, stunned by the opulence of the luxury hotel, bracketed the suffering of Kashmiri Muslims with that of the Palestinians at the hands of Israel. Yelling at his frightened captives, a terrorist yelled, "Did you know that a Zionist general [Avi Mizrahi] visited Kashmir two months ago?"[18]

The prime minister rushed to Mumbai on November 28 and spent the day presiding over a meeting of top state officials and visiting the injured in hospitals.

At the Taj Mahal Hotel, a denouement was reached when the attackers set off six explosions—one in the lobby, two in the elevators, and three in the restaurant. This led to the NSG mounting its Operation Black Tornado to flush out the attackers. They all ended up dead, either as victims of the security forces' fire or as suicides. The extraordinarily savage episode ended at eight AM on November 29.

Blood tests on the terrorists showed they had taken cocaine and LSD to help them sustain their energy and stay awake for two-and-a-half days. Police claimed to have found syringes at the scenes of the carnage.

By the time the sixty-hour outrage ended, 166 people, including 28 foreigners, including 6 Americans, were killed. Of the 293 injured, all but 37 were Indian. The military-style terrorist attack in Mumbai became known as 26/11 in India.

An unprecedented feature of 26/11 was the widespread use of social networks to communicate information about the violent act being televised nonstop. It became the most well-documented terrorist attack to date. In diplomatic terms, it wiped out the trust and confidence the two neighbors had built up in stages since 2004. Indo-Pakistan relations became inextricably tied to the progress made by Pakistan to bring the perpetrators of the 26/11 attack to justice.

DELHI-ISLAMABAD RELATIONS IN DEEP FREEZE

The bloody Mumbai saga set off a cascade of diplomatic activity, with telephone lines between Delhi, Washington, and Islamabad buzzing, and US secretary of state Condoleezza Rice acting as the key player. The frantic conversations between the top officials in these capitals resulted in crossed wires and confusion, which raised the prospect of a hot war between the nuclear-armed neighbors.

Acting on the cumulative evidence provided by Kasab and intercepts of the conversations between the terrorists and their handlers in Karachi, Singh called his Pakistani counterpart, Gilani, on November 28. He suggested the dispatch of ISI chief Lieutenant General Ahmed Shuja

Pasha to Delhi to see India's evidence of the LeT's links with the terrorists. Gilani agreed. But when he approached Pasha's superior, COAS General Kayani, and President Zardari, they overruled sending the ISI director-general to Delhi. A compromise followed. Gilani settled for dispatching a lesser representative of the ISI instead.

Islamabad maintained that the LeT had nothing to do with the Mumbai outrage, which the Pakistani media, briefed by officials, attributed to Bangladeshi and Indian criminals. When the Indian authorities revealed that the arrested suspect was a son of Amir Shahban Kasab from Faridkot, the Islamabad government insisted that such a person did not exist in Pakistan. In stark contrast, investigative journalist Saeed Shah traveled to Faridkot to try to track down Ajmal Amir Kasab's family.[19] Shah then consulted the electoral rolls for Faridkot and found the names and national identity card numbers of Kasab Senior and his wife, Noor Illahi. Several other reporters followed his lead. On the night of December 3 the Kasab couple would disappear mysteriously.

On November 29 Singh chaired a meeting of the military high command and intelligence chiefs. Air Chief Marshal Fali Homi Major strongly advocated surgical strikes at the terrorist training camps in Pakistani Kashmir. The prime minister promised to discuss this option at the next meeting of the Cabinet Committee on Security, which tilted toward hitting the camps. Armed with a clandestine report on this high-level debate, the CIA station chief in Delhi concluded that India was about to attack Pakistan. He instantly reported this to the CIA director, General Michael Hayden, who conveyed this information to President George W. Bush.

The previous day, India's foreign minister, Pranab Mukherjee, and his Pakistani counterpart, Mukhdoom Shah Mahmood Qureshi, who happened to be in Delhi during the Mumbai attacks, had a heated telephone conversation. After stating that "all options" were open to India to avenge the Mumbai carnage, Mukherjee added that "they [Pakistanis] were leaving us no choice but to go to war."[20] Qureshi interpreted Mukherjee's words as a warning of an upcoming war and informed Prime Minister Gilani.

In Washington, a White House aide anxiously called Rice to inform her that "the Pakistanis say that the Indians have warned them that they've decided to go to war." Surprised, she said, "What?" and added, "That isn't what they're telling me. In my many conversations with the Indians over the [past] two days, they'd emphasized their desire to defuse the situation and their need for the Pakistanis to do something to show that they accepted responsibility for tracking down the terrorists." She then asked the operations center at the State Department to get Mukherjee on the phone. It failed to contact him. "I called back again," Rice continued. "No response. By now the international phone lines were buzzing with the news. The Pakistanis were calling everyone—the Saudis, the Emiratis, the Chinese. Finally Mukherjee called back. I told him what I'd heard." He explained that Qureshi had taken his stern words over the phone "the wrong way." At the State Department, Rice received frantic calls from the US ambassadors in New Delhi and Islamabad. "Ambassador (David) Mulford's [in Delhi] message was stark. 'There is war fever here. I don't know if the Prime Minister can hold out. Everyone knows that the terrorists came from Pakistan.'" She then talked to Ambassador Anne Patterson in Islamabad. "Her message was just as clear. 'They have their heads in the sand,' she said." This version appeared in Rice's book *No High Honor: A Memoir of My Years in Washington*.[21]

These developments were enough to set the alarm bells ringing in Washington. On November 30 (the next day) Bush instructed Rice to rush to South Asia.

Rice arrived in Delhi on December 3. In her meetings with top officials, she conveyed the condolences of the US administration to the Indian government and people. With Rice standing by his side, Mukherjee told reporters that undoubtedly the terrorists who struck Mumbai came from Pakistan and that they were coordinated there. "The government of India is determined to act decisively to protect its territorial integrity and the right of our citizens to a peaceful life with all the means at our disposal," he added.[22] "Pakistan needs to act with urgency and with resolve and cooperate fully and transparently [with India]," said Rice. "The response of the Pakistan government should be one of cooperation and action. That is what we expect and we have been sending that message."[23]

In Islamabad Rice conferred with the highest civilian and military leaders. "The Pakistanis were at once terrified and in the same breathe dismissive of the Indian claims," she noted in her memoirs. "President Zardari emphasized his desire to avoid war but couldn't bring himself to acknowledge Pakistan's likely role in the attacks." Having listened to a long explanation by Prime Minister Gilani that those who had launched the Mumbai attacks had nothing to do with Pakistan, Rice said, "Mr Prime Minister . . . either you're lying to me or your people are lying to you. I then went on to tell him what we—the United States—knew about the origins of the attack. I didn't accuse Pakistan's government of involvement; that wasn't the point. But rogues within the security services might have aided the terrorists. It was time to admit that and to investigate more seriously." In her book she mentioned that General Kayani was "the one person who, even if he couldn't admit responsibility, understood that Pakistan would have to give an accounting of what had happened."[24]

Rice's comparatively mild statement issued at the Chaklala Airbase before her departure from Islamabad was at odds with the report published by the Karachi-based *Dawn*. In her talks with Pakistani officials she referred to "irrefutable evidence" of the involvement of elements in Pakistan in the Mumbai attacks and that Pakistan needed to act urgently and effectively to avert a strong international response.[25]

In her interview with Wolf Blitzer of CNN on December 7, Rice summed up her conclusion thus: "I don't think that there is compelling evidence of involvement of Pakistani officials. But I do think that Pakistan has a responsibility to act, and it doesn't matter that they're non-state actors."[26]

President Zardari had taken to using the term "nonstate actors" to deny any complicity by the Pakistani state. But that did not exempt Islamabad from investigating the hard facts supplied by Delhi. By contrast, Prime Minister Singh claimed solid evidence of a Pakistani connection and warned that India would not tolerate use of the territories of its neighbors to mount attacks on his country and that there would be a "cost" to it.

Hot on Rice's heels, Senator John McCain, the unsuccessful Republican presidential candidate, arrived in Delhi. He met Singh and then flew to Islamabad on December 5 to confer with Gilani. At an informal lunch with senior journalists and politicians in Lahore, he informed his audience that "a visibly angry" Singh had told him that they had enough evidence of the involvement of former ISI officers in the planning and execution of the Mumbai attacks, and if the Pakistani government failed to act swiftly to arrest the people involved, India would be left with no option but to conduct aerial operations against select targets in Pakistan. "The democratic government of India is under pressure and it will be a matter of days after they have given the evidence to Pakistan [that they decide] to use the option of force if Islamabad fails to act against the terrorists," said McCain, according to Ejaz Haider, a senior editor at the *Daily Times*, who attended the lunch. "We were angry after 9/11. This is India's 9/11. We cannot tell India not to act when that is what we did, asking the Taliban to hand over Osama bin Laden to avoid a war and waging one when they refused to do so."[27]

PAKISTAN BENDS—IN STAGES

The joint Washington-Delhi pressure worked. On December 7, Pakistani troops raided the LeT base at Shawai Nullah near Muzaffarabad, the capital of the Pakistan-controlled Azad Kashmir. They arrested twenty LeT activists as well as Lakhvi, the alleged mastermind of the Mumbai attacks, and Zarrar Shah, another LeT leader.[28] Simultaneously, Islamabad declared that even surgical strikes against suspected terrorist training camps in Pakistani Kashmir would be considered an attack on Pakistan's sovereignty and that it would retaliate with "all its might."

On December 10 the UN Security Council designated the Jamaat ud Dawa (JuD), the front organization for the LeT, a terrorist faction. And the Council's Al Qaida and Taliban sanctions committee declared that Lakhvi, Muhammad Hafiz Saeed, and two other leaders of the LeT were terrorists subject to sanctions. Pakistan placed Saeed under house arrest under the Maintenance of Public Order law, which allowed the authorities to detain temporarily those who were deemed likely to create disorder. That and Islamabad's statement that it would ban the JuD were welcomed by Delhi.[29]

To deprive India of a rationale to carry out a surgical strike on the headquarters of the LeT/JuD at Murdike, twenty miles north of Lahore, the Pakistani government pressured LeT/JuD management to let an Indian reporter of the Delhi-based magazine *Tehelka*, Harinder Baweja, visit the premises in mid-December. She was given a guided tour of the educational complex, attended by very few people because of the Eid festival break, with the JuD spokesman, Abdullah Muntazir, insisting that the JuD was a charitable organization. On further questioning, he conceded that "we used to provide logistical help to the Lashkar [LeT], collect funds for them and look after their publicity," and added that "they must have bought weapons with the money we gave them."[30]

But these gestures were not enough for India to end its week-old state of war readiness for its air force and navy. However, its decision not to mobilize its ground forces remained unchanged. "Pakistan has one of the best armies of the world," declared Gilani on his arrival in Multan, the base of one of Pakistan's corps. "The nation should not be worried. . . .

Pakistan is a responsible state. Being a nuclear power, we are cautious in reaction." Islamabad put its naval forces on alert in response to the redeployment of India's warships. Equally, its air force confirmed reports of "increased vigilance" on its part.[31]

Though limping along during its last days, the Bush administration strongly advised the quarrelling neighbors to cool it. Its counsel fell on receptive ears. "We are not planning any military action," said the Indian defense minister, Arackaparambil Kurien Antony, on December 16. "At the same time, unless Pakistan takes actions against those terrorists who are operating in their soil against India, and also against all those who are behind this Mumbai terrorist attack, things will not be normal."[32]

Mukherjee qualified Antony's statement a week later. He explained that India had not ruled out military operations against terrorists in Pakistan if its government failed to curb those based on its own soil. "If you ask about military conflict, nobody will say about it in the media. [But] we have kept our options open."[33]

On December 16 Islamabad placed its air force on high alert and conducted aerial surveillance of all its sensitive sites likely to be targeted by India. It also mobilized its ground troops along the LoC and the international border to protect vital points. To Washington's distress, it moved a fifth of its troops deployed in the tribal areas along the Pakistan-Afghan border to its frontier with India. In response, Delhi redeployed its soldiers along the Pakistani border. This led Washington to resort to public diplomacy and urged increased cooperation between the sparring nations in investigating the Mumbai attacks, which India squarely blamed on Pakistan-based militants.[34]

"I propose to India to de-activate forward air bases," said Qureshi on December 30. "I also propose to India to re-locate its ground forces to peace time positions. These measures will reduce tension and we will move forward in a positive way." Mukherjee referred to the Indian army's statement that its movements were part of its "normal winter exercise." As for his own stance, he said, "From day one I am saying this is not an India-Pakistan issue. This is an attack perpetrated by elements emanating from the land of Pakistan, and Pakistan government should take action."[35]

Defying overwhelming evidence to the contrary, Islamabad had disowned the Pakistani nationality of Ajmal Amir Kasab for weeks. Then on January 7 it conceded that he was a Pakistani national and went on to file a case against him. This pacified Indians to some extent.

A week later India's COAS, General Deepak Kapoor, said that he considered war "the last resort." In response Gilani argued that with India and Pakistan being nuclear powers, there was no possibility of war between them. He explained to his compatriots that Indian leaders were issuing strong statements to satisfy outraged public opinion at home.[36]

Though the two neighbors once again avoided hot war, the process of normalization of relations went into a deep freeze following the Mumbai outrage. For several weeks they communicated with each other on different wavelengths. At the root of this noncommunication was Pakistan's outright denial of any involvement even by nonstate agents operating on its soil. Its leaders feared that if they conceded any link between their country and the Mumbai attacks in the emotionally charged atmosphere prevailing at the UN Security Council after 26/11, the Council would impose sanctions on Pakistan. So they dragged their feet to let passions cool. They took ten long weeks to even confirm Kasab's Pakistani nationality.

But by sticking to the denial mode for so long, Pakistani officials stoked tensions between Delhi and Islamabad; they kept their respective air forces and navies on high alert. India went on complaining bitterly that Pakistan was not doing enough to arrest those behind the attacks, despite the voluminous evidence it had received from India.

The situation suddenly eased on February 12, 2009. "Some part of the conspiracy [to mount the Mumbai attacks] has taken place in Pakistan," conceded Pakistani's interior minister, Rehman Malik. He added that eight suspects from the banned LeT had been detained. "We have lodged an FIR [first information report by police] into the case."[37]

Even though disappointed that the suspects' list did not include Hafiz Muhammad Saeed, the cofounder of the LeT, the Indians were gratified that finally they had succeeded in getting the Pakistanis on the same page with them. Malik had owned up to only "part" of the conspiracy relating to Pakistan, chiefly to validate Islamabad's claim that the plotters had the active cooperation of some Indian Muslims, who among other things had secured SIM cards for the terrorists' mobile phones.

A GLACIAL THAW

By the time the Pakistani authorities brought the case for trial, it was April. The next month the Congress Party–led coalition in Delhi led by Manmohan Singh was reelected. On June 24 Singh met President Zardari on the margins of the Shanghai Cooperation Organization summit in Yekaterinburg, Russia. They decided to overcome the factors holding up the "composite dialogue" between their countries.

On the sidelines of the Non-Aligned Movement summit in Sharm-el-Sheikh, Egypt, Singh met Gilani on July 16. "Prime Minister Gilani assured that Pakistan will do everything in its power in this regard [of combating terrorism]," read their joint communiqué. "He said that Pakistan had provided an updated status dossier on the investigations of the Mumbai attacks and had sought additional information/evidence." After stating that "the two countries will share real time, credible and actionable information on any future terrorist threats," the communiqué added that "Prime Minister Gilani mentioned that Pakistan has some information on threats in Baluchistan and other areas." Lastly, both leaders recognized that "action on terrorism should not be linked to the composite dialogue process and these should not be bracketed. Prime Minister Singh said that India was ready to discuss all issues with Pakistan, including all outstanding issues."[38]

Different interpretations of the statement followed. In Islamabad, the de-linking of action on terrorism from the composite dialogue was hailed as a diplomatic victory for Pakistan, eager to sidestep the fallout from the Mumbai episode. Also, the Pakistani media interpreted the mere mention of Baluchistan in the joint communiqué as evidence of India's clandestine assistance to Baluchi insurgents battling Islamabad in their quest for independence.

In Delhi, Singh was taken to task by the opposition Bharatiya Janata Party (BJP). Decrying the joint communiqué as "surrender" by India, and fulminating at the reference to Baluchistan in the document, it staged a walkout from Parliament. In reply, Singh argued on July 30 that de-linking the composite dialogue from action by Pakistan against terrorism strengthened India's commitment, and that "meaningful process of engagement cannot move forward unless and until Pakistan takes measures to control terrorism." He added, "When I spoke to Prime Minister Gilani about terrorism from Pakistan, he mentioned to me that many Pakistanis thought that India meddled in Baluchistan. I told him that we have no interest in destabilizing Pakistan. . . . If Pakistan has any evidence . . . we are willing to look at it because we have nothing to hide." Rounding off his argument, he said, "Unless we want to go to war with Pakistan, dialogue is the only way out but we should do so on the basis of trust but verify."[39]

The diametrically opposite interpretations of the Singh-Gilani state-ment by the politicians and press of India and Pakistan illustrated the wide chasm that persisted between their respective popular perceptions.

All the same, in August, Delhi provided further evidence on the in-volvement of Saeed in the 26/11 outrage. In response, following their meeting in New York during the UN General Assembly session in Sep-tember, Qureshi assured the Indian foreign minister Somanahalli Mal-laiah Krishna of "doing everything" to bring to justice the perpetrators of the Mumbai attacks.

Both Delhi and Islamabad were pressured by President Barack Obama's administration to resume the peace process. Secretary of State Hillary Clinton considered reconciliation between India and Pakistan es-sential to achieving Washington's overarching aim of turning war-ravaged Afghanistan into a stable, democratic political entity. Despite opposition at home, Singh bit the bullet and initiated talks at the highest bureaucratic level of foreign secretary. Pakistani officials gloated that "India had been brought to its knees." In return, India threatened to cancel the talks if Islamabad did not cease "grandstanding."

And yet the differences in perception persisted. Whereas Delhi in-sisted that these were to be "talks about talks," with one item on the agenda—terrorism—the Pakistanis said they wanted to discuss several issues, including Kashmir.[40]

India's Nirupama Rao and her Pakistani counterpart, Salman Bashir, held a four-hour session in New Delhi on February 25, 2010. Bashir stressed that Pakistan was a victim, not a sponsor, of terrorism. More than five thousand Pakistanis had been killed and nearly thirteen thou-sand injured in terrorist attacks there since 2008. He accused India of supporting "militants and terrorists" in Afghanistan, which endangered the security of Pakistan.[41]

On her part, Rao presented Bashir with three dossiers on fifty senior Islamist militants based in Pakistan and urged greater efforts by Islam-abad to hunt for the perpetrators of the Mumbai terror attacks. She expressed her frustration that the LeT's Saeed was a free man. In early June 2009 the Lahore High Court had declared his detention unconsti-tutional and ordered his release. A month later the Pakistani government appealed this decision. It lost. On October 12 the Lahore High Court quashed all cases against Saeed and set him free. The court also ruled that the JuD was not a banned organization and could work freely in Pakistan.[42]

Following the well-worn pattern, the leaders of India and Pakistan used a summit of the South Asian Association for Regional Cooperation (SAARC) to meet informally on the sidelines. At this regional conference in Thimphu, Bhutan, at the end of April, Singh had an hour-long, one-on-one conversation with Gilani. No joint statement ensued, but it was reliably learned that they decided that their foreign ministers should work out the "methodology" to carry forward the composite dialogue process.[43]

Pakistan listed its steps to curb the activities of the banned JuD. "We have frozen 16 bank accounts of Jamaat ud Dawa, blocked six websites, cancelled all arms licenses issued to the outfit, detained 71 activists, placed the names of 64 activists on the Exit Control List, put over 63 madrassas of the JuD under government control and confiscated all its publications and papers," said Interior Minister Malik in early May. The government had also appealed to the Supreme Court over the release of Saeed and awaited its verdict.[44] On May 26 the Supreme Court dismissed the prosecutor's case and upheld the lower court's decision to release Saeed.

In June India's home minister Palaniappian Chidambaram met Malik in Islamabad on the margins of the SAARC interior ministers' meeting. While providing further leads on the Mumbai attacks, he expressed his dissatisfaction at the glacial pace of the trial of the seven suspects by an antiterrorism court in Rawalpindi. He noted that on May 9 the defense lawyers filed an application in which they argued that the government was resorting to various tactics to delay the trial. They referred to its application to the Indian authorities seeking access to Kasab. It was bound to be rejected because on May 6 Kasab had been found guilty of eighty-six charges and given capital punishment. According to the Article 403 of Pakistan's Code of Criminal Procedure and Article 13 of its constitution, a person once convicted or acquitted cannot be tried for the same offense again.[45]

At the end of a twenty-five-minute telephone conversation between him and Krishna on how to narrow the "trust deficit," the Pakistani foreign minister Qureshi invited Krishna to Islamabad. But any goodwill created so far evaporated following a revelation by India's home secretary, Gopal Krishna Pillai, on the eve of Krishna's departure on July 14. It was based on the full confession made by David Coleman Headley in May 2010 as part of his plea bargain to be spared capital punishment after his arrest in Chicago in October 2009. In June he spent thirty-four hours talking to Indian investigators in the presence of FBI agents. Pillai said that fresh evidence provided by Headley showed that the ISI and Saeed played a "much more significant" role in planning and executing the 26/11 terrorist attack than was known before.[46] (In October India released a 109-page summary of David Coleman Headley's confession.)

Though Krishna went through his scheduled meetings, including the one with Qureshi—joined by Interior Minister Malik, who summarily dismissed Headley as "an unreliable witness"—the chance of any diminution in mutual trust deficit had practically vanished. At the joint press conference Krishna looked on stony-faced as Qureshi said that besides terrorism the two delegations had discussed Kashmir, Sir Creek, and Siachen Glacier. He complimented this by mentioning Pakistan's assurance that it would seriously follow up the leads given to it earlier by Chidambaram.[47] From Delhi's perspective, however, the latest development was nothing more than the continuation of "talks about talks."

Pakistan decided to call India's bluff that no composite dialogue would be resumed until and unless there was a substantive delivery on 26/11 and cross-border terrorism. All it had to do was to spin out the trial of the seven suspects, which started in April 2009 and went through four changes of judge. The ploy worked. The Indian government concluded that it could not just continue "nonengagement," and that it needed to engage with Pakistan in the hope that it would yield the result that refusal to talk did not. It put that policy into practice at the foreign secretaries' meeting in Thimphu on February 6, 2011.

However, discernible movement did not occur until March 27. On that day Singh invited Gilani to witness the India-Pakistan World Cup semifinal cricket match in Mohali, a small town in Punjab a few miles from the Pakistan border, on March 30. Gilani agreed. And in a major confidence-building gesture, his government decided to let Indian investigators travel to Pakistan to probe the Mumbai attacks.

On March 30 security was tight in Mohali. Indian army helicopters and antiaircraft guns imposed a no-fly zone over the Mohali stadium to ward off any potential attack by militants. Singh and Gilani spent eight hours watching a cricket match. The broad "agenda," according to Rao, was to "understand each other better, resolve outstanding issues and at the core of the dialogue . . . normalize relations."[48] India won, scoring 260 runs for 9 wickets, with Pakistan all out at 231.

A new round of talks ensued between foreign secretaries. On June 24, at long last, Pakistan agreed to include nonstate actors and safe havens for terrorists as part of the terrorist infrastructure to be addressed.[49]

A quid pro quo followed. After deliberations with his new Pakistani counterpart, Hina Rabbani Khar, on July 27 in New Delhi, Krishna implicitly acknowledged participating in a "composite dialogue" with Pakistan. Their joint communiqué expressed satisfaction at the holding of meetings on counterterrorism (including progress on the Mumbai trials) and narcotics control, as well as such other issues as economic cooperation, Siachen Glacier, and above all the Kashmir dispute. They settled for continued discussions, in a purposeful manner, with a view to finding a peaceful solution by narrowing divergences and building convergences. They agreed on measures to liberalize cross-LoC trade and travel.[50]

This was the first substantial foreign ministers' meeting after the November 2008 Mumbai terrorist attacks. And they were right to define it as a foundation for a "new era" in bilateral links.

SIGNS OF BUDDING GOODWILL

A dramatic illustration of the improved relations came on October 23. An Indian military helicopter with a colonel and two majors on board lost its bearings in bad weather and strayed twelve miles into Pakistani Kashmir from its base in the India-controlled region. The mishap had the potential of spiraling into a major spat requiring high-level political intervention. Instead, Pakistan's military escorted the intruding aircraft after ordering it to land, questioned the crew politely, and discovered nothing more than the standard engineering equipment aboard. This information was conveyed to the highest military authority in Islamabad. It activated the hotline to Delhi. As a result, the Indian crew was released, and their helicopter was refueled. Within five hours it was back at its base.[51]

A week later Islamabad announced its intention to normalize commercial ties with India by extending it most-favored-nation status (MFN)—meaning that it was ready to give India a trade advantage by offering low tariffs—by January 1, 2013, thus reciprocating Delhi's gesture dating back to 1996. This was a major concession by Islamabad—up to that point it had insisted that improvement in trade relations and people-to-people contacts should come only after an amicable resolution of the Kashmir dispute.

With relations thawing slightly, Singh and Gilani had an hour-long meeting on the margins of the SAARC summit in Addu City, Maldives, on November 10. They discussed terrorism, trade, and the divided territory of Kashmir. "The time has come to write a new chapter in the history of our relationship," Singh said, standing beside Gilani at a joint press conference. Foreign Minister Khar was realistic. "We have many, many long miles to move ahead still," she said.[52]

During her visit to Delhi on April 3, 2012, US undersecretary of state Wendy Sherman told the Indians that Washington had placed a $10 million bounty on the capture of Saeed for his alleged role in the 2008 Mumbai attacks.[53] Only three other extremists, including Taliban leader Mullah Muhammad Omar, carried such a staggering figure with their seizure.

A defiant Saeed held a press conference in a hotel just across the street from the headquarters of Pakistan's Army in Rawalpindi—a symbolic gesture suggesting that his close ties with the ISI remained intact. "I am living my life in the open and the US can contact me whenever they want." The Americans knew where he was, he added. "This is a laughable, absurd announcement. . . . Here I am in front of everyone, not hiding in a cave."[54]

During a heated debate in the National Assembly on the subject, Gilani warned that the American reward was a "negative message" and would "further widen the trust deficit" between Washington and Islamabad. He described Saeed as "a domestic matter." Opposition MPs called the award "mind boggling" and "ridiculous." Outside Parliament, right-wing lawyers in Lahore pointed out that courts in Pakistan had cleared him of all charges.[55]

The media in Pakistan and India were abuzz with the implications of the bounty on Saeed, as President Zardari prepared for a private pilgrimage to the shrine of the Sufi saint Khwaja Moinuddin Chishti in Ajmer, Rajasthan, on April 8. He had planned this trip much earlier to fulfill a *mannat*,[56] or vow, he had made during his long incarceration on corruption charges. He was invited to lunch in Delhi by Premier Singh, and accepted.

On the eve of his departure for India, he chatted with reporters. "My stance on Saeed is not different from that of my government," he told them. "My visit to India is of a religious nature and I do not think Manmohan Singh will make me sit [and discuss only] this issue."[57] Indian officials tried to downplay the luncheon reception for Zardari, at which the wide-ranging cuisine included the Kashmiri delicacy of *Goshtaba*, meatballs in curd-based curry. But the significance of the first visit by the Pakistani president to India in seven years was hard to underestimate.

Further news of a warming of relations came on April 13. On that day the trade ministers of India and Pakistan inaugurated an enlarged border commercial terminal at Wagah with a capacity to handle six hundred trucks a day. This was done to help bolster bilateral trade, which had risen to $2.6 billion a year, up from $300 million in 2004. Simultaneously, India decided to lift its ban on foreign direct investment by Pakistan.[58]

Singh and Zardari met again on the margins of the Non-Aligned Movement summit in Tehran on August 30, 2012. "We have covered a lot of ground but we still have to go a long way," remarked Zardari at the joint press conference. He added that Pakistan was keenly looking forward to a visit by Premier Singh, born in the Pakistani Punjab village of Gah, which in his view was "long overdue." But the Indian leader was coy, covering himself in the diplomatic language of traveling to Islamabad at the "appropriate time." Briefing the Indian media, his foreign secretary, Ranjan Mathai, said: "Prime Minister Singh pressed for an expeditious conclusion of the 26/11 trial and said action taken in this sphere would be a major confidence building measure." It would help to bridge the trust deficit and build public support for the kind of relationship India would like to see between the two nations, he added.[59]

In short, Delhi's bottom line had not changed. There would be no "business as usual" until and unless Pakistan brought to justice the perpetrators of the Mumbai attack.

On the eve of his departure for Islamabad for the third round of high-level talks on September 8, Krishna stressed the same point in an exclusive interview to the Press Trust of India. Given the numerous adjournments of the case, the Indians' patience was running thin. A frustrated Singh referred to "increased attempts by militants to cross the LoC." In other words, India continued to treat terrorism as the number one item on the agenda. All the same, the two governments signed a new visa regime. Among other changes, the agreement exempted travelers over sixty-five, children under twelve, and businessmen from reporting to the police during their travels.[60]

On the other hand, yielding to the pressure of the Islamist groups and the farm lobby, the Pakistani government failed to keep its promise of granting India MFN status by December 31, 2012. And the New Year started with a sudden rise in tension in Kashmir. Minor incidents across the LoC were commonplace; they did not threaten the cease-fire signed in November 2003. The eighty-odd instances of minor technical violations by both sides in 2012 were considered routine.

In the violence that erupted during January 6–8 near Mendhar, 140 miles north of Jammu, the killing of one Pakistani soldier by the Indians allegedly in retaliation for the Pakistanis' cease-fire violations led to the further killing of two Indian troops. One of them, Lance Naik Hemraj, was beheaded by a cross-border raiding party. "After this barbaric act there cannot be business as usual with Pakistan," declared Singh. "What happened at the LoC is unacceptable; those who are responsible should be brought to book." In reply Pakistan's foreign minister Khar said, "We have ordered an independent investigation, but we are offering more, let a third party investigate the issue." India did not take up her offer. "It [the beheading] was stage-managed and pre-planned," claimed the Indian COAS, General Bikram Singh. "India reserves its right to retaliate at the time and place of its choice. The important thing now is to ensure that morale among commanders in Kashmir remains high."[61]

Following this saber rattling, however, India's director general of Military Operations, Lieutenant General Vinod Bhatia, conferred with his Pakistani counterpart. They reached an understanding to lower the temperature.

Soon after, popular attention in South Asia turned to the impending general election in Pakistan. To ensure a level playing field, Mir Hazar Khan Khoso, a retired judge, was sworn in as the caretaker prime minister on March 25, 2013.

THE RETURN OF NAWAZ SHARIF

In the National Assembly poll held on May 11, the Pakistan Muslim League (N), led by Muhammad Nawaz Sharif, a pro-business conservative, won 166 seats, reducing the incumbent PPP to a fraction of its previous size. With 18 independent members of the National Assembly joining the PML (N), Sharif secured a comfortable majority in the 374-strong chamber. Having survived all criminal convictions (subsequently overturned), six months in jail during the dictatorship of Musharraf, and seven years of exile in Saudi Arabia—where, given a government loan, he set up a steel plant—and Britain, he was back at the helm at home.

Singh congratulated him and his party on their "emphatic victory," hoping to work with him to chart "a new course for the relationship" between their countries. Surprisingly, the BJP president, Rajnath Singh, followed Prime Minister Singh's example. "Mr. Sharif's statements on rebuilding relations with India are a positive sign," he remarked. Referring to Sharif's statement "to pick up the pieces of 1999 peace process," he added that "keeping in view our past experiences with Pakistan, the BJP views Mr. Sharif's statements with cautious optimism."[62]

Sharif was sworn in as prime minister on June 5, after he had secured a record 244 votes in the National Assembly. He set another record by becoming the first prime minister in his country's sixty-five-year history to take over from an elected government that served a full five-year term, an unprecedented achievement. "The democratic transition of government in Pakistan is a welcome development," noted the BJP leader.[63]

Such bonhomie did not last long, thanks to the tit-for-tat violence that erupted again at the LoC at the end of July. Indian soldiers killed four men from Pakistani Kashmir, alleging that they were infiltrators. This claim ran contrary to the fact that among them they had only one assault rifle and no grenades or communications equipment. Islamabad contended that they were local peasants who in the process of picking herbs had strayed close to the LoC when they were abducted by the Indians.

These killings set off a fresh round of bloodletting. Some analysts believed that such attacks were deliberately orchestrated by elements within the Indian and Pakistani forces opposed to rapprochement between their governments.

Accusations and counteraccusations were hurled when India said five of its soldiers guarding the LoC were killed on the night of August 6. On August 7 hundreds of Indian Youth Congress activists staged a violent protest near the Pakistani high commission in Delhi. There were anti-Pakistan demonstrations in other major Indian cities. Noting the street uproar, Defense Minister Antony told Parliament that "specialist troops of the Pakistan army were involved in this attack," thus directly implicating the government. "We all know that nothing happens from the Pakistani side of the Pakistan Line of Control without support, assistance, facilitation and often, direct involvement of the Pakistan army."[64]

In Islamabad, addressing government officials, Sharif expressed "his sadness over the recent incidents," and added, "It is incumbent upon the leadership of both sides not to allow the situation to drift and to take steps to improve the atmosphere."[65] Later that month, in his interview with David Blair and David Munk of the *Daily Telegraph* of London, Sharif said, "We didn't have any India-bashing slogans in the elections. There have been such slogans in the past—10 years ago, 20 years ago, 30 years ago—but not now. In fact, I very clearly spoke about good relations with India even before the elections were happening."[66]

Sharif kept up this theme when he addressed the UN General Assembly on September 27. "We stand ready to re-engage with India in a substantive and purposeful dialogue," he declared. "We can build on the Lahore Accord signed in 1999, which contained a road map for the resolution of our differences through peaceful negotiations. I am committed to working for a peaceful and economically prosperous region. This is what our people want and this is what I have long aspired for."[67]

By contrast, the following day Manmohan Singh lashed out at Pakistan in his address to the Assembly: "State-sponsored cross-border terrorism is of particular concern to India, also on account of the fact that the epicenter of terrorism in our region is located in our neighborhood in Pakistan." Expressing his willingness to peacefully resolve all issues, including Kashmir, with Pakistan, he said, "However, for progress to be made, it is imperative that the territory of Pakistan and the areas under its control are not utilized for aiding and abetting terrorism directed against India. It is equally important that the terrorist machinery that draws its sustenance from Pakistan be shut down."[68]

All the same, as agreed before, Singh and Sharif had an hour-long meeting over breakfast at a New York Hotel on September 29. Militants' attacks on a police station and an army base in Indian Kashmir on September 26, resulting in thirteen deaths, were designed to derail the prime ministers' meeting but failed in their political objective. The leaders agreed that they needed to stop the recent spate of attacks in the Kashmir region in order for peace talks to advance. They instructed their senior military commanders to find a way to shore up the LoC.[69]

Two days earlier, Singh had had a luncheon meeting with President Obama at the White House. "They reaffirmed their commitment to eliminating terrorist safe havens and infrastructure, and disrupting terrorist networks including Al Qaida and Lashkar-e Taiba," read their joint communiqué. "The Leaders called for Pakistan to work toward bringing the perpetrators of November 2008 Mumbai attacks to justice."[70]

Despite repeated urgings by Delhi to speed up the trial of the suspects involved in the Mumbai attacks, the case in the antiterrorism court of Judge Malik Muhammad Akram in Islamabad had moved at a snail's pace for a variety of reasons, technical and others. In May 21013 the chief prosecutor, Chaudhry Zulfiqar Ali, was gunned down by suspected militants in Islamabad, where the case had been transferred from Rawal-pindi, whose Adiala jail held the suspects.

In February 2014, Sartaj Aziz, advisor to Sharif on national security and foreign affairs, assured India's foreign minister, Salman Khurshid, that a verdict was likely in a couple of months.[71] His prediction proved grossly optimistic. On March 3 in an attack on a district court in Islamabad, ter-rorists killed twelve people, including two judges. The latest judge on the case, Atiqur Rehman, demanded deployment of commandos for his secu-rity. When the government refused, he stopped his weekly trips to Adiala jail. The case came to a virtual halt. So far the court had cross-examined only thirty-two of the sixty prosecution witnesses.[72]

In the final analysis the 2008 Mumbai carnage was linked to the un-resolved Indo-Pakistani dispute about Kashmir, which was grounded in the partition of the subcontinent. But there was another rivalry between the twin states that originated with the division: Afghanistan. As long as Britain ruled the Indian subcontinent as part of its empire, Afghanistan served as a buffer between its most prized colony and Russia, governed first by the czars and then by the Bolsheviks. The partition of British India wrought a radical geopolitical change.

18

Competing for Kabul

The historic link between the Indian subcontinent and Afghanistan dates to the reign of Emperor Zahiruddin Muhammad Babur. A man of middle stature, stout, fleshy faced, with a scanty beard, Babur founded the Mughal Empire in the subcontinent in 1526. Before capturing the Delhi Sultanate he had ruled the Domain of Kabul—today's eastern and southern Afghanistan—for twenty-one years. And honoring his wish, his successor in Agra transported his corpse to Kabul for burial a decade after his death in 1530. His enclosed tomb sits at the top of a hill transformed into a walled and terraced garden, called Bagh-e Babur, which is now a popular picnic site.

This shared history shattered with the partition of British India, with Pakistan sharing its western frontier with Afghanistan. The birth of Pakistan revived an old dispute about the Durand Line, which in 1893 defined the border between British India and Afghanistan, with all the passes of the Suleiman Mountains placed under British jurisdiction. It argued that Pakistan was not a successor state to Britain but a new state carved out of British India. Therefore whatever treaty rights issued from the Durand Agreement expired. Pakistan's governor-general Muhammad Ali Jinnah rejected this argument summarily.

The other contending issue was the movement for creating independent Pashtunistan out of parts of North-West Frontier Province (later Khyber Pakhtunkhwa) and Federally Administered Tribal Agencies (FATA), forming one-fifth of West Pakistan. Kabul supported this campaign, which Pakistan derided as "an Afghan stunt." Afghanistan's animus toward Pakistan was so strong that it cast the only negative vote on the newborn state's admission to the United Nations on September 30, 1947.[1]

Noting the discontent among the Pashtun tribes along the Afghan-Pakistan border, who had enjoyed semiautonomous status under the British, Jinnah conducted talks with their leaders to work out a new modus vivendi. These failed. Tensions remained high. In June 1949 Pakistan's planes attacked an Afghan village. Though the government apologized, periodic border incidents continued.

Animosity toward Pakistan led Afghanistan and India to sign a Treaty of Friendship in January 1950. It alluded to "the ancient ties which have existed between the two countries for centuries." Indian scholars familiar with the *Arthashastra* (Sanskrit: literally, text on wealth), a manual on statecraft by Chankaya Kautilya around 300 BCE, approvingly quoted his axiom: "A ruler with contiguous territory is a rival. The ruler next to the adjoining is to be deemed a friend."

In modern times, however, governing a landlocked country sharing a long frontier with Pakistan limited the area of maneuver for Afghan king Muhammad Zahir Shah. Geography trumped international politics. The Afghan government signed the Transit Trade Agreement with Pakistan in late 1950. It won Afghanistan the right to import duty-free goods through Karachi.

After founding the South-East Asia Treaty Organization (SEATO) with Thailand and the Philippines in September 1954, Pakistan succeeded in getting SEATO to endorse the Durand Line. This angered Kabul. In March 1955 it cautioned the Pakistani government not to include the Pashtun area into the proposed single unit of West Pakistan. Its warning was ignored.

Six years later, after the Pakistani army carried out a major offensive in its turbulent tribal belt, Afghanistan protested. On August 22 Pakistan shut its consulates in Afghanistan and demanded that Kabul should do the same. It refused. Pakistan closed its border with Afghanistan and cut diplomatic links with it.

The loss of its concomitant commercial ties with Pakistan compelled Afghanistan to strengthen its trade links with the Soviet Union, three of whose constituents—Turkmenistan, Uzbekistan, and Tajikistan—abutted Afghanistan. This persuaded Pakistan to restore its ties with its western neighbor. Their reconciliation happened in May 1963. In 1965 they signed a fresh Transit Trade Agreement, which restored the situation before the latest spat. Nonetheless, Kabul-Moscow trade would expand to the extent that by the mid-1970s Afghanistan's commerce with the Soviet Union would account for nearly half of its foreign trade.

AFGHANISTAN LOOMS LARGE IN POST-1971 PAKISTAN

The loss of the eastern wing of Pakistan traumatized the leaders in Islamabad. They vowed to protect the remaining wing with utmost vigilance from the malevolent designs of India, whose military planners no longer had to have a strategy for combating Pakistan on two fronts. With the generals in Delhi now free to focus on a single front, it became incumbent on their Pakistani rivals to ensure active cooperation of Kabul in case of war with Delhi. The long, porous Afghan-Pakistan border offered an escape route for Pakistan's civilian and military leaders as well as its troops and war materiel. Having a friendly government in Afghanistan, ruled by royals since 1747, became an absolute necessity.

But, unexpectedly, the situation in Kabul underwent a sea change. In July 1973 Prime Minister General Muhammad Daoud Khan overthrew his cousin Zahir Shah and declared Afghanistan a republic. To consolidate his power he revived the issue of Pashtunistan with Pakistan. His officers started training twelve thousand irredentist Pashtun and Baluch volunteers to harass Pakistan's army. In return, Pakistani prime minister Zulfikar Ali Bhutto sponsored an unsuccessful anti–Daoud Khan coup in July 1975. Mediation by Shah Muhammad Reza Pahlavi of Iran eased tensions by 1977. But normal relations between Kabul and Islamabad were disrupted in April 1978, when Marxist military officers mounted a coup against Daoud Khan, who was assassinated. They renamed the country the Democratic Republic of Afghanistan (DRA).

During these tumultuous events, India was a bystander. It recognized the DRA, whereas Pakistan did not. Following the Kremlin's military intervention in Afghanistan in December 1979, Delhi continued to have cordial relations with the government in Kabul. Indeed, given its 1971 Friendship and Cooperation Treaty with Moscow, it increased its stake in Afghanistan. It cooperated with Kabul in industrial, irrigation, and hydroelectric projects. In the mid-1980s it emerged as the single largest donor to Afghanistan.[2] In 1988, for instance, India-based WAPCOS Ltd (Water and Power Consultancy Services) started to reconstruct the Salma Dam on the Hari River in Herat province.

Contrary was the case with Pakistan. It became the frontline state in Washington's drive to expel the Soviets from Afghanistan. After the withdrawal of Soviet troops in February 1989, to the chagrin of Islamabad, the government of the leftist Muhammad Najibullah in Kabul did not fall. India stood by Najibullah until he was killed by the victorious Islamist mujahedin in April 1992. It was to Delhi that he had dispatched his family on the eve of the fall of his regime. And it was his failure to catch a flight to the Indian capital at the last minute that led to his mutilation and murder at the hands of the mujahedin.

During the civil war that erupted in Afghanistan along ethnic lines after the spring of 1992, Pakistan played an active role in conciliating the warring parties. Its efforts failed. It therefore decided to back a new faction, called the Taliban, beginning in 1994. With its active economic and military assistance, the Taliban started to gain control of Afghanistan gradually. It captured Kabul on September 26, 1996. On the eve of its triumphant storming of the Afghan capital, India closed its embassy. In marked contrast, jubilant Pakistan prepared to open its embassy in Kabul.

Islamabad worked hard to gain the Taliban regime diplomatic recognition. The next five years marked the zenith of its influence in Afghanistan, with the Taliban controlling 95 percent of the country. Yet the one-eyed Taliban leader Mullah Muhammad Omar refused to accept the Durand Line, arguing that "between the [Islamic] Umma [world community] there could be no borders."[3]

In sharp contrast, India backed the Northern Alliance (NA), led by Ahmad Shah Masoud, an ethnic Tajik, which was formed to oppose the Taliban by all means. Controlling a tiny area in northern Afghanistan, it maintained its headquarters in the town of Khwaja Bahuddin with a secure base in the adjoining Tajikistan.

Russian and Iran were the other two major backers of the NA. Though the Kremlin supplied heavy weapons and helicopters to the NA through Tajikistan, it respected the NA's opposition to allowing the presence of Russians among its militiamen, who had spent years fighting the Soviets in Afghanistan.

That created an opening for the Indians, who had been using Soviet-made military hardware for decades. India dispatched technicians to repair and maintain the NA's Soviet-made weapons. It also provided the NA with arms and other war materiel as well as military advisers. Its Research and Analysis Wing (RAW) intelligence agency sought the permission of Tajikistan to use Ayni Air Base near its capital, Dushanbe, and Farkhor Air Base, eighty-one miles southeast of Dushanbe, to ferry military equipment to the NA; service its tanks, helicopters, and artillery guns; and collect intelligence. It succeeded, but only after Moscow intervened on its behalf.[4]

Over the years the Indian armed forces gradually upgraded the Ayni and Farkhor Air Bases, and set up a secret field hospital at Farkhor to treat the NA's fighters. The hospital received its most prominent patient, Masoud, on September 9, 2001, when he was ferried in by helicopter with shrapnel lodged deep into his brain. At the NA headquarters in Khwaja Bahuddin, he had been taping a TV interview with two Moroccans, Karim Taizani and Bakem Bakkali, posing as journalists with Belgian passports, when Bakkali triggered explosives attached to the videotape as well as to Taizani's body. He died instantly while Bakkali was killed by Masoud's bodyguards. Masoud breathed his last at the Indian-run field hospital a few hours after his arrival.[5]

Two days later came the September 11 terrorist attacks on New York and Washington. These outrages orchestrated by Al Qaida leader Osama bin Laden from Afghanistan led President Bush to declare a global "war on terror." India backed the campaign. Pakistani president Pervez Musharraf prevaricated. But facing the prospect of Pakistan being bracketed with the Taliban-ruled Afghanistan, he cut his ties with the Taliban and cooperated with the United States. Later events would show, however, that Musharraf's U-turn on the Taliban was in essence a temporary adjustment to regain Washington's trust and support.[6]

Following the eight-week-long US-led Operation Enduring Freedom, launched on October 7, 2001, which overthrew the Taliban regime, Hamid Karzai, an ethnic Pashtun, was named Afghanistan's interim president by an International Conference on Afghanistan in Bonn, Germany, on December 5.

POST-TALIBAN AFGHANISTAN

The fourth son of Abdul Ahad Karzai, a politician and leader of the Popalzai tribe, Hamid graduated from high school in Kabul in 1976 at the age of nineteen. He was then accepted as an exchange student by the Himachal Pradesh University in Shimla, India. He obtained his master's degree in International Relations and Political Science in 1983.[7] During his seven years in India, he acquired fluency in Urdu/Hindi and became addicted to North Indian cuisine and Bollywood movies. Three decades later, during an interview with a British historian, he was reported to be moved "almost to tears" while recalling "the sound of monsoon rain hitting the tin roof of his student lodgings [in Shimla] and the sight of the beautiful cloud formations drifting before his windows."[8]

He then traveled to Pakistan and joined the mujahedin fighters resisting the Soviet military presence in Afghanistan. In 1985, he traveled to Lille, France, to attend a three-month journalism course. When he returned to Peshawar, he served as deputy director of the political office of the National Liberation Front of Afghanistan, a traditional, pro-monarchist religious body, led by Professor Sibghatullah Mujadidi.

When the mujahedin government was established in Kabul in 1992, Karzai was appointed deputy foreign minister. Two years later, when the civil war between the various mujahedin groups started, he resigned from his post and began to work actively for convening a national Loya Jirga (Pashto: Grand Council). In August 1999, his father, who had been organizing anti-Taliban resistance from his base in Quetta, was assassinated by Taliban agents and their Pakistani backers. He then took over the leadership of the Popalzai tribe and organized its affairs from a refugee camp in Pakistan. At the time of the Pentagon's war on Taliban-ruled Afghanistan, he was inside the country trying to bolster anti-Taliban resistance.

On December 22, 2001, both India and Pakistan sent their foreign ministers to Kabul to witness the handover of power by President Burhanuddin Rabbani, a Tajik leader of the NA, to Karzai. The next day India's foreign minister, Jaswant Singh, reopened the Indian embassy in Kabul and announced that the Indian consulates in Jalalabad, Kandahar, Mazar-e Sharif, and Herat would reopen in "the next few months."[9] These missions were meant to help build contacts with local leaders, facilitate trade and investment, and acquire better understanding of regional developments. Also, the state-run Air India assisted the Karzai government in returning the ailing Ariana Afghan Airlines to a healthy state by donating a few aircraft and helping it relaunch its international service suspended during Taliban rule.

Pakistan reopened its embassy in Kabul a month later. It and India each pledged $100 million in aid to Afghanistan at a January 2002 donors' conference. But given its earlier experience in developing Afghanistan's infrastructure, India soon outpaced Pakistan in this race. Much to Islamabad's frustration, an Indian company won the contract to build a road from the border town of Spin Boldak to Kandahar.

Violating its promise to President Musharraf not to deal with the NA, the Bush administration oversaw the NA's cooption in the administration of Karzai, much to the delight of Delhi.

With seven-eighths of the UN-sponsored Loya Jirga delegates voting for Karzai in June 2002, he had his interim presidency confirmed. The Indians were joyous to see an Indophile like Karzai confirmed as president. He envisaged India, a stable, comparatively well-developed democracy, as an ideal partner for his underdeveloped, struggling country. His twenty-nine-strong cabinet maintained the status quo, with General Muhammad Qasim Fahim, a Tajik, as defense minister and other Tajiks retaining among others foreign, interior, and intelligence ministries. The job of the National Directorate of Security (NDS) chief went to Muhammad Arif Serwari, the NA's erstwhile chief intelligence official.

As in the past, he maintained a suspicious eye on Pakistan and its intelligence network in Afghanistan. He looked benignly on India, allowing it to set up its own intelligence network. RAW agents cooperated actively with NSD operators to monitor pro-Pakistan and pro-Taliban elements.

THE KICKING CONJOINED TWINS

The Taliban announced its rebirth dramatically a week before the first anniversary of 9/11—a bomb explosion in Kabul, which caused fifteen fatalities, and an assassination attempt on Karzai during his visit to Kandahar.[10] While the Pentagon trumpeted its swift victory in Iraq during March and April 2003, the Taliban staged guerrilla assaults in the southern provinces of Helmand and Zabul adjoining Pakistan—the Taliban's prime source of volunteers, cash, and arms, and the site of several training camps.

During his visit to America in the last week of June 2003, Musharraf was received by Bush at Camp David, indicating that he was being treated as "a close friend" of the US president. When questioned by reporters about cross-border attacks on Afghanistan from Pakistan, he replied that the writ of Karzai did not run beyond the edges of Kabul. This remark angered Karzai. On July 7 he accused Musharraf of interference in Afghanistan's domestic affairs.

At the same time reports circulated in Kabul that Pakistani forces had intruded sixteen miles into Nangarhar province along their common border. This led to protests in Kabul outside the Pakistani embassy the next day. A well-organized mob, armed with sticks, stones, and sledge hammers vandalized the mission while the staff locked themselves in the basement. Pakistan closed its embassy in Kabul as well as its consulate in Jalalabad.[11]

Zalmay Khalilzad, an Afghan-American serving as the special US presidential envoy for Afghanistan, intervened to cool passions. Karzai apologized for the damage done to the Pakistani mission and agreed to compensation. The representatives of the United States, Afghanistan, and Pakistan together decided to send a joint team to investigate reports of border clashes between Pakistani and Afghan forces. Pakistan reopened the embassy on July 23. On the source of the extremists' cross-border attacks on Afghanistan, however, Khalilzad was unequivocal: "We know the Taliban are planning [attacks] in Quetta."[12]

During the diplomatic spat, Karzai stressed the vital importance of Pakistan to his country. "We are like conjoined twins, and like such twins sometimes we cannot stop kicking each other," he said in his interview with Ahmed Rashid, a Pakistani journalist and author. Regretfully, Karzai realized that the "brotherly feeling" between him and Musharraf was evaporating. "We have one page where there is a tremendous desire for friendship and the need for each other. But there is the other page of the consequences if intervention continues. . . . Afghans will have no choice but to stand up and stop it."[13]

In a move designed to put both Karzai and India, governed by Prime Minister Atal Bihari Vajpayee, on the defensive, on July 27 Islamabad expressed its "deep concerns" about Delhi's activities along the Pakistan-Afghan border. It alleged that the Indian consulates had "less to do with humanitarian aid and more to do with India's top-secret intelligence agency, the Research and Analysis Wing." A hand-grenade assault on India's Jalalabad consulate on September 1 drew the attention of the international media. In a subsequent report for the Boston-based *Christian Science Monitor*, filed from Jalalabad, Scott Baldauf summarized Pakistan's claims. It held the Indian consulates responsible for printing fake Pakistani currency and orchestrating acts of sabotage and terrorism on Pakistani territory. It accused Delhi of establishing networks of "terrorist training camps" inside Afghanistan—at the military base of Qushila Jadid, north of Kabul; near Gereshk in Helmand province; in the Panjshir Valley northeast of the capital; and at Kahak and Hassan Killies in the Nimruz province. During his visit to Jalalabad, however, Baldauf found the consulate "swamped with delegations of Indian diplomats and businessmen who were snapping up many of the lucrative projects to rebuild the roads and infrastructure of Afghanistan."[14]

Having maintained for a long time that the Baluchistan Liberation Army was a fiction, Chief Minister Jam Muhammad Yousaf announced in mid-August 2004 that India's RAW was running forty terrorist camps in the province.[15] As the Baluch insurgency, led by Sardar Akbar Bugti, intensified, it became routine for the Pakistani media to refer to the involvement of the Indian consulates in Afghanistan and claim that evidence had been found. But it was never made public. The insurgency reached a peak in the summer of 2006.

KARZAI'S FIRST TERM AS PRESIDENT

In the October 2004 election held under the new constitution, Karzai was elected president by 55 percent of the ballots on a voter turnout of an impressive 73 percent. His vice presidents were Fahim, a Tajik, and Karim Khalili, a Shia Hazara.

During the two-day visit to Kabul in August 2005, Indian prime minister Manmohan Singh led a foundation-stone-laying ceremony for the Afghan parliament complex, which was to be financed by Delhi. It was to be built opposite the ruinously damaged Dar ul Aman royal palace on the outskirts of the capital. Singh hoped the seed of democracy in Afghanistan would grow into a robust tree. As a result of the inordinate delays in starting the construction, the original cost of Rs 3 billion ($60 million) would balloon to Rs 7.1 billion ($140 million) in eight years.

Such a gesture—graphically highlighting India's generosity toward Afghanistan while underscoring its commitment to democracy—caused heartburn among Pakistani policy makers, then facing rising insurgency in Baluchistan as well as FATA. In March 2006, when Pakistan's troops encountered considerable resistance to their offensive against militants in North and South Waziristan Agencies, an unnamed official in Islamabad claimed that Pakistan had collected "all required information about the involvement of India in fomenting unrest in North and South Waziristan." He alleged that "the Indian consulates in Southern Afghanistan have been supplying money as well as arms and ammunition to the militants that has added to the trouble and violence in the tribal belt."[16]

In his interview with Delhi-based *Outlook* magazine in April 2006, Mushahid Hussain Sayed (aka, Mushahid Hussain), chair of the Pakistan

Senate's foreign relations committee, claimed that RAW had established training camps in Afghanistan in collaboration with the NA's remnants. "Approximately 600 Baluch tribal dissidents are getting specialized training to handle explosives, engineer bomb blasts, and use sophisticated weapons in these camps." He added that "the Indian consulates in Kandahar and Jalalabad and their embassy in Kabul are used for clandestine activities inside Pakistan in general and the Federally Administered Tribal Areas and Baluchistan in particular." According to Sayed, "Indian diplomatic and RAW officials have significant ingress in the Afghan ministry of tribal affairs, and they are exploiting it to conduct covert activities. Indian agents are instrumental in arranging meetings of tribal elders and Afghans with dual nationalities with Indian consulate officials in Jalalabad, and assisting them in spotting and recruiting suitable tribal elders from Jalalabad and Pakistan's North and South Waziristan Agencies for covert activities." He added that "meetings of tribal elders are arranged by the Afghan intelligence agency [Riyast-i-Amniyat-i-Milli] at the behest of those RAW officials who serve in different diplomatic offices of India in Afghanistan. Indian agents are carrying out clandestine activities in the border areas of Khost and in Pakistan's tribal areas of Miranshah with the active support of Afghan Border Security Force officials."[17]

Years later a former Indian consul general in Kandahar "privately" admitted to a Delhi-based interviewer that "he had met with Baluchi leaders at his consulate there" while claiming that his ambassador gave him "strict instructions not to aid them in any way against Pakistan." He "hinted" that "RAW personnel were present among the staff at the Kandahar and Jalalabad consulates."[18]

The truth was hard to determine. What really mattered was the extent and intensity of the insurgent operations sponsored by India. These could be rationalized as Delhi's quid pro quo to Islamabad's involvement in stoking the separatist movement in Indian Kashmir, even though RAW's activities never rivaled those of the ISI in India-held Kashmir. On the other hand, just as Pakistan condemned India periodically for its egregious human rights violations in Kashmir, Delhi expressed concern at the fighting in Baluchistan and recommended dialogue. Overall, it is fair to say that even without the subversive activities of RAW, Islamabad would have encountered security problems in its tribal belt and Baluchistan, both of which had a long history.

By attributing the violent anti-Pakistan activities in FATA to India working in cahoots with Afghanistan, Islamabad motivated its forces during its later offensives against the militant jihadists in FATA. They were made to believe that in the final analysis their campaign in FATA was against their number one enemy, India, which has been the unchanging doctrine of the Pakistani military.

As the Afghan Taliban regrouped, and insurgency gathered momentum especially in southern Afghanistan in early 2006, relations between Karzai and Musharraf turned testy. To defuse the situation the Afghan president met his Pakistani counterpart in Islamabad in mid-February. Among other things he handed his interlocutor a list of Afghan Taliban militants allegedly living in Pakistan, including their leader, Mullah Omar. When no action followed, Kabul leaked the list to the media. Musharraf would later claim that "much of the information was old and useless."

On his part, Musharraf complained of an anti-Pakistan conspiracy hatched by the defense and intelligence agencies of Afghanistan run by ethnic Tajiks—Fahim and Serwari respectively—one-time stalwarts of the pro-Delhi NA. "[Karzai] better set that right," he said.[19] His hectoring angered Karzai, who regarded it as open interference in Afghanistan's internal affairs.

During Bush's brief visits to Kabul, Delhi, and Islamabad in early March, the strained Afghan-Pakistan relations were discussed. An unnamed senior Pakistani official close to Musharraf told Agence France-Presse: "We have provided sufficient evidence to President Bush what certain Afghan officials are doing to fund and supply arms to militants in Pakistan. . . . One Afghan commander in Jalalabad is sending arms into Pakistani areas, for example. As a result our soldiers are dying and their soldiers are dying too."[20]

Jalalabad figured as prominently in Pakistan's accusations against the Karzai regime as it did in the case of the Singh government in Delhi.

Meanwhile, resurgence of the Taliban led to intense fighting in the southern Afghan provinces of Kandahar and Helmand. Suicide bombings exacted heavy losses among British and Canadian forces operating under the aegis of the US-led NATO. By the summer of 2006, NATO intelligence had obtained irrefutable evidence of the ISI's alliance with the Afghan insurgents, covering recruitment, training, and arming and dispatching of partisans as well as overseeing their leadership.

By contrast, in his interview with Fareed Zakaria, editor of *Newsweek International*, on September 19, Musharraf claimed that Mullah Omar was in Kandahar and therefore "the center of gravity of this [Taliban] movement is in Afghanistan." Two days later, in his interview with

Zakaria, Karzai retorted: "Mullah Omar is for sure in Quetta in Pakistan. . . . We have even given him [Musharraf] the GPS numbers of his house—of Mullah Omar's house, and the telephone numbers . . . when we had a nasty meeting that day [in February] and subsequent to that as well."[21]

Bush invited Karzai and Musharraf to a working dinner at the White House on September 27, 2006, at which he hoped to help the feuding duo turn the page. When Karzai complained bitterly about Pakistan's policy of harboring the Afghan Taliban, Musharraf accused him of basing his allegations on "outdated" intelligence and kowtowing to India. Despite the many billions the US treasury had poured into Afghanistan since 2002, and the $5.5 billion given to the Pakistani army to assist the Pentagon's operations in Afghanistan, the American president failed abysmally to reconcile his quarrelling chief guests.

DURAND LINE DISPUTE—CONTINUED

The ill-defined Afghan–Pakistan border continued to be a running source of tension and periodic skirmishes. For instance, during an armed confrontation in September 2005 precipitated by the posting of a Pakistan flag inside Afghanistan, 120 Afghan soldiers gathered on the border in Khost province. They threatened to attack Pakistani soldiers if the latter did not abandon a disputed checkpoint. It required intervention by an American officer to calm the disputants.[22]

In May 2007 Afghan troops assaulted Pakistan's military outposts, which they claimed were illegally built on their soil, and killed eight Pakistani soldiers. In response Pakistan's artillery fire on targets in Afghanistan led to seven deaths among the Afghan forces.

Almost a year later 150 paramilitaries from Pakistan's Frontier Corps crossed into Afghanistan near Khost and exchanged fire with Afghan border guards. Later that day two separate groups of Afghan soldiers, each 30 strong, retaliated by targeting Pakistani border posts. The firefights ended only when the tribal elders from both sides met at the frontier and resolved the dispute.[23]

In mid-May there was a three-day exchange of fire between Afghan and Pakistani troops in the Aryub Zazai district of Afghanistan's Paktia province. It left seven Pakistanis and eight Afghans dead. The clash was triggered by the demolition of Afghan security checkpoints by Pakistanis, who wanted to build their own posts.[24]

This was a spillover from the disturbed conditions in FATA. Afghan-Pakistan tensions inflamed to the point at which Karzai warned Islamabad that if it did not repress the jihadists in FATA, he would dispatch Afghan troops into Pakistan to accomplish the task.

DEADLY ATTACK ON INDIAN EMBASSY IN KABUL

The lethal car bomb attack on the Indian embassy in Kabul on July 7, 2008, set a new low in Indo-Pakistan and Afghan-Pakistan relations. It killed 58 people, including the Indian defense attaché Brigadier Ravi Datt Mehta and Indian foreign service officer V. Venkateswara Rao, and injured more than 140. The suicide bomber struck just as the embassy's main gate was opened to let in a car carrying Mehta and Rao.

"The sophistication of this attack and the kind of material that was used in it, the specific targeting, everything has the hallmarks of a particular intelligence agency that has conducted similar terrorist acts inside Afghanistan in the past," said Karzai's spokesman, Humayun Hamidzada. "We have sufficient evidence to say that."[25] This was a thinly disguised reference to the ISI. Hamidzada thus implicitly rejected the Taliban's claim that it had carried out the terror attack. Karzai waded in. "The killings of people in Afghanistan, the destruction of bridges in Afghanistan . . . are carried out by Pakistan's intelligence and Pakistan's military departments," he asserted.[26]

A few weeks later India pointed its finger at the ISI for its role in the blasting of its embassy. Its spokesman referred to the analysis of the explosives used in the terrorist act by forensic experts of the NATO-led International Security Assistance Force (ISAF) in Afghanistan. ISAF had concluded that these originated from the Pakistan Ordnance Factories (POF) in the northern Pakistani garrison city of Wah.[27]

In their report for the *New York Times* of August 1, 2008, Mark Mazzetti and Eric Schmitt said that US intelligence agencies had concluded that ISI personnel helped plan the bombing of India's embassy. This was based on intercepted communications between ISI officers and militants, belonging to the North Waziristan–based, Al Qaida–affiliated Jalaluddin Haqqani network, which caused the massive bomb blast.[28] The conclusion of US intelligence agencies dovetailed with the findings of Afghanistan's NSD.

Further details and evidence became available when Carlotta Gall, a senior reporter with the *New York Times*, published her book *The Wrong*

Enemy: America in Afghanistan, 2001–2014 in March 2014. "The embassy bombing was no operation by rogue ISI agents acting on their own. It was sanctioned and monitored by the most senior officials in Pakistani intelligence," she noted. "American and Afghan surveillance intercepted phone calls from ISI officials in Pakistan and heard them planning the attack with the militants in Kabul in the days leading up to the bombing," she added. "At the time, intelligence officials monitoring the calls did not know what was being planned, but the involvement of a high-level official in promoting a terrorist attack was clear." But, she continued, "The evidence was so damning that the Bush administration dispatched the deputy chief of the CIA, Stephen Kappes, to Islamabad to remonstrate with the Pakistanis." However, the bomber struck before Kappes reached Pakistan. "Investigators found the bomber's cell phone in the wreckage of his exploded car. They tracked down his collaborator in Kabul, the man who had provided the logistics for the attack. That facilitator, an Afghan, had been in direct contact with Pakistan by telephone. The number he had called belonged to a high-level ISI official in Peshawar. The official had sufficient seniority that he reported directly to ISI headquarters in Islamabad."

The ultimate purpose of the operation transcended damaging Indian interests. "The [overarching] aim was to make the cost too high for everyone to continue backing the Karzai government," Gall concluded. "The ISI wanted them all to go home." As the authorities in Kabul investigated the attack, they became convinced that the "ISI was working with Al Qaida, the Taliban, the Haqqanis, and Pakistani groups such as Lashkar-e Taiba, which was behind most of the attacks on Indian targets."[29]

After this outrage, India advised Karzai to set up a foreign intelligence agency, just as it had done in 1968. He agreed. The subsequent Research and Analysis Milli Afghanistan (RAMA), formed with the active assistance of RAW, started functioning a year later. Rama is the name of a Hindu god. That provided enough ammunition to Pakistani commentators to attribute evil designs to the newly established Afghan agency, the principal one being to destabilize their country.

As in the past, the summit of the South Asian Association for Regional Cooperation, held in Colombo on August 2, 2008, provided a chance for the prime ministers of India and Pakistan to confer with each other. Singh broached the bombing of the Indian embassy in Kabul with his counterpart, Yusuf Raza Gilani, who promised to investigate but later asked Singh to provide "concrete evidence."[30]

Meanwhile, much to the chagrin of Islamabad, Kabul's economic relations with Delhi blossomed. Protected by the three-hundred-strong contingent of the Indo-Tibetan Border Force, the Indian Army's Roads Organization completed the building of the 150-mile Zaranj-Delaram Road, which linked with the Kushka-Herat-Kandahar Highway, by the end of 2008. It did so in the face of assaults by the Taliban. Indian engineers built digitized telecommunications networks in eleven Afghan provinces. And one thousand Afghan students were offered scholarships to Indian universities annually.[31] Emulating its earlier practice, India channeled its development aid for mutually agreed-on wells, schools, and health clinics into the Afghan government's budget.[32] This procedure was dramatically different from the one followed by the United States and its allies, who paid the civilian contractors directly or the approved local and foreign nongovernmental organizations.

KARZAI'S CHANGING PAKISTANI INTERLOCUTORS

Facing impeachment for violating the constitution by the six-month-old democratically elected coalition government in Islamabad, Musharraf resigned as president on August 18, 2008. While the Indian cabinet withheld comment, Karzai hoped Musharraf's departure would boost democracy in both countries.

The Afghan president called Prime Minster Yusuf Raza Gilani "a good man" with "the right intentions." He welcomed General Ashfaq Parvaz Kayani, Pakistan's army chief, during the latter's visit to the US Air Force base at Bagram on August 19. "Afghanistan cannot achieve peace or prosperity without friendly relations with Pakistan," he told Kayani. Speaking to Aryn Baker of *Time*, Karzai said, "I hope [Kayani] recognizes that what they are doing [in terms of supporting militancy in Afghanistan] is causing immense damage to Pakistan itself. Someone has to recognize this need for change and for a modern relationship with Afghanistan, a civilized relationship. I hope it will occur."[33]

Karzai's hope was unfulfilled. Kayani was committed to upholding the Pakistani military's doctrine that India is its number one enemy and that makes it mandatory for Pakistan to acquire strategic depth in case of an Indian invasion by securing unrivaled influence in Kabul. Karzai, on the other hand, was scathing about both the concept of strategic depth and the means being deployed by Islamabad to achieve it. "If Pakistan is using radicalism as a tool of policy for strategic depth in Afghanistan, well, I wish to tell them that it won't work," Karzai averred.[34]

Once Asif Ali Zardari was elected president by the provincial and federal lawmakers in September 2008, a civilian democratic system was fully in place in Islamabad as the final arbiter of power—in theory. In reality, though, as before, real power in national security affairs rested with the military. Zardari had neither the intelligence nor the charisma of his wife, Benazir Bhutto, nor the political cunning of Muhammad Nawaz Sharif. However, he held moderate views about both Afghanistan and India.

He met Karzai in Ankara on December 5 at the initiative of Turkey's president Abdullah Gul. At the end of the trilateral summit, Karzai said that relations between Afghanistan and Pakistan had improved extremely well since the election of Zardari as president. Both of them discussed fresh ways of curbing Islamist extremists and pledged stronger cooperation against terrorism. "The foreign ministers of Afghanistan and Pakistan are now working together and developing joint strategy against Al Qaida and other terrorist groups [operating in our border regions]," stated their joint communiqué.[35]

As a follow-up, Karzai and Zardari met again in Ankara, hosted by Gul, on April 1, 2009, to boost military cooperation against militant Islamists. But civilian control over the military was lacking in Pakistan. This became crystal clear in May 2009, when Zardari transferred the ISI from the military to the interior ministry. General Kayani rejected the order. Within hours, Zardari backtracked.

The change in Islamabad's official stance on the Karzai government had no impact on Afghans' popular perception of Pakistan. According to the February 2009 opinion poll by the Kabul-based Afghan Centre for Socio-Economic and Opinion Research for the BBC, ABC News, and ARD (Germany), 91 percent had somewhat or very unfavorable view of Pakistan. The corresponding figure for India was 21 percent, with 74 percent having a somewhat or very favorable view of that country.[36] Part of the reason was the popularity of Bollywood movies and Indian TV soap operas shown widely on Afghan TV channels often dubbed in Dari, the state language of Afghanistan.

Unsurprisingly, Zardari had failed to convince the Obama administration that Pakistan's security services had ceased their traditional backing for the militant groups fighting NATO and local forces in Afghanistan.

The second terror assault on the Indian embassy in Kabul on October 8, 2009, showed that not much had changed. A massive bomb carried in a sport utility vehicle killed seventeen police officers and civilians, wounded seventy-six people, and destroyed vehicles and buildings. The explosion was heard across the capital, as shock waves shattered windows and a huge plume of brown smoke rose hundreds of feet. But because after the July 2008 attack, India had fortified its embassy with high blast walls, heavy steel gates, and a more circuitous entrance, the mission building was un-scathed. As in the case of the earlier terror assault, the Taliban claimed responsibility. And as before, this turned out to be a feint. The finger was pointed at the ISI with the telephone intercepts recorded by Washington's National Security Agency providing the evidence.[37]

KARZAI'S SECOND TERM OF OFFICE

In the August 20, 2009, presidential election, marred by wide-scale fraud, the all-Afghan Independent Election Commission (IEC) declared Karzai the winner with 54.7 percent of the vote. Facing a flood of complaints, the IEC audited the results thoroughly. In mid-October it awarded Karzai 49.67 percent of the ballots, a shade below the 50 percent plus one vote required for the win. But the second round was called off on November 2, when his rival, Abdullah Abdullah, pulled out. Karzai was victor by default. He took his oath of office on November 19.

While US-led NATO forces were engaged in fighting Taliban in-surgents and training rapidly expanding Afghan troops and policemen—called Afghan National Security Forces (ANSF)—their political masters had to devise and implement an exit strategy. This was the main purpose of the International Conference on Afghanistan in London on January 28, 2010. "We must reach out to all of our countrymen, especially our disenchanted brothers, who are not part of Al Qaida, or other terrorist networks, who accept the Afghan constitution," said Karzai. He agreed to establish a "national council for peace, reconciliation and reintegration," and reinvigorate peace overtures to senior Taliban leaders with the help of Saudi king Abdullah. Washington backed his move. "The starting premise is you don't make peace with your friends," said US secretary of state Hillary Clinton. "You have to be able to engage with your enemies."[38]

The 2009 BBC/ABC News/ARD opinion poll showed that 64 percent of Afghans favored talks with the Taliban.[39] Though India attended the London conference, the prospect of the Karzai government, encouraged by the United States, negotiating with the Taliban worried its policy makers.

There was no love lost between India and the Taliban. Fresh evidence of the Taliban's hostility toward Delhi came on February 26, 2010, with a terrorist attack on an Indian target in Kabul. This time it was the Arya Guesthouse, home to Indian doctors, near the luxury Safi Landmark Hotel in central Kabul. It was demolished by Taliban bombers equipped with suicide vests and automatic rifles. The occupants of the guest house were army doctors. But respecting Islamabad's touchiness about Delhi providing Afghanistan with military assistance, all army doctors and nurses working at the Indira Gandhi Child Health Institute were dispatched to Kabul, unarmed and in civilian dress. Nine Indian physicians perished in the attack, and many more were injured.

The assault started at six thirty AM, when a car bomb exploded outside the target. The powerful blast razed the building. Then a suicide bomber detonated his vest of explosives outside the crumbling structure. Among the survivors was Dr. Subodh Sanjivpaul. He locked himself in his bathroom for three hours. "When I was coming out, I found two or three dead bodies," he said at the military hospital in Kabul. "When firing was going on the first car bomb exploded and the roof fell on my head."[40] Karzai went out of his way to condemn the terror attack and thank India for the assistance it was offering his republic.

Yet at the same time, Karzai tried to lure Taliban leaders to the negotiating table, an enterprise that had Islamabad's enthusiastic backing. On the eve of his meeting with General Kayani and the ISI director-general Lieutenant General Ahmed Shuja Pasha on June 28 in Kabul, Karzai sacked his NSD chief, Amrullah Saleh. Like his predecessor Serwari, he was an unashamedly pro-India Tajik and was viewed by the Taliban and the ISI as their most vocal antagonist.[41] Kayani and Shuja reportedly urged Karzai to give the Taliban a place in a future political settlement. Delhi immediately conveyed its unease at a possible Taliban power-sharing deal, which among other things would block civilian aid and investment by India.[42]

Given the zero-sum relationship between the major South Asian nations regarding Afghanistan, a diplomatic setback for Delhi was an automatic gain for Islamabad, which wanted to see the peace process advance in Afghanistan but only under its tutelage. The latest development also highlighted the fact that when it came to reconciling the Kabul government with Taliban insurgents, India had no role to play except to raise objections.

The high officials in Delhi were also irritated when in the ongoing negotiations between Afghanistan and Pakistan to update their 1965

Transit Trade Agreement, India's interests were overlooked. Islamabad agreed to Kabul's request to allow Afghan trucks to proceed to the Indian border at Wagah as well as to the ports of Karachi and Gwadar. This was incorporated in the Memorandum of Understanding that Pakistan and Afghanistan signed in July 2010. In marked contrast, Islamabad summarily rejected Delhi's proposal to let Indian trucks drive through its territory to deliver goods in Afghanistan. Pakistan was Afghanistan's leading export partner and second most important import partner after the United States. Intent on maintaining its current commercial hegemony over Afghanistan, it wanted to rule out India as a competitor.

Afghanistan's transit trade through Pakistan was also a lucrative source of revenue for the Karachi port, through which most of Afghanistan's external trade passed, and for Pakistani road transport companies, many of which were owned by the army. Furthermore, Pakistani officials feared that if they allowed direct Afghan-India commerce through their country, the Afghans might start using the Mumbai port for part of their foreign trade, thereby curtailing Pakistan's revenue.

In November 2010, Afghanistan and Pakistan formed a joint chamber of commerce to expand trade. Official commerce between Afghanistan and Pakistan commerce had been rising steadily, from $830 million in 2006 to $2.5 billion in 2012. The informal trade, including smuggling, in that year amounted to $2 billion.[43]

Denied the use of Pakistani territory for its commerce with Afghanistan, the Indians resorted to making greater use of Iran as a route to trade with Afghanistan. As a result of the 2003 Indo-Afghan Preferential Trade Agreement, which reduced customs duty on a range of goods, bilateral trade increased to $600 million in 2011.[44]

In the political arena, to Delhi's relief, rapprochement between Karzai and Kayani fell apart after about a year for reasons beyond their control. The Obama administration had been increasingly using drone attacks to carry out targeted killings of jihadist militants in Pakistan. On May 2, 2011, US troops, acting unilaterally, killed Osama bin Laden in the Pakistani city of Abbottabad. Though Washington had allocated $20 billion in aid to Pakistan since 9/11,[45] it could not rely on its government to cooperate in strict secrecy in the capture or assassination of the Al Qaida chief.

The Pentagon's operation enraged the Afghan Taliban as well as the four-year-old Pakistani Taliban. The latter vowed to avenge bin Laden's murder by escalating violence in the Afghan-Pakistan tribal belt and eastern Afghanistan. Also, before withdrawing from bordering provinces of

Afghanistan to let local forces deal with security, US-led NATO commanders encouraged Afghan soldiers to attack Pakistani border posts. As a result, cross-border shelling increased sharply.

On June 26, Karzai claimed that Pakistan had fired 470 rockets into two eastern Afghan provinces, evacuated by NATO troops, over the past three weeks, killing thirty-six people. He held Islamabad responsible for this bombardment even if regular Pakistani soldiers were not involved.[46]

The Pakistan military's artillery backing for the Afghan Taliban's operations illustrated partly a lack of civilian control over the armed forces in Islamabad and partly Pakistan's continued double-dealing with the United States regarding the Afghan Taliban.

As a consequence, the Afghan-Pakistan border region remained unstable. On September 25 Kabul claimed that more than 340 rockets had been fired over four days from Pakistan. Two weeks later Pakistan's security forces claimed that they had killed thirty Afghan militants when a group of two hundred insurgents from Afghanistan crossed the border into Pakistan.[47]

Following the September 20, 2011, suicide bombing in Kabul, which killed former Afghan president Burhanuddin Rabbani, the Tajik head of the High Peace Council (HPC), the Karzai government accused the ISI of involvement. In its view, Islamabad resorted to this tactic when it realized that it was being excluded by the HPC while pursuing peacemaking with the Taliban. By so doing, Pakistan underscored its control over the reconciliation process and its assertion of a key role in any talks on ending violence as well as its ability to sabotage the peace negotiations when it was sidelined.

KABUL'S STRATEGIC PARTNERSHIP WITH DELHI

On October 4, 2011, Karzai and Indian prime minister Singh signed the Agreement on Strategic Partnership between India and the Islamic Republic of Afghanistan. It was the first pact of its kind that Kabul signed after its treaty with the Soviet Union in 1979. Significantly, this document referred to the 1950 Treaty of Friendship between the two countries and stated that it was "not directed against any other State or group of States." Under its "Political and Security Cooperation" provision, India agreed to "assist, as mutually determined, in the training, equipping and capacity building programs for Afghan National Security Forces." The bulk of the agreement covered cooperation in trade and economic development. The strategic partnership was to be supervised by a Partnership Council, co-chaired by the foreign ministers of the two countries.[48]

At the joint press conference Singh said that violence in Afghanistan was undermining security in South Asia and that India would "stand by Afghanistan" when foreign troops withdrew from the country by December 2014. He pointedly made no reference to Delhi's commitment to increase its training of Afghan security forces, including the police.[49] The next day Karzai explained that the accord simply made official the years of close ties between India and Afghanistan's post-Taliban government, with Delhi providing a significant amount of civilian aid to Kabul since 2002.

Pakistan responded in a convoluted fashion. Stressing that this was "no time for point scoring, playing politics or grandstanding," its Foreign Ministry spokeswoman added, "At this defining stage when challenges have multiplied, as have the opportunities, it is our expectation that everyone, especially those in position of authority in Afghanistan, will demonstrate requisite maturity and responsibility." By contrast, Talat Masood, a retired Pakistani general and a frequent commentator on national security, was direct. Alluding to Pakistan's long-held perception that "it is being encircled by India from both the eastern and western borders," he said that "the agreement will heighten Pakistan's insecurities." The influential *Dawn* newspaper expressed concern that the pact could lead to "ill-advised efforts to ramp up Pakistani involvement in Afghanistan."[50]

Islamabad's fear was enhanced when the Coulsdon-based *IHS Jane's Defence Weekly* published the details of India's promised military assistance provided by its Delhi correspondent Rahul Bedi on November 29. The plan was to fly twenty to thirty thousand Afghan recruits over the next three years for training in regimental centers in the north and east of India. The most promising troops would receive further training at the army's Counter Insurgency Jungle Warfare School in the northeastern state of Mizoram. The Afghan trainees would be equipped with assault rifles and other small arms, with the possibility of transferring rocket launchers, light artillery, and retrofitted Soviet T-55 tanks to them later.[51]

The figure of twenty to thirty thousand Afghan trainees turned out to be wildly inflated. During Karzai's visit to India in December 2013, the two governments announced that India would raise the number of ANSF trainees each year to one thousand, with the focus of the training being on counterinsurgency and counterterrorism operations.[52]

Around the same time, the Karzai government decided to allocate three of the four iron ore blocks, containing 1.8 billion tons of iron, in central Afghanistan to the Afghan Iron and Steel Consortium of Indian companies, led by the state-owned Steel Authority of India Limited. The deal required an investment of $10.3 billion, the largest in the war-torn country so far.[53] But two years later, unable to raise capital on favorable terms and facing increased security risks, the consortium considered slashing its initial outlay to $1.5 billion.[54]

To balance his pro-India bias, Karzai suggested a Strategic Partnership Agreement (SPA) with Pakistan during the Afghanistan-Pakistan-Britain summit chaired by British prime minister David Cameron on September 27, 2012, on the sidelines of the UN General Assembly session in New York. This was warmly welcomed by President Zardari. On his return to Kabul, however, Karzai came up with a precondition. Pakistan, he said, must stop "the export of terrorism, suicide bombers, interference and all the other things which result in killing and disturbing the Afghan people's tranquility and [is] destabilizing Afghanistan."[55] This unexpected move by Karzai slowed progress toward an SPA between the two neighbors.

All the same, in November, Afghanistan's HPC leaked its document "Afghan Peace Process Roadmap to 2015" to Pakistan's high officials. It envisaged direct talks between the Kabul government and the Taliban in early 2013, with a Saudi city as the preferred venue, and a truce soon thereafter, followed by arrangements for the insurgents to be reintegrated and their leaders given a share of power. It seemed more a wish list than a realistic plan.

However, what stood out was its acknowledgment of the centrality of Pakistan in the peace process, a point the Karzai government had been reluctant to concede so far. This was enough to alarm India. Its national security advisor, Shiv Shankar Menon, referred to the red lines agreed on by the London Conference on Afghanistan in January 2010, which required the Taliban to cut all links with Al Qaida and other terrorist organizations and respect the values and ideals enshrined in Afghanistan's constitution, including women's rights.[56]

In any case, despite repeated promises to conclude the envisaged SPA by a certain date, nothing definite materialized because of the trust deficit between the neighbors. Nor was there any discernible progress in the peace process with the insurgents. Given the exit date of December 2014 for foreign forces, Taliban leaders saw no need to negotiate with Karzai, whom they routinely described as a puppet of America. Lack of progress in these areas suited Delhi.

KARZAI THE JUGGLER

As NATO forces' withdrawal date approached, Karzai urged Delhi to step up its assistance to bolster security within the framework of the 2011 Indo-Afghan SPA. During his visit to India from May 20 to 22, 2013, his twelfth since assuming office, he submitted his wish list to boost the security and counterterrorism capability of Afghanistan. It included a supply of attack helicopters, rocket launchers, light and heavy artillery, retrofitted Soviet T-55 tanks, and transport aircraft.

The Indian government needed to mull over Karzai's request, taking into account the electoral victory of Nawaz Sharif's party in Pakistan. Sharif's return to power in Islamabad augured well for an improvement in Indo-Pakistan relations, with a positive impact on the Afghan situation. Equipping Kabul with heavy weaponry was likely to be seen as provocative by Islamabad. Therefore the Singh government prevaricated, claiming that it needed the Kremlin's permission before transferring its Soviet-era arms to Afghanistan. There was also concern in Delhi that the successor to Karzai after the 2014 presidential election would be less pro-India than Karzai.

Back-channel efforts to bring the Karzai government and the Taliban leadership to the negotiating table in Doha collapsed in June 2013, when the Taliban called its newly opened office in the Qatari capital the Embassy of the Emirate of Afghanistan, flaunting the Taliban flag. Karzai was livid.

As before, Karzai walked a tightrope, intent on showing that Afghanistan's relations with India were not at the expense of Pakistan's. During his one-day trip to Islamabad on August 25 to confer with Nawaz Sharif, his session went so well that he extended his stay by a day. Sharif added $115 million to Pakistan's aid to Kabul, pushing the total to $500 million. At a joint press conference Karzai said that he wanted the Pakistani government to play a mediating role with the Taliban, with whom it had "a high degree of influence." In return, Sharif repeated Pakistan's mantra that the Afghan peace and reconciliation process must be "Afghan-owned and Afghan-led."[57]

Responding to Karzai's request that Mullah Abdul Ghani Baradar, a moderate deputy of Mullah Omar who had been arrested in Karachi in

February 2010, be released, Sharif did so the next month. But there was no change in the Taliban's official policy of refusing to confer with the Karzai government.

The Taliban's violent activities included sabotaging the fruits of India's $2 billion sanctioned civilian aid, of which 70 percent would be allocated by the end of 2013. The comparative statistic for Pakistan's $500 million was only 40 percent. Moreover, Islamabad had failed to construct a road, college, or health clinic that could be a visible example of its openhandedness.[58]

At the same time, in the absence of proper auditing and monitoring, the end result was far from the rosy picture painted by Indian officials. For instance, a visit by a Reuters reporter to the village of Achin in southeast Afghanistan found "a gaping hole in the roof of [an India-funded] school, cracked walls and broken desks and chairs." Its headmaster was surprised that records in Kabul showed that the school was completed.[59]

It was worth noting that as of June 2011, India had not launched any major initiatives for the previous two to three years. And the Indian-built Zaranj-Delaram Road, passing through the Taliban-dominated Nimroz province, had become pockmarked by the craters created by the improvised explosive devices (IEDs) detonated by the Taliban.[60] The ambitious four-year, $300 million Salma Dam project in Herat, initiated in 2006, remained unfinished in mid-2013 because of the repeated attacks on construction workers with IEDs and because of budget overruns. When commissioned, the dam will irrigate seventy-five thousand acres of land in Herat and generate forty-five megawatts of electricity.[61]

Overall, competition between India and Pakistan in Afghanistan covered not only geopolitics and commerce but also soft power.

SOFT POWER COMPETITION: ONE-SIDED

In the field of soft power, India was miles ahead of its rival Pakistan. This was most obvious in television. Starting with Tolo TV (Dari: Sunrise), which went on air in October 2004, commercial TV flourished in Afghanistan, where under the Taliban rule it had been outlawed. Tolo provided a large variety of shows. Among these, Indian soap operas, dubbed in Dari, with an episode aired daily often during prime time, when the power supply was reliable, proved popular. By early 2008 Tolo was broadcasting three Indian soap operas daily, with some rival channels showing six, attracted by their low cost and addictive appeal.

Of the Indian television dramas on Tolo, *Kyunki Saas Bhi Kabhi Bahu Thi* (Hindi: Mother-in-Law Was Once Daughter-in-Law)—popularly known as *Tulsi*, the first name of the daughter-in-law Tulsi Viran—was hugely popular. Its audience of ten million in a country of thirty million was a record. Afghans became so hooked on the drama that almost all activities ceased in the country for half an hour beginning at eight thirty PM. "It's like an addiction," said the twenty-three-year-old policeman Nasrullah Mohammadi.[62] The cultural impact on the population was so strong that, imitating their Indian peers, Afghan teenagers took to touching their elders' feet as a sign of respect, a novelty in Afghanistan.

Several factors explained the phenomenon. Overall, Afghans and Indians shared similar family and cultural norms and traditions. For instance, the archetypical mother-in-law was demanding and oppressive toward her young, diffident daughter-in-law because that was how she was treated by her mother-in-law when she was a young wife living in a joint family. There was total absence of entertainment outside the house, particularly for women. "People in other countries have others means of enjoyment and having fun, but we have nothing," said twenty-three-year-old Roya Amin, mother of a young daughter, in Kabul, who watched three Indian TV dramas daily.[63] These entertaining episodes also helped Afghans forget the endless violence and woes in their country.

The same reasoning applied to Bollywood movies. Before the advent of the Taliban, these films were the staple of local moviegoers for decades. "Our culture is so similar and the best part is that most of us learn Hindi watching Bollywood movies," said Afghan actress Vida Samadzai during her visit to Delhi in 2010. "Even before coming to India, I was quite fluent in Hindi, 80 percent of my language was just perfect, thanks to Bollywood movies."[64]

At present, although Kabul had some functioning movie theaters, the Bollywood movies being shown there were pirated because the local distributors lacked funds. Tickets often cost less than half a US dollar. In some cases Indian producers sent prints as gifts to Afghan distributors. The pirated prints were also aired on TV channels.

"I like Indian dance and song very much and I come to cinema at least once a week to watch Indian movie," said Abdul Wahid, a twenty-year-old student and a breadwinner of his family. "Hard study at school in the morning and boring work in the afternoon to support my family have sandwiched me. To forget the pain, a rational way is to watch Indian movies in cinema."[65] There was also a strong vicarious element at work.

"The larger-than-life representations of the Bollywood heroes, in sharp contrast to their stark reality, provide them a vicarious opportunity to immerse themselves into the grandiose reel life fantasies," explained Sujeet Sarkar in his book *In Search of a New Afghanistan.* "The chart-busting music is another addictive element."[66]

Compared to the number of TV viewers, the movie audience was miniscule. The unprecedented popularity of *Tulsi* and other similar Indian serials raised concern among Afghan officials and religious leaders. They objected to the shots of Hindu idols and the worship of them, which clashed with Islam's strict ban on idol worship, as well as the plunging necklines and bare midriffs, shoulders, and arms of sari-clad Indian actresses.

In early April 2008 the Ministry of Information and Culture ordered four TV channels, including Tolo, to take five Indian soap operas off the air by mid-April. All complied except Tolo. It chose to pixilate the contentious images. Yet that was not enough. In early May the parliament passed a law banning *Tulsi* and four other Indian serials. Since then TV channels have employed censors who pixilate any content that could be objectionable.

As for Bollywood movies, the official censors ordered cuts before giving the distributor the license to exhibit the film. This applied to Pakistan as well, where Bollywood films continued to cast a spell on the public despite the four-decade-long ban on their (official) import in the wake of the 1965 Indo-Pakistan War on Kashmir.

19

Shared Culture, Rising Commerce

In his quest for a subcontinent homeland for Indian Muslims, Muhammad Ali Jinnah had their general welfare uppermost in mind. He had envisaged the existing Punjab and Bengal to become part of Pakistan. As for the bulk of provinces where Muslims were a minority, he imagined that their safety would be guaranteed by the presence of Hindus and Sikhs in the two wings of Pakistan. That is, each independent country would hold the minority community within its frontiers as an effective bargaining chip with the other. That did not happen. As a result of the partition of Punjab, and the subsequent communal bloodbath perpetrated almost wholly in villages, its Pakistani part was cleared of Hindus and Sikhs and its eastern section of Muslims. In the postindependence period, therefore, there were no Hindu or Sikh families separated by the border. Initially, any migration of Hindus and Muslims in divided Bengal was limited.

The separation of families occurred in the case of those Muslims in the minority provinces who chose to migrate to Pakistan, seeking better economic prospects for themselves and life in an Islamic environment. Most of this voluntary movement was limited to Delhi, United Province, and part of Bombay, especially its capital city and the Gujarati-speaking section of the province. These Muslim migrants were invariably literate and engaged in commerce or government service. They were the ones who complained loudly about the creeping restrictions on Indo-Pakistan travel that followed from the mid-1950s onward.

The province of Sindh, which remained undivided, had a population of only five million, a quarter of them Hindu. Mainly urban dwellers, they made their living as traders or professionals, forming a large part of the civil service, and had little social intercourse with local Muslims. In the absence of Hindu peasants, there was no large-scale violence in Sindh. However, as the number of immigrants from the Muslim minority provinces of India swelled in Karachi and Hyderabad, the second largest city in Sindh, the authorities let anti-Hindu violence erupt briefly in these cities. That was enough to result in an orderly exodus of about a million Hindus over the next few years to different parts of India, from Delhi in the north to Kolhapur south of Bombay. There was thus no rupture in the families of Sindhi Hindus.

Any common sharing of cultural values between Hindus and Muslims was limited to Hindustani movies made in Bombay. (The term "Bollywood" is a much later construct.) Since movie theaters existed only in large towns and cities, proportionately fewer Muslims visited them than Hindus.

All the same, such Indian movie stars as Raj Kapoor and Dilip Kumar (birth name: Muhammad Yusuf Khan) enjoyed equal fame in Pakistan and India. Raj Kapoor's 1951 movie *Awara* (Hindustani: "Tramp"), in which he plays the lead role with Nargis, a Muslim, was as much of a hit in West Pakistan as in India. The healthy rivalry between him and Dilip Kumar as versatile actors ended in 1960, with Dilip Kumar's dazzling lead performance in *Mughal-e-Azam* ("The Great Mughal"), which broke box office records on both sides of the border.

The shutters came down after the September 1965 Indo-Pakistan War. President Field Marshal Muhammad Ayub Khan issued a presidential order declaring Indian movies, which had been exhibited regularly in Pakistan up until then, "enemy property." The Martial Law Order (MLO) 81 issued by Zia ul Haq regarding registration of cinematographic film decertified all Indian movies released between 1947 and 1981.[1] Also Islamabad's trade protocol prohibited the import of any film whose language or actors originated in India or Pakistan.

During his rule, Zia ul Haq made two exceptions: *Noor Jehan* and *Kashish* (Hindi: Attraction). *Noor Jehan*, a filmic extravaganza based on the life story of a Mughal empress, was released in India in 1967. Its poor box office returns bankrupted its actor-producer, Shaikh Mukhtar. Driven to desperation, he migrated to Pakistan with the prints of all seven movies he had produced. Over the years his pleas with Pakistani officials to certify the release of one or more of his productions were ignored—until he persuaded Zia ul Haq to see *Noor Jehan*. He liked it. By a cruel irony of fate, the day the censors gave the green light for its exhibition—May 11,

1980—Mukhtar died of a heart attack. The movie premiered on May 23 and was a roaring success.

The next break in Pakistan's blanket ban on Indian films came with another historical tale, *Mughal-e-Azam*. Directed by Karimuddin Asif, it was the tale of Emperor Akbar and the illicit love affair between Crown Prince Salim (later Emperor Jahangir) and Anarkali, a courtesan. Released in black and white in 1960, it was by far India's biggest and grandest epic movie, with A-list actors and sumptuous sets and costumes. Its revival came in November 2004, when its digitally colored version, produced by Shapoorji Mistry, a grandson of the original producer, Shapoorji Pallonji Mistry, was screened nationwide in India to great acclaim and a strong box office.

The next month, Akbar Asif, the London-based son of the director Karimuddin Asif, presented a print of the colored movie to Pakistani president General Pervez Musharraf as a gift. Musharraf gave permission for its exhibition in May 2005.[2] During the Pakistani president's London visit in late 2005, Asif and the producer met him and offered to donate the box office takings in Pakistan to the survivors of the October 8 earthquake in Kashmir.[3]

Mughal-e-Azam premiered in Lahore on April 22, 2006. "The move to ensure that *Mughal-e-Azam* turned out to be the cultural bridge between India and Pakistan was to fulfill my father's dream of getting it to be the first film to get permission to be screened in Pakistan," said Asif.[4] As the first Indian movie to be shown officially in Pakistani movie theaters after forty-one years, it acquired an unrivaled status.

A few days later another Bollywood flick, *Taj Mahal: An Eternal Love Story*, produced in 2005, opened in Lahore. Musharraf made an exception because the movie pertained to the Mughal period, and the lead role of Empress Mumtaz Mahal, in whose memory the world famous monument was built, was played by Sonya Jehan, a Pakistani actress whose mother was French.

India's tourism and culture minister, Ambika Soni, joined the Indian delegation in Lahore on the opening night. "It is a welcome beginning," she said, and she hoped *Taj Mahal* would pave the way for an eventual lifting of Pakistan's ban. Islamabad's official stance was that screening Indian movies would be permitted only after all unsettled issues with India had been resolved. Soni pointed out that Delhi did not impose any restrictions on Pakistani films and artists performing in India.[5] In June 2006, a Statutory Regulatory Order issued by the Pakistani government allowed the import and exhibition of Indian and other foreign films and serials.[6]

By then, with the advent of VHS tapes and then DVDs from the mid-1990s, piracy of Indian and other foreign movies had become commonplace. At local markets in Pakistan, the DVD trader selling the latest Hollywood and Bollywood blockbusters was a familiar sight. The distributors in Pakistan also managed to import Indian films by producing documents that showed that their country of origin as Britain or the United Arab Emirates (UAE). According to an unofficial estimate in 2006, every day an estimated fifteen million people in Pakistan watched a Bollywood movie—10 percent of the population.[7]

In 2008, the blockbuster *Race*, a comic thriller and action film set mostly in Dubai and Durban, gave the Pakistani exhibitors a mouthwatering taste of box-office success scored by an imported Indian film. The resulting upsurge in movie attendance figures reversed the downward trend that had seen the number of movie theaters plunge from 1,300 in the 1970s to 270, leading to the rise of new multiplexes.[8]

In his petition to the Lahore High Court in November 2012, Mubashir Lucman, a TV talk host, challenged the smuggling of Indian films and their exhibition in Pakistani theaters. He claimed that since June 2006 at least 213 Indian movies had been shown in Pakistan under a false certificate of origin. The court ordered that the Central Board of Film Censors should not certify films that lacked proper import documents.[9]

Though Urdu is the mother tongue of only 5 percent of Pakistanis, it is the official language of the state and is taught in schools nationwide. Most Pakistanis are therefore bilingual. Urdu is one of the eighteen officially recognized languages of India, where Hindi is the primus inter pares among the native tongues. It is taught in non-Hindi-speaking areas, except in Tamil Nadu. Spoken Hindi is akin to spoken Urdu, and that language is often called Hindustani. Bollywood's screenplays are written in Hindustani.

"The common man in Pakistan wants entertainment and Indian movies provide them with a source of getting away from the [mundane] routines of life," said Irfan Ashraf, a Pakistani film critic. "Cinema owners in Pakistan understand this aspect of the political economy of the media and therefore [most of them] want Indian movies though a few among the local movie producers, directors would always resist [Indian content]."[10]

The release of *Dhoom 3* (Hindi: Uproar 3), a Bollywood action thriller with a record budget of $21million, on December 19, 2013, in India, and then in Pakistan a week later, introduced a new element in the tangled tale of the Indian film industry and Pakistan. Written and directed by Krishna Acharya, the lead was played by the superstar Aamir Khan. On the first day the movie racked up box office receipts of Rs 20 million from fifty-six screens in Karachi, beating the record of Rs 11.4 million set by the Pakistani film *Waar* (Urdu: The Strike) in the previous month. The craze in the port city reached such heights that the multiplexes ran *Dhoom 3* on all their screens with five shows a day per screen. Nadeem H. Mandviwalla, the distributor, was ecstatic. "2013 was a great year for exhibitors and distributors, and the success of *Chambeli*, *Man Hoon Shahid Afridi* [Urdu: I am Shahid Afridi, cricket's superstar], *Waar*, *Chennai Express* and *Dhoom 3* showed Pakistani and Indian films could co-exist on screen."[11]

Actually, such coexistence had officially come to pass. On December 16, Lucman, who had sought a ban on Indian films before a High Court in Lahore and had the backing of those who feared the decline of the domestic industry in the face of Bollywood imports, withdrew his petition following a compromise. He and the Pakistan Cinema Owners' Association and film distributors signed a Memorandum of Understanding whereby movie theaters in Pakistan were to be permitted to give equal screening time to Indian and Pakistani movies.[12]

This pragmatic attitude in the business community was at odds with the prevalent view in political and military circles.

TOOLS OF PSYCHOLOGICAL WARFARE

The hard-liners in the political-military establishment fretted about the insidious influence of Indian films and broadcasting media in shaping public opinion in Pakistan. Major General Muhammad Asif, in his essay in the latest edition of Pakistan's biennial journal *Green Book*, published by the General Headquarters, Rawalpindi, for the officer corps, lamented the fact that because of the lack of credibility in the Pakistani media, many people turned to All India Radio, the BBC, and Indian satellite channels for news, particularly during Indo-Pakistan crises.[13]

The 2010 *Green Book*, published in 2012, covered information warfare. In the opening essay, "Treatise on India-backed Psychological Warfare Against Pakistan," Brigadier Umar Farooq Durrani stated that India's Research and Analysis Wing (RAW) funded many newspapers and even TV channels, such as Zee TV, which is "considered to be the India's media headquarters to wage psychological war." However, according to Durrani, the most subtle form of psychological warfare "is found in movies where Muslim and Hindu friendship is screened within the backdrop of melodrama. Indian soaps and movies are readily welcomed in most households in Pakistan. The effect desired to be achieved through this is to undermine the Two National Theory as being a person[al] obsession of [Muhammad Ali] Jinnah." In his foreword to the book, Chief of Army Staff (COAS) General Ashfaq Parvez Kayani described the essays as providing "an effective forum for the leadership to reflect on, identify and define the challenges faced by the Pakistani army and share ways of overcoming them."[14]

As for Pakistan's movie industry—based in Lahore and called Lollywood—it had recovered from the trough it had hit during the rule of Zia ul Haq. But it was a minnow compared to Bollywood. With its revenue of $3 billion in 2011, Bollywood was expected to generate income of $4.5 billion by 2016.[15]

Where Pakistanis could console themselves in their competition with Indians in popular culture was cricket. There the odds favored them.

CRICKET: SPECTACULAR ARENA FOR ONE-UPMANSHIP

One consequence of the partition was greater sports rivalry, which was spectacularly expressed on the cricket oval. Though Pakistan became a permanent member of the International Cricket Council (ICC) in 1948, it acquired test status four years later. In the following six decades, it played 58 tests with India. It won 11 tests and lost 9, with the rest being draws.[16] On the other hand, the Indians won the ICC's World Cup at the Lord's in London in June 1983, nine years before the Pakistanis, captained by Imran Khan, did in Melbourne. Starting in October 1978, the two neighbors' national squads competed against each other in One Day International (ODI) in multinational tournaments and Twenty20 contests.[17] In 126 such encounters until March 2014, Pakistan won 72 and India 50, with 4 declared draws.[18]

Pakistan's first series of test matches with India started in October 1952. Its team lost the first test in Delhi. Then it fought back with verve in Lucknow, inflicting a humiliating defeat on its host by an inning. Whereas its performance buoyed the spirits of Pakistanis at home, the Indian spectators at the stadium were so furious that they booed and mocked their players. By winning the next match, the Indians saved their sports honor.

But the abuse that was hurled at the Indian cricket squad in Lucknow left an indelible mark. The message was: there is a lot more at stake than just cricket. A match between the two national teams was to be treated as a battle fought on the pitch—a war without the shooting. Indeed, the term "clash" replaced the normal "match" in the case of India and Pakistan. This forced the two captains and their squads to follow defensive tactics. Hence the 1954–1955 test series hosted by Pakistan and the 1960–1961 series by India were draws.

The sports and trade break caused by the Kashmir War in 1965 continued well past the next armed conflict in 1971. It was only in 1978, when the heads of government in Delhi and Islamabad—Morarji Desai and General Zia ul Haq respectively—had not been the direct participants in the 1971 war, that cricketing ties were restored. In November 1978 the sixteenth Indo-Pakistan test match was played in Faisalabad, Pakistan. The Indo-Pakistan cricket test series became an annual event.

One-day matches were also played in some tournaments, such as the short-lived Austral-Asia Cup, which was staged in the United Arab Emirates. Because of their brevity, these games are very exciting. The most memorable one between India and Pakistan was played in Sharjah in 1986 for the Austral-Asia Cup Final. Pakistan needed 4 runs off the last ball to win. Javed Miandad, a legendary batsman, hit a 6 when his strike sent the ball over the boundary marker and into the crowd. Pakistan went into an ecstatic frenzy while its archrival was shattered. This was Pakistan's first victory in a one-day tournament and the consequent depression it caused among Indians lingered a long time. Indeed, the shock of triumph or defeat was so intense that several people died of heart attacks on both sides of the border.[19]

The next year Indian prime minister Rajiv Gandhi broke new ground by inviting Zia ul Haq to watch a match with him in February 1987 to defuse the tension caused by India's Operation Brasstacks war games. With that, the term "cricket diplomacy" entered the diplomatic lexicon in South Asia. Later, the worsening of Delhi-Islamabad relations because of the insurgency in Kashmir ended the countrywide tours by the competing squads, the forty-fifth test match in Sialkot, Pakistan, in mid-December 1989 being the last during the twelve-year period. It was in a game played against the Pakistani team in Karachi a month earlier that the sixteen-year-old Sachin Tendulkar, who would be hailed as the greatest postwar batsman, made his debut in a test series.

On the one hand test matches aroused partisan passions on both sides of the Indo-Pakistan border; on the other they enabled people-to-people contact. "I remember in the 1989 Test at Lahore, people came from New Delhi and Amritsar," recalled Rameez Raja, the chief executive of the Pakistan Cricket Board (PCB). "Likewise when Pakistan played in India, people from Pakistan went to Chandigarh and other Indian cities."[20]

With the Kashmiri separatists' insurgency gathering pace in the early 1990s and the Indian government using an iron fist to squash it, relations between Delhi and Islamabad became frosty. The cricket test match series was suspended.

At the initiative of Sahara India, a business conglomerate, the PCB and the Board of Control for Cricket in India (BCCI) signed a five-year contract in 1995 to play five annual ODIs in Toronto, a neutral venue. In the three seasons from September 1996 to September 1998, Pakistan won the tournaments. By then, with cable TV making inroads in India, more Indians had access to watching cricket played overseas. Betting on cricket, although illegal, became widespread in both India and Pakistan. The remaining two ODIs fell by the wayside when, in the wake of the Kargil War in the spring of 1999, Sahara India ended its sponsorship.[21]

As for the Indo-Pakistan test matches, on the eve of Indian premier Atal Bihari Vajpayee's bus journey from Delhi to Lahore in February 1999, the forty-sixth Indo-Pakistani test match was played in Chennai. Pakistan won by 12 runs. The return tour of the Indian squad failed to materialize because of the Kargil War, which resulted in yet another break in official bilateral cricket links.

On June 8, 1999, while Indian and Pakistani soldiers were fighting in Kargil, the contest between the cricket teams of the warring nations in the World Cup tournament in Manchester, England, became the most watched segment of the tournament. Though Pakistan was beaten by India, it had done so well in earlier matches that it went on to the semifinal.

In the aftermath of the terrorist attack on the Indian parliament in December 2001, Delhi broke off diplomatic ties with Islamabad. Mutual relations, including sports, remained frozen until August 2003. Six months later, India played the first of its three tests, despite security concerns, and as many ODIs. "Our public has been starving to see India play in Pakistan for nearly 14 years," said Raja. "I think eight international matches would generate huge excitement and interest, while almost every [sports] centre will also get its due share [of hosting the game]."[22] The Indians won the series, 2 to 1. By then airing the matches on TV had become big business. So the pressure on players to win intensified.

Predictably, the terror attacks on Mumbai in November 2008 ruptured Indo-Pakistan cricket ties. In the wake of a terror attack on the visiting Sri Lankan team in Lahore in March 2009, the ICC cancelled Pakistan's cohosting of the 2011 Cricket World Cup. The headquarters of the organizing committee was shifted from Lahore to Mumbai. With Pakistan no longer hosting games, eight of the games were played in India, four in Sri Lanka, and two in Bangladesh. This was a major blow to Pakistan from which it has yet to recover fully.

A CRICKET BATTLE ON THE PLAINS OF PUNJAB

When the Indian and Pakistani teams found themselves facing each other in the ICC's 2011 semifinal in the stadium in Mohali, a satellite town of Chandigarh, passion rose in both nations—and with it the size of betting, now running into billions of rupees. An extra element of drama was added when Indian prime minister Manmohan Singh invited his Pakistani counterpart, Yusuf Raza Gilani, to watch the daylong battle on a cricket pitch on March 30.

On the eve of this momentous event, the Mohali stadium was surrounded by contingents of policemen in khaki, antiriot paramilitaries in blue fatigues, commando units in black overalls, and regular troops in full battle uniform. They were aided by bomb disposal squads with sniffer dogs and helicopters in the air. Those entering the stadium went through a metal detector and were given vigorous pat-downs by security guards.

With only half of the twenty-eight thousand stadium seats available to the public—the other half reserved for celebrities, diplomats, and officials from both countries—demand far exceeded supply, with tickets selling for up to ten times the official price. Those desperate to gain entrance had started lining up thirty-six hours before the event. Belying the reports that Indian visas had been given to thousands of Pakistanis, there was only a trickle crossing the Wagah border post. Most Pakistanis chose to watch the event live on TV.

In Karachi, the home of the cricket captain Shahid Afridi, the authorities erected giant screens at venues across the city, while car owners draped their vehicles with the national flag and posters of the players. In a rare goodwill gesture, prison officials arranged a special screening of the match for their Indian inmates and provided them with the Indian tricolor to cheer their side. In Chandigarh, Punjab's deputy chief minister

Sukhbir Singh Badal urged residents to open their "hearts and homes to our brothers from across the border." They were generous to the Pakistani visitors, up to a point. "They can come, they can play but they cannot win," said an ardent fan of the Indian squad. "This is India's match."[23]

And so it turned out. India won by 29 runs. Three Pakistanis died of heart attacks caused by the shock of defeat. One of them was fifty-five-year-old Liaquat Soldier, an actor-writer-director who collapsed while participating in a TV show in Karachi organized for the much-hyped match. "The whole nation . . . simply got disappointed," read the editorial of the Lahore-based *Dunya* (World) newspaper. "Fans watching live screening returned to their homes during the last overs of the match."[24]

India went on to challenge Sri Lanka in the final, played in Mumbai. It triumphed, beating its rival by 6 wickets. It became the first country to win the ICC's World Cup final on home soil. With a record 67.6 million people watching the gripping final—most of them poised on the edge of their seats—it also became one of the most viewed sporting events on television.

INDIA'S STATUS ON THE RISE

By now there was a mismatch in the international standing of the Indian and Pakistan teams. This stemmed from the improving quality of India's players and the emergence of India as the thriving commercial hub of international cricket. The realization that failure to play against India was excluding Pakistan's squad from the most lucrative hub led the PCB to urge the BCCI to resume sports links, reiterating its long-held stance that politics should not interfere with sporting ties. The BCCI invited the Pakistani team to tour India for three ODIs and two Twenty20s in late December 2012 and early January 2013.

During its first tour of India in five years, Pakistan came out even in the Twenty20 series but won the ODI series, 2–1, its first victory since 2005. Its cricketers and media exhibited a true spirit of sportsmanship when Tendulkar, a cricketing phenomenon, retired from the sport after nearly a quarter century. Among other things, the Pakistani media covered Tendulkar's farewell speech live on November 16, 2013. Newspapers and cricketers showered praise on the sports icon. Calling him "the most complete batsman of his age," the *Express Tribune* and *Daily Times* explained that he had the rare skill of repelling bowling attacks of all sorts and tailoring his natural aggression to suit the needs of his team. The glowing tributes to Tendulkar went on for so long that they annoyed the leadership of the Pakistani Taliban. In a video message its spokesman urged Pakistan's media to stop praising the Indian batsman.[25]

Such an attitude was alien to the PCB, which was keen to see the BCCI accept its invitation for a bilateral cricket tour of Pakistan by India, the last one having been in 2006. The BCCI failed to oblige. Frustration in the PCB built up. In December 2013 its acting chair, Najam Sethi, an eminent journalist-businessman, said that Pakistan was more than willing to tour India. "If they are not coming to Pakistan, we are willing to tour them." He explained that "India owe us two home series as per the Future Tour Program, and India-Pakistan series is the most sought after, millions of people are waiting for it." But he also pointed out that being the financial hub and one of the most solicited teams, India had a busy cricket schedule—a fact that militated against its team playing a long series with an archrival such as Pakistan.[26] In other words, India's growing economic clout was becoming a factor in shaping its cricketing relations with its leading South Asian neighbor.

India achieved an average of 8 percent growth in its economy between 2004 and 2011, whereas Pakistan's GDP expansion declined from 7.4 percent during that period to 2.8 percent.[27] The lower 5 percent increase in India's GDP in 2013 was still twice as much as that of its feisty rival. As it was, the weakness of Pakistan's economy compared to India's was noted at Pakistan's inception.

UPS AND DOWNS OF BILATERAL TRADE

Taking into account the gross imbalance in the GDPs of India and Pakistan in 1947, the General Agreement on Trade and Tariffs (GATT) allowed the new nation to impose restrictions on its trade with India. GATT's successor, the World Trade Organization (WTO), followed suit in 1995. That was why when Delhi accorded Pakistan most-favored-nation (MFN) status—meaning that it was ready to give Pakistan a trade advantage by offering low tariffs—in 1996, the WTO exempted Islamabad from reciprocating, which is the common practice.

Partition placed the jute-growing area into East Pakistan and the cotton-growing Sindh into West Pakistan, whereas jute and textile mills were in West Bengal and Bombay respectively. Therefore 56 percent of

Pakistan's exports went to India, whereas only 32 percent of India's finished goods exports were destined for the opposite direction. Before 1965, West Pakistan and India used eleven land routes for bilateral trade: eight in Punjab and three in Sindh.[28] With the prices of commodities rising as a result of the Korean War (1950–1953), Pakistan had favorable trade with India. This continued for some years after the end of that conflict. During 1957–1963 bilateral trade balanced out. Later the situation favored Pakistan. In fiscal 1964, for instance, Pakistani goods worth $46 million were shipped to India, which earned only $27 million for its exports to Pakistan.[29]

After the 1965 Indo-Pakistan War, bilateral trade ceased. Prior to the conflict, passenger and freight trains used to run between Jodhpur in Rajasthan and Karachi. In the aftermath of the armed conflict, rail tracks were uprooted between Munabao in Rajasthan and Khokharapar in Sindh. It was only after four decades—in February 2006—that the railway stations of Munabao and Khokharapar would be reconnected.[30] Travel across the international border virtually ceased after the 1965 war because even the issuing of single-entry visas by the neighboring countries became rare. Pakistanis needed a separate visa for each Indian state, and every time they traveled to a different state they had to report to its police department. The same procedure applied to Indians visiting Pakistan.

In early 1971, Delhi and Islamabad inked a trade agreement. It fell apart in December with the outbreak of the Bangladesh War. It was only in 1975 that the two nations signed a fresh commercial protocol valid for three years. During this period the bilateral commerce favored India. Over the next twelve years, the total volume of trade varied between $31 million and $87 million, with Pakistan selling more goods than India. But as Pakistan raised the number of items on its positive list for imports to eight hundred in 1996 (when India granted it MFN status), two-way commerce, totaling $241 million, favored India to the tune of $168 million.[31]

Later, the size of the cross-border trade became susceptible to whatever diplomatic sensitivities prevailed between Delhi and Islamabad. The bilateral trade during fiscal 1999 shrank by 43 percent from the previous year's $319.5 million because of the Kargil War. Conversely, as a consequence of the composite dialogue for peace agreed by Vajpayee and Pakistani President Pervez Musharraf in January 2004 at the South Asian Association of Regional Cooperation (SAARC) summit in Islamabad, there was a pick-up in bilateral commerce. In fiscal 2004 it rose by 76 percent from $476 million in the previous year.[32] The leaders decided to reopen closed rail and air routes.

The Wagah-Attari border crossing along the historic Grand Trunk Road in Punjab was the natural choice. But the implementation came in stages, with Pakistan being slow to reciprocate, allowing only fourteen Indian items to be imported by road. In 2005 the two sides signed a protocol to trade via this frontier post so long as the trucks were unloaded in the country of origin, with porters carrying the goods across the frontier.

UPGRADING THE WAGAH-ATTARI BORDER CROSSING

It was only on October 1, 2007, that Islamabad and Delhi agreed to trucks crossing the border and depositing their consignments at the other country's customs house, to be reloaded into local vehicles after inspection. On that day, the mood on India's Attari side was festive, with national flags flying amid cheerfully worded banners, and gaily dressed farmers singing and dancing. Indian Punjab's chief minister Badal sent off the first cargo of tomatoes in a decorated truck. By contrast, the atmosphere on the other side was lukewarm. Disappointingly, Badal's counterpart in Pakistani Punjab, Shahbaz Sharif, failed to reciprocate his gesture.[33]

India's exports to Pakistan jumped from $547 million in fiscal 2004 to $1.7 billion three years later. But Pakistani shipments to India stagnated around $300 million because most of its exports consisted of traditional textiles, leather products, sports goods, chemicals, and cement.[34] In June 2008 the two governments decided to increase the frequency of Delhi-Lahore freight trains from two to five a week to cope with the steady rise in commerce.[35]

Interestingly, contraband trade through smuggling and third-country routing exceeded legitimate transactions. It was comprised not only of audio and video cassettes but also India-made machinery and spare parts, especially for the textile industry, and newsprint, which were bought by Pakistanis through the (UAE) or Singapore. Given Islamabad's tenuous foreign exchange reserves, the government ignored the illicit trade—until 9/11. Then, thanks to Washington's generous aid to Islamabad for the latter's participation in its war on jihadist terrorism, Pakistan's foreign exchange reserves expanded nearly sevenfold. With that the need for third-country imports from India slackened.[36]

The bonhomie between Indian prime minister Singh and Pakistan president Asif Ali Zardari, displayed at the end of their meeting in New York in September 2008, augured well for stronger economic ties. The next month India and Pakistan permitted limited commerce across the Line of Control in Kashmir on the Uri-Muzaffarabad and Poonch-Rawalakot trade routes. But the terror attacks in Mumbai reversed the upward trend in commerce. The bilateral trade in fiscal 2008 fell by $440 million.

Though the South Asian Free Trade Area (SAFTA) treaty, specifying reduction of customs duty on all traded goods to zero by 2016 for SAARC members,[37] had become operational on January 1, India and Pakistan ratified it only in 2009. As a result, Indo-Pakistan commerce received a boost. In fiscal 2010 two-way commerce increased by a third, to a little over $2 billion. Yet Pakistan accounted for less than 0.5 percent of India's overall trade, and India just over 1 percent of Pakistan's.[38]

India urged Pakistan to reciprocate by according it MFN status. But its government failed to respond positively to Delhi's call because of considerable opposition at home. It came mainly from the farm lobby, fearing competition from Indian agriculture, and textile manufacturers. Focused primarily on foreign markets, Pakistani mill owners by and large produced better quality cloth, whereas their Indian counterparts, catering for the vast domestic market, prioritized cheap, lower-quality textiles. Pakistani manufacturers were thus vulnerable to imports of India's low-priced cloth. Unable to overcome resistance rooted in economics, combined with opposition from Islamist groups on ideological grounds, Pakistan's government dithered.

Nonetheless, hopeful of improved economic relations with Islamabad, the Indian cabinet decided to build an Integrated Check Point (ICP) at Attari on a plot of 118 acres in February 2010. Eighteen months later, in August 2011, it removed Pakistan from the negative list under the Foreign Exchange Management Act, paving the way for investment from Pakistan. In November 2011 Pakistan decided to grant India MFN status in principle.[39]

PAKISTAN'S QUALITATIVE SHIFT RAMPS UP TRADE

On March 21, 2012, Pakistan made a major policy shift. So far it had kept a positive list of goods that could be imported from India. It now replaced that with a negative list for Indian imports, with all other unspecified items allowed entry into the country. By so doing the number of allowable Indian items leapt from 1,956 to 6,800. This helped Pakistani industrialists, who were now free to import raw materials from India except those produced domestically.[40] Significantly, the 1,209 banned items were in agriculture, textiles, pharmaceuticals, and automobiles.[41]

Islamabad's liberalized protocol was expected to reduce the import of Indian goods through third countries, such as the UAE, which jacked up prices. Shipping Indian goods through Dubai was three times more expensive than transporting them overland to Pakistan. For instance, a bicycle tire, which had been on Pakistan's positive list for trade with India, shot up to 600 Pakistani rupees from the original 250 Indian rupees (1 Indian Rupee = 1.6 Pakistani Rupee) by the time it reached Pakistan through Dubai.[42]

On April 13, 2012, Attari was a beehive of activity. Since it was Baisakhi, a harvest festival coinciding with the New Year of Punjabis, the mood in the province was festive. That was the day India's home minister, P. Chidambaram, chose to inaugurate the Attari ICP, constructed at a cost of Rs 1,500 million ($30 million) and guarded by the Border Security Force, part of the home ministry. Pakistan's ICP at Wagah, built earlier on nine acres of land, was guarded by the Pakistan Rangers, a paramilitary force maintained by the interior ministry.

A structure of yellow and pink stone, the Attari ICP housed state-of-the-art facilities for security, customs, and immigration requirements for passenger and cargo traffic by rail and road. Its two-story passenger terminal resembled an airport terminal, with waiting areas, restaurants, rest rooms, and duty-free shops. The cargo terminal was constructed like an office complex, with different areas earmarked for government agencies, cargo handling agents, banks, and so on. Its parking area had space for five hundred trucks, and its warehouses, including cold storage places, were meant for receipt, inspection, trans-shipment, and delivery of imported goods. The prominently marked trade and passenger gates across the dust-blown arches completed the new, efficient arrangement. Such facilities were expected to reduce dramatically the delay of up to one week truck drivers had often experienced before.

Dressed in immaculate Tamil dress of white, open-neck shirt and a long flowing *lungi*, Chidambaram unveiled the ten-foot-high plaque, inscribed in Hindi, Punjabi, and English, dedicated to "the nation, and peace and harmony with Pakistan"—as Badal and his counterpart from Pakistan, Shahbaz Sharif, and Indian commerce minister Anand Sharma and his Pakistani counterpart, Makhdoom Amin Fahim, clapped enthusi-astically.[43] On the previous day Sharma and Pakistan's commerce secretary Zafar Mahmood had inaugurated the Lifestyle Pakistan 2012 exhibition, displaying fashion textiles, jewelry, and designer furniture in Delhi. India had reduced the number of items prohibited for import from Pakistan by a third.

At Attari, speeches by the dignitaries followed. When Fahim ended his speech with the instantly coined slogan "Pakistan-Hindustan *dosti zindabad*" (Long live the Pakistan-Hindustan friendship), he got an en-thusiastic response from the audience. Badal demanded that the ICP be allowed to handle all 6,800 items traded between Karachi and Mumbai, not just 137, as was the case then.[44]

Six months later Delhi agreed to curtail its sensitive list, allowed un-der SAFTA, to 100 items from the present 614 by April 2013, whereby a SAARC member was allowed to maintain high tariffs. Islamabad con-sented to phasing out its negative list in December 2012 and cutting its sensitive list of 950 items to 100 within five years.[45]

By April 2013, the Indo-Pakistan trade by road though Attari-Wagah almost doubled. And each day some three hundred people crossed the border.[46] In fiscal 2012 the volume of bilateral commerce reached a record $2.6 billion. But that was far less than the Indo-Pakistan trade through third countries, estimated at more than $4 billion.[47]

The Pakistan People's Party (PPP)–led government in Islamabad failed to keep its promise to confer MFN status on India by the end of 2012. It justified its failure by pointing out that India did not address its concerns about nontariff barriers (NTB) erected by Delhi. Actually, India had argued that its NTBs did not apply exclusively to Pakistan and that this subject fell within the purview of SAFTA. In any case, Islamabad's noncompliance stemmed from the resistance of its automobile and phar-maceutical industries as well as the farm lobby, and the forthcoming gen-eral election in May 2013. Since the PPP was accused of being pro-Delhi by the opposition, its according of MFN on India would have played into the hands of its rivals.

MOST FAVORED NATION BY ANOTHER TITLE

Following the parliamentary election, Pakistan Muslim League (Nawaz), or PML (N), led by Muhammad Nawaz Sharif, formed the government in June 2013 after being overthrown in a military coup in October 1999. In their meeting on January 17, 2014, the commerce ministers of India and Pakistan—Sharma and Khurram Dastgir Khan respectively—agreed on a protocol of nondiscriminatory market access on a reciprocal basis, because in Pakistan the term "most favored nation" had become politically charged. Islamabad consented to trimming its negative list of trade items with India while maintaining one hundred items on the sensitive list, on which an additional tariff was allowed.[48]

The ministers also decided to keep the Wagah-Attari border crossing open around the clock instead of twelve hours a day. Islamabad agreed to allow the import of all products from India at its Wagah ICP. These changes were expected to divert trade from the complicated sea route to a simplified one by land. And the declaration of Wagah and Attari as dry ports set the stage for shipping cargo by container, which would reduce transportation and handling costs.[49]

These steps boosted cross-border commerce. One of the main hurdles to further expansion of trade was the poor infrastructure on the Pakistani side of the land frontier. Its ICP at Wagah was a fraction of the size of India's at Attari.

In addition, bureaucratic and other procedures in Pakistani were far more arduous than in India. A Pakistani exporter had to deal with the paramilitary Pakistan Rangers; the military's National Logistic Cell, charged with crisis management and logistics emergency; the customs department; and the Anti-Narcotics Force, with overlapping responsibilities. Pakistan's railway infrastructure was also in a worse state than India's. And with Karachi being the only major Pakistani port so far, transportation by sea was constrained by limited port facilities, cumbersome customs procedures, and bureaucratic red tape. In addition, because of currency restrictions, all payments had to be made in a hard currency.

On the other hand, political opposition to normalization of commercial relations between the two neighbors was on the wane, while lobbying for it by businesses became more vigorous. In February 2014, Malik Tahir Javaid, chair of the Pakistan Industrial and Traders Associations Front, urged the government to allow the import of all those items not manufactured in Pakistan to be imported from India.[50]

Were this to happen, annual bilateral trade could easily reach $10 billion before the end of the decade. Other estimates put the figure at $20 billion under "normal" commercial relations between Islamabad and Delhi. After the Islamabad-Beijing free trade agreement went into effect in July 2007, the bilateral commerce increased more than threefold in six years—from $4.1 billion in fiscal 2006.[51]

When the governments in Beijing and Delhi embarked on economic liberalization in 1991–1992, they decided to set aside their border disputes, which had led to war thirty years back, and tighten commercial ties. Within a decade, their bilateral trade ballooned from $265 million to $4.95 billion. During the subsequent decade the growth rate accelerated. With bilateral commerce amounting to $74.7 billion in fiscal 2012, China became India's number one trading partner.[52]

The moral is that if Pakistan and India were to follow the example of China and India, they would both gain materially. Thriving commerce may well bring about the end to the Longest August between the two neighbors by helping to create mutual prosperity underpinned by continued peaceful coexistence. This would require putting the Kashmir issue on the back burner the way Beijing and Delhi did with their border dispute and focusing on forging strong economic links.

20

Overview and Conclusions

India and Pakistan, born as twins in August 1947, are now respectively the second and the sixth most populous nations on the planet. They also belong to the exclusive nine-member nuclear arms club. In terms of GDP estimates based on purchasing power parity, India is number three after the United States and China. And it has the distinction of being the world's largest democracy. These facts underscore the importance of its relations with its neighbor, Pakistan, which also shares borders with China, Afghanistan, and Iran. Twice, between 1999 and 2002, India and Pakistan came close to a nuclear confrontation.

The partition of the Indian subcontinent was the culmination of a process that started when Afghanistan-based Muhammad Ghori, commanding an army of Afghans, Arabs, Persians, and Turks, gained control of the Indus Valley basin in 1188. Four years later he defeated Prithvi Raj in the Second Battle of Terrain, paving the way for his leading general, Qutbuddin Aibak, to annex Delhi. Out of this was born the Delhi Sultanate. It lasted until 1526, when it gave way to the Mughal Dynasty, which ended in 1807. What distinguished the Afghans and Mughals from the earlier invader-conquerors of the subcontinent was that they were the followers of Islam. Their beliefs and religious practices clashed with those of the indigenous Hindus.

The rise of the British Empire on the ashes of the Mughal Dynasty put both the Hindu majority and the Muslim minority under the common yoke of a foreign power with its home base in distant Britain, a Christian country. While the Muslim elite's loss of power left it sulking,

413

upper-caste Hindus adjusted readily, switching from learning Persian to English to help the new rulers administer the subcontinent.

Preeminent among those Muslim aristocrats who accepted the unpalatable reality was Sir Syed Ahmed Khan, who urged his coreligionists to learn English. He also understood the importance of nationalism, a nineteenth-century construct originating in Europe. According to him, Muslims in India were a nation, and so were Hindus.

Within a few years of the founding of the Indian National Congress in 1885, calling for an increased role in the government by Indians, Sir Syed foresaw its modest demand escalating to a campaign to expel the British from India. "Is it possible that under these circumstances [of British withdrawal] two nations—the Mohammedans and the Hindus—could sit on the same throne and remain equal in power?" he asked rhetorically in 1888.[1]

His argument was flawed. It failed to recognize that universal suffrage in an independent India would deprive the minority Muslims of being "equal in power." This is the point Muhammad Ali Jinnah articulated four decades later. Alluding to the historical oppression of minorities by majorities, he demanded legal safeguards for the Muslim minority in his address to the Congress session in 1928. He pleaded that Muslims, forming a quarter of the population, should be allocated a third of political power. The overwhelmingly Hindu leadership of the Congress prepared to concede only 27 percent. This was the first of the landmark events that led to the division of the subcontinent.

THE CONGRESS PARTY'S BLUNDERS

The next such event occurred in 1937. After the Muslim League had won two-thirds of the Muslim seats in the Bombay legislature and two-fifths in United Provinces', Jinnah offered the League a partnership with the Congress. But Vallabhbhai Patel, who controlled the party machine, demanded the merger of League legislators with the Congress before any of them could be appointed minister. The haughty behavior of Congress officials made even neutral Muslim leaders suspicious of their real intentions toward Muslims.

Leaving aside the exceptional case of the small, Muslim-majority North-West Frontier Province, the Congress won an average of one Muslim seat in each of the ten provinces. With practically no Muslim lawmakers on its benches, the Congress ruled six provinces. This made non-League Muslim legislators realize that the Congress would exercise power on the basis of a majority in the general (Hindu) constituencies. Non–Muslim League leaders started collaborating with the League.

The performance of the Congress ministries provided examples of insensitivity toward Muslims' beliefs and feelings. Congregational singing of "Vande Mataram" (Sanskrit: I bow to Mother) as part of the official protocol in schools, colleges, and elsewhere was one. According to Rabindranath Tagore, a nationalist poet and philosopher, the core of "Vande Mataram" was a hymn to the goddess Durga. In Islam, deifying or worshiping anyone or anything other than the One and Only (unseen) God constitutes idolatry and is forbidden.

The two-year-plus rule of the Congress gave Muslims a foretaste of what to expect in an independent India. Support for the Muslim League grew rapidly. In the 1945–1946 elections, it garnered all 30 Muslim places in the Central Legislative Assembly, securing 87 percent of the Muslim vote. In the provincial legislatures its size quadrupled to 425 out of 485 Muslim seats.[2]

By then the League's resolution asserting that Muslims were "a nation by any definition," and that the Muslim-majority areas in the northwestern and eastern zones of India, "should be grouped to constitute Independent States in which the constituent units will be autonomous and sovereign,"[3] was six years old.

More significantly, the term "Pakistan" had become irresistibly attractive to Muslims of all classes and persuasions. Orthodox Muslims envisaged a Muslim state run according to the Sharia. Muslim landlords felt assured of the continuation of the *zamindari* (landlord) system, which the Congress had vowed to abolish. Muslim businessmen savored the prospect of fresh markets in Pakistan free from Hindu competition. Civil servants foresaw rapid promotion in the fledgling state. These perceptions among Muslims grew in an environment in which Hindus were much better off economically than Muslims.

Astonishingly, there was a singular lack of perception among Congress leaders of the economic factors bolstering the League's appeal. Jawaharlal Nehru made passing remarks about peasants, whether Muslim or Hindu, suffering at the hands of landlords. Mahatma Mohandas Gandhi failed to grasp that it was that section of the Muslim population that felt it could not compete with Hindus in getting government jobs and in commerce and industry that backed the League.

On the political front, what made partition inevitable was Nehru's boastful declaration on July 8, 1947, about Britain's Constitutional Award of May 16. It envisaged united India with a constituent assembly, elected by existing provincial legislatures, convening briefly in Delhi, and then dividing into Sections A (Hindu majority), B (Muslim-majority, northwestern region), and C (Muslim-majority, Bengal-Assam) to frame a constitution for three subfederations into which federal, independent India was to be divided. Nehru announced that the Congress had agreed to participate in the Constituent Assembly and, once convened, the Assembly would have the power to change the Constitutional Award's provisions, if it so wished, and that the grouping scheme would most likely not survive. This led Jinnah to withdraw the League's acceptance of the Constitutional Award.

The savage butchery that Muslims and non-Muslims—Hindus and Sikhs—perpetrated on one another in Punjab left five hundred thousand to eight hundred thousand people dead and caused the largest mass exodus in history. When communal frenzy gripped Delhi, with Muslims bearing the brunt, Nehru stuck firmly to his secular beliefs, while Patel and Rajendra Prasad disapproved of the Indian army protecting Muslim citizens.

Moreover Patel and his cohorts in Nehru's government were hell-bent on strangling Pakistan at birth. Jinnah complained about this to British prime minister Clement Attlee and vowed that the Dominion of Pakistan would "never surrender." Despite his failing health, he helped the incipient Pakistan, composed of two wings separated by a thousand miles, to find its infant feet.

JINNAH FAILS TO WOO THE MAHARAJA

While acting as the chief executive of Pakistan, Jinnah dealt directly with the tribal areas adjoining Afghanistan and the princely states. He realized that failure to persuade the Hindu Maharaja Sir Hari Singh of the predominantly Muslim Jammu and Kashmir to accede to Pakistan would be a severe blow to his two-nation theory. An opponent of Jinnah's thesis, the maharaja rebuffed his friendly approaches.

Jinnah then assigned the Kashmir portfolio to Prime Minister Liaquat Ali Khan. He complemented his strategy of taking charge of the Azad Army formed independently by Kashmiri Muslims with a plan to secure Srinagar by deploying armed irregulars from the tribal areas. He informed Jinnah of the first track but not the second.

When the invasion of the tribal irregulars led to the airlifting of Indian troops to Srinagar in October 1947, following the maharaja's accession to India, Jinnah was distraught. His unease increased when Pakistan's commander in chief General Sir Frank Messervy refused to obey his order to deploy Pakistani troops. Sir Frank argued that implementing Governor-General Jinnah's order would result in British officers commanding their respective Indian and Pakistani contingents in a fight against each other.

Jinnah's dream of incorporating all of Jammu and Kashmir into Pakistan withered, accelerating his physical decline. He died in harness only a year after the birth of Pakistan.

The outbreak of war with India in Kashmir within months of Pakistan's inception gave its military a primacy it has maintained since then, monopolizing the drafting and implementation of national security policies after the assassination of Ali Khan in October 1951. With his death the nation lost the remaining cofounder of Pakistan. The Muslim League started to unravel, while differences between the eastern and western wings sharpened on the status of Bengali, the mother tongue of the majority of Pakistani citizens. Urdu remained the sole official language. The ongoing squabbling between politicians led to the seizure of power by General Muhammad Ayub Khan in 1958.

This highlighted the contrasting development of Pakistan and India, where two general elections held under a republican constitution and universal suffrage returned the Congress to power, with Nehru as prime minister and foreign minister. His policy of nonalignment with the power blocs contrasted with Pakistan's alignment with the United States. Pakistan acquired the distinction of being a member of the anticommunist South-East Asia Treaty Organization as well as the Central Treaty Organization.

As head of a stable military administration in Pakistan, Ayub Khan was able to reach a deal on the distribution of Indus waters once the World Bank persuaded the United States and Britain, along with Australia and New Zealand, to finance the construction of canals and storage facilities in India to transfer water from the eastern Indian rivers to West Pakistan.

Arriving at an enthusiastic reception in the Pakistani capital of Karachi in September 1960, Nehru cosigned the Indus Waters Treaty with Ayub

Khan. The successful conclusion to a long-running economic dispute encouraged Ayub Khan to broach the subject of Kashmir. But when, in the Presidential Lodge in scenic Murree, he initiated a conversation on the subject, Nehru turned his eyes away, toward the stunning scenery. He concluded the session by stating that any change in the status quo would face serious domestic opposition, and referred to the violent public reaction to China's occupation of India's territory.

NEHRU'S TUSSLE WITH CHINA

By then China had become an integral element in the Indo-Pakistan equation because of its occupation of a part of Kashmir, as alleged by Delhi. Nehru raised the issue with Ayub Khan of Pakistan's boundary with China. He told Nehru that they did not claim any area not covered by the actual Line of Control, as determined by their experts. On his return to Delhi, Nehru criticized Pakistan for having approached the Chinese to demarcate the border.

Nehru was suffused with self-righteousness. This attitude had its merits when it came to sticking to such progressive concepts as secularism and democracy in India, where he enjoyed unrivaled mass popularity. But it was ill suited to diplomacy, where give and take is the universally accepted currency. This became apparent in his dealings with Pakistan on Kashmir and then with China on the border issue. Some analysts attributed self-righteousness to Nehru's Brahminical lineage. Brahmins had claimed and exercised monopoly over knowledge in the caste-ridden Hindu society.

To resolve the border dispute through negotiations, China's premier Zhou Enlai suggested to Nehru that their troops should retreat for twelve miles from the border. Nehru rejected the proposal. Nonetheless, China unilaterally pulled back its soldiers for twelve miles. India interpreted this as China's weakness. It occupied 1,540 square miles of Chinese territory and set up sixty forward posts, forty-three of them north of the McMahon Line in the eastern sector. On September 11, 1962, Delhi permitted all forward posts and patrols to fire on any armed Chinese who entered India's claimed territory. This was tantamount to a declaration of war.

On October 18, Chairman Mao Zedong addressed the Politburo of the Communist Party of China on this subject. "Now that Nehru is determined to fight us, we have no way out but to keep him company," he said. "However, our counter-attack is only meant to serve a warning to Nehru and the Government of India that the boundary question cannot be resolved by military means."[4]

The second part of Mao's statement proved to be the key to understand why at midnight on November 20, having established its superiority in weaponry, strategy, communications, logistics, and planning in the month-long war, China declared a unilateral cease-fire, and added that after their withdrawal, the Chinese frontier guards would be far behind their positions held prior to September 8, 1962.

As wars go, this was a minor affair in which neither side deployed its air force. But it opened a new chapter in India's foreign policy and relations between the United States and the Soviet Union. These superpowers set aside their rivalry and backed India, treating Communist China as their common foe. This radical realignment affected Indo-Pakistan relations. The pro-Washington Pakistan was alarmed and angered to see India being armed heavily by the United States as well as Britain—both of which had persuaded Ayub Khan not to open a battlefront against India in Kashmir or elsewhere on its western frontier during the Sino-Indian War.

Though Nehru went through the motions in his government's talks with Pakistan on Kashmir, nothing came of it. He had no intention of altering his stance that the current cease-fire line in Kashmir should be turned into an international border. This was unacceptable to Pakistan, which demanded a plebiscite, as Nehru had agreed initially. Nehru considered revising his policy on Kashmir only when massive anti-India demonstrations took place in Srinagar in December 1963.

His release of the Kashmiri leader Shaikh Muhammad Abdullah from jail in the spring of 1964 and Abdullah's flight to Rawalpindi to meet Ayub Khan showed promise. But Nehru died of heart failure in May, while Abdullah was in Pakistan. With that died the prospect of a satisfactory resolution of the Kashmir conundrum during Nehru's lifetime.

Overall Nehru's inflexible stance on Kashmir for seventeen years had stoked frustration among Pakistani leaders. When they could no longer contain it, they tried to change the status quo through force. Given India's military superiority, these attempts would fail. The setbacks in Kashmir altered Pakistan's history radically, with the 1965 war leading to the secession of East Pakistan, and the 1999 Kargil conflict resulting in the termination of democracy. The Pakistani leadership also tried to achieve its aim by using armed infiltrators to destabilize Indian Kashmir. Delhi reacted with a ferocious response, using torture and extrajudicial killings on an industrial scale. After 9/11, however, as a victim of cross-border terrorism, India gained widespread Western sympathies, which improved its diplomatic clout.

SECOND INDO-PAKISTAN WAR

In the aftermath of the Sino-Indian War, Anglo-American military aid to India started tilting the balance of power in South Asia in India's favor. Ayub Khan used force to expel India from the 48 percent of Jammu and Kashmir it occupied.

The strategy he deployed was a repeat of what Ali Khan had done eighteen years earlier. Under Operation Gibraltar, Pakistan-trained militias infiltrated Indian Kashmir in August 1965, followed by the involvement of regular troops invading Indian Kashmir on September 1. The three-week-long armed conflict, which spread to Pakistani and Indian Punjab, ended with a UN-brokered cease-fire. The fear of China opening a front on India's eastern frontier was an important factor in Delhi accepting the truce.

There were substantial losses in men and military hardware on both sides. By frustrating Pakistan's objective to alter the status quo in Kashmir, India scored a success. The domestic consequences of Ayub Khan's failure were far reaching. During the conflict people in East Pakistan, lightly defended by their troops, were exposed. Their fear and helplessness increased their alienation from West Pakistan and boosted Bengali nationalism, which achieved its aim in the form of the sovereign state of Bangladesh, created out of East Pakistan. The controlled media in Pakistan had made people believe that their armed military was doing wonderfully well. If so, why did Ayub Khan accept the UN cease-fire resolution?, most Pakistanis wondered aloud. The military dictator's credibility plunged, paving the way for his exit in 1969.

But his successor, General Yahya Khan, failed to honor the result of the general election held October through December 1970 in Pakistan under universal suffrage, which entitled the Bengali nationalist Awami League leader Shaikh Mujibur Rahman to premiership. Instead he unleashed a reign of terror in East Pakistan.

The subsequent crisis caused by the flight of millions of East Pakistanis provided the government of Indira Gandhi with an opportunity.

Through adroit moves in diplomacy, training of guerrillas to undermine East Pakistan's government, and superb military tactics, combined with breaking the Pakistani army's code, Gandhi brought about the signing of the surrender document by General Amir Abdullah Khan Niazi in Dacca on December 17, 1971.

The predominantly Hindu Indians tapped into their religious mythology to crown their triumph. They conferred the sobriquet of Goddess Durga (Sanskrit: Inaccessible) on Indira Gandhi. According to Hindu lore, Durga is a warrior goddess who decapitates the buffalo-demon Mahisasura. Now Gandhi slew the evil of the two-nation theory on which Jinnah had built Pakistan with its two far-flung wings.

East Pakistan's secession proved that a common religion was not a strong enough glue to hold together two societies with different languages, dress, and cultures. The trumping of religion by ethnic nationalism was a bitter pill to swallow, not only for West Pakistanis but also for those in Indian Kashmir who advocated accession to Pakistan.

The third Indo-Pakistan War closed a tumultuous period in the postindependence history of South Asia.

POST-1971 PAKISTAN

India now had to deal with a Pakistan that had lost more than half of its population but was more cohesive racially and religiously, with its Hindu minority reduced to less than 2 percent. It was ruled by the popularly elected Zulfikar Ali Bhutto, who had built up the Pakistan People's Party (PPP) from scratch.

At the summit in Shimla in June 1972, he faced the victorious Gandhi, whose leading aim was to bring the Kashmir dispute to an official close. Bhutto was opposed to this. When their respective delegations reached a deadlock, he had a one-on-one meeting with Gandhi. He convinced her that after the loss of East Pakistan, if he were to abandon his country's claims to Kashmir, he would be thrown out by the military. Having agreed earlier to convert the 1949 UN cease-fire line into the LoC, Bhutto seemed willing to let it morph into an international frontier without a written declaration. On Gandhi's insistence the final draft committed both sides to settle all their differences "by peaceful means through bilateral negotiations or by other peaceful means mutually agreed upon," thus ruling out third-party mediation. And it listed a final settlement of

Jammu and Kashmir "as one of the outstanding questions awaiting settlement."[5] In the subsequent decades, the 1972 Shimla Accord continued to be the basis of all Indo-Pakistan talks.

But progress on normalizing relations and resuming trade and economic cooperation got sidetracked by turmoil in India's and Pakistan's domestic scenes. Bhutto faced insurgency by nationalists in Baluchistan. In June 1975, a court invalidated Gandhi's parliamentary seat won on the corrupt practice of using government facilities and resources during her 1971 election campaign. Instead of stepping down, she imposed an emergency and ruled by decree.

In Pakistan, the rigged March 1977 general election gave the PPP a large majority. The opposition, rallying behind the Pakistan National Alliance, resorted to massive demonstrations. Army Chief General Muhammad Zia ul Haq intervened by mounting Operation Fair Play on July 5, arrested Bhutto, and promised fair elections within ninety days. That never happened.

An Islamist to the core, Zia ul Haq clung to power until August 1988, when he was killed, along with twenty-seven others, by an explosion in the transport plane ferrying them near the Bahawalpur airport. During his rule Pakistani state and society had undergone Islamization and drifted further away from secular, democratic India.

Any ill will that Zia ul Haq had generated for his military dictatorship in the United States evaporated when Soviet troops moved into Afghanistan on Christmas Day 1979 to bolster the twenty-month-old Marxist regime in Kabul. Whereas India had recognized the leftist regime in Afghanistan, Pakistan had not. When President Jimmy Carter offered $400 million in aid to Islamabad to shore up armed Islamist resistance to the Afghan government, Zia ul Haq called it "peanuts"[6] and rejected it.

His prospect brightened when Ronald Reagan became US president in 1981. Washington poured funds and weapons for the Afghan mujahedin through Pakistani army's Inter-Service Intelligence (ISI) directorate. Reagan persuaded Congress to sanction $3.2 billion aid to Islamabad over the next six years, arguing that arming Pakistan with modern US weaponry would reduce the chance of its pursuing the nuclear option. In practice, Pakistan forged ahead on both armament fronts, conventional and nuclear.

Shaken by India's detonation of a "nuclear device" in May 1974, Pakistan had initiated a clandestine program to catch up with its arch rival in this regard. Given Beijing's overarching aim to deprive India of becoming the hegemonic power in South Asia, it surreptitiously aided Islamabad in its nuclear arms program. To this quadrilateral linkage was added another actor: Israel. Committed to thwarting the nuclear weapons ambition of any Muslim country, Israel offered to work with Delhi to bomb the Kahuta nuclear facility, located twenty miles from Islamabad and run by Abdul Qadeer Khan. By late 1982, a joint Indo-Israeli plan to raid Kahuta was hatched. During their clandestine trip to Tel Aviv in early 1983, Indian military officers purchased electronic equipment to jam Kahuta's air defenses.

On the surface, Gandhi and Zia ul Haq maintained cordial relations. On the margins of the seventh Non-Aligned Movement summit in Delhi in March 1983, they agreed to set up the Joint Indo-Pakistan Commission, with subcommissions for trade, economics, information, and travel. This double-dealing became an abiding feature of Delhi-Islamabad relations.

The Indo-Israeli plot against Pakistan did not remain secret from the ISI for long. In the autumn of 1983 its chief sent a message to its counterparts in India's Research and Analysis Wing foreign intelligence agency. This brought about a meeting between Munir Ahmad Khan, head of the Pakistan Atomic Energy Commission (PAEC), and Raja Ramanna, head of the Bhabha Atomic Research Centre, Trombay, in a Vienna hotel. Khan warned Ramanna that if India alone, or in collusion with Israel, attacked Kahuta, Pakistan would hit India's nuclear facility in Trombay on the outskirts of Mumbai.[7] This compelled Gandhi to hesitate. In addition, Pakistan's ambassador in Delhi conveyed the same message to India's Ministry of External Affairs.[8]

This maneuver helped Zia ul Haq achieve his twin objectives of signaling that Islamabad's nuclear program was unstoppable, thus gaining international acceptance by stealth, and issuing a stern warning to Gandhi. She revoked her earlier go-ahead to Israel's hawkish defense minister Ariel Sharon.

Militant Sikhs' violent agitation for an independent homeland, called Khalistan, appealed to Zia ul Haq since it was based on religious grounds. At his behest, the ISI aided the extremist Sikhs with training and weapons. The activists of the Khalistan movement turned the Sikhs' holiest complex, the Golden Temple in Amritsar, into an armed fortress. To destroy this base, Gandhi ordered the storming of the Golden Temple by the army in June 1984. The military succeeded at the cost of shedding much blood and alienating the Sikh community nationwide. In retaliation, two of Gandhi's Sikh bodyguards assassinated her in October.

She thus became the second Indian leader to fall victim to violence stemming from religious fanaticism, the earlier example being that of Mahatma Mohandas Gandhi, who was assassinated by a Hindu supremacist for urging the Indian government to meet its financial obligations to Pakistan.

THE RACE FOR NUCLEAR ARMS

Rajiv Gandhi, the only surviving son of Indira, who succeeded her as prime minister, was untutored in politics or administration. Nonetheless, after his meeting with Zia ul Haq in December 1985 in Delhi, they agreed not to attack each other's nuclear facilities as a confidence-building measure. Crucially, though, they disagreed on the nature of their nuclear programs, both of them professing a peaceful use, a facade that would crack in 1987.

In December 1986 Gandhi gave a green light to the Indian Army chief, Lieutenant General Krishnaswamy Sundararajan, to stage the war game code-named Brasstacks to test his innovative concept of combining mechanization, mobility, and air support. The operation involved mobilizing nearly three-quarters of the Indian army in Rajasthan and putting them on high alert. As a model for a full-scale invasion, it revived Pakistani leaders' long-held nightmare that their country would be annihilated by India.

In retaliation, Zia ul Haq, as army chief, extended the military's winter exercises in Punjab, mobilized the army in Karachi and the Southern Air Command, and deployed armored and artillery divisions as part of a pincer to squeeze Indian Punjab, where the Sikh insurgency had revived.

In an astutely planned maneuver, Qadeer Khan gave an interview to Indian journalist Kuldip Nayar on January 28, 1987, in Islamabad. If India pushed Pakistan into a corner, "we will use the bomb," he told Nayar. "We won't waste time with conventional weapons."[9] While Nayar's scoop was held up by the London-based *Observer*, a Sunday newspaper, awaiting authentication by different sources, the story leaked.

To defuse the festering crisis, Gandhi invited Zia ul Haq to witness the second day's play in the five-day cricket match in Jaipur on February 22. He accepted the invitation. Sitting next to Gandhi, he reportedly whispered that if India's forces crossed the border, Indian cities would be "annihilated." A pro forma denial of the statement by Islamabad followed.

All the same, from then on the media in India routinely said that Pakistan was "within a few turns of a screwdriver" of assembling an atom bomb.

In short, after four decades of living in fear of India's overwhelming military superiority, Pakistan achieved parity with its rival in nuclear deterrence. Nevertheless, it did not lay to rest Pakistani leaders' fears of India becoming the unchallenged regional power in South Asia.

Initially, Gandhi and the democratically elected Pakistani prime minister Benazir Bhutto got along well. On the sidelines of the summit of the South Asian Association for Regional Cooperation (SAARC) in Islamabad in late December 1988, Bhutto had a meeting with Gandhi. She pledged to choke off Pakistan's aid to Sikh separatists. In return, Gandhi promised to withdraw Indian troops from the contested Siachen Glacier in Kashmir, which he failed to do because of his party's defeat in the 1989 general election.

On the last day of 1988 the two leaders signed the "Agreement on Prohibition of Attack against Nuclear Installations and Facilities" to become effective beginning January 27, 1991. Earlier in 1988, sticking to the practice of following underhanded policies, common to both rivals, Gandhi had ordered the upgrading of the nuclear testing site in Pokhran, Rajasthan, first used in 1974, to make it suitable for detonation on short notice.

Indo-Pakistan relations soured as the separatist insurgency in Kashmir intensified from 1989 onward and Delhi resorted to brutish methods to squash it. Bhutto and her successor, Muhammad Nawaz Sharif, protested, but to no avail.

Following Rajiv Gandhi's assassination in May 1991, the leadership of the Congress Party passed to P. V. Narasimha Rao. During his five years in office, the international scene changed radically. The Soviet Union's disintegration in December 1991 signaled US victory in the forty-five-year-long Cold War.

Delhi strengthened its ties with Washington, which saw no need to downgrade its historic links with Pakistan.

Once India had established full diplomatic relations with Israel in 1992, at a time when the Islamist insurgency in Kashmir had risen sharply, that small but militarily powerful nation with long experience in tackling terrorism became a factor in determining Delhi's relations with Islamabad.

In sum, within half a century of their establishment, India and Pakistan found their bilateral relations being forged by multiple factors, involving the United States, the Soviet Union, China, Israel, and Afghanistan.

In 1995 Narasimha Rao decided to conduct underground tests on nuclear weapons. Preparations built up to a climax in early December. These were picked up by four powerful American spy satellites. President Bill Clinton urged him to abandon the plan. He did so, but instructed nuclear scientists to be ready for tests within a month of receiving an executive order.[10] By radically altering their pattern of work—such as laboring only at night—at Pokhran, the Indians managed to defeat US spy satellites.

In March 1998, when Bharatiya Jan Sangh (BJP) leader Atal Bihari Vajpayee became prime minister as head of the BJP-led National Democratic Alliance with a slim majority, he ordered nuclear tests to consolidate the loyalty of the non-BJP members of the alliance.

On May 11, he announced three underground nuclear tests, including one involving a thermonuclear device. Two more tests of smaller bombs followed on May 13. These explosions were received with widespread enthusiasm, making Indians feel proud of their scientists and engineers for their mastery of high technology.

Across the border, prime minister Sharif faced a quandary. Given the dire state of Pakistan's economy, he was vulnerable to US sanctions, and Clinton urged him to refrain from testing a nuclear bomb. But once the Islamist parties mounted pro–nuclear test demonstrations on May 15, Sharif had no choice but to fall in line with popular sentiment.

Two days later, he ordered the PAEC chair, Ishfaq Ahmed, to "conduct the explosions!"[11] These were conducted in the Ras Koh mountain range in Baluchistan on May 28. "We have settled a score and have carried out five successful nuclear tests," he declared on Pakistan TV. To beat India, he ordered one more test on May 30.

FRIENDLY SIGNS BLOSSOM—BRIEFLY

These explosions boosted both Sharif's and Vajpayee's popular standing, giving them the confidence to stop flexing their muscles and start mending fences. At their meeting on the margins of the UN General Assembly in New York they decided to resume bus service between Delhi and Lahore to encourage people-to-people contact.

The star passenger on the inaugural bus trip on February 20, 1999, was Vajpayee. He was received at the Wagah border crossing by Nawaz Sharif and senior cabinet ministers in the full glare of the international media. The high point of his stay in Lahore was the laying of a wreath at the Minar-e Pakistan, at the site where on March 23, 1940, the All India Muslim League passed its resolution for a homeland for the Muslims of India. In the visitors' book, Vajpayee wrote: "A stable, secure and prosperous Pakistan is in India's interest. Let no one in Pakistan be in doubt. India sincerely wishes Pakistan well."[12] Coming from a Hindu nationalist leader, such a statement was received with a full-throated cheer by Pakistani politicians and media.

The two prime ministers signed the Lahore Declaration. It stated that the possession of nuclear weapons by both nations required additional responsibility to avoid conflict and promote confidence-building measures. To avoid accidental or unauthorized use of nuclear weapons, the signatories agreed to give each other advance notice of ballistic missile flight tests and accidental or unexplained use of nuclear arms in order to stave off nuclear conflict. They also agreed to discuss their nuclear doctrines and related security issues.[13]

But Sharif's hope that Pakistan and India would be able to live as friendly neighbors like America and Canada would prove wildly optimistic barely three months later.

ON THE BRINK OF A NUCLEAR CLASH, TWICE

Without even informing Sharif, Army Chief Pervez Musharraf violated the Shimla Agreement by attempting to change the status quo in Kashmir by using force in the Kargil region. The initial claims of Islamabad that the fighting there was being done by local Kashmiri mujahedin collapsed when intercepts of conversations between Musharraf, then visiting Beijing, and the chief of the general staff, Lieutenant General Muhammad Aziz Khan, in Rawalpindi were released by the Indian authorities.

On June 13 Vajpayee told Sharif that only when Pakistan had withdrawn its troops would he be ready to talk. Clinton intervened. He advised Vajpayee not to open a new front in Kashmir. Remarkably, China called for the withdrawal of Pakistan's forces to the LoC and settling its border issues with India peacefully.

India declared that it would not be the first to use nuclear weapons, but on June 23 Pakistan's information minister Mushahid Hussain, appearing on a BBC program, refused to give the same guarantee.[14]

On the battlefront, Indians started expelling Pakistanis from their occupied outposts in Kargil. Facing an imminent defeat, Musharraf would most likely open new fronts in Kashmir, Sharif calculated. The resulting strong response by India would lead to a full-scale war, a calamitous prospect. In Washington, Clinton fretted when his study of the National Security Agency's intercepts of satellite images showed the unveiling of nuclear-tipped missiles at Sargodha Air Force Base, ordered by Musharraf for possible use in an outright war with India.

Eager to prevent a nuclear holocaust in South Asia, Clinton summoned Sharif and Vajpayee to Washington. Vajpayee declined, aware that attending a tripartite meeting on Kargil would violate India's position that Kashmir was a bilateral issue.

After tense negotiations on America's Independence Day, 1999, Sharif signed a joint statement with Clinton. It specified an agreement to restore the LoC, thus facilitating a cease-fire, seen as a preamble to the resumption of bilateral talks to resolve all Indo-Pakistan disputes. Sharif doubted that his army would see the statement as "the right thing for Pakistan and the world."

His hunch proved prescient. He was toppled by Musharraf in October. As in the case of the 1965 Indo-Pakistan War in Kashmir, which led to the overthrow of General Ayub Khan, the Kargil conflict produced a similar upset, the only difference being the army chief (Yahya Khan) replacing military president Ayub Khan, and not a popularly elected politician.

As before with military dictators, once Musharraf had consolidated his power, he tried to tackle the Kashmir issue. He displayed flexibility by inviting solutions other than a plebiscite in his talks with Vajpayee in Agra in July 2001, only to find him and his senior BJP cabinet ministers insisting on Musharraf stopping cross-border terrorism and illegal infiltration into Indian Kashmir.

The 9/11 attacks strengthened the hands of BJP leaders in Delhi at the expense of Musharraf. The daring terrorist assault on the Parliament House in Delhi in December raised India's moral high ground further. Yet it required relentless pressure by President George W. Bush and the mobilization of the Indian army to get Musharraf to ban five extremist organizations in mid-January 2002. While so doing, he agreed to offer Kashmiris nothing more than "moral, political and diplomatic support."

As in the past, the resulting thaw in Delhi-Islamabad relations proved transitory. An audacious terrorist attack on May 14, 2002, on the army camp at Kaluchak in Kashmir, killing thirty men, women, and children, roiled Indian leaders as never before.

Vajpayee authorized the bombing of training camps in Pakistan-held Kashmir. But the air force lacked enough laser-guided bombs and night-vision pods to accomplish the task. By the time these arrived from Israel, it was June 5. In the interim, Army Chief General Sundararajan Padmanabhan had moved eight of the ten strike divisions of the army to jumping-off points near the Pakistani border. His Pakistani counterpart, Musharraf, moved an attack force of armored and motorized infantry divisions into combat readiness positions.

Alarm bells rang in Washington and London. The CIA chief informed Bush's War Cabinet that his analysts believed that given the confusion among decision makers in Delhi and Islamabad as to when and how a conventional war could escalate to a nuclear confrontation, there was a serious risk of the first nuclear strike since World War II.[15] Washington and London advised around sixty thousand Americans and twenty thousand Britons to start leaving India beginning on May 31.

Stock markets in India and Pakistan plunged. That shook the two governments, more so the one in Delhi. The pro-business, BJP-led cabinet wanted to propel India beyond the sluggish GDP growth rates of the past. The abrupt loss of Western confidence in India's fast-expanding economy gave Vajpayee pause.

The threat of an imminent nuclear clash between the neighbors passed. But the two armies remained battle-ready. Feeling the economic pain of maintaining its forces across the LoC on high alert, Musharraf saw merit in pragmatism. On December 17, 2003, he said his government was prepared to drop its long-standing demands for a plebiscite on Kashmir to end the fifty-six-year-old dispute. This required both sides to be flexible.

The slow process of bilateral talks gathered pace after the return of the Congress-led government in Delhi in May 2004, under the premiership of Manmohan Singh. Musharraf and Singh set up a backchannel to resolve the Kashmir conundrum away from the prying eyes of the media.

After many meetings in hotels around the world, their envoys—Tariq Aziz and Satinder Lambah—agreed on a plan. Musharraf gave an inkling of it in his December 2006 interview with Delhi-based NDTV. Pakistan, controlling more than one-third of Kashmir, would give up its claim to Indian-administered Kashmir, occupying about half of the original princely state,[16] if people from both regions had freedom of movement through open borders. There would be phased withdrawal of troops from both sides of the LoC.[17]

Since this formula did not require a change in the border, it interested Indian leaders, but they feared that the withdrawal of their army from their region would allow separatists to thrive. They were also not sure Musharraf had the consent of senior generals on a subject that was the defining element in the history of Pakistan's military. They had to weigh the chances of Musharraf being elbowed out by the armed forces' high command, as it had Ayub Khan. Lastly, would any deal agreed to by the Musharraf government remain intact in the post-Musharraf era?

On November 28, 2007, Musharraf had to resign as army chief before being sworn in for a second term as civilian president. And on August 18, 2008, he stepped down as president to spare himself impeachment by Parliament, which was dominated by anti-Musharraf parties following the general election in February. With this, the two South Asian rivals lost yet another opportunity for a peaceful settlement of the Kashmir dispute.

Three months later the sixty-hour siege of luxury hotels in Mumbai by Pakistani terrorists, recruited to bring about the liberation of Indian Kashmir, damaged Indo-Pakistan relations gravely. It took two-and-a-half years for the return of diplomatic conversation between the two capitals. Initially, India insisted that no progress could be made in normalizing relations until the perpetrators of the Mumbai attack were brought to justice. Later it relented.

INCREASED TRADE HOLDS PROMISE

As the signatories of the South Asian Free Trade Area treaty, specifying reduction of customs duty on all traded goods to zero by 2016 for the eight-member SAARC, India and Pakistani started liberalizing mutual trade from 2009 onward.

But the PPP-led government failed to fulfill its promise to confer most-favored-nation (MFN) status on India by the end of 2012. Delhi had accorded MFN status to Pakistan in 1996. However, in March 2012 Islamabad replaced its positive list of goods that could be imported from India with a negative list. That raised the number of allowable Indian items by three-and-a-half times, to 6,800.

Following the return of Sharif to power in May 2013, India and Pakistan agreed on a nondiscriminatory market access protocol, thus skirting the term "most favored nation," which had become politicized in Pakistan. During the fiscal year ending in April 2013, Indo-Pakistan commerce, at

$2.6 billion, was way below the $4 billion worth of trade that Indians and Pakistanis conducted via third countries.

It is worth recalling that after signing the Lahore Declaration in early 1999, Sharif had expressed the hope in Vajpayee's presence that "Pakistan and India will be able to live as the United States and Canada."[18] So cordial are the relations between these neighbors in North America that their 1,538-mile-long border is militarily undefended. Sadly, Sharif's sentiment remains just that: a well-meaning thought stemming from infectious goodwill. All the same, it provides a glimpse of what could be—a notion of an alternative scenario for the twins of South Asia based on ongoing, mutual cooperation and benevolence leading to prosperity and peace.

Regretfully, the two neighbors' pursuit of generally hostile bilateral policies, rooted in the intractable Kashmir dispute, have diverted scarce resources from advancing health, education, and social welfare to building up the military and the concomitant arms industry. With its 74 percent literacy rate in 2011, India—where education is a fundamental right according to its constitution—was way behind its officials' often repeated aim of achieving universal literacy.[19] In Pakistan, only 21 percent were literate in 2012.[20] This was a dismal statistic for a country capable of manufacturing nuclear arms and engaged in a nuclear arms race with neighboring India.

Epilogue

Following the landslide victory of the National Democratic Alliance—led by the Hindu nationalist Bharatiya Janata Party (BJP)—in India's general election, BJP head Narendra Modi invited the seven other leaders of the South Asian Association for Regional Cooperation to his inauguration as Indian prime minister on May 26, 2014.

The generals in Islamabad advised Prime Minister Sharif to decline the invitation. He disregarded their counsel. The generals resented this because, to them, India remained at the core of Pakistan's national security concerns, and that entitled them to have the last word in this arena. Determined to underline his supreme authority, on the eve of his departure for Delhi, Sharif ordered the release of 151 Indian fishermen arrested for fishing in Pakistani waters as a goodwill gesture.[1]

On May 27, Sharif had an hour-long one-on-one meeting with Modi, during which he invited his host to Pakistan. Their warm handshake in front of the cameras seemed to offer a promise of improved Indo-Pakistan relations. Sharif said that their top diplomats would meet soon to take their dialogue forward. As pro-business leaders they resolved to pursue normalization of trade relations. According to Barkha Dutt of Delhi-based NDTV, "Sharif said this strong mandate frees up leaders on both sides . . . to actually turn a new page in the history of India and Pakistan."[2] Sharif was thus referring to the large majority his party had won in Pakistan's general election a year earlier.

Responding to Modi's gift of a shawl for Sharif's mother, Shamim Akhtar, the Pakistani leader presented a white sari for his Indian counterpart's mother, Heeraben Modi, in early June.

However, as had happened before, violations along the Line of Control (LoC) in Kashmir increased in the wake of lowered diplomatic tensions. Between early June and early August, India identified more than thirty violations of the LoC, and Pakistan reported fifty-seven violations.[3]

On August 12, Modi visited Kargil in Kashmir to inaugurate a power plant. "Pakistan has lost strength to fight conventional war, but continues to engage in a proxy war through terrorism," he said. Earlier that day, while addressing soldiers in the regional capital of Leh, he informed them that Indian troops were "suffering more casualties from terrorism than from war."[4]

As if Modi's statements were not enough to dissipate the Indo-Pakistan goodwill generated in the spring, Sharif faced a challenge to his office from a street protest in Islamabad that would last several weeks.

Starting on August 14, Pakistan's independence day, the opposition leader Imran Khan led a protest march from Lahore to Islamabad, calling for Sharif's resignation on the grounds that his party had rigged votes in the 2013 general election. Another procession was led by Muhammad Tahirul Qadri, a cleric whose Pakistan Awami Tehreek (Urdu: People's Movement) was a broad alliance of moderate Sunnis and persecuted Shias. His party had boycotted the parliamentary election the previous year. Qadri advocated genuine democracy that empowers the underprivileged.

Sharif ordered a cordoning of the administrative heart of the capital with barbed wire and shipping containers, calling it the Red Zone.

When, on August 19, protestors tore down the barricades and entered the Red Zone, Army Chief General Raheel Sharif called on the government to negotiate with the protesters. But when the government appointed a team of politicians to talk to the protest leaders, Khan insisted that the prime minister must resign first. This was unacceptable to Sharif as well as all other opposition groups. While the military high command seemed unwilling to seize power, it was glad to see the Sharif government weakened.

Meanwhile, the Foreign Office had scheduled August 25 as the date for the arrival of India's foreign secretary, Sujatha Singh, for talks with her Pakistani counterpart, Aizaz Chaudhry. Among other things, they were expected to prepare the agenda for a Modi-Sharif meeting in New York in late September. But a hitch developed.

According to Islamabad, it had been a "long-standing practice" ahead of Indo-Pakistan talks for Pakistan's high commissioner in Delhi to hold meetings with dissident Kashmiri leaders in order to "facilitate meaningful discussion on the issue of Kashmir."[5]

When India learned of an upcoming meeting of Shabir Ahmad Shah, a Kashmiri separatist leader, with the Pakistani high commissioner Abdul Basit, Foreign Secretary Singh advised Basit to cancel the appointment. Basit ignored the advice, as instructed by his Foreign Office. Given the street challenge Sharif faced at the time, he could not afford to be seen to be "subservient" to India. The Basit-Shah meeting went ahead on August 18. Pakistan's spokesperson, Tasnim Aslam, argued that Kashmir was a disputed territory and that Pakistan was a "legitimate stakeholder" in the Kashmir dispute.[6]

The Modi government described the Pakistani envoy's action as interference in India's domestic affairs. It cancelled the foreign secretaries' talks. By refusing to overlook Pakistan's open contacts with the Kashmiri separatists, as the previous governments had done in order to preserve the peace process, Modi drew a fresh red line. He thus struck a blow against the renewed peace efforts he had initiated after his inauguration.

While still facing a crisis created by protests that had paralyzed the Pakistani capital, Sharif made a move to break the diplomatic stalemate with Delhi. In early September he sent a box of the choicest Pakistani mangoes to Modi. He also dispatched mangoes to India's foreign minister, Sushma Swaraj, as well as President Pranab Mukherjee and Vice President Hamid Ansari, both of them veteran Congress Party members.[7] The gesture implied an offer of sweetness.

This gesture proved insufficient to revive cordiality. Addressing the UN General Assembly on September 26, Sharif expressed his disappointment at the cancellation of the foreign secretary–level talks. "The core issue of Jammu and Kashmir has to be resolved," he said. "This is the responsibility of the international community. . . . Pakistan is ready to work for resolution of this problem through negotiations." Meanwhile, he declared, "we cannot draw a veil over the issue of Kashmir, until it is addressed in accordance with the wishes of the people of Jammu and Kashmir."[8] Soon after delivering his speech, he returned to Islamabad to defuse the ongoing political crisis there.

The next day Modi told the General Assembly that, with far more pressing problems facing South Asia and the world, "raising [the Kashmir dispute] at the UN won't resolve bilateral issues." He added, "We want to promote friendship with Pakistan too, but we can only talk without the shadow of terrorism over us."[9]

In short, the decades-long Kashmir dispute remained frozen.

By contrast, a steady improvement in trade and cultural relations between the two neighbors continued. On September 11, High Commissioner Basit, who had been at the core of the cancellation of foreign secretary–level meetings, inaugurated the Pakistan Lifestyle Exhibition in New Delhi. It showcased Pakistani products in textiles, marble, and leather.[10] More importantly, two weeks earlier the Automotive Component Manufacturers Association of India and the Pakistan Association of Automotive Parts and Accessories Manufacturers signed a memorandum of understanding in Lahore to set up testing facilities in Pakistan and work together on skills development.[11]

In the cultural field, an important development had occurred in June. Zee Entertainment Enterprises Limited (Zeel) launched a new channel, Zindagi (Hindi/Urdu: Life) TV, to make some of Pakistan's best syndicated shows—comedies, one-off TV films, and dramas revolving around a household of characters—available to TV audiences across India. Zeel's executive, Shailja Kejriwal, said that Indians were "deeply curious" about life in Pakistan. "It is quite startling that post-independence, the Indian viewer has never actually seen Pakistan visually. Test audiences were sort of stunned and excited when we revealed these places were in Pakistan because they felt so familiar to them."[12]

The opening up of a vast TV market provided an enormous opportunity for Pakistan's media business. It was also significant that during his visit to Delhi in late May, Sharif had a meeting with Subhash Chandra—chair of the conglomerate Essel Group, which includes Zeel—to discuss the content of Zindagi TV. Within weeks, Zindagi TV's Pakistani fare proved popular, partly because, in the words of an Indian television critic, "the simple and straight to the point way of telling the stories in these Pakistani serials is a welcome change from the otherwise suffocating, never-ending Indian shows."[13]

All in all, therefore, while the Kashmir dispute shows no sign of progress toward resolution, Indo-Pakistani relations in the realm of commerce and cultural exchange are on a steady course of improvement.

Notes

INTRODUCTION

1. Jonathan Marcus, "The World's Most Dangerous Place?," BBC News, March 23, 2000.

2. Vinay Kumar, "LoC Fencing in Jammu Nearing Completion," *Hindu*, February 1, 2004.

3. Athar Parvaiz, "INDIA: Kashmir's Fence Eats Crops," *IPS News*, October 31, 2011, http://www.ipsnews.net/2011/10/india-kashmirs-fence-eats-crops.

4. Ibid.

5. Dilip Hiro, *The Timeline History of India* (New York: Barnes & Noble, 2006), 242.

6. R. Shayan, "Sir Syed Ahmed Khan," Agnostic Pakistan (blog), December 14, 2008, http://agnosticpakistan.blogspot.co.uk/2008/12/sir-syed-ahmed-khan.html.

7. Ashish Vashi, "Gandhi-Jinnah, Hindu-Muslim: Godhra Created Many Rifts," *DNA India*, February 18, 2012.

8. Meena Menon, "Chronicle of Communal Riots in Bombay Presidency (1893–1945)," *Economic & Political Weekly*, November 20, 2010.

9. Cited in Jaswant Singh, *Jinnah: India–Partition–Independence* (New Delhi: Rupa and Company, 2009), 86, citing *Mohammed Ali Jinnah—An Ambassador of Unity: His Speeches and Writings, 1912–1917, with a Biographical Appreciation by Sarojini Naidu* (Lahore, Pakistan: Atish Fishan, 1989), 11.

10. Hiro, *The Timeline History of India*, 249.

CHAPTER 1: THE MODISH DRESSER MEETS THE MAHATMA

1. Jaswant Singh, *Jinnah: India—Partition—Independence* (New Delhi: Rupa and Company, 2009), 68–69. Watson's Hotel, built in 1863, survives as Esplanade Mansion near Rajabai Clock Tower in South Bombay.

2. Dilip Hiro, *The Timeline History of India* (New York: Barnes & Noble, 2006), 247.

3. Singh, *Jinnah*, 86.

4. Cited by Tim Leadbeater, *Britain and India 1845–1947* (London: Hodder Education, 2008), 38.

5. Cited in Singh, *Jinnah*, 100–101.

6. "Gurjar Sabha, January 14, 1915, citing *The Collected Works of Mahatma Gandhi*, Vol. 14, 342," *Bombay Chronicle*, January 15, 1915, posted by Arun, September 9, 2012, http://thepartitionofindia.blogspot.co.uk/2012/09/gurjar-sabha-january-14-1915-from-cwmg.html.

7. "Mohandes Gandhi Travels to South Africa to Work Under a Year-Long Contract with Dada Abdulla & Co., an Indian Firm" (April 1893), World History Project, http://worldhistoryproject.org/1893/4/mohandes-gandhi-travels-to-south-africa-to-work-under-a-year-long-contract-with-dada-abdulla-co-an-indian-firm.

8. Louis Fischer, *Gandhi: His Life and Message for the World* (New York: Mentor Books, 1954), 43. As a pious Hindu, Gandhi believed in the myriad myths of Hinduism, including the one that bathing in the Ganges, consecrated by Lord Shiva, washed away all sin.

9. This episode was presented as a powerful flashback in the 1983 Academy Award–winning biopic *Gandhi*, directed by Sir Richard Attenborough. Today a bronze statue of the semi-clad Mahatma Gandhi, with his right arm raised in blessing, stands in the city center of Pietermaritzburg.

10. Fischer, *Gandhi*, 25.

11. Cited in ibid., 28.

12. "Bambatha Rebellion 1906," South African History Online, n.d., http://www.sahistory.org.za /topic/bambatha-rebellion-1906.

13. Sanskrit: steadying.

14. Fischer, *Gandhi*, 41.

15. After failing to get Africans to work in mines or on sugar or cotton plantations, British owners used Indian agents in southern India to recruit rural, lower-caste, Hindu landless laborers on a small, fixed wage for a five-year contract. The agreement included an option for a further five years' employment for the indentured laborer before being repatriated at the employer's expense. The Indian government outlawed the indentured laborer contracts in 1916.

16. Sushila Nayar, *Mahatma Gandhi, Satyagraha at Work* (Ahmedabad: Navajivan, 1989), 678–679, 684.

17. Cited in Singh, *Jinnah*, 604.

18. Fischer, *Gandhi*, 60.

19. Barbara Crossette, "Pakistan's Father: What Mohammed Ali Jinnah Accomplished, and What Might Have Been Had He Lived Longer," *New York Times*, December 14, 1997.

20. Cited in Fischer, *Gandhi*, 80.

21. Motihari has the distinction of being the birthplace of Eric Arthur Blair, who acquired the pen name of George Orwell in 1933.

22. Rajendar Prasad, *Satyagraha in Champaran* (Ahmedabad: Navajivan, 1949), 115–116.

23. Fischer, *Gandhi*, 59.

24. Ashish Vashi, "Gandhi-Jinnah, Hindu-Muslim: Godhra Created Many Rifts," *Daily Bhaskar*, February 18, 2012.

25. Gail Minault, *The Khilafat Movement: Religious Symbolism and Political Mobilization in India* (New York: Columbia University Press, 1982), 57.

26. Singh, *Jinnah*, 96.

27. Stanley Wolpert, *Jinnah of Pakistan* (New Delhi: Oxford University Press, 1985), 40.

28. Kathryn Tidrick, *Gandhi: A Political and Spiritual Life* (London: I. B. Tauris, 2006), 122–124.

29. Mani Bhavan, "Chronology/Time Line, 1915–1932," 2004, http://www.gandhi-manibhavan .org/aboutgandhi/chrono_detailedchronology_1915_1932.htm.

30. Perry Anderson, "Gandhi Centre Stage," *London Review of Books*, July 5, 2012, 3–11.

31. Singh, *Jinnah*, 106.

32. Though Brigadier General Reginald Dyer was relieved of his command and shipped to Britain on sick leave, he was never disciplined. In March 1920 the House of Commons condemned Dyer by 230 votes to 129, but the House of Lords declared by 129 votes to 86 that he had been treated unjustly. He died in 1927. Thirteen years later, Udham Singh, a Sikh resident of Coventry, England, shot dead Sir Michael O'Dwyer, who had described Dyer's massacre as "the correct action," at the Royal Albert Hall, London, and was hanged.

33. Cited in Hiro, *The Timeline History of India*, 251.

34. "Jinnah of Pakistan: Calendar of Events, 1919," Humsafar.info, n.d., http://www.humsafar .info/1919.php.

CHAPTER 2: GANDHI'S ORIGINAL SIN

1. Gail Minault, *The Khilafat Movement: Religious Symbolism and Political Mobilization in India* (New York: Columbia University Press, 1982), 72.

2. Ibid., 56.

3. Ibid., 76.

4. Cited in Jaswant Singh, *Jinnah: India—Partition—Independence* (New Delhi: Rupa and Company, 2009), 124–125.

5. Sanjeev Nayyar, "Khilafat Movement," March 2001, http://www.esamskriti.com/essay-chapters/Khilafat-Movement-2.aspx.

6. Minault, *The Khilafat Movement*, 77–78.

7. "Jinnah of Pakistan: Calendar of Events, 1919," Humsafar.info, n.d., http://www.humsafar.info/1919.php.

8. Taimoor Gondal, "The Khilafat Movement," CSS Forum, December 16, 2011, http://www.cssforum.com.pk/386748-post13.html.

9. Rajmohan Gandhi, *Gandhi: The Man, His People and the Empire* (London: Haus, 2010), 133.

10. Cited in Louis Fischer, *The Life of Mahatma Gandhi* (London: Granada, 1982), 66–67.

11. Cited by Dilip Hiro, *The Timeline History of India* (New York: Barnes & Noble, 2006), 256.

12. Cited by Perry Anderson, "Gandhi Centre Stage," *London Review of Books*, July 5, 2012, 3–11.

13. "'I regard the Ramayana of Tulasidas as the greatest book in all devotional literature'—Mahatma Gandhi," quoted on National Hindu Students Forum UK, *Sixth Form*, no. 4, December 2010, http://www.nhsf.org.uk/sixth-form/newsletter/issue4.html.

14. See Chapter 1, p. 22.

15. Dr. Yogendra Yadav, "Cows Protection and Mahatma Gandhi," Peace & Collaborative Development Network, July 20, 2012, http://www.internationalpeaceandconflict.org/profiles/blogs/cows-protection-and-mahatma-gandhi, citing Gandhi's speech at the opening ceremony of a cow shelter in Bettiah, North Bihar, on December 8, 1920.

16. Kruthi Gonwar, "Who Gave the Title of Mahatma to Gandhiji?," *New Indian Express*, June 26, 2012.

17. Francis Robinson, *Separatism Among Indian Muslims: The Politics of the United Provinces* (Cambridge: Cambridge University Press, 2007), 314.

18. Ibid., 317.

19. Cited by Anderson, "Gandhi Centre Stage."

20. Robinson, *Separatism*, 318.

21. "The Khilafat Movement (1919–1924)," Quaid-e-Azam Mohmmad Ali Jinnah (blog), 2008, http://m-a-jinnah.blogspot.co.uk/2010/04/khilafat-movement-1919-1924.html.

22. Ibid.

23. Ibid.

24. Fischer, *Life of Mahatma Gandhi*, 72.

25. Cited in Singh, *Jinnah*, 124.

26. Evelyn Roy, "The Crisis in Indian Nationalism," *Labour Monthly* (London), February 1922.

27. "Non-Cooperation Movement 1920," *General Knowledge Today*, October 25, 2011.

28. Roy, "The Crisis in Indian Nationalism."

29. Ibid.

30. Equally, despite calls from many to refer to Muhammad Ali Jauhar as "Maulana," he refused. Rajmohan Gandhi, *Understanding the Muslim Mind* (New Delhi: Penguin Books, 2000), 135.

31. Akhila Mol, "Biography of Madan Mohan Malviya," *Preserve Articles*, n.d., http://www.preservearticles.com/201103034355/biography-of-madan-mohan-malviya.html.

32. Cited in Hiro, *The Timeline History of India*, 255.

33. Cited in Fischer, *Life of Mahatma Gandhi*, 252–253.

34. Vinay Lal, "'Hey Ram': The Politics of Gandhi's Last Words," *Humanscape* 8, no. 1 (January 2001), citing Mohandas Gandhi, *Autobiography or the Story of My Experiments with Truth* (Ahmedabad: Navajivan, 1940 [1927]), 371.

35. Cited by Anderson, "Gandhi Centre Stage."

36. "The Mind of Mahatma Gandhi," *Young India*, April 3, 1924, 114.

37. Cited by Anderson, "Gandhi Centre Stage."

38. Louis Fischer, *Gandhi: His Life and Message for the World* (New York: Mentor Books, 1954), 72.

39. "Madan Mohan Malaviya: Gaya Presidential Address Hindu Mahasabha 1923," http://14.139.41.16/mahamana/images/stories/gaya.pdf.

40. Ibid.

41. Cited by Fischer, *Gandhi*, 78. Gandhi had made this argument as early as October 1917 in a speech on cow protection in Bettiah, North Bihar. See Yadav, "Cows Protection and Mahatma Gandhi."

42. Cited in Fischer, *Gandhi*, 75.

43. Purist Hindus call Hinduism *Santan Dharma*, Eternal Law.

44. Singh, *Jinnah*, 119.

45. Fischer, *Gandhi*, 79.

46. Cited in Yadav, "Cows Protection and Mahatma Gandhi."

47. Singh, *Jinnah*, 120.

48. Cited in Gandhi, *Understanding the Muslim Mind*, 137.

49. Cited by Hiro, *The Timeline History of India*, 257.

50. Jamil-ud-din Ahmad, *Middle Phase of the Muslim Political Movement* (Lahore: Publishers United, 1969), 138–139.

51. Hector Bolitho, *Jinnah: Creator of Pakistan* (Westport, CT: Greenwood, 1982), 94–95.

52. Cited in Fischer, *Gandhi*, 94.

53. Though fifteen in number these were later presented as Jinnah's Fourteen Points to chime with the Fourteen Point declaration of US president Woodrow Wilson.

54. Stanley Wolpert, *Jinnah of Pakistan* (New Delhi: Oxford University Press, 1985), 96–105.

55. Cited in Fischer, *Gandhi*, 95.

56. Other members of the delegation included Motilal Nehru, Vithalbhai Patel (Speaker of the Central Legislative Assembly), and Sir Tej Bahadur Sapru, a leading constitutional lawyer.

57. Hiro, *The Timeline History of India*, 258.

58. Cited in Fischer, *Gandhi*, 96.

59. National Gandhi Museum, "Salt Satyagraha and Dandi March," n.d., http://www.mkgandhi.org/articles/salt_satya.htm.

60. Webb Miller, *I Found No Peace: The Journal of a Foreign Correspondent* (New York: Simon & Schuster, 1936), 193–195, 446–447.

61. Ibid., 198–199.

62. William Roger Louis, *Adventures with Britannia: Personalities, Politics, and Culture in Britain* (London: I. B. Tauris, 1997), 154.

63. Fischer, *Gandhi*, 100; Hiro, *The Timeline History of India*, 257.

CHAPTER 3: THE TWO-NATION THEORY

1. Cited in Stanley Walport, *Jinnah of Pakistan* (New Delhi: Oxford University Press, 1985), 122.

2. Cited in Dilip Hiro, *The Timeline History of India* (New York: Barnes & Noble, 2006), 258.

3. Jaswant Singh, *Jinnah: India—Partition—Independence* (New Delhi: Rupa and Company, 2009), 182.

4. "Gandhi—A Pictorial Biography: Gandhi-Irwin Pact," Mahatma Gandhi Website, n.d., http://www.mkgandhi.org/biography/gndirwin.htm.

5. Louis Fischer, *The Life of Mahatma Gandhi* (London: Granada, 1982), 358–359.

6. Sankar Ghose, *Mahatma Gandhi* (New Delhi: Allied, 1991), 206.

7. Louis Fischer, *Gandhi: His Life and Message for the World* (New York: Mentor Books, 1954), 151.

8. Ghose, *Gandhi*, 208.

9. Joya Chatterji, *Bengal Divided: Hindu Communalism and Partition, 1932–1947* (Cambridge: Cambridge University Press, 2002), 20.

10. "Jinnah of Pakistan, Calendar of Events, 1935," Humsafar.info, n.d., http://www.humsafar.info/1935.php.

11. Complete text at http://www.mediamonitors.net/noworNever.html or http://en.wikisource.org/wiki/Now_or_Never;_Are_We_to_Live_or_Perish_Forever%3F.

12. Khursheed Kamal Aziz, *Rahmat Ali: A Biography* (Lahore: Vanguard, 1987), 85.

13. Jamil-ud-din Ahmad, ed., *Some Recent Speeches and Writings of Mr. Jinnah*, vol. 1 (Lahore: Ashraf, 1952), 555–557.

14. "Gandhi Gives Notice of 21 Days' Fast," *Barrier Miner* (New South Wales, Australia), May 2, 1933, http://trove.nla.gov.au/ndp/del/article/48429154.

15. "Central Legislative Assembly Etectorate [*sic*]," November 10, 1942, Commons and Lords Hansard: Official Report of Debates at Parliament, http://hansard.millbanksystems.com/written _answers/1942/nov/10/central-legislative-assembly-etectorate.

16. Rajmohan Gandhi, *Understanding the Muslim Mind* (New Delhi: Penguin Books, 2000), 143.

17. For several reasons, elections to the proposed Federal Legislative Assembly and Council of State were not held.

18. Cited in "Presidential Address by Muhammad Ali Jinnah to the Muslim League, Lucknow, October 1937," http://www.columbia.edu/itc/mealac/pritchett/00islamlinks/txt_jinnah_lucknow_1937 .html.

19. See Joseph E. Schwartzberg, ed., *A Historical Atlas of South Asia* (Minneapolis: University of Minnesota Press, 1978), 222, reprinted at http://dsal.uchicago.edu/reference/schwartzberg/pager .html?object=260&view=text.

20. Sir Edward Blunt, "Indian Elections: Congress Policy," *Spectator* (London), February 26, 1937.

21. The actual figures were: Bihar 91/152, Bombay 88/175, Central Provinces 71/112, Madres 159/215, Orissa 36/60, and United Provinces 134/228.

22. See Fischer, *Life of Mahatma Gandhi*, 428, and "From a Letter of Jawaharlal Nehru to M. A. Jinnah (6 April 1938)," Nehru-Jinnah Correspondence, Office of the General Secretary of the Indian National Congress, 1938, http://cw.routledge.com/textbooks/9780415485432/43.asp.

23. B. R. Nanda, "The Ghost of a Missed Chance," *Outlook*, January 24, 1996.

24. Riaz Hussein, "Revival of Punjab Muslim League: Jinnah-Iqbal Collaboration," *Iqbal Review* 28, no. 3 (October 1987).

25. Cited in Singh, *Jinnah*, 250.

26. Perry Anderson, "Gandhi Centre Stage," *London Review of Books*, July 5, 2012, 3–11.

27. Singh, *Jinnah*, 232.

28. Cited in Penderel Moon, *Divide and Quit* (Berkeley: University of California Press, 1962), 16.

29. Cited in Singh, *Jinnah*, 248.

30. Muhammad Ali Jinnah, presidential address to the Muslim League, Lucknow, October 1937, http://www.columbia.edu/itc/mealac/pritchett/00islamlinks/txt_jinnah_lucknow_1937.html.

31. K. Datta and A. Robinson, eds., *Selected Letters of Rabindranath Tagore* (Cambridge: Cambridge University Press, 1995), Letter 314.

32. "From a Letter of Jawaharlal Nehru to M. A. Jinnah (6 April 1938)." These stanzas are:

> Mother, I salute thee!
> Rich with thy hurrying streams,
> bright with orchard gleams,
> Cool with thy winds of delight,
> Dark fields waving Mother of might,
> Mother free.
> Glory of moonlight dreams,
> Over thy branches and lordly streams,
> Clad in thy blossoming trees,
> Mother, giver of ease
> Laughing low and sweet!
> Mother I kiss thy feet,
> Speaker sweet and low!
> Mother, to thee I salute.
> Who hath said thou art weak in thy lands
> When the sword flesh out in the seventy million hands
> And seventy million voices roar
> Thy dreadful name from shore to shore?
> With many strengths who art mighty and stored,

To thee I call Mother and Lord!
Though who savest, arise and save!
To her I cry who ever her foeman drove
Back from plain and sea
And shook herself free.

33. Azad, meaning "free" in Urdu and Hindi, was Maulana Abul Kalam Muhiyuddin Ahmed's pen name.

34. Cited in Hiro, *The Timeline History of India*, 261.

35. Quaid-i-Azam Muhammad Ali Jinnah, address to Lahore Session of Muslim League, March 1940, Ministry of Information and Broadcasting, Government of Pakistan, Islamabad, 1983, http://www .columbia.edu/itc/mealac/pritchett/00islamlinks/txt_jinnah_lahore_1940.html.

36. Cited in Fischer, *Gandhi*, 79.

37. Jaswant Singh, *Jinnah*, 287–288.

38. Warren Kimball, ed., *Churchill and Roosevelt: Complete Correspondence*, vol. 1 (Princeton, NJ: Princeton University Press, 1984), 374.

39. Patrick French, *Liberty or Death: India's Journey to Independence and Division* (London: Harper-Collins, 1997), 138.

40. Cited in Alan Hayes Marriam, *Gandhi vs. Jinnah: The Debate over the Partition of India* (Calcutta: Minerva Associates, 1980 / Thousand Oaks, CA: Sage, 1982), 81.

41. Cited in ibid., 80–81.

42. Hiro, *The Timeline History of India*, 286.

43. *Quit India, 30 April–21 September 1942*, vol. 2 in *Constitutional Relations Between Britain and India: The Transfer of Power 1942–7*, ed. Nicholas Mansergh (London: HMSO, 1970–1983), 853.

44. Cited in Fischer, *Gandhi*, 135.

45. Gandhi, *Understanding the Muslim Mind*, 159.

46. Hector Bolitho, *Jinnah: Creator of Pakistan* (Westport, CT: Greenwood, 1982), 146, 147.

47. "India: Simla Conference," *Time*, July 9, 1945.

48. In reply to a letter from Maulana Azad, recently elected president of the Congress Party, which asked for his cooperation in pressing for an expanded central cabinet, Jinnah had sent a telegram on July 12, 1940: "I refuse to discuss with you in correspondence or otherwise. Can't you realize you are made a Muslim 'show boy' Congress President? If you have self-respect, resign at once" (cited in Gandhi, *Understanding the Muslim Mind*, 155).

CHAPTER 4: A RISING TIDE OF VIOLENCE

1. Patrick French, *Liberty or Death: India's Journey to Independence and Division* (London: Harper-Collins, 1997), 210, citing *The Post-War Phase: New Moves by the Labour Government, 1 August 1945–22 March 1946*, vol. 6 in *Constitutional Relations Between Britain and India: The Transfer of Power 1942–7*, ed. Nicholas Mansergh (London: HMSO, 1970–1983), 279–280.

2. Cited in Mohandas K. Gandhi, *The Collected Works of Mahatma Gandhi* (New Delhi: Publications Division, Ministry of Information and Broadcasting, Government of India, 1972–1978), vol. 83, 135.

3. "1946: Naval Ratings Mutiny Shakes the British: Mutiny Suppressed," *Sainik Samachar*, January 2009, http://sainiksamachar.nic.in/englisharchives/2009/jan15-09/h25.html.

4. Ibid.

5. Dhananjaya Bhat, "RIN Mutiny Gave a Jolt to the British," *Sunday Tribune* (Delhi), February 12, 2006.

6. Arun, "Provincial Elections India 1946," Wake Up, Smell the Coffee (blog), January 27, 2011, http://observingliberalpakistan.blogspot.co.uk/2011/01/provincial-elections-india-1946.html.

7. Hamadani, "Muslim League 100 Years Old: 1945–1946 Elections," Naseeb.com, January 1, 2007, http://www.naseeb.com/journals/muslim-league-100-years-old-1945-1946-elections-135962.

8. Allen Hayes Merriam, *Gandhi vs Jinnah: The Debate over the Partition of India* (Calcutta: Minerva Associates, 1980 / Thousand Oaks, CA: Sage, 1982), 91–92.

9. Naseer Ahmad Faruqui, "Recollections of Maulana Muhammad Ali: Memories of My Beloved," 1962 (revised 2011), http://www.ahmadiyya.org/books/m-kabir/mjk4-4.htm.

10. Rajmohan Gandhi, *Understanding the Muslim Mind* (New Delhi: Penguin Books, 2000), 165.

11. "Parliament of India: Some Facts of Constituent Assembly," n.d., http://parliamentofindia.nic .in/ls/debates/facts.htm; "First Constituent Assembly of Pakistan (1947–1954)," HistoryPak.com, August 8, 2012, http://historypak.com/first-constituent-assembly-of-pakistan-1947-1954.

12. Cited in Louis Fischer, *Gandhi: His Life and Message for the World* (New York: Mentor Books, 1954), 157.

13. Cited in ibid., 157–158.

14. Gandhi, *Understanding the Muslim Mind*, 166.

15. Ibid., 170, citing Jamil-ud-din Ahmad, *Creation of Pakistan* (Lahore: Publishers United, 1976), 278.

16. Gandhi, *Understanding the Muslim Mind*, 170.

17. Louis Fischer, *The Life of Mahatma Gandhi* (London: Granada, 1982), 538.

18. Ibid., 542–544.

19. Claude Markovits, "The Calcutta Riots of 1946," *Online Encyclopedia of Mass Violence*, July 24, 2008, http://www.massviolence.org/The-Calcutta-Riots-of-1946?artpage=2-5.

20. Gandhi, *Understanding the Muslim Mind*, 170, citing Durga Das, ed., *Sardar Patel's Correspondence* (Ahmedabad: Navajivan, n.d.), vol. 3, 40.

21. The cabinet ministers were Jawaharlal Nehru, Vallabhbhai Patel, Rajendra Prasad, Chakravarti Rajagopalachari, Asaf Ali, Sarat Chandra Bose, John Matthai, Baldev Singh (a Sikh), Sir Shafaat Ahmad Khan, Jagjivan Ram, Ali Zaheer, and Cooverji Hormuji Bhabha (a Parsi).

22. Dennis Kux, *India and the United States: Estranged Democracies, 1941–1991* (Washington, DC: National Defense University Press, 1992), 50.

23. Gandhi, *Understanding the Muslim Mind*, 171, citing Ahmad Jamil-ud-din, ed., *Historical Documents of the Muslim Freedom Movement* (Lahore: Publishers United, 1973), 545–546.

24. Fischer, *Gandhi*, 164.

25. Ibid., 163; Ian Stephens, *Pakistan* (New York: Praeger, 1963), 111.

26. Cited in Kenton J. Clymer, *Quest for Freedom: The United States and India's Independence* (New York: Columbia University Press, 1995), 266.

27. Cited in French, *Liberty or Death*, 270.

28. Papiya Ghosh, *Partition and the South Asian Diaspora: Extending the Subcontinent* (London: Routledge, 2007), 3.

29. Fischer, *The Life of Mahatma Gandhi*, 569.

30. Fischer, *Gandhi*, 167.

31. Wasio Abbasi, "Chronicles of Pakistan: Sindh's Ethnic Divide and Its History—Part 1," Reason Before Passion (blog), October 12, 2012, http://wasioabbasi.wordpress.com/2012/10/12/chronicles -of-pakistan-sindhs-ethnic-divide-and-its-history-part-1.

32. Clymer, *Quest for Freedom*, 266.

33. In 1943 Mridula Gandhi, born in 1929, was invited from Karachi—where her widowed father, Jaisukhlal, a nephew of the Mahatma, worked for a shipping company—to Pune to look after the ailing Kasturbai Gandhi in jail. After Kasturbai's death she returned to her parental home.

34. Cited by Jad Adams, "Thrill of the Chaste: The Truth About Gandhi's Sex Life," *Independent* (London), April 7, 2010.

35. Uday Mahurkar, "Mahatma & Manuben," *India Today*, June 7, 2013.

36. Cited by Adams, "Thrill of the Chaste."

37. Rajmohan Gandhi, *Gandhi: The Man, His People, and the Empire* (Berkeley: University of California Press / London: Haus, 2010), 552.

CHAPTER 5: BORN IN BLOOD

1. Jinnah demanded that imperial Britain dissolve the unitary system in India; and create Pakistan, composed of the Muslim-majority provinces in the northwest and the northeast, and Hindustan, as

separate dominions within the British Commonwealth; and then leave it to them to form a confederation on an equal basis or sign a treaty as sovereign states. But his time frame of ten years proved unrealistic when the British government decided to withdraw from India by June 1948.

2. Penderel Moon, ed., *Wavell: The Viceroy's Journal* (New York: Oxford University Press, 1997), 406.

3. Patrick French, *Liberty or Death: India's Journey to Independence and Division* (London: Harper-Collins, 1997), 334, citing *The Mountbatten Viceroyalty, Princes, Partition, and Independence, 8 July–15 August 1947*, vol. 12 in *Constitutional Relations Between Britain and India: The Transfer of Power 1942–7*, ed. Nicholas Mansergh (London: HMSO, 1970–1983), 214.

4. "Note by Sir E. Jenkins," April 16, 1947, https://sites.google.com/site/cabinetmissionplan/punjab-february---march-1947.

5. General Sir Frank Messervy, "Some Remarks on the Disturbances in the Northern Punjab," in *The Fixing of a Time Limit, 4 November 1946–22 March 1947*, vol. 9 in Mansergh, ed., *Constitutional Relations Between Britain and India*, 898–899.

6. Cited in Ayesha Jalal, *The Sole Spokesman: Jinnah, the Muslim League and the Demand for Pakistan* (Cambridge: Cambridge University Press, 1994), 245–246n1.

7. Louis Fischer, *The Life of Mahatma Gandhi* (London: Granada, 1982), 577.

8. Cited in Louis Fischer, *Gandhi: His Life and Message for the World* (New York: Mentor Books, 1954), 171.

9. Fischer, *Gandhi*, 173.

10. French, *Liberty or Death*, 302.

11. Cited in Fischer, *Gandhi*, 170.

12. Ian A. Talbot, "Jinnah and the Making of Pakistan," *History Today* 34, no. 2 (1984).

13. Transcript of Muhammad Ali Jinnah's speech of June 3, 1947, released by All India Radio, Delhi, http://omarrquraishi.blogspot.co.uk/2013/09/transcript-of-mohammad-ali-jinnahs.html.

14. "The Plan of June 3, 1947," Quaid-e-Azam Mohammad Ali Jinnah (blog), 2008, http://m-a-jinnah.blogspot.co.uk/2010/04/plan-of-june-3-1947.html.

15. Alex von Tunzelmann, *Indian Summer: The Secret History of the End of an Empire* (London: Simon & Schuster, 2008), 203.

16. Cited by French, *Liberty or Death*, 306.

17. "Sylhet Referendum 1947," *Banglapedia: National Encyclopedia of Bangladesh*, 2012, http://www.banglapedia.org/HT/S_0653.htm.

18. Muhammad Iqbal Chawla, "Mountbatten and the NWFP Referendum: Revisited," *Journal of the Research Society of Pakistan* 48, no. 1 (2011).

19. The Congress-dominated cabinet decided to retain the name India, discarding the option of Hindustan as a counterpoint to Pakistan.

20. *The Mountbatten Viceroyalty, Princes, Partition, and Independence*, 512.

21. By June 1947, the British troops in India numbered only four thousand.

22. Cited in Rajmohan Gandhi, *Understanding the Muslim Mind* (New Delhi: Penguin Books, 2000), 175.

23. A. Read and D. Fisher, *The Proudest Day: India's Long Road to Independence* (New York: W. W. Norton, 1997), 490.

24. *The Mountbatten Viceroyalty, Princes, Partition, and Independence*, 475, 709.

25. "Mr. Jinnah's Presidential Address to the Constituent Assembly of Pakistan, August 11, 1947," http://www.pakistani.org/pakistan/legislation/constituent_address_11aug1947.html.

26. Lionel Baixas, "Thematic Chronology of Mass Violence in Pakistan, 1947–2007: Mass Violence Related to the State's Formation," *Online Encyclopedia of Mass Violence*, June 27, 2008, http://www.massviolence.org/Thematic-Chronology-of-Mass-Violence-in-Pakistan-1947-2007.

27. M. J. Akbar, *India: The Siege Within* (Harmondsworth, UK: Penguin Books, 1985), 146.

28. "On This Day: India Gains Independence from Britain," *Finding Dulcinea*, August 15, 2011, http://www.findingdulcinea.com/news/on-this-day/July-August-08/On-this-Day--India-Gains-Independence-from-Britain.html.

29. Von Tunzelmann, *Indian Summer*, 236.

30. Baixas, "Mass Violence Related to the State's Formation."

31. But it was only in 1998 that *Train to Pakistan* was made into a movie.

32. Ramchandra Guha, *India After Gandhi: The History of the World's Largest Democracy* (London: Macmillan, 2007 / New York: Harper Perennial, 2008), 15n19.

33. Cited in by Z. H. Zaidi, ed., *Quaid-i-Azam Mohammad Ali Jinnah Papers: Volume I* (New York: Oxford University Press, 1994), 459.

34. *Times of India*, September 10, 1947.

35. The figure of 330,000 comprised 90 percent of the Muslim residents of New Delhi and 60 percent of Old Delhi's.

36. Sunil Khilnani, *The Idea of India* (London: Penguin Books / New York: Farrar, Straus and Giroux, 1998), 31.

37. Cited in von Tunzelmann, *Indian Summer*, 280.

38. Sankar Ghose, *Jawaharlal Nehru: A Biography* (Bombay: Allied, 1993), 170–171.

39. Ghose, *Jawaharlal Nehru*, 170–171.

40. Alan Campbell-Johnson, *Mission with Mountbatten* (London: Robert Hale, 1951), 200–201.

41. Cited in by Zaidi, *Quaid-i-Azam*, 476.

42. Col. Dr. Dalvinder Singh Grewal, "The Making of Refugees," SikhNet, February 28, 2013, http://www.sikhnet.com/news/making-refugees.

43. Cited in Guha, *India After Gandhi*, 15.

44. Kuldip Nayar, *Beyond the Lines: An Autobiography* (New Delhi: Roli Books, 2012), 10.

45. Martin Frost, "Frost's Meditations: Partition of India," August 2007, http://www.essaysyards.blogspot.com/2011/06/frosts-meditations.html.

46. Richard Symonds, *In the Margins of Independence: A Relief Worker in India and Pakistan, 1942–1947* (Karachi: Oxford University Press, 2001), 116.

47. Von Tunzelmann, *Indian Summer*, 279.

48. Ibid., 280.

CHAPTER 6: THE INFANT TWINS AT WAR

1. Z. G. Muhammad, "Stories Retold: Of Some Historical Narratives About Kashmir," *Punchline*, March 11, 2013, http://www.greaterkashmir.com/news/2013/Mar/11/stories-retold-27.asp.

2. The year 1934 saw the launching of the first English-language weekly, the *Kashmir Times*, a decade after the founding of the Hindi newspaper *Ranbir* in Jammu.

3. In his autobiography, Shaikh Muhammad Abdullah revealed that his grandfather was a Hindu named Ragho Ram Kaul.

4. Soon after, the Congress Party set up the All India States People's Conference to agitate for democratic representation in the princely states.

5. Victoria Schofield, *Kashmir in Conflict: India, Pakistan and the Unending War*, rev. ed. (London: I. B. Tauris, 2003), 41.

6. Jagmohan, *My Frozen Turbulence in Kashmir*, 8th ed. (New Delhi: Allied, 2007), 78.

7. Alarmed by the rising protest against his regime, the maharaja refrained from integrating soldiers demobilized after World War II into his army.

8. Jagmohan, *My Frozen Turbulence in Kashmir*, 78.

9. Christopher Snedden, "The Forgotten Poonch Uprising of 1947," *Eye on Kashmir* 643 (March 2013), http://www.india-seminar.com/2013/643/643_christopher_snedden.htm.

10. Ian Stephens, *Pakistan* (London: Ernest Benn, 1963), 200.

11. Cited in "Tribal Invasion: An American Reportage," *Kashmir Sentinel*, 2012, http://kashmirsentinel.org/tribal-invasion-an-american-reportage.

12. Cited in Schofield, *Kashmir in Conflict*, 43.

13. Snedden, "The Forgotten Poonch Uprising."

14. Schofield, *Kashmir in Conflict*, 46.

15. Schofield, *Kashmir in Conflict*, 46, citing *Quaid-i-Azam Mohammad Ali Jinnah: Speeches and Statements, 1947–1948* (Karachi: Government of Pakistan, 1989), 91–92.

16. Alex Von Tunzelmann, *Indian Summer: The Secret History of the End of an Empire* (London: Simon & Schuster, 2008), 288.

17. Chaudhuri Muhammad Ali, *The Emergence of Pakistan* (New York: Columbia University Press, 1967), 292.

18. Cited in Khalid Hasan, "The Other Khurshid Anwar," *Friday Times* (Lahore), February 11, 2005.

19. "27 October 1947," Truth by KBaig (blog), October 26, 2013, http://www.truthbykbaig.com /2013/10/27-october-1947-day-when-indian-forces.html.

20. J. C. Aggarwal and S. Agrawal, *Modern History of Jammu and Kashmir: Ancient Times to Shimla Agreement* (New Delhi: Concept, 1995), 41–43.

21. India's commander in chief, General Sir Robert Lockhart, was also subordinate to Field Marshall Sir Claude Achinleck.

22. Cited in "Tribal Invasion."

23. "Chapter VI: Pacific Settlement of Disputes," Charter of the United Nations, http://www .un.org/en/documents/charter/chapter6.shtml.

24. Dr. Justice Adrarsh Sein Anand, "Accession of Kashmir—Historical & Legal Perspective," *Supreme Court Cases* 4, no. 11 (1996), http://www.ebc-india.com/lawyer/articles/96v4a2.htm.

25. John Connell, *Auchinleck: A Critical Biography: A Biography of Field-Marshal Sir Claude Auchinleck*, 2nd ed. (London: Cassell, 1959), 920.

26. See Chapter 5, p. 110.

27. Prof. Dr. Yogendra Yadav, "The Facts of Rs 55 Crores and Mahatma Gandhi," Peace & Collaborative Development Network, September 16, 2012, http://www.internationalpeaceandconflict.org /profiles/blogs/the-facts-of-55-crores-and-mahatma-gandhi.

28. Dilip Simeon, "Gandhi's Final Fast," Akshay Bakaya's Blog, March 22, 2010, http://www.gandhi topia.org/profiles/blogs/gandhis-final-fast-by-dilip.

29. Ibid.

30. Ibid.

31. Because the Indian government made its decision during Mahatma Gandhi's fast, some historians have wrongly attributed his fasting to the issue of the cash payable to Pakistan.

32. "Gandhi Shot Dead," *Hindu*, January 31, 1948.

33. Nathuram Vinayak Godse was convicted as the killer of Mahatma Gandhi and his chief coplotter, Narayan Dattatraya Apte, as the leader of the assassination team. Both received the death penalty and were hanged at the central jail in Ambala, East Punjab, on November 15, 1949.

34. Responding to the reports of the RSS killing Muslims, Vallabhbhai Patel expressed his favorable opinion of the RSS on January 8 and added, "You cannot crush an organization by using *danda* [a stick]." He considered the reports of its violent activities as "somewhat exaggerated." Patrick French, *Liberty or Death: India's Journey to Independence and Division* (London: HarperCollins, 1997), 359–360.

35. See Chapter 1, p. 11.

36. "Quaid-i-Azam Corner, Jinnah's Condolence Message on the Death of Gandhi," *Republic of Rumi*, January 30, 1948, http://pakistanspace.tripod.com/archives/jinnah19480130.htm.

37. "Jinnah's Speech to Sind Bar Association, Karachi," *Dawn* (Karachi), January 26, 1948.

38. Jinnah of Pakistan, "Speeches & Statements: Selfless Devotion to Duty," Humsafar.info, n.d., http://www.humsafar.info/480221_sel.php.

39. Muhammad Ali Chaudhri, *The Emergence of Pakistan* (New York: Columbia University Press, 1967), 297.

40. By early April 1948 India had transferred only one-sixth of the share Pakistan was entitled to. It failed to deliver any of the 249 tanks allocated to Pakistan. Pervaiz Iqbal Cheema, *The Armed Forces of Pakistan* (New York: New York University Press, 2001), 18.

41. "Resolution 47 (1948)," https://www.mtholyoke.edu/acad/intrel/kashun47.htm.

42. Cited in Stanley Wolpert, *Jinnah of Pakistan* (New Delhi: Oxford University Press, 1985), 361.

43. Hector Bolitho, *Jinnah: Creator of Pakistan* (Westport, CT: Greenwood, 1981), 223.

44. Jaswant Singh, *Jinnah: India—Partition—Independence* (New Delhi: Rupa and Company, 2009), 470–474, summarizing Dr. Illahi Bux's description in his book *With Quaid-i-Azam During His Last Days*.

45. Cited in ibid., 476.

CHAPTER 7: GROWING APART

1. For the text of the story, visit http://www.punjabiportal.com/articles/punjabi-short-stories-saadat -hassan-manto. On the fiftieth anniversary of the death of Saadat Hassan Manto, an eighteen-minute film titled *Toba Tek Singh*, directed by Afia Nathaniel, was shown at the New York Asian American International film festival 2005.

2. "The Prime Minister of India, Pandit Jawaharlal Nehru Addressed a House Reception, October 13, 1949," US House of Representatives, http://history.house.gov/HistoricalHighlight/Detail/36630 ?ret=True.

3. "Liaquat Ali Khan Goes to the US (1950)," *Friday Times* (Lahore), September 30–October 6, 2011.

4. "Resignation Letter of Jogendra Nath Mandal, 8 October 1950," http://en.wikisource.org/wiki /Resignation_letter_of_Jogendra_Nath_Mandal.

5. Ibid.

6. Tridib Santapa Kundu, "The Partition and the Muslim Minorities of West Bengal, 1947–1967," Partition Studies (blog), August 23, 2009, http://bengalpartitionstudies.blogspot.co.uk/2009/08/partition -and-muslim-minorities-of-west.html.

7. Though Indo-Pakistan trade resumed in 1951, both the volume and the value of bilateral commerce declined steadily, with the two neighbors expanding the new foreign commercial ties they had forged.

8. Kundu, "The Partition and the Muslim Minorities of West Bengal."

9. Shahid Saeed, "Murder at Company Bagh," *Friday Times* (Lahore), March 25–31, 2011.

10. "Report of Inquiry Commission on Assassination of Mr. Liaquat Ali Khan," *Keesing's Record of World Events* 8–9 (August 1952): 12426.

11. Valmiki Choudhary, ed., *Dr Rajendra Prasad: Correspondence and Select Documents Vol. 21* (New Delhi: Allied, 1995), 91.

12. Dilip Hiro, *Inside India Today* (London: Routledge and Kegan Paul, 1976 / New York: Monthly Review Press, 1977), 211–212.

13. *US News & World Report*, November 13, 1953, cited by Hamid Hussain, "Tale of a Love Affair That Never Was: United States-Pakistan Defense Relations," *Defence Journal* (June 2002).

14. *Keesing's Contemporary Archives*, Vol. 9: 1952–1954, 13461, cited by Zulfikar Ali Bhutto, *The Myth of Independence* (Oxford: Oxford University Press, 1969), 44–45.

15. *Keesing's Contemporary Archives*, Vol. 9: 1952–1954, 13462, cited by Bhutto, *The Myth of Independence*, 45.

16. Bhutto, *The Myth of Independence*, 44.

17. Dennis Kux, *India and the United States: Estranged Democracies, 1941–1991* (Washington, DC: National Defense University Press, 1992), 124–125.

18. SEATO members were Australia, France, New Zealand, Pakistan, Philippines, Thailand, United Kingdom, and the United States.

19. Claire Provost, "Sixty Years of US Aid to Pakistan: Get the Data," *Guardian* (London), July 11, 2011.

20. "Telegram from the United States Mission at the United Nations to the Department of State," January 10, 1957, *Foreign Relations of the United States, 1955–1957*, Vol. 8: South Asia, Document 40, US Department of State, Office of the Historian, http://history.state.gov/historicaldocuments /frus1955-57v08/d40.

21. In his book *Glimpses* (Lahore: Jang, 1992), Syed Amjad Ali states that H. S. Suhrawardy's personal assistant advised the embassy staff of the prime minister's agreement to the US facility on Pakistan soil.

22. Farooq Hameed Khan, "Badaber to Shamsi," *Nation* (Lahore), July 8, 2011.

23. "Summary of US Aid to Pakistan, 1948–2010," *Guardian* (London), July 11, 2011.

24. Yasmeen Yousif Pardesi, "An Analysis of the Constitutional Crisis in Pakistan (1958–1969)," *Dialogue* 7, no. 4 (October–December 2012).

25. Dilip Hiro, *A Comprehensive Dictionary of the Middle East* (Northampton, MA: Interlink, 2013), 271.

26. Yousaf Saraf, "Bogra-Nehru Accord," Kashmiri Info, October 27, 2006, http://www.kashmiri .info/Kashmir-Fight-for-Freedom-by-Yousaf-Saraf/bogra-nehru-accord.html.

27. Ibid.; "Bogra-Nehru Negotiations," *Story of Pakistan*, June 1, 2003, http://storyofpakistan.com /bogra-nehru-negotiations.

28. S. Gopal, H. Y. Sharada Prasad, and A. K. Damodaran, eds., *Selected Works of Jawaharlal Nehru: Volume 19* (New Delhi: Oxford University Press, 1996), 322. This letter came to light forty-eight years after it was penned.

29. Sumanta Bose, *Kashmir: Roots of Conflict, Paths to Peace* (Cambridge, MA: Harvard University Press, 2005), 72.

30. Arvind Lavakare, "Forgotten Day in Kashmir's History," *Rediff News* (Mumbai), March 8, 2004, citing *Hindu*, February 17, 1954.

31. "Not Even Abdullah," *Spectator* (London), January 17, 1958, 6.

32. Jawaharlal Nehru had first visited the USSR along with his father, Motilal, in 1927, when they attended the tenth anniversary of its founding.

33. Cited in Bose, *Kashmir*, 71.

34. "Telegram from the United States Mission at the United Nations to the Department of State."

35. Article 37, "Chapter VI: Pacific Settlement of Disputes," Charter of the United Nations, http:// legal.un.org/repertory/art37/english/rep_supp2_vol2-art37_e.pdf.

36. *Pakistan's Foreign Policy, 1947–2005: A Concise History* (Karachi: Oxford University Press, 2007), 57.

37. A. G. Noorani, "Planning Foreign Policy," *Dawn* (Karachi), October 3, 2009.

38. Paul M. McGarr, *The Cold War in South Asia: The United States and the Indian Subcontinent, 1945–1965* (New York: Cambridge University Press, 2013), 77–78.

39. Rajeshwar Dayal, *A Life of Our Times* (Delhi: Orient Longman, 1998), 301, 303.

40. A. G. Noorani, "Lessons of Murree," *Frontline* (Chennai), June 19–July 2, 2010.

41. Muhammad Ayub Khan, *Friends Not Masters: A Political Biography* (Berkeley: University of California Press / Karachi: Oxford University Press, 1967), 124–125.

42. Ibid., 126.

CHAPTER 8: NEHRU'S "FORWARD POLICY": A STEP TOO FAR

1. The far more detailed map signed only by Henry McMahon and Lonchen Shatra on March 25, 1914, showed the McMahon Line. On April 28, following the instructions of the Beijing government, Chen Ivan withdrew his initial from the earlier draft of the Simla Convention. Neither draft identified present-day Arunachal Pradesh, previously called North-East Frontier Agency (NEFA), as "British India" or something similar.

2. It was only in October 1951 that the Dalai Lama endorsed the pact.

3. "Major Bob Khathing: A Legend," *Assam Rifles*, February 29, 2012, http://assamrifles.gov.in /news_view.aspx?id=1300; Neville Maxwell, *India's China War* (New York: Pantheon Books, 1970 / Harmondsworth, UK: Penguin Books, 1972), 66.

4. Sir Charles U. Aichison, *A Collection of Treaties, Engagements and Sanads Relating to India and Neighbouring Countries, Volume XII* (New Delhi: Foreign and Political Department of the Government, 1931), 5.

5. Karunakar Gupta, *Spotlight on Sino-Indian Frontiers* (Calcutta: New Book Centre, 1982), 82.

6. Shastri Ramachandran, "Nehru's Stubbornness Led to 1962 War with China?," *Times of India*, December 19, 2010.

7. Cited in A. G. Noorani, "Nehru's China Policy," *Frontline* (Chennai), July 22–August 4, 2000.

8. Dilip Hiro, *Inside India Today* (London: Routledge & Kegan Paul, 1976 / New York: Monthly Review Press, 1977), 248–249.

9. Cited by Noorani, "Nehru's China Policy."

10. Ravinder Kumar and H. Y. Sharada Prasad, eds., *Selected Works of Jawaharlal Nehru*, 2nd series, vol. 26 (New Delhi: Jawaharlal Nehru Memorial Fund, Distributed by Oxford University Press, 2000), 477.

11. Cited by Noorani, "Nehru's China Policy."

12. Cited in Claude Arpi, "Talks Between Mao and Nehru, October 1954," http://www.claudearpi .net/maintenance/uploaded_pics/195410TalksMaoNehru.pdf.

13. B. N. Mullik, *My Years with Nehru: The Chinese Betrayal* (Bombay: Allied, 1971), 183.

14. Cited in M. L. Sali, *India-China Border Dispute: A Case Study of the Eastern Sector* (New Delhi: APH, 1998), 81.

15. A. G. Noorani, "The Truth about 1962," *Hindu*, November 30, 2012.

16. "Dalai Lama Escapes to India," BBC News, March 31, 1959.

17. Cited in Maxwell, *India's China War*, 282.

18. Nehru restrained the Dalai Lama from setting up a government in exile. Kuldip Nayar, *India: The Critical Years* (London: Weidenfeld & Nicolson, 1971), 143.

19. Mark A. Ryan, David M. Finkelstein, and Michael A. McDevitt, *Chinese Warfighting: The PLA Experience Since 1949* (Armonk, NY: M. E. Sharpe, 2003), 177.

20. Cited by Noorani, "Nehru's China Policy."

21. The Indian government went on to name October 21 Police Commemoration Day.

22. Cited by Noorani, "Nehru's China Policy."

23. Ananth Krishnan, "China Files: Crossing the Point of No Return," *Hindu*, October 25, 2012.

24. See Chapter 7, p. 157.

25. *Washington Post*, October 22, 1960, cited in Mike Gravel, *The Pentagon Papers: The Defense Department History of United States Decision-Making on Vietnam*, vol. 2 (Boston: Beacon, 1971), 799.

26. Noorani, "Nehru's China Policy," citing the US Central Intelligence Agency Staff Study for the Department of Defense, "The Sino-India Border Dispute, from 1950 to 1962," May 2007.

27. Cited by Noorani, "Nehru's China Policy."

28. Neville Maxwell, "China's India War: How the Chinese Saw the 1962 Conflict," *East Asia Forum*, August 2, 2011.

29. "Nixon's China Game," PBS, June 26, 1961, http://www.pbs.org/wgbh/amex/china/timeline /timeline4nf.html.

30. Maxwell, "China's India War."

31. Cited by Ye Zhengjia, "Clearing the Atmosphere," *Frontline* (Chennai), October 10–23, 1998, citing Major General Lei Yingfu, *My Days as a Military Staff in the Supreme Command* (in Chinese) (Nanchang: Baihuazhou Culture and Arts, 1997), 210.

32. Nayar, *India*, 172–173.

33. John Kenneth Galbraith, *Ambassador's Journal: A Personal Account of the Kennedy Years* (Boston: Houghton Mifflin, 1969), 388.

34. Ibid., 383.

35. Ibid., 376.

36. Ibid., 387.

37. Jeff M. Smith, "A Forgotten War in the Himalayas," *Yale Global*, September 14, 2012.

38. Maxwell, *India's China War*, 448–449.

39. Cited in Nayar, *India*, 179.

40. See Chapter 7, p. 157.

41. *Haqeeqat* won the National Film Award for the second best feature film in 1965.

42. Cited by Nayar, *India*, 190.

43. A. G. Noorani, "Kashmir Resolution: Never Before So Close," *Daily Times* (Lahore), June 25, 2008.

44. Later the US gave India an $80 million loan to finance the construction of a nuclear power station at Tarapur in Bombay province by American corporations, powered by low-enriched uranium supplied by the US government.

45. Harold Gould, *The South Asia Story: The First Sixty Years of U.S. Relations with India and Pakistan* (New Delhi: Sage, 2010), 64, 68.

46. Praveen Swami, "India's Secret War in Bangladesh," *Hindu*, December 26, 2011.

47. Yousaf Saraf, "Kashmir Fight for Freedom," Kashmiri Info, October 27, 2006, http://www .kashmiri.info/Kashmir-Fight-for-Freedom-by-Yousaf-Saraf/sh-abdullah-in-pakistan.html.

48. Cited by Bal Raj Madhok, *Kashmir: The Storm Center of the World* (Houston: A. Ghosh, 1992), citing *Aatish-e Chinar* (in Urdu) (Srinagar: Ali Muhammad & Sons, 1982).

49. Victoria Schofield, *Kashmir in Conflict: India, Pakistan and the Unending War*, rev. ed. (London: I. B. Tauris, 2003), 106.

50. All that made Jammu and Kashmir different from other states of the Indian Union was its red flag with a plow and three vertical stripes and the ban on non-Kashmiris buying property in the state or settling there.

51. Sheikh Mohammad Abdullah, "Kashmir, India and Pakistan," *Foreign Affairs* (April 1965).

52. India protested to the United States against the use of these US-supplied arms; Washington fired off a protest in turn. But nothing changed.

53. In February 1968, the arbitration committee awarded 10 percent of the Rann of Kutch to Pakistan.

54. Cited in G. M. Hiranandani, "Chapter 3: The 1965 Indo Pakistan War," in *Transition to Triumph*, October 15, 1999, http://indiannavy.nic.in/book/1965-indo-pakistan-war.

55. Hiranandani, "The 1965 Indo Pakistan War."

CHAPTER 9: SHASTRI'S TALLEST ORDER: PAKISTAN'S NIGHTMARE COMES ALIVE

1. Gibraltar is the Spanish derivative of the Arabic name Jabal Tariq, meaning "Mountain of Tariq," an Arab general, who captured it in 711. It thus symbolizes the victory of Muslims over nonbelievers.

2. Cited in Mahmood Shaam, "We Won the 1965 War, Not India," *Rediff India Abroad*, September 6, 2005.

3. "Battle of Hajipir Pass 1965," Pakistan Defence, February 27, 2011, http://defence.pk/threads /battle-of-hajipir-pass-1965.95263. To maintain the utmost secrecy, Pakistan's Inter-Services Intelligence Directorate did not take the pro-Pakistan elements in Kashmir into confidence, thus depriving the infiltrators of vital intelligence.

4. Cited in Kuldip Nayar, *India: The Critical Years* (London: Weidenfeld & Nicolson, 1971), 214.

5. Cited in G. M. Hiranandani, "Chapter 3: The 1965 Indo Pakistan War," in *Transition to Triumph*, October 15, 1999, http://indiannavy.nic.in/book/1965-indo-pakistan-war.

6. Cited in ibid., quoting P. V. R. Rao, the defense secretary.

7. A. H. Amin, "Grand Slam—A Battle of Lost Opportunities," *Defence Journal* (Karachi), September 2000.

8. Cited in Chintamani Mahapatra, "American Activism on the Kashmir Question," *Strategic Analysis* 21, no. 7 (October 1997): 987–997.

9. Cited in Nayar, *India*, 218.

10. Cited in Farzana Shaikh, *Making Sense of Pakistan* (London: Hurst & Company, 2009), 160.

11. In any case, the term "international communism" lost its monolithic connotation in 1963, when China started challenging the Soviet occupation of part of its border areas, and the communist neighbors started beefing up their forces in the disputed frontier regions.

12. Shaam, "We Won the 1965 War."

13. Later, September 6 was named Defense Day in Pakistan, when homage is paid to the martyrs of the 1965 conflict at the war memorials built in most cities, with the electronic media airing special programs and newspapers publishing bulky supplements to remember the war dead.

14. Harshvardhan Pande, "The Battle of Asal Uttar—1965," Great Indian War Stories (blog), May 14, 2010, http://greatindianwarstories.blogspot.co.uk/2010/05/battle-of-asal-uttar-1965.html. Thirty-two tanks, including twenty-eight Pattons, were in working condition.

15. Harbakhsh Singh, *In the Line of Duty: A Soldier Remembers* (Delhi: Lancer, 2000), 253.

16. Shaam, "We Won the 1965 War."

17. Nayar, *India*, 237.

18. Ramachandra Guha, *India After Gandhi: The History of the World's Largest Democracy* (London: Macmillan, 2007 / New York: Harper Perennial, 2008), 398.

19. Shaam, "We Won the 1965 War."

20. George Ginsburgs and Robert M. Slusser, eds., *A Calendar of Soviet Treaties: 1958–1973* (Rockville, MD: Sijthoff & Noordhoff, 1981), 319.

21. Of the Security Council's eleven members, only one—Jordan—abstained.

22. Herbert Feldman, *From Crisis to Crisis: Pakistan, 1962–1969* (Karachi: Oxford University Press, 1972), 146.

23. The breakdown of India's gain in Pakistan was the following: the Sailkot sector, 180 square miles; the Lahore sector, 140 square miles; and Sindh, 150 square miles.

24. David Van Praagh, *The Greater Game: India's Race with Destiny and China* (Montreal: McGill-Queen's University Press, 2003), 294.

25. Cited in Adrian Levy and Catherine Scott-Clark, *Deception: Pakistan, the United States and the Secret Trade in Nuclear Weapons* (New York: Walker & Company, 2007), 18.

26. Nayar, *India*, 240.

27. The exchange rate of Rs 5 = US$1 changed to Rs 7.576 = US$1. India's defense spending in 1965–1966 rose sharply, to 24 percent of its total expenditure.

28. Bound by a no-war pact, India might have thought twice before waging a war in East Pakistan in 1971.

29. Katia Zatu Liverter, "Part 1: Russia as Mediator: Imperial and Soviet Times," *RT Comment*, July 15, 2011.

30. Altaf Gauhar, *Ayub Khan, Pakistan's First Military Ruler* (Lahore: Sang-e-Meel Publications, 1993), 386–387.

31. His newly acquired fondness for the Soviet Union led Ayub Khan to ban the showing of the anti-Russian James Bond movie *From Russia with Love*.

32. "Official Text of the Tashkent Declaration 1966," http://www.stimson.org/research-pages/tashkent-declaration.

33. Cited in Lubna Abid Ali, "Towards the Tashkent Declaration," *South Asian Studies* 28, no. 2 (2008).

34. Mohammed Asghar Khan, *The First Round, Indo-Pakistan War 1965* (New Delhi: Vikas, 1979), 120–121.

35. Nayar, *India*, 252.

36. Ibid., 250.

37. Ibid., 254.

38. Kuldip Nayar, "The Night Shastri Died and Other Stories," *Outlook* (Delhi), July 9, 2012.

39. Cited in Abid Ali, "Towards the Tashkent Declaration."

40. Whereas Rawalpindi was the executive capital of Pakistan, Dacca was its legislative capital.

41. Siyasi Mubassir, "Zulfikar Ali Bhutto Revisited Part I (1956–1966)," *Pakistan Link*, February 5, 2005, http://pakistanlink.org/Opinion/2005/Feb05/24/03.htm.

42. A. G. Noorani, "Lyndon Johnson and India," *Frontline* (Chennai), May 12–25, 2001.

43. See Chapter 8, p. 174.

44. B. Raman, *The Kaoboys of R&AW: Down Memory Lane* (New Delhi: Lancer, 2008), 127.

45. Ashok Raina, *Inside RAW: The Story of India's Secret Service* (New Delhi: Vikas, 1981), 53–54.

46. "1970 Polls: When Election Results Created a Storm," *Dawn* (Karachi), January 8, 2012.

47. Cited in Ramchandra Guha, *India After Gandhi: The History of the World's Largest Democracy* (London: Macmillan, 2007), 453, quoting a secret report by RAW in January 1971, entitled "Threat of Military Attack or Infiltration Campaign by Pakistan."

48. Later Yahya Khan would also jail Zulfikar Ali Bhutto after the latter had criticized him for mishandling the situation in East Pakistan.

CHAPTER 10: INDIRA GANDHI SLAYS THE TWO-NATION THEORY

1. Cited in Vivek Guamste, "The Hindu Genocide That Hindus and the World Forgot," *India Tribune*, 2012.

2. Cited in A. G. Noorani, "The Mystique of Archives," *Hindu*, March 1, 2003.

3. Cited in Ramchandra Guha, *India After Gandhi: The History of the World's Largest Democracy* (London: Macmillan, 2007 / New York: Harper Perennial, 2008), 452.

4. A. A. K. Niazi, *Betrayal of East Pakistan* (New Delhi: Manohar Books, 1998), 78.

5. Born to Christian parents in the Western Indian city of Belgaum, Anthony Mascarenhas graduated from St. Patrick's College in Karachi and settled in the city after partition, starting out as a journalist with the state-owned Associated Press of Pakistan.

6. Cited by Mark Dummett, "Bangladesh War: The Article That Changed History," BBC News, December 16, 2011.

7. Dummett, "Bangladesh War." While working for the *Sunday Times* in London, Anthony Mascarenhas published his book *Rape of Bangladesh* in 1972.

8. "Nixon's Dislike of 'Witch' Indira," BBC News, June 29, 2005.

9. "Sino-Soviet Border Clashes," Global Security, n.d., http://www.globalsecurity.org/military /world/war/prc-soviet.htm.

10. Praveen Swami, "India's Secret War in Bangladesh," *Hindu*, December 26, 2011.

11. Indian military trainers set up six camps for recruiting and training volunteers as saboteurs. At one camp, some three thousand young men had to wait up to two months for induction. Claude Arpi, "1971 War: How the US Tried to Corner India," *Rediff India Abroad*, December 26, 2006.

12. Cited in Guha, *India After Gandhi*, 456.

13. By then, the Soviet Union had become India's largest supplier of arms while becoming the biggest single buyer of Indian goods. Dilip Hiro, *Inside India Today* (London: Routledge & Kegan Paul, 1976 / New York: Monthly Review Press, 1977), 251.

14. Cited in ibid., 251.

15. Arpi, "1971 War."

16. Cited in Guha, *India After Gandhi*, 455.

17. "Mukti Bahini," *Banglapedia: National Encyclopedia of Bangladesh*, n.d., http://www.bpedia.org /M_0380.php.

18. Arpi, "1971 War."

19. Noorani, "The Mystique of Archives."

20. Richard Nixon, "Remarks of Welcome to Prime Minister Indira Gandhi of India, November 4, 1971," http://www.presidency.ucsb.edu/ws/?pid=3208.

21. "Nixon's Dislike of 'Witch' Indira."

22. Arpi, "1971 War."

23. Adrian Levy and Catherine Scott-Clark, *Deception: Pakistan, the United States and the Secret Trade in Nuclear Weapons* (New York: Walker & Company, 2007), 61.

24. Praveen Swami, "Fighting Pakistan's 'Informal War,'" *Hindu*, July 15, 2008.

25. Praveen Swami, "India's Secret War in Bangladesh," *Hindu*, December 26, 2011.

26. Sarmila Bose, "The Courageous Pak Army Stand on the Eastern Front," *Mianwali Online*, n.d., http://www.mianwalionline.com/personalities/genniazi/AAKNiazi.shtml#Op-Ed.

27. Blema S. Seinburg, *Women in Power: The Personality and Leadership Style of India Gandhi* (Montreal: McGill-Queen's University Press, 2008), 36.

28. Cited in Noorani, "The Mystique of Archives."

29. Ibid.

30. Anatoly Dobrynin, *In Confidence: Moscow's Ambassador to Six Cold War Presidents* (New York: Crown, 1995), 237.

31. Sajit Gandhi, ed., "The Tilt: The US and the South Asian Crisis of 1971," *National Security Archive Electronic Briefing Book* No. 79, December 16, 2002, http://www2.gwu.edu/~nsarchiv/NSAEBB /NSAEBB79/.

32. Later this became known as the Blood Telegram. It would be used as the title of a book by Gary J. Bass in 2013.

33. Ghazala Akbar, "Why the Seventh Fleet Was Sent to the Indian Ocean in 1971," Pakistan Link, January 2012, http://pakistanlink.org/Commentary/2012/Jan12/20/01.HTM.

34. Swami, "India's Secret War."

35. "Niazi Signed the Instrument of Surrender with General Aurora on December 16, 1971, at Dacca," *Daily Star* (Bangladesh), May 4, 2005.

36. Bose, "The Courageous Pak Army."

37. "The Rediff Interview: Lt Gen A. A. Khan Niazi," *Rediff News* (Mumbai), February 2, 2004.

38. Cited in Tariq Ali, *The Duel: Pakistan on the Flight Path of American Power* (New York: Scribner, 2008), 206.

39. Official websites of the Indian and Pakistani defense ministries are www.mod.nic.in and www.mod.gov.pk, respectively.

40. *The Report of the Hamoodur Rehman Commission of Inquiry into the 1971 War* (Lahore: Vanguard, 2001), 317, 340.

41. David Frost interview with Shaikh Mujibur Rahman aired on January 18, 1972; see http://groups.yahoo.com/neo/groups/mukto-mona/conversations/topics/5108.

42. Richard Sisson and Leo E. Rose, *War and Secession: Pakistan, India, and the Creation of Bangladesh* (Berkeley: University of California Press, 1990), 360n24.

43. Sarmila Bose, *Dead Reckoning: Memories of the 1971 Bangladesh War* (New York: Columbia University Press, 2011), 181.

44. Ziad Obermeyer, Christopher J. L. Murray, and Emmanuela Gakidou, "Fifty Years of Violent War Deaths from Vietnam to Bosnia: Analysis of Data from the World Health Survey Programme," *British Medical Journal*, June 26, 2008.

45. F. B. Ali, "The Coup of 19 December 1971: How General Yahya Was Removed from Power," Pakistan Patriots (blog), June 21, 2013, http://pakistanpatriots.wordpress.com/2013/06/21/the-coup-of-19-december-1971-how-general-yahya-was-removed-from-power/.

46. Syed Badrul Ahsan, "Pakistan in December 1971," *Daily Star* (Bangladesh), December 19, 2012.

47. Tammy Kinsey, "Garam Hawa," *Film Reference*, n.d., http://www.filmreference.com/Films-Fr-Go/Garam-Hawa.html.

CHAPTER 11: ZULFIKAR ALI BHUTTO: THE SAVIOR OF WEST PAKISTAN

1. See p. 196.

2. Syed Badrul Ahsan, "Pakistan in December 1971," *Daily Star* (Bangladesh), December 19, 2012.

3. Adrian Levy and Catherine Scott-Clark, *Deception: Pakistan, the United States and the Secret Trade in Nuclear Weapons* (New York: Walker & Company, 2007), 19–20.

4. "When Benazir Bhutto Enjoyed *Pakeezah* in Shimla," IANS, May 13, 2012, http://www.ummid.com/news/2012/May/13.05.2012/benazir_bhutto_in_shimla.htm.

5. Cited in Victoria Schofield, *Kashmir in Conflict: India, Pakistan and the Unending War*, rev. ed. (London: I. B. Tauris, 2003), 127.

6. Manish Chand, "40 Years Later, Shimla Accord Haunts India-Pakistan Ties," *South Asia Monitor*, July 1, 2012.

7. "Simla Agreement, July 2, 1972," http://www.jammu-kashmir.com/documents/simla.html.

8. Ab Qayoom Khan, "Sheikh Abdullah: A Political Sufferer-II," *Kashmir Observer*, September 10, 2012.

9. Dilip Hiro, *Inside India Today* (London: Routledge & Kegan Paul, 1976 / New York: Monthly Review Press, 1977), 254.

10. Cited in Dorothy Norman, ed., *The First Sixty Years: Presenting in His Own Words the Development of the Political Thought of Jawaharlal Nehru and the Background Against Which It Evolved* (London: Bodley Head, 1965), 186.

11. Both suppliers had stipulated that CIRUS was to be used only for peaceful purposes.

12. See Chapter 9, p. 188.

13. Levy and Scott-Clark, *Deception*, 30.

14. "Nuclear Technology 1970–1974," Bhutto.org, 2014, http://www.bhutto.org/article21.php.

15. Ahmadis are the followers of Mirza Ghulam Ahmad (1835–1908), born in the village of Qadian in Punjab. Their belief that Ahmad is the Messiah in succession to Lord Krishna, Jesus Christ, and the Prophet Muhammad contradicts mainstream Muslims' tenet that Muhammad is the last and final prophet. They formed 2.3 percent of Pakistan's population.

16. Christina Lamb, *Waiting for Allah: Pakistan's Struggle for Democracy* (London: Hamish Hamilton, 1991), 84.

17. Levy and Scott-Clark, *Deception*, 62.

18. Apparently, URENCO stands for uranium (UR) enrichment (EN) company (CO). In 2013, it was the globe's second largest vendor of nuclear fuel, selling its products to fifty countries.

19. Levy and Scott-Clark, *Deception*, 60, citing Zulfikar Ali Bhutto, *If I Am Assassinated* (Delhi: Vikas, 1979), 138.

CHAPTER 12: ISLAMIST ZIA UL HAQ, BUILDER OF THE A-BOMB

1. When Muhammad Zia ul Haq visited his alma mater in Delhi in 1983, he was shown his application to the principal for leave. He had misspelled his name as "Zai ul-Haq." "Glimpses of St. Stephen's College," St. Stephen's College, http://www.ststephens.edu/archives/history2.htm.

2. Cited in Shahid Javed Burki and Craig Baxter, eds., *Pakistan Under The Military: Eleven Years of Zia Ul-Haq* (Boulder: Westview, 1991), 5.

3. Cited in Josy Joseph, "MEA Totally Misread General Zia-ul-Haq's Intentions After Coup, Show Declassified Papers," *Times of India*, November 7, 2011.

4. Protesting against Britain's recognition of Bangladesh, Pakistani president Zulfikar Ali Bhutto withdrew Pakistan from the Commonwealth. Pakistan's later application for readmission to the Commonwealth was accepted in 1988. Among Commonwealth members, diplomatic mission heads are called high commissioners instead of ambassadors.

5. Cited in Joseph, "MEA Totally Misread General Zia-ul-Haq's Intentions."

6. Robert Hutchinson, *Weapons of Mass Destruction: The No-Nonsense Guide to Nuclear, Chemical and Biological Weapons Today* (London: Weidenfeld and Nicolson, 2003), 112.

7. B. Raman, *Kaoboys of R&AW: Down Memory Lane* (New Delhi: Lancer, 2008), 113.

8. Nuclear reprocessing technology was developed to separate and recover fissionable plutonium from irradiated nuclear fuel. Initially, reprocessing was used to extract plutonium for producing nuclear weapons. Later, reprocessed plutonium was alternatively recycled back into MOX nuclear fuel for thermal reactors.

9. Dilip Hiro, *Apocalyptic Realm: Jihadists in South Asia* (New Haven, CT: Yale University Press, 2012), 58.

10. Ardeshir Cowasjee, "A Re-Cap of Soviet–Pakistan Relations," *Dawn* (Karachi), December 3, 2011.

11. Meeting President Nur Muhammad Taraki in the capital city of Kabul would have implied de facto recognition of the Democratic Republic of Afghanistan, which Zia ul Haq was unwilling to do.

12. General Khalid Mahmud Arif, *Working with Zia: Pakistan Power Politics 1977–1988* (New York: Oxford University Press, 1995), 307.

13. Dilip Hiro, *War Without End: The Rise of Islamist Terrorism and Global Response* (London: Routledge, 2002), 211.

14. In practice, only the penalties involving lashing were implemented.

15. In June 1980, BBC TV's documentary *Project 706: The Islamic Bomb* provided the fullest account of Pakistan's uranium enrichment program.

16. A separate arrangement was made for Pakistan's purchase of forty versatile F-16 fighter aircraft manufactured in the United States, much to Delhi's alarm.

17. Hiro, *Apocalyptic Realm*, 322n23; "Pakistan Nuclear Weapons," Global Security, n.d., http://www.globalsecurity.org/wmd/world/pakistan/nuke.htm.

NOTES

18. V. D. Chopra, ed., *Significance of Indo-Russian Relations in the 21st Century* (New Delhi: Kalpaz, 2008), 85.

19. William K. Stevens, "Pakistan's Leader to Confer in India," *New York Times*, October 31, 1982.

20. Adrian Levy and Catherine Scott-Clark, *Deception: Pakistan, the United States and the Secret Trade in Nuclear Weapons* (New York: Walker & Company, 2007), 104.

21. "Pakistan Nuclear Weapons—A Chronology," Federation of American Scientists, June 3, 1998, http://www.fas.org/nuke/guide/pakistan/nuke/chron.htm.

22. Levy and Scott-Clark, *Deception*, 104–105.

23. Hiro, *Apocalyptic Realm*, 122.

24. Levy and Scott-Clark, *Deception*, 105–106.

25. Ibid., 106.

26. Ibid., 105; see also "Adrian Levy Interview with Amy Goodman," *Democracy Now!*, November 19, 2007.

27. Stephen Zunes, "Pakistan's Movement for the Restoration of Democracy (1981–1984)," Nonviolent Conflict, 2009, http://www.nonviolent-conflict.org/index.php/movements-and-campaigns/movements-and-campaigns-summaries?sobi2Task=sobi2Details&sobi2Id=24.

28. Suranjan Das, *Kashmir and Sindh: Nation-Building, Ethnicity and Regional Politics in South Asia* (New Delhi: Anthem, 2001), 144.

29. Partha Sarathy Ghosh, *Cooperation and Conflict in South Asia* (Chennai: Technical Publications, 1989), 42.

30. Jarnail Singh Bhindranwale was the leader of the Damdami Taksal, a fundamentalist sect within Sikhism.

31. In one of his speeches Prime Minister Rajiv Gandhi admitted to having lost more than 700 soldiers in Operation Blue Star. On October 31, 2009, CNN-IBN reported the army losing 365 commandos.

32. Khushwant Singh, *A History of the Sikhs, Volume II: 1839–2004*, 2nd ed. (New Delhi: Oxford University Press, 2012), 364.

33. Marc Kaufman, "India Blames Pakistan in Sikh Conflict," *Philadelphia Inquirer*, June 19, 1988.

34. Indira Gandhi and P. V. Narasimha Rao, "Debate on the White Paper on the Punjab Agitation, Monsoon Session of Parliament, 1984: Interventions by Prime Minister and Home Minister," Ministry of External Affairs, 1984.

35. Singh, *A History of the Sikhs, Volume II*, 378.

36. Reginald Massey, "Khushwant Singh Obituary," *Guardian* (London), March 20, 2014.

37. The elections in Punjab and Assam, then under emergency, were held almost a year later.

38. According to Milton Beardon of the CIA, by the time the Soviets left Afghanistan in early 1989, the CIA had spent $6 billion and Saudi Arabia $4 billion. Cited by Stephen Kinzer, "How We Helped Create the Afghan Crisis," *Boston Globe*, March 20, 2009.

39. Stephen R. Wilson, "India and Pakistan Pledge Not to Destroy Each Other's Nuclear Plants," Associated Press, December 17, 1985.

40. Ibid.

41. Because of their black uniforms, the commandos of the National Security Guards were popularly called Black Cats.

42. Hiro, *War Without End*, 220.

43. Abdul Sattar, *Pakistan's Foreign Policy, 1947–2005: A Concise History* (Karachi: Oxford University Press, 2007), 194, 195.

44. J. Bandhopadhyay, *The Making of India's Foreign Policy* (New Delhi: Allied, 1991), 272.

45. Levy and Scott-Clark, *Deception*, 151.

46. Shafik H. Hashmi, "The Nuclear Danger in South Asia," citing the *Atlantic*, November 2005, 82, http://www.cssforum.com.pk/css-compulsory-subjects/current-affairs/3803-nuclear-danger-south-asia.html.

47. Cited in Levy and Scott-Clark, *Deception*, 151. The *Observer* paid Kuldip Nayar a miserly £350 ($500) for his sensational exclusive story.

48. Levy and Scott-Clark, *Deception*, 152.

49. Steven R. Weisman, "On India's Border, a Huge Mock War," *New York Times*, March 5, 1988.

50. Terry Atlas, "Terror Attacks on U.S. Down Sharply in 1987," *Chicago Tribune*, January 18, 1988.

51. Ravi Shankar, "Spy Wars," *New Indian Express*, May 16, 2012.

52. In December 2006, a court in New York convicted Khalid Awan, a Pakistani national, of providing money and financial services to the Khalistan Commando Force chief Paramjit Singh Panjwar in Pakistan. "Pakistani Convicted for Financing Sikh Militant Group," *Rediff News* (Mumbai), December 21, 2006.

53. Marc Kaufman, "In the Punjab's Golden Temple, Sikh Militants Rule Once More," *Philadelphia Inquirer*, February 12, 1988.

54. Anant Mathur, "Secrets of COIN Success: Lessons from the Punjab Campaign," *Faultlines* 20 (January 2011).

55. Kaufman, "Punjab's Golden Temple."

56. Kaufman, "India Blames Pakistan."

57. Barbara Crossette, "Who Killed Zia?" *World Policy Journal* 22, no. 3 (Fall 2005).

58. Cited in Edward Jay Epstein, "Who Killed Zia?," *Vanity Fair*, September 1989.

59. Epstein, "Who Killed Zia?"

60. Crossette, "Who Killed Zia?"

61. Epstein, "Who Killed Zia?"

62. Fatima Bhutto, *Songs of Blood and Sword: A Daughter's Memoir* (London: Jonathan Cape, 2010 / New York: Nation Books, 2010), 281.

63. Cited in Epstein, "Who Killed Zia?"

64. Crossette, "Who Killed Zia?"

65. Bhutto, *Songs of Blood and Sword*, 282.

66. Robert D. Kaplan, "How Zia's Death Helped the US," *New York Times*, August 23, 1989.

67. Crossette, "Who Killed Zia?"

68. Ibid.

69. Atul Sethi, "20 Years On, Zia's Death Still a Mystery," *Times of India*, August 17, 2008, citing Edward Jay Epstein on the twentieth anniversary of Zia ul Haq's assassination.

70. *A Case of Exploding Mangoes* was long-listed for the prestigious Booker Prize in Britain in 2008.

CHAPTER 13: RAJIV-BENAZIR RAPPORT—CUT SHORT

1. Cited in "Benazir Bhutto: Oxford Party Girl Cursed by Blood-Soaked Family Dynasty," *Daily Mail* (London), December 28, 2007.

2. G. Parthasarathy, "Rumblings in Pakistan: Zardari Is Indeed on a Slippery Slope," *Tribune* (Chandigarh, India), October 2, 2008.

3. Unlike the bygone years, when Muhammad Yusuf Khan had to change his name to Dilip Kumar, a Hindu name, to win popular accolade, none of the latter-day Khans had felt the need to do so. This was a measure of how secularism was taking root in India, with most Indians regarding religion as a strictly personal matter with no professional or political implication.

4. Meena Gopal, "Benazir Bhutto Riposte: 'I Kept My Word, Rajiv Didn't,'" *Outlook India*, December 31, 2007.

5. Cited in Madhu Jain, "French Leave: Rajiv Gandhi Embarks on Giddy Five-Day Three-Nation Tour," *India Today*, August 15, 1989.

6. "Editorial: The Brothers Hinduja and the Bofors Scandal," *Frontline* (Chennai), October 28–November 10, 2000.

7. The *Hindu* was edited by Narasimha Ram, a graduate of Columbia University's School of Journalism in New York.

8. In 2012 the Supreme Court ruled that Ishaq Khan, General Aslam Beg, and Lieutenant General Asad Durrani, the ISI chief, had conspired to provide financial assistance to the IJI. See "Asghar Khan Short Order, Full Text," *Express Tribune* (Karachi), October 19, 2012; and Husain Haqqani, *Pakistan: Between Mosque and Military* (Washington, DC: Carnegie Endowment for International Peace, 2005), 248.

9. Cited in Haqqani, *Pakistan*, 294.

10. Haqqani, *Pakistan*, 296.

11. Barbara Crossette, "Assassination in India: A Blast, and Then the Wailing Started," *New York Times*, May 21, 1991.

12. Most of her twenty-six coplotters were sentenced to death by the trial court seven years later. Upon appeal, in January 2014 the Supreme Court commuted the capital punishment sentences of fifteen of them to life imprisonment. The next month it did the same in the case of three others. "Rajiv Gandhi Murder: India Court Suspends Plotters' Release," BBC News, February 20, 2014.

13. Shekhar Gupta, "India in the Dock: Babri Masjid Demolition 1992: How the World Reacted," *India Today*, December 5, 2011.

14. "Pakistanis Attack 30 Hindu Temples," *New York Times*, December 8, 1992.

15. Adrian Levy and Catherine Scott-Clark, *Deception: Pakistan, the United States and the Secret Trade in Nuclear Weapons* (New York: Walker & Company, 2007), 240.

16. Harinder Baweja, "Get America Out of the Way and We'll Be OK," *Tehelka*, February 2, 2008.

17. "The RAW: Understanding India's External Intelligence Agency," *Indian Defence Forum*, September 29, 2009, http://defenceforumindia.com/forum/defence-strategic-issues/5670-raw-understanding-indias-external-intelligence-agency.html.

18. Hamish Telford, "Counter-Insurgency in India: Observations from Punjab and Kashmir," *Journal of Conflict Studies* 21, no. 1 (Spring 2001).

19. Victoria Schofield, *Kashmir in Conflict: India, Pakistan and the Unending War*, rev. ed. (London: I. B. Tauris, 2003), 172.

20. The Armed Forces (Special Powers) Act (AFSPA) was first passed in 1958 to cover the "disturbed" areas in northeast India. It still remains in force there.

21. Jason Burke, "Indian Officers Named in Report on Kashmir Abuses," *Guardian* (London), December 6, 2012.

22. Basharat Peer, *Curfewed Night* (Noida: Random House India, 2009) / *Curfewed Night: One Kashmiri Journalist's Frontline Account of Life, Love, and War in His Homeland* (New York: Scribner, 2010) / *Curfewed Night: A Frontline Memoir of Life, Love and War in Kashmir* (London: Harper, 2010), 143.

23. Dilip Hiro, *Apocalyptic Realm: Jihadists in South Asia* (New Haven, CT: Yale University Press, 2012), 103.

24. Schofield, *Kashmir in Conflict*, 176, 177, 183.

25. Hiro, *Apocalyptic Realm*, 104.

26. Cited in Schofield, *Kashmir in Conflict*, 194.

27. Levy and Scott-Clark, *Deception*, 255–256.

28. "Pakistan Against Forces of Extremism: PM," *Dawn* (Karachi), April 6, 1995.

29. Cited by A. G. Noorani, "The Truth About the Lahore Summit," *Frontline* (Chennai), February 16–March 1, 2002.

30. Ibid.

31. "Pakistan Nuclear Weapons—A Chronology," Federation of American Scientists, June 3, 1998, https://www.fas.org/nuke/guide/pakistan/nuke/chron.htm.

CHAPTER 14: GATE-CRASHING THE NUCLEAR CLUB

1. Every year, at a grand ceremony, each recruit of the Rashtriya Swayamsevak Sangh made his donation to the leader of his branch.

2. "'The Sangh Is My Soul,' Writes Atal Bihari Vajpayee, the First Swayamsevak Who Became Prime Minister," *Samvada*, December 24, 2012, http://samvada.org/2012/news/the-sangh-is-my-soul-writes-atal-bihari-vajpayee-the-first-swayamsevak-who-became-pm.

3. Carey Sublette, "India's Nuclear Weapons Program: The Momentum Builds: 1989–1998," Nuclear Weapon Archive, March 30, 2001, http://nuclearweaponarchive.org/India/IndiaMomentum.html.

4. T. V. Paul, "The Systemic Bases of India's Challenge to the Global Nuclear Order," *Nonproliferation Review* (Fall 1998).

5. Cited in ibid.

6. Cited in Sublette, "India's Nuclear Weapons Program."

7. See Chapter 11, p. 222.

8. "Weapons of Peace: How the CIA Was Fooled," *India Today*, May 17, 1999.

9. "On This Day, 11 May 1998: India Explodes Nuclear Controversy," BBC News, 2003.

10. Tim Weiner, "Nuclear Anxiety: The Blunders: US Blundered on Intelligence, Officials Admit," *New York Times*, May 13, 1998.

11. Cited in Reem Siddiqi, "Nuclear Arms in India: A Weapon for Political Gain," *Monitor: Journal of International Studies* 7, no. 1 (Fall 2000).

12. Thomas Blom Hansen, *The Saffron Wave: Democracy and Hindu Nationalism in Modern India* (Princeton, NJ: Princeton University Press, 1999), 3. A few opinion polls showed 92 percent favoring India going nuclear. "India Focus: Strategic Analysis and Forecast," *India Focus: Strategic Analysis and Forecasts*, May 1998, http://www.indiastrategy.com/may98.htm.

13. John F. Burns, "Nuclear Anxiety: The Overview: Pakistan, Answering India, Carries out Nuclear Test'; Clinton's Appeal Rejected," *New York Times*, May 29, 2013.

14. Rai Muhammad Saleh Azam, "When Mountains Move—The Story of Chagai," *Defence Journal*, June 2000.

15. In a cold test, a nuclear bomb is triggered without the fissile material required to detonate it.

16. Carey Sublette, "Pakistan's Nuclear Weapons Program: 1998: The Year of Testing," Nuclear Weapon Archive, September 10, 2001, http://nuclearweaponarchive.org/Pakistan/PakTests.html.

17. "US Offered $5 Bn to Refrain from Nuclear Tests: Nawaz Sharif," *Times of India*, May 28, 2010.

18. Sublette, "Pakistan's Nuclear Weapons Program."

19. Raj Chengappa and Zahid Hussain, "Bang for Bang: Pokhran Tests Fallout," *India Today*, June 8, 1998.

20. Christopher Walker and Michael Evans, "Pakistan Feared Israeli Raid: Missiles Were Put on Alert to Counter Strike at Nuclear Sites," *Times* (London), June 3, 1998.

21. Cited in Sublette, "Pakistan's Nuclear Weapons Program."

22. Burns, "Nuclear Anxiety."

23. John Ward Anderson and Kamran Khan, "Pakistan Declares Intention to Use Arms in Self-Defense," *Washington Post*, May 30, 1998.

24. *Bulletin of the Atomic Scientists* (July 1998): 24.

25. "Arms Control and Proliferation Profile: India," Arms Control Association, July 2013, http://www.armscontrol.org/factsheets/indiaprofile.

26. Husain Haqqani, *Pakistan: Between Mosque and Military* (Washington, DC: Carnegie Endowment for International Peace, 2005), 248, 247.

27. Farhan Bokhari, Stephen Fidler, and Roula Khalaf, "Saudi Oil Money Joins Forces with Nuclear Pakistan," *Financial Times*, August 5, 2004.

28. Cited in Amjad Abbas Maggsi, "Lahore Declaration February, 1999: A Major Initiative for Peace in South Asia," *Pakistan Vision* 14, no. 1 (2013): 183–201.

29. Amit Baruha, *Dateline Islamabad* (New Delhi: Penguin Books, 2007), 119.

30. A. G. Noorani, "The Truth About the Lahore Summit," *Frontline*, February 16–March 1, 2002.

31. Ibid.

32. Haqqani, *Pakistan*, 363n205.

33. Pamela Philipose, "The Symbol of Pakistan," *Indian Express*, February 22, 1999.

34. "Lahore Declaration," http://www.nti.org/treaties-and-regimes/lahore-declaration. The Indian and Pakistani foreign secretaries had prepared the draft of this agreement a month earlier.

35. Kenneth J. Cooper, "India, Pakistan Kindle Hope for Peace," *Washington Post*, February 21, 1999.

36. Philipose, "The Symbol of Pakistan."

37. Cited in Ranbir Vohra, *The Making of India: A Historical Survey* (Armonk, NY: M. E. Sharpe, 2000), 309.

38. "Clinton Welcomes Meeting Between Vajpayee and Sharif," press release, February 22, 1999, http://www.fas.org/news/india/1999/99022301_nlt.htm.

39. After the coup in October 1999, General Pervez Musharraf sacked Air Chief Pervez Mahdi Qureshi.

40. Praveen Swami, "Pakistan Revisits the Kargil War," *Hindu*, June 21, 2008. See also "The Musharraf Tapes—II," Moral Volcano Daily Press (blog), January 11, 2004, https://moralvolcano.wordpress.com/tag/musharraf; Haqqani, *Pakistan*, 252.

41. Praveen Swami, "Pakistan Revisits the Kargil War," *Hindu*, June 21, 2008; Malik Zahoor Ahmad, "The Unsung Hero of Kargil," *News* (Karachi), February 20, 2013.

42. "G8 Statement on Regional Issues," June 20, 1999, http://www.g8.fr/evian/english/navigation/g8_documents/archives_from_previous_summits/cologne_summit_-_1999/g8_statement_on_regional_issues.html.

43. "Pakistan Warns of Kashmir War Risk," BBC News, June 23, 1999.

44. "Pervez Musharraf Claims 1999 Kargil Operation Was a Big Success for Pak Army," *India Today*, February 1, 2013.

45. Rezaul H. Laskar, "Sharif After Kargil: 'Mr President, Pak Army Will GET Me,'" *Rediff News* (Mumbai), February 26, 2013.

46. "Pakistan Warns of Kashmir War Risk."

47. Bruce Riedel, "American Diplomacy and the 1999 Kargil Summit at Blair House," Occasional Paper No. 17, Fifth Annual Fellows' Lecture, April 17, 2002, http://media.sas.upenn.edu/casi/docs/research/papers/Riedel_2002.pdf.

48. Malik Zahoor Ahmad, "The Unsung Hero of Kargil," *News International* (Karachi), February 20, 2013.

49. Ibid.

50. Zahoor Ahmad, "The Unsung Hero of Kargil."

51. A. G. Noorani, "Kargil Diplomacy," *Frontline* (Chennai), July 31–August 13, 1999.

52. Riedel, "American Diplomacy and the 1999 Kargil Summit."

53. Cited in Graham Bowley and Jane Perlez, "Musharraf Prepares to Drop Army Role," *New York Times*, November 28, 2007.

54. Dilip Hiro, *Apocalyptic Realm: Jihadists in South Asia* (New Haven, CT: Yale University Press, 2012), 107.

55. Cited in Noorani, "The Truth About the Lahore Summit."

56. "Pak Army Defeated by Indian Media," December 15, 2013, http://defence.pk/threads/pak-army-defeated-by-indian-media.291310. Major General Muhammad Azam Asif's essay on the media was part of the biennial *Green Book*, published by the Pakistani Army for serving officers; the 2010 edition focused on information warfare.

57. Rajiv Tikoo, "The Larger Than Life Director," *Financial Express*, February 19, 2000.

58. Ihsan Aslam, "Bollywood's Kargil," *Daily Times* (Lahore), June 24, 2004.

59. "Prominent Writer, Actor, Rauf Khalid Dies in Road Accident," *Dawn* (Karachi), November 25, 2011.

60. Cited in Dilip Hiro, *War Without End: The Rise of Islamist Terrorism and Global Response* (London: Routledge, 2002), 285.

61. Ibid., 277.

62. James Risen and Judith Miller, "Pakistani Intelligence Had Links to Al Qaeda, U.S. Officials Say," *New York Times*, October 29, 2001.

63. Ansar Abbasi, "Musharraf Had Given Authority to Three Generals to Overthrow Nawaz," *News* (Karachi), October 27, 2013.

64. "How the 1999 Pakistan Coup Unfolded," BBC News, August 23, 2007.

65. Gwen Ifill, "Pakistan After Coup," *PBS Newshour*, October 19, 1999; "Transcript of Address to the Nation in English by the Chairman Joint Chiefs of Staff Committee and Chief of the Army Staff, General Pervez Musharraf," Pakistan News Service, October 12, 1999.

66. Of the 545 members, 2 belonging to the Anglo-Indian community are nominated by the president of the Republic of India.

67. Sanjoy Majumder, "India Wary of Pakistan Army," BBC News, October 13, 1999.

68. Zahid Hussain, "Freed Militant Surfaces," Associated Press, January 5, 2000.

CHAPTER 15: GENERAL MUSHARRAF BUCKLES UNDER US PRESSURE

1. "Jammu and Kashmir Backgrounder," South Asia Terrorism Portal, 2001, http://www.satp.org/satporgtp/countries/india/states/jandk/backgrounder/index.html.

2. Jonathan Marcus, "Analysis: The World's Most Dangerous Place?," BBC News, March 23, 2000.

3. Mike Wooldridge, "Analysis: Clinton's Disappointments in South Asia," BBC News, March 26, 2000.

4. Bill Sammon, "Clinton Uses Decoy Flight for Security," *Washington Times*, March 26, 2000; James Risen and Judith Miller, "Pakistani Intelligence Had Links to Al Qaeda, U.S. Officials Say," *New York Times*, October 29, 2001.

5. "Clinton Addresses Pakistani People," CNN, March 25, 2000.

6. "Pakistan Court Limits Army Rule," BBC News, May 12, 2000.

7. Sridhar Krishnaswami, "Vajpayee's American Yatra," *Frontline* (Chennai), September 30–October 13, 2000.

8. "Annan's No to UN Resolution on Kashmir," *Tribune* (Chandigarh, India), March 11, 2001.

9. "Activities of Secretary-General in India, 15–18 March 2001," United Nations, 2001, http://www.un.org/News/Press/docs/2001/sgt2270R.doc.htm.

10. Aijaz Ahmad, "Of What Went Wrong at Agra," *Frontline* (Chennai), July 21–August 3, 2001.

11. Ibid.

12. Rahul Bedi, "The Tel Aviv Connection Grows," *India Together*, July 26, 2002, http://www.indiatogether.org/govt/military/articles/isrlbuy02.htm.

13. Ed Blanche, "Mutual Threat of Islamic Militancy Allies Israel and India," *Jane's Terrorism and Security Monitor*, August 14, 2001.

14. "Text of Bush's Act of War Statement," BBC News, September 12, 2001.

15. Dilip Hiro, *War Without End: The Rise of Islamist Terrorism and Global Response* (London: Routledge, 2002), 314.

16. Jane Perlez, "A Pakistani Envoy in Britain Defuses Cultural Land Mines," *New York Times*, August 4, 2007.

17. Hiro, *War Without End*, 314n38.

18. Ibid., 314n36.

19. Ibid., 314n37.

20. Rory McCarthy, "Pakistani Leader's Attempt to Rein in Militants Is Met with Defiance," *Guardian* (London), May 26, 2002.

21. "Context of September 15, 2001: Head of ISI Argues Pakistan Should Side with Taliban, but Musharraf Agrees to Help US as Opportunistic Necessity," History Commons, n.d., http://www.historycommons.org/context.jsp?item=a0901musharrafmeeting.

22. Hiro, *War Without End*, 315n40.

23. "Musharraf Rallies Pakistan," BBC News, September 19, 2001.

24. Hiro, *War Without End*, 315n39.

25. Ibid., 315.

26. Ibid., 316n42.

27. "Militants Attack Kashmir Assembly," BBC News, October 1, 2001.

28. "Indian Parliament Attack Kills 12," BBC News, December 13, 2001.

29. Steve Coll, "The Stand-Off: How Jihadi Groups Helped Provoke the Twenty-First Century's First Nuclear Crisis," *New Yorker*, February 13, 2006.

30. Ibid.

31. Hiro, *War Without End*, 374n3.

32. "2002—Kashmir Crisis," Global Security, 2011, http://www.globalsecurity.org/military/world/war/kashmir-2002.htm.

33. "International Concern over Danger of Conflict in South Asia," *Disarmament Diplomacy* 62 (January–February 2002).

34. Hiro, *War Without End*, 380; "Pakistan Moves Nuclear Weapons," *Washington Post*, November 11, 2001.

35. Praveen Swami, "Gen. Padmanabhan Mulls over Lessons of Operation Parakram," *Hindu*, February 6, 2004.

36. Coll, "The Stand-Off."

37. Cited in Hiro, *War Without End*, 381.

38. Javed Naqvi, "Musharraf Offers Sustained Talks: Handshake with Vajpayee Charms SAARC," *Dawn* (Karachi), January 6, 2002.

39. Sridhar Krishnaswami, "A Balancing Act," *Frontline* (Chennai), January 19–February 1, 2002.

40. Cited in Scott D. Sagan, "The Evolution of India and Pakistan Nuclear Doctrine," speech to the Belfer Center for Science and International Affairs, Harvard University, May 7, 2008, http://belfercenter .ksg.harvard.edu/files/uploads/Sagan_MTA_Talk_050708.pdf.

41. Hiro, *War Without End*, 382; Ahmed Rashid, *Descent into Chaos: How the War Against Islamic Extremism Is Being Lost in Pakistan, Afghanistan and Central Asia* (London: Allen Lane, 2008 / New York: Penguin Books, 2009), 146.

42. Adrian Levy and Catherine Scott-Clark, *Deception: Pakistan, the United States and the Secret Trade in Nuclear Weapons* (New York: Walker & Company, 2007), 323.

CHAPTER 16: NUCLEAR-ARMED TWINS, EYEBALL-TO-EYEBALL

1. "2002—Kashmir Crisis," Global Security, 2011, http://www.globalsecurity.org/military/world /war/kashmir-2002.htm.

2. When India Almost Went to War with Pakistan," Inside Story (blog), *Hindustan Times*, November 2, 2011, http://blogs.hindustantimes.com/inside-story/2011/11/02/when-india-went-to-war-with -pakistan-twice/.

3. Steve Coll, "The Stand-Off: How Jihadi Groups Helped Provoke the Twenty-First Century's First Nuclear Crisis," *New Yorker*, February 13, 2006.

4. 2002—Kashmir Crisis."

5. Coll, "The Stand-Off."

6. Cited in Scott D. Sagan, "The Evolution of India and Pakistan Nuclear Doctrine," speech to the Belfer Center for Science and International Affairs, Harvard University, May 7, 2008, http://belfercenter .ksg.harvard.edu/files/uploads/Sagan_MTA_Talk_050708.pdf.

7. See Chapter 14, p. 279.

8. "India Draft Nuclear Doctrine," *Disarmament Diplomacy 39* (July–August 1999).

9. Mark Fitzpatrick, A. I. Nikitin, and Sergey Oznobishchev, eds., *Nuclear Doctrines and Strategies: National Policies and International Security* (Amsterdam: IOS Press, 2008), 131.

10. Cited in Sagan, "The Evolution of India and Pakistan Nuclear Doctrine."

11. "Musharraf Refuses to Renounce First Use of Nuclear Weapons," *Irish Examiner*, June 5, 2002.

12. Coll, "The Stand-Off."

13. "Leaders Agree on Using Peaceful Means: Putin," *Dawn* (Karachi), June 4, 2002; "Musharraf Refuses to Renounce First Use of Nuclear Weapons."

14. "Almaty Summit Leads to Creation of Asian Security Organization," Conference on Interaction and Confidence-Building Measures in Asia, June 4, 2002, http://prosites-kazakhembus.homestead.com /Special_Report_CICA.html.

15. Coll, "The Stand-Off."

16. "2002—Kashmir Crisis."

17. "Joint Indo-US Naval Exercise," BBC News, May 5, 2002.

18. "Powell Press Conference in New Delhi, July 28, 2002," http://www.usembassy.it/viewer/article .asp?article=/file2002_07/alia/A2072601.htm&plaintext=1.

19. Ela Dutt, "Pervez Firm on Ending Infiltration: Powell," *Tribune* (Chandigarh, India), August 1, 2002.

20. Dilip Hiro, *Apocalyptic Realm: Jihadists in South Asia* (New Haven, CT: Yale University Press, 2012), 111.

21. Aditi Phadnis, "Parakram Cost Put at Rs 6,500 Crore," *Rediff News* (Mumbai), January 16, 2003.

22. Praveen Swami, "Gen. Padmanabhan Mulls over Lessons of Operation Parakram," *Hindu*, February 6, 2004.

23. Prime Minister's Office, "Cabinet Committee on Security Reviews Progress in Operationalizing India's Nuclear Doctrine," press release, January 4, 2003, http://pib.nic.in/archieve/lreleng/lyr2003/rjan2003/04012003/r040120033.html.

24. Pronounced *jiiyo* in Urdu, *Geo* means "keep living."

25. Amy Waldman, "Pakistan TV: A New Look at the News," *New York Times*, January 25, 2004.

26. Reporters Sans Frontières, "Pakistan—2003 Annual Report," http://archives.rsf.org/article.php3?id_article=6480.

27. Husain Haqqani, *Pakistan: Between Mosque and Military* (Washington, DC: Carnegie Endowment for International Peace, 2005), 260.

28. Of the 342 National Assembly seat, 271 were contested, with the remainder allocated to different groups according to the popularly won places.

29. Haqqani, *Pakistan*, 306, citing his interview with an ISI official in Islamabad in January 2005.

30. Suman Guha Mozumder, "Not Keen to Meet Vajpayee: Musharraf," *Rediff News* (Mumbai), September 25, 2003.

31. "Near Miss for Musharraf Convoy," BBC News, December 14, 2003.

32. Salman Masood, "Pakistani Leader Escapes Attempt at Assassination," *New York Times*, December 26, 2003.

33. Bill Roggio, "Assassination Attempt Against Pakistan's President," *Long War Journal*, July 6, 2007.

34. "2002—Kashmir Crisis."

35. "Chief Minister Hails Musharraf's Statement," *Tribune* (Chandigarh, India), December 19, 2003.

36. "Musharraf Says History Made Between India and Pakistan," *Daily Jang* (Islamabad), January 6, 2004.

37. T. R. Ramachandran, "Need to Understand Each Other's Concerns, Says PM," *Tribune* (Chandigarh, India), January 5, 2004.

38. "Did Brajesh Mishra Meet ISI Chief?," *Tribune* (Chandigarh, India), January 6, 2004.

39. Shashank Joshi, "India and the Four Day War," Royal United Services Institute, April 7, 2010, http://www.rusi.org/analysis/commentary/ref:C4BBC50E1BAF9C.

CHAPTER 17: MANMOHAN SINGH'S CHANGING INTERLOCUTORS

1. "India and Pakistan Set Up Hotline," BBC News, June 20, 2004.

2. See Chapter 7, p. 151.

3. The India-administered regions are the Hindu-majority part of Jammu, Muslim-majority Jammu, Muslim-majority Kashmir Valley, Kargil, and Ladakh.

4. Syed Rifaat Hussain, "Pakistan's Changing Outlook on Kashmir," *South Asian Survey* 14, no. 2 (December 2007): 195–205.

5. "PM Invites Musharraf to Watch Cricket," *Rediff News* (Mumbai), March 10, 2005.

6. Gautaman Bhaskaran, "India and Pakistan Play Political Cricket," April 26, 2005, http://www.gautamanbhaskaran.com/gb/cricketdiplomacy.html.

7. Rifaat Hussain, "Pakistan's Changing Outlook on Kashmir."

8. Cited in A. G. Noorani, "A Step Closer to Consensus," *Frontline* (Chennai), December 15–30, 2006.

9. Jyoti Malhotra, "Kashmir: Is Solution in Sight?," BBC News, December 7, 2006.

10. Steve Coll, "The Back Channel," *New Yorker*, March 2, 2009.

11. Dilip Hiro, *Apocalyptic Realm: Jihadists in South Asia* (New Haven, CT: Yale University Press, 2012), 211–212.

12. For the complete text of the email of the Indian Mujahedin's Ahmedabad blasts, see http://deshgujarat.com/2008/08/02/full-text-of-indian-muajahideens-ahmedabad-blasts-email.

13. Jason Burke, "Mumbai Spy Says He Worked for Terrorists—Then Briefed Pakistan," *Guardian* (London), October 18, 2010. The ISI also instructed David Coleman Headley to recruit Indian agents to inform about Indian troop movement and levels.

14. For the story of Ajmal Amir Kasab, http://chauhansaab.blogspot.co.uk/2012_11_01_archive.html; see also "I Am Going Away for Jihad: Kasab Told His Mother in Pak," *Indian Express*, December 13, 2008.

15. Catherine Scott-Clark and Adrian Levy, *The Siege: 68 Hours Inside the Taj Hotel* (New York: Penguin Books, 2013) / *The Siege: Three Days of Terror Inside the Taj* (London: Viking, 2013), 55.

16. Alastair Gee, "Mumbai Terror Attacks: And Then They Came After the Jews," *Times* (London), November 1, 2009.

17. Lydia Polgreen and Vikas Bajaj, "Suspect Stirs Court by Confessing," *New York Times*, July 20, 2009.

18. Hiro, *Apocalyptic Realm*, 114.

19. Saeed Shah, "Revealed: Home of Mumbai's Gunman in Pakistan Village," *Guardian* (London), December 7, 2008.

20. "Post-26/11, Pranab Mukherjee's Words Rattled Pakistan: Condoleezza Rice," *Economic Times*, October 28, 2011.

21. Ibid.

22. "2008—Mumbai Attack 22/11," Global Security, 2011, http://www.globalsecurity.org/military/world/war/indo-pak_2008.htm.

23. China Hand, "The Mumbai Paradox," China Matters (blog), December 4, 2008, http://chinamatters.blogspot.co.uk/2008/12/mumbai-paradox.html.

24. Post-26/11, Pranab Mukherjee's Words Rattled Pakistan."

25. Nirupama Subramanian, "McCain Warns Pakistan of Indian Air Strikes," *Hindu*, December 7, 2008.

26. *Late Edition with Wolf Blitzer*, CNN, December 7, 2008, http://edition.cnn.com/2008/POLITICS/12/07/rice.mumbai.

27. Subramanian, "McCain Warns Pakistan of Indian Air Strikes."

28. Tariq Naqash and Syed Irfan Raza, "Operation Against LeT-Dawa Launched in AJK," *Dawn* (Karachi), December 8, 2008.

29. "UN Bans Jamaat ud Dawa; Declares It a Terror Outfit," *Times of India*, December 11, 2008.

30. Harinder Baweja, "Into the Heart of Darkness," *Tehelka*, December 20, 2008.

31. "2008—Mumbai Attack 22/11."

32. Ibid.

33. Ibid.

34. Ibid.

35. Ibid.

36. Ibid.

37. "Pakistan Admits India Attack Link," BBC News, February 12, 2009.

38. "Text of India-Pakistan Joint Statement in Sharm-el-Sheikh Between Manmohan Singh and Pakistan PM Syed Yusuf Raza Gilani on July 16, 2009," Islamic Terrorism in India (blog), July 18, 2009, http://islamicterrorism.wordpress.com/2009/07/18/text-of-india-pakistan-joint-statement-in-sharm-el-sheikh-between-manmohan-singh-and-pakistan-pm-syed-yusuf-raza-gilani-on-july-16-2009/.

39. Sana Qamar, "Sharm El-Sheikh Meeting: An Analysis," *Reflections* 4 (2009).

40. "South Asia Rivals' Differing Agendas," BBC News, February 23, 2010.

41. Jason Burke, "India-Pakistan Talks Centre on Terrorism but Fail to Make Progress," *Guardian* (London), February 25, 2010.

42. Ibid.

43. Sachin Parashar, "High-Level Visits in Bid to Restore Full-Scale Dialogue," *Times of India*, July 10, 2010.

44. "Pakistan Asks India to Give Access to Kasab," NDTV/PTI, May 3, 2010, http://www.ndtv.com/article/world/pakistan-asks-india-to-give-access-to-kasab-20871.

45. "Pak Court Adjourns 26/11 Case to May 22," *Hindu*, May 9, 2010.

46. "ISI Behind 26/11, from Start to End: Home Secy," *Indian Express*, July 14, 2010.

47. Nissar Ahmad Thakor, "Everything Including Kashmir Discussed: Qureshi," *Greater Kashmir*, July 15, 2010.

48. Neeta Lal, "Will Manmohan Singh's Invitation to His Pakistani Counterpart to Watch an India vs Pakistan World Cup Tie Help Ties?," *Diplomat*, April 1, 2011.

49. "Indo-Pak Ties Not a Profit or Loss Statement: Rao," IBN Live, July 3, 2011, http://ibnlive.in.com/news/indopak-ties-not-a-profit-or-loss-statement-rao/164704-3.html.

50. "Text of the Joint Statement by Foreign Minister Hina Rabbani Khar and Indian Minister of External Affairs S.M. Krishna, New Delhi; 27 July 2011," http://www.piia.org.pk/images/document/text-of-the-joint-statement-by-foreign-minister-hina-rabbani-27-july-2011..pdf.

51. Mark Magnier, "Indian Helicopter Strays into Pakistan-Held Part of Kashmir," *Los Angeles Times*, October 24, 2011.

52. "India Pakistan Relations: Prime Minister Manmohan Singh Calls for a New Chapter," *Huffington Post*, November 10, 2011.

53. Assad Kharal, "US Announces $10 Million Bounty on Hafiz Saeed: Report," *Express Tribune*, April 3, 2012.

54. Stephanie Kennedy, "Pakistan Militant Taunts US over $10m Bounty," ABC News, April 5, 2012.

55. Salman Masood, "Pakistani Lawmakers Criticize US Reward for Militant Leader," *New York Times*, April 5, 2012.

56. *Mannat* is a popular practice in Sufism, when a believer vows to visit a shrine of an eminent Sufi saint or give money or food to the needy if their wish is fulfilled.

57. "Delicacies Await Zardari at Dr Singh's Lunch, BUT . . . ," *Rediff* (Mumbai), April 7, 2012.

58. Annie Banerji, "India to Allow FDI from Pakistan, Open Border Post," Reuters, April 13, 2012.

59. "Both Leaders Stick to Their Stands," *Dawn* (Karachi), August 30, 2012.

60. Salman Masood, "India and Pakistan Sign Visa Agreement, Easing Travel," *New York Times*, September 8, 2012.

61. "From Bashir to Khurshid: Who Said What on the LoC Crisis," *First Post* (Mumbai), January 17, 2013.

62. "Statement by BJP President, Shri Rajnath Singh on Mr. Nawaz Sharif's Win in Pakistan Polls," http://www.bjp.org/index.php?option=com_content&view=article&id=8732:press—shri-rajnath-singh-on-mr-nawaz-sharifs-win-in-pakistan-polls&catid=68:press-releases&Itemid=494.

63. Ibid.

64. Jon Boone, "Kashmir Tensions Threaten to Return India and Pakistan to Vitriolic Past," *Guardian* (London), August 8, 2013.

65. Ibid.

66. David Blair and David Munk, "If Pakistan Is to Prosper, We Must Stop Bashing India," *Daily Telegraph* (London), August 24, 2013.

67. "Pakistan Committed Against Extremism, but Drones Must Stop: Nawaz at UN," *Express Tribune*, September 27, 2013.

68. Elizabeth Roche, "Manmohan Singh at UN: Pakistan Should Dismantle Terror Machinery," *Live Mint* (Delhi), September 28, 2013.

69. "Nawaz, Manmohan Agree to Reduce Kashmir Tensions," *Dawn* (Karachi), September 29, 2013.

70. "Joint Statement on Manmohan Singh's Summit Meeting with President Obama in Washington," *Hindu*, September 27, 2013.

71. "26/11 Mumbai Attacks: Trial Against Pak Suspects Adjourned," *First Post* (Mumbai), March 5, 2014.

72. Malik Asad, "Trial of Mumbai Attack Case Suspects Stalled," *Dawn* (Karachi), April 4, 2014.

CHAPTER 18: COMPETING FOR KABUL

1. Fazal-ur Rahim Marwat, "The Durand Line Issue," *Frontier Post* (Peshawar), October 17, 2003.

2. William Dalrymple, "A Deadly Triangle," Brookings Institution, June 25, 2013, http://www.brookings.edu/research/essays/2013/deadly-triangle-afghanistan-pakistan-india-c.

3. Najmuddin A. Shaikh, "What Does Pakistan Want in Afghanistan?," *Express Tribune* (Karachi), December 27, 2011.

4. It was only in 2002 that Delhi acknowledged setting up an airbase in Farkhor.

5. Dilip Hiro, *War Without End: The Rise of Islamist Terrorism and Global Response* (London: Routledge, 2002), 297–298.

6. Husain Haqqani, *Pakistan: Between Mosque and Military* (Washington, DC: Carnegie Endowment for International Peace, 2005), 262.

7. Himachal Pradesh University conferred an honorary doctorate on Hamid Karzai in 2002.

8. Dalrymple, "A Deadly Triangle."

9. "Alongside Its Embassy in Kabul, India Will Open Consulates in Four Afghan Cities," *Pravda*, December 24, 2001.

10. Ahmed Rashid, *Descent into Chaos: How the War Against Islamic Extremism Is Being Lost in Pakistan, Afghanistan and Central Asia* (London: Allen Lane, 2008 / New York: Penguin Books, 2009), 143–144.

11. Ahmed Rashid, "Pakistan Closes Its Embassy in Afghanistan amid Escalating Diplomatic Tension," *RefWorld* (UNHCR), July 8, 2003.

12. Ahmed Rashid, "Islamabad's Lingering Support for Islamic Extremists Threatens Pakistan-Afghanistan Ties," *RefWorld* (UNHCR), July 23, 2003.

13. Ibid.

14. Scott Baldauf, "India-Pakistan Rivalry Reaches into Afghanistan," *Christian Science Monitor*, September 12, 2003.

15. "Image of the Beast," There Are No Sunglasses (blog), January 9, 2010, https://therearenosunglasses.wordpress.com/2010/01/09.

16. Shaiq Hussain, "Pakistan to Ask India to Rein in Afghan Consulates," *Nation* (Islamabad), March 18, 2006.

17. Mariana Baabar, "RAW Is Training 600 Baluchis in Afghanistan," *Outlook* (Delhi), April 24, 2006.

18. Dalrymple, "A Deadly Triangle."

19. "Pakistan's Musharraf Slams Afghanistan's Karzai," *Afghanistan News Center*, March 6, 2006.

20. Ibid.

21. "Afghanistan President Hamid Karzai with Fareed Zakaria, Editor, *Newsweek International*," Council on Foreign Relations, September 21, 2006, http://www.cfr.org/afghanistan/afghanistan-president-hamid-karzai-rush-transcript-federal-news-service/p11507.

22. "Seven Pakistani Troops Dead as Border Clash Continues," *Nawaaye Afghanistan*, May 15, 2008.

23. Ibid.

24. Ibid.

25. "Embassy Attack in Kabul Highlights Pakistan-India Rivalry," EurasiaNet, July 8, 2008, http://www.eurasianet.org/departments/insight/articles/pp070208.shtml.

26. Sayed Salahuddin, "Karzai Says Pakistan Behind Indian Embassy Bomb," *Afghan News Bulletin* no. 2105, July 15, 2008.

27. Some of the grenades used in the 2008 Mumbai terror attacks were also traced back to the POF unit in Wah. The grenades were manufactured by POF under license from an Austrian firm.

28. Mark Mazzetti and Eric Schmitt, "Pakistanis Aided Attack in Kabul, US Officials Say," *New York Times*, August 1, 2008.

29. "ISI Nailed in Kabul Embassy Outrage: 2008 Bombing Plan WAS Hatched in Pakistan, New Book Claims," *Mail Today Bureau* (Delhi), March 23, 2014; "2008 Indian Embassy Attack in Kabul Sanctioned by ISI, New Book Claims," *Times of India*, March 23, 2014.

30. Kuldip Nayar, "ISI Playing a Dangerous Game with Taliban," *Sunday Times* (Delhi), August 17, 2008.

31. Bhashyam Kasturi, "India's Role in Afghanistan," State of Pakistan, February 20, 2012, http://www.stateofpakistan.org/indias-role-in-afghanistan.

32. "India and Pakistan Ramp Up Aid as They Jostle for Influence in Kabul," Reuters, March 4, 2014.

33. Aryn Baker, "Karzai on Musharraf: Good Riddance," *Time*, August 19, 2008.

34. Ibid.

35. "Turkey, Afghanistan, Pakistan to Strengthen Anti-Terrorism Co-op," Xinhua Net, December 5, 2008.

36. "Afghanistan: National Opinion Poll" for BBC, ABC News, and ARD, http://news.bbc.co.uk/1/shared/bsp/hi/pdfs/05_02_09afghan_poll_2009.pdf.

37. Dalrymple, "A Deadly Triangle."

38. Julian Borger, "UN in Secret Talks with Taliban," *Guardian* (London), January 28, 2010.

39. Afghanistan: National Opinion Poll.

40. "9 Indians Among 17 Dead as Taliban Bombers Attack Kabul," *Times of India*, February 26, 2010.

41. Karzai appointed his brother-in-law Ibrahim Spinzada as the new NSD director temporarily, and replaced him with Rahmatullah Nabil, a Pashtun politician.

42. "Amid Pakistani Moves, Krishna to Attend Kabul Meet," *Thaindian News*, July 10, 2010.

43. "Expert Discuss Ways to Promote Pak-Afghan Trade," *Express Tribune* (Karachi), August 24, 2013.

44. Larry Hanauer and Peter Chalk, "India's and Pakistan's Strategies in Afghanistan: Implications for the United States and the Region," Occasional Paper, Center for Asia Pacific Policy, RAND, 2012, http://www.rand.org/content/dam/rand/pubs/occasional_papers/2012/RAND_OP387.pdf, 16n35.

45. Susan Cornwell, "Factbox: US Has Allocated $20 billion for Pakistan," Reuters, April 21, 2011.

46. Solomon Moore and Rahim Faiez, "Hamid Karzai: Pakistan Firing Missiles into Afghanistan," *Huffington Post*, June 28, 2011.

47. "30 Afghan Militants Killed After Cross Border Raid," *Express Tribune* (Karachi), October 10, 2011.

48. "Text of Agreement on Strategic Partnership between the Republic of India and the Islamic Republic of Afghanistan," October 4, 2011, http://im.rediff.com/news/2011/oct/04indo-afghan-strategic-agreement.pdf.

49. "Afghanistan and India Sign 'Strategic Partnership,'" BBC News, October 4, 2011.

50. Sebastian Abbot, "Pakistan Warns Afghanistan After Pact with India," Associated Press, October 6, 2011.

51. "India Plans to Train 30,000 Afghan Soldiers," *National* (Dubai), December 3, 2011, 3; Rahul Bedi, "India Steps Up Afghan Troop Training," *IHS Jane's Defence Security Report*, November 29, 2011.

52. Richard Weitz, "Afghanistan and India Deepen Strategic Cooperation," CACI Analyst, January 22, 2014. According to Afghanistan's ambassador to India, about 350 Afghan army officers receive annual training in India, with a total of 1,400 trained since 2003.

53. "Indian Consortium Wins $10bn Afghanistan Mines Deal," BBC News, November 29, 2011.

54. "SAIL-Led Consortium to Cut Spend on Afghan Iron Ore Mine," *Live Mint* (Delhi), November 11, 2013.

55. Huma Imtiaz, "New York Summit: Zardari, Karzai and Cameron Discuss Afghan Endgame," *Express Tribune* (Karachi), September 27, 2012; "Accusations of Afghan President Termed 'Totally Misplaced,'" *Express Tribune* (Karachi), October 9, 2012.

56. Anirban Bhaumik, "India Concerned over Leaked Afghan Peace Road Map," Taand.com, January 4, 2013, http://www.english.taand.com/index.php?mod=article&cat=articles&article=2280.

57. "Karzai Calls for Pakistan Role in Afghan Peace Process," BBC News, August 26, 2013.

58. "Afghanistan Aid" (graph), Reuters, March 4, 2014.

59. "India and Pakistan Ramp Up Aid."

60. Hanauer and Chalk, "India's and Pakistan's Strategies in Afghanistan."

61. "India Vows to Complete Salma Dam Project Within a Year," *Tolo News*, August 24, 2013.

62. Aryn Baker, "Afghanistan Unplugs Bollywood's Siren Song," *Time*, May 8, 2008.

63. Alisa Tang and Rahim Faiez, "TV Stations Defy Afghan Government Ban on Indian Soap Operas," Associated Press, April 23, 2008.

64. Robin Bansal, "Afghanistan Crazy About Bollywood, but Lacks Official Market," IANS, April 18, 2010, http://www.bollywood.com/afghanistan-crazy-about-bollywood-lacks-official-market.

65. Abdul Haleem, Chen Xin, "Feature: Jobless Young Afghans Find Escape in Bollywood Movies," Xinhua Net, June 17, 2012.

66. "Afghanistan and the Popularity of Bollywood Are Inseparable," *Economic Times*, June 17, 2012.

CHAPTER 19: SHARED CULTURE, RISING COMMERCE

1. Pending Proceedings Order, Martial Law Order No. 107 (December 30, 1985), http://pakistan constitutionlaw.com/pending-proceedings-order-martial-law-order-no-107-30th-of-december-1985.

2. Taran Adarsh, "Mughal-e-Azam Censored in Pakistan," *Sify Movies*, February 13, 2006, http://www.sify.com/movies/mughal-e-azam-censored-in-pakistan-news-bollywood-kkfvtdefjcd.html.

3. "Pakistan Clears Bollywood Films," BBC News, February 8, 2006.

4. "Mughal-e-Azam Releases in Pakistan: Will Others Follow Suit?," *One India News*, April 23, 2006.

5. "Taj Film Set for History in Pak," *Telegraph* (Kolkata), April 25, 2006.

6. M. Zulqernain, "Pakistani Court Stops Airing of Indian, Foreign Films on TV," *Rediff News* (Mumbai), December 11, 2013.

7. "Mughal-e-Azam Releases in Pakistan."

8. Ibid.

9. "Ban on Indian Movies," *Dawn* (Karachi), December 6, 2012.

10. Palash Ghosh, "Bollywood Boom and 'Dhoom': Indian Films Wildly Popular in Pakistan Despite 'Ban' on Their Exhibition," *International Business Times*, January 7, 2014.

11. "Amir Khan's 'Dhoom 3' Breaks Box Office Records in Pakistan," *Indian Express*, December 26, 2013.

12. "Pakistan's Ban on Bollywood Films Withdrawn," *Financial Express*, December 17, 2013.

13. "Pak Army Must Acquire a Television Channel," *Siasat Daily* (Hyderabad), December 17, 2013.

14. Praveen Swami, "*Green Books*, Red Herring and LoC War," Hindu, January 16, 2013.

15. Ghosh, "Bollywood Boom and 'Dhoom.'"

16. "India vs Pakistan: Cricket History," NDTV Cricket, December 10, 2012, http://sports.ndtv.com/india-vs-pakistan-2012/about/200488-india-vs-pakistan-cricket-history.

17. A Twenty20 game, introduced in 2003 in England and Wales, involves two teams; each has a single innings and bats for a maximum of 20 overs.

18. Statistics from ESPN's Cricinfo, http://stats.espncricinfo.com/ci/engine/stats/index.html?class=2;filter=advanced;opposition=7;orderby=won;team=6;template=results;type=team.

19. Kanishkaa Balachandran, "Going, Going . . . Gone, Following Shivnarine Chanderpaul's Heroics, Cricinfo Looks Back at Similar One-Day Thrillers," ESPN Cricinfo, April 10, 2008.

20. "Resumption of India-Pakistan Matches Moves Closer," ESPN Cricinfo, October 22, 2003.

21. "Sahara India to Sponsor India, Pakistan Matches in Canada," ESPN, July 15, 1996, http://www.espncricinfo.com/page2/content/story/72440.html.

22. "Resumption of India-Pakistan Matches Moves Closer."

23. Sanjoy Majumder, "India-Pakistan Cricket Battle at Mohali Raises Passions," March 30, 2011.

24. "Heartbreak in Pakistan, Three Die over Defeat," NDTV, April 1, 2011, http://www.ndtv.com/article/world/heartbreak-in-pakistan-three-die-over-defeat-95531.

25. "Stop Praising Sachin Tendulkar, Taliban Warn Pakistan Media," *Times of India*, November 28, 2013.

26. "Pakistan Ready to Tour India for Cricket Revival: Sethi," *Dawn* (Karachi), December 18, 2013.

27. "Gross Domestic Product (GDP) in Pakistan," Kushnirs, n.d., http://kushnirs.org/macro economics/gdp/gdp_pakistan.html.

28. Mubarak Zeb Khan, "MFN Status for India on the Cards," *Dawn* (Karachi), January 26, 2014.

29. *MNF Status and Trade Between Pakistan and India*, Pakistan Institute of Legislative Development and Transparency, January 2012.

30. Vimal Bhatia, "Road Link Likely Between India and Pakistan Soon," *Times of India*, September 23, 2012.

31. *MNF Status and Trade Between Pakistan and India.*

32. Ibid.

33. "Tomato-Laden Truck Covers New Ground for India-Pakistan Trade," *DNA India*, October 1, 2007.

34. *MNF Status and Trade Between Pakistan and India.*

35. "Pakistan, India to Increase Frequency of Freight Trains," *Nation* (Islamabad), June 20, 2008.

36. B. Raman, "Indo-Pak Economic Ties: Ground Realities," Observer Research Foundation, November 26, 2004, http://orfonline.org/cms/sites/orfonline/modules/analysis/AnalysisDetail.html?cmaid=2252&mmacmaid=197.

37. The eight members of the South Asian Association of Regional Cooperation in 2007 were Afghanistan, Bangladesh, Bhutan, India, Maldives, Nepal, Pakistan, and Sri Lanka.

38. Mohsin S. Khan, "Improving India-Pakistan Relations Through Trade," East Asia Forum, April 19, 2010, http://www.eastasiaforum.org/2010/04/19/improving-india-pakistan-relations-through-trade.

39. "India-Pakistan Events," Reuters, August 4, 2012.

40. "Pakistan Notifies Negative List for Trade with India," *Economic Times*, March 21, 2012.

41. "Modi Uses Business the Way Out with Pak," *Siasat Daily* (Hyderabad), May 28, 2014.

42. "Pak Trade Barrier Holds Indian Bicycle Industry," *Hindustan Times*, April 6, 2014.

43. Sarabjit Pandher, "Attari Integrated Check Post to Open Tomorrow," *Hindu*, April 12, 2012.

44. Sarabjit Pandher, "New Liberal Visa Regime with Pakistan Soon: Chidambaram," *Hindu*, April 13, 2012.

45. "India to Cut List to 100 from 614 Items," *Nation* (Islamabad), October 22, 2012.

46. Nazar Ul Islam, "Trading with the Enemy," *Newsweek*, December 17, 2013.

47. "Trade Between India and Pakistan Surges 21% to $2.4 Billion," *Express Tribune*, May 14, 2013.

48. "Govt to Curtail Negative List of Trade Items with India," *Express Tribune*, January 23, 2014.

49. "India, Pakistan Need to Take Steps to Boost Trade," *Economic Times*, January 21, 2014; Zeb Khan, "MFN Status for India on the Cards."

50. "Importable Items from India: PIAF Asks Government to Cut Down Negative List," *Business Recorder*, January 2, 2014.

51. Aamir Shafaat Khan, "Trade Deficit with China Up 58pc," *Dawn* (Karachi), February 10, 2013.

52. "Economic and Trade Relations between China and India," Economic and Commercial Section of the Consulate General of the People's Republic of China in Mumbai, December 15, 2004, http://bombay2.mofcom.gov.cn/article/bilateralcooperation/inbrief/200412/20041200010319.shtml; "Total Trade, Country-wise," Ministry of Commerce & Industry, Government of India, http://commerce.nic.in/eidb/Default.asp.

CHAPTER 20: OVERVIEW AND CONCLUSIONS

1. R. Shayan, "Sir Syed Ahmed Khan," Agnostic Pakistan (blog), December 14, 2008, http://agnosticpakistan.blogspot.co.uk/2008/12/sir-syed-ahmed-khan.html.

2. Arun, "Provincial Elections India 1946," Wake Up, Smell the Coffee (blog), January 27, 2011, http://observingliberalpakistan.blogspot.co.uk/2011/01/provincial-elections-india-1946.html.

3. Cited in Dilip Hiro, *The Timeline History of India* (New York: Barnes & Noble, 2006), 261.

4. Cited by Ye Zhengjia, "Clearing the Atmosphere," *Frontline* (Chennai), October 10–23, 1998, citing Major-General Lei Yingfu, *My Days as a Military Staff in the Supreme Command* (in Chinese) (Nanchang: Baihuazhou Culture and Arts, 1997), 210.

5. "Simla Agreement, July 2, 1972," http://www.jammu-kashmir.com/documents/simla.html.

6. Muhammad Zia ul Haq missed the irony of using the term "peanuts": Jimmy Carter was a peanut farmer before being elected governor of Georgia in 1970.

7. Adrian Levy and Catherine Scott-Clark, *Deception: Pakistan, the United States and the Secret Trade in Nuclear Weapons* (New York: Walker & Company, 2007), 104–105.

8. Ibid., 106.

9. Ibid., 151.

10. T. V. Paul, "The Systemic Bases of India's Challenge to the Global Nuclear Order," *Nonproliferation Review* (Fall 1998).

11. Rai Muhammad Saleh Azam, "When Mountains Move—The Story of Chagai," *Defence Journal* (June 2000).

12. Pamela Philipose, "The Symbol of Pakistan," *Indian Express*, February 22, 1999.

13. "Lahore Declaration," http://www.nti.org/treaties-and-regimes/lahore-declaration. The Indian and Pakistani foreign secretaries had prepared the draft of this agreement a month earlier.

14. "Pakistan Warns of Kashmir War Risk," BBC World, June 23, 1999.

15. Steve Coll, "The Stand-Off: How Jihadi Groups Helped Provoke the Twenty-First Century's First Nuclear Crisis," *New Yorker*, February 13, 2006.

16. The remainder of the pre-1947 Jammu and Kashmir was controlled by China.

17. Jyoti Malhotra, "Kashmir: Is Solution in Sight?," December 7, 2006, BBC News.

18. Kenneth J. Cooper, "India, Pakistan Kindle Hope for Peace," *Washington Post*, February 21, 1999.

19. "Literacy in India," Census of India 2011, http://www.census2011.co.in/literacy.php.

20. "Pakistan Ranks 180 in Literacy: UNESCO," *Pakistan Today*, December 4, 2013.

EPILOGUE

1. Saba Imtiaz, "Fishermen Cross an Imperceptible Line into Enemy Waters," *New York Times*, August 24, 2014. Between 2008 and 2013, India had released 353 Pakistani fishermen.

2. Hilary Whiteman and Harmeet Shah Singh, "India, Pakistan Leaders Meet, Signal Steps to Rebuild Trust," CNN, May 27, 2014.

3. Hari Kumar, "Premier Denounces Pakistan for 'Proxy War,'" *New York Times*, August 12, 2014.

4. Ibid.; "Narendra Modi Accuses Pakistan of Waging Proxy War in Kashmir," *Guardian* (London), August 12, 2014.

5. Biplob Ghosal, "Geelani Meets Pakistani High Commissioner, Says India's Decision to Cancel Talks 'Childish,'" Zee Media Bureau, August 19, 2014, http://zeenews.india.com/news/nation/geelani-meets-pakistani-high-commissioner-says-indias-decision-to-cancel-talks-childish_955441.html.

6. "Pakistan Says It Is 'Not Subservient' to India," *Times of India*, August 19, 2014.

7. Sachin Prashar, "Nawaz Sharif Seeks to Sweeten India-Pakistan Ties with Mangoes to Narendra Modi," *Times of India*, September 5, 2014.

8. "Pakistan Can't Draw Veil over Kashmir Issue: PM," *Daily Times* (Lahore), September 27, 2014.

9. Chidanand Rajghatta, "At UN General Assembly, PM Narendra Modi Rebukes Pakistan for Its Kashmir Obsession," *Times of India*, September 27, 2014.

10. "Time for 'New Beginning' in Bilateral Ties: Pakistani High Commissioner to India," *Express Tribune* (Karachi), September 11, 2014.

11. Indian Council for Research on International Economic Relations (ICRIER), "India-Pakistan Auto Makers Ink Co-operation Agreement, August 27, 2014," http://indiapakistantrade.org/recent Developments.html#automakers.

12. Jon Boone and Rupam Jain, "Indians to Get Peek into Daily Lives of Pakistanis with New Soap Opera Channel," *Guardian* (London), June 23, 2014.

13. Nandini Sharma, "Gear Up for Two New Shows on Zindagi," *Business Insider*, July 12, 2014.

Select Bibliography

Adams, Jad. *Gandhi: Naked Ambition*. London: Quercus, 2010.

Ahmed, Akbar S. *Pakistan and Islamic Identity: The Search for Saladin*. London: Routledge, 1997.

Akbar, M. J. *India: The Siege Within*. Harmondsworth, UK: Penguin Books, 1985.

Ali, Tariq. *The Duel: Pakistan on the Flight Path of American Power*. New York: Scribner, 2008.

———. *Pakistan: Military Rule or People's Power*. London: Jonathan Cape, 1970.

Anderson, Perry. *The Indian Ideology*. Gurgaon: Three Essays Collective, 2012.

Aziz, Khursheed Kamal. *Rahmat Ali: A Biography*. Lahore: Vanguard Books, 1987.

Bandhopadhyay, J. *The Making of India's Foreign Policy*. New Delhi: Allied, 1991.

Bhutto, Fatima. *Songs of Blood and Sword: A Daughter's Memoir*. London: Jonathan Cape, 2010 / New York: Nation Books, 2010.

Bhutto, Zulfikar Ali. *If I Am Assassinated*. New Delhi: Vikas, 1979.

———. *The Myth of Independence*. London and Karachi: Oxford University Press, 1969.

Blackburn, Robin, ed. *Explosion in a Subcontinent: India, Pakistan, Bangladesh and Ceylon*. Harmondsworth, UK: Penguin Books, 1975.

Bolitho, Hector. *Jinnah: Creator of Pakistan*. Westport, CT: Greenwood, 1981.

Bose, Sumanta. *Kashmir: Roots of Conflict, Paths to Peace*. Cambridge, MA: Harvard University Press, 2005.

Chatterji, Joya. *Bengal Divided: Hindu Communalism and Partition, 1932–1947*. Cambridge: Cambridge University Press, 2002.

Chaudhri, Muhammad Ali. *The Emergence of Pakistan*. New York: Columbia University Press, 1967.

Fischer, Louis. *Gandhi: His Life and Message for the World*. New York: Mentor Books, 1954.

———. *The Life of Mahatma Gandhi*. London: Granada, 1982.

French, Patrick. *Liberty or Death: India's Journey to Independence and Division*. London: HarperCollins, 1997.

Galbraith, John Kenneth. *Ambassador's Journal: A Personal Account of the Kennedy Years*. Boston: Houghton Mifflin / London: Hamish Hamilton, 1969.

Gandhi, Rajmohan. *Gandhi: The Man, His People and the Empire*. Berkeley: University of California Press / London: Haus, 2010.

———. *Understanding the Muslim Mind*. New Delhi: Penguin Books, 2000.

Ghose, Sankar. *Jawaharlal Nehru: A Biography*. New Delhi: Allied, 1993.

———. *Mahatma Gandhi*. New Delhi: Allied, 1991.

Gould, Harold. *The South Asia Story: The First Sixty Years of U.S. Relations with India and Pakistan*. New Delhi: Sage, 2010.

Guha, Ramchandra. *India After Gandhi: The History of the World's Largest Democracy*. London: Macmillan, 2007 / New York: Harper Perennial, 2008.

Gulhati, Niranjan D. *The Indus Waters Treaty: An Exercise in International Mediation*. Bombay: Allied, 1973.

Hansen, Thomas Blom. *The Saffron Wave: Democracy and Hindu Nationalism in Modern India*. Princeton, NJ: Princeton University Press, 1999.

Haqqani, Husain. *Pakistan: Between Mosque and Military*. Washington, DC: Carnegie Endowment for International Peace, 2005.

Hiro, Dilip. *Apocalyptic Realm: Jihadists in South Asia*. New Haven, CT: Yale University Press, 2012.

———. *Inside India Today*. London: Routledge & Kegan Paul, 1976 / New York: Monthly Review Press, 1977.

———. *The Timeline History of India*. New York: Barnes & Noble, 2006.

———. *War Without End: The Rise of Islamist Terrorism and Global Response*. London: Routledge, 2002.

Hutchinson, Robert. *Weapons of Mass Destruction: The No-Nonsense Guide to Nuclear, Chemical and Biological Weapons Today*. London: Weidenfeld & Nicolson, 2003.

Jagmohan. *My Frozen Turbulence in Kashmir*. 8th edition. New Delhi: Allied, 2007.

Jalal, Ayesha. *The Sole Spokesman: Jinnah, the Muslim League and the Demand for Pakistan*. Cambridge: Cambridge University Press, 1985.

Khilnani, Sunil. *The Idea of India*. London: Penguin Books, 1998 / New York: Farrar, Straus and Giroux, 1998.

Kux, Dennis. *India and the United States: Estranged Democracies, 1941-1991*. Washington, DC: National Defense University Press, 1992.

Lamb, Christina. *Waiting for Allah: Pakistan's Struggle for Democracy*. London: Hamish Hamilton, 1991.

Levy, Adrian, and Catherine Scott-Clark. *Deception: Pakistan, the United States and the Global Nuclear Weapons Conspiracy*. London: Atlantic Books, 2007 / New York: Walker & Company, 2007.

Lieven, Anatol. *Pakistan: A Hard Country*. London: Allen Lane, 2011.

McGarr, Paul M. *The Cold War in South Asia: The United States and the Indian Subcontinent, 1945–1965*. Cambridge: Cambridge University Press, 2013.

Merriam, Allen Hayes. *Gandhi Versus Jinnah: The Debate over the Partition of India*. Calcutta: Minerva Associates, 1980 / Thousand Oaks, CA: Sage, 1982.

Michel, Aloys Arthur. *The Indus Rivers: A Study of the Effects of Partition*. New Haven, CT: Yale University Press, 1967.

Moon, Penderel. *Divide and Quit*. Berkeley: University of California Press, 1962.

———, ed. *Wavell: The Viceroy's Journal*. New York: Oxford University Press, 1997.

Nayar, Kuldip. *Beyond the Lines: An Autobiography*. New Delhi: Roli Books, 2012.

———. *India: The Critical Years*. London: Weidenfeld & Nicolson, 1971 / New Delhi: Vikas, 1971.

Peer, Basharat. *Curfewed Night*. Noida: Random House India, 2009. / *Curfewed Night: One Kashmiri Journalist's Frontline Account of Life, Love, and War in His Homeland*. New York: Scribner, 2010. / *Curfewed Night: A Frontline Memoir of Life, Love and War in Kashmir*. London: Harper, 2010.

Prasad, Rajendra. *Satyagraha in Champaran*. Ahmedabad: Navajivan, 1949.

Raman, B. *The Kaoboys of R&AW: Down Memory Lane*. New Delhi: Lancer, 2008.

Sattar, Abdul. *Pakistan's Foreign Policy, 1947–2005: A Concise History*. Karachi: Oxford University Press, 2007.

Schofield, Victoria. *Bhutto: Trial and Execution*. London: Cassell, 1977.

———. *Kashmir in Conflict: India, Pakistan and the Unending War*. Revised edition. London: I. B. Tauris, 2003.

Scott-Clark, Catherine, and Adrian Levy. *The Siege: 68 Hours Inside the Taj Hotel*. New York: Penguin Books, 2013. / *The Siege: Three Days of Terror Inside the Taj*. London: Viking, 2013.

Singh, Jaswant. *Jinnah: India—Partition—Independence*. New Delhi: Rupa and Company, 2009.

Singh, Khushwant. *A History of the Sikhs: Volume 2, 1839–2004*. New Delhi: Oxford University Press, 2012.

———. *Train to Pakistan*. New Delhi: Penguin Books, 2009.

Snedden, Christopher. *Kashmir: The Unwritten History*. New Delhi: HarperCollins India, 2013.

Stephens, Ian. *Pakistan*. London: Ernest Benn, 1963.

Tidrick, Kathryn. *Gandhi: A Political and Spiritual Life*. London: I. B. Tauris, 2006.

Verghese, B. G. *Waters of Hope*. New Delhi: Oxford and IBH, 1990.

Von Tunzelmann, Alex. *Indian Summer: The Secret History of the End of an Empire*. London: Simon & Schuster, 2008.

Ziring, Lawrence. *The Ayub Khan Era: Politics in Pakistan 1958–1969*. Syracuse, NY: Syracuse University Press, 1971.

———. *Pakistan in the Twentieth Century*. Karachi: Oxford University Press, 1997.

Index

Aatish-e-Chinar, 176
A B Bofor, 267
Abbas, Chaudhury Muhammad, 176
Abbas, Ghulam 112
Abbottabad, 118, 119, 387
ABC News (US), 384, 385
Abdullah, Farooq, 277, 279
Abdullah, Shaikh Muhammad, 112,
    178, 181, 277
  and Ayub Khan, Muhammad, 176
  and Bangladesh War, 227
  and Gandhi, Indira, 228
  and Jinnah, Muhammad Ali, 113,
    116
  and Nehru, Jawaharlal, 112, 116,
    151, 176
  and Pakistan, 153, 176, 359
  and plebiscite, 177
  and Singh, Sir Hari, 113, 116, 121
  and Zhou Enlai, 177
  as Chief Administrator, 123
  as Chief Minister, 228
  as Prime Minister, 130, 142
  biography and character of,
    112–113
  imprisonment of, 143, 150, 153, 178
  trail of, 153, 174–175
Abdullah, Shiraz, 47
Abdullah Abdullah, 385
Abdullah bin Abdul Aziz (Saudi
    Crown Prince), 289, 385
Abraham (Prophet), 4
Abraham Lincoln (US warship), 303
Abu Dhabi, 305

A Case of Exploding Mangoes, 262
Acharaya, Krishna, 399
Achin, 392
Addu City, 362
Advani, Lal Krishna, 314, 315,
    325–326
Afghan Mujahedin, 238, 241, 252–253
Afghan-Soviet Treaty of Friendship
    and Cooperation, 238
Afghan Taliban, *see* Taliban
Afghanistan and Afghans, 4, 5, 299,
    369, 422
  and Britain, 369
  and Carter, Jimmy, 237, 326
  and India, 238–239, 359, 371,
    372–373, 374, 375–376, 377, 378,
    381–382, 383, 384, 385–386, 387,
    390, 391, 392–393, 422
  and North Atlantic Treaty
    Organization NATO), 379
  and Pakistan, 238, 370–371, 372,
    374, 375–376, 377, 378, 380–381,
    384, 386–387, 389, 390, 416, 422
  and Russia, 372
  and Soviet Union, 238, 253, 258,
    370–371, 372
  and Taliban, 372, 385, 386, 390,
    391, 392
  and United Nations, 375
  and United States, 237, 252, 316,
    326, 359, 372, 375, 376, 383, 385,
    387
  civil war in, 372
  Marxist coup in, 237–238, 368, 371

Afridi, Aleem, 217
Afridi, Shahid, 403
Afridi tribe, 118
Afzal, Muhammad, 321
Aga Khan, 6
Agra, 213, 309, 314, 369, 428
Agreement on Prohibition of Attacks Against Nuclear Installations and Facilities (India-Pakistan), 266, 323, 425
Agreement on Strategic Partnership between India and Islamic Republic of Afghanistan, 388–389
Ahmad, Aziz, 194
Ahmad, Fakhruddin Ali, 232
Ahmad, Qazi Hussein, 292
Ahmad Khan, Munir, 190, 222, 244, 423
Ahmadis, 229
Ahmed, Imtiaz, 264
Ahmed, Ishaq, 285
Ahmed, Khwaja Ihsan, 293
Ahmed, Mahmood, 299, 304, 305, 306, 316, 317, 319
Ahmed, Shamshad, 290
Ahmedabad, 17, 21, 23, 36, 85
Ahmedabad Mill Owners Association (AMOA), 21–22
Ahmedabad Textile Labor Association, 23
Aichison's Treaties, 160
Aibak, Qutbuddin, 413
Air India, 374
Ajmer, 363
Akal Fauj, 100
Akali Dal, 252
Akali Party, 79
Akbar (Emperor), 397
Akbar, Saad, 140–141
Akbar, Zahid Ali, 230
Akhnoor, 179, 181, 183, 184, 328
Akhtar, Farhan, 302
Akhtar, Javed, 301, 302
Akram, Malik Muhammad, 367
Aksai Chin, 154, 160, 165, 167

Al Furqan, 337
al Libi, Abu Faraj, 338
al Nahyan, Shaikh Zayed bin Sultan, 305
Al Qaida, 304, 310, 316, 317, 322, 338, 348, 363, 373, 382, 384, 385, 387, 390
Al Zulfikar, 261
Alexander, Albert Victor, 79
Algiers, 177
Ali, Chaudhry Zulfikar, 267
Ali, Muhammad Akbar, 234
Ali, Chaudhri Muhammad, 119, 129, 147
Ali, Asaf, 85, 113, 124
Ali, Syed Ajmad, 148
Ali, Choudhry Rahmat, 56–57
Ali, Shaukat, 28, 29, 30, 31, 32, 42–43
Ali Brothers, 27–28, 29–30, 35, 38
Ali Khan, Liaquat, 58, 85, 87, 93, 94, 96, 98, 105, 115, 130, 303
    and China, 138
    and Kashmir, 115, 116, 117, 119, 122, 123, 124, 133, 142, 416–417
    and Nehru, Jawaharlal, 132, 133, 138, 139–140
    and United States, 138
    assassination of, 140–141, 417
    biography and character of, 31–32
All India Congress Committee (AICC), 53, 60, 70, 71, 76, 81, 88, 97
All India Cow Protection Organization, 42
All India Hindu Mahasabha, see Hindu Mahasabha
All India Khilafat Conferences, 26, 27, 29, 30
All India Muslim League, see Muslim League
All India Sikh Students Federation, 252
All India Trade Union Congress, 23
Allama, Ghulam Ali, 88
All Parties Conference, 44
All Parties Hurriyat Conference (APHC), 277, 314, 342, 349

All Tripura Tiger Force, 197

Alling, Paul H., 110

Almaty, 330

Almelo, 231

Ambassador's Journal, 170

Ambedkar, Bhimrao Ramji, 54, 67

America and Americans, *see* United
    States

Amjad, Syed Muhammad, 312

Amin, Hafizullah, 238

Amin, Nurul, 139, 210

Amin, Roya, 393

Amman, 257

Amnesty International, 277

Amritsar, 24, 25, 26, 40, 248, 249, 256,
    423

Amsterdam, 231

*An Outsider Everywhere: Revelations of
    an Insider*, 223

Anada Math, 64

Anarkali, 397

Anderson, Jack, 212

Anglo-Indians, 51

Ankara, 384

Annan, Kofi, 313

"Ansar," 276

Ansari, Maulavi Abbas, 339

Ansari, Mukhtar Ahmad, 30, 34

Antony, Arackaparanibil Kurien, 356,
    366

Anwar, Khurshid, 117–118, 119,
    129–121

ARD (Germany), 384, 385

Ariana Afghan Airlines, 374

Armed Forces (Jammu and Kashmir)
    Special Powers Act (AFJKSP),
    275–276

Armitage, Richard, 316, 324

Arthashastra, 370

Arya Samaj, 29, 40, 41

Aryub Zazai, 380

Asian Games, 247

Asiatic Registration Bill, 12, 14, 15

Asif, Akbar, 397

Asif, Irfan, 398

Asif, Karimuddin, 397

Asif, Muhammad Azam, 301

Aslam, Ihsan, 302

Assam, 159

Associated Press of India, 117

Ataturk, Mustafa Kemal, 40

Atlantic Charter, 69

Attari, 303, 403, 409, 410

Attenborough, Richard, 25, 49, 106

Attlee, Clement, 74, 76, 77, 79, 87, 90,
    91, 94, 110, 113, 125, 416

Atwal, Avtar Singh, 248

Auchinleck, Sir Claude, 77, 100, 122,
    125

Aurora, Jagjit Singh, 209, 214, 215

Australia, 18, 152, 155, 417

Austro-Hungarian Empire, 11

Awami League (Pakistan), 147, 196,
    198, 199, 201, 202, 222

Awara (movie), 396

Axis Powers, 69, 75

Ayni Air Base, 372

Ayodhya, 272, 281

Ayub Khan, Gohar, 288

Ayub Khan, Muhammad, 146, 345,
    417, 428, 430
    and Abdullah, Shaikh Muhammad,
       176
    and Bhutto, Zulfikar Ali, 221, 179,
       180, 188, 294
    and China, 188
    and India, 396, 419
    and India-Pakistan War (1965),
       185, 187, 189–190, 420
    and Inter-Services Intelligence
       (ISI), 197
    and Kashmir, 155, 156–157, 170,
       173, 179, 180, 185, 196, 418
    and Kennedy, John F., 171, 174
    and Mao Zedong, 188
    and Nehru, Jawaharlal, 154, 155–
       57, 166, 170–171, 176, 417–418
    and Operation Desert Hawk, 179
    and Operation Gibraltar, 182–183
    and Operation Grand Slam, 179, 183
    and Shastri, Lal Bahadur, 174, 179,
       194

Ayub Khan, Muhammad *(continued)*
  and Soviet Union, 187–188,
    191–192
  and Tashkent Declaration, 195
  as Chief Martial Law
    Administrator, 149
  as Deputy Prime Minister, 210
  as President, 149, 153–154,
    155–157, 233
  biography and character of, 156
  resignation of, 196, 420
Azad, Maulana Abdul Kalam
    Muhiyuddin Ahmed, 48, 68, 72,
    74, 75, 78, 79, 80, 97, 126
Azad Army (Kashmir), 115, 117, 118
Azad Jammu and Kashmir, *see* Azad
    Kashmir
Azad Kashmir, 120, 123, 129, 133,
    142, 180, 189, 211, 215, 227, 268,
    270, 276, 342, 343, 355
Azhar, Maulana Masoud, 308, 320,
    337
Azhar, Muhammad Ibrahim, 508, 323
Aziz, Sartaj, 291, 295, 368
Aziz, Shahid, 287, 299, 304
Aziz, Shaukat, 337, 339
Aziz, Tariq, 342, 344, 345, 429
Aziz Khan, Muhammad, 294,
    295–296, 299, 304, 305, 317, 319,
    427
Azizabad, 348

Babri Mosque, 272, 281
Babur, Zahiruddin Muhammad, 4,
    272, 369
Badaber, 148
Badal, Sukhbur Singh, 404, 407, 409,
    410
Bahawalpur, 259, 422
Bakem, 373
Baker, Aryn, 383
Baker, James, 270
Baldauf, Scott, 376
Baltistan, 142
Baluchistan and Baluchis, 97, 226,
    228, 256, 274, 286, 358, 377–378

Baluchistan Liberation Army, 377
Bandar (Saudi Prince), 297, 298
Bandipora, 3
Bangkok, 342
Bangladesh, 189, 217, 222, 227, 420
Bangladesh Liberation War, *see*
    Bangladesh War
Bangladesh War, 200, 209–214, 217,
    220, 227, 303, 406
Banihal Pass, 119
Baradar, Abdul Ghani, 391
Baramulla, 3, 119, 120, 123
Barco, James W., 152
Bardoli, 37, 46
Bari, Maulana Abdul, 29
Barisal, 139
Barnala, Surjit Singh, 252
Bashir, Salman, 359
Batra, R. L., 120
Baweja, Harinder, 355
BBC, 261, 272, 301, 384, 385, 399
Beas River, 98, 154
Bedi, Rahul, 389
Beg, Mirza Aslam, 259, 264
Beg, Mirza Afzal, 153
Beijing, 147, 162, 188, 196, 200, 204,
    208, 233, 295
Bengal, 55, 57, 78, 95–96, 97, 395
Bengal Tenancy Act, 1885, 19
Bengali (language), 147, 417
Berger, Sandy, 298
Besant, Annie, 23, 33
Betrayal of East Pakistan, 202
Bhabha, Homi J., 228, 229
Bhabha Atomic Research Center, 229,
    423
Bhakar, Sarwant Singh, 249
Bharatiya Jan Sangh (BJS), 143, 145,
    280, 281
Bharatiya Janata Party (BJP), 272, 279,
    280, 281, 284, 300, 315, 331, 340,
    358, 366, 426
Bhatiya, Vinod, 365
Bhatt, Touseef, 3
Bhindranwale, Jarnail Singh, 248, 250,
    252

Bhindranwale Tiger Force, 257
Bhutan, 159
Bhutto, Amir, 221
Bhutto, Benazir, 263–264, 266, 278, 345
  and Gandhi, Rajiv, 265, 266, 267, 425
  and general elections, 264–265, 273, 274
  and India, 273
  and Indian Kashmir, 269, 274
  and Narasimha Rao, Pamulapartu Venkata, 274
  and Nawaz Sharif, Muhammad, 273
  and nuclear program, 277–278, 285
  and Sikh militancy, 266, 425
  and Taliban, 274
  and United States, 278
  and Zia ul Haq, Muhammad, 263
  as Prime Minister, 265, 268, 269, 273–274
  assassination of, 141, 347
  biography and character of, 221, 223–224
Bhutto, Fatima, 261
Bhutto, Khurshid, 230
Bhutto, Murtaza, 261, 262
Bhutto, Nusrat Begum, 221, 264, 265
Bhutto, Sir Shah Nawaz, 221, 230
Bhutto, Zulfikar Ali, 173, 174, 176, 192, 211, 218, 230, 265
  and Afghanistan, 237, 371
  and Ahmadis, 229
  and Ayub Khan, Muhammad, 221, 179, 180, 188, 294
  and Baluchistan, 226, 228
  and Bangladesh War, 212
  and China, 188, 208
  and Gandhi, Indira, 223–225, 421–422
  and India, 191, 229
  and India-Pakistan War (1965), 190
  and Kashmir, 192, 225, 227, 229, 65
  and Mao Zedong, 188, 230
  and nuclear program and weapons, 190, 222, 229, 230, 231, 283, 288
  and Pakistan National Alliance, 232
  and Pakistan People's Party, 196, 198, 421
  and Rahman, Shaikh Mujibur, 198, 199, 222
  and Shimla Agreement, 225, 421–422
  and Soviet Union, 187, 191
  and Tashkent Declaration, 195
  and United Nations Security Council, 189, 224
  and United States, 185, 191
  and West Pakistan, 220–233
  and Yahya Khan, Agha Muhammad, 222
  and Zia ul Haq, Muhammad, 233, 234, 235, 263, 422
  biography and character of, 221, 224, 230
  hanging of, 235
  military coup against, 232, 235–236
Bihar, 86
Bin Laden, Osama, 299, 300, 303, 304, 306, 316, 317, 319, 323, 326, 355, 373, 387
Birkenhead, Lord, 43, 44
Birla, Ghanshyam Das, 107
Birmingham, 285
Blackwill, Robert, 321, 330
Blaine, John J., 49
Blair, David, 366
Blitzer, Wolf, 354
Blood, Archer K., 212
Board of Control for Cricket in India (BCCI), 402, 404
Boer War, 12, 13
Bogra, Muhammad Ali, 144, 146, 149–151, 152, 157, 170, 173, 221
Bollywood, 396, 400
Bombay, 6, 8, 9, 10, 17, 36, 76, 85, 134, 221, 228, 310. See also Mumbai
Bombay Khilafat Committee, 27
Bomdi La, 171
Bonn, 373
Bose, Sarat Chandra, 85
Bose, Sarmila, 216

Bose, Subash Chandra, 75, 76, 77
Bose, Vimal, 89, 90–91
Bosnia, 217
Boston Tea Party, 52
Botha, Louis, 16
Bourke-White, Margaret, 123
Brahmaputra River, 159
Brezhnev, Leonid, 219, 240, 241
Britain and British, 4, 5, 11, 14, 21, 25, 28, 30, 34, 35, 37, 38, 39, 51, 54, 58, 61, 69, 70–71, 74, 79–80, 133, 141, 152, 155, 158, 170, 174, 185, 320, 331, 365, 368, 369, 379, 398, 413, 417
Brownlee, Les, 322
Buch, M. Yusuf, 119
Budap, 3
Buddhism, 32
Bugti, Sardar Akbar, 377
Bukhari, Fazi, 291
Bulganin, Nikolai, 152
Bulletin of Atomic Scientists, 289
Bureau of Alcohol, Firearms and Tobacco (US), 261
Burma, 158, 159, 163
Burrow, Sir John, 84
Bush, George Herbert Walker, 210, 328
Bush, George W., 3, 316, 317, 322, 323–324, 325, 328, 329, 332, 353, 373, 375, 376, 379, 380
Butt, Ziauddin, 304, 305
Bux, Illahi, 130, 131

Calcutta, 7, 10, 27, 36, 40, 47, 83–84, 103, 105, 139, 198, 201, 203. *See also* Kolkata
Cameron, David, 390
Camp Bonifas, 1
Canada, 18, 293, 379, 427, 431
Cape Colony, 16
Caroe, Olaf, 159, 160
Carter, Jimmy, 237, 238, 239, 240, 310, 422
Casey, William, 241
Cawthorne, Robert, 197

Celeste, Richard, 310
Central Intelligence Agency (CIA), 174, 197, 206, 210, 238, 239, 241, 245, 255, 262, 284, 286, 303, 316, 326, 329, 336, 338, 356, 382, 429
Central Khilafat Committee, 32, 33, 35, 36
Central Legislative Assembly, 40, 43, 58
Central Treaty Organization (CENTO), 146, 417
Ceylon, *see* Sri Lanka
Chagai Hills, 286
Chagai II, 288
Chambeli (movie), 399
Chamberlain, Neville, 67
Chamdo, 160
Champaran, 18, 19, 23
Champaran Agrarian Law, 23
Chandigarh, 252, 402, 403
Chandrashekhar, Maradadam, 271
Chattopadhyay, Bankim Chandra, 64
Chaudhuri, Jayanto Nath, 183
Chaudhry, Iftikhar Muhammad, 345
Chauri Chaura, 27
Chelmsford, Lord, 24, 25, 30, 33
Chen Ivan, 158
Chenab River, 98, 99, 154, 183
Chennai Express (movie), 399
Cherenenko, Konstantin, 251
Chhindwara, 28
Chicago Tribune, 248
Chidambaram, Palaniappian, 360, 361, 409
China and Chinese, 159, 161, 162, 413
    and India, 137, 145, 154, 157, 158–166, 167–172, 188, 201, 208, 233, 412, 418
    and India-China War, 169–172, 185, 233
    and Kargil War, 296
    and nuclear program and weapons of, 184, 208, 229, 245, 280
    and Pakistan, 138, 147–148, 157, 170, 173, 195, 197, 201, 205, 206, 230, 231, 241, 243, 244, 296, 312, 411–412, 422, 427

and Soviet Union, 163, 165, 204
and United Nations, 200
and United States, 163, 168, 204, 208, 211–213, 293
Chishti, Khwaja Moinuddin, 363
Chishti, Khwaja Qutb-ud-din, 125, 126
Chitral, 129
Chittagong, 47
Chittagong, Hill tract, 209
Christian Science Monitor, 376
Christianity and Christians, 5, 53, 55, 229, 231
Chugh, R. N., 193–194
Chughtai, Ismat, 219
Chotani, Muhammad, 27
Chuckraborty, P. V., 77
Chundrigar, Ismail Ibrahim, 118
Churchill, Sir Winston, 52, 69, 70, 71, 74, 87, 94, 112, 172
Civil and Military Gazette, 115, 117
Clinton, Bill, 2, 278, 282, 297
  and India, 285, 310
  and Kargil War, 295, 296, 297, 298–300
  and Musharraf, Pervez, 311
  and Nawaz Sharif, Muhammad, 285, 286, 287, 297, 298–300, 303, 304, 427
  and nuclear tests by India and Pakistan, 285, 289
  and Pakistan, 290, 311, 312
  and Taliban, 299
  and Vajpayee, Atal Bihari, 296, 299, 310, 312, 427–428
  on Gandhi, Mohandas Karamchand, 312
  on Kashmir, 3, 309, 311
Clinton, Chelsea, 310
Clinton, Hillary, 363, 385
CNN, 354
Cochin, 76
Coll, Steve, 331
Cologne, 296
Colombo, 198, 304, 305, 392
Communal Award (1932), 55

Communalism and communal violence, 6, 40, 41–43, 84, 85, 86–87, 88–89, 91–92, 99–100, 103, 105, 126, 139, 395, 416
Communist parliamentarians (India), 285
Communist Party of China, 229
Communist Party of East Pakistan, 138
Communist Party of India (CPI), 23, 145, 168, 223, 232
Comrade (weekly), 27
Conference on the Freedom of the Seas, 221
Conference on Interaction and Confidence-Building Measures in Asia, 330
Congress Party
  Colonial India, 5, 7, 10, 11, 17, 24, 25, 28, 30, 34–35, 44, 52, 53, 54, 55, 57, 59, 60–61, 64, 67, 70, 73, 77–78, 79, 81, 93–94
  Independent India, 141, 149, 175, 177, 194–195, 219, 228, 232, 247, 250, 267, 271, 274, 284, 333, 340, 341, 357, 414–415, 429
Congress Working Committee (CWC), 34, 53, 55, 67, 81
Constitutional Award (1946), 79–80, 81, 415, 416
Cricket, 255
  Diplomacy, 255, 343, 361, 491, 403, 424
  Matches: One-day International, 400, 401; Test, 255, 361, 400, 401; Twenty20, 400
Council of State, 25
Cripps, Sir Stafford, 70, 79, 81
Cronkite, Walter, 166
Crossette, Barbara, 259–260, 261, 271
Cuban Missile Crisis (1962), 169, 171, 299, 332
Cunningham, Sir George, 118, 119

Dacca, 6, 139, 187, 195, 198, 199, 201, 205, 210, 212, 214, 215, 227, 303. *See also* Dhaka

Dada Abdulla & Company, 11–12
Daily Telegraph, 366
Daily Times, 354, 404
Dalai Lama, 158, 159, 164
Damascus, 261
Damdani Taksal, 252
Dandi, 47, 48
Daoud Khan, Muhammad, 237, 371
Dar as Islam, 303
Dari (language), 384, 392
Das, Tulsi, 33
Datta, Veena, 223, 224
Dawn, 72, 84, 223, 354, 389
Dayal, Rajeshwar, 155
Dead Reckoning: Memories of the Bangladesh War, 215
Dean, John Gunther, 261
Defence Journal (Pakistan), 115
Defence Research and Development Organization (DRDO), 283
Defense of India (Criminal Law Amendment) Act, 20, 24
Defense Intelligence Agency (DIA), 330
Dehlavi, Jamil, 132
Delhi, 7, 8, 24, 28, 103, 205, 247, 330, 333, 363, 372, 395, 396, 400, 413
  anti-Sikh pogrom in, 249–250
  communal violence in, 105–106
  terrorist attacks in, 320–322, 324, 335, 429
Delhi Sultanate, 4, 369, 413
Delhi-Lahore Bus Service, 290, 291, 312
Democratic Republic of Afghanistan (DRA), 37
Desai, Morarji, 233, 236, 238, 286, 401
Deve Gowda, Haradanahalli Doddegowda, 277, 288
Devi, Rani Chib, 111
Devi, Tara, 114
Devnagri script, 66
Dhaipai, 108
Dhaka, 227, 309
Dhar, Durga Prasad, 43, 205

Dharasana, 48, 49
Dhoom 3 (movie), 398, 399
Dixon, Owen, 142
Dixit, Jyotindra Nath, 307, 342
Dobrynin, Anatoly, 211, 212
Doha, 391
Domel, 119
Donkers, Hendrina, 230
Douglas-Home, Sir Alec, 223
Dras sector, 295
Dubai, 335, 342, 346, 398, 409
Dulles, John Foster, 142, 143, 145
Dunham, Phyllis, 130, 131
Dunya, 404
Durand Line, 369, 372
Durban, 12, 398
Durga (goddess), 64, 65, 66, 218, 415
Durrani, Muhammad Ali, 260, 262, 269
Dutt, Batukeshwar, 46
Dyer, Reginald, 24, 25, 31, 33
Dykes, D.O., 121

East Bengal, 85, 86, 97
East India Company, 4, 19, 55
East Pakistan, 97, 109, 139, 140, 188, 190, 195, 199, 205, 207, 209, 419, 420, 421
  estimates of violent deaths in 1971, 216–217
East Punjab, 102, 105, 122
Edward VIII (King), 35–36
Egypt, 107
Eisenhower, Dwight, 141–142, 143, 144, 148, 165, 310
English (language), 5, 7, 21, 147, 414
Epstein, Edward Jay, 259, 260, 261, 262
Evans, Harold, 203, 204
Express Tribune, 404

Fahim, Makhdoom Amin, 440
Fahim, Muhammad Qasim, 375, 377, 379
Faisalabad, 401
Farooq, Amjad, 338
Faruqi, Naseer Ahmad, 79

Federal Bureau of Investigation (FBI), 262, 360
Federally Administered Tribal Agencies (FATA), 237, 238, 369, 377, 378, 379, 381
Faridkot (Pakistan), 343, 352
Faridkot (Princely) State, 109
Farkhor Air Base, 373
Feldman, Herbert, 189
Ferozepur, 100, 107, 109, 190
Fifty Day War (Stage play), 302
Film and television industry, 134, 175, 219, 224, 265–266, 302
  in Afghanistan, 393, 396–399
  in India, 384, 396–399
  in Pakistan, 394, 398–399
Financial Express, 302
First Gujarat Political Conference, 21
Fischer, Louis, 54, 82–83
Flames of Chinar, 176
Fleischer, Ari, 331
Ford, Gerald, 237
Foreign Affairs (Journal), 178
France, 30
Friends Not Masters, 156
Frontline, 291
Frost, David, 216, 277

G8 summits, 285, 296
Gaddafi, Muammar, 229
Gah, 364
Gait, Sir Albert, 20
Galbraith, John, 170, 173
Gall, Carlotta, 380–382
Gallup Poll (Pakistan), 319
Gandhi (movie), 25, 49, 106, 132
Gandhi, Abdullah, 62
Gandhi, Feroze, 194
Gandhi, Harilal, 13, 62
Gandhi, Indira, 250
  and Abdullah, Shaikh Muhammad, 228
  and Bangladesh War, 210, 215, 224, 421
  and Bhutto, Zulfikar Ali, 223–225, 421–422

and East Pakistan, 204, 440–421
and Kashmir, 225, 228
and Khalistan movement, 248
and Nixon, Richard, 207–208
and nuclear program and weapons, 228
and Pakistan, 241–242, 244, 235, 246
and Research and Analysis Wing, 197
and Shimla Agreement, 225, 421–422
and Soviet Union, 207, 240, 241
and United States, 197, 207–208
and Zia ul Haq, Muhammad, 241–242, 244, 266, 423
as Goddess Durga, 218
assassination of, 249, 271, 423–424
biography and character of, 194–195, 224, 247, 250
emergency declared by, 232, 281, 422
Gandhi, Jaisukhlal, 89
Gandhi, Karamchand, 12
Gandhi, Kasturbai, 11, 12, 48, 72
Gandhi, Laxmidas, 13
Gandhi, Mohandas Karamchand, 8, 10–11, 21, 58, 60, 61, 194, 312, 313, 415
  and Ahmedabad textile workers strike, 22
  and Champaran indigo farmers, 18–23
  and communalism and communal violence, 41, 42–43, 87, 103, 105, 126
  and Congress Party, 34–35, 43, 53, 57
  and cow protection, 32, 35, 38, 41
  and Hinduism, 16, 28, 31, 32, 38–39, 47, 49, 62, 89
  and Irwin, Lord, 52–53
  and Jinnah, Muhammad Ali, 11–12, 21, 22–23, 25, 33–34, 36–37, 46, 49–50, 61–62, 68, 71, 72–73, 78, 82–83, 85, 90, 128

Gandhi, Mohandas Karamchand
(continued)
and Kashmir, 114
and Khilafat movement, 29–30, 31,
32
and Mountbatten, Lord Louis, 93,
95, 103
and Muslim refugees, 107
and Nehru, Jawaharlal, 63, 87,
94–95, 127
and non-cooperation campaign
(1920–1922), 33–38, 40
and non-violent tactics, 15–16, 223
and Pakistan, 125
and Patel, Vallabhbhai, 89, 107, 127
and Quit India campaign, 71
and Round Table Conferences, 46,
53–55
and Rowlatt Act, 24–25
and Salt Tax protest march, 46–47,
52
and sexual abstinence experiments,
89–90
and Untouchables, 43, 57
assassination of, 126–127, 424
biography character of, 12–13, 21,
49–50, 78
in South Africa, 12–17
on economic development model,
45, 132
on Hindu-Muslim unity, 89, 94–95
on Indian National Army, 76
on Islam, 62, 82
on Jallianwala Bagh massacre, 25,
31
on partition, 94
on religion and politics, 28, 31, 38
on Two Nation Theory, 69
on World War II, 67–68, 70–71
fasting by, 22, 23, 39, 42, 57, 125
Gandhi, Mridula, 89, 127
Gandhi, Putlibai, 12
Gandhi, Rajiv, 269, 278
and Bhutto, Benazir, 265, 266, 267,
425
and Hassan bin Talal, 257

and nuclear program and weapons,
251, 266, 282, 424, 425
and Pakistan, 254, 255, 258, 261,
288
and Sikh militancy, 252
and Zia ul Haq, Muhammad,
251–252, 255, 259, 266, 401, 424
assassination of, 271
biography and character of,
250–251
cricket diplomacy by, 255
Gandhi, Priyanka, 250
Gandhi, Rahul, 250
Gandhi, Sanjay, 250
Gandhi, Sonia, 250, 265
Garm Hava (movie), 219
Geo TV, 335
George V (King), 91, 98
George VI (King), 91, 98
Gereshk, 376
Germany, 7, 11, 67
Ghori, Muhammad, 4, 413
Gilani, Daood Sayed, 347–348
Gilani, Syed Salim, 347
Gilani, Yusuf Raza, 345, 351–352, 353,
355, 357, 358–359, 360, 361, 362,
382, 383, 403
Gilgit Agency, 142
Gilgit Wazarat, 111, 114
Girdharidas, Mangaldas, 11
Glimpses of World History, 156
Godfrey, J. H., 76
Godhra, 6, 21
Godse, Nathuram Vinayak, 127
Gojra, 108
Gokhale, Gopal Krishna, 10–11, 12,
16
Golden Temple, 248, 252, 256, 257,
258, 423
Gorbachev, Mikhail, 258, 267
Gore-Booth, Sir Paul, 170, 173
Goss, Peter, 316
Government of India Act (1919), 25,
39
Government of India Act (1935), 56,
58–59, 94

Gracey, Sir Douglas, 43, 129
Graham, Bob, 316
Green Book, 399
Grewal, Dalvinder Singh, 107
Gromyko, Andrei, 191, 205
Gujarati (language), 21
Gujral, Inder Kumar, 278–279, 282–283
Gul, Abdullah, 384
Gul, Hamid, 257, 264, 274
Gul, Muhammad Shah, 141
Gulmarg, 124
Gurdaspur, 99, 116
Gurez, 3
Gurjar Sabha, 11, 128
Gwadar, 387
Gyasto, Tenzin, 159

Haidar, Ejaz, 354
Haig, Alexander, 211, 212, 241
Hailey, Sir Malcolm, 51
Haji Pir Pass, 182, 183, 192, 193
Haksar, Parmeshwar Narayan, 223
Halfway to Freedom, 123
Hamdard, 28
Hamdoon Rahman Inquiry Commission, 216
Hamid Khan, Abdul, 209, 214, 217
Hamidzada, Humayun, 381
Hanif, Muhammad, 262
Hansen, Thomas Blom, 284
Haq, Ehsan ul, 292, 299, 304, 305, 319, 335
Haq, Ijaz ul, 261
Haqeeqat (movie), 172
Haqqani, Jalaluddin, 381
Hardinge, Lord, 17
Hari River, 37
Harijan, 57, 58, 76, 89
Harkat al Jihad Islami (HuJI), 346
Harkat ul Ansar, 294, 308
Harkat ul Mujahedin, 294, 304, 307–308
Harriman, Averell, 173
Haryana, 248, 252
Hashimi, Abdul Rahman, 348

Hassan, Gul, 182, 217, 218
Hassan, Killies, 376
Hassan, Mashood, 260
Hassan bin Talal (Jordanian Prince), 348
Hayden, Michael, 352
Headley, David Coleman, 348, 360–361
Headley, Serrill, 347
Hekmatyar, Gulbuddin, 237
Helmand, 375, 379
Helms, Richard, 210
Hemraj, Naik, 365
Herat, 374, 392
Hersh, Seymour, 323
Heycock, W. B., 20
Hidayatullah, Sir Ghulam Hussein, 79, 87, 88
Hind Swaraj, 31
Hindi (language), 65, 393, 398
Hindu, 267, 269, 329
Hindu Mahasabha, 39, 66, 126, 127
Hindu Rashtra, 127
Hinduism and Hindus, 4, 5, 6, 7, 11, 16, 31, 32, 40, 41–43, 51, 55, 65, 68–69, 91, 101–102, 140, 201, 206, 219, 227, 229, 231, 242, 257, 271–281, 346–347, 394, 395–396, 413, 418, 421
Hindustan Times, 284
Hindustani (language), 44, 65, 66, 134, 396, 398
Hizb ul Mujahideen, 268, 307
Hoare, Sir Samuel, 55
Home Rule League, 18
Huang Hue, 208, 210–211
Hunter, Lord William, 30, 32, 33
Hunza, 142
Huq, Abul Kasem Fazlul, 61, 63, 64, 66
Husain, Aamir Reza, 301
Hussain, Mushahid, 279, 291, 297, 377–378
Hussain, Riaz, 181
Hussein, Wajahat, 320
Hyderabad (India), 98, 310
Hyderabad (Pakistan), 396

If I am Assassinated, 231
Iftikharuddin, Mian, 109, 115, 117
IHS Jane's Defence Weekly, 389
Ikramullah, Sarvath, 257
Imam, Sir Ali, 6, 44
Immigration Regulation Act, 16
Imperial Legislative Assembly, 10, 24, 25
Imperial Legislative Council, 10
In Confidence, 212
In the Line of Duty, 186
In the Line of Fire: A Memoir, 344
In Search of a New Afghanistan, 394
India: The Critical Years, 187, 194
India and Indians, 2, 3, 4, 8, 24, 103, 109
  and 9/11, 318, 428
  and Afghanistan, 238–239, 359, 371, 372–373, 374, 375–376, 377, 378, 380, 381–382, 383, 384, 385–386, 387, 388, 389, 390, 391, 392–393, 422
  and Baluchistan, 358, 377–378
  and China, 137, 145, 154, 157, 158–166, 188, 201, 208, 233, 412
  and East Pakistan, 209
  and Israel, 243, 244, 250, 287, 315, 323, 328, 423, 425
  and Kashmir, 278–279, 326, 366. *See also* India-Administered Kashmir
  and Pakistan, 125, 126, 127, 128, 204, 206, 207, 240, 243, 246, 251, 254, 271, 274–275, 285, 287, 308, 310, 312, 319, 321–322, 323, 326, 328, 331, 332, 333, 336, 358, 367
  and Soviet Union, 152, 153, 211–212, 215, 239, 419
  and Taliban, 307, 383, 385–386
  and United Nations, 125, 152–153, 287
  and United States, 136, 145, 165, 170, 174, 185, 190, 205, 206, 229, 318, 321, 322, 323, 419, 425
  broadcasting media in, 314–315, 335, 350
  economy of, 312, 331, 405, 413, 429
  military doctrine of, 334, 340, 355
  nuclear doctrine of, 329, 330, 331, 334, 339, 341, 429
  nuclear program and weapons of, 184, 222, 243, 251, 253, 280, 281–285, 289, 291–292, 293, 297, 413, 422–423, 426, 427
India Councils Act, 6, 7
India Independence Act (1947), 98
India Salt Act, 46
India Today, 267
India-Administered Kashmir, 269, 274, 278–279, 366
  and Research and Analysis Wing, 275
  and Soviet Union, 152, 227
  constitutions of, 142, 151, 152, 177–178
  elections in, 142–143, 153, 175, 276–277, 333–334
  separatist movement in, 268–269, 272, 309, 326, 419–420
  terrorism in, 320, 322
  torture in, 275–276
India-China Boundary Problem, 1846–1947: History and Diplomacy, 160
India-China War, 169–172, 185, 233
India-Pakistan Trade Relations, 405–412, 430–431
  contraband trade, 407
India-Pakistan War (1965), 185, 187, 189–190, 420
India-Pakistan War (1971), *see* Bangladesh War
India-Pakistan War (1999), *see* Kargil War
Indian Airlines, 374
  Indian Airlines plane hijacked, 307–308, 323, 335
  See also Air India
Indian Atomic Energy Commission, 229
Indian Mujahedin (IM), 346–347
Indian Home Rule, 31

Indian Kashmir, *see* India-
Administered Kashmir
Indian National Army (INA), 75, 76
Indian National Congress, *see*
Congress Party
Indian Opinion, 14
Indian Relief Act, 11, 16
Indian Youth Congress, 366
Indo-Soviet Treaty of Friendship and
Cooperation, 205, 206, 363, 371
Indus River, 98, 154
Indus River basin, 331, 413
Indus Waters Treaty, 155, 221, 266
Inter-Dominion Accord, 154
Inter-Services Intelligence (ISI), 181,
196, 197, 198, 233, 236, 239, 244,
246, 247, 252, 256, 257, 265, 268,
269, 270, 271, 275, 276, 297,
299, 304, 310, 319, 335, 337, 340,
347–348, 351–352, 354, 361, 363,
378, 379, 381, 382, 384, 386, 388,
422, 423
Interlaken, 257
International Atomic Energy Agency,
196
International Cricket Council (ICC),
400
International Monetary Fund (IMF),
270, 285, 290, 300, 317
Iqbal, Javed, 47
Iqbal, Sir Muhammad, 51, 56, 65
Iran, 145, 204, 238, 372, 387
Isaacs, Rufus Daniel, 35
Ishaq Khan, Ghulam, 259, 264, 265,
269, 273
Islam, 4, 35, 40, 43, 65, 128, 147, 231,
232, 235, 275, 288, 347, 394, 413,
415
Islamabad, 231, 239, 254, 259, 265,
267, 305, 306, 310–311, 339, 343,
368, 406
Islami Jamhoori Ittihad (IJI), 264,
265, 269
Islamic atom bomb, 229, 288
Islamic Conference Organization, 227
Islamic Republic of Pakistan, 227

Ismay, Hastings, 105
Ispahani, Nusrat, 221. *See also* Bhutto,
Nusrat Begum
Israel and Israelis, 231, 241, 243, 261,
287, 315, 323, 328, 350, 413
Israelites, 107
Italian Fascist Party, 280

Jagmohan, 268–269
Jahan, Akbar, 177
Jahan, Nur, 185
Jahangir (Emperor), 397
Jainism, 39
Jaipur, 255, 310
Jaish-e Muhammad (JeM), 320, 321,
322, 326, 337
Jalalabad, 374, 376, 378, 370
Jalandhar, 274
Jallianwala Bagh massacre, 25, 31, 134
Jamaat-e Islami (JeI), (Jammu
and Kashmir) 247, 258, 268,
(Pakistan), 268, 270, 273, 276,
292
Jamaat ud Dawa (JuD), 348, 355, 359,
360
Jamali, Zafarullah Khan, 336
Jamiat Ulema-e Islami (JUeI),
273–274
Jammu, 3, 111, 116, 170
Jammu and Kashmir, *see* Kashmir
Jammu and Kashmir Liberation Front
(JKLF), 247, 268
Jammu Region, 99, 111, 143, 250
Jamuna River, 99, 143, 250
Jamnagar, 245
Jamwal, Rajinder Singh, 115, 119,
122, 327
Janata Alliance, 233, 236, 281
Jane's Terrorism and Security Monitor,
315
Japan, 69, 70, 72, 159
Jasaulipatti, 19
Jauhar, Muhammad Ali, 27–28, 30,
34–35, 40, 42, 44, 58
Javaid, Malik Tahir, 411
Jehan, Sonya, 397

Jenkins, Sir Evan, 91, 92, 99, 100–101
Jeremiah, David, 284
Jewish and Jews, 229, 231, 350
Jha, Lakshmi Kant, 179
Jhelum River, 98, 133, 154
Jinnah (movie), 132
Jinnah, Dinah, 37, 54
Jinnah, Fatima, 54, 100, 130
Jinnah, Maryam, 23, 37, 43, 45
Jinnah, Muhammad Ali, 7, 8, 11, 13,
    21, 25, 33, 34, 76, 87, 93, 96, 109,
    123, 132, 148, 303, 369, 400, 414,
    416
  and Abdullah, Shaikh Muhammad,
    113, 116
  and Azad, Maulana Abul Kalam 74,
    75, 79
  and Central Legislative Assembly,
    40, 58
  and Congress ministries, 63, 67
  and Congress Party, 10, 17, 44, 45,
    71, 82, 414
  and Constitutional Award, 80, 81,
    416
  and Cripps Plan, 70
  and Direct Action, 81
  and Gandhi, Mohandas
    Karamchand, 11–12, 21, 22–23,
    25, 33–34, 36–37, 46, 49–50,
    61–62, 68, 71, 72–73, 78, 82–83,
    85, 90, 128
  and Home Rule League, 18, 23
  and Imperial Legislative Assembly,
    10, 24
  and Kashmir, 113, 115–116, 118,
    119, 122–123, 129, 130, 133,
    416–417
  and Mountbatten, Lord Louis, 93,
    94, 95–96
  and Muslim League, 10, 17, 41, 43,
    44, 57, 58, 60, 63–64
  and Nehru, Jawaharlal, 65–66, 83,
    131–132
  and Pakistan foreign policy, 110
  and role of religion in Pakistan, 101,
    128
  and Round Table Conferences, 51,
    55, 56
  and Royal Indian Navy mutiny, 77
  and Two Nation theory, 68, 218,
    421
  as Governor-General of Pakistan,
    79, 97, 100, 109, 110, 118
  as President of Constituent
    Assembly, 100
  biography and character of, 9–10,
    21, 50, 135
  Fourteen points of, 45, 51
  ill-health and death of, 73, 129,
    130–131
  marriage of, 23–24, 230
  on communal violence, 86, 109
  on Government of India Act
    (1935), 59
  on Khilafat movement, 29
  on non-cooperation campaign, 33,
    40
  on Pakistan, 57, 96, 97, 395
  and Pakistan's constitution, 128–129
  on Quit India campaign, 71
  on World War II, 67, 72
  residency in London residence, 54,
    56–57
Jodhpur, 406
Johannesburg, 14, 15, 16
John Glenn Amendment to Foreign
    Assistance Act (US), 236
Johnson, Lyndon, 179, 185, 191, 197
Joint Defense Council of India and
    Pakistan, 124
Joint Indo-Pakistan Commission
    (1983), 423
Jordan, 234, 257
Junagarh, 98
Junejo, Muhammad Khan, 251, 254

kaMancinza, Bambatha, 14
Kabul, 237, 308, 319, 369, 372, 374,
    375, 381, 386, 388, 393
Kahak, 376
Kahuta, 239, 243, 345, 423
Kahuta Research Laboratory, 244, 261

Kak, Ram Chandra, 113, 114
Kakar, Wahid, 273
Kalimpong, 161, 163
Kallenbach, Hermann, 15
Kalshura, 138
Kaluchak, 428
Kandahar, 303, 307, 308, 319, 374, 378, 379
Kanjarkot, 178
Kant, Krishna, 320
Kao, Rameshwar Nath, 197, 209
Kapoor, Deepak, 357
Kapoor, Raj, 396
Kappes, Stephen, 382
Karachi, 8, 47, 76, 100, 102–103, 130, 131, 148, 149, 155, 195, 210, 211, 221, 224, 231, 256, 273, 275, 278, 288, 395, 306, 335, 348, 387, 396, 399, 403, 406, 411
Karakoram Highway, 208
Karamat, Jehangir, 286, 288, 290
Kargil, 2, 191
Kargil War, 294–300, 301–302, 313, 329, 332, 333, 334, 335, 337, 342, 402, 406, 419, 427–428
Karia, 23
Karmal, Babrak, 238
Kasab, Amir Shahban, 352
Kasab, Muhammad Ajmal, Amir, 348, 349, 351, 352, 356, 357, 360
Kasauli, 164
Kashmir and Kashmiris, 2–3, 4, 98, 110, 111, 112, 113, 114, 115–116, 117, 118, 119, 120, 121, 122–123, 124, 128, 129, 133, 142–143, 150–151, 153, 155, 156–157, 170, 173, 175, 176, 179, 180, 185, 192, 196, 208, 225, 227, 229, 268, 277, 294, 295, 311, 314, 315, 324, 326, 332, 334, 337, 338, 342, 343, 344, 361, 362, 364, 366–367, 397, 412, 416–417, 418, 419, 429
Kashmir Ki Kali (movie), 175
Kashmir Times, 117
Kashmiri, Ilyas, 348

Kasuri, Khurshid Mahmood, 341–342, 345
Kasuri, Muhammad Khan, 235
Kathua, 116
Katmandu, 307, 324, 325
Kaufman, Marc, 258
Kautilya, Chanakya, 379
Kaw, M. K., 223, 224
Kayani, Ashfaq Parvez, 344, 345, 352, 354, 383, 384, 386, 387, 400
Karzai, Abdul Ahad, 373, 374
Karzai, Hamid, 375
    and Bush, George W., 380
    and Gilani, Yusuf Raza, 383
    and India, 375, 380, 382, 385, 386, 388, 389, 390, 391, 392
    and Kayani, Ashfaq Parvez, 383, 387
    and Musharraf, Pervez, 375, 379
    and Nawaz Sharif, 391
    and Omar, Mullah Muhammad, 380
    and Pakistan, 376, 381, 383, 388, 390, 391
    and Singh, Manmohan, 388
    and Taliban, 372, 385, 386, 390, 391, 392
    as President of Afghanistan, 373, 375, 377, 385
    biography and character of, 373–374
Kennedy, John F., 166
    and Ayub Khan, Muhammad, 171, 174
    and India, 170, 172
    and Nehru, Jawaharlal, 167, 171, 173
    and Soviet Union, 332
KGB, 256, 261
KHAD, 242, 256, 261
Khaksars, 97
Khalid, Abdul Rauf, 302
Khalid, Kidwai, 330
Khalili, Karim, 377
Khalilzad, Zalmay, 376
Khalistan Commando Force, 257

Khalistan movement, 242, 246, 248, 251–252, 254, 257, 258, 423
Khan, Aamir, 266, 399
Khan, Abdul Hamid, *see* Hamid Khan, 209, 214, 217
Khan, Abdul Jabbar, 118
Khan, Abdul Qayyum, 117, 118, 119
Khan, Abdur Rahman, *see* Rahman Khan, Abdur
Khan, Abu Dera Ismail, 348
Khan, Asghar, 192, 269
Khan, Muhammad Daoud, *see* Daoud Khan, Muhammad
Khan, Ghazanfar Ali, 88
Khan, Ghulam Ishaq, *see* Ishaq Khan, Ghulam
Khan, Ghulam Jilani, 233
Khan, Hakim Ajmal, 36
Khan, Imran, 400
Khan, Khurram Dastgir, 411
Khan, Liaquat Ali, *see* Ali Khan, Liaquat
Khan, M. S., 72
Khan, Mazhar Ali, 109, 223
Khan, Mirdad, 156
Khan, Muhammad Musa, *see* Musa Khan, Muhammad, 182, 183
Khan, Muhammad Akbar, 115, 117, 128, 198
Khan, Muhammad Ayub, *see* Ayub Khan, Muhammad
Khan, Sir Muhammad Hamidullah, 85
Khan, Muhammad Tikka, *see* Tikka Khan, Muhammad
Khan, Muhammad Yahya Khan, *see* Yahya Khan, Muhammad
Khan, Muhammad Yusaf, *see* Yusaf Khan, Muhammad
Khan, Muhammad Yusuf, 396
Khan, Munir Ahmad, *see* Ahmad Khan, Munir
Khan, Sir Osman Ali, 110
Khan, Abdul Qadeer, *see* Qadeer Khan, Abdul
Khan, Raana, 58
Khan, Rahim, 214, 218
Khan, Salman, 266
Khan, Shah Nawaz, 75, 76
Khan, Shah Rukh, 266
Khan, Shahzada Yaqub, 265
Khan, Sir Sikandar Hayat, 63, 64
Khan, Sir Syed Ahmad, 5, 414
Khan Research Laboratories (KRL), 286
Kiani, Jamshaid Gulzar, 219, 317, 319
Khar, G. M., 218
Khar, Hina Rabbani, 362, 363, 365
Kharan, 288, 289
Khathing, Ralengnao, 160
Khem Karan, 109, 186–187, 189
Kher, Bal Gangadhar, 61
Khilafat Manifesto, 29, 30
Khilafat movement, 29–30, 31, 32, 33–35, 36
Khilnani, Sunil, 106
Khokhar, Riaz, 340
Khokharpar, 406
Khomeini, Ruhollah, 238
Khoso, Mir Hazar, 365
Khost, 304, 378, 380
Khunjerab Pass, 173, 208
Khurshid, Salman, 284–285, 368
Khrushchev, Nikita, 152, 165, 171, 332
Khwaja Bahuddin, 372, 373
Khyber Pakhtunkhwa, 369
Kim Jong-Un, 1
Kipling, Rudyard, 36, 184
Kissinger, Henry, 167, 201, 204, 205–206, 208, 210, 211–213
Kochi, 332
Kohat, 41–42
Kolhapur, 396
Kolkata, 346
Korean War (1950–1953), 137, 145, 149, 406
Kosygin, Alexei, 187, 189, 190–191, 193, 204, 205
Kripalani, Jiwatram Bhagwandas, 95
Krishak Praja Party, 61
Krishna, Lord, 33

Krishna, Somanahalli Mallaiah, 359, 360, 361, 362, 364
Krishna Rao, K. V., 275, 279
Kumar, Dilip, 397
Kumari, Meena, 224
Kumari, Raj, 281
Kushka-Herat-Kandahar Highway, 383

Laag (television series), 302
Ladakh, 167, 177
Ladakh Wazarat, 111
Laghari, Farooq, 278
Lahore, 99, 134, 184, 185, 187, 195, 196, 215, 227, 256, 263, 264, 288, 291, 292, 314, 331, 400, 412, 413
Lahore Declaration, 293, 312, 314, 367, 417
Lakhi Bai, 229
Lakhvi, Zaki ur Rahman, 348, 355
Lakshmi (goddess), 65
Lall, Arhur, 152
Lambah, Satinder, 342, 344, 345, 429
Lanpher, Gibson, 296
Larkana, 221, 263
Lashkar-e Taiba (LeT), 260, 270, 273, 321, 322, 326, 337, 346, 347, 348–350, 352, 355, 367, 382
League of Nations Supreme Council, 30
Lee, Christopher, 132
Leh, 294
Leigh-Croft, Sir Fredrick, 9
Lhasa, 164
Liberation Tigers of Tamil Eelam (LTTE), 271
Libya, 229
Life, 123
Lille, 374
Line of Control (LoC), 2–3, 225, 309, 342, 343, 366, 367, 408, 421, 428, 429
Linlithgow, Lord, 58, 67, 69, 71
LoC Kargil (movie), 302
Lodhi, Mahila, 316
Lollywood, 400

London, 9, 13, 30, 51, 203, 222, 263, 264, 342, 385
Lone, Rashid, 3
Longju, 164
Lop Nor, 184, 208, 245
Lucknow, 17, 400, 401
Lucknow Pact, 17, 28
Lucman, Mubashir, 398, 399
Lyallpur, 107

MacDonald Ramsay, 45, 52, 53, 54, 55
Macmillan, Harold, 170, 172, 174
Madaripur, 205
Madras, 13, 30, 47
Mahajan, Mehr Chand, 117, 120, 121, 128, 130
Mahal, Mumtaz (Empress), 397
Mahisasura, 218, 421
Mahmood, Sultan Bashiruddin, 221, 231
Mahmood, Zafar, 410
Mahsud tribe, 118
Maino, Antonia Eduige Albina, 250. *See also* Gandhi, Sonia
Majid, Caliph Abdul, 40
Major, Fali Homi, 352
"Major Iqbal," 348
Makhanji, Kasturbai, 12. *See also* Gandhi, Kasturbai
Malabar, 39
Malaviya, Madan Mohan, 23, 33, 39, 66
Malaya, 70
Maldives, 270
Male, 270
Malik, Akhtar Hussain, 180, 183
Malik, Rehman, 357, 360, 361
Mamdot, Iftikhar Hussain Khan, 91, 117
Man Hoon Shahid Afridi (movie), 399
Manchester, 54, 402
Mandal, Jogindar Nath, 85, 139
Mandviwalla, Nadeem, H., 399
Manekshaw, Sam Hormusji Jamshedji, 200, 215
Mano Majra, 104

Manto, Sadat Hassan, 134–135
Manto, Safiya, 135
Mao Zedong, 162, 168, 169, 172, 184, 188, 230, 418–419
Markovitz, Claude, 84
Marriam, Alan Hayes, 78
Mary (Queen), 55
Mascarenhas, Anthony, 201, 202
Mascarenhas, Yvonne, 202
Masood, Talat, 389
Masoud, Ahmad Shah, 319, 372, 373
Mashruwala, Kishorelal, 89
Mathai, Ranjan, 364
Maxwell, Neville, 171
Mazar-e Sharif, 374
Mazzetti, Mark, 381
McCain, John, 354–355
McConaughy, Walter, 170
McCurry, Mike, 287
McLaughlin, John, 329
McMahon, Sir Henry, 158
McMahon Line, 159, 163, 167, 168, 172, 418
Mecca, 41, 177
Medina, 41
Meghna River, 214
Mehdi of Pirpur, Muhammad, 67
Mehmet VI (Sultan-Caliph), 26, 28–29, 30, 31
Mehran Bank, 269
Mehrauli, 125
Mehta, J. S., 235
Mehta, Ravi Datt, 381
Mendhar, 181, 365
Menon, Shiv Shankar, 390
Menon, Vapal Pangunni, 94, 98, 120, 121
Menon Plan, 94, 95, 96
Mere Sanam (movie), 175
Messervy, Sir Frank, 92, 122–123, 417
Mexico, 15
Miandad, Javed, 401
Miller, Web, 48, 49
Minar-e Pakistan, 292, 427
Miranshahi, 378
Mirpur, 118

Mishra, Lalit, 331, 339
Mishra, Rishi Kumar, 293–294
Mission Fateh: Real Stories of Kargil Heroes (television series), 301
Mistry, Shapoorji, 397
Mistry, Shapoorji Pollanji, 387
Mirza, Iskander Ali, 146, 147, 148–149, 153
Mirza, Salim, 219, 220
Mizoram, 389
Mizrahi, Avi, 351
Mohali, 361, 403
Mohammad, Khalid Shaikh, 338
Mohammadans, see Muslims
Mohammadi, Nasrullah, 393
Montagu, Edwin, 21, 25, 38, 40
Mopilas, 39
Morning News, 201, 203
Moscow, 191, 207, 233, 251, 267
Mossad, 197, 243, 244, 261, 336
Motihari, 19, 20
Mountbatten, Lady Edwina, 93, 102
Mountbatten, Lord Louis, 91, 93, 94, 95–96, 102, 103, 107, 114, 120, 121–122, 123, 124, 125, 251
Movement for Restoration of Democracy (MRD), 246, 247
Mubarakmand, Samar, 286
Mudi, Sir Francis, 79
Mughal Dynasty, 413
Mughal Empire, 7
Mughal-e Azam (movie), 396, 397
Mughals, 4, 5
Muhajir Qaumi Mahaz (MQM), 165, 269
Muhammad (Prophet), 4, 175
Muhammad, Bakshi Ghulam, 116, 143, 150, 163, 175, 177
Muhammad, Ghulam, 110, 146
Muhammadan Educational Conference, 5, 6
Mujadidi, Sibghatullah, 374
Mukherjee, Pranab, 3, 282, 352, 353, 354, 356
Mukhtar, Shaikh, 396–397
Mukti Bahini, 201, 206, 207, 209, 210

Mulford, David, 353
Mullik, B. M., 163
Multan, 40, 92, 234, 236
Mumbai, 407, 410. *See also* Bombay
Mumbai 2008 Terrorist Attack, 346, 347, 348, 349–351, 352–354, 355, 356–357, 403, 430
Munabao, 406
Munir, Muhammad, 141
Munk, David, 366
Muntazir, Abdullah, 355
Muridke, 355
Murree, 55, 232, 418
Musa Khan, Muhammad, 182, 183
Musharraf, Sehba, 304, 313
Musharraf, Pervez, 320, 347, 397, 430
  and Bush, George W., 317, 322, 323–324, 328, 373, 375, 376, 379, 380
  and Clinton, Bill, 311
  and cricket diplomacy, 343
  and India, 308, 318
  and Kargil War, 294, 295–296, 297, 298, 299, 313, 332, 338, 342, 427–428
  and Karzai, Hamid, 375, 379
  and Kashmir, 294, 314, 324, 343, 344, 366–367, 429
  and Nawaz Sharif, Muhammad, 290, 298, 304–306, 309, 365, 428
  and nuclear program and weapons, 297, 298, 302, 307, 309, 323, 325, 330–331
  and Powell, Colin, 324, 334
  and Singh, Manmohan, 342, 343, 388, 429
  and Taliban, 209, 318
  and Vajpayee, Atal Bihari, 291, 307, 313, 314, 324–325, 331, 406, 428
  as Chief Executive of Pakistan, 307, 312
  as President, 313, 319
  assassination attempts on, 337
  coup by, 304–306
  emergency declared by, 345
  on terrorism, 325, 326, 328, 428

  resigns as Army Chief, 345
  resigns as President, 346, 383, 430
Muslim Conference (Jammu and Kashmir), 112, 113, 115, 153, 176, 415
Muslim League
  India, 6, 7, 10, 11, 17, 18, 25, 27, 30, 34, 40, 41, 44, 45, 51, 55, 57, 58, 60, 61, 63–64, 68, 77–79, 83–84, 88, 91, 93–94, 96, 147, 219
  Pakistan, 131, 146, 148, 233
Muslim League National Guard (MNG), 83, 84, 92, 97, 100, 118, 140
Muslims, 4, 5, 6, 7, 11, 17–18, 26, 28, 30, 31, 33, 35, 38, 39, 40, 41–42, 44, 51, 55, 57, 58, 63, 68–69, 70, 72, 91, 101–102, 128, 140, 219, 272, 292, 318, 391, 395, 415
Muttahida, Majlis-e Amal (MMA), 336
Mutual Security Act (US), 137, 138
Muzaffarabad, 118, 119, 124, 133, 176, 343, 348, 408
Muzaffarpur, 19

Nagar, 142
Nagasaki, 286
Nagpur, 36, 37
Naidu, Sarojini, 48
Naik, Niaz Ahmad, 293–294, 300
Nairobi, 393
Najibullah, Muhammad, 372
Nanak Dev, Guru, 100, 242
Nankana Sahib, 100
Naoroji, Dadabhai, 9, 10
Narainganj, 181
Narasimha Rao, Pamulapartu Venkata, 240, 271–272, 274, 282, 285, 426
Nawa-i Waqt, 185
Narayan, Jaya Prakash, 232
Narayanan, Kicheri Raman, 295, 313
Nargis, 396
Naseerullah, Babur, 274
Natal Indian Congress, 13
Nath, Ram, 193

National Agriculturist Party, 60

National Awami League, 226

National Conference (Jammu and Kashmir), 112, 143, 153, 175, 177, 228, 268, 277, 333–334

National Democratic Alliance (NDA), 279, 280, 300, 340

National Democratic Front of Bodoland, 197

National Front, 267

National Liberation Front of Afghanistan, 374

National Security Agency (NSA), 148, 283, 296, 297, 385

Nationalist Muslim Conference, 75, 78, 79

Nawabshah, 305

Nawaz Sharif, Muhammad, 264, 269, 289, 340, 345, 384
  and Bhutto, Benazir, 273
  and Clinton, Bill, 285, 286, 287, 297, 298–300, 303, 304, 427
  and Gujral, Inder Kumar, 278
  and India, 270, 273, 288, 391, 430
  and, Ishaq Khan, Ghulam, 273
  and Kargil War, 295–300, 303, 307, 427–428
  and Karzai, Hamid, 391
  and Kashmir, 270, 293–294, 425, 427–428
  and Lahore Declaration, 293, 312
  and military High Command, 299, 300, 303–306
  and Musharraf, Pervez, 290, 298, 304–306, 309, 365, 428
  and Narasimha Rao, Pamulapartu Venkata, 272
  and nuclear program and weapons, 279, 285–289, 426
  and Singh, Manmohan, 365, 367
  and United States, 270, 273
  and Vajpayee, Atal Bihari, 290, 291–292, 295–297, 313, 426–427
  and Zia ul Haq, Muhammad, 270
  as Prime Minister, 269, 365, 410

biography and characters of, 269–270

overthrown by a military coup, 306

Nayala, 310

Nayar, Kuldip, 187, 194, 254–256, 424

Nazarbayev, Nur Sultan, 331

Nazimuddin, Khwaja, 131, 141

NDTV, 429, 344

Nehru, Kamala, 59, 194

Nehru, Jawaharlal, 38, 46, 47, 59, 62, 63, 66, 72, 94, 95, 100, 107, 127, 41, 149, 172, 176, 194, 416, 417
  and Abdullah, Shaikh Muhammad, 112, 116, 151, 176
  and Ali Khan, Liaquat, 132, 133, 138, 139–140
  and Ayub Khan, Muhammad, 154, 155–57, 166, 170–171, 176, 417–418
  and Bogra, Muhammad Ali, 149–151, 157
  and China, 157, 160–172, 418
  and communal violence and communalism, 63, 86, 87, 105, 106
  and Constitutional Award, 81, 416
  and Dalai Lama, 164
  and Eisenhower, Dwight, 144, 148
  and Gandhi, Mohandas Karamchand, 63, 87, 94–95, 127
  and Indian National Army, 76
  and Jinnah, Muhammad Ali, 65–66, 83, 131–132
  and Kashmir, 111, 112, 113, 114, 116, 120, 121, 122, 123–124, 142, 150–151, 143, 155–156, 173, 175, 176, 208, 342
  and Kennedy, John F., 167, 171, 173
  and Koran War (1950–1953), 145
  and Mao Zedong, 162, 418–419
  and nuclear program and weapons, 229
  and Princely States, 98
  and secularism, 106–107, 128, 416
  and Soviet Union, 124, 152, 171, 188

and Truman, Harry, 136
and United States, 85, 144–145, 171–172
and Vande Matram (song), 65–66
and Zhou Enlai, 169, 170, 418
as President of Congress Party, 60, 80
as Vice-President of Executive Council, 85
biography and character of, 106, 112, 132, 151, 156, 161, 174, 177
foreign policy of, 85, 144, 151, 166, 417
on Government of India Act (1935), 59
on Pakistan, 94, 125, 150–151, 155, 157
on Two Nation theory, 69
Nehru, Motilal, 38, 44, 47, 177
Nehru Report, 44, 45, 54
Nepal, 158, 163
New Delhi, *see* Delhi
New York, 273
New York Times, 136, 204, 256, 271, 282, 324, 381
New Yorker, 323, 331
New Zealand, 18, 155, 41
Newcastle (South Africa), 16
Newsweek International, 379
Niazi, Amir Abdullah Khan, 202, 207, 209–210, 214, 215, 217, 421
Nimitz, Chester, 150
9/11, 316, 323, 336, 338, 354, 420, 428
Nishtar, Abdur Rab, 86, 95
Nixon, Richard, 196, 202, 206, 207–208, 211, 215, 219, 221, 267, 293, 310
No Higher Honors: A Memoir of My Years in Washington, 353
Noakhali, 86
Non-Aligned Movement summits, 244, 358, 364, 423
Non-Proliferation Treaty (NPT), 243, 251, 278, 284
Nonproliferation Act (US), 236
Noon, Firoz Khan, 147, 148

Noor Jehan (movie), 396
Nooran, 104
Noorani, A. G., 160
Noorani, Zain, 254
North Atlantic Treaty Organization (NATO), 145–146, 379, 381, 384, 385, 388, 391
North Korea and North Koreans, 136–137, 278
North Waziristan, 118, 377, 378
North-East Frontier Agency (NEFA), 158, 159
North-East Frontier Tract, 158
North-West Frontier Province (NWFP), 60, 61, 62, 96, 97, 118, 237, 269, 274, 369, 414
Northern Alliance, 373, 374, 375
Northern Areas (Kashmir), 133, 142, 227, 392
Nuclear Club, 280
Nuclear Proliferation Prevention Act (US), 284
Nuclear Weapons and Foreign Policy, 167
Nusserwanjee, Jamshed, 45

Obama, Barack, 3, 359, 367, 387
Obermeyer, Ziad, 217
Observer, 255, 424
O'Dwyer, Sir Michael Francis, 24
Omar, Mullah Muhammad, 316, 319, 338, 363, 372, 379, 380, 391
One Day International (cricket matches), 400
Operation Badr, 294, 295, 300, 301
Operation Black Thunder, 252
Operation Black Thunder II, 258
Operation Black Tornado, 373
Operation Blue Star, 248–249
Operation Brasstacks, 253–254, 401, 424
Operation Chanakaya, 275
Operation Chengiz Khan, 209
Operation Cyclone, 238
Operation Desert Hawk, 252
Operation Enduring Freedom, 373

Operation Fair Play, 232, 422
Operation Gibraltar, 179, 180, 182, 183, 420
Operation Grand Slam, 179, 180, 183, 184
Operation Gulmarg, 119, 120
Operation Prakaram, 322
Operation Searchlight, 199, 203
Operation Shakti, 283
Operation Shop, 249
Operation Vijay, 295, 300
Operation Woodrose, 249
Orange Free State, 13
Osirak Contingency (India), 243
Osmani, Muhammad Abdullah Gani, 201
Otacamund, 178
Ottoman Empire, 11, 27, 30
Ottoman Turkey, 7
Outalha, Faiza, 348
Outlook, 377
Oxford, 54

Padmanabhan, Sunderarajan, 322, 324, 325, 326, 334, 429
Paghman, 237
Pahwa, Madan Lal, 126
Pahlavi, Muhammad Reza, 145, 238, 371
Pakeezah (movie), 223, 224
Pakistan (book), 115
Pakistan and Pakistanis, 2, 3, 4, 52, 57, 78, 96, 97, 249, 288, 395
  and Abdullah, Shaikh Muhammad, 153, 176, 359
  and Afghanistan, 238, 370–371, 372, 374, 375–376, 377, 378, 380–381, 384, 386–387, 389, 390, 416, 422
  and Bangladesh, 226, 227
  and Central Treaty Organization (CENTO), 145–146, 149, 417
  and China, 138, 147–148, 157, 170, 173, 195, 197, 201, 205, 206, 230, 231, 241, 243, 244, 296, 312, 411–412, 422, 427
  and Clinton, Bill, 289, 290, 311, 312
  and Gandhi, Indira, 241–242, 244, 235, 246
  and Gandhi, Mohandas, 125
  and Gandhi, Rajiv, 254, 255, 258, 261, 288
  and India, 125, 126, 127, 128, 204, 206, 207, 240, 243, 246, 251, 254, 271, 274–275, 285, 287, 308, 310, 312, 319, 321–322, 323, 326, 328, 331, 332, 333, 336, 358, 367
  and Islam, 128, 147, 201, 227, 232, 235
  and Karzai, Hamid, 376, 381, 383, 388, 390, 391
  and Kashmir, 279, 416. *See also* Pakistan-Administered Kashmir
  and Khalistan movement, 248, 257, 258
  and Mumbai 2008 Terrorist Attack, 352–354
  and Mutual Defense Assistance Agreement (1954), 144
  and South-East Asian Treaty Organization (SEATO), 145, 152, 185, 187, 370, 417
  and Soviet Union, 132, 190, 191, 192, 193, 241
  and Taliban, 274, 303, 317, 322, 337, 372, 373, 379, 380, 381
  and United Nations, 125, 152–153, 287
  and United States, 110, 128, 137, 143, 144, 145, 148, 149, 153–154, 157, 179, 185, 187, 196, 204, 222, 237, 241, 243, 244, 246, 251, 253, 270, 272, 278, 287, 307, 309, 310, 311, 316–318, 326, 332, 336, 363, 373, 376, 380, 387, 407, 417, 422, 426
  birth of Pakistan, 102–103
  broadcasting media in, 301, 335, 399
  constitutions of, 227, 269
  economy of, 10, 289, 290, 300, 318, 405, 407, 426
  Hindus in, 140, 201, 227, 273, 421

military and its doctrine, 143–144,
  145–146, 190, 226, 230, 306, 337,
  340, 355–356, 371, 378–379,
  383–384, 389, 418
nuclear doctrine of, 329, 330–331
nuclear program and weapons of,
  140, 222, 230, 236, 241, 244, 245,
  251, 285–289, 291–292, 293, 297,
  299, 325, 331, 337, 341, 356, 413,
  422–23, 425, 427, 431
origins of terrorist attacks in, 258,
  266, 299, 311, 312, 321–322, 337,
  358, 367
victim of terrorist attacks, 256, 258,
  259
Pakistan-Administered Kashmir, *see*
  Azad Kashmir, Baltistan, and
  Northern Areas (Kashmir)
Pakistan Atomic Energy Commission
  (PAEC), 222, 285–286, 288, 413
Pakistan Communist Party, 223
Pakistan Constituent Assembly
  (1947), 101, 103
Pakistan Cricket Board (PCB), 400,
  404, 405
Pakistan Electronic Media Regulatory
  Authority (PEMRA), 335
Pakistan People's Party (PPP), 196,
  198, 222, 226, 232, 233, 234, 235,
  246, 262, 264–265, 273, 292, 336,
  345, 347, 410, 422
Pakistan Muslim League–Nawaz
  Sharif (PML-N), 269, 278, 336,
  345, 365, 410
Pakistan Muslim League–Quaid-i-
  Azam (PML-Q), 336, 345
Pakistan National Alliance (PNA),
  231, 232, 234
Pakistan Times, 109, 116
Pakistan-US Cooperation Agreement,
  153–154, 185
Pakistani Taliban, 387, 404
Pakka Anna, 108
Pan Tsue-li, 164
Panchgani, 85
Panchsheel, 161, 163

Pandit, Vijay Lakshmi, 124, 136
Panjshir Valley, 376
Panjwar, Paramjit Singh, 257
Panmunjom, 1
Pannikar, K. M., 137
Parasuram, R. P., 89
Parikh, Narhari, 89
Paris, 30, 267
Parsis, 11
Partition Council, 96, 129
Parvaiz, Athar, 3
Pasha, Ahmed Shuja, 351–352, 386
Pashban-e Ahl-e Hadith, 337
Pashtunistan, 369, 371
Patel, Vallabhbhai, 60–61, 62, 66, 77,
  84, 89, 95, 96, 120, 121, 125, 127,
  414, 416
Pathankot, 116
Patiala, 100
Patil, Shivraj, 350
Patna, 86
Patterson, Anne, 353
Pearl Harbor, 69
Peer, Basharat, 276
Pentagram rock band, 301
People's Democratic Alliance, 269
People's Democratic Party, 333–334
People's Republic of China (PRC), *see*
  China
Permanent Settlement Act (1793), 19
Persian (language), 5, 7, 239, 414
Persian Gulf, 227
Peshawar, 112, 148, 187, 188, 237, 303
Pethick-Lawrence, Lord, 79, 81
Petit, Sir Dinshaw, 18
Petit, Rattanbai (Ruttie), 18, 23–24.
  See also Jinnah, Maryam
Philadelphia Inquirer, 258
Philippines, 370
Phoenix Settlement, 14, 15
Pietermaritzburg, 13
Pillai, Gopal Krishna, 360
Pirbhoy, Adamjee, 6
Plebiscite Front, 153, 181, 228
Pokhran, 228, 229, 282, 283, 286, 289,
  425, 426

Poland, 67

Poonch, 118, 122, 294, 408

Poonch-Mirpur area, 114, 114, 117

Poonch-Uri, 191

Poonja, Jinnahbhai, 9

Poonja, Mithi Bai, 9, 69

Popalzai tribe, 373, 374

Porbandar, 12, 349

Powell, Colin, 324, 325, 326, 333

Praagh, David van, 189

Prasad, Rajendra, 96, 106, 141, 143, 416

Pressler, Larry, 245

Pressler Amendment (US), 246, 278

Pretoria, 16

Princely States, 51, 53, 59, 79, 87, 98

Pugwash Conference on Jammu and Kashmir, 343

Punjab
  Colonial India, 55, 88, 95–96, 97, 395
  communal holocaust in, 101–102, 104–105, 416
  Independent India, 242, 247–248, 252, 256, 274
  population exchange in, 107–108, 109
  Pakistan, 274

Pushtu (language), 239

Putin, Vladimir, 331

Puzanov, Alexander, 237

Qadeer Khan, Abdul, 230–231, 244, 245, 254–255, 256, 288, 423, 424

Qazi, Ashraf Jahangir, 314

Qazi, Javed Ashraf, 356

Quetta, 97, 130, 303, 374, 376

Quit India campaign (1942), 71, 77

Quit Kashmir campaign (1946), 113

Quran, 42, 346

Qureshi, Makhdoom Shah Mahmood, 352, 353, 356, 360, 361

Qureshi, Pervez Mahdi, 291, 294, 295

Qureshi, Shuaib, 44

Qushila, Jadid, 376

Rabbani, Burhanuddin, 374, 388

Radcliffe, Sir Cyril, 99, 100

Radhakrishnan, Servpalli, 143

Rafiuddin, Maulavi, 10

Raghavan, N., 160–161

Raghunath, Krishnan, 290

Ragi, Darshan Singh, 256

Rahman, Fazlur, 274

Rahman, Hamdoon, 222

Rahman, Shaikh Mujibur, 196, 198, 199, 201, 215, 216, 222, 227

Rahman Khan, Abdur, 241, 244, 259, 262

Raj, Prithvi, 4, 413

Raja, Rameez, 402

Rajagopalachari, Chakravarti, 70–71, 72, 84

Rajaratnam, Thenmozhi, 271

Rajasthan, 253, 254, 256

Rajkot, 12

Ram, Chhotu, 64

Ram Raj, 43, 53

Rama, Lord (Hindu god-king), 16, 43, 272, 281, 382

Rama Janam Bhoomi Mandir, 281

Ramadan (month), 109, 337, 342

Raman, Bahukutumbi, 236

Raman, Venkat, 193

Ramanna, Raja, 243, 244, 423

Ramayana, 33

Ramganj, 86

Rampur, 27

Rangoon, 70

Rann of Kutch, 178

Rao, Nirupama, 359, 361

Rao, Pamulapartu Venkata Narasimha, *see* Narasimha Rao, Pamulapartu Venkata

Rao, V. Venkateswara, 381

Raphel, Arnold, 259

Rashid, Ahmed, 376

Rashtriya Swayamsevak Sangh (RSS), 88, 126, 127, 280–281, 284

Rattam, 107, 108

Ravi River, 98, 116, 154

Rawalakot, 408

Rawalpindi, 92, 140, 170, 187, 209, 259, 317, 338, 368
Reading, Lord, 35, 38, 46
Reagan, Ronald, 240–241, 243, 244, 246, 253, 254, 263, 422
Rees, Thomas Pete, 100
Rehman, Atiq, 368
Reliance World Cup (cricket), 255
Report of the Committee Appointed by the Government of India to Investigate the Disturbances in the Punjab etc., 30, 32
Republic of China (Taiwan), 168, 200
Republican Party (Pakistan), 147, 148
Research and Analysis Milli Afghanistan (RAMA), 382
Research and Analysis Wing (RAW), 197, 206, 399
  and Afghanistan, 372–373, 376, 377
  and assassination of Zia ul Haq, Muhammad, 262
  and Awami League, 198
  and Counter Intelligence Team–J (CIT–J), 252, 274, 279
  and Counter Intelligence Team–X (CIT–X), 252, 256, 274, 279
  and East Pakistan, 198, 201
  and Indian Kashmir, 275
  and Inter-Services Intelligence, 244, 257, 275
  and KHAD, 242
  and Mossad, 197, 244
  and Pakistan, 236, 245, 266, 275–275
  and Kargil War, 296
  and Shin Beth, 250
  and Sikh militancy, 266
Rice, Condoleezza, 325, 351, 352–354
Riedel, Bruce, 298, 300
Rodham, Dorothy, 310
Rome, 218
Roosevelt, Franklin, D., 69
Rose, Leo E., 216
Roshan, Hrithik, 302
Round Table Conferences (London), 50, 51, 53

Rowlatt, Sidney, 24
Rowlatt Act, 24, 27, 28
Royal Indian Navy mutiny (1946), 76, 77
Ruskin, John, 4
Russia, 372

Sadiq, Ghulam Muhammad, 116, 175, 177
Saeed, Hafiz Muhammad, 321, 355, 357, 359, 360, 361, 363
Sahai, Jagan Nath, 193, 194
Sahara India, 402
Sahara TV, 301
Sahgal, Prem, 75
Sajjad, Wasim, 273
Saleh, Amrullah, 386
Salim (Prince), 397
Salt March, 46–49, 50
Samadzai, Vida, 293
Sanatan Dharm Sabha, 41
Sandys, Duncan, 173
Sanjivpaul, Subodh, 386
Sarabhai, Ambalal, 21–22
Sargodha Air Force Base, 298, 428
Sarkar, Sujeet, 394
Sarvar Upazila, 227
Sathyu, Mysore Shrinivas, 219, 220
Sattar, Abdul, 253
Saudi Arabia, 227, 239, 275, 289, 365
Savage, Gerald, 100
Sayed, Mushahid Hussain, *see* Hussain, Mushahid
Sayeed, Mufti, 339
Schmitt, Eric, 381
Scott, H. L., 113
Se-La Pass, 159, 160, 171
Seoul, 1
Serwani, Muhammad Arif, 375, 379
Sethi, Najam, 405
Shaam, Mahmood, 185
Shah, A. K., 117
Shah, Sir Sultan Muhammad, 6, 56
Shah, Zarrar, 355
Shahi, Agha, 236
Shaikh, Ahmed Umar, 308

Shamsuddin, Khwaja, 175
Shanghai Cooperation Organization, 358
Sharif, Muhammad, 304
Sharif, Shahbaz, 304, 407, 409
Sharjah, 401
Sharma, Anand, 409, 410, 411
Sharm-el-Shaikh, 358
Sharon, Ariel, 243, 245, 423
Shashank, 340
Shastri, Lal Bahadur, 176
　　and Ayub Khan, Muhammad, 179, 194
　　and China, 188
　　and Kashmir, 182, 184, 190, 215
　　and Kosygin, Alexei, 191
　　and Operation Desert Hawk, 179
　　and nuclear program and weapons, 184, 229
　　and Soviet Union, 187, 188, 190–192
　　as Prime Minister, 176
　　death of, 192, 193–194
　　biography and character of, 177, 182
Shatra, Lonchen, 159
Shaw, George Bernard, 13
Shawai Nullah, 355
Shekhar, Chandra, 270
Shergill, Karan, 302
Sherman, Wendy, 363
Shias, 275
Shimla, 223, 314, 373
Shimla Agreement, 225, 226, 228, 276, 314, 421–422
Shin Beth, 250
Shradhanad, Swami, 29
Shukla, Pandit Raj Kumar, 18, 19
Siachen Glacier, 2, 251, 257, 266, 279, 295, 340, 361, 362, 425
Sialkot, 184, 254, 401
Sikhs, 53, 55, 91–92, 99–100, 111–112, 242, 247–250, 251–252, 254, 257–258, 266, 274, 395, 425
Simla Convention (1913), 159
Simon, John, 43, 44

Simon Commission, 44
Sindh, 78, 87–88, 97, 102, 109, 246–247, 269, 273, 275, 395–396
Sindh Assembly Coalition Party, 48
Sindhi (language), 247
Singapore, 70, 407
Singh, Sir Amar, 111
Singh, Baldev, 85, 87, 95, 96, 121
Singh, Beant, 249
Singh, Beant (Chief Minister), 274
Singh, Bhagat, 46
Singh, Bikram, 365
Singh, Bishan, 135
Singh, Dilbagh, 243
Singh, Gobind, 92
Singh, Gulab, 113
Singh, Gurbaksh, 186
Singh, Gurbaksh Dhillon, 75
Singh, Harbakhsh, 184
Singh, Sir Hari, 110, 111–112, 119–120, 121, 142, 416
Singh, Janak, 114, 117
Singh, Jaswant, 10, 62, 293, 308, 314, 324, 329, 331, 374
Singh, Juggat, 104
Singh, Karan, 142, 143
Singh, Khushwant, 104, 249
Singh, Krishna, 96
Singh, Kunwar Natwar, 341
Singh, Mangal, 44
Singh, Manmohan, 340
　　and Afghanistan, 377, 388–389, 391
　　and Gilani, Yusuf Raza, 351, 358–359, 360, 361, 363, 382, 403
　　and Karzai, Hamid, 388
　　and Kashmir, 342, 365, 367
　　and Mumbai 2008 Terrorist Attack, 350, 351, 352, 354
　　and Musharraf, Pervez, 342, 343, 388, 429
　　and Nawaz Sharif, Muhammad, 365, 367
　　and Obama, Barack, 367
　　and Pakistan, 359, 367
　　and Zardari, Asif Ali, 358, 363, 364, 408

as Prime Minister, 340, 341, 357
biography and character of, 364
Singh, Partap, 111
Singh, Rajnath, 365
Singh, Ranjit, 92
Singh, S. K., 254
Singh, Swaran, 73, 173, 205, 240
Singh, Tara, 92
Singh, Vishwanath Pratap, 267, 268
Sinkiang-Uighur Autonomous
    Region, 160, 163
Sino-India War, *see* India-China War
Sir Creek, 279, 340, 361
Sisson, Richard, 215
Smith, David, 328
Smuts, Jan, 14, 16
Solanki, Amar Singh, 349
Solarz Stephen, 246
Soldier, Iqbal, 404
Soni, Ambika, 397
Soomro, Muhammad Mian, 346
South Africa, 11, 16, 18, 231
South Asian Association for Regional
    Cooperation (SAARC), 242,
    265, 270, 278, 290, 312–313, 324,
    339, 361, 381, 406, 408, 410, 425
South Asian Free Trade Area
    (SAFTA), 408, 410, 430
South Korea and South Koreans, 1,
    137
South Waziristan, 118, 377, 378
South-East Asia Treaty Organization
    (SEATO), 145, 152, 185, 187,
    320, 417
Soviet Central Asia, 148
Soviet Union, 124, 152, 153, 161, 162,
    163, 165, 167, 188–189, 191, 204,
    205, 207, 422
    and Afghanistan, 238, 253, 258,
    370–371, 372
    and Bangladesh War, 210
    and United States, 167, 169, 171,
    188–189, 210–213, 238, 240, 272,
    332
Special Frontier Force, 174, 197, 206
Spin Boldak, 374

Sri Lanka, 168, 271, 290, 404
Srinagar, 3, 111, 120, 121, 175, 182,
    294, 320, 343, 416, 417, 419
Stalin, Joseph, 151
Stars for Another Sky, 135
Statesman, 86
Stephens, Ian, 115
Sudhan clan, 294
Sudhir, 108
Sufis, 31, 88, 265
Suhrawardy, Hussein Shaheed, 78,
    83–84, 103, 147, 148, 257
Sunday Times (London), 203
Sunderarajan, Krishnaswamy, 253,
    254, 424
Sunnis, 275
Suntook, Nowsher F., 244
Sutlej River, 98, 99, 100, 154
Swat Valley, 183
Swatantra, 109
Syed, Ghulam Murtaza, 247
Sylhet, 97
Symington, Stuart, 236
Symington Amendment (US), 236,
    240, 241, 231
Szulc, Ted, 204

Tagore, Rabindranath, 32, 65, 66, 415
Tahiliani, Hariram Radhakrishna, 253
Taiwan, 103, 168, 201
Taizani, 373
Taj Mahal, 219, 309, 314
Taj Mahal: The Eternal Love Story
    (Movie), 397
Taj Mahal Palace Hotel, 348, 350, 351
Tajikistan, 370
Tajiks, 375
Taliban, 3, 295, 299, 303, 307–308,
    382, 393
    and Afghanistan, 372, 385, 386, 390,
    391, 392
    and Al Qaida, 390
    and Bhutto, Benazir, 372, 385, 386,
    390, 391, 392
    and Clinton, Bill, 299
    and India, 307, 383, 385–386

Taliban *(continued)*
  and Karzai, Hamid, 372, 385, 386, 390, 391, 392
  and Musharraf, Pervez, 209, 318
  and Pakistan, 274, 303, 317, 322, 337, 372, 373, 379, 380, 381
  and United States, 317, 322
  resurgence of, 375, 379
Tamewali, 259, 260
Tanmurg, 124
Taraki, Nur Muhammad, 237–238
Tarar, Muhammad Rafiq, 287, 307, 316, 313
"Tariq, General," 115
Taseer, Muhammad Din, 116
Tashkent, 188, 190, 191
Tashkent Declaration, 192, 193, 195
Tawang, 160, 169, 170, 171, 181
Tawi River, 183
Tehelka, 355
Tel Aviv, 243, 423
Tendulkar, Sachin, 401, 404–405
Tenet, George J., 284
Tezpur, 164, 171
Thagla Ridge, 168
Thailand, 145, 370
Thatcher, Margaret, 267
The 9/11 Commission Report, 316
The Discovery of India, 156
The Emergence of Pakistan, 119
The Story of My Experiments with Truth, 10
The Wrong Enemy: America in Afghanistan, 381–382
Thendup, Gyalo, 161
Thoreau, Henry David, 13, 15
Thimayya, K. S., 154
Thimpu, 360, 361
Thussu, Swarupram, 177
Tibet, 158–162
Tikka Khan, Muhammad, 199, 202, 207
Tilak, Bal Gangadhar, 23
Time, 136, 187, 383
Tippera, 86
Tiscenka, Vera, 147

Tiwana, Sir Khizr Hayat, 79, 88, 91
Toba Tek Singh, 135
Tolo TV, 392, 393, 394
Tolstoy, Leo, 13
Tolstoy Farm, 16
Toronto, 404
Train to Pakistan, 104
Transvaal Immigration Restriction Act, 15, 16
Transvaal Republic, 13
Treaty of Friendship and Cooperation (Afghan-Soviet), 238
Treaty of Friendship between India and Afghanistan (1950), 370, 388
Treaty of Peace with Japan, 137
Treaty of Sevres, 33
Trelford, Donald, 255
Trombay, 229, 244, 423
Troti, 183
Truman, Harry, 136, 137, 138, 141
Tulsi (television serial), 3893, 394
Turki bin Faisal (Saudi Prince), 241
Turkey, 28, 145, 171, 204
Turkmenistan, 370
26/11, 351, 357, 361, 364
Two Nation theory, 5, 68, 69, 218, 414
Tyabji, Abbas, 48
Tyabji, Badruddin, 10

U Thant, 184, 188
Uban, Sujan Singh, 179, 209
Union of South Africa, *see* South Africa
Unionist Party, 61, 79, 91
United Arab Emirates, 289, 398, 401, 407, 409
United Front (East Pakistan), 146, 278
United Press International, 48
United Nations (UN), 1, 124, 150, 200, 250, 277, 287, 313, 370, 375
United Nations Military Observer Group in India and Pakistan (UNMOGIP), 133, 184

United Nations Commission on India and Pakistan (UNCIP), 133, 136, 143, 151

United Nations Security Council, 1, 124, 129–130, 136–137, 152–153, 184, 188, 200, 210, 282–283, 294, 355, 357

United Progressive Alliance (UPA), 340, 341

United Province, 395

Unto This Last, 14

United States, 15, 21, 55, 152, 155, 293, 303, 332, 363, 350

  and 9/11, 316

  and Afghanistan, 237, 252, 316, 326, 359, 372, 375, 376, 383, 385, 387

  and Ali Khan, Liaquat, 138

  and Bhutto, Benazir, 278

  and Bhutto, Zulfikar, 185, 191

  and China, 163, 168, 204, 208, 211–213, 293

  and Gandhi, Indira, 197, 207–208

  and India, 136, 145, 165, 170, 174, 185, 190, 205, 206, 229, 318, 321, 322, 323, 419, 425

  and Israel, 243

  and Nawaz Sharif, Muhammad, 270, 273

  and Nehru, Jawaharlal, 85, 144–145, 171–172

  and Pakistan, 110, 128, 137, 143, 144, 145, 148, 149, 153–154, 157, 179, 185, 187, 196, 204, 222, 237, 241, 243, 244, 246, 251, 253, 270, 272, 278, 287, 307, 309, 310, 311, 316–318, 326, 332, 336, 363, 373, 376, 380, 387, 407, 417, 422, 426

  and Soviet Union, 167, 169, 171, 188–189, 210–213, 238, 240, 272, 332

  and Taliban, 317, 322

  Nonproliferation Act of, 236

  Nuclear Proliferation Prevention Act of, 284

Untouchables (Hindu), 43, 53, 54, 55, 57

Upadhaya, Deen Dayal, 281

Urdu (language), 65, 66, 147, 398, 417

URENCO, 231

Uri, 3, 119, 120, 124, 408

US-Pakistan Mutual Security Pact, 157

Usmani, Muzaffar, 305, 317, 319

USSR, *see* Soviet Union

Uzbekistan, 188, 370

Vaishya (movie), 302

Vajpayee, Atal Bihari, 233, 289, 334, 376

  and Clinton, Bill, 296, 299, 310, 312, 427–428

  and Indian Airlines plane hijacked, 307–308

  and Kargil War, 295–296, 298–301

  and Kashmir, 293, 337

  and Lahore Declaration, 293, 312

  and Musharraf, Pervez, 291, 307, 313, 314, 324–325, 331, 406, 428

  and Nawaz Sharif, Muhammad, 290, 291–292, 295–297, 313, 426–427

  and nuclear doctrine, 329

  and nuclear program and weapons, 280, 281–82, 283, 426

  and Pakistan, 292, 293, 322–323, 325, 427, 429

  and terrorist attacks in Delhi, 320–322, 324, 335, 429

  biography and character of, 280–281

Vajpayee, Krishna Bihari, 280

Vajpayee, Namita, 292

Vale of Kashmir, 120, 129, 133, 142, 157, 175, 277, 295

Vance, Cyrus, 236

Vande Matram (song), 64–66, 415

Vanity Fair, 259

Vedic Hinduism, 31, 32

Venkataraman, Ramaswamy, 259

Verma, A. K., 257

Victoria (Queen), 349

Vienna, 196, 423

Vietnam, 217
Vij, Nirmal Chander, 334
Vijaypur, 327
Vishakhapatnam, 76, 327
Vohra, Gulab, 62
Voice of Kashmir radio, 182
Vorontsov, Yuli, 211

Waar (movie), 399
Wagah, 187, 291, 364, 387, 403, 407,
    409, 411, 416
Wah, 381
Wahhabis, 275
Wahid, Abdul, 393
Walong, 171
*War and Secession: Pakistan, India and
    the Creation of Bangladesh*, 216
Warsaw, 168
Washington, 1, 85, 138, 196, 207, 261,
    267, 325
Wassom, Herbert M., 259
Wavell, Archibald Lord, 71, 72, 73, 79,
    80, 81, 83, 85, 87
Weisman, Steven R., 25
Welwyn Garden City, 247
West Bengal, 109, 139, 140, 217
West Pakistan and West Pakistanis,
    134, 140, 146, 217, 219
West Punjab, 102, 105, 118, 119
Weston, D., 19
Willingdon, Lord, 55
Wilson, Harold, 178
Wilson, Woodrow, 21
Wisner, Frank, 282
Wolport, Stanley, 21
World Bank, 154–155, 266, 270, 285,
    417
World Policy Journal, 260
World Sindhi Conference, 247
World Trade Center (New York), 273,
    316
World War I (1914–1918), 7–8, 11,
    22, 24, 26, 28
World War II (1939–1945), 67–68,
    70–71, 72
Wullar Barrage, 279, 340

Xinjiang Autonomous Region, 160,
    173, 204
Xinjiang-Tibet Highway, 166, 167

Yahya Khan, Agha Muhammad, 183,
    196, 198, 201, 217, 420, 428
    and Ayub Khan, Muhammad, 196,
        420
    and Bangladesh War, 209–210, 213,
        214, 217
    and Bhutto, Zulfikar Ali, 222
    and East Pakistan, 199, 205, 207
    and Nixon, Richard, 196, 202,
        207
    and Operation Grand Slam, 183
    general election under, 197–198
    resignation of, 218
Yaqoob, Abdul Razak, 335
Yamuna River, *see* Jamuna River
Yaron, Amos, 328
Yeh Khamoshi Kahan Tak?, 297
Yekaterinburg, 358
Young India, 35, 36, 38, 39, 41, 42
Yousaf, Jam Muhammad, 277
Yuan Zhongxian, 159
Yusaf Khan, Muhammad, 320, 323,
    328, 345

Zabul, 375
Zaheer, Sajjad, 223
Zahid, Anwar, 293
Zahir Shah, Muhammad (King), 237,
    370, 371
Zakaria, Fareed, 379–380
Zaki, Akram, 273
Zardari, Asif Ali, 224, 264, 265, 266,
    268, 347, 352, 353, 354, 357, 358,
    363, 364, 384, 390, 408
Zardari, Hakim Ali, 224, 266
Zawahiri, Ayman, 228
Zee TV, 399
Zhou Enlai, 147–148, 161, 162, 163,
    165–166, 202, 204, 233, 418
    and Abdullah, Shaikh Muhammad,
        177
    and Kissinger, Henry, 205–206

and Nehru, Jawaharlal, 169, 170, 418

Zia ul Haq, Muhammad, 141, 238, 258, 318, 400, 401, 423

and Afghanistan, 237, 238, 239, 258

and Bhutto, Benazir, 263

and Bhutto, Zulfikar Ali, 233, 234, 235, 263, 422

and Gandhi, Indira, 241–242, 244, 266, 423

and Gandhi, Rajiv, 251–252, 255, 259, 266, 401, 424

and India, 235, 236, 246, 247, 254, 396

and Inter-Services Intelligence, 239–240, 257

and Kashmir, 268, 326

and Khalistan movement, 251–252

and Movement for Restoration of Democracy, 246, 247

and nuclear program and weapons, 236, 240–241, 251–252, 254–255, 423, 424, 425

and Pakistan People's Party, 233

as Army Chief, 233, 254, 429

assassination of, 258–260, 262, 263, 276, 422

biography and character of, 234–235, 251, 262

general elections under, 251, 270

Islamization by, 238, 239, 258, 265, 268, 275–276, 292

military coup against Bhutto, Zulfikar Ali, 232, 235–236

Ziarat, 130

Zinni, Anthony, 296

Zinta, Priety, 302

Zira, 100

Zoroastrians, 194

Zulu rebellion, 12, 14

DILIP HIRO is one of the world's leading experts on South Asian, Central Asian, and Middle Eastern affairs. His thirty-four books include *Inside India Today*, *Inside Central Asia*, *The Timeline History of India*, *War Without End*, and *Apocalyptic Realm: Jihadists in South Asia*. He contributes to the *New York Times*, *Guardian*, *Washington Post*, *Observer*, and *Nation*, as well as *Salon*, *TomDispatch*, and *YaleGlobal* online magazines. He is a commentator for CNN, the BBC, and Al Jazeera English.

NATION
BOOKS

The Nation Institute

Founded in 2000, **Nation Books** has become a leading voice in American independent publishing. The inspiration for the imprint came from the *Nation* magazine, the oldest independent and continuously published weekly magazine of politics and culture in the United States.

The imprint's mission is to produce authoritative books that break new ground and shed light on current social and political issues. We publish established authors who are leaders in their area of expertise, and endeavor to cultivate a new generation of emerging and talented writers. With each of our books we aim to positively affect cultural and political discourse.

Nation Books is a project of The Nation Institute, a nonprofit media center dedicated to strengthening the independent press and advancing social justice and civil rights. The Nation Institute is home to a dynamic range of programs: the award-winning Investigative Fund, which supports ground-breaking investigative journalism; the widely read and syndicated website TomDispatch; the Victor S. Navasky Internship Program in conjunction with the *Nation* magazine; and Journalism Fellowships that support up to 25 high-profile reporters every year.

For more information on Nation Books, The Nation Institute, and the *Nation* magazine, please visit:

www.nationbooks.org

www.nationinstitute.org

www.thenation.com

www.facebook.com/nationbooks.ny

Twitter: @nationbooks